Advance praise for Jerry Hopkins' book

"Jerry Hopkins was the first serious journalist to take Elvis seriously, writing the first biography. The Elvis bookshelf is crowded now, but don't let that put you off. This thoroughly revised and updated version of his two classic books deserves a shelf of its own."
—*Jann Wenner,* founder and editor of *Rolling Stone*

"Jerry Hopkins long ago established the ground rules for serious biographical consideration of Elvis Presley. With a rare combination of seat-of-the-pants reporting and thoughtful portraiture, he creates a richly nuanced picture of a world in flux, both for Elvis himself and for the broad range of humanity that was—and continues to be—so indelibly affected by his music."
—*Peter Guralnick,* author of *Last Train to Memphis* and *Careless Love: The Unmaking of Elvis Presley*

"In 1975, when I began to study Elvis Presley as an agent for social change, there was but a single serious biography available, *Elvis: A Biography* by Jerry Hopkins. (Today, books about Elvis exceed 500.) Jerry Hopkins got there first and established a foundation for all who followed. Based on numerous interviews with a wide variety of people who knew Presley at various times and contexts of his life, Hopkins gives us a picture of Elvis unaffected by the posthumous legends and interpretations that now go on and on. It is a sympathetic, unassuming, yet journalistically sound picture that has weathered a stormy test of time. Sound Elvis scholars like Peter Guralnick and Michael Bertrand have drawn from his research, and I still tell those who want an introduction to Elvis they should start with Jerry Hopkins. Hopkins remains a pioneer who recognized the influence of popular culture on the whole of American life and that from the mid-fifties and beyond Elvis Presley was its king."
—*John Bakke,* University of Memphis Professor Emeritus

Praise for Jerry Hopkins' previous books on Elvis,
*Elvis: A Biography* and *Elvis: The Final Years.*

"In *Elvis: The Final Years, Rolling Stone* contributing editor Jerry Hopkins supplements his *Elvis: A Biography* published in 1971 and now out of print, rather successfully, to present a 'balanced view' of the Memphis Myth's latter-day paranoia, pettiness, generosity, childishness and artistic decline, his fondness for drugs, guns, jewels, police paraphernalia and pretty women, his death and funeral and the continuing commercial exploitation of everything that he left behind."—*New York Times*

"A well-told Horatio Alger story that shows how a sexy barefoot boy from Mississippi became the most enduring and successful show business personality ever known. There are over 250 million records, 31 movies; according to Gallup, his first name is better known than any two names in the world."
—*New York Magazine*

"Excellent. Hopkins is a meticulous reporter, and he tells his story with a loving flair that matches his extraordinary subject."—*Chicago Daily News*

"Virtually all that is known about Elvis Presley is collected in one place. . .a valuable volume, a must inclusion in any rock and roll library."
—*Record World*

"*Elvis: A Biography* is exciting throughout."—*L.A. Free Press*

"A graphic word show about Elvis the man and Elvis the performer. It is so inclusive. . ."—*Columbus Dispatch*

# ABOUT THE AUTHOR

Jerry Hopkins wrote *Elvis: A Biography*, the first biography of the King, published in 1971. A sequel, *Elvis: The Final Years*, followed in 1980. Both were *New York Times* bestsellers. Long out of print, the two books are here completely revised and updated in one volume with the addition of all new material, and a new final chapter that goes inside the Elvis Presley Estate, revealing how he became Forbes magazine's "No.1 Richest Dead Celebrity" five years in a row.

Hopkins is the author of more than 30 books, including the best-selling biography of Jim Morrison, *No One Here Gets Out Alive,* which was No. 1 on the *New York Times* bestseller list and has more than two million copies in print. He also has written biographies of Jimi Hendrix, David Bowie, and Yoko Ono, and for 20 years was a correspondent and contributing editor for *Rolling Stone.* His Elvis archives at the University of Memphis serve as a primary resource for serious Elvis scholars. Hopkins now resides in Thailand.

# ELVIS
## The Biography

# Jerry Hopkins

Plexus, London

All rights reserved including the right of
reproduction in whole or in part in any form
Copyright © 2007, 2010 by Haku 'Olelo
Published by Plexus Publishing Limited
The Studio, Hillgate Place
18-20 Balham Hill
London, SW12 9ER
www.plexusbooks.com

British Library Cataloguing in Publication Data
A catalogue record for this book is available from the British Library

ISBN 978-0-85965-454-8

Cover design by Coco Wake-Porter
Printed in Great Britain by Bell & Bain Ltd

This book is sold subject to the condition that it shall
not by way of trade or otherwise be lent, re-sold, hired out
or otherwise circulated without the publisher's prior consent
in any form of binding or cover other than that in which it
is published and without a similar condition including this
condition being imposed on the subsequent purchaser.

# CONTENTS

# ACKNOWLEDGEMENTS

For the first half of this book, there were more than a thousand sources: dozens of books, plus all the articles in all the magazines, with special thanks to the offices (and the files) of *Billboard* and *The Hollywood Reporter*, plus all the newspapers, with the most help coming from the files of the *New York Times* (1956-70), the *Los Angeles Times* (1956-70), the *Nashville Tennessean* (1956-70), the *Memphis Press-Scimitar* (1954-70) and the *Daily Journal* in Tupelo (1930-70). Thanks, too, to the Tupelo Public Library and the Library of the Academy of Motion Picture Arts and Sciences in Hollywood.

Approximately seventy-five individuals were interviewed for the second part of this book. Most of them hadn't been interviewed by anyone else before. Many gave me exclusive access.

One of these was Colonel Tom Parker, who never really gave me an interview, providing instead what took the form of low-key, rambling monologues. To him I offer my special thanks for allowing me to clear so many fences merely by dropping his name.

Others deserving deepest appreciation include Grelun Landon, Jerry Schilling, John Wilkinson, T.G. Sheppard and John Bakke, for their unstinting time and support.

There were many warm and co-operative people who gave their time, shared their memories and granted interviews.

In Tupelo: Mayor James Ballard, Mr. and Mrs. J. C. Grimes, Mrs. Faye Harris, Mrs. Tressie Miller, the Reverend Eugene Moffat, Buck Presley, Hershell Presley, J. M. (Ikey) Savery and John Tidwell.

In Memphis: Ginger Alden, Jo Alden, Jackson Baker, Mrs. Ruby Black, James Blackwood, Melissa Blackwood, Pat (Medford) Booth, Stanley Booth, T. C. Brindley, Ray Brown, Bill Burk, Marian Cocke, Richard Davis, JoCathy (Brownlee) Elkington, Maurice Elliott, Buzzie Forbess, Mrs. Elgie Forbess, Alan Fortas, Maggie (Smith)Glover, Arthur Groom, Lowell Hays, Jr., Milo High, Edwin Howard, W. J. Huettel, Bob Johnson, Stan Kesler, James Kingsley, George Klein, Jerry Lee Lewis, Marion Keisker MacInnes, Elsie

Marmann, Howard Massey, Mike McMahon, Chips Moman, B. P. (Buddy) Montesi, Bill Morris, Herbie Omell, Gary and Mr. and Mrs. Sterling G. Pepper, Sam Phillips, Tom Phillips, Dee Presley, Vester Presley, Mrs. Jane Richardson, Kang Rhee, Billy Ray Schilling, Mildred Scrivener, Willie Smith, David Stanley, James and Gladys Tipler and Bobby (Red) West.

In Nashville: Roy Acuff, Chet Atkins, Mae Axton, Jerry Carrigan, Jack Clement, Betty Cox, Oscar Davis, Bobby Emmons, D. J. Fontana, Steve Goldstein, Jack Hurst, Juanita Jones, the Jordanaires (Gordon Stoker, Neal Matthews, Hoyt Hawkins, Ray Walker), Larrie Londin, Joe Mescale, Scotty Moore, Bob and Helen Neal, Minnie Pearl, Pete Peterson, Webb Pierce, Cecil Scaife, Diana Shepard, Dolores Watson Siegenthaler, Shelby Singleton, Mrs. Jo Walker, Bill Williams, Happy Wilson and Bobby Wood.

In Shreveport: Frank Page.

In New York: Fred Bienstock, Otis Blackwell, David Dalton, Ahmet Ertegun, Jerry Leiber, Mort Shuman and Mike Stoller.

In Los Angeles: Bob Abel, Gerald Drayson Adams, Steve Allen, Wally Beene, Bill Belew, Steve Binder, Bill Bixby, Robert (Bumps) Blackwell, Hal Blaine, Dudley Brooks, Stan Brossette, Tony Brown, Walter Burrell, James Burton, Mrs. Virginia Coons, Yvonne Craig, Ken Darby, Joan Deary, Mac Davis, Dolores (Dee) Fuller, Pat (Perry) Gerson, Billy Goldenberg, Jack Good, Charles Greene, Glenn D. Hardin, Jon Hartmann, Bones Howe, Rick Husky, Ron Jacobs, Pete Johnson, Sam Katzman, Jerry Knight, Antonia Lamb, Malcolm Leo, Lance LeGault, Frank Lieberman, Larry Muhoberac, Gene Nelson, Rick Nelson, John O'Grady, Bill O'Hallaren, Johnny Otis, Matty Pasetta, Joe Pasternak, Little Richard Penniman, Gerald Peters, Ellen Pollon, Jim Rissmiller, Johnny Rivers, Denis Sanders, Mario Sanders, Jerry Scheff, Sol Schwartz, Phil Spector, Gary Smith, Myrna Smith, Andy Solt, Cliffie Stone, Sam Theaker, Linda Thompson, Dean Torrance, Del Trollope, Moe Weise, Ben Weisman, John Wilson and Steve Wolf.

In Las Vegas: The employees and officers of the International Hotel, Bruce Banke, Sam Belkin, Gene Dessell, Joe Guercio, Marty Harrell, Bill Jost, Henri Lewin, and Artie Newman.

In Honolulu: Phil Arnone, Ron Rewald, Eddie Sherman, Kalani Simerson.

Another large debt is owed to RCA Records, whose Los Angeles office opened its files, provided a desk, a telephone, and the unlimited use of a photocopy machine, as well as a complete set of Elvis's records.

For assistance in understanding the inner workings of the Elvis Presley estate, I am deeply grateful to Jack Soden, Todd Morgan, Jerry Schilling, Gary Hovey, Andrew Solt and the musicians, singers and crew of the Elvis Presley in Concert mixed-media tour.

Thanks also to the dozens more who talked off the record or asked not to be quoted. As is usual with such sources, if there seemed to be an ax to grind, the information was discounted.

And all the fans, especially Bill Kaval, and Rex Martin, for providing so many rare audio tapes.

A number of previously published books about Elvis also were consulted, occasionally for direct quotation or information, more often for confirmation of material obtained in interview. They included: *Elvis: What Happened?* by Red West, Sonny West and Dave Hebler as told to Steve Dunleavy; *Inside Elvis* by Ed Parker; *My Life With Elvis* by Becky Yancey and Cliff Linedecker; *I Called Him Babe* by Marian J. Cocke; *Elvis: Portrait of a Friend* by Marty Lacker, Patsy Lacker and Leslie S. Smith; *Elvis and Me* by Priscilla Beaulieu Presley with Sandra Harmon; *Elvis by the Presleys* by Priscilla Presley and Lisa Marie Presley; *Me and a Guy Named Elvis* by Jerry Schilling.

Thanks to my publisher Sandra Wake for inviting me to create this volume and for being instrumental in making it happen; thanks also to her editorial team, Julia Shone, Richard Porter and Paul Woods and to the design team, Rebecca Longworth and Coco Wake-Porter.

Photos courtesy of the Gilloon Agency, United Press International, Lillian Foscue Vann, 20th Century-Fox Film Corporation, Paramount Pictures Corporation, Metro-Goldwyn-Mayer Studios, National General Corporation, National Broadcasting Company, U.S. Army, Elvis Presley Enterprises, Inc., RCA, Wide World photos, and National Film Archive.

And finally, thanks to Jann Wenner and *Rolling Stone*, for the impetus and continued support.

JERRY HOPKINS

To
Jim Morrison, for the idea.

# INTRODUCTION

I n 1969, when I was interviewing Jim Morrison for *Rolling Stone*, he said he'd read a paperback history of rock and roll that I'd written and wondered if I was planning another book. I said I was thinking about writing a biography of Frank Zappa. He said, "I'd like to read a book about Elvis."

I'd had no idea that Jim was an Elvis fan, and I confess that I hadn't been one at all. In fact, when he first appeared in 1956, I listened only to jazz. A year later, when the kid in the next room in my university fraternity house played Elvis's second album over and over, I grumbled to my roommate, "If I hear 'Old Shep' one more time, I'm going over there and break that record and the kid's neck, not necessarily in that order!"

Six years later, Steve Allen asked me to write and produce a television special that would introduce jazz to kids. I decided the best way to do that was to show the common roots that jazz and rock had in the blues. I also figured I should start listening to rock radio. Not long after that, the Beatles stormed America and I never looked back. By 1966 I was writing for *Rolling Stone*, and by 1969 I was researching Elvis's life, on Jim's advice. At the time, Elvis was still making all those sappy movies. The Beatles, the Rolling Stones, Bob Dylan and others seemed far more relevant to what was happening. Many of the people I approached for interviews asked, "What do you want to write about him for?" Subsequently, Elvis left Hollywood behind him, started appearing in Las Vegas and went on the road, then everyone understood what Jim Morrison was talking about.

Hunter Davies had written a biography of the Beatles, but in 1969, the rock biography as a genre did not exist. *Elvis: A Biography* was published by Simon and Schuster in 1971. Six years later, when Elvis died, it was still the only biography in print, despite his successful comeback. In the year following Elvis's death, the *New York Times* reported 3.5 million sales of my book.

At the same time, dozens of Elvis's so-called friends and exploitative journalists hacked out lurid memoirs and exposés, focusing on the sex, the guns, the drugs. I thought some balance was needed, as people were forgetting what

Elvis represented, not just musically but historically. So I set forth again and, in 1980, St Martin's Press published *Elvis: The Final Years*, covering the last six years of his life and the first year or so of posthumous madness.

This time, I had the help of many insiders who wouldn't talk the first time around—including Colonel Tom Parker, who opened several doors for me. This book also sold well.

Since then, some five hundred books about Elvis have been published. There's even one volume that does no more than catalog all of the other books. Eventually, both of mine went out of print, and my research material was moved to the Mississippi Valley Collection at the University of Memphis, on loan. There it became a resource for some of the newer, more serious investigations into Elvis's life and music.

Now I've been asked to edit the two original manuscripts so they can be republished in a single volume, and add a new final chapter that takes a look at what put Elvis at the top of *Forbes* magazine's "Top-Earning Dead Celebrities" list for five years in a row. What is it that kept a wildly successful video-plus-live-band show—*Elvis: The Concert*—on the road for ten years, playing twice at London's Wembley Arena? How is it that Elvis grossed between five and six million dollars a year when he was alive and at his peak in the 1960s, and in 2005 earned as much as $70 million? I thought that a story worth telling.

In order to compress my two books into one, I've cut some of the original text. But I've also added new material based upon information that's come to light since the original books were published, as well as new interviews conducted specifically for this publication.

It's now more than seventy years since Elvis was born, fifty since he introduced himself to so many of us with "Heartbreak Hotel," "Love Me Tender," "Hound Dog" and "All Shook Up." For another twenty years, he ruled the rock and roll roost, becoming one of the most influential personalities of the twentieth century. It has been thirty years since he died, yet the impact of his life and music remains a driving force.

Those of us who dismissed him then, or do so now, were and are mistaken. Like Elvis or not, praise him or damn him, none of us can say he didn't change our world.

Jerry Hopkins
Bangkok, Thailand, 2007

# Chapter 1

# TUPELO

Tupelo is the seat of Lee County, one of several poor rural counties in the northeastern corner of Mississippi, about halfway between Memphis and Birmingham, where, roughly, the rich farming soil of the Midwestern prairie meets the harsh brick-colored soil of the Southeast. Oldtown and Mud creeks bisect the town and dozens more vein the rolling countryside, many of them carrying Indian names.

The Indians brought seed corn and introduced farming to the area, and the years passed with only occasional visitors, among them the Spanish explorer Hernando de Soto and the Sieur de Bienville, the French colonial governor who had founded New Orleans and Mobile to the south. Both were run off by the Indians.

In 1801 a treaty was signed between the white man and the Chickasaw, and farmers, mostly Scotch-English, began to till the land. Then in 1832, with the signing of another treaty, the Indians agreed to return to the land of their ancestors, Oklahoma. Now the settlers came in a rush and land prices soared to five dollars an acre. By 1850 the leading community was Harrisburg, named for a prosperous farmer, but when the Mobile and Ohio laid its tracks through the rich bottom land a few miles away, the citizens of Harrisburg deserted the town and built beside the railroad. The new town was called Gum Pond and then Tupelo, from the Chickasaw word *topala*, meaning "lodging place." The tupelo gum trees provided dense foliage that shed water, their leaves were aromatic and possessed healing qualities, and their trunks yielded a chewing gum.

Soon thereafter, the last Civil War battle fought in Mississippi was staged on the Tupelo slopes. Sherman was marching toward Georgia from Tennessee, and he dispatched General Andrew J. Smith and 14,000 Union troops to confront General Nathan Bedford Forrest and 6000 Confederate cavalry who endangered Sherman's flanks. The Southern forces were beaten three times in two days and then the Yankees burned the town to the ground.

Tupelo was rebuilt slowly after the war. It became the seat of Lee County, named for Robert E. Lee. In the years that followed, Tupelo became one of the first communities in the South to diversify its agricultural base, importing what was the nation's first pure-bred Jersey herd to do so. With this development, Carnation erected a huge plant, its first in the South. This, with three textile plants, gave Tupelo needed industry. A few years later, in 1936, Tupelo became the first city in the nation to acquire electrical power from the Tennessee Valley Authority. Back in 1910, Memory E. Leake, who owned a lumberyard, built some of the first houses in the country to be sold on the long-term installment plan. The city's public library bookmobile was Mississippi's first.

Then came the Great Depression, and no matter how progressive Tupelo was, it didn't help. A large part of the economy still was rooted in the rich bottom land surrounding the town, and when orders began to fall off at the textile plants, profits declined and workers were forced into what was called the stretch-out system, whereby they would operate several times as many machines as they'd manned before, with only a minimal increase in pay, or sometimes no raise at all. In Lee County, farmers and part-time farmers and their families supplied most of the labor in local industry. Tupelo was the principal trading center for a five-county rural area, and when jobs became scarce in town, it meant the income of the farm family was cut. And when the plants didn't have orders for clothes, it meant they wanted to buy less cotton, or pay less for it, so again the farmers were hurt. Fully half of the farm families in the Tupelo area were tenant farmers, living on someone else's land, or sharecroppers, sometimes living elsewhere—all working the fields for a share of profits. First the profits disappeared and then the jobs.

Tupelo had fewer than six thousand people when the Depression began, the more prosperous of whom lived in white one-story clapboard homes with green roofs and shutters, or two-story homes faced with red brick. South of Main Street, near the textile plants and cotton mill, was another residential neighborhood, a section of yellow and white four- and five-room plank houses that sat behind sagging wire and wood fences, perched on pilings along unpaved streets. This was Mill Town, or South Tupelo, where all the houses were built by the mill owners and rented to their employees.

The town's business section was on Main Street, which was lined with two- and three-story red brick buildings with stores on the street level and small factories or offices in the upper stories.

Beyond the stores and Mill Town were the tracks of the Mobile and Ohio and the St. Louis and San Francisco (Frisco) railroads, and beyond the tracks lay a section called Shakerag. This is where most of Tupelo's Negro cooks, nurses and house servants lived in weathered shacks.

A quarter mile past Shakerag, on a hilly rise the other side of Mud and

Oldtown creeks, was the small neighboring community of East Tupelo, then separate from the town from which it took its name. It was cut in two parts by the Birmingham highway, with most of the tiny shotgun-style homes and the schoolhouse south of the highway, and only nine houses, one grocery store and the First Assembly of God Church on the other side.

It was on this side of town, literally the poor side of the Tupelo tracks, that there lived a young farm worker named Vernon Elvis Presley and a teenaged sewing machine operator named Gladys Smith.

# Chapter 2

# THE CHILD

Mrs. Faye Harris was Gladys Presley's closest friend in East Tupelo. A widow, she and her sister, Mrs. Tressie Miller (another widow), lived in the same small home on Adams Street for close on half a century. The house was directly across from the First Assembly of God Church and backed up to the bottom land, which flooded fairly regularly, sometimes rising so much that Mrs. Harris's furniture sat more than two feet deep in muddy water.

"There wasn't one thing I knowed Gladys didn't know it too, and the other way around," she said. "Mr. Presley used to kid us about that. He'd come in and say, 'I got somethin' to tell you. Glad'—he called her Glad—'but you'll have to go tell your buddy down the street, won't you?'

"Gladys's parents farmed some. I never did know what they did, but her mother moved near to me when the kids got grown some. Gladys had five sisters and three brothers. It was a big family. And Gladys was the fifth girl. She only had one younger sister and that was Cletis.

"Gladys didn't meet a stranger. She could meet anybody and be ready for a big laugh. When things began to get dull, we said we have to go see Gladys and get cheered up.

"Mr. Presley was more distant. I didn't know him so well. He lived the other direction from me, but close by. He had one brother, Vester, and three sisters. After you knew Mr. Presley, he was friendly, but at first he was a little more distant to folks."

Gladys lived with her parents, brothers and sisters in a house just a little larger, on a corner lot on lower land closer to the church, on Berry Street, two and a half blocks away.

"We all knew each other," said Mrs. Harris. "I remember seeing Mr. Presley. He used to run around with my nephews a lot, sometimes spend the night right here in this house. He was going with other girls at the time. Then he and Gladys got to going together, going in to the roller rink in town or having picnics over to the fish hatchery. The hatchery was one of the nicest places we had in those days, with trees to sit under and a nice lake to look at. They didn't go together too long until they got married. They went down in Verona, about five miles from here. They just run off and did it one day. They sure was a handsome couple—him so blond and her so dark—and both of them happy as kids on the day that school lets out."

Vernon was just seventeen, a minor, so he added five years and said he was twenty-two, while Gladys subtracted two from her to nineteen. The $3 fee they borrowed from friends.

(A few years later, Gladys's younger sister Cletis married Vernon's brother Vester.)

It was 1933. Vernon was seventeen and working a nearby farm with his father, down on the rich land called East Bottom. They were, like most in East Tupelo, hoeing cotton and corn and peas for a share of the season's profits.

Gladys was four years older than Vernon, twenty-one, and worked as a sewing machine operator next to her friend Faye Harris at the Tupelo Garment Company in Mill Town. Each morning at six, the same time her husband began working the fields, she reported for work at her machine. She worked by the piece and she worked twelve hours a day, five or six days a week, and according to Faye Harris, if each of them grossed thirteen dollars for the week, it was a good paycheck. "On top of that," said Mrs. Harris, "the company had a quota you had to meet each day of production, and if you didn't meet it, you were laid off."

On the first floor of the plant a keen-bladed electric knife cut cloth to pattern. The material was then sent upstairs, where it was to be stitched on machines by women operators. Sometimes Gladys moved over to the next most responsible position, that of inspector, and checked all the shirts as they came by for the right number of buttons and buttonholes. Some time later Gladys left the Tupelo Garment Company for Reed's, which occupied the second and third floors of a three-story red brick building nearby and produced women's work dresses, smocks and aprons. There again she ran a sewing machine.

For a time Vernon and Gladys lived with their in-laws, first with the Smiths and then with the Presleys. When Gladys learned she was pregnant, in the summer of 1934, she quit her job at the garment factory. It was, Faye Harris said, "a hard pregnancy and she couldn't work, couldn't work at all." At the time, Vernon was driving a truck, delivering milk from door to door in East Tupelo. His boss was Orville S. Bean, who had a dairy farm a quarter of a mile from where the Presleys lived, and Vernon thought perhaps Mr. Bean could help him get a new house.

"Orville Bean had money and he loant money," said Mrs. Harris. "Mr. Presley went to him and asked him to help him build a house. Him and Gladys wanted a little place of their own now they was raising a family. So he financed the house, then rented it to them. He did that a lot in the neighborhood."

The house was like tens of thousands built in the South in the 1920s and 1930s to house the poor, both black and white. It was in the shotgun-style, oblong with frame side-walls, a peaked roof and a small covered porch. Inside was a brick fireplace, with a chimney running up the middle of the house. It was thirty feet long—just ten man-sized steps from the front door to the rear—and half that in width, divided equally into two perfectly square rooms.

(Years later Elvis wondered aloud in his twenty-three-room mansion in Memphis if the entire place wouldn't fit in the mansion's living room.)

The front room was the bedroom, where there was an iron bedstead with a lumpy mattress. On one side of the bed was the small iron-grated fireplace, on the other the front door. There were three windows, one at the head of the bed, another across the room at the other side of the house, the third facing the porch. Overhead was a single electric outlet. The floors were bare.

The back room, the kitchen-dining room, was where friends and family were entertained. It was furnished with a stove, table, chairs and a cabinet. Again there were the three windows, one overhead outlet and a rear door. There was no running water. Outside there was a pump, some distance from the outhouse.

There were two fair-sized trees in front of the house, another three to one side, a sixth in the back, offering some shade in summer and places for kids to climb. Nearby was a stand of young long-needled pine, and down Old Saltillo Road were some narrow streams and broad pasture land.

The house sat on ground higher than most in East Tupelo, but like all the one-story homes in the neighborhood it rested on tired stumpy legs made of concrete block and brick—protection against flooding and heavy rain. Below the house and off west toward Tupelo the creeks flooded their banks, and behind the house was a severely eroded clay hillside; when it rained, as it often did, mud slid past and underneath the house to the road below.

The second week of January 1935 County Superintendent W. A. Roper left for the state capital to beg emergency relief financing for the county's schools, because if funds weren't forthcoming, classes would have to shut down six months a year instead of the customary three. It was announced that the cannery operated under President Roosevelt's Federal Emergency Relief Act, which had opened only a month earlier, would close within the week, leaving 160 persons unemployed. J. E. Riley, Lee County's head of the Rural Rehabilitation Division, said 146 farm families would be selected from the relief rolls, provided (on a loan basis) with eighteen acres in cotton, corn, hay, feed and food crops, along with a home, water and wood, to help them toward self-sufficiency . . . Reed's department store was having a "gigantic sale" offering women's coats for $3.98 and dress oxfords for $1.47 . . . Francis Lederer, Joan Bennett, Charles Ruggles and Mary Boland were featured at the Strand Theatre in *The Pursuit of Happiness* . . . And Elvis Aron Presley was born.

He was born shortly after noon on January 8.

"They didn't have insurance and the doctor didn't believe in carrying his expectant mothers to the hospital, so Gladys stayed at home," said Mrs. Harris. "All along Gladys told everybody she was going to have twins, but the doctor wasn't having any of it. Elvis was borned, they had done washed him and she said she was still in labor. The doctor said he didn't think so.

"Gladys said, 'Well, it's the same pain.'

"Finally a neighbor said, 'Doctor, there's another baby got to come out of there.'"

The second child was stillborn. ("We matched their names," Mrs. Presley said years later. "Jesse Garon and Elvis Aron.") When Faye Harris came rushing up to the Presley home from work at the garment plant, little Jesse Garon was laid out in a tiny coffin in the front room.

The baby was buried the next day in an unmarked grave on a hillside in the Priceville Cemetery a few miles to the north and east.

Elvis was to be an only child, and he was as spoiled as the meager family budget could afford.

"Gladys thought he was the greatest thing that ever happened and she treated him that way," said Mrs. Harris. "She worshiped that child from the day he was borned to the day she died. She'd always keep him at home, or when she let him go play, she always was out seeing about him, making sure he was all right. And wherever she went, visiting family or down to Roy Martin's grocery store, she always had Elvis with her. She wouldn't go nowheres without Elvis. Elvis'd get out of her sight and you could hear her hollerin' and cryin' and carryin' on to plumb down here, afraid he'd got lost or something."

If Mrs. Presley treated Elvis as a mother bear cossets her only cub, spoiling him, she also gave him a means of earning respect from others, feeding him something that seemed a cross between Emily Post and a rigid sort of Christianity.

"One time he found a Coca-Cola bottle on my porch and he carried it home with him," said Mrs. Harris. "She spanked him and sent him back. He said, 'Miz Harris, I done wrong and my mama whipped me for it, so here's your Coca-Cola bottle back.' I gave it back to him and gave him some cookies besides. He told Gladys, 'Mother, I told you she didn't care if I took it.' And she told Elvis, 'But you didn't ask her first.'"

Elvis himself once said, "My mama never let me out of her sight. I couldn't go down to the creek with the other kids. Sometimes when I was little I used to run off. Mama would whip me, and I thought she didn't love me."

Mrs. Presley was once quoted as saying she tried to teach Elvis and his little friends not to fight but to be happy. She said that once in a while a bully came along and then Elvis's daddy would have to show him how to stand up for himself. She said Elvis won most of the fights.

The Presleys also taught their son to say "sir" and "ma'am," to stand when an elder (Grandma, Uncle Vester, Aunt Delta Mae) entered the room. Not to interrupt or argue. And if you don't have nothing nice to say, don't say nothing at all. So well did they impress the young Elvis with these simple rules that years later, even after he had worked with movie directors and recording executives only a few years older than he was, and they insisted he use their first names, he continued to call them Mr. or Mrs. and to say "yes, sir" and "yes, ma'am," and "please." Elvis was, if nothing else, polite.

And as his parents loved him, he returned their love. Both his parents told stories about how upset he got when his father plunged into a lake to swim or rushed into a burning building to help save a neighbor's furniture. (The home of his Uncle Noah, Aunt Christine and his playmate and cousin Bobby was one of several that burned in East Tupelo, and another fire gutted the church.) His parents said Elvis was afraid of losing his father, that's why he cried so much.

Elvis also cried, years earlier, when in 1938 Vernon, Gladys's brother, and another man entered Mississippi's notorious Parchman Farm to serve three years for forging a check made out to Vernon over his employer Orville Bean's name. The Presleys lost their home and although Vernon was released after only eight months—at Bean's request—it was an incident that marked Vernon and his family for the rest of Elvis's life.

In the 1930s and early 1940, the First Assembly of God Church in Tupelo was a small one-story structure on Adams Street, just a block and a half from where the Presleys lived. It was there Elvis heard his first music.

In later years, Mrs. Presley liked telling a story about Elvis's behavior in church: "When Elvis was just a little fellow, he would slide off my lap, run down the aisle and scramble up to the platform of the church. He would stand looking up at the choir and try to sing with them. He was too little to know the words, of course, but he could carry the tune."

As Elvis grew, he and his parents would sing together at camp meetings, revivals and church conventions, but only as part of the congregation, never as a "popular trio" or in the church choir, as has been reported in several magazines. Nor, apparently, were the Presleys quite the churchgoers legend has it they were. Mrs. Harris, who said she never missed a service (and it's difficult to doubt anything she said), claims the Presleys were "regular but not fanatical; they'd miss a service ever' now and then."

The Assemblies of God churches, founded only twenty-five years earlier, in 1914, were at the time part of the evangelical movement that swept most of the South and Midwest during the roaring twenties and depressing thirties. Like other white Pentecostal church groups (many shared the same basic beliefs but adhered to different founders and names), those who took their prayers to the Assembly of God held a conservative interpretation of the Bible, believing among other things that the wicked would be judged and on dying be consigned to everlasting punishment in the lake which burneth with fire and brimstone. The simple message: Be good or go to hell.

The Sunday services usually opened with song, the Presley family joining the congregation and choir. Behind the altar would be the pastor and his lay associates, dressed much as the congregation in inexpensive but "decent" dress. Later one of the laymen would lead the congregation in silent prayer and likely as not the pastor, sitting quietly to one side, his hands folded in his lap, would begin to speak "in tongues," a phenomenon that purportedly represented direct contact with God as God speaks through the individual in a language unknown to him. Among white Pentecostals the speaking-in-tongues experience has virtually no high emotional content. In contrast with Negro churches of similar stripe, the white congregation remains calm; it is taken as matter-of-factly as the condemnation to hell for wickedness.

Which is not to say the Presley congregation was lethargic. Anything but. During much of the service the mood was formed by the minister, who when not speaking in tongues was praying fervently—providing a noisy lead for those others present who wished to cry aloud, "Praise God . . . thank you, Lord . . . I love you. Lord!"—and stalking the aisle of the church delivering a fire-and-brimstone sermon. During the sermon the pastor's voice rumbled and shook, carrying equal parts of threat and hope. Filling the small plank church in East Tupelo with a flood of words that coiled and uncoiled in measured cadence, exhortations and chastisements that came in a rush, followed by whispers of spiritual ecstasy.

"They was good revivals," said Mrs. Faye Harris. "Lots of people was saved."

Years later, when asked where he got his wiggle, Elvis said, "We used to go to these religious singin's all the time. There were these singers, perfectly fine singers, but nobody responded to them. Then there was the preachers and they cut up all over the place, jumpin' on the piano, movin' ever' which way. The audience liked 'em. I guess I learned from them."

Elvis was not a handsome boy. What is probably the earliest photograph shows him at two or three—huge eyes looking off to the left, a twisted, flattened nose, drooping lips, all round and soft and looking rather like an infant doing an impression of Edward G. Robinson; there's even a hat with a brim, worn a little cockeyed, leaning to Elvis's right.

In another early photograph, taken when he was six, there is no hat and his platinum blond hair is parted as if with a garden hoe, cut close at the sides, a few strands falling over his prominent forehead. His eyes are outsized and heavily lidded, his nose flat and off-center, his thick lips even then twisted in the lopsided leer that later would become world famous.

In both these pictures it was as if his head hadn't yet grown enough to match the prominent features. Dressed in a loose sweater pulled over a cotton shirt, one collar-point in, one out, Elvis looks in the second photograph almost as much the perfect waif as he seemed in the earlier one.

A later picture, taken outside his home with his parents, shows Elvis wearing a white long-sleeved shirt open at the neck, the sleeves about two inches too short, white and brown shoes, suspenders yanking his trousers halfway up his chest. His father is wearing a white shirt, a leather jacket and loose-fitting slacks, his mother a dotted print dress, belted at the waist.

In none of the photographs is anyone smiling.

When Elvis was five, his mother began walking him to class (a practice she would continue through part of his high school days in Memphis) across Highway 78 into the main section of the little town to the simple wooden frame buildings that served as the East Tupelo Consolidated School. All twelve grades were being taught and the school had a high school accreditation, the first high school graduation having been held six years earlier, in 1934, when there were nine teachers and just four students in the senior class. By the time Elvis was in fourth grade there were seven hundred students at East Tupelo and twenty-six teachers.

No one associated with the school system remembers much about Elvis before he was in the fifth grade, when Mrs. Oleta Grimes was his homeroom teacher. She lived less than a hundred yards from the Presleys on Old Saltillo Road and had introduced herself to Gladys when she'd been told they were related distantly.

"He was a good student," said Mrs. Grimes. "You remember if they're not. I knew him that well, I'd remember that. Sweet, that's the word. And average. Sweet and average.

"There were about thirty in each of the homerooms and each morning we'd have chapel," she said. "Devotions. Well, two mornings in a row I asked my children if anybody could say prayer. No one said anything. Then on the third day Elvis put up his hand. He said he could say prayer. And he said prayer and he sang several songs he knew. I remember one of them and it wasn't really right for chapel, but Elvis sang it so sweetly, it liked to make me cry. That was 'Old Shep.' [A popular song recorded by Red Foley about a boy and his dog.] Mr. J. D. Cole was the principal at the time and I asked him to listen to Elvis sing. And Mr. Cole was so impressed he carried Elvis to the Mississippi-Alabama Fair and entered him in the annual contest."

The Mississippi-Alabama Fair and Dairy Show was organized in 1904 as the Lee County Fair and was municipally owned and operated as a non-profit event for the farmers of the area. There were horse shows and cattle auctions and, later, beauty contests at which Miss Mississippi and Miss Alabama were selected for the Miss America Pageant in Atlantic City. In the 1940s, talent contests were held, with local winners coming from the two states to compete for an annual prize. Elvis was ten when Mr. Cole entered him to represent East Tupelo, which was only half a mile from the fairgrounds.

Elvis sang "Old Shep" at that fair, standing on a chair and reaching for the microphone, unaccompanied, because the guitar players present were reluctant to give help to any of the competition. Elvis won second prize—five dollars and free admission to all the amusement rides.

"My husband Clint had a furniture store at the time," said Mrs. Grimes, "and I had Elvis to come by and sing 'Old Shep' for him, because he couldn't get away to see him at the fair. Elvis sang his song and Clint gave him a nickel for a soda.

"I didn't think Elvis'd ever amount to anything, of course."

As Elvis was growing up, his father moved from job to job, leaving the milk delivery route when there weren't customers enough to continue it, working crops in the bottom, sorting lumber and hiring out as an apprentice carpenter at the Leake and Goodlett Lumberyard in Tupelo. Tupelo served as headquarters for eighteen counties in the administration of President Roosevelt's New Deal projects, and so Vernon also found himself doing carpentry for the Works Progress Administration (WPA), eventually becoming a foreman. Whatever he could get he took—like other men during the Depression.

"They moved several times," said Mrs. Harris. "They lived in several houses this side of the highway, on Kelly Street, then on Berry. Later the house on Berry was condemned. They was real poor. They just got by."

At least they ate regularly. The food may not have been the most nutritious, but it was regular. Mrs. Harris said there wasn't much meat, though. "You had to buy your meat," she said. "A few had hogs in the yard, but most had to buy their meat and that was expensive. So we mostly relied on vegetables. Peas, cornbread, okra, tomatoes, lettuce, radishes, boiled corn when we had it, and in the wintertime we'd have dried stuff and canned peaches and apples. We never went real hungry, but we worked at it sometimes."

Times were equally tough on Tupelo. The year Elvis was born, cotton growers were predicting the South's first billion-dollar crop, but if this represented prosperity for some, little of it reached the common man. And the weather, always unpredictable in northern Mississippi, only made matters worse. Often the creeks would flood the bottom land and many of the small homes in East Tupelo. And in 1936 one of history's most deadly tornadoes came whirling out of neighboring Harrisburg into Tupelo, killing two hundred and sixteen, injuring more than a thousand, and destroying nine hundred homes—all in just thirty-two seconds. In East Tupelo, where damage was by contrast minimal, the Presleys watched roofs torn off and walls warped so they'd never settle straight up and down again and there'd always be cracks and leaks.

There were no tornado cellars in East Tupelo. The land was too low and water would have seeped into them. So on the hot dry days when the sky suddenly went black and the woolly stillness of the afternoon air was torn by the cry of wind, Elvis was rushed some distance by his mother to a storm shelter cut in a distant hillside, to wait hours before it seemed safe to leave.

One of those days Vernon was at work and Elvis and his mother were in the shelter alone, singing at first to keep from being so frightened, then talking about the singing Elvis'd been doing and how well he had done at the fair. Elvis told his mother he wanted a bicycle. Mrs. Presley knew this and Mr. Presley had priced bicycles and the fifty-five-dollar tag was too high. So Mrs. Presley asked her son wouldn't he rather have the ($12.95) guitar in the same window with the bike; after all, it would help him with his singing, and maybe later he could have the bike. The way the story goes, Elvis said if he got the guitar, he wouldn't ask for the bicycle again for a year.

In the months following, Elvis taught himself how to play the guitar—with a little help from his uncles, Johnny Smith and Vester Presley, who showed him several chords—and began listening to the radio, trying to copy the sounds he heard. He listened to the popular country music vocalists—Roy Acuff, Ernest Tubb, Ted Daffan, Bob Wills and Jimmie Davis, along with the records of the man generally recognized as the Father of Country Music, Jimmie Rodgers, who had been from Meridian, Mississippi, a hundred or so miles from Tupelo.

He also listened to the blues singers who were from the same neighborhood, Mississippi's cotton bottom, stretching west to the Mississippi River and south to New Orleans—people like Booker (Bukka) White, Big Bill Broonzy, Otis Spann, B. B. King, John Lee Hooker (who wrote a song called "Tupelo Mississippi Flood"), Chester (The Howlin' Wolf) Burnett, Jimmy Reed, Earl Hooker, and McKinley (Muddy Waters) Morganfield. And on Sundays and Wednesdays—Wednesdays being revival days at the First Assembly of God Church—Elvis learned to sing spirituals.

Slowly the style was formed.

"In the afternoons we'd bunch up, go to one house, talk, listen to the radio and entertain ourselves," said Mrs. Harris. "In the spring we went to the woods out behind his house. Me and Gladys would sit and gossip while the kids rolled down the hill. They loved to gather the wild flowers—the dogwood and the honeysuckle. Gladys liked to have flowers in the house."

Just as often Elvis's friends would come over to the Presley house to sit on the hill behind it and listen to Elvis slowly pick out the songs he knew.

Elvis never wanted for friends, company at the house, or people to visit nearby. Besides his school chums, there were the large Presley and Smith families, and elsewhere in the county were *more* relatives—cousins of cousins of cousins and such. Buck Presley was first cousin to Elvis's grandfather, for one example, and he and his wife Alice and their seven sons lived and farmed in Richmond, eight miles away. Buck and his wife and two of his boys, Hershell and J. W., lived in small sparsely furnished homes in Nettleton.

"We would ride over to Tupelo on the school bus," Buck said. "Go to visit Elvis and all—go to shows, fight, everything else. I remember a lot of times we used to jump that fence to go to the fair. We got caught one time and that broke it up. Those guys with the clubs they had around the fence like to scare us to death."

"I remember Elvis used to carry that ol' gi-tar around," said Hershell. "He loved that gi-tar. It didn't have but three strings on it most of the time, but he sure could beat the dickens outa it."

During World War Two, when Elvis was in his first years of school, before he won the fair contest and got his guitar, his father went to work in a munitions plant in Memphis, a hundred miles to the northwest. He came home every weekend he could, and when the war ended he moved back. He had hoped to take his family to Memphis, but the housing was inadequate or unavailable and when the war ended there was no job.

In 1946 the East Tupelo Consolidated School was merged with the Tupelo School District. (The two towns merged in 1948.) This meant that in June 1947 Elvis's school held its last high school graduation ceremonies. From then on the eleventh and twelfth grades were bussed to class in Tupelo.

About the same time, the Presleys moved into town, settling near the Fairgrounds and opposite Shakerag, Tupelo's black ghetto, and Elvis was enrolled at Milam Junior High School. Soon after, in 1948, when Elvis was thirteen, the Presleys left town. "We were broke, man, broke, and we left Tupelo overnight," Elvis said years later. "Dad packed all our belongings in boxes and put them on the top and in the trunk of a 1939 Plymouth. We just headed to Memphis.

"Things had to be better."

# Chapter 3

# HIGH SCHOOL

T hings weren't any better in Memphis, not at first. If anything, they were worse. The living quarters in East Tupelo and Tupelo had never been spacious or especially comfortable, but compared to what they found in Tennessee's largest city (population then about 300,000) they seemed almost palatial.

At first they packed themselves into one room of a large box-like home at 572 Poplar Avenue, a mile from where the Mississippi River flanked the city's business center. It was a once-exclusive neighborhood considered part of North Memphis and, like many just outside the city's commercial core, it was inhabited almost exclusively by the poor. At one time the house may have been elegant, but in 1948 it was cut up into greasy one-room apartments. There were no kitchen facilities and the Presleys shared a bath with three other families. There were sixteen high-ceilinged rooms in the building, providing shelter for no less than sixty individuals. The electrical wiring was a daily threat. Heating was totally inadequate. There were holes in the walls, and wherever there wasn't a hole there was dirt. The Presleys slept, cooked (hauling water from the bathroom, to prepare meals over a hotplate) and ate in the one room. It was not the sort of home you invited your friends to see.

Initially Elvis had no friends. Largely this was because of his reticence, his shyness. A new boy in any neighbourhood undergoes a period of painful adaptation, and when it is a thin, polite country boy from a farm town in Mississippi moving to Memphis, a city he'd only heard about (and might have feared because his father hadn't found work all that easily), the pain became acute, the strangeness and bigness nearly overwhelming. The L. C. Humes High School Elvis was taken to his first week in Memphis, for instance, had more than 1600 students in its six classes (seventh through twelfth), more pupils than there were people in East Tupelo.

Years later Vernon Presley talked about that first day of school, when he took Elvis to class, left him outside the principal's office, and no sooner was he back home than Elvis was back home too. Vernon said Elvis was so nerv-

ous he was bug-eyed, and when he asked what was wrong, Elvis said he was-
n't sure about where things were and there were so many kids . . . he was afraid
the kids would laugh at him.

Elvis returned the following day and slowly he found his way, while his
father worked in a tool company and drove a truck for a wholesale grocer and
his mother sometimes worked in a curtain factory or as a waitress in a downtown cafeteria. The combined Presley family income came to about $35 a week.

No one outside the Presley family recalls much about that first year in
Memphis. Elsie Marmann remembers Elvis was in her eighth-grade music class
and said he really didn't show much promise. "He wasn't in my glee club," she
said, "he didn't have the kind of voice I could use in a glee club." Mrs. Tressie
Miller, who'd followed the Presleys to Memphis from Mississippi to live in the
same house on Poplar Avenue, said there was a big yard in front of the house
and after school Elvis sometimes entertained friends, picking and singing the
songs he knew. Others comment on how serious Elvis was, or how quiet, or
how polite. Everyone said he loved his mother—no, worshiped her. And that's
about it. It would be a year before any of his teachers or classmates knew Elvis
well enough to talk about. And even then, most at Humes seldom if ever really recognized Elvis. All high schools have students who go nearly unnoticed.
Elvis was one of those.

In February 1949, Vernon began working as a laborer at the United Paint
Company, packing cans of house paint into boxes for shipment. United's factory, in a five-story brick building that had been a brewery in pre-Prohibition
times, a cotton warehouse after that, was only a few blocks from where the
Presleys lived. Vernon was paid eighty-three cents an hour, grossing $38.50 on
the good weeks, when he picked up five hours of overtime. He held the job for
five years.

On June 17 the same year, Elvis and his mother had a caller at their one
room—Mrs. Jane Richardson, who was one of two home service advisers
working for the Memphis Housing Authority. The Presleys had applied for
assistance, and Mrs. Richardson was there to determine whether or not they
were qualified.

"They were just poor people," said Mrs. Richardson. "I interviewed Mrs.
Presley and Elvis and at that time I said he was a very nice boy. They seemed
nice and deserving. Those were my remarks from my investigation of their living conditions before they moved into the project."

Her report, which described the Poplar Avenue residence as "infested" and
"in need of major repairs," was submitted. Vernon's salary at United Paint was
checked; it was determined he sent ten dollars a month to his mother in West
Point, Mississippi; it was noted he had a 1937 Pontiac that operated rather fit-

fully; and it was suggested the Presleys be accepted for residence at the Lauderdale Courts, the federally funded housing project in the same neighborhood and near Vernon's work.

Three months later, in May, as Elvis was completing his first year at Humes High, the Presleys moved into a two-bedroom, ground-floor apartment in the Lauderdale Courts at 185 Winchester Street.

The red brick project was one of several constructed in the mid-thirties by the federal government, and it had been operated since that time by the city. It was designed for low-income families, and rent traditionally had been adjusted to how much the individual family could afford to pay. The Presleys were asked to pay thirty-five dollars a month initially.

"Most of the people who lived here came from slum areas, substandard housing," said Mrs. Richardson. "That was the requirement then that we'd move them in here. Our slogan was 'From slums to public housing to private ownership.' And we have had a number of people who have lived here who have saved enough to make a down payment on a small home."

There was a quiet anguish hovering over the dry grass lawns, the harsh symmetrical walks and anonymous brick buildings. The 433 units in the project—some in one-story structures with wrought iron trim, others in three-story monoliths—were kept as neatly as the housing authority insisted, but money for individual comfort and decoration was scarce. The Presleys lived in one of the monoliths, and across the street were grey leaning shacks housing some of the city's poorest blacks, a drugstore and a beer parlor, and beyond that the United Paint Company and St. Joseph's Hospital. A half mile to the south was dark and scabrous Beale Street, the legendary home of the blues. The Lauderdale Courts had been open just eleven years and the housing was better than adequate, but the neighborhood was not the best.

The first day in the apartment Vernon filled out a report describing the condition of the living room, two bedrooms, a separate kitchen and private bath. Carefully making check marks on the form and adding his comment in a neat, legible hand in pencil, he wrote, "Wall around bath tub need repair . . . apartment in need of paint job . . . one shade will not roll in bed room . . . light in front hall will not stay on . . . oven door will not shut tight . . . one leg [of dresser] broke off . . . bathroom sink stopped up . . . faucet in kitchen sink needs repairs."

Still, it was a decided step up from the place on Poplar. From slum to public housing. The Presleys lived in the project apartment three and a half years, and during that time Mrs. Richardson or someone else from the Housing Authority came through two or three times a year to see how the linoleum and woodwork were holding up, as well as to check on income and other meager facts of life. It was noted by Mrs. Richardson in the first home service report, made Thanksgiving week of 1949, that the Presley car had given out, that there was no telephone in the apartment, and that Vernon remained at United Paint with an estimated annual income of $2080.

Even with Elvis in high school now, his parents continued to coddle him. "They treated him like he was two years old," said Mrs. Ruby Black, the mother of the late Bill Black, who played bass for Elvis's first records and concerts. "Mrs. Presley talked about her twin babies and she just lived for Elvis. Years later he called her every night when he was touring and Mrs. Presley couldn't go to sleep until she'd heard from him." Elvis himself once recalled that his mother walked him to school until he was fifteen.

"That only happened some of the time," said Evan (Buzzy) Forbess, one of Elvis's closest friends at Humes. "Most of the time he went with us."

Buzzy lived with his sisters and mother in the same building the Presleys lived in. His father had run off with a waitress soon after he was born, and since that time his mother had been working in a curtain factory. It was, in fact, Mrs. Forbess who got Gladys her job sewing curtains. Buzzy was a year behind Elvis, but for four years they were practically inseparable.

"It was a lower poverty-type school, one of the lowest in Memphis," said Buzzy. "I wouldn't have taken much for that school and I don't think Elvis would've, either. He said so several times. In that neighborhood the fact that Elvis got through without getting into serious trouble was an accomplishment."

Buzzy talked about the fights Elvis was in. He tells about how there was a scrap after a football game and Elvis was one who "jumped a rope and joined right in." When Elvis was in the tenth grade and someone from the opposing team cussed out Humes's coach from a parked school bus, and Elvis "threw his bony ol' arm up there, right through the open window of the bus, and clipped that boy on the nose, and that ended it."

Buzzy said football was Elvis's consuming interest. One time, he said he and Elvis and some others went over to the waterworks to play ball with a bunch of "nigras." "Man, they had the craziest way of snapping the ball," Buzzy said. "We were used to numbers, like four, thirty, eighteen, five, snap! And the center would hike the ball to the quarterback. With this colored team the center would bend over the ball and the quarterback would start shouting something like 'Beans, maters, taters . . .' They'd be hollering vegetables and we'd be falling down laughing. We'd still be on our fannies laughing and they'd've scored a touchdown."

For a year Elvis played ball for the Humes High Tigers. "He went out in the eleventh grade and made the team all right," said Buzzy. "He didn't play in twelfth grade, but eleventh, junior year, he did. He was a little small and not used to organized ball, but he never shied away from sticking his nose in. He played end. He played a few games of the ten or so we had that year. He didn't score any touchdowns. He usually played defense. He did score a lot in sandlot games. He had real good hands and he was fast. But he was just too small for organized ball games."

Bobby (Red) West was another high school friend. He was a year ahead of Elvis at Humes and lived in another, nearby government housing project, Hurt Village. Like Buzzy, Red was a varsity regular on the football team. "Elvis had his hair real long in those days," Red said. "He was the only guy. The rest of us had crew cuts. I remember once when all the guys were gonna get him and cut his hair. I helped him escape from that. He had trouble with his hair when he was playing ball. He just played one year and the coach told him to cut his hair or get off the team. That's about what it boiled down to. He wore the loud clothes, the pink and black. He was just different. It gave the people something to do, to bother him."

Elvis once said he had to let his hair and sideburns grow to look like a truck driver, to make him seem older. He never really talked much about why he dressed so loudly; it was merely something he did.

"I would see them leave every Sunday morning for church," said Buzzy Forbess's mother. "He was so cute. One Sunday he'd have a pink pair of pants on and a dark coat. Next Sunday it'd be the dark pants and the pink coat."

Down on Beale Street, at the corner of Second Street, there was a men's clothing store owned by the Lansky Brothers, who specialized in selling vibrant yellow suits and pink sport coats with black lightning streaks, white shoes, and glittery men's accessories. Whenever the country musicians came to Memphis from Nashville, this was one of the stops they made. It also was a favorite of the blacks who lived in the neighborhood. Elvis seldom had much money to spend on clothing, but whenever he did, it was spent there.

Through football, his hair style and manner of dress, Elvis was developing an identity, slowly building a confidence, a sense of personal security. Yet he remained shy, and oddly enough it was his music about which he was most reticent.

Elvis wasn't reluctant to sing for his friends, picking out the few basic chords he knew on the guitar, but when it came to performing in front of anyone else, he backed down. Buzzy Forbess said, "He and I had biology together and it came time for a Christmas party. Elvis was in the tenth grade and we wanted to get Elvis to sing. He was scared to death and he left his guitar behind on purpose, so he could say he couldn't sing."

Another classmate, Mona Raburn Finley, once said that when Elvis did bring his guitar to school, she and her friends sometimes would beg him for an hour to sing, then when he started, the bell would ring and class would be over.

Not until Mildred Scrivener, a history teacher at Humes High, put Elvis in the school's variety show did he begin to walk away from his timidity.

"I never knew Elvis could sing until someone in my class said Elvis should bring his guitar to our homeroom picnic," she said. "Elvis did bring his guitar, and while everybody else was running around doing what young people do, Elvis sat quietly by himself playing and singing to the few who gathered around him. Slowly, other students began to come to him. There was something about his plaintive singing which drew them like a magnet."

Miss Scrivener was Elvis's homeroom teacher in his senior year, and when the school's 1600 students crammed the auditorium for the variety show, Elvis was on the program. The show was held to raise money for a special school fund and no one would dare miss it. Most pupils at Humes were from poor homes, and if ever a boy or girl couldn't afford to attend a dance, or lacked money enough for lunch or clothing, he or she had a quiet talk with Tom Brindley, the school's principal, who would pull enough money from the fund, and no one was the wiser.

"There were three teachers in charge of the show," Miss Scrivener said, "and I was the one appointed to be producer. That meant I was the one to make up the program. The year when Elvis performed, I remember there were more than thirty acts—nearly more acts than there was time to show them properly. And what about encores? When a student did well, he or she was entitled to an encore. I solved that problem by calling everyone together and saying we just didn't have as many minutes, so there would be only one encore—the person who got the most applause could go out again at the end of the show.

"The tension was there that night, more than ever before. As the students finished their little act—singing or dancing or playing the piano or doing a recitation—they'd come off stage and say, 'Boy, was I lousy!' and another student would say, 'No, you were the most.' But a teacher knows her students and I could tell—every one of them was hoping to be the one to get the encore. You know who got it. Elvis was standing at the edge of the stage, half hidden by the curtain, when I told him, 'It's you, Elvis. Go on out there and sing another song.'

"I'll never forget the look on his face when he came off the stage from doing the encore. 'They really liked me. Miss Scrivener,' he said. 'They really liked me.'"

"One of my sisters had given me a red flannel shirt and he liked it, so I let him wear it for the show," said his friend Buzzy. "He sang a love song first and the teachers started to cry. Really. They just started to boo-hooing. He sang a couple of songs more and about the third one he dedicated it to me. I wondered why. Afterward he gave me my shirt back and he showed me where he had made a little tear in it, closing it in a car door. He was buttering me up by dedicating the song to me."

Buzzy said the only other times Elvis performed "publicly" for strangers was when he joined the Odd Fellows' local boys' club, which urged its members to participate in charitable activities in exchange for the use of game and meeting rooms. Buzzy was a member, he said, and he would do a little improvisational dancing and fooling around while Elvis played his guitar and sang when they visited the patients at the Memphis Veterans Hospital.

In November 1950 one of the home service reports shows that Elvis was working as an usher at Loew's State Theater downtown from five to ten each night at $12.75 a week. It was a job he quit soon thereafter because he was falling behind in his studies. He resumed it the following summer, only to be fired. Arthur Groom, the theater manager, said the girl who sold candy and popcorn in the lobby was slipping Elvis some stuff on the side and the other usher snitched on Elvis, so Elvis took a punch at him and Elvis was canned.

His next job was working a full shift, from three in the afternoon until eleven-thirty at night, at the Marl Metal Products Company. He began to fall asleep in class—something Miss Scrivener said she overlooked, knowing the circumstances. "That's too much for any young boy," Gladys said a few years later. "It got so hard on him—he was so beat all the time—we made him quit, and I went to work at St. Joseph's Hospital."

The home service report of June 19, 1951, shows Vernon had received a $10-a-week raise to $48.50, counting the five hours of overtime. And the rent was bumped accordingly, seven more dollars to forty-three. It was the next report, filed in December, that included Mrs. Presley's income as a nurse's aide, and although this was only four dollars a day, it proved to be a problem. The Housing Authority worked on annual income figures, not daily or weekly figures, so when her projected yearly income came to $1248 and this was added to her husband's yearly sum, the total exceeded the maximum permitted by the city.

. "Have had illness in family, wife is working to help pay out of debt. Bills pressing—and don't want to be sued," were the words on another report filed in December in an attempt to explain why Mrs. Presley had taken a job. The illness was Vernon's; he'd hurt his back at work and the medical costs were piling up. It didn't matter. Still the projected family income was beyond the $3000 ceiling. That meant the Presleys had to be evicted.

A short time later Mrs. Presley quit work at the hospital, the Presley income was re-examined and the eviction notice was withdrawn.

However strapped the Presleys were economically, still there seemed to be enough in the family budget to keep Elvis reasonably content. "His parents gave him money for a push lawn mower," said Buzzy, "and Elvis paid them back out of his earnings. We usually mowed just enough to get the money for what we wanted—movies, carnivals and so on. Except for those two jobs he had, he didn't work too much. His parents provided well enough, considering how poor they were." Buzzy scoffed at a story about Elvis once selling a pint of his blood. "He didn't need to," he said. "He never had a need for money. He didn't need much and if he did, his parents took care of him. Any story you hear like that, stack it up against the Lincoln Coupe they bought him. It was an old car, but that's how good his parents were to him. His father used the car too, of course, but really it was bought for him."

Mr. Presley once told a story about Elvis and that car, which was then more than ten years old. It was a hot summer night and residents of the project gathered outside to sit on porches and under the scattered trees, looking for some cool breeze and friendly gossip. "That ol' car sure could eat gas and I suppose Elvis was worried I'd not have enough to get to work," Vernon said. "So he come running up yelling, 'Hi, Dad. I put fifteen cents' worth of gasoline into the car.' Everyone laughed and he like to died of embarrassment."

The Presleys were like family to Buzzy. "One time I hurt my arm," he said. "I fell on concrete playing basketball and a little later I was at Elvis's house, my arm all bruised. Tears come to Mrs. Presley's eyes when she saw my arm. She was a soft-hearted woman, that's all she was."

Sometimes, Buzzy said, usually on Friday or Saturday nights, the Presleys walked to a movie theater in the neighborhood, the Suzore No. 2, turning the apartment over to Elvis and Buzzy for a party. "They weren't noisy parties, nothing like that," said Buzzy. "Instead of records, Elvis would play and sing, but it wasn't noisy." (Mrs. Richardson said that only once did someone have to run over and tell Elvis that the tenants were beginning to complain, so he'd have to play and sing more quietly.) "Elvis was always doing that at parties and so we learned to dance before he did. We were conforming to the dances of the time. The bop was big—and slow dances. This was right after the jitterbug went out. Elvis had his own movements, of course, and eventually we all came around to his way. I remember seeing him in front of a jukebox one time, listening to the record and imitating playing a guitar and doing those moves. Another time we went to a party and there was a piano there. He started fooling around and the first thing you know he was beating out a song. He never had any training, on the piano or the guitar, so far as I know. He picked it up by ear. He had the feel for it.

"He dated pretty good. He liked to date. He wasn't the sort to just walk up and ask for dates right off, though. And the girls he did go out with, they were pretty affectionate; they really cared for him. At parties he'd be there. He wasn't that shy. And if we talked him into being the life of the party, he'd be that. He wouldn't let a party drag on."

On most dates, Buzzy said, they doubled and went to movies or to local carnivals to throw balls at milk bottles and ride the rides. "I remember one time we were gonna rent a truck for a hayride," he said. "We all chipped in fifty cents apiece but we were a little short. So Elvis went down to the record store next to the Suzore and made an announcement that we were having a hayride and we had a truck outside. Pretty soon we had a truck full and enough money to pay for it."

Friday and Saturday nights when Elvis didn't have a date, usually he'd see a movie with some of the guys from the neighborhood. The Suzore No. 2 was one of those large old theaters found in poorer Southern neighborhoods in the 1950s—two ancient heaters huffing and puffing to keep things barely tolerable in winter, two creaky fans for the blistering summer heat, and the roof leaked. Buzzy said Elvis tried to see at least one movie a week and that he liked Tony Curtis best. At the time, Curtis was becoming a favorite with the teenagers, usually appearing in swashbucklers and adventure flicks.

In school Elvis liked shop and ROTC the best, although that was where Red West said he suffered some of the roughest harassment concerning his clothes and hair. In shop Elvis made a cutting board and a salad bowl for his mother. And so much did he like ROTC, that after he had made some money from his first records, he returned to Humes High (something he did often the first few years) and spent $900 on uniforms for the school's ROTC drill team. One of the few pictures taken at the time, in fact, shows him standing proudly in his khaki uniform, overseas cap at a cocky angle on his blond head, and under that a lopsided grin.

In the Humes High yearbook, *The Herald*, for 1953, there is only one picture of Elvis, showing him in a dark coat, a white shirt, a light tie, acne, prominent sideburns, hair long at the sides and slicked back into a classic ducktail, the top pompadoured and swirled and stacked just so, a spit curl hanging over his forehead. Next to the picture it said:

> PRESLEY, ELVIS ARON
> Major: Shop, History, English
> Activities: R.O.T.C., Biology Club,
> English Club, History Club, Speech Club.

The only other mention of Elvis in the book is in the class will, where it said, "Donald Williams, Raymond McCraig and Elvis Presley leave hoping there will be some one to take their places as 'teachers' pets'??????" (Buzzy said he has no idea what that means, unless it's a reference to Elvis's making the teachers cry when he sang.) He was not voted most popular, most talented, most charming, most outstanding, or most likely to succeed. He was not voted most anything.

"He was like the rest of us," said Buzzy. "He wasn't an A student because he didn't want to be. He was plenty smart enough, but I don't remember many times where we'd carry books home. We all passed with Bs and Cs, that's all."

Vernon's salary continued to creep upward, but it never was enough. In the spring of 1952, the Presleys fell behind in their rent and utilities and they received a notice from the Housing Authority that they were delinquent in the amount of $43.74, and a fine of a dollar a day was being imposed, effective immediately.

In August the same year a report filed by United Paint Company showed Vernon was earning an average of $53.22 a week, and a week after that Vernon filed a report with the Housing Authority saying it wasn't true, he didn't average that much.

In November Gladys returned to St. Joseph's Hospital as a nurse's aide, the family income again passed the maximum allowed, and once more the Presleys received a letter of eviction. They were told they had until February 28, 1953, to get out.

The Presleys spent the Christmas and New Year's holidays in the project and on January 7, the day before Elvis's eighteenth birthday, moved into a small apartment at 398 Cypress Street, closer to the center of the city. It was a seven-room house that had been cut into four apartments. It didn't look much better than the room they lived in on Poplar Avenue. And it cost them $52 a month.

On June 3, 1953, in a ceremony in the city's Ellis Auditorium, where all local high school graduations were held, Elvis was given his diploma. A few days later, he joined several of his classmates in asking the Tennessee employment authority to help him find work.

# Chapter 4

# SUNRISE

That summer, Elvis worked first at the M. B. Parker Machinists' Shop and then at the Precision Tool Company, factory jobs that were as forgettable as the work was tedious. More important to Elvis was his meeting Dixie Locke. She was three years younger than Elvis, a sophomore in high school, when they met at the Assembly of God Church on McLemore in South Memphis.

"He was just so different, all the other guys were like replicas of their dads," Dixie told Peter Guralnick for his Elvis biography, *Last Train to Memphis*. "To watch him, you would think, even then, he was really shy. What was so strange was that he would do anything to call attention to himself, but I really think he was doing it to prove something to himself more than to the people around him. Inside, even then, I think he knew that he was different. I knew the first time I met him that he was not like other people."

An evening followed at the Rainbow Rollerdrome, a popular weekend hangout for Memphis teenagers, and sooner than both expected, they took each other home to meet the parents, who naturally disapproved. She was too young and he had all that hair and wore bolero shirts and pegged pants with a strip down the side. Yet there was no stopping it. In the evenings and on weekends they were inseparable. They went to church together, they babysat Dixie's cousins together, they went to movies and the all-night gospel shows at Ellis Auditorium, double-dated with Elvis's cousin Gene Smith (who was going with Dixie's sister Juanita), and according to Dixie, Elvis poured his heart out, talking as she suspected he'd never talked to another friend, telling her that what he wanted most in the world was to sing. They also talked about running off to Mississippi and getting married.

About the same time, Elvis was sent for an interview at the Crown Electric Company, an electrical contracting firm that wired churches, schools, industrial plants, shops and residences. There were forty-five electricians on the payroll then and Elvis was hired to run materials out to the jobs in a truck and sometimes helped keep stock in the warehouse. He made $1.25 an hour. After taxes it worked out to about $41 a week. He took out a little for gas for the old car his family had bought, plus enough for movies with Dixie, a little more for food, and gave the rest to his father, unemployed now with a bad back.

The job was a good one for Elvis, for then Crown was situated in a two-story stucco building at 353 Poplar Avenue, hiking distance from the apartment on Cypress where the Presleys now lived—only a block from their original Memphis home and three from the Lauderdale Courts, so Elvis was close to friends. Elvis usually *did* walk to Crown, checking in about eight in the morning. The working owners, James and Gladys Tipler, remembered how he first came to them.

"We called Tennessee unemployment," said Mrs. Tipler, "and when I talked to the lady, she told me she had a very nice boy, but not to be—these were exactly the words she used—don't be fooled by his appearance. And when he walked in and I seen him, if she hadn't-a said that, I think I would-a told him to take to the door. Because I mean his hair was long! Even though he was a clean-cut-lookin' kid, I just wasn't used to that."

Mr. Tipler added, "Elvis used to like that hair. He'd wear it way back there! He'd come back from a run in the truck, and he'd go right to a mirror to comb his hair. Wouldn't be a time when he didn't do that, combing the hair just so."

"He was neat in appearance," said Mrs. Tipler. "Even if I wasn't used to that long hair, you know. Now it wouldn't make any difference."

Mr. Tipler kidded his wife: "You made his appointments for him to go to the beauty shop!" Then, confidentially, joshing her: "She made all his appointments for him to get his hair fixed. He went to the beautician, you know, to get his hair trimmed. He didn't go to a reg'lar barber. He was way ahead of those other fellas, even way back yonder."

Elvis was Crown's youngest employee, and as such he came in for some good-natured kidding from some of the older electricians. "They used to play jokes on him," said Mrs. Tipler. "He came in from a job one day, I'll never forget it. He came in and he said, 'Miz Tipler, I have to have some sky hooks.' Him and I both looked in that warehouse I don't know how long for some sky hooks, until Tip come in and I said, 'Tip, they need some sky hooks out at East School,' and Tip laughed at us both and he said, 'How crazy can you be? You don't put any hooks in the sky.'

"Sometimes when he'd come in, he was supposed to be here earlier. This one day he had already blew a tire out on the truck. Instead of stoppin', he drove on in with it like that. And he had that ol' gi-tar of his and I said, 'Elvis, put down that gi-tar.' I said, 'It's gonna be the ruination of you. You better make up your mind what you're gonna do.' And he laughed at me."

The truck Elvis drove was a Ford pickup with a carry-back for equipment, and sometimes on his way to pick up or deliver supplies he'd pass the Memphis Recording Service, a small but lucrative sideline to the Sun Record Company, both of which had been founded and were being operated by Sam Phillips.

At the time, Sun was being run as an independent production company, and Sam was selling and leasing his tapes to other companies, operating on a profit margin thinner than the aluminum discs he used to make the master records. The Memphis Recording Service provided added income by recording bar mitzvahs and weddings and making off-the-air transcriptions for local radio stations and personal records for the walk-in trade. Elvis had known about this service—make your own record, two songs for four dollars—and when he had the money saved, he parked the truck in the neighborhood during a lunch hour and went in. Running the office that day was Marion Keisker, a gregarious woman in her thirties who had been a local radio personality since childhood. She recently had retired as "Miss Radio of Memphis" to serve as Sam's office manager.

"It was a Saturday afternoon, a busy, busy afternoon, and for some reason I happened to be alone in the office," she said. "The office was full of people wanting to make personal records. It was a stand-and-wait-your-turn sort of thing. He came in, said he wanted to make a record. I told him he'd have to wait and he said okay. He sat down. Of course he had his guitar. They all had their guitars in those days.

"While he was waiting his turn, we had a conversation I had reason to remember for many years afterward, because later I had to tell the story so often. He said he was a singer. I said, 'What kind of a singer are you?' He said, 'I sing all kinds.' I said, 'Who do you sound like?' He said, 'I don't sound like nobody,' I thought, Oh yeah, one of those. I said, 'Hillbilly?' He said, 'Yeah, I sing hillbilly.' I said, 'Who do you sound like in hillbilly?' He said, 'I don't sound like nobody.'"

The Ink Spots were among Elvis's favorite singers in 1953 and it was one of their songs, "My Happiness," that Elvis had decided he wanted on a record as a present for his mother. The second song was "That's When Your Heartaches Begin," a weepy ballad that was part recitation. On both songs he accompanied himself on his battered guitar, sounding, he said years later, like "somebody beating on a bucket lid."

Marion Keisker remembered, "When we went back to make the record, a ten-inch acetate, he got about halfway through the first side and I thought, I want to tape this.

"Now this is something we never did, but I wanted Sam to hear this. He was out at the time and the only thing I could find was a crumply piece of tape and by the time I got it set up, I'd missed part of the first song. I got maybe the last third of it and all the second song. I don't even know if Elvis knew I was taping it."

In explaining why she made a tape copy, Marion told something about Sam Phillips that Sam himself never told—and explained part of the motivation for Sun Records. First, she said, you had to understand Sam's background.

Sam was raised on his father's Alabama plantation, she said, where Uncle Silas Payne, a black, held him on his knee and sang the blues to him. In school Sam learned how to play the sousaphone and drums, and following college he became a radio announcer, moving to Memphis, where he coordinated the broadcast of orchestra music from one of the city's hotels. He was making $150 a week and had a wife and two young sons when he quit to open his own studio. Marion said the music Sam had been programming bored him.

"It seemed to me that the Negroes were the only ones who had any freshness left in their music," Sam himself once said, "and there was no place in the South they could go to record. The nearest place where they made so-called 'race' records—which was soon to be called 'rhythm and blues'—was Chicago, and most of them didn't have the money or time to make the trip to Chicago."

Memphis long had been of major importance in the history of the blues. It was the world's leading cotton marketplace, serving the rich broad Mississippi delta country to the south, and for years had been a magnet to the bluesmen of the cotton country. Many blacks settled on and around Beale Street—only a few blocks from Sam's studio—to pick and sing in back rooms and local beer parlors.

In the first years of Sam's independence, from 1951 to 1953, he recorded several of the finest singers in Memphis—Bobby Bland, Jackie Brenston (whose "Rocket 88" was a hit in the Negro market and was covered a year later by Bill Haley and the Comets), Chester (The Howlin' Wolf) Burnett, and Doc Ross—peddling the aluminum masters to Chess and Checker Records in Chicago. He recorded Joe Hill Louis, B. B. King and Big Walter Horton and sold their songs to Modem and RPM Records, small blues labels in Los Angeles.

Then in 1953, before Elvis walked in to make his four-dollar record, Sam began issuing the first 78-rpm records to carry the bright yellow and orange Sun label. He released two regional hits, "Love My Baby" by Little Junior Parker and "Just Walking in the Rain" by the Prisonaires, the latter being a group formed when its members were in the Tennessee State Penitentiary. (The song later was a hit for Johnny Ray.) None of the artists Sam recorded ever had been recorded before; he took pride in being first.

All of which brings us back to Marion Keisker and Elvis Presley. She said, "The reason I taped Elvis was this: Over and over I remember Sam saying, 'If

I could find a white man who had the Negro sound and the Negro feel, I could make a billion dollars.' This is what I heard in Elvis, this . . . what I guess they now call 'soul,' this Negro sound. So I taped it. I wanted Sam to know."

Marion said that when Sam returned, she fed the crumpled tape through the studio's one-track recording system. Sam said he was impressed, but the boy needed a lot of work. He asked her if she'd written down his name and address. She said yes and showed him the slip of paper on which she'd written "Elvis Pressley [sic]. Good ballad singer. Hold." The address showed he was living at 462 Alabama Street, a modest two-story brick home set back from the street and flanking the Lauderdale Courts. The telephone number was that of a friend on the same block who'd come and get him if anyone ever called.

Months passed and on January 4, 1954, a Friday, Elvis visited the Memphis Recording Service a second time, when Marion was out and Sam was in. Elvis told Sam his name and asked if Marion had mentioned him. Sam said yes, Marion had spoken highly of him and yes, he liked the tape she had made and he hoped Elvis was getting along tolerably, but no matter how much he wanted to do something, he just couldn't, not right away. Sam was a gentle, charming man, somewhat absent-minded but usually sensitive in his contact with the public. Elvis shuffled nervously, ran his hands through his hair and said he wanted to cut another four-dollar record. Sam nodded and Elvis made his second "demo," pairing Joni James's "I'll Never Stand in Your Way," and an old Jimmy Wakely tune, "It Wouldn't Be the Same Without You." According to Marion, Sam was equally impressed by Elvis and he, too, noted his name and a phone number in the cluttered files. And he told Elvis he'd call.

Often during his lunch break while at Crown, Elvis would run past one of the local radio stations, WMPS, to watch the live broadcast of the *High Noon Roundup*. Country artists were featured on the first half of the hour-long program, the Blackwood Brothers Quartet and other gospel groups on the second half. The show's master of ceremonies was Bob Neal, a disc jockey with a deep, deep voice who would become Elvis's personal manager; but that was more than a year away.

About the same time, Elvis almost joined one of the Blackwood family's vocal groups. The leader of the quartet, James Blackwood, told the story: "When Elvis was eighteen, when he was driving the truck, my nephew Cecil and three other boys had a gospel quartet they called the Songfellows. They thought one of the boys was gonna leave, and so Elvis auditioned and he would-a joined them in singing around the Memphis area, except the other boy changed his mind. That finished it, and I think Elvis was disappointed, but he still sang with the boys from time to time during rehearsals. And he often came to our all-night gospel sings at the auditorium."

At the all-night sings, a tradition in the South, Elvis sometimes got up and sang spirituals as a solo vocalist. With the Blackwoods backing him harmonically, and singing the songs he loved best, he seemed to find unusual confidence. James Blackwood said Elvis kept his eyes closed most of the time when he sang. He also said Elvis moved his hips in a manner not totally suited to spirituals, but he wrote it off to enthusiasm.

"Elvis liked to sing, you could see that," he said. "Singing came natural to Elvis, all right."

Marion Keisker said of this period: "Every time a song came up, I'd say to Sam, 'How about the kid with the sideburns? Why don't we give him a chance?' And Sam'd say, 'I'm afraid he's not ready yet' or 'How do we get in touch with him?' and by the time I'd say, 'Here's the number,' Sam'd be into something else again. Well, this little game went on and on."

Then one day—in 1954, approximately eight months after Elvis had first visited the Memphis Recording Service—Sam got a demonstration record he liked, a dub that had been made in Nashville. For most of a day Sam had been on the telephone trying to learn who the singer was, because he wanted to get permission to release the dub as is.

"It was a single voice with a single guitar, a simple lovely ballad," said Marion. "Sam couldn't find out who the singer was, he was told it was just a Negro kid hanging around the studio when the song came in, and so he said, 'If I can't find him, I'll have to find somebody else, because I want to release the song.' I told Sam, 'What about the kid with the sideburns?'

"Sam said, 'Oh, I don't know how to get in touch with him. I've even forgotten his name.' I said, 'I just have the card right here.' I pulled out my little piece of paper. Again it was a Saturday afternoon, and Sam said, 'If you can get him over here . . .' So I called and they went up the street and called Elvis to the phone. It was like 'Mr. DeMille will see you now.' I was still standing there with the telephone in my hand and here comes Elvis, panting. I think he ran all the way."

Sam played the dub for Elvis. It was called "Without You." Elvis tried it and was awful. He tried it again and again, and there was minimal, if any, improvement.

"We were taking a break," said Marion, "and Sam said, 'What can you do?' Elvis said, 'I can do anything.' Sam said, 'Do it.' So he started playing, just snatches of anything he knew—religious, gospel, western, everything. Real heavy on the Dean Martin stuff. Apparently he'd decided, if he was going to sound like anybody, it was gonna be Dean Martin. We stayed there I don't know how many hours, talking and playing. Elvis said he was looking for a band. Sam said maybe he could help him, he wasn't sure."

What Sam did next was call Scotty Moore, a twenty-one-year-old guitar player who'd come to Memphis from the armed forces two years earlier to work in his brother's dry cleaning plant and organize a hillbilly band called the Starlight Wranglers. Scotty was thin, boyish and enthusiastic, willing to fit into any slot offered him, so long as he could play his guitar and be with people he liked. In later years Sam Phillips, and many others, would say it was Scotty more than anyone who provided and/or influenced much of the "Elvis Presley sound," that Scotty was the Great Unsung Hero in Elvis Presley's life.

Scotty recalls, "We were playing several honky-tonks around town and I went in to see Sam, realizing that anybody had to have a record to get any-where. We became close. In fact, Sam was lookin' for somebody that was willing to work, so we more or less donated the band. He did put out a record on ourselves, I guess he probably pressed fifty, maybe a hundred copies. We sure didn't sell any more than that."

Scotty laughed when he recalled his inauspicious start. "We tried backing up different people," he said. "I can't remember any names now. Everybody in the band had daytime jobs and were doing this on the side. The job I had got through about two in the afternoon and I'd go down and Sam and I would go next door to Miss Taylor's restaurant, sit there and drink coffee for a couple hours, you know . . . discuss what could we do, do this, do that, and so forth. Finally he mentioned Elvis's name."

Sam told Scotty who Elvis was and said he might have some potential. "I said, 'Well, call him. Let's get him in and work with him,'" said Scotty. "Every day for two solid weeks I'd go down there in the afternoon and talk with Sam. I'd say, 'Did you call this guy? Did you call Elvis?' Because Elvis sounded like a name outa science fiction. And he'd say, 'No, no, I haven't done it yet.' I think Marion heard us talking and she finally went and dug through the files, pulled out his card and said, 'Here, call!'"

Sam said no, he didn't want to make a big thing of it and suggested Scotty telephone, maybe make a date for the weekend, listen to the kid on his own ground, or maybe at Scotty's house, and report back with what he thought. Scotty said okay and he called Elvis early Saturday night, identifying himself as "Scotty Moore of Sun Records." Elvis was at a movie, his mother said, but she'd go get him. Elvis then called Scotty and they made plans to get together at Scotty's house the following afternoon.

Elvis was wearing pink slacks, a pink shirt and white buck shoes, the way Scotty remembers it, and after the initial awkwardness had passed, Elvis and Scotty began playing their guitars, with Elvis singing several songs recently popularized by Eddy Arnold and Hank Snow, two established country artists, and Billy Eckstine, one of Elvis's favorite popular black artists. Bill Black, a bass player who lived just three doors away from Scotty, wandered in about halfway through the two-hour session and after listening for a short time wandered out again, returning after Elvis had left.

"I said, 'Well, what did you think?' Bill said, 'Well, he didn't impress me too damned much.' You know—snotty-nosed kid come in here with the wild clothes. We didn't think much about it at all. So I called Sam Sunday afternoon, I told him, 'Well, the boy's got a good voice . . .' I told him the songs that Elvis did and I said, 'He didn't do them any better than the originals did.' And so forth. Sam said, 'Well, tell you what. I'll call him and we'll set up an audition for tomorrow night, Monday night. We won't bring the whole band in, the hillybilly group with the steel guitar, the whole thing.' He said, 'Just you and Bill come over, something for a little rhythm. We'll put down a few things and we'll see what he sounds like coming back off the tape recorder.' I said okay."

What followed was not a simple audition but several months of hard work. No one seems to remember precisely how many months. Almost every day, after they finished work, Bill and Scotty and Elvis met in the small Sun studio to rehearse, to (quoting Marion) "develop a style." Elvis appeared with Scotty's full band in a local club a few times, but Sam said he didn't sound right with that much instrumentation behind him.

"Mostly I think they were coming in every afternoon to please Sam," said Marion. "He kept saying, 'Keep it simple, keep it simple.' Sam was listening while doing other things. They were trying to evolve something that was different and unique. Finally one night—I don't know whether Sam decided he was ready or he had finally heard something—he said, 'Okay, this is the session.'"

"The first thing that was put on tape was 'I Love You Because,'" said Scotty. "Then he did a couple of those country-orientated things. They were all right. Little while later we were sitting there drinking a Coke, shooting the bull, Sam back in the control room. So Elvis picked up his guitar and started banging on it and singing 'That's All Right, Mama.' Jumping around the studio, just acting the fool. And Bill started beating on his bass and I joined in. Just making a bunch of racket, we thought. The door to the control room was open, and when we was halfway through the thing, Sam come running out and said, 'What in the devil are you doing?' We said, 'We don't know.' He said, 'Well, find out real quick and don't lose it. Run through it again and let's put it on tape.' So to the best of our knowledge, we repeated what we just done and went through the whole thing."

"That's All Right [Mama]" was a song written and originally recorded for RCA Victor's Bluebird subsidiary in the 1940s by Arthur (Big Boy) Crudup, a black country blues singer who was one of Elvis's vocal influences. (Years later Elvis would finance some recording sessions for Crudup, although in 1969

Crudup said he still had never met Elvis.)

"We spent three or four nights trying to get a back side in the same vein," said Scotty. "We finally did 'Blue Moon of Kentucky' and this came about the same way. We'd gone through this song, that song, and I don't think any of them were on tape. Then Bill jumped up, started clowning with his bass and singing 'Blue Moon of Kentucky' in falsetto, mimicking Bill Monroe [the bluegrass musician who wrote the song]. And Elvis started banging on his guitar. And the rhythm thing jelled again.

"That was the first record."

What had been cut in the tiny studio was in many ways historic: Elvis and his two backup musicians combined the sounds of white country and black blues to form what would be called "rockabilly." On "That's All Right [Mama]," the blues song, the instrumentation gave the version a country sound, and on Bill Monroe's bluegrass hit, Elvis sang the blues.

Scotty said he and Bill shook their heads as they listened to the songs played back through Sam's recording system, agreeing that, yes, the sound was exciting enough, "But, good God, they'll run us outa town when they hear it."

Sam said he was going to take the record to Dewey Phillips, a white disc jockey who talked like a hick and devoted his WHBQ radio show *Red Hot and Blue* to records by black blues artists. It seemed the only place to go. At the time, mixing black and white music wasn't as acceptable as it would be just a few years later.

Dewey Phillips was one of those classic "good ol' boys" who followed the broken trail so many country singers blazed, marked by amphetamines and alcohol. In August 1954, when "That's All Right [Mama]" was released, he was one of the top disc jockeys in Memphis. He was a tall wavy-haired man with a soft voice, a bit of a paunch, a ready grin, and sitting in his shirtsleeves listening to his friend Sam, and then to Elvis's record, he said yes, he liked it too, and he'd sure give it a spin. Dewey was not related to Sam, but as Sam became better known, Dewey seldom denied it if someone said he was. Deep down, he said, they must have been cousins at least.

The night Dewey played the record, Elvis tuned the family radio to WHBQ and ran to his favorite escape, the Suzore No. 2 theater. His parents said later he was too nervous, or shy, to be where he might hear his own record. Elvis probably didn't remember which film he was watching that night, because his parents walked the aisles to find him before the movie was over. Dewey had played the record, the listeners had begun to call in their enthusiastic reaction. Dewey played it again and again, and now he wanted to interview Elvis on the air.

Not long before he died, Dewey told what happened during that interview.

Elvis arrived out of breath and Dewey said, "Sit down, I'm gone interview you." And according to Dewey, Elvis said, "Mr. Phillips, I don't know nothing about being interviewed."

"Just don't say nothing dirty," Dewey said back.

"He sat down and I said I'd let him know when we were ready to start," Dewey recalled. "I had a couple of records cued up, and while they played, we talked. I asked him where he went to high school and he said Humes. I wanted to get that out, because a lot of people listening had thought he was colored. Finally I said, 'All right, Elvis, thank you very much.' 'Aren't you gone interview me?' he asked. 'I already have,' I said. 'The mike's been open the whole time.' He broke out in a cold sweat."

Within a few days, there were orders for five thousand records sitting on Marion Keisker's desk. "We hadn't even cut a master when he took the dub to Dewey," Marion said. "We were back-ordered on a brand new artist with a brand new type of thing before we could get our mastering done and get some pressings from Plastic Products. It was that immediate."

It was not all that immediate for Elvis. Next day he reported for work at Crown Electric same as the day before, and he began appearing at local night clubs, not for a star's wages but for whatever he could get.

One of Elvis's first jobs was singing at the Eagle's Nest, a spacious ball-room on Lamar Avenue that featured country swing bands and was tied in with a motel and swimming pool. An early Sun recording artist named Malcolm Yelvington had a band playing weekends in the club, and Marion said Sam per-suaded Malcolm to let Elvis sing with him a couple of times. And then Elvis appeared in the club with another band, one headed by Jack Clement. Clement was the band's vocalist and Elvis was what Clement calls "the floor show," singing between regular sets. A local disc jockey called Sleepy Eyed John (Lepley) booked the place and Elvis was paid $10 a night.

In time, of course, Elvis appeared more often with his friends Scotty Moore and Bill Black, who were having trouble with the rest of their band. Scotty said, "Bill and I still had the Starlight Wranglers and we were playing two or three clubs around town. You can imagine the jealousy factor that jumped real quick as soon as that record popped out—from a rehearsal. The whole band would-a been on it had it been a regular record session. Elvis played the Bon Air Club with us a couple of weeks. He was the guest artist and there was a conflict right away."

Scotty said audience reaction to Elvis at the Bon Air was minimal. "There was a little response, but it was more like 'What's he doing? Show time, folks, it's show time!'" But when Elvis, Scotty and Bill helped open the Katz family's first drugstore on Lamar, Scotty said an entire parking lot full of teenagers "just went crazy."

About the same time, the Starlight Wranglers finally broke up, and Elvis and Scotty and Bill agreed to split whatever they earned three ways—25 per cent for Bill, the same share for Scotty, 50 per cent for Elvis. It was the end of July 1954 and "That's All Right [Mama]" was in the number three position on the Memphis country and western sales chart, where it remained for two weeks, then bounced in and out of first position for a while, hovered around the fifth and sixth places for a longer period, and finally disappeared in December. It also appeared briefly on charts in Nashville and in New Orleans, but total sales were well under twenty thousand. *Billboard*, the country's leading music publication, praised the record, calling Elvis, in the magazine's quaint vocabulary, a "potent new chanter who can sock over a tune for either the country or the r&b markets." Still, the record was only a hit regionally. It was an encouraging beginning but not an exceptional one.

Said Marion Keisker: "On that first record of Elvis's we sent a thousand copies to disc jockeys and I bet nine hundred went into the trash can, because if a rhythm and blues man got it and heard 'Blue Moon of Kentucky' [the blue-grass number], he tossed it away . . . same thing if the country man heard 'That's All Right.' Later, of course, they all wrote back and wanted second copies. All Sam ever said was 'Play it once, just play it once.' Trouble was, nobody listened."

One of Sam's brothers, Tom Phillips, was working for the Scott Paper Company in Mobile, Alabama, and carrying Sam's records around from radio station to radio station, traveling an area that covered much of his own state, south-eastern Louisiana (including New Orleans) and the southern half of Mississippi. "Everybody told me to take them back," said Tom laconically. "All I could do was leave my number."

And so it went nearly everywhere.

"You can't believe how much criticism I got from my friends in the disc jockey business," said Sam Phillips. "I recall one jockey telling me that Elvis Presley was so country he shouldn't be played after five A.M. And others said he was too black for them."

In the South in July 1954, just two months after the U.S. Supreme Court banned racial segregation in public schools, it was not easy to sell a singer whose voice was "integrated."

On July 31, he appeared at the Overton Park Shell in Memphis at an all-country music show. Marion Keisker said, "This was the first time Elvis had ever come on a stage before a big audience on a commercial show. And there was such a stage presence, such fantastic ease, what's called charisma today. I remember talking with a woman and I asked her, 'Who'd you come to hear?' She said, 'Marty Robbins, I never miss Marty Robbins. Who'd you come to see?' I said, 'Elvis Presley.' She said, 'Who?' I said, 'After this show, you won't ask me again.'

"By this time the union had heard of Elvis and he was not a union member, because Sun wasn't a union company. They refused to let him go on stage. So there was a great scrambling around, everybody taking up money, trying to get enough to make the initiation fee so he could go on and sing. He finally made it and one of the songs he sang was 'I'll Never Let You Go, Little Darling.' He'd sung that in the studio and looked at me. Now I'm a restrained person, in public anyway, and I heard somebody screaming, just keening, and I discovered it was me, the staid mother of a son. I was standing out there screeching like I'd lost my total stupid mind."

Dewey Phillips was another who was there that day and the way he told the story, Elvis sang country ballads during the afternoon show and the audience didn't react. So Elvis went to Dewey, who had spent part of the afternoon with Sam, and they told Elvis to forget the country songs that night and sing "Good Rockin' Tonight," one of the faster songs in his repertoire. Dewey said that when Elvis sang that song, and started to shake, the place came apart. Dewey said he was standing at one end of the stage watching it and went out to walk Elvis off. When they passed Webb Pierce, an established country headliner who was waiting in the wings to go on, Dewey said he smiled at Webb and Webb snarled back at him, "You sonofabitch!"

This, of course, gave the record another big push. It sold well in Memphis, where the public was given a chance to hear it and thereby decide for itself whether or not it was worth buying, and this provided the Presleys with some needed money. Sun wasn't a rich company and Elvis hadn't received any advance against future royalties when he'd signed a contract, but when the record began to sell, he was given a hundred dollars here, two hundred there when he needed it. The record also helped get him on two of the nation's most revered country radio programs, Nashville's *Grand Ole Opry* and Shreveport's *Louisiana Hayride*.

Sam Phillips arranged the *Opry* booking, calling friends he had known in Nashville when he was in radio. (The *Opry* is an official function of radio and television station WSM.) Marion Keisker said she and Sam closed the Sun office and drove the winding two-lane highway, four hours to Nashville, for the show, with Elvis, Scotty and Bill in another car behind them.

"For all of us," Marion said, "the *Grand Ole Opry* was the summit, the peak, the show you hoped you'd get eventually—not when you had just one record out."

Almost since its inception in 1925 the *Opry* had been a target for every hopeful in the country and western field. Over the years the Saturday night show had been broadcast from a number of locations, ranging in size from a crowded neighborhood movie house (the Hillsboro Theater) to the huge Greek-columned War Memorial Auditorium, which seated 2200, to the Ryman Auditorium, which was the largest hall in central Tennessee and had seats for over 3500. No matter where the *Opry* was staged, there were long lines waiting to get in and hundreds, sometimes thousands, were turned away. Payment to musicians appearing on the show traditionally had been union scale—about thirty dollars for a star the year Elvis was there, a third that for sidemen—but the Ryman Auditorium, better known as the Opry House, was no less than country music's Carnegie.

The way Marion Keisker told it, Elvis wandered around the afternoon of the show, amazed at how shabby the building was. It had been built in 1892—same year as Carnegie Hall—and didn't look as if it'd been painted since. Marion said Elvis kept saying, "You mean this is what I've been dreaming about all these years?"

They were greeted by Jim Denny, who headed the *Opry* talent office, booking all the acts for the show. Marion said, "He was very incensed. He said, 'I wanted the full band that's on the record. Our agreement was we were gonna have the performance just like it's on the record.' What he was objecting to was the only musicians he saw were Scotty and Bill and he thought there should be more. This was one of the great mysteries that perplexed everyone—how Sam got that sound. He made such a big sound, everybody thought there was a big band on the records. Jim Denny thought he was getting at least four or five people besides Elvis."

The *Opry* was divided into half-hour segments, each with a different host, and the star who introduced Elvis in 1954 was Hank Snow, a singer who'd recently had a number one hit on all the country charts ("I Don't Hurt Anymore") and who asked Elvis as he was going on, "What's your name again?"

"Elvis Presley, sir."

"No," said Hank, "not that. I mean what name do you sing under?"

"Elvis Presley, sir."

And then he went out there and sang "That's All Right [Mama]" and "Blue Moon of Kentucky."

When it was all over, Jim Denny went up to Elvis and told him he might consider trying driving a truck again. Marion said they were so upset at this, they drove off and left a suitcase full of Elvis's clothing in a gas station on the way out of town. And according to Gordon Stoker of the Jordanaires, a gospel quartet then appearing on the *Opry* every week, "Elvis cried all the way home. It took him days, weeks, to get over it. Much later Jim Denny threw his arm around Elvis at a social occasion and said to the people present, 'I always knew this boy had it in him to make it.' Elvis said, 'Yes, sir, thank you, sir,' then said out of the side of his mouth to friends, 'The sumbitch don't remember when he broke my heart.' Elvis wasn't being a hypocrite saying 'yes, sir, thank you, sir.' He was first of all a gentleman. But his heart was broken in Nashville that night."

(Marion offered a footnote: "That same day we went over to the *Opry*, Sam had a piano player he wanted to check out in a little bistro over there. Elvis came in with us, turned around, was very uncomfortable, finally said he'd wait for us outside. Sam said, 'Why?' He said, "Cause my mama wouldn't want me in a place like this.' That was reason enough to Elvis not to be there. So he went outside and waited on the sidewalk. People said it was just publicity about how he felt about his mother and all. Elvis's reaction to this was: Well, doesn't everyone do like this? It was unthinkable to him that everyone didn't love his parents, didn't want to do everything for his parents. Here's a young man so pure, so sweet, so wonderful, that he's unbelievable.")

The second radio booking, on the *Louisiana Hayride*, was more successful. This too had been arranged by Sam, and early the day of the appearance in October Scotty, Elvis and Bill set out for Shreveport in Scotty's Chevrolet, the vehicle they used for most of their early out-of-town dates. (Neither Bill nor Elvis owned a car.) The *Hayride* was only six years old when Elvis sang the songs from his first record on it, but the program already figured significantly in the careers of several country personalities (Hank Williams, Jim Reeves, Webb Pierce, and Kitty Wells among them), and so this booking too was considered a plum.

Frank Page, one of the *Hayride*'s two announcers, introduced Elvis effusively: "Just a few weeks ago a young man from Memphis, Tennessee, recorded a song on the Sun label and in just a matter of a few weeks that record has sky-rocketed right up the charts. It's really doing well all over the country. He is only nineteen years old. He has a new, distinctive style—Elvis Presley. Let's give him a nice hand . . ."

The announcer paused as Elvis stepped forward, then said, "Elvis, how are you this evening?"

"Just fine. How are you, sir?"

"You all geared up with your band . . ."

"I'm all geared up."

". . . to let us hear your songs?"

Then Elvis nervously said, "Well, I'd like to say how grateful we are to be out here. It's a real honor for us to have . . . get a chance to appear on the *Louisiana Hayride*. And we're going to do a song for you . . ." He paused.

"You got anything else to say, sir?"

"No, I'm ready."

"We're gonna do a song for you we got on the Sun record, it goes something like this."

Elvis was invited back and then was given a year's contract to appear on the show each week. He became so much a regular, he even warbled one of the show's commercial spots, a practice that was fairly common for country singers on the jamboree type of show: "You can get 'em pipin' hot after four P.M. / You can get 'em pipin' hot / Southern Made Doughnuts hits the spot / You can get 'em pipin' hot after four P.M."

"We would do the show in segments," said Frank Page, who went on to become the *Hayride*'s producer. "One half hour would be sponsored by Lucky Strike, another half hour by Jax Beer, and so on. They wanted different commercial voices, so that's why there were two of us announcers. It ran eight to eleven—three hours long. Most of the acts appeared twice, early in the show and late.

"Elvis was popular on the *Hayride*. We filled it up every Saturday night. We had filled it up with Hank Williams before, we filled it up with Johnny Cash later on. Usually some of the 3500 seats were empty, but not when Elvis was there.

"For the record, we never had one minute's trouble with Elvis. I recall only one time he had a fight with a boy who was jealous. It was a non-performer, backstage. And Elvis laid him out."

Another new friend was Pappy Covington, who had a country swing band and ran the *Hayride*'s artist service bureau, booking small country shows throughout what was called the "Ark-La-Tex area," which included the seventy-some counties in south-western Arkansas, northern Louisiana and east Texas covered by KWKH. Elvis and Scotty and Bill worked several of Pappy's package tours, with Elvis often appearing as the "Hillbilly Cat" or "The King of Western Bop." In Texas, rhythm and blues was called "cat music," and the phrase "western bop" combined the two sounds he had mixed.

In time, the *Hayride*'s staff drummer, D. J. Fontana, joined Elvis's backup band, at first when Elvis worked the Shreveport area, later wherever Elvis went. He remembers one of the early jobs: "For years they were used to havin' a country band at this place on weekends. Friday and Saturday night you couldn't stir 'em with a stick, that's how crowded it was. This was at the Lakecliff, a combination night club and motel shack-up place. So we went on and I guess they thought their regular band was comin' on after us and they looked at us, wonderin' what we were gonna do. So we started hooting and hollering and jumping and I have to say it thinned out sharply. Those people looked at us and said, 'That's not Hoot and Curly.' And they left. By the time we got through, there wasn't five or six people left. They wasn't ready for it, man. They never did book us back in there again. Said we ruint the place. Noooo way! Get out! Wouldn't even let us stay in the motel."

Another in the list of all-time Elvis shows—depressing then, funny in retrospect—was described by Columbia Records executive Cecil Scaife, then a disc jockey in Helena, Arkansas. He remembered when Elvis and Scotty and Bill worked in Helena on a twelve-dollar guarantee, performing on a flat-bed truck.

"We had two shows planned," Cecil said, "one at two-thirty in the afternoon, the other at seven or eight. Elvis came by to look at the radio station on his way to the first show and then he stopped at the drugstore next to the station and bought some Havana sweets . . . smoked one . . . had two chocolate milkshakes . . . and smoked a second cigar. Then he started turning green and after he finished vomiting and so on, we didn't know if we had an act or not. Scotty found an extra pair of pink pants that'd been on a coat hanger in the car, 'cause Elvis had ruined the first pair. And they'd been hanging down at one end of the hanger, so when Elvis put them on, they looked like they were gathered at the knees. He looked just awful, but he went on and did the show."

By now Elvis had quit his job at Crown Electric. His old boss, James Tipler, said, "He come to us finally and he said he didn't think he could keep on working nights, playing his music and singing, and still give us a good day's work, too, so he left us."

A few months later the nation's country music disc jockeys were getting a questionnaire from *Billboard* asking them, among other things, "Whom do you consider the most promising new hillbilly or country and western artists coming up at the present time?" The vote was to be based on the period from the first of the year (1954) through the first week of October. Elvis finished eighth, an exceptional showing for someone who'd never been heard of in July and who had but one record release at the time the poll was taken.

Even with acceptance like this, Elvis's income was minimal. Screaming crowds, a favorable vote from disc jockeys and a contract with the *Louisiana Hayride* notwithstanding, things were rough. The bookings had been few and, literally, far between, with Scotty, Elvis and Bill (and sometimes D.J.) pushing their car all over the South, working for little more than would get them a starchy meal and gasoline enough to reach the next town. And in time, they couldn't even count on the transportation, the 1954 Chevrolet Bel Air they'd bought on the credit Scotty's wife had by working at Sears back home in Memphis. The car worked well enough at first, of course, but the back roads and long-distance driving pointed it toward one of those Southern automobile graveyards long before its time.

Said Scotty: "My wife was working to pay the car and we were sleeping in the back of it, starving to death. It finally said flooooooomph and fell all to pieces."

It was time to find a manager.

Although few know it, Elvis actually had three managers, the first being his guitar player, Scotty Moore. "Sleepy Eyed John Lepley was after him," Scotty said, "and two, three other—I can't say crooked, but, well—people we didn't know, that really were jumpin' up and down trying to get him. It was Sam's suggestion: Sign him to a management contact and this will squelch all this activity. Then, if somebody asks, you can say he's got a manager and you won't be lying or anything. So I did. I signed him to a year contract."

Scotty worked hard to find dates for Elvis and his band, usually in school-houses, at civic club meetings, and hospitals—anything for exposure and to give them the experience they all wanted.

The contract was a one-page document drawn up after consultation with a local attorney and identified W. S. Moore III as a "band leader and booking agent" and Elvis as a "singer of reputation and renown [who] possesses bright promises of large success." Scotty was to receive ten per cent of all earnings from any appearance Elvis made, so long as Scotty had made the booking. The contract was signed by Scotty, Elvis and both his parents July 12, 1954, nearly a month before "That's All Right [Mama]" was released.

Scotty doesn't regret giving the contract away six months later. He said that when the right man came along, he happily filed the contract with his souvenirs.

"I was interested in playing, not booking show dates and telling anybody how to sing," he said.

The manager who got Elvis next was Bob Neal (born Robert Neal Hobgood), the disc jockey whose mid-day show Elvis had visited alone and with Dixie as a fan before he cut his first record. Bob, then in his middle thirties, was raised in Kentucky but had been in Memphis since 1942. In the years following he served in every capacity except station manager at WMPS, then one of the leading hillbilly broadcast operations in the mid-South. Initially, he had the five to eight A.M. show starting in 1948, spinning records, playing a ukulele and telling corny jokes to help the farmers and factory people off to work. Bob also began staging small concerts, using his program to promote them. He was married and had five sons, some of them teenagers.

Said Bob, "We worked out just a simple thing without consulting attorneys, just a simple management-type contract. Of course he was under age, so his mother and Vernon approved the thing when we started."

In return for fifteen per cent of Elvis's earnings, off the top, before taxes (if anybody bothered to take them out) and expenses. Bob was to handle all the bookings. Another ten per cent was put into a fund for promotional expenses.

And Scotty went back to picking guitar.

Because of the earlier connection, for Elvis it was like going into business with an old, respected friend. Indeed, Bob Neal and his wife Helen often spoke of Elvis as their sixth son.

Elvis's second record had been released by the time he had signed with Bob, in January 1955. This was a song the blues singer Wynonie Harris released in 1949 and the song he sang to get the crowd moving at the Shell, "Good Rockin' Tonight." On the back side of the record was "I Don't Care if the Sun Don't Shine," a song recorded in 1950 by Patti Page and Elvis's idol, Dean Martin—one verse of which was written by Marion Keisker because Elvis didn't know all the lyrics. The original composer, Mack David, agreed to the record's release when it was promised Marion's name would be left off the label and she wouldn't share in royalties. It earned one of *Billboard*'s spotlight positions and Elvis was called "a sock new singer." More important, *Billboard* said Elvis could appeal to country and rhythm and blues and pop. All three. Few records before had earned that distinction. Elvis was now being recognized as a man in a special category.

Strangely, the record didn't sell as well as the first, rising no higher than number three in Memphis, appearing not at all on the country music charts in other cities.

Even this early in his career a pattern had formed in Elvis's recording sessions that would continue with only minor variations throughout his career. "Every session came hard," said Marion. "He never had anything prepared, and the sessions always went on and on and on. First thing, he'd always want to cover some record he'd heard on the jukebox. And Sam would have to persuade him he couldn't do that. He'd have to do something new and different and let the people try to cover *him*. Elvis was different from the other Sun artists who came later. He did not write his own songs. We had to create them on the spot or take somebody else's song from our stable of writers. And he'd never rehearse. The others would get back from shows on the road and rehearse until they thought they had something presentable, and *then* go to Sam. Not Elvis. Elvis never had *anything* ready. It was always a case of the same thing we did when we first called him in—sitting down and letting him go through everything he knew or he would like to do, and we'd pick things to concentrate on."

Marion said she recalled times when everyone was "so tired, and then some little funny thing would set us off—I'd see Elvis literally rolling around on the floor, and Bill Black just stretched out with his old broken-down bass fiddle, just laughing and goofing off. It was a great spirit of—I don't know, everyone was trying very hard, but everyone was trying to hang very loose through the whole thing. [Sometimes] if Elvis would do something absolutely extraordinary and somebody would hit a clinker or something would go wrong before the tape was completed, Sam would say, 'Well, let's go back, and you hold on to what you did there. I want that.' And Elvis would say, 'What did I do? What did I do?' Because it was all so instinctive that he simply didn't know."

With Bob Neal in charge, it began to build. Elvis and Scotty and Bill—now being billed as the Blue Moon Boys—were playing essentially the same type of show, but they were playing more often. Bob Neal explained that most of the bookings followed the format he had set in the past: "Going out and working shows in the territory. Having a good following on WMPS," Bob said, "I could cover a range of a hundred and fifty to two hundred miles around town, and I would simply set a date for a schoolhouse, basically do all the advertising on my radio show, sometimes buy a few window cards, and that was it. We'd do three or four shows a week. My wife Helen'd go along and stand at the door with a cigar box and sell the tickets, and I'd get up and tell a few of my jokes, M.C. the show. Usually we took in about three hundred dollars. And if we sold dates outright to other promoters, maybe farther away from Memphis than I thought I could handle, we'd ask two, three, four hundred dollars, whatever we thought we could get."

"We'd go in and get things set up," said Scotty. "Fifteen minutes before the show it was like an avalanche. Wooooomp! They'd be hanging from the rafters."

Some of the early attraction was Bob Neal, not Elvis, but in a short time the number of Presley fans increased to a point where Elvis began to command enough money for his manager to re-evaluate the financial arrangement Elvis had with Scotty and Bill. So far, Elvis had been pocketing fifty per cent, but Bob apparently felt that was unfair and that Elvis should be getting more. Sam Phillips said Elvis owed as much to Scotty Moore for his musical style as he owed to anyone—and it was generally acknowledged that Bill Black's clowning, his riding that battered stand-up bass around the stage as if it were a horse, had been a large part of the show Elvis had to offer an audience—yet Elvis was the star, and as such, Bob believed he deserved a larger cut. Slowly, then more quickly and noticeably, it was Elvis and his contribution, musical and physical, that pulled the audiences into the school gymnasiums and auditoriums, and it was Elvis's voice, not Scotty and Bill's music, that made Horace Logan extend the *Hayride* contract from a year to eighteen months. So Bob had a talk with Elvis and it was decided that Scotty and Bill would have to take a cut in pay.

"I remember there was quite a bit of unhappiness about this at that time," said Bob. "That they would quit and so on. But they stayed on. The same thing happened later with Johnny Cash and the Tennessee Two. It was impossible to say to the musicians in the beginning, 'I'll pay you such and such,' because no one had any money. Then when success began to come, it had to be changed.

"The eventual basic decision to change from a percentage to a salary was Elvis's. We talked about it, he and I, and we talked about it with his parents and decided it had to be done. It was my job to carry the word [to Scotty and Bill]."

Between weekend appearances on the *Hayride*—and to make some of them, Elvis and the boys had to race across much of Texas, driving all night and all day—and well-scattered schoolhouse shows, Elvis returned to the cramped twelve-by-twelve-foot Sun studio at 706 Union Street. Sun was a small company, so poor that when they'd run low they'd take the unsolicited tapes they received from hopeful singers in the Louisiana bayou country or the Georgia farm lands or wherever else they came from in the morning mail, splice them together and record Sun releases over them.

There was a shipping room toward the rear, and the back room was being subleased to an auto upholstery firm. The walls were covered with acoustic tile (Carl Perkins later would call it the "pokey-dot room"), painted institutional green and all the woodwork was white. Marion Keisker said she papered the bathroom herself.

Elvis was here to cut his third record, one side of which started out as one of those smooth, shuffling blues ballads, and then Elvis said, "Hold it, fellas. That don't move me. Let's get real, real gone." And then the song, "Milkcow Blues Boogie," began to rock. It had been recorded originally in 1930 by blues singer Sleepy John Estes, again in 1938 by another blues vocalist, Joe Williams. On the other side of Elvis's record was "You're a Heartbreaker," a typical hillybilly weeper given a rocking beat.

This record wasn't even mentioned in *Billboard* and it sold poorly.

Even so, Elvis was building a following of sufficient size and ardor to warrant a fan club and attract the first of what would be a long series of paternity suits. Paternity suits are a hazard faced by almost all male performers and the first to hit Elvis came in 1954, when a teenager in Mississippi said Elvis had done her wrong. The suit was dismissed. Dixie was still his girl, but she told friends she was feeling doubts. She feared Elvis would change with success and as the road trips lengthened and became more frequent, their relationship suffered. When it came time to form the first Elvis Presley fan club, a contest was held, with the presidency going to the fan who wrote the best letter explaining why he or she wanted that honor. Marion said there was no question but that Dixie's was the most convincing letter of the hundreds received. It didn't seem to help.

Sometime during the winter of 1954-55, before Bob Neal signed Elvis—the principals involved don't have any more specific remembrance than that—a man named Oscar (The Baron) Davis came to Memphis to promote an Eddy

Arnold Show for his boss, Colonel Tom Parker, a flashy personal manager who reminded most of his friends of something between W. C. Fields and P. T. Barnum. In those days Oscar was nearly as colorful as the Colonel. He was a thin, white-haired dude who, if you believed the stories, had earned a million dollars in country music and spent a million and a half.

Oscar was working as Tom Parker's advance agent, handling Eddy Arnold's publicity. "I was in Memphis to cut my spots, the transcriptions for selling the show, at WMPS, and Bob Neal was the big disc jockey there," Oscar said. "I had heard much about Elvis. I asked Bob if he had the Elvis records and he said he did. He played them for me. He said, 'I can't play them on this station because they're barred here.' Bob was playing sweet country, good listening music, and Elvis was too raucous.

"Then he said, 'Incidentally, he's playing at the Airport Inn if you'd like to see him.' I said I'd be glad to. We went out to the airport and he just had the two boys with him, a guitar player and a bass player. The place was full of women. It seated only around sixty people, but they were screamin' their heads off. I said, 'Bob, this guy is sensational. I'd like to meet him. Introduce me to him.' He said, 'I can't. He hates my guts because I can't play his records.' I said, 'Well, I'm going to meet him.' And I brought him over to the table. Now, Scotty Moore, the guitar player, was acting as the manager at that time. So we made a tentative deal and they were somewhat excited about getting me in the picture with them. We agreed to meet the following Sunday when Eddy Arnold would be in town and I would be back.

"It was a rather cold day and around eleven o'clock in the morning they showed up. I steered them to the coffee shop across the street from the auditorium, not telling Colonel Parker anything about Elvis. Then, after I got through setting up the box office, everything ready, I started across the street. The Colonel followed me.

"I didn't want him to know about Presley. I was working for him. I was doing the exploitation for him. But I didn't want him to know. He said, 'Where you going?' I couldn't say, 'I'm going nowhere,' so I said, 'I'm going over to have a cup of coffee.' So we went over there, and Elvis and Judd Phillips and Bill Black and Scotty Moore were in the restaurant, waiting for me to come and make a deal. So Tom entered into the negotiations and the first thing he said was 'Well, the guy will get nowhere on Sun Records. This is the first thing.' And Judd Phillips, who is Sam's brother, said, 'Well, he's not going off Sun Records and that's for sure.' Because they were beginning to get a little action. So Tom brought up a lot of other objections to handling Elvis, and I proceeded almost at that time to be discouraged about the whole thing. We went back and we had a few arguments about Elvis, Tom and I. Finally I was riding with

him, we were coming back to Nashville, and Roy Acuff called me up. He wanted me to exploit him and Kitty Wells and Johnny and Jack as a package. So I
proceeded to forget about Elvis."

The Colonel apparently did not forget. First he wanted to see how well Elvis
would do on the record charts and then he waited for reports from the field. The
*Billboard* award—eighth place in the "most promising" category—made Elvis
a "possible." The Memphis sales charts designated him a "local hero." The
reports from the field, and personal observation of the audience reaction, tagged
him a "potential smash." (In even the most rural corners of show business there
are well-defined categories of success and near success.) Elvis was big on the
*Louisiana Hayride*, but they hated him on the *Grand Ole Opry*. You could pay
your money or take your choice. The Colonel split it down the middle. He made
no move of commitment but started to get involved in a small way by helping
Bob Neal make a deal for a concert in Carlsbad, New Mexico. This was in
February 1955, just one month after Neal got involved.

# Chapter 5

# THE COLONEL: 1

Once upon a time (the way the Colonel tells the story) a younger, thinner Tom Parker was working the foot-long-hot-dog concession on a carnival runway. The buns were a foot long, but there was no more than a little piece of wiener sticking out of each end, while the rest was filled with the cheaper condiments. If anyone complained about being cheated (the Colonel said), why he'd just point to the piece of hot dog he'd dropped in the sawdust that morning and say, "You dropped your meat, boy. Now move along, you dropped your meat."

Another time, he said he filled a barrel with hose water, added a packet of citric acid and a lot of cheap white sugar, cut up a single lemon to float on the top, and sold the swill as lemonade.

Once upon a third time he caught sparrows, dyed them yellow and sold them as canaries.

It was also customary that during show intermissions, as the audience left the tent or schoolhouse for a smoke and a stretch, he sent a small boy inside to pick up the souvenir books the people had left on or under their seats, books they'd purchased on entering.

In 1955 Colonel Tom Parker already was something of a legend. Not only had he managed two of the top country singers, Eddy Arnold and Hank Snow, he'd left that stack of amazing stories behind him, piling up like jokes in a nightclub comic's monologue. Or, more accurately, like the anecdotes in a book that certainly must have been one of the Colonel's then-recent favorites, H. Allen Smith's *The Compleat Practical Joker*.

The biggest joke was never revealed, at least not for many years. The truth was, the Colonel himself was phonier than those fake canaries.

The man who called him Thomas Andrew Parker, who said he was born in West Virginia, where his parents were traveling with a carnival, and orphaned in the fifth grade, was, in fact, born Andreas ("Dries") Cornelis van Kujik in 1909 in Breda, the Netherlands, the son of a liveryman. After dropping out of school at about age thirteen, he worked on the docks, then for the Holland-America Line. By the time he was twenty, he had virtually disappeared, cutting off all contact with his family and reappearing, we now know, in Atlanta, Georgia, where he enlisted in the U.S. Army, using the name Andre Van Kujik.

Following service in Hawaii—where he adopted the name of his commanding officer, Captain Thomas R. Parker—he was transferred to a post in Florida. A knee injury earned him a discharge and he settled in Tampa, known as a winter home for carnival workers. While still in Holland he had trained his father's horses, and an early fascination with local shows led him to teach a pet goat to climb a ladder. So it seemed logical when he went to work for the Royal American Shows.

The Colonel's close friend Oscar Davis said, "This was the granddaddy of all the traveling shows—a railroad show, as opposed to a truck show. It was headquartered in Tampa. He handled the food—what they call the 'pie car' on the train, where all the carnival people ate as they went from town to town. He also ran a 'mitt camp' for reading palms. He was almost psychic, that man. Upon occasion he would do the palm reading himself. All in a humorous spirit, of course."

In a sense it was a wonderful world for Tom Parker, for nowhere else could his imagination be so rapidly expanded, so readily applied. On all sides he was surrounded by super-salesmen and easily exploitable freaks. The voluptuous snake charmer slept with her pet python, the sword swallower was one of the few in the world who swallowed fluorescent light bulbs and then turned them on so you could see his chest glow, geeks bit heads off live chickens, the tattooed lady invited you to examine almost all of her body, midgets ran between the barker's legs, and dozens of fast-talking conmen invited thousands of passers-by to step right up and pitch pennies, throw baseballs, shoot rifles, have their fortunes told, watch kootch dancers and buy canaries, lemonade and foot-long hot dogs.

Another of the Colonel's friends said, "There was one time when everybody called a meeting in the cookhouse. They'd been charging fifty cents admission and the meeting was to discuss lowering the price to twenty-five. The Colonel said no and they fought him. But he said he had a better idea, if they'd just let him try it one day. What he did was have a sign painted that said, 'Admission $1.00. If not satisfied, half your money back.' Of course no one admitted to being satisfied and they all asked for, and got, half their money back. But the gimmick worked. There were crowds and they hadn't lowered their price."

To milk a final nickel from his customers, the Colonel introduced a variation on the old P. T. Barnum "Egress" stunt. (Barnum had trouble getting people to leave his exhibits and posted a huge sign over a door that said, "This way to the Egress." People thought it was another freak or weird animal, not knowing "egress" was just another word for "exit.") The Colonel's improvement came in charging his customers to leave. He had rented a cow pasture and kept cows on the only road through the pasture all the preceding night, so that by the time the carnival opened its tent flaps, the road was knee-deep in manure. After the show the customers were led to the road, the only exit. They could then walk a quarter mile through soft fresh cow manure or pay the Colonel a nickel to ride a pony through.

"It was day-to-day living," said the Colonel's friend. "Sometimes he didn't have food for he and his wife Marie and her son from an earlier marriage. He smoked cigars even then and did most of his shopping in the gutters of the cities he visited. When he found a cigar butt more than an inch long, it was a good day."

In the late 1930s, Tom was working for Tampa's humane society and promoting anyone he could get to hire him. One month it might be sending feature stories about a circus to newspapers, the next a series of concerts for Gene Austin, the popular singer who'd had such a big hit with "My Blue Heaven," the next raising money for a new kennel or dog catcher's truck. And when some of the headline country artists came through Florida from Nashville, he'd help them. Minnie Pearl, the country comedienne, who met Parker when she played Tampa with Roy Acuff in the early forties, said, "We went down there and he tied our show in with some chain, like Kroger, and it was smart promotion because it filled the house several times. It was a point-of-purchase thing, where you clip the coupon and go to the store to get tickets at a discount. The store paid for the newspaper advertising that way, and many more tickets were sold, because every Kroger cashier in a three-county area was working what amounted to a box office. The man was thinking even then."

(Similarly, the Colonel later would take Eddy Arnold's first radio sponsor, the Ralston Purina Company, and book Eddy and his band to play at dozens of mill openings and Purina feed and seed dealers' conventions. He had a genuine fondness for involving commercial enterprises outside show business, knowing it always broadened the record market while diminishing immediate costs and boosting the take at the till.)

Minnie Pearl said, "Shortly after that we went on a tent show with Eddy Arnold and his band and Jam-Up and Honey [a blackface team] and Uncle Dave Macon. And Tom became connected with the tent show as an advance agent. Instead of working auditoriums, we took a tent along with us and played all these little tiny towns. The tent seated three thousand. We couldn't do twenty miles a day, because we'd 'strike the rag' at night after the show and then have to put it back up again in the next town. We all traveled in cars. Tom stayed ahead of us, but every now and then he'd jump back and travel with us for a while."

What the portly cigar-smoking advance agent was doing this summer was lining up the radio and newspaper advertising, placing posters on walls and in store windows, and trying for some local publicity, a radio interview or a news story in the local weekly. He may not have admitted it then, but he was preparing himself for a move to Nashville and a full-time commitment to the country music field, while getting to know Eddy Arnold, the man he would serve as personal manager.

Roy Acuff, soon to be the patriarch of the multimillion-dollar Acuff-Rose complex of record companies, talent agencies and music publishing firms, said, "I presume I was the first one ever to invite Tom to Nashville. He had helped me sell a flour company I had behind me then, helpin' to advertise it in the state of Florida. I suggested he come to Nashville, meet the boys."

Acuff said Parker wanted to manage him, but "he wouldn't take anyone who just wanted to stay with the *Grand Ole Opry*, and I wanted to stay with the *Opry*. He wanted to have complete control. I wanted to go on as I was doin'."

So Tom looked around Nashville and finally signed Eddy Arnold, who then was making his first feature appearance on the *Opry* as a soloist. Eddy had been born on a farm near Henderson, Tennessee, in 1918, the son of a onetime country fiddler who encouraged him to learn the guitar when he was ten. He dropped out of school in the 1930s to help on his family farm, and for years all he played for were local dances, usually traveling to and from the jobs on a mule. He made his living on the farm and as an assistant in a Henderson mortuary. He made his radio debut in 1936 on a radio station in nearby Jackson and then joined Pee Wee King's Golden West Cowboys Band, singing in a style reminiscent of Gene Autry. He was calling himself the "Tennessee Plowboy" when Tom persuaded Eddy to leave the *Opry* and go with him.

Up to and after World War Two most country and western talent scheduling was handled by radio station talent bureaus which were designed to use the singers and musicians on the station's programs while booking them over that area covered by the station's transmitter. At the end of the war, however, several individuals like Tom Parker came along who ignored the radio station stranglehold on talent and announced themselves as "independent bookers and promoters." Now it was possible for talent to work the entire South through one office, rather than jump from station to station, and to avoid working for any one station in an area to the exclusion of all others. In this way Tom Parker became one of the true pioneers in country music.

According to Eddy Arnold, he was a good manager in other ways. "When

*Above: Two-year-old Elvis with parents Gladys and Vernon Presley, and his Senior picture at Humes High School, aged 18. Right: Elvis Presley Birthplace and Community Centre, now a public park and recreation facility, Tupelo. Below: Lauderdale Courts neighbourhood in Memphis; the Presleys lived in the centre, ground floor apartment, 1949-53.*

*Above left: outside the legendary Sun Recording Studio. Above right: Sam Phillips of Sun Records, 1954. Left: inside the Sun Recording Studio, Elvis (centre) with Bill Black (left) and Scotty Moore in their first publicity photograph, 1954. Below left: singing with his parents at home, 1956.*

*A picture from Elvis's personal publicity file, taken in the Speer studio, Memphis, 1954.*

*Above: Sun Records' "million-dollar-quartet"—Elvis at the piano with (from left to right) Jerry Lee Lewis, Carl Perkins and Johnny Cash joining him in an informal gospel sing, 1956. Below: Hysteria in a Miami movie house, 1956.*

SUNDAY - FEB. 6
TWO SHOWS ★ 3:00 p.m. & 8:00 p.m.
**AUDITORIUM**
MEMPHIS, TENN.
**FARON YOUNG**
★ "IF YOU AIN'T LOVIN'"
**MARTHA CARSON**
★ BEAUTIFUL GOSPEL SINGER
**FERLIN HUSKEY**
THE HUSHPUPPIES
Doyle and Teddy
**WILBURN BROTHERS**
Plus... MEMPHIS' OWN
**ELVIS PRESLEY**
SCOTTY and BILL
He'll Sing "HEARTBREAKER" - "MILK COW BOOGIE"
**MANY MORE...**

*Above left: an early recording session, 1955. Above right: at home with his own little hound dog. Left: Elvis's first single, "That's All Right (Mama)" released on Sun Records, July 5th, 1954. Below: Elvis signs for RCA, 1955, from left: Colonel Parker, Elvis's mom, Elvis, and Elvis's dad with two RCA executives.*

*Above: "If I stand still when I sing, I'm dead . . ." Left and opposite: instant Presley-mania took over. "If I just stood out there and sang and never moved, people would say 'Well, my goodness, I can stay home and listen to his records.' But you have to give 'em a show, somethin' to talk about."*

*Left: Elvis and his manager,*
*Colonel Tom Parker*
*Below: with Richard Egan*
*in his first film,* Love Me
Tender, *1956.*

he managed me, it was always exclusive management by Thomas A. Parker," he said in his autobiography, *It's a Long Way from Chester County.* "When Tom's your manager, he's all you. He lives and breathes his artist. I once said to him when he was managing me, 'Tom, why don't you get yourself a hobby—play golf, go boating, or something?' He looked me straight in the eye and said, 'You're my hobby.'"

Parker managed Eddy for most of a decade, taking him to a point where he eclipsed Roy Acuff's record on the top of what *Billboard* called "the H.B. [for hillbilly] talent heap." In 1944 he took Eddy to RCA Victor to record, and Eddy began to crank out hits, reaching the first of a series of peaks in 1947, when Victor released the million-selling "Bouquet of Roses." He also kept Eddy on the road, knowing that one of the best ways to build, and keep, a record audience was through saturation "personals," appearing everywhere there was a schoolhouse or room to pitch a tent.

Said Hubert Long, later one of Nashville's top talent manipulators but then apprenticed to Parker as an advance agent: "I'd go out alone in front of a tour a week or ten days to see everything was in order—the interviews, the accom- modations and so on. I'd talk to him on the phone or I'd leave an envelope with all the information in it—who'd be stopping by to see him, that sort of thing. Besides Eddy, he had the Willis Brothers, then called the Oklahoma Wranglers, Guy, Chuck and Skeeter Willis—those three musicians along with Roy Wiggins on steel guitar—a girl singer or a comedian, or maybe a girl comedi- an. A well-rounded country show. He put the package together and I will say this: He left no stone unturned. When Eddy came to a town, whether it had five thousand or five million people, everyone knew he was coming. I think if there's any one thing that led to his success, it's the promotion."

It also was an ability to wheel and deal, making outrageous demands. When Eddy Arnold first appeared in Las Vegas, for example, Parker went to the William Morris Agency, which was handling the deal, and insisted on getting the two weeks' pay in advance. Oscar Davis said, "They tried to argue him out of it. He said, 'I don't know these people; they might go outa business.' And they said, 'But, Tom, they buy the biggest acts in the nation. They won't go out of business.' He said, 'Well, if they don't want to okay it, you okay it and you'll be responsible for the money.' William Morris said it couldn't do that, some- thing about policy. And Tom said, 'Well, if you can't be responsible, there must be an element of doubt.' Tom got his money."

In the early 1950s the Colonel and Eddy Arnold split up. Oscar Davis hinted there were a number of incidents leading to the break, but said it was an argu- ment in Las Vegas that made the relationship collapse. Parker had been laying out a two-page newspaper advertisement as a surprise to Eddy, he said, and when Eddy walked into the Colonel's room unexpectedly, Parker quickly hid the layout, Eddy accused him of doing something behind his back, one thing led to another and pretty soon Eddy was without a manager, Parker was without a star.

Bill Williams, then a newsman for the *Grand Ole Opry*'s radio station, WSM, and later *Billboard*'s man in Nashville as well as an officer in the Country Music Association, remembered what happened to the Colonel next. "It was very hard for a man like the Colonel to make any headway then," he said. "There was a time when independent promoters had influence and the time would come again, but in the early fifties the *Opry* was the thing and no one functioned much without reaching the *Opry* or being booked by the Artists Service Bureau, which was run by Jim Denny right there in the *Opry* office. Sometimes if an artist felt the Service Bureau was slighting him, he'd latch onto one of the loose promoters and managers, who'd get them a few bookings and then they'd find it wasn't the way they thought it was, so they'd run right back to the *Opry* again." Williams said it was during this time that Parker, along with Oscar Davis and others, operated from WSM's lobby, using the lobby telephone. "The Colonel and the others would report in each morning at nine, shortly after the work staff came in, sit down on the sofas, and start calling all over the South booking their acts. When the phone rang, by agreement whoever was closest answered it by the number, fearing they might lose a booking if someone calling Tom got Charley Brown on the phone instead and Charley said it was Brown Productions instead of Tom's company. It was quite complicated, but they had it all worked out. And between them they lined up more clients and did more business than the *Opry*'s Service Bureau, which was directly across the hall . . . while WSM blithely picked up the tab—for years!"

The time came, of course, when the free phone was cut off, when an aggressive new assistant to the president was brought in to cut costs and he discovered all those hundreds of dollars being charged each month to the telephone in the lobby. This forced the Colonel and his pals into the station announcer's booth, where there was another telephone, and then into the studios themselves. Finally a system was installed whereby no one could call out unless he went through a newly installed switchboard. It came as such a shock, two of the promoters quit show business altogether, went home to Missouri and reportedly entered politics.

After he left the WSM lobby, it was from his one-story eleven-room flagstone home on the Gallatin Road north of Nashville in Madison that Parker ran his company, Jamboree Attractions. The house was situated on former grazing land and in a few years would be worth an enormous sum, just as the land across the highway would rise in price fast enough to convince its owner, Eddy Arnold, to sell it to Sears. The actual business the Colonel ran from the basement and then the garage he converted into offices, the walls of which were covered with posters, photographs and souvenirs, including the certification of his honorary colonelcy, presented by Tennessee's Governor Frank G. Clement in 1953.

Working with Parker was a small, cordial, almost penguin-like man with sandy hair, Tom Diskin. He had come to the Colonel from Chicago when Parker had Eddy Arnold, and the Colonel put Diskin's sisters—who sang and called themselves the Dickens Sisters—on several of his shows. Diskin joined Parker as his right-hand man, handling most of the dirtier office work at first and then taking over management of the tours, which meant he accompanied the acts and was responsible for much of the menial back-breaking work that went with being on the road.

In 1954, one of the artists the Colonel represented from Madison was Hank Snow, a short, almost scrawny forty-year-old who had been on his own since he was fourteen, singing in his native Nova Scotia, Canada, where he built a following that attracted the attention of RCA Victor. At first his records were available only in Canada, but after 1949, Hank began to sell in the United States, which brought him to Nashville to appear on the *Opry*. Among the big hits that followed was "I Don't Hurt Anymore," the number one country and western song of 1954, the song that was in the number one position in Memphis the week Elvis's first record made its first appearance (at number three). Less than two months later Hank signed with the Colonel, giving him exclusive personal appearance booking rights. A month later Parker had taken over administration of Hank Snow Enterprises, the loosely organized business umbrella over Hank and all his publishing, recording, radio, television and film activities. Once again Tom Parker was in control of the South's leading country and western singing star.

It was shortly after that the Colonel began helping Bob Neal with Elvis's bookings in the South and Southwest.

# Chapter 6

# SUNSET

Immediately following the show in Carlsbad, New Mexico, Elvis and Scotty and Bill joined Hank Snow, touring the Southwest, closing ten days later in Bastrop, Louisiana. Elvis was billed beneath Snow, Hank's son Jimmy, the Duke of Paducah, Mother Maybelle and the Carter Sisters, and the Jimmie Rodgers Show. Then he went to Cleveland with Bob Neal to appear at the Circle Theater, one of three houses competing for the city's Saturday night country music market. The same week Bob began advertising in the music trade publications, asking night club and concert promoters to call him for bookings, urging disc jockeys to get in touch if they wanted records. (Sun's distribution setup left much to be desired and this was the only way some jockeys could get Elvis's records.) Mike Michael of KDMS in El Dorado, Arkansas, reported in *Billboard* that Elvis was "just about the hottest thing around these parts. His style really pleases the teenagers." In Dallas, where Elvis was putting in a return appearance at the Big D Jamboree, the press agent for the Sportatorium, home of the Big D, said Elvis was just terrific, they wanted him back again.

The only rejection Elvis received during this time came when Bob Neal flew the boys to New York to audition for Arthur Godfrey's *Talent Scouts*, then the most popular, and therefore important, new talent showcase on television. It was Elvis's first airplane flight and his first time in New York. Elvis didn't like New York and Godfrey didn't like Elvis; the *Talent Scouts* said no.

In May Elvis went on what Bob Neal calls "his first big tour," a three-week sweep through the South, again with Hank Snow's Jamboree, starting in New Orleans May 1, jumping from city to city in Louisiana, Alabama, Florida, Georgia, Virginia and Tennessee, closing in Chattanooga on the twentieth. Snow was the headliner. Others were Faron Young, the Wilburn Brothers, Slim Whitman, Martha Carson, the Davis Sisters, Mother Maybelle and the Carter Sisters, Onie Wheeler and the Jimmie Rodgers Show. All country. Except for Elvis. Booked and promoted by the general manager of Hank Snow's production company, Tom Parker.

It was while Elvis was on this tour that his fourth record from Sun was released. "Baby, Let's Play House" was a blues song that introduced the hic-cupping glottis strokes for which Elvis would become famous, backed by "I'm Left, You're Right, She's Gone," a country song written a few weeks earlier by a Memphis steel guitar player named Stan Kesler.

It would be nearly two months before the songs appeared on the record charts, and in the meantime Elvis made another week's sweep in another direc-tion with Hank Snow and Ferlin Husky, the Carlisles, Maxine and Jim Ed Brown, and Onie Wheeler. The third week in the month he slid into Meridian, Mississippi, for the Jimmie Rodgers Memorial Celebration. In connection with this performance, Bob Neal took out a quarter-page advertisement in the trade magazines calling Elvis "the freshest, newest voice in country music." There was a picture of Elvis in a white shirt, dark coat and necktie, a mention of his new Sun record, a mention of his weekly *Hayride* appearances, and Elvis said, "Howdy to all my friends at the Jimmie Rodgers Memorial." The same week, "Baby, Let's Play House" and "I'm Left, You're Right, She's Gone" got a sev-enty-seven (good) rating from *Billboard*, a B (very good) from *Cash Box*. The next week "I'm Left . . ." appeared in the number eight position in Memphis, and Elvis began touring Texas and Oklahoma again.

The money was coming in now and Elvis was buying Cadillacs for his per-sonal use, in pink and pink and black. Country musicians loved Cadillacs and Elvis was no exception. A year or so later when Sun Records had added Johnny Cash, Carl Perkins and Jerry Lee Lewis, among others, to its impressive ros-ter, someone would say you could find Sun by looking for the chicken coop nested in Cadillacs.

Then Elvis began to have trouble with his road cars. "When the Chevy finally give out, Elvis went and bought a 1951 Lincoln Continental," said Scotty Moore. "Bill wrecked that one. We were doing a date in Arkansas and a truck pulled out and he run it under the truck and totaled the thing out. That's when Elvis bought the '54 Cadillac. That's the one that burned up, near Texarkana, Arkansas. What happened was the wheel bearing went out. His chick was with him. They were comin' behind us. He wasn't payin' no damn attention to the car and all of a sudden he realized the damn thing was on fire. He couldn't put it out. All he could do was open the trunk and throw our clothes and instruments out all over the road.

"So we rented a small plane," he said, "loaded all the instruments in it and barely got off the ground the next day, going to Sweetwater, Texas. Elvis had bought his folks a '54 pink and white Ford at the same time he bought the Cadillac, and somebody brought it to us in Sweetwater so we could finish the tour."

Elvis was energetic, almost to a nervous fault, often keeping his closest friends—in those days, Scotty and Bill and D. J.—awake all night talking and clowning. Said Scotty: "We'd have to throw him outa the car practically. He'd catch me or Bill or D. asleep and he'd take off one of our shoes and toss it out the window. We'd have to stop and go back and find it. Another time he threw out the car keys. At night! He had so much nervous energy we'd have to sit up nights to wear him out so we could go to sleep. There'd be pillow fights. We'd wrestle. Anything we could think of. It like to wore us out, and every day, every night was the same."

He chewed his fingernails, drummed his hands against his thighs, tapped his feet, and every chance he got he ran a comb through blond hair that, quoting Marion Keisker, "had so much goop in it, it looked dark."

It seemed somehow that all this energy was but a prelude to what came on stage. Just as there would be during the 1970s—in Las Vegas, primarily—little introduction to Elvis's performance, there was little then. It was possible someone would introduce him, but likely as not Scotty and Bill and D. J. would be set up, having provided the backup music for another singer on the show. Then Elvis would come out and go right into one of his ballads. Draped in black slacks with a pink stripe down the sides, a pink shirt with the collar turned up catching the ends of his longish hair, and a pink sport jacket with big black teardrops on the front and back, he *was* the Hillbilly Cat, he was the King of Western Bop. He leaned forward, legs braced, guitar hung around his neck, hands clutching the stand microphone. He looked at the girls in the front row with lidded eyes, eyebrows forming a loving and woeful arch. During the song's instrumental break he gave them that lopsided grin and maybe twitched one leg. Once.

The next song might be a rocker, giving Elvis a chance to show the folks what they'd come to see. Now both legs were twitching—jerking and snapping back into that original braced position. It's not likely Elvis was thinking of the Pentecostal preachers of his Tupelo childhood at moments like this, but it was apparent he hadn't forgotten them. All he'd done was translate hellfire and damnation into "Good Rockin' Tonight." His arms flailed the inexpensive guitar, pounding the wood on the afterbeat and snapping strings as if they were made of cooked spaghetti. From one song right into another, most of them already recorded for Sun or soon to be released. Country songs. With a beat. The girls began to squirm and move; it was music that made their behinds itch.

"You'd see this frenzied reaction, particularly from the young girls," said Bob Neal. "We hadn't gone out and arranged for anybody to squeal and scream. Not like Frank Sinatra did in the forties. These girls screamed spontaneously. Nowadays it seems to be fashionable for the teenyboppers when they see the act, they know they're supposed to squeal and quiver and so forth. Back in that time there'd been a long period when nobody'd done that—not since Sinatra . . . and that was fifteen years earlier. For Elvis they just did it automatically.

"Plus," Elvis's former manager added, "it was almost frightening, the reaction that came to Elvis from the teenaged boys. So many of them, through some sort of jealousy, would practically hate him. There were occasions in some towns in Texas when we'd have to be sure to have a police guard because somebody'd always try to take a crack at him. They'd get a gang and try to waylay him or something. Of course, Elvis wasn't afraid of them and was quite willing to defend himself—and did on occasion.

"I remember one night in Lubbock, Texas, we were on a series of one-nighters out there and we worked this deal with the radio station where they said they could get us four or five hundred extra dollars for doing a deal at some club in town. So Elvis thought that was fine. At that time picking up an extra four or five hundred was very helpful. The day before we got there, though, the station people called me, out on the road somewhere, and said they'd had an awful lot of threats from guys about what they were going to do to Presley. So they'd arranged for police protection for Elvis all day long. I explained this to Elvis and he said, 'Oh, I don't need that.' I told him he better listen. So sure enough, all day, all afternoon, all night, they were there—policemen and plain-clothesmen. We got in about three in the afternoon, spent a little time at the motel and then went to the auditorium. Then later he went to the club. The sheriff's deputies took over out there. Along about twelve or twelve-thirty, everything had been very peaceful so far, and the deputies said, 'I guess we can leave.' And I said, 'Go ahead. Everything's okay.' We were walking out to the car in the parking lot when somebody called, 'Hey, Elvis, come here.' Friendly. Elvis walked over, grinning, figuring somebody just wanted an autograph. It was somebody waiting for him. And the guy sitting there in the car just reached out and hit him in the face as hard as he could and drove off. Elvis ran back and got in our car and said he'd recognize him and made us drive around Lubbock until five o'clock in the morning. He was determined he was going to find somebody and fix him up.

"He was naturally pleased to get a reaction from an audience," Bob said. "He got a real kick from it. He really enjoyed the reaction from the girls, but he asked me, 'Why do those guys want to be like that?' He considered himself a regular fella, just as much an ordinary-type stud as any of them, but they were mad at him. I explained and others explained, but he just didn't seem to understand. He said it didn't seem logical.

"On the little shows in the area Elvis was getting top billing. We'd just say we're bringing the Elvis Presley Show to you. But naturally when we were working some of the big packages—the things Colonel Parker was putting together—he'd get more or less minor billing. One thing that always happened, though, after the first night of a tour, Presley would always close the show. No matter what, nobody wanted to follow him.

"I remember one time we had a package playing six or eight days out in Texas and I'd set the show with Elvis on last. After the first show Ferlin Husky approached me and said he thought he should close the show, being the headliner and all. I said if he wants to take the chance, okay, so the next night I switched it around. I told Elvis and he just laughed, said it didn't make any difference to him. Sure enough, Ferlin followed Elvis. It was pitiful. Ferlin did everything he could. He was a fine performer. But the audience was screaming bring back Presley, where's Elvis! Plus: leaving. So the next morning Ferlin conceded there was no way to follow Elvis. He came to me and said, 'I think we better go back to the way you had the show set up the first time.'"

Bob said Elvis couldn't stand to see an audience sit on its hands. "He threw everything into it, trying to break that audience down, trying to get it with him. He'd always react to audience reaction and in the rare instances when he'd be placed on the show early, I always felt he kind of outdid himself, making it tough for the guy to follow. He was a very competitive showman. He was greatly anxious for success. Helen used to talk with him on the way back from one-nighters in the Memphis area, and she said he talked not in terms of being a moderate success. No—his ambition and desire was to be big in movies and so forth. He'd ask her did she think he could make it. She said he could go as far as he wanted to. From the very first he had ambition to be nothing in the ordinary but to go all the way. He was impatient. He would say, 'We got to figure out how to do this, we got to get ahead.'"

At the beginning of the third week of June Elvis was in Beaumont, Texas, playing a police benefit with Marty Robbins, the Maddox Brothers and Rose and Retta (Maddox), Sonny James, the Belew Twins and the Texas Stampers. Twenty-four hundred seats were sold five times in two days, with the top ticket price at one dollar. On June 26 he was in Biloxi, Mississippi, the next two days at Keesler Air Force Base nearby, the next two at Curtis Gordon's Club in Mobile, Alabama. On July 1 he was playing Baton Rouge, Louisiana's capital, and on the third he was in Corpus Christi, Texas. He was singing at a picnic in De Leon, Texas, on July 4, along with his old friends the Blackwood Brothers and the Statesmen, and a bunch of the usual country acts.

There seemed to be no end to it.

It was when Elvis first appeared in Jacksonville that he experienced his first "riot." It was here that teenagers tore his clothes off, shredded his pink shirt and white jacket, and ripped his shoes from his feet, actually putting Elvis himself in physical danger, although at the time he laughed it off.

Previews of coming attractions.

"They loved him in Florida," said Oscar Davis, who promoted the concert for the Colonel. "I guess we put more emphasis on Florida, because Tom was acquainted with the state and he wanted to show him off down there. So we devoted more time in Tampa and Orlando and Jacksonville."

The same week *Billboard* again reviewed Elvis's fourth record, saying, "In the past few weeks, various Southern territories have been seeing nice action with this disk. After a strong kick-off in the Memphis area, it has begun to sell well in Houston, Dallas, New Orleans and Nashville and is moving out now in Richmond, St. Louis and the Carolinas."

In the middle of July another important mark was made, when "Baby, Let's Play House" became Elvis's first record to appear on one of the national best-seller charts. Previously he had been on regional charts only, but now he was on the chart drawn on the basis of dealer reports throughout the nation with a high volume in country and western sales. And the next week the record was on *two* national charts—number fifteen on the best-selling country list, number eleven on the list of country records that got the most air play by country disc jockeys.

As this record worked its way up the charts, Elvis's fifth, and last, for Sun Records was released. This was "Mystery Train"—a song written by Sam Phillips and a black blues singer named Little Junior Parker and had been a rhythm and blues hit by Parker on Sun a few years earlier—backed with "I Forgot to Remember to Forget," a country song written by Stan Kesler, who'd previously written "I'm Left, You're Right, She's Gone."

As the record was being shipped to record stores, Colonel Parker and his assistant, Tom Diskin, began meeting with Bob Neal, Elvis and Elvis's father to discuss their fall and winter plans. At these meetings, the first that would be talked about publicly as "policy meetings," it was agreed that Elvis probably would do very well in all the polls to be announced during November's disc jockey convention in Nashville and that it would be announced soon that Elvis would leave Sun Records for a larger company.

"In practically all of 1955, there were negotiations of one sort or another going on," said Bob Neal. "Some people thought I had an interest in Sun, and I'd get a call from some company asking can we buy the Presley contract, how much is it? I'd say, 'Let me see, I'll check with Sam Phillips and let you know.' I know when it started off it would have taken only four or five thousand dollars, but I recall one time later when Mitch Miller, who was with Columbia, called me. We were out on a tour in Texas and he said how much is the contract? I said I'd check. By that time Sam was asking eighteen or twenty thousand. I called Mitch back and he said, 'Forget it. No artist is worth that kind of money.'"

The bidding continued. Ahmet Ertegun, president of Atlantic Records, essentially a rhythm and blues and jazz label, offered $25,000. "That was everything we had, including my desk," Ahmet said. "I figured we'd get Elvis, we'd have a star and we'd take off in the country field. But going from Sun to Atlantic was like trading an Austin for a Morris. Besides, the Colonel said he had to have forty-five thousand, which at the time was not only outrageous but silly."

Arnold Shaw, later a writer, in 1955 was associated with the Edward B. Marks Music Corporation, a song-publishing outfit in New York, and he claimed he was the cause of some of the Presley excitement. He said he first heard Elvis's records in the summer when he visited Colonel Parker in Madison. Then he returned to New York, where he played them for Bill Randle, a disc jockey whose program was broadcast there and in Cleveland. He said Randle was afraid to break the records in New York but was willing to give them a try in Ohio. And the response to *this* was enough to cause Randle—who'd discovered the Crew Cuts and therefore commanded a lot of respect in the cash-register if not the creative end of the record business—to start hyping Elvis to record companies in New York. That, said Arnold Shaw, had dozens of labels in the city wondering how much Elvis's Sun contract actually might be worth.

The Colonel went to New York and took a small suite in the Hotel Warwick. With him he had a long telegram from Elvis's parents that empowered the Colonel to find a buyer. Among the many he met were his old friends at RCA Victor, Steve Sholes, who was head of the company's artist and repertoire department in Nashville, and Frank Folsom, Victor's president. The Colonel had known these men for years, largely through his dealings with Eddy Arnold and Hank Snow, both RCA recording artists. He also met with Jean and Julian Aberbach, the German-born brothers who operated Hill and Range Music, Inc., the young, aggressive music publishing company then taking over much of the country and western market.

Sam Phillips flew to New York to hear Victor's final offer: $35,000 in cash for Elvis's contract (which had about a year to run) and rights to all his released and unreleased material—with another $5000 going to Elvis as a bonus for signing. In today's highly competitive record market $40,000 isn't pocket change, but in 1955 it was regarded as something decidedly larger than a king's ransom. Sun was to retain the rights to press records to fill all orders until the first of the year, after which RCA had exclusive rights to everything Elvis had recorded or would record—for a period of three years. Sam said it seemed fair, contracts should be drawn up and probably they would be signed during the disc jockey convention in Nashville, then only a few weeks away.

It had been determined a short time earlier that Hill and Range would publish the Elvis Presley song folio, and during these later negotiations the Aberbachs bought the rights to Hi Lo Music, a subsidiary of Sun Records Sam had formed to publish several of the songs his artists recorded. These included three of Elvis's: "Mystery Train," "I'm Left, You're Right, She's Gone" and "You're a Heartbreaker." Hill and Range also agreed to set up Elvis Presley Music, Inc., to publish songs Elvis would record, sharing the publisher's royalties with Elvis on a fifty-fifty partnership for a period of five years.

RCA said it hoped to have the first Presley record—a reissue of one of Sun's records—out by early December, and that the company would promote Elvis not just in the country market but in the three existing fields simultaneously—country, rhythm and blues, and pop.

Hill and Range said it would have the first Presley song folio—words and music to Elvis's recorded songs—ready for release by December 10.

Back in Memphis, Elvis's relationship with Dixie was limping toward its end. Although it was no secret among those close to Elvis that he rarely turned away the women who made themselves available to traveling performers, it was he who accused her of going out on him when he was on the road. He took her to her junior prom, but then took his class ring back. Sometimes in his absence, with Elvis's parents' permission, she stayed overnight with them, sleeping in his bed. But she rarely slept with him again. By September 1955, she told Elvis's mom it was over and they had a good cry.

Bob Neal continued to serve as Elvis's "official" manager and he opened a small record shop on Main Street, Memphis, using it as a ticket location for the occasional concerts he was staging locally. The Elvis Presley Fan Club (answering all letters on black and pink stationery) and out-of-town bookings were run from an office on Union Street not far from Sun Records. And, of course, he still had that early morning show on WMPS.

There was another accident on September 2, as Elvis and Scotty and Bill and D. J. were driving from New Orleans to Texarkana, which caused a thousand dollars in damage to one of their Cadillacs, but no one was hurt. Elvis then worked his way through Arkansas, parts of Missouri, much of Mississippi (beating it back to Shreveport each week for his *Hayride* appearances), then made one of his rare airplane trips to Norfolk, where he joined Hank Snow's All-Star Jamboree for a tour that took him to Asheville in the western North

Carolina mountains and to Roanoke, Virginia. After that Elvis headlined a smaller unit—with the Louvin Brothers and Cowboy Copas—that criss-crossed the same two states, closing in Kingsport, Tennessee, a twelve-hour drive from home.

All the audience records were being broken now and by mid-September Elvis had three songs on the national country music charts: "Mystery Train," "Baby, Let's Play House" and "I Forgot to Remember to Forget." And a month after that, in mid-October, Elvis went out with his own jamboree, headlining over Jimmy Newman, Jean Shepard, Wanda Jackson, Bobby Lord, Floyd Cramer (who also now sometimes played piano for Elvis) and his new pal from Sun Records, Johnny Cash. The tour started in Abilene and closed two weeks later in St. Louis. Then, in mid-November, Elvis interrupted his touring to attend the country and western disc jockeys' convention in Nashville.

"They had him on display," said Minnie Pearl. "That was the first time I ever saw Elvis, although I had heard about him before that. Believe me, they had him on display."

They also held him up for considerable praise. "Baby, Let's Play House" ranked sixteenth in the year's country and western song category, the same position Elvis himself occupied in the disc jockey's favorite artists list. He was named the thirteenth most played artist on radio and whereas he had been eighth most promising country artist in 1954, now he was number one.

And it was announced that Elvis was leaving Sun Records for RCA Victor.

A lot of thought had gone into Sam Phillips's decision to sell, much of it prompted by Tom Parker, who had been weaning Elvis away from Sun (and Bob Neal) for some time.

"Colonel Tom had been working on Mr. and Mrs. Presley for about a year, in the most polished and Machiavellian way," said someone who was in a position to watch. "You wouldn't believe it. You just couldn't believe it. Mrs. Presley, God rest her soul, she was just a mother, that's what she was. And the Colonel'd go to her and say, 'You got the finest boy in the world, Miz Presley, and it's terrible the way they're makin' him work.' He'd go to them and sweet-talk them. Mrs. Presley, she didn't know. Colonel Tom knew they were"—and here the voice drops, sadly— "poor white trash, and he told them her son was working too hard and Elvis was entitled to *some* leisure after all. He had a farm up in Madison, he said, with horses and all, and he gave the Presleys $200, told them to send Elvis up there to relax, ride the horses."

The observer said, "Colonel Tom was a salesman. I'll give him that. He sure knew how to sell." Marion Keisker's observations meshed with these. "The Colonel had completely won Vernon Presley over to his side. And of course, Colonel Parker didn't think he could continue with Sam, that they could do business together. He envisioned bigger things, more money."

Having won Elvis's father, Marion said, Elvis's father changed. "Mr. Presley had become very antagonistic, and whereas a year earlier Elvis had stood there with tears streaming down his face, saying, 'This is what I've always wanted, my very own record with my very own name on it,' all of a sudden, under the suggestion of the Colonel, *we* had become totally dependent upon Elvis . . . *we* had no studio without Elvis . . . and so on and so on. He became quite demanding. Very difficult. And, of course, Elvis wanting to do what his parents wanted, this put him under a strain too."

Still another factor, Marion said, was the trouble involved in recording Elvis. "We knew his potential," she said, "but each record was sweated out with hours of do it again and hold onto that little thing there. Every session came so hard. He didn't have anything prepared. He wasn't like Johnny [Cash] and the ones who came later, like Jerry Lee [Lewis] and Carl [Perkins], who always had material prepared, who always were ready to record.

"Elvis was out for fun. He never rehearsed. He was nineteen and he had a motorcycle and he liked to ride the streets, looking for excitement. So often I'd see him zipping along Union Street, a new girl on the back of that motorcycle, or walking with two or three girls at once. Later he'd tell me, 'I'm sorry I didn't introduce you, Marion. I didn't know their names.'

"One day we had him and one day we didn't. He'd left us. And I had written the original contract."

Marion was emotional about Elvis's departure from Sun. But she seemed equally realistic. "By this time we'd have had to go out and spend more money and be a big company, or we had to fall back to being a nothing company," she said. "It was a moment of decision. Sam decided, and I think wisely, that he could use the money. He could make other stars just as he made Elvis. And it wasn't six weeks later we came out with 'Blue Suede Shoes.' Of course a lot of disc jockeys then said it wasn't Carl Perkins, but Elvis. They said we were just calling him something else and trying to put something over on Victor.

"I can tell you this, it was Carl Perkins, all right. Victor got every one of our tapes. That's my only regret: Sam gave Victor all the out-takes. There must have been—easy!—fifty or seventy-five cuts, different versions of the same song in many cases, dozens and dozens of tapes. They were songs we wouldn't release—because we didn't think they were good enough or fresh enough, or Scotty broke a string or Elvis flatted or something. We never intended to release them. By George, Victor released them. All of them. I'd have destroyed them. Sam just gave them to Victor. He didn't have to. It was a gesture."

Chapter 7

# HYSTERIA: 1

R CA re-released the five Sun records on its own label within a few weeks of the contract signing, so that in the winter of 1955 Elvis was in a unique position—that of having two record companies behind him, both selling the same product. And then advertisements began appearing in the music trade publications listing Bob Neal as Elvis's manager—"under the direction of Hank Snow Jamboree Attractions . . . Col. Tom Parker, General Manager." So, in a way, Elvis now had two managers working for him as well.

Actually it was the Colonel, not Neal, who now was guiding Elvis's career. Neal had been active in the negotiations with Victor, helping to make final arrangements for the contract signing in Nashville, but it was the Colonel who had done all the bargaining. And it was the Colonel who had eased Elvis out of his *Louisiana Hayride* contract, trading the remaining six months for a free concert appearance, held December 17 as a benefit for the Shreveport YMCA. The *Hayride*, helpful in the early days, had too parochial an audience and it committed Elvis every Saturday night, the biggest night of the week for personal appearances as well as a popular network television night; the Colonel wanted Saturdays free.

"The Colonel was setting bookings and he'd send the papers to me for the Presleys' signatures," said Bob Neal. "So I wasn't really devoting full time to it by any means. It was a partial-type thing. I still did the morning show and ran the record shop. The Colonel did all the basic negotiation. I stayed away from that."

As was Elvis's custom, he returned home to Memphis for the Christmas and New Year's holidays, then on January 10, 1956, two days following his twenty-first birthday, he went into the studio that RCA shared with the Methodist Church in Nashville to cut some new material. The facilities at 1525 McGavock Street were owned by the Methodist TV, Radio and Film Commission and were so primitive the stairwell in the rear of the building doubled as an echo chamber and whenever anyone pulled a Coke from the soft drink machine at the foot of the stairs, that sound was included on the recording.

The Elvis session went smoothly and seemed, on the surface at least, to be little different from most country sessions: three hours, in and out, with a minimum of fooling around. But if anyone had taken a picture—and no one did, apparently—it would have been not only a historical one but one which clearly revealed the brain trust that was forming around Elvis, an efficient mix of flashy hard-nosed salesmanship and musical and professional expertise that would help make Elvis king.

One of those sitting in the cramped control room was Steve Sholes, the bulky and somewhat rumpled forty-five-year-old father figure and head of Victor's artist and repertoire department in Nashville. He had begun what was to be a forty-year association with RCA when he was in high school in New Jersey. He was one of the first record producers to see the potential in Nashville and more than anyone else had built the label's enviable country and western roster—finding, signing, recording and/or promoting Chet Atkins, Elton Britt, Jim Ed and Maxine Brown, Hank Locklin, Hank Snow, Homer and Jethro, Jim Reeves, Pee Wee King, Roy Rogers, and the Sons of the Pioneers before Elvis had come along. Even with his enviable track record, Sholes said later that over Elvis he practically had put his job on the line.

"We had never bought up any contracts before, or masters or anything like that," he told writer David Dalton. "The money we paid, which seems like peanuts today, was pretty big, and they called me in and wanted me to assure them that they would make their money back in the first year. I gulped a little and said I thought we would. How the heck was I to know? A story was going around Nashville that I was the biggest fool that ever came down the pike, because we would never be able to make the kind of records he made for Sam Phillips over in Memphis. The truth of the matter is we didn't. By the time we got around to making 'Heartbreak Hotel' for Victor, his style had evolved a lot. We were making a new sound that was different even from the very original sound that Elvis had put together."

Also in the control room were Colonel Parker and his assistant, Tom Diskin, and an engineer. And in the small studio were Elvis and the musicians—Scotty and Bill and D. J. and a group of hand-picked musicians and backup singers, including guitarist Chet Atkins and Gordon Stoker of the Jordanaires, one of the top vocal groups in the gospel and country fields, the quartet serving as regulars on the *Grand Ole Opry* when Elvis appeared on that show a year earlier. He was booked for the session with two members of the Speer Family Gospel Quartet, another recent RCA acquisition.

The first of three songs completed at that session was "Heartbreak Hotel," which had been written by Mae Boren Axton (mother of folk singer Hoyt Axton), who had worked for Hank Snow as a publicist a year earlier and then was teaching school in Florida. The building's bizarre echo chamber came in for heavy use on this song, so much in fact, at times it almost sounded as if Elvis were hollering from the bottom of a well, with the rest of the ballad coming in a deeper, slurring, nearly hiccupping tone. All of which was punctuated by assertive guitar chords, an occasional tinkle from a piano and a barely discernible bass. The second and third songs were "I Want You, I Need You, I Love You," Elvis's second Victor release (to be dropped on the market after "Hotel" had peaked), and "I Was the One," to be released as the back side of "Hotel." On both of these the Jordanaires contributed a series of "wah-wah's" or "oooooh's" and "aaaaaaaah's," giving the songs a fuller, softer sound.

Steve Sholes said Elvis's style had evolved in the months since he'd recorded in Memphis and if these songs were any criterion, it was true. Much of the biting edge of Scotty's country guitar and nearly all the pelvic boogie beat had been neatly removed. All the songs were ballads. Floyd Cramer played piano, an instrument Elvis himself played on later recording dates, but which made this one sound almost cocktail-partyish—if you could forget, for a moment, the voice. Elvis's rhythmic, fluid tenor—dipping toward baritone—voice and the amazing vocal gimmickry remained distinctly his own, but the over-all impression was he had abandoned rockabilly for pop.

Gordon Stoker said, "After the session, Elvis said if any of the songs went big, he wanted all the Jordanaires to record all his stuff with him. We didn't think they'd go big. We didn't think much about it at all. We didn't even remember Elvis's name, really. It was just another job for us."

Chet Atkins, one of the most admired guitarists in Nashville and an idol to Scotty Moore, felt differently. As Peter Guralnick noted, the usually calm and unaffected man was so impressed by Elvis's performance in the studio he called his wife and told her to come down to the studio immediately. "I told her she'd never see anything like this again, it was just so damn exciting."

Elvis was back on the road with Scotty and Bill and D. J. and his buddies Red West and Bitsy Mott, still plugging away in the South, when it was announced that he had been booked for a series of four Saturday night appearances (at $1,250 apiece) on the Tommy and Jimmy Dorsey *Stage Show*, a half-hour program produced by Jackie Gleason and carried by CBS-TV preceding Gleason's comedy series *Honeymooners* and opposite the first half of *The Perry Como Show*. The Dorseys had been having rating troubles and Gleason's executive producer, Jack Philbin, said at the time that he and Gleason had been on a somewhat desperate search for something to help the show when he was shown a picture of Elvis and decided "this kid is the guitar-playing Marlon Brando." Gleason himself never said more than "If I booked only the people I

like, I'd have nothing but trumpet players on my show. It was and is our opinion that Elvis would appeal to the majority of the people."

It was rainy and cold on January 28, the date of Elvis's first appearance, and
in the otherwise puffy liner notes on Elvis's first album—released three months
later—"very few braved the storm. The theater was sparsely filled with shiv-
ering servicemen and Saturday nighters, mostly eager for the refuge from the
weather. Outside, groups of teenagers rushed past the marquee to a roller-skating rink nearby. Just before show time, a weary promoter returned to the box
office with dozens of tickets, unable even to give them away on the streets of
Times Square." The theater was in mid-Manhattan's West Fifties, New York's
theatrical district, and although Elvis's name was on the marquee, it attracted
little attention. He may have been causing riots in the deep South, but in New
York only a few in the music business had heard of him.

He was introduced with the same professional enthusiasm given all television guest stars, and in living rooms all over the country the small-screen television sets went dark for a second and when the picture returned, Elvis was
standing center stage, gazing into the camera with his dark lidded eyes. He
moved his shoulders slightly, adjusting the draped sport jacket he was wearing,
relaxed his wide-spread legs, snapping his right knee almost imperceptibly.
"Wellllll, since mah beh-bee left me / Ah've found a new place to dwell / It's
down at the end of Lonely Street / It's Heartbreak Hotel . . ." As Scotty came
in on guitar, Elvis's legs jerked and twisted. He thumped his own guitar on the
afterbeat, using it as a prop and almost never playing it now. He bumped his
hips. He moved his legs in something that seemed a cross between a fast shuf-
fle and a Charleston step. He sneered, dropped his eyelids and smiled out of the
left side of his mouth. He used every physical trick that had come to him in the
sixteen months since his first record was released, tricks which were polished
by repeated use, but still natural and spontaneous. The television audience had
never seen anything like it. After all, the most popular programs of the period
were Ed Sullivan's *Toast of the Town*, *$64,000 Question*, *I Love Lucy* and *You Bet
Your Life*, none of which did much to affect, or mirror, the American libido.
And now Elvis Presley was "doing it." On television. Coast to coast.

Mail for that Dorsey show far surpassed anything in the program's experience.

"Heartbreak Hotel" was released the same week and *Billboard* noted, wisely, that "Presley is riding high right now with network TV appearances and the
disk should benefit from all the special plugging." A week later *Billboard* noted
that sales of the record had "snowballed," and in listing some of the top markets for the record, showed that Elvis now was a smash on the West Coast as
well as throughout the South. By February the record was in *Billboard*'s Top
100, the major national tabulation of record hits. And the following week it

jumped forty places to number twenty-eight—on its way to number one.

Elvis was a national hit, but it appears he was one of the last to know. Scotty Moore said, "We were working near every day. We'd pull into some town, go to the hotel room and get washed up or go right to the auditorium or movie house, and after we played our shows, we'd get back in the cars and start driving to the next town. We never saw any newspapers. We didn't know we were getting big write-ups. They told us the record was going good, but we'd heard that before and even if it was, we weren't seeing any money from it. And we didn't hear much radio, because it was drive all night, sleep all day, and there wasn't much radio at night.

"There was a lot of crowd reaction, but we'd been seeing that for a year. How were we to know? All we knew was drive, drive, drive."

Red West said the schedule was so tight at the time, Elvis and the boys used somebody else's instruments on the Dorsey shows while he drove with their instruments to the city where the Sunday concert was to be. Then Elvis and Scotty and Bill and D. J. would fly to that city as soon as the Saturday Dorsey show ended.

"The next weekend it'd be the same thing all over again," Red said. "We'd be in some city somewhere and they'd go off to New York and I'd start driving to where they'd meet me the next day. I remember one show we were in Virginia somewhere and they flew from there to the show and I drove all the way to West Palm Beach, Florida. I was by myself. I drove straight through because we didn't have that much time. There was a show the next night. I took No Doz and kept going. I'll never forget it. I was really fightin' it to stay awake. But the TV shows was what did it. That's what sent him on his way."

The worst was yet to come, in March, when following the last Dorsey show, Scotty and Bill and D. J. and Elvis left New York in a snowstorm, drove to Los Angeles to play the Coliseum and then drove to San Diego to appear with Milton Berle on an aircraft carrier, and from there drove straight to Denver for another concert. So demanding was the pace, Elvis finally collapsed and was taken to a Jacksonville, Florida, hospital. Although he had a fever and doctors said he should rest for at least a week, Elvis got dressed and walked out of the hospital the following morning, to resume the current tour.

During this same period, Elvis went back into the studio, usually in New York, where RCA had its most modern facilities. It was there he recorded much of the material that went into his first album. There were twelve songs on the album, several of them already familiar in the rock and rhythm and blues markets. He sang Carl Perkins's song "Blue Suede Shoes" (released as a single in Canada and England, where it became a hit nearly equal to "Heartbreak Hotel" in the U. S.; he promised Sam Phillips he would not release it in competition with the original); "Tutti Frutti," which had been a hit for its author, Little Richard Penniman, as well as for Pat Boone; "I'm Counting on You," a song written by Don Robertson, who soon would record a national hit of his own ("Happy Whistler") and later would crank out dozens of songs for Elvis's movies; and, added from Elvis's first recording session for RCA in Nashville, Ray Charles's "I Got a Woman" and the Drifters' "Money Honey," both staples in his live performances. There was also an old standard, "Blue Moon," by Richard Rodgers and Lorenz Hart, one of four songs on the album from those RCA had inherited from Sun. The other three—all considered inappropriate for release by Sam Phillips because Elvis or Scotty or Bill had flatted or blown a note—were "Just Because," "I'll Never Let You Go" and "I Love You Because." However weak Sam may have thought the Sun leftovers were, they did still have the recognizable rockabilly beat that made Elvis, and Sun, so famous and, in fact, still were stronger than some of the newer songs. Thus it seemed Elvis had at least partially returned to the sound that had established him. But it never was mentioned publicly that anything on the album wasn't new.

The cover of the album showed Elvis (in a black and white photograph) playing his guitar, his thin, boyish face twisted in the pain of screaming a gutsy blues. Running down the side of the album was Elvis's first name in large pink letters, across the bottom his last name in large green letters. It was released in mid-March and went immediately into the eleven spot on *Billboard*'s best-selling album chart.

"When we first started recording," Steve Sholes said of this period, "the way he held the guitar was pretty close to where his mouth was, and we were trying to record him vocally at the same time because we didn't do tracking in those days. The guitar was so loud you couldn't hear his voice. We moved the mike around and so forth, and we finally ended up using a ukulele pick, a felt pick. He played the guitar so hard that every two or three takes he would break a string. And even after we got the ukulele pick, he was still breaking strings. I remember one take we were doing, he dropped the ukulele pick in the middle of a take, but he kept on banging the thing with his fingers. Jesus, when we got done with the take, his fingers were bleeding, so I said to him, 'Why didn't you quit?' 'Oh,' he said, 'it was going so good, I didn't want to break it up.'

"In the early days we would make a lot of takes and we would get to the point where I thought we had a pretty good one. And I'd say, 'I think we got it pretty good there, Elvis.' And he would say, 'I think I can do a little better.' He never criticized anybody else. If anyone made a mistake on a number, he would never point it out to them. He'd just say, 'Let's try it again, I think I was a little flat on that one,' until the musician picked up on it himself. A lot of artists are the reverse. You have to keep driving them—'Make one more take, I think

you can get this a little better.' Some of them are so gosh-darned big-headed
that you can't even say that to them, you have to say, 'The third trumpet player was flat,' or something like that. It's a lie, just to get him to sing a little more,
because if you told him he was flat, he'd get hysterical and walk out. When you
get an artist of Elvis's caliber, one who analyzes himself as closely as Elvis does,
and is willing to keep working as hard as Elvis, you know that all these things
added together are what made him successful."

Of course there was that voice. "Bill Haley and the people who preceded
Elvis had a very primitive sound, comparatively," Sholes said. "Elvis has a fine
musical ear and a great voice, a much better voice than people really think he
has. He has a feel for popular music much greater than other people at that time
had. That's why he was able to groove it in a direction that the kids liked,
because that was the way *he* liked it."

At the same time that Elvis's first album was released, RCA spat out a couple of what were called "extended play" records, which were the size of 45-rpm
records but had two or more songs per side. These EPs also went to the top of
the best-seller charts.

There was another development in March as Bob Neal's contract had
expired and the Colonel took control, becoming Elvis's "sole and exclusive
Advisor, Personal Representative and Manager in any and all fields of private
entertainment"—in exchange for 25 per cent of Elvis's total earnings before
taxes and other deductions, as was usual in such arrangements.

Bob Neal was not left like a beached fish in this transfer of "property." He
still had his morning radio show, the record store, the occasional concerts in the
area; and a short time later he became president of Stars, Inc., a management
company he formed with Sam Phillips to handle all of Sun's still-impressive
roster of artists: Carl Perkins, Johnny Cash, Warren Smith (then being
described as a possible successor to the Presley crown), Eddie Bond, Jack
Earls, Roy Orbison and his band, the Teen-Kings.

"My contract with Elvis was to expire and I simply let it go," Bob said. "The
only further thing: I received some small amount of commissions and royalties
from the initial period. There wasn't anything involved in a continuing commission or share. I hadn't asked for anything and hadn't tried to negotiate anything. I could have. But I didn't try to."

Late the same month, Elvis went to Hollywood for a screen test at Paramount
Studios, flying there at the invitation of Hal Wallis, a producer of films that
ranged all over the creative map from *Casablanca* and *The Maltese Falcon* to the
Martin and Lewis quickies. He had called the Colonel about the screen test after
seeing Elvis on one of the Dorsey shows and getting reports from the

Paramount-controlled movie theaters where Elvis had been appearing recently.

"Tom wanted to pursue a career in motion pictures for Elvis," said Oscar Davis, "so he played the Florida State theaters and the various theater chains on the East Coast, with Elvis singing between movie showings—starting at two and working until about eleven at night. I exploited the dates and we packed the theaters everywhere. Hollywood became aware of Elvis this way. These were all Paramount-controlled theaters, so Paramount became interested. Hal Wallis entered the picture and made the deal with Tom."

Elvis played a scene with veteran character actor Frank Faylen in the test. He was wearing jeans and a work shirt and was told to run through a few emotions, which he did—gesturing wildly and fervently, shouting at Faylen at one moment, poking a cigar in his mouth the next moment as he tapped the older actor on the chest to emphasize a point he'd just made. Faylen, knowing he shouldn't attempt to upstage Elvis—for the singer was an amateur, no matter how assured he seemed—did little more than react.

Although Elvis made it clear to the Colonel that he didn't want to sing in the movies, he wanted to act—like his heroes, Marlon Brando, James Dean, Richard Widmark and Tony Curtis—he went along when given a guitar and told to lip sync to his recording of "Blue Suede Shoes." Then, almost as if it were something to make him feel better, Wallis had him do two scenes from *The Rainmaker*, a Broadway play that Wallis then had in pre-production. However, there was never any hope extended that Elvis might join the cast led by Burt Lancaster and Katharine Hepburn. Elvis's musical performance was considered a success—it made the leap to film, which is sometimes difficult—and his acting efforts were considered amateurish but enthusiastic, as were Wallis's and Paramount's aspirations.

Wallis reviewed the results and offered the Colonel a three-film contract, the first to be made in the fall, possibly in early winter, depending upon how rapidly a script, director and supporting cast could be arranged. For his services, Elvis was to be paid $100,000 and for subsequent films this figure was to be increased, to $150,000 for the second and $200,000 for the third, large figures for the time. The Colonel was further triumphant in making the contract non-exclusive, freeing the Colonel to make other deals.

While in California, Elvis made another network appearance, on *The Milton Berle Show*, broadcast from aboard the U.S.S. *Hancock*, an aircraft carrier docked in San Diego. Predictably, he sang his first hit, "Heartbreak Hotel," along with "Blue Suede Shoes."

"You know how he moves around all the time," said Neal Matthews, one of the Jordanaires. "He's hard to contain, hard to keep in one position. Milton and the producer and director kept telling Elvis to stay on the chalk line. And Milton said, 'You or me, one, is gonna be outa the camera and it's not gonna be me.'"

Elvis also appeared in a sketch that, in time, made clear much of the main-stream entertainment world's lack of respect for this new thing called rock and roll. In a comedy sketch, Berle played Elvis's twin brother, speaking in a New Yorker's version of a Southern drawl, wearing clown-sized blue shoes, pant legs rolled up, yet claiming to have taught the singer everything he knew. They then sang "Blue Suede Shoes" together, the comedian behaving like an absolute fool to get the same big laughs he got when he wore a dress, another common ploy.

Elvis played along. "I owe it all to you, Melvin," he said.

The show was aired April 3, with an estimated 40 million in the audience, a figure that represented one out of every four people in the U.S.

His records continued to dominate the charts, making it seem as if someone had taken a rubber stamp to all the music trades: no matter where you looked, it said ELVIS PRESLEY. The first album passed the 100,000 mark and went to the number three position the second week—behind Harry Belafonte's first album and the soundtrack from *The Man with the Golden Arm*. By month's end, both the album and "Heartbreak Hotel" were on top. "A Howling Hillbilly Success" was the way the headline read in *Life*, Elvis's first national magazine spread, "Young Elvis Presley's Complaint Becomes Nation's Top Pop Tune."

In Amarillo, Texas, where Elvis had been interviewed by *Life*, fans kicked through a plate glass door to offer him bits of underwear to autograph. In San Diego it was necessary to call out the Shore Patrol to bolster local police security.

"From then on it became a battle," said D. J. Fontana. "Hard to get into the auditorium, hard to get out. The Colonel had it set up security-wise. Nobody got in anywhere. Lotta times we'd go in two or three hours ahead of time to set up and they wouldn't let us in. So we'd set there and wait until somebody came out that knew us. Same way getting out. Soon as he'd get through his act, they'd have a police car or something there and he was gone. We'd pack up and two or three hours later they'd let us out. We'd stick our heads out of the door and the kids would say, 'Is he in there?' We'd say, 'No, he's gone.' They'd say, 'You're lying.' They just didn't believe us. We had a heck of a time getting out of those buildings."

By now the touring conformed to a pattern shaped by the Colonel years earlier. Oscar Davis described the pattern: "First we had the country music acts. And then we had a different format, more in the pop field. But we never had any names. Frankie Conners, an Irish tenor . . . Phil Maraquin, a comic from Detroit . . . various acts out of Chicago. It was a hodgepodge show, but it made Elvis look good. When he came out, it was dynamite.

"We had trouble," Oscar said. "It was hard for the early acts, because the audience'd yell for Presley. This caused a lot of confusion. So I got out in the beginning and I explained that we had policemen and firemen there and in the event anyone left their chairs, we would stop the show immediately, so if you want to see Elvis, stay in your chairs. And I said all acts on the first part of the bill, you're gonna see these, and they're all friends of Elvis and Elvis asked that you treat them as kindly as you would treat him. And any outburst, we stop the show and you don't see Elvis.

"Sometimes it worked, sometimes it didn't, and when it didn't, that's when the newspapers wrote it up big, made it seem a riot. Of course sometimes it *was* a riot, but not as often as most people think."

On April 23, Elvis went into Las Vegas for two weeks at the New Frontier Hotel. It was, in retrospect, a mistake; the bunch that kept Las Vegas alive was not Elvis's crowd. The middle-aged marrieds from middle America celebrating twentieth wedding anniversaries, the Eisenhower Republicans, the rich vacationers and gamblers and tourists—these weren't the ones who swooned when they heard the first words of "Heartbreak Hotel" or kicked through a door to offer Elvis a well-filled teenaged brassiere and a ball-point pen for an autograph. Only curiosity kept the Venus Room open where Elvis was appearing—with the Freddie Martin Orchestra and comedian Shecky Greene. Thanks to the publicity or to their own kids, these people knew about Elvis, but that didn't mean they liked him. Elvis never played to an empty house, and there were *some* matrons who went for Elvis in a manner that rivaled the pubescent attacks from their daughters. But most entered the huge showroom hating Elvis, and no matter how hard he tried, he couldn't get them off their hands. Curious, they'd come to see what he was all about and they'd paid the sums asked by the hotel, but that didn't mean they'd scream, applaud or faint. From what Bill Black said afterward, according to friends, it was so quiet at the hotel when they performed, for the first time they heard the musical clinkers. Prior to that time the noise of the audience had drowned out any mistakes.

When Elvis opened, it was his name that appeared at the top of the marquee outside the hotel. A few days later Shecky Greene's name was on top and Elvis had been put on the bottom, beneath the name of the orchestra leader.

The Colonel and the people at the New Frontier met and agreed the best thing to do was to tear up the $8500-a-week contract and forget about the whole thing. The Vegas booking seemed like a good idea a week earlier, but now it was a big mistake.

"Heartbreak Hotel" was in the number one spot—where it stayed for eight weeks—when Elvis's second RCA single was released in early May. This was one of the songs he'd recorded in that first Victor session in January, "I Want You, I Need You, I Love You," backed with "My Baby Left Me," an up-tempo blues written by Arthur Crudup, the black blues singer who'd written "That's All Right [Mama]."

That same week both *Time* and *Newsweek* greeted Elvis with columns of hesitant praise. *Time* called him the "teeners' hero," said his voice was rich and round, his diction poor, his movements sexy. Teenaged girls went wild when they saw him, the magazine said, and as a result Elvis was pocketing $7500 in profits each week. *Newsweek* put Elvis on its "Music" page, a subdivision of "The Arts" (he shared the page with a review of a Broadway play, *Most Happy Fella*), and offered a number of "typical female comments," all making some reference to Elvis either being a dope peddler or a jailbird, or looking like a snake. Both magazines had him owning three Cadillacs and a three-wheeled motorcycle.

With all these vehicles, Elvis also had bought a new home in Memphis, a $40,000 one-story green-and-white-trimmed ranch house at 1034 Audubon Drive in one of the city's better neighborhoods, not far from Audubon Park. The house sat in the center of a wide plot, with a thick stand of trees in the rear giving privacy to the swimming pool Elvis had built. There were three bedrooms, a game room, a sitting room, dining room and living room, furnished with large cheap pieces of elusive period and taste. On the walls were scattered some of Elvis's early publicity photographs and souvenirs he bought on his tour trips.

It was a quiet neighborhood, until Elvis arrived. Then the home became a target for Memphis teenagers, so much so, in fact, that Elvis had a brick wall built to separate the house from the street and then added tall metal spikes—none of which did any good. The girls only trespassed more aggressively, pulling up blades of grass from the lawn, pressing their noses against the windows, even scraping dust from the Cadillacs into small envelopes.

Said Buzzy Forbess, Elvis's friend from his project and high school days: "I remember so many teenagers were coming by, the neighbors began to complain, and then when Mrs. Presley began hanging the wash out on the line . . . whooooeee, boy, they really howled. They said it wasn't that kind of neighborhood. People just don't hang their wash out on Audubon Drive. Well, Elvis just told them what for. Said it was his house and his parents could do anything they wanted. And the way it came out in the papers, it was the only house on the block that was paid for. Elvis had paid cash and his neighbors was still making payments, or renting."

Mr. and Mrs. Presley seemed little changed by this. They kept their old friends in the Lauderdale Courts; the only difference was when they got together, the Presleys would sometimes drive to the project in one Cadillac, bring friends to the house for a visit, then return them in a second car.

Elvis, meanwhile, still visited *his* old friends, stopping by at Sun—once joining Carl Perkins, Johnny Cash and Jerry Lee Lewis (all of whom were on the label then) in an impromptu gospel sing around the studio piano—or revisiting his teachers at Humes High. On one of these visits he performed at the annual talent show, the same show he had sung at during his senior year.

For recreation he'd visit the amusement park at the county fairgrounds. Because of his popularity, it was impossible for him to attend during the park's normal hours, so he'd rent the park after it closed, inviting friends to accompany him. When Elvis had a date, this is where he usually took her. His touring had ended an eighteen-month-long relationship with Dixie Locke and Elvis didn't date any one girl regularly.

Most of these girls he met on the road. Ralph Gleason, critic for the *San Francisco Chronicle*, said of Elvis's visit to Oakland in 1956: "Before he made the run to the car, an occasional chick would get past the cops and bust all the way through to the dressing room door. He was sweet to them as earlier he had baited them as they hung over the railing or, when he was onstage, they ran up to the line of cops. He'd slap his crotch and give a couple of bumps and grinds and half grin at the insane reaction it produced each time.

"It was the first show I'd seen that had the true element of sexual hysteria in it."

# Chapter 8

# HYSTERIA: 2

E lvis was bouncing all over the country now. His appearances early in the
year mainly were in the South, even during the months when
"Heartbreak Hotel" was becoming a national hit, but now instead of moving
from city to city he was jumping from state to state. In mid-May he was headlined over Hank Snow and the Jordanaires at the Cotton Pickin' Jamboree in
Memphis, part of the annual Cotton Carnival, a show promoted by Bob Neal.
The first week of June he was back in California, making his second appearance on *The Milton Berle Show*. Then he was in Colorado and then he was
signed to appear on Steve Allen's new Sunday night show being broadcast live
from New York.

It was after he'd appeared on the Berle show again on June 6 that Elvis collected some more of the criticism that now seemed as much a part of the act as
the wiggle and the voice. It was Jack Gould, television critic for the *New York
Times*, who delivered the longest and most virulent blast:

"Mr. Presley made another television appearance last night on the Milton
Berle show over Channel 4. Indeed, the entire program revolved around the
boy. Attired in the familiar oversize jacket and open shirt which are almost the
uniform of the contemporary youth who fancies himself as terribly sharp, he
might possibly be classified as an entertainer. Or, perhaps quite as easily, as an
assignment for a sociologist.

"Mr. Presley has no discernible singing ability. His specialty is rhythm
songs which he renders in an undistinguished whine; his phrasing, if it can be
called that, consists of the stereotyped variations that go with a beginner's aria
in a bathtub. For the ear he is an unutterable bore, not nearly so talented as
Frankie Sinatra back in the latter's rather hysterical days at the Paramount
Theater. Nor does he convey the emotional fury of a Johnnie Ray.

"From watching Mr. Presley it is wholly evident that his skill lies in
another direction. He is a rock-and-roll variation of one of the most standard
acts in show business: the virtuoso of the hootchy-kootchy. His one specialty is an accented movement of the body that heretofore has been primarily

identified with the repertoire of the blonde bombshells of the burlesque run-way. The gyration never had anything to do with the world of popular music and still doesn't.

"Certainly Mr. Presley cannot be blamed for accepting the adulation and economic rewards that are his. But that's hardly any reason why he should be billed as a vocalist. The reason for his success is not that complicated."

The man second to Gould in television criticism was Jack O'Brien of the *New York Journal-American*, and it seemed as if he had written his review while looking over Gould's shoulder: "Elvis Presley wiggled and wriggled with such abdominal gyrations that burlesque bombshell Georgia Sothern really deserves equal time to reply in gyrating kind. He can't sing a lick, makes up for vocal shortcomings with the weirdest and plainly planned, suggestive animation short of an aborigine's mating dance."

Nor was this the end of it. During the next few months, Elvis appeared on television again and again, and each time the reviews were more anatomical than musical.

It was the first of July when Elvis was in New York for the second show of Steve Allen's new variety series, initiated by NBC-TV in an attempt to bump off the CBS opposition, Ed Sullivan. Steve debuted his show a week earlier with Kim Novak, Vincent Price, Wally Cox, Dane Clark, Sammy Davis and the Will Masten Trio among the notables, and in this show Elvis was to share the music and laughs with Imogene Coca and Andy Griffith. Steve admitted he was going for names—at the network's insistence—to assure some impressive ratings. It worked. Steve got more than 55 per cent of the audience, while Sullivan was left with a meager 15 per cent.

What Steve did to earn this astonishing figure was to put Elvis in a silly satire of deep South country music shows, such as Elvis had played for years. It opened with "your old partner, Big Steve," a six-gun strapped around his waist, making a speech to all his friends and neighbors, with Elvis and Imogene Coca and Andy Griffith standing behind him in western clothing. The set itself looked much like the *Louisiana Hayride* set. For most of the sketch Elvis, designated as a part of the "gang," did little more than contribute a few "yahoos." Finally, he was introduced as Tumbleweed.

"Tumbleweed is a trick rider," said Steve. "Yes, sir, you ain't seen trick ridin' till you've seen Tumbleweed. Yesterday he went across the range at a full gallop, blindfolded . . . he picked up a rattlesnake with his teeth, jumped four fences, and dropped that snake in a gopher hole—all at a full gallop. Tell 'em why it was so tough, Tumbleweed."

Elvis stepped forward and said, deadpan, "I don't use no horse!"

It went on like that for a while, Steve delivering set-up lines, his guests coming in with the punch lines, and the skit closed with Big Steve introducing a cowboy song, with each of the guests taking a verse. When it came Elvis's turn, he blinked his eyes, plunked his guitar and sang: "I got a horse, I got a gun / I'm goin' out and have some fun / But I'm a-warnin' you galoots / Don't step on my blue suede boots."

A little later in the show Elvis sang "Hound Dog," a rhythm and blues hit from 1952 that he had picked for his next single release. The way Steve told it, "We'd recognized the controversy that was building around Elvis and so we took advantage of it, putting him in a tuxedo—white tie and tails—and taking away his guitar. We thought putting Elvis in formal wardrobe to sing the song was humorous. We also asked him to stand perfectly still, and we positioned a real hound dog on a stool next to him—a dog that had been trained to do nothing but sit and look droopy. I must say Elvis took it quite naturally, and good-naturedly."

The fans did not take it so well. They began picketing the Steve Allen Theater the following morning, carrying signs that said "We want the real Presley."

Said John Lardner in *Newsweek*: "Allen was nervous, like a man trying to embalm a firecracker. Presley was distraught, like Huckleberry Finn when the widow put him in a store suit and told him not to gape or scratch."

The same week, Ed Sullivan began negotiating with the Colonel for Elvis. He previously had said he wouldn't touch Elvis with a long stick, but when he saw Steve's ratings, there was a certain amount of hemming and hawing and before it was over, he'd promised Elvis $50,000 for three performances, the first in September, the others at eight-week intervals. Per show, this more than tripled the previous high Sullivan had ever paid—$5000—and more than doubled Steve Allen's fee of $7500.

Steve said, "We could have engaged in bidding against Ed, but it wouldn't have proved anything. It would have given our show a higher rating, but it would have been Elvis's rating, not ours."

Elvis's first appearance on Sullivan's *Toast of the Town* was on September 9, when he helped Ed corner 82.6 per cent of the audience, equal to about 54 million people, a record that stood until 1964, when Sullivan coaxed the Beatles onto his show. What was most remarkable was that Elvis was shown on the home screen from the waist *up*. The only way anybody at home could tell his hips were moving was to listen to the screams from the girls in the studio audience.

That must have made Jack Gould of the *Times* happy, right? Wrong.

The following day Gould wrote, "Elvis Presley made his appearance on the Ed Sullivan Show over Channel 2 and the National Broadcasting Company didn't even bother to compete. It gave Steve Allen the night off and ran an

English film. From his extensive repertoire of assaults on the American ear, Mr. Presley included 'Hound Dog.' The maidens in the West Coast studio audience squealed appreciatively over their idol's mobility. On the East Coast, Charles Laughton, substituting for Mr. Sullivan, patiently waited until it was all over." That was the complete review.

And if that weren't enough, Gould then wrote a much longer article, which appeared in the *Times* the following Sunday. He first recalled Elvis's "strip tease behavior" on Milton Berle's show, applauded a "much more sedate" appearance on the Allen program, but then said that Elvis "injected movements of the tongue and indulged in wordless singing that was singularly distasteful" on the Sullivan show.

"Quite possibly Presley just happened to move in where society has failed the teen-ager. Certainly, modern youngsters have been subjected to a great deal of censure and perhaps too little understanding. Greater in their numbers than ever before, they may have found in Presley a rallying point, a nationally prominent figure who seems to be on their side.

"Family counselors have wisely noted that ours is still a culture in a stage of frantic and tense transition. With even sixteen-year-olds capable of commanding $20 or $30 a week in their spare time, with access to automobiles at an early age, with communications media of all kinds exposing them to new thoughts very early in life, theirs indeed is a high degree of independence. Inevitably it has been accomplished by a lessening of parental control.

"Small wonder, therefore, that the teenager is susceptible to over-stimulation from the outside. It is at an age when the awareness of sex is both thoroughly natural and normal, when latent rebellion is to be expected. But what is new and a little discouraging is the willingness and indeed eagerness of reputable businessmen to exploit these critical factors beyond all reasonable grounds.

"When Presley executes his bumps and grinds, it must be remembered by the Columbia Broadcasting System that even the twelve-year-old's curiosity may be over-stimulated.

"In the long run, perhaps Presley will do everyone a favor by pointing up the need for early sex education so that neither his successors nor TV can capitalize on the idea that his type of routine is somehow highly tempting yet forbidden fruit.

"A perennial weakness in the executive echelons of the networks is their opportunistic rationalization of television's function. The industry lives fundamentally by the code of giving the public what it wants. This is not the place to argue the artistic foolishness of such a standard; in the case of situation comedies and other escapist diversions it is relatively unimportant.

"But when this code is applied to teenagers just becoming conscious of life's processes, not only is it manifestly without validity but also it is perilous. Catering to the interests of the younger generation is one of television's main jobs; because those interests do not always coincide with parental tastes should not deter the broadcaster. But selfish exploitation and commercialized over-stimulation of youth's physical impulses is certainly a gross national disservice."

What Gould was saying, once all the verbiage had been thinned, was he thought Ed Sullivan and CBS were going too far in putting Elvis on television at eight o'clock, when impressionable youngsters might have their libidos stroked unnecessarily. More simply, the television industry was presenting something definitely obscene and thereby forgetting it was, after all, a public trust.

Earlier the "Threat" had been Frank Sinatra and bubble gum and Communists writing film scripts in Hollywood and flying saucers and televi-sion itself and, going back, the horseless carriage and the flying machine and jazz and the Charleston and Roosevelt and the WPA and rumble seats. Later it would be beatniks and peaceniks and the Beatles and the twist and hippies and all of California and marijuana. Always there was something or someone, real or fictional, responsible for the imminent destruction of Society As We Know It. In 1956 it was Elvis and rock 'n' roll.

All across America the edicts were posted. In San Antonio, Texas, rock 'n' roll was banished from city swimming pool jukeboxes because, according to the city council, the music "attracted undesirable elements given to practicing their spastic gyrations in abbreviated bathing suits." In Asbury Park, New Jersey, newspapers reported that twenty-five "vibrating teenagers" had been hospitalized following a record hop, prompting Mayor Roland Hines to prohib-it all future rock concerts in the city's dance halls. Which in turn spurred offi-cials in nearby Jersey City to cancel a rock show at the 24,000-seat Roosevelt Stadium. In San Jose, California, it was said teenagers repelled seventy-three peace-keeping policemen, injuring eleven and causing $3000 in damage to the auditorium—which caused neighboring Santa Cruz to ban all concerts from its civic buildings. In Boston, following a "riot" by students at the Massachusetts Institute of Technology, a specially appointed committee organized to study the music branded disc jockeys "social pariahs" and banned them from partic-ipating in record "hops" and other public entertainment. In two other Massachusetts towns, Somerville and Medford, there were stabbings, and a local district attorney, Garret Byrne, said, "Tin Pan Alley has unleashed a new monster, a sort of nightmare of rhythm. Some of our disc jockeys have put emotional TNT on their turntables. Rock 'n' roll gives young hoodlums an excuse to get together. It inflames teenagers and is obscenely suggestive." The *New York Daily News* said the rioting stretched from "puritanical Boston to julep-loving Georgia" and accused record makers and disc jockeys of "pandering to the worst juvenile taste." The paper then recommended a "crackdown on riotous rock 'n' roll," describing the music as a "barrage of primitive jungle-beat rhythm set to lyrics which few adults would care to hear," and advocated banning all teenagers from dancing in public without the written consent of their parents, along with a midnight curfew for everyone under twenty-one.

Concentrating their attack on Elvis specifically, in Syracuse, New York, a group of women circulated petitions demanding that Elvis be barred from television and sent them to the three networks. In Romeo, Michigan, a sixteen-year-old high school student was expelled for refusing to have a local barber cut his sideburns and Elvis ducktail, while in Knoxville, Tennessee, three crew-cropped football players set up their own barbershop and trimmed all the Elvis hair styles in sight, whether or not the owners liked it. Elvis was hung in effigy in Nashville and burned in absentia in St. Louis. In Ottawa, Canada, eight students of the Notre Dame Convent were expelled for disobeying a school edict to stay away from one of Elvis's local concerts. At Yale University two students formed the national I Like Ludwig [Beethoven] Fan Club and started handing out "I Like Ludwig" buttons to counter all the "I Like Elvis" buttons; three of the Ludwig buttons eventually found their way onto the lapels of violinist Isaac Stern, Philadelphia's conductor Eugene Ormandy and cellist Pablo Casals.

Although men from every professional walk of life joined the massive assault, it was the religious fraternity that seemed the most incensed. Said the Reverend William Shannon in the *Catholic Sun*: "Presley and his voodoo of frustration and defiance have become symbols in our country, and we are sorry to come upon Ed Sullivan in the role of promoter. Your Catholic viewers, Mr. Sullivan, are angry; and you cannot compensate for a moral injury, not even by sticking 'the Little Gaelic Singers of County Derry' on the same bill with Elvis Presley." Evangelist Billy Graham said he'd never met Elvis and didn't know much about him, but "From what I've heard, I'm not so sure I'd want my children to see him." Cardinal Spellman, in a sermon in New York during a "Pageant of Prayer" marking the close of the Tenth National Confraternity of Christian Doctrine, quoted at length from one of Jack Gould's articles. Downtown in Greenwich Village—where you'd think there'd be some liberalism—the Reverend Charles Howard Graff of St. John's Episcopal Church called Elvis a "whirling dervish of sex."

It shouldn't have surprised anyone that this sort of reaction to popular music occurred. Thirty years earlier, public reaction to jazz was, as in 1956 with rock 'n' roll, more "violent" than the music itself. At that time, in the 1920s, the *Ladies Home Journal* said jazz was Bolshevik-inspired and constituted a replacement for sex and marriage that would reduce the birth rate. Articles of the period were titled "The Jazz Path of Degradation," "It Is Worse Than Saloon and Scarlet Vice," "Unspeakable Jazz Must Go" and "Does Jazz Put the Sin in Syncopation?" Said the *Journal* in one of its more acerbic onslaughts: "Jazz originally was the accompaniment of the voodoo dancer, stimulating the half-crazed barbarian to the vilest deeds. The weird chants, accompanied by the syncopated rhythm of the voodoo invokers, have also been employed by other barbaric people to stimulate brutality and sensuality. That it has a demoralizing effect on the human brain has been demonstrated by many scientists."

In 1956 much the same sort of public hysteria prevailed.

Elvis was granting occasional interviews in those days, and invariably this criticism would crop up during the questioning. One of those interviews was released as a 45-rpm record, in cooperation with *TV Guide*. First he was asked what he thought about the nickname he'd been given, "Elvis the Pelvis."

"I don't like to be called 'Elvis the Pelvis,' but, uh . . . I mean, it's one of the most childish expressions I ever heard comin' from an adult. 'Elvis the Pelvis.' But, uh, if they want-a call me that, I mean there's nothing I can do about it, so I just have to accept it. You have to accept the good with the bad, the bad with the good."

Elvis next was asked about the predominantly adult criticism he'd been getting.

"As a rule, most of the adults are real nice," Elvis said. "They're understanding. They . . . they . . . uh, I've had 'em to come round to me by the hundreds and say, 'I don't personally like your kind-a music, but, uh, uh, my children like it and so on, and, and if they like it, well I ain't got any kick about it, 'cause when I was young I liked the Charleston. I liked the fox trot. I liked this and that.' They, uh, they're adults with a little intelligence. I mean, you know, they don't run people into the ground for havin' a nice time."

Elvis's voice came rolling out like syrup on an autumn day: thick and smooth and sweet, with a soft bite. He sounded like a hillbilly James Stewart, with a slur that ran into a twang. He was asked, "When you hear rock 'n' roll, it just gets you on fire?"

"Oh, I, uh . . . not when I just hear it on the radio. When I do it on a stage, you have to put on a show for the people. In other words, people can buy your records and hear you sing, 'cause they don't have to come out to hear you sing, you have to put on a show to draw a crowd. If I just stood out there and sang and never moved, people would say, 'Well, my goodness, I can stay home and listen to his records.' But you have to give 'em a show, somethin' to talk about."

And finally: "How did that rockin' motion get started?"

"The very first appearance after I started to record, I was on a show in Memphis where I started doin' that," he said, referring to the concert in the

Overton Park Shell. "I was on the show as an extra added single . . . a big jamboree in an outdoor theater . . . uh . . . outdoor auditorium. And, uh, and I came
out on stage and, uh, uh, I was scared stiff. My first big appearance, in front of
an audience. And I came out and I was doin' a fast-type tune, uh, one of my
first records, and ever'body was hollerin' and I didn't know what they was hollerin' at. Ever'body was screamin' and ever'thing, and, uh, I came off stage and
my manager told me they was hollerin' because I was wigglin'. Well, I went
back out for an encore and I, I, I kind-a did a little more. And the more I did,
the wilder they went."

Elvis certainly wasn't naïve. He had many things going for him in
1956—timing, good looks, a rich and versatile singing talent, a crafty manager—but he also was quick enough to know when he had (however naturally)
stumbled onto a good thing, a show business gimmick that might win him an
enthusiastic following. He was too modest when he told a writer, "I'm not kid-
din' myself. My voice alone is just an ordinary voice. What people come to see
is how I use it. If I stand still while I'm singin', I'm dead, man. I might as well
go back to drivin' a truck." But there was some truth in what he said, just as
there was truth in the advertising slogan "It's the sizzle that sells the steak."

Still, Elvis was not a pushy or cocky young man. He was many things, but
he was not overly aggressive; he was not the raving egotist many with sudden
wealth and fame become. He owned a fleet of Cadillacs and a small parking lot
full of other assorted vehicles, he had a wardrobe that included thirty sport
coats and forty sport shirts, and his fingers and wrists were hung with diamonds and sapphires, but this wasn't ostentation, not in the usual sense. It was
just his way of conforming to the customs of that peculiar cultural group from
which he recently had graduated, the country and western singer. Back home
in Tennessee, as soon as any of those good ol' boys got a few dollars together,
they bought Cadillacs and fancy duds and flashy jewelry; that didn't mean they
gave up grits. And in Elvis's case, the *first* thing he bought was a house for his
parents.

"When you come right down to it," said Bob Neal, "I think it was a matter
of his wanting to accomplish a great deal of this for his mother, to make her
comfortable and happy."

"That's right," said Mrs. Gladys Tipler, Elvis's old boss at Crown Electric.
"Before he ever knew he was going to make a nickel, one day he set here in our
office and he said to Tip, 'If I ever get my hands on any money, Mr. Tipler, I'm
gonna buy my mother a home.' He stated that, he sure did. And that was the
first thing he did when he did get some money. That's no come-on stuff."

When you put it together, it made perfect newspaper copy—and Elvis had
been cast in the perfect mould. He was six feet tall and quick to punch a boy out

if he got out of line. His hair was worn long and slicked back and his sideburns came all the way down to the bottom of his ears. He rolled the sleeves on his short-sleeved sport shirts three times to show the biceps, wore his collar pulled up in back, and slipped a half-inch leather belt into two-inch loops and shoved the buckle over one hip. He liked to drive flashy cars, race motorcycles, shoot pool and lay girls. (Said Johnny Cash: "He had a project to see how many girls he could make. He did okay.") He was what "good girls" called a hood. But he was Southern, dripping manners and charm. He loved—no, worshiped—his mother; he wouldn't do anything that would embarrass her. He addressed everyone as Mr. or Mrs.; his sentences were punctuated with "sir" and "ma'am."

Within a week of Elvis's first Sullivan show, RCA released seven of his records simultaneously, all of them 45s. No one had done anything like this before. (One could imagine the Colonel shouting in a carnival bally: "Seven—count 'em, folks!—seven amazing singles at once!") It was considered foolish, even suicidal; the public would be confused, and no one record could ever rise above the massive choice facing the radio programmer and record buyer. Sure, RCA had reissued all five of Elvis's Sun records less than a year earlier, but that had been regarded as a move executed to take advantage of Sun's final sales push and to fill the time between Elvis's signing and the recording and release of new material.

Said *Billboard*: "Fourteen tunes, formerly available on Presley's LPs or EPs, now available on seven singles, within reach of any kid with eighty-nine cents." It was saturation marketing. So what if none of the seven rushed to the top of the charts, every one of them sold at least 100,000 copies—which, multiplied by six or seven cents per record (Elvis's cut, including performance fees and publishing or writing royalties), added up to an impressive figure. Besides that, one of the two songs Elvis sang on the Sullivan show was "Love Me Tender." In introducing this song, he said it was the title tune from his first picture—then two months from release—and he hoped everybody liked it. This and this alone created such a demand—orders for 856,327 copies a week *before* shipping—that RCA had to put it out earlier than originally planned. This gave Elvis *eight* new singles.

The bizarre thing about all this was that "Hound Dog" was, in early September, in the number one spot for the sixth week in a row, and it was abundantly clear that the next week it would be succeeded by "Don't Be Cruel," the song on the other side of the same record. And chances were good that the latter would stay on top for several more weeks. So who needed "Love Me Tender?"

What happened was Elvis had three number one hits in a row. Two million kids bought "Hound Dog" and then *another* two million went in and bought "Don't Be Cruel." (Even if it was the same record.) And after that more than a million went back and bought "Love Me Tender." From August, when the run started, until December nobody but Elvis was going to be at the head of the charts. No one. In the autumn of 1956, as teenagers returned to school, the saturation gamble paid off.

Bones Howe was a onetime jazz drummer who later could boast number one records with the regularity and apparent ease most men display in knotting neckties and shoelaces. From 1965, he produced more hits than most producers have in a lifetime—"It Ain't Me, Babe" and "You Baby" for the Turtles, "Windy" for the Association, "Stoned Soul Picnic" and "Aquarius / Let the Sunshine In" for the Fifth Dimension, and several of Diana Ross's solo records, to name a few. In the late summer of 1956 he was a $72-a-week recording apprentice and serving, he said, as bottom-rung engineer for Elvis's first recording sessions in Hollywood.

"They would come to town and take an entire floor at the Roosevelt Hotel on Hollywood Boulevard, or the Plaza near Hollywood and Vine, and later the Knickerbocker on Ivar, just north of the boulevard," he said. "They had to take a whole floor because they couldn't guard his room otherwise. Girls would be crawling up the fire escapes. And Elvis would encourage them. Finally I think they threw him out of one of the hotels. Anyway, they'd come to Hollywood, travelling in one of those Cadillacs with an extra section in the middle—you know the kind, four doors on each side—driving here from Memphis—Scotty and Bill and D. J. and Elvis and a few of the other guys, his bodyguards. And in the morning, from the time they got up, they'd drive up and down Hollywood Boulevard. They'd pull up to a stop light and just before the light changed, if there were girls standing on the corner, Elvis would roll the window down, take his sunglasses off and say hello. And then the light would change and they'd take off, leaving hundreds of people wandering around in the intersection screaming and jumping up and down and chasing the Cadillac down the street. Elvis just loved it."

Bones said afternoons were spent in the large room that was Studio B in Radio Recorders at 7000 Santa Monica Boulevard, a few blocks from Hollywood High School. At the time it was one of the most popular recording facilities in Los Angeles. Henry Mancini cut his *Peter Gunn* album in that room. Norman Granz took Ella Fitzgerald and Stan Getz and Gerry Mulligan there. Columbia Records used the studio to record most of its artists. But when Elvis came to town, said Bones, no one else got near the place. For Elvis, it was booked not by the hour, but by the week.

"Everything had to be left alone," said Bones. "They'd come in the first day and they didn't move the drums or anything for two weeks sometimes. Fifteen hours a day, seven days a week. It was all up to Elvis how long the sessions ran. They'd run all night if he felt like it. He was the barometer. If he felt good, we'd get things done. If he didn't feel good, or couldn't get into it in an hour or so, that's all."

Those in the control room with Bones included most of the regulars—the Colonel, Steve Sholes, some of Elvis's pals—along with Thorne Nogar, whose studio it was, usually somebody from RCA, and either Jean or Julian Aberbach or their right hand in running Hill and Range Songs and the manager of Elvis's music publishing company, Freddy Bienstock. Bienstock, a cousin of the Aberbachs, had joined the Elvis team during his second recording session for RCA in New York the preceding spring, and by summer his role was clearly defined. It was Freddy Bienstock who would for the next twelve years collect all the material from which Elvis would select songs for his records; Bienstock was then the equivalent of Elvis's A&R (artist and repertoire) man. Ordinarily this responsibility should have gone to Steve Sholes, who was head of A&R for RCA, but by now Sholes was becoming less and less involved. His presence at recording sessions continued, of course, and he still was the label's "representative," but he seldom had much, or anything, to say about how the session was conducted. In time he would even talk to Elvis not directly but through the Jordanaires.

"We had a number of writers under contract," Freddy said, his Swiss childhood still coloring his speech. "We would suggest they write some material for Elvis. People like Otis Blackwell, Doc Pomus, Mort Shuman, Joy Byars in Nashville, Sid Tepper and Roy Bennett. And more would arrive unsolicited, naturally, hundreds of songs each week. I was like a clearing house for Elvis, so that after a while even RCA was sending me songs."

Bones said that all of this material was brought to the sessions by Bienstock or one of the Aberbachs on "dubs" or demonstration records, which were precisely what they are purported to be: records made to demonstrate a song's values, or lack of them. Almost all of them had been semi-professionally produced (at worst) and many could have been released commercially as is, if anyone wished. The instrumentation was seldom changed, and usually Elvis would sing the song the way the singer on the demo sang it—largely because *that* singer was doing it the way he thought Elvis would.

Said Bones: "They'd come in with these stacks of dubs, stacks that were twenty inches high sometimes. Elvis hadn't heard them before arriving at the studio. He'd come in with his entourage. Usually they'd all be dressed alike: dark pants and a loud sport shirt. Sometimes all the guys would be wearing 'I Like

Elvis' buttons. It was a carnival. Then when it finally settled down, my job was to play disc jockey . . . to play these dubs out into the studio, where there were big speakers, and Elvis and the guys would be. I'd put a record on and Elvis would listen and at some point or other he'd signal take it off and I'd stick it on the 'out' pile. If he liked it, he'd tap the top of his head, meaning play it again from the top. He'd listen to it two or three times, and if it was something he really thought he wanted to record, we'd play it over and over again until everybody knew the song. And then Elvis would sing it as the group played behind him."

His schedule had made it difficult to get Elvis into the studio and his habit of refusing to review material beforehand and insisting upon working from "head arrangements" worked out on the spot made RCA nervous. But the sessions, held over a long weekend, produced "Love Me" (by Jerry Lieber and Mike Stoller, who'd written "Hound Dog"), three songs by Little Richard (for which Freddy Bienstock secured co-publishing rights), and a handful of country tunes, including "Old Shep," the Red Foley song about a boy and his dog that Elvis had sung at the State Fair when he was ten.

Bones said, "He might make thirteen or fourteen takes and he'd go back and listen to the early ones. He'd say, 'I think we had one back there that was better . . .' And we'd go back and listen. And when he listened, he'd dance, work out, with the tape playing real loud . . . the same way he usually performed when he was singing. With Elvis every take was a performance. The same way as on stage."

According to Steve Sholes, when Elvis danced in the studio it created a problem. "In the session I'd say, 'Elvis, can't you stand still?' And he'd say, 'No, I can't. I'm sorry. I start playing and the movements are involuntary.' The reason I wanted him to stand still was because he kept getting off-mike."

Elvis eventually stopped playing the guitar and merely thumped it on the side or back on the afterbeat. This often was added as an "overdub," in another session, which made it easier for Sholes and the others to record his voice.

"Fantastic thing about Elvis was that after one playing of the record he would have the thing in mind, the melody perfect, the chords all down. This isn't too amazing for a country singer," Sholes said, "but the thing that killed me was that he generally had most of the lyrics too, sometimes all of them. The second time through he'd have all the lyrics. Sometimes we'd be making a take and I'd say, 'Gee, Elvis, I think you made a mistake in the lyrics there.' And he'd say, 'I don't think I did, Mr. Sholes.' And I'd look at the damn sheet and I'd find he was right. He has something close to photographic memory."

Bones Howe said, "So what it really boiled down to was Elvis produced his own records. He came to the session, picked the songs, and if something in the arrangement was changed, he was the one to change it. Everything was

worked out spontaneously. Nothing was really rehearsed. Many of the important decisions normally made previous to a recording session were made *during* the session.

"What it was," said Bones, "was a look at the future. Today everybody
makes records this way. Back then Elvis was the only one. He was the forerun-
ner of everything that's record production *these* days. Consciously or uncon-
sciously, everyone imitated him. People started doing what Elvis did."

For years things would be in disarray in Nashville, thanks to Elvis. The regulars on the *Grand Ole Opry* didn't just dislike Elvis's music, they disliked him.
It was bad enough he'd bastardized country music, they said, but then it
became popular, which meant their own records weren't selling as well as they
had. Before Elvis a hit for Hank Snow sold maybe half a million copies, but
now Hank, and most others, couldn't get half that. This caused a split in the
country ranks. In rejecting rock 'n' roll, some went even more "country" than
they had in the past. Others jumped aboard the rockabilly bandwagon rolling
through town, so many that by 1957 the record charts were nearly dominated
by former good ol' country boys—Jerry Lee Lewis, Johnny Cash, Sonny
James, Marty Robbins, George Hamilton IV, Conway Twitty and the Everly
Brothers among them. In the meantime about a hundred country radio stations
changed formats and went rock. And so did a lot of the fans. Never before had
there been so much pickin' and grinnin' on the best-seller charts, and at the
same time never before had the source of this sound taken such a beating.

Things also changed regarding black music. Early in his career Elvis had
displayed an open respect for black music and black musicians. He wasn't the
first to record songs written or originally recorded by Negroes, but most of
*that* action in the middle fifties came when somebody like Bill Haley "covered"
Big Joe Turner's "Shake, Rattle and Roll" or Georgia Gibbs took "Jim Dandy"
from LaVern Baker. Those singers were taking established rhythm and blues
hits and cleaning them up for the white pop market. Elvis may have wanted to
cover some rhythm and blues songs he heard while at Sun, but he never did.
And when he included songs by Little Richard and Ray Charles and others on
his RCA albums, it was long after the originals had been hits. Elvis wasn't taking songs from the blacks for gain, but because he honestly respected the music.
And so others began to show respect.

Sort of parallel to this was the increased respect the black market began to
manifest for the white artist. Elvis wasn't the first Caucasian to appear on the
rigidly segregated rhythm and blues chart, but he was the first to appear there
consistently and his presence made it simpler for others to follow. Country
music and the blues never had been so far apart, really, and all Elvis was doing
was bringing them together in a way that might be palatable to both sides. Said

Paul Ackerman, *Billboard*'s music editor and one of rock's earliest chroniclers: "Often the difference between a country side and an r&b side is merely the use of strings as against the use of horns. The Presley sound—it is pointed out—might be called r&b without horns, but with strings."

There were many other ways in which Elvis changed the shape of popular tastes. Guitar sales climbed astronomically. Elvis also changed the style of stardom, making it—among other things—more commercial than it previously had been, while establishing once and for all the enormous weight and power of what is now called the "youth market." It would be some time before all these patterns of change would be acknowledged and quantified, but no question, Elvis changed the face and sound of his generation in ways that could only be called revolutionary.

The man responsible for so much of this, of course, was the illegal Dutch immigrant of carnival fame. He wasn't quiet while Elvis was becoming the biggest single attraction in the history of popular music. He stood in the wings at every turn. It is idle to discuss whether or not Elvis would have been as big without the Colonel's help, but there is no doubting that the Colonel earned much of the credit for making him a superstar so fast. Just as Gladys Presley had held her son close to her ample bosom, so did the Colonel—guiding him, advising him and protecting him.

"Elvis trusted the Colonel explicitly," said Oscar Davis. "He was a young man and he flared up a little bit, but Tom was a strong man and he'd lay the law down and that's the way Elvis went. He trusted Tom to do what was right for him."

First he saw that Elvis was comfortable, that he had everything he wanted—cars, clothes, jewelry, a new home each year.

Then he had some of Elvis's pals put on the payroll—people like Red West and Lamar Fike and Bitsy Mott and his cousin Gene Smith, who'd been tagging along as company anyway. Now they were being paid to continue to keep Elvis company and to serve as personal security guards.

He continued to shove Elvis's concert price up. Said Oscar Davis, still doing the Colonel's advance promotion during this period: "It jumped to $25,000 a night. That's not phenomenal nowadays, but before Elvis, probably the top money paid to artists was to Dean Martin and Jerry Lewis, who were getting $10,000. When the Colonel was offered that sum in New York and Chicago, he turned it down flat.

"What did he need it for?" Oscar said. "As Elvis got larger, we discontinued the use of radio and used only newspapers to promote the concerts. When we played Chicago, Fort Wayne and St. Louis, Toronto, Ottawa and Philadelphia, we used nothing but newspapers . . . and the disc jockeys. We'd take the leading teenage disc jockey in every market and let him M.C. the show. He'd love it, he'd talk about it all the time. We'd also arrange a dinner date for a girl, which they'd select, running a contest and things like that. It became very easy to sell him."

And he promoted Elvis as no singer had been promoted before. Sometimes this was as simple a thing as tipping the radio and press whenever Elvis made a move, so that they would notify the teenagers Elvis was going to make that move and then would go out and report on how many teenagers were there. Steve Sholes's secretary, Juanita Jones, said, "Whenever Elvis came to town, we had to promise complete security, not to tell anyone. Then Colonel Parker would tip the press and the kids would tear the place apart. Elvis'd live in a railroad car or in a trailer bus or have a room at the Anchor Motel and it was supposed to be a big secret, but later we'd find out the Colonel had told everybody."

Falling back on his carnival habits, he rented elephants and advertised Elvis with posters hanging from their flanks. He wore shirts that had Elvis's name stitched across the back and front. And in a stroke of bizarre genius, he hired all the midgets in Hollywood—most of them Munchkins left over from *The Wizard of Oz*—to parade through town as the Elvis Presley *Midget* Fan Club.

It was in August that the Colonel announced what would be one of his more extravagant—and profitable—schemes. That was when he said he had engaged Howard Bell and Hank Saperstein of Special Projects, Inc., in Beverly Hills to handle all his product merchandising. Saperstein, through his own company, H. G. Saperstein and Associates, previously had licensed and promoted merchandising for several television shows—*Super Circus*, *Ding Dong School*, *Lassie*, *The Lone Ranger*, *Jim Bowie* and *Wyatt Earp* among them. While Howard Bell brought with him experience in merchandising Peter Pan, Mickey Mouse and Davy Crockett, all for Walt Disney. Before it was all over, there were no less than seventy-eight different Elvis Presley products being sold—and sales were reported in the millions of dollars each month.

So pervasive was the marketing, if one of Elvis's fans bought one of everything, she could, upon arising in the morning, pull on some Elvis Presley bobbysox, Elvis Presley shoes, an Elvis Presley skirt and Elvis Presley blouse, an Elvis Presley sweater, hang an Elvis Presley charm bracelet from her wrist, put an Elvis Presley handkerchief in her Elvis Presley purse and head for school, where she might swap some Elvis Presley bubble gum cards before class, where she would take notes with an Elvis Presley pencil. After school she might change into Elvis Presley Bermuda shorts, Elvis Presley blue jeans (which were not blue but black, trimmed in white and carried Elvis's face on a pocket tag) or Elvis Presley toreador pants, and either write an Elvis Presley pen pal (whose address she got from an Elvis Presley magazine) or play an Elvis Presley game, while drinking an Elvis Presley soft drink. And before going to bed in her Elvis Presley knit pajamas, she might write in her Elvis Presley diary, using an Elvis Presley ball-point pen, listen to "Hound Dog" a final ten times, then switch out the light to watch the Elvis Presley picture that glowed in the dark.

That wasn't all. There were Elvis Presley photographs (glossy eight-by-tens and wallet size), belts, bolo ties, gloves, mittens, novelty hats, T-shirts, neckerchiefs, necklaces, statues and plaster-of-Paris busts, bookends, guitars, lipstick (in Hound Dog Orange, Heartbreak Hotel Pink and Tutti Frutti Red), colognes, stuffed hound dogs, dancing dolls, greeting cards, pins, sneakers, buttons, photograph albums, phonographs, Ivy League pants, Ivy League girls' shirts, pillows, combs, hairbrushes and twenty-nine other items of essential teenaged consequence. All sold at Sears, Roebuck, Montgomery Ward, W. T. Grant, Woolworth's, Kresge, AMC Stores, Macy's, Allied Department Stores, H. L. Green, Rexall and Whelan drugstores. Or available by mail, much of it advertised in Elvis Presley magazines.

For every item in the Presley line, Elvis and the Colonel collected a royalty of four to eleven per cent of the manufacturer's wholesale price. This probably didn't come to more than two to five cents for each dollar item, but when that was multiplied by several million, it was like having another number one record.

Saperstein also agreed to take over administration of the Elvis Presley National Fan Club, which had been operating at a loss for several months. There were 250,000 members in the U. S., another 150,000 elsewhere, and until now the 3-4000 letters that arrived daily were being answered from Madison, Tennessee, where the Colonel kept his office. Anyone who wrote got a free membership card and was offered three different Elvis Presley souvenir packages, costing a quarter, fifty cents, or a dollar. The cheapest package included two small photographs and a button, the next size a couple of larger pictures and a button, the most expensive package even larger photographs and a button, plus a songbook and a picture book.

Elvis's mother was beginning to feel the pressure. Her close friend Mrs. Faye Harris said, "They'd take little pieces of brick and pull up the grass and swarm all over the house, peeking in windows. She was so glad when we come for a visit. She said, 'Thank God, you're here to answer the doorbell.' We had to stay under lock all the time we was there. We couldn't walk in the yard and if we went for a ride, they followed us.

"Gladys tol' me one day, she was settin' there, the checks was comin' in, 'I wish Elvis would quit right now and marry a girl and have a child. That'd make me so happy. He's got enough comin' in from his hits and his cosmetics and things, he could retire right now. He could put himself in a furniture store and really mop up. If he did that, I'd be so happy, I don't know whether Memphis could hold me or not.'"

Apparently Mrs. Presley never told her son how she felt.

Elvis was back in Tupelo for a model homecoming, so clichéd as to defy credibility. Already Elvis represented the all-American prototype, the Horatio Alger hero of the South: the son of a dirt-poor sharecropper who sang in his mama's church and went on to wealth and fame. Providing the irony that is so much a part of so many clichés was the fact that Elvis would be appearing at the Mississippi-Alabama Fair and Dairy Show, where he'd sung "Old Shep" a decade earlier.

The fact that only a few individuals honestly remembered the thin, flat-nosed towhead with the lidded eyes from the wrong side of the G.M.& O. and Frisco tracks did not in any way deter anyone in Tupelo from turning out or in some way contributing to the day's events. September 26 was declared Elvis Presley Day and a banner was hung across Main Street. The merchants decorated their shop windows in what the local boosters called an "Elvis Presley Theme," with most of the displays taking their direction from the titles of Elvis's records. A parade was planned. And just before the afternoon show Mayor Jim Ballard, who began his political career as a restaurateur and ran for city clerk the year the Presley family moved to Memphis, gave Elvis a three-foot-long guitar-shaped key to the city. "This town's proud to call you its son," he said. And Mississippi Governor James P. Coleman had come up from Jackson to tell him, "This state and the nation admire you."

J. M. (Ikey) Savery, head of the oldest insurance agency in Mississippi and president of the fair the past twenty years, said, "It was unbelievable. Buses came from Atlanta, Birmingham, Jackson. There were girls who'd been here two or three days, from Philadelphia and Boston and New York. I guess there were fifteen or twenty thousand. We had to put out chairs and bleachers in front of the grandstand. We had the local police, county sheriffs and the highway patrol there in the afternoon, and the girls went right over them. That night we had the National Guard, and the girls went over *them*."

On his way back out of town, Elvis autographed the $10,000 check he got for his performance and gave it back to Tupelo.

# Chapter 9

# HOLLYWOOD: 1

E lvis had begun work on his first film, *Love Me Tender*, on August 22. He was away from Hollywood for the Tupelo appearance in September but returned to stay at the Knickerbocker Hotel through mid-October. Originally the film was titled *The Reno Brothers* and there were no songs, but when it became apparent even to the most cynical Hollywood producer that Elvis represented enormous box office potential, three songs were hurriedly shoved between the pages of the script and the title of the film was changed to *Love Me Tender*, a rewrite of the Civil War ballad "Aura Lee." (Elvis was given 50 per cent of the authorship of the songs, a common practice at the time.)

Elvis has two brothers in the film, the oldest played by Richard Egan, and the way the story went, everybody but Elvis goes off to fight the Yankees in the war, leaving him back on the farm to look after Mother (Mildred Dunnock). Word comes that Egan is dead, and Elvis and Debra Paget marry. Debra had been Egan's fiancée before he was "killed," although Elvis doesn't know that. Then Egan returns and Elvis solves the problem by dying. The film ends with Elvis's face superimposed against the sky singing the title song again. Thus, every time the record was played, it plugged the film and every time someone saw the movie, the song was plugged.

The producer of *Love Me Tender* was David Weisbart, who had been producer of James Dean's most popular film, *Rebel Without a Cause*, in 1955. Because Dean was the only other teen icon to emerge in the 1950s, numerous comparisons were made. On Elvis's first day on the set, in fact, part of the talk between Elvis and his producer was devoted to whether he might not be right for the leading role when Hollywood got around to producing *The James Dean Story*, a film concept much discussed in 1956, the year following Dean's death. In the end, it was not dramatized but released instead as a documentary.

Another connection with Dean was made when Elvis met and became friends with three members of the *Rebel Without a Cause* cast, Dennis Hopper, Nick Adams and Natalie Wood. The latter two were with Elvis when he dropped in unannounced at the home of Louella Parsons, the gossip columnist, who seemed to be totally charmed by him—as was the young actress who had grown up in Hollywood. Natalie later said, "He was the first person of my age group I had ever met who said to me: 'How come you're wearing makeup? Why do you want to go to New York? Why do you want to be on your own?' It was like having the date I never ever had in high school."

Elvis enjoyed Hollywood. He had his guys around for jokes and any errands he wanted taken care of. The studio gave him a secretary. And the writers and photographers stood in line. One of these was a little girl named Patricia Vernon, who wrote for the *New York Herald Tribune*: "A press agent came by to tell me I had had enough time with Elvis. I started to leave and Elvis, who was still sprawled on the couch, darted out his hand and caught my foot. 'Maybe she's shy; maybe she'd like to be alone with me,' he said. The press agent shrugged and left. I asked Elvis to take his hand off my foot. 'Okay,' he said, looking up under heavy lids. 'Ah'm just spoofing you.' I asked Elvis how he felt about girls who threw themselves at him. Again the heavy-lidded look. 'Ah usually take them,' he said, watching my face for the shock value of his words. He grinned. 'Hell,' he said, 'you know, Ah'm kind of having fun with you because you're so smart.'" And when she asked Elvis if he thought he was a sex symbol to kids, as some psychiatrists were saying, he said something that would be quoted for years: "They all think I'm a sex maniac. They're just frustrated old types, anyway. I'm just natural." It was apparent in nearly every way that Elvis was having fun.

By the time Elvis was making *Love Me Tender*, the Army had become a part of his life. On October 24 his draft board in Memphis said yes, it was true that he had been sent a questionnaire to "bring his status up to date." Lots of young men didn't report address changes, marital status and other relevant facts, a draft board spokesman said, so occasionally what is called a Selective Service Dependency Questionnaire was sent to all registrants. But there was nothing to worry about, the board's chairman, Milton Bowers, told newsmen. Elvis was 1-A but there were several hundred able-bodied men ahead of him.

It was then, in October, that *Billboard* published a frontpage story of Elvis's draft call in such detail it was generally regarded as true. It said that he was going into the Special Services, or entertainment branch, of the Army, that he would be reporting for duty at Fort Dix, New Jersey, and that he would be allowed to continue his television and recording dates and probably would be granted an early six-week furlough to make another film. The story was totally inaccurate, but before it could be denied, a former *Billboard* staff writer, Steve Schickel, then with radio station WGN in Chicago, recorded a song that was inspired by this premature call: "Leave My Sideburns Be."

Songs like this were one of the stranger phenomena associated with Elvis's hysterical success. In 1956 and 1957 there were dozens about Elvis or inspired by him. Humorist Stan Freberg had the first and most successful, his satiric version of "Heartbreak Hotel." The others were more flattering. Janis Martin, a South African vocalist, recorded "My Boy, Elvis," a song whose lyric contained the titles of Elvis's first six or seven singles. "Dear Elvis" was sung by somebody identified only as Audry and took the form of a gushy fan letter using lines from current hit records. "To me, Elvis, you are the dreamiest," said Audry. "Ohhhhh, you've got the magic touch," sang the Platters from their hit "Magic Touch." Billy Boyle contributed a plaintive wail whose message was in its title, "My Baby's Crazy 'Bout Elvis." Peter de Bree and his Dutch backup band, the Wanderers, shouted a biographical thank-you called "Hey, Mr. Presley." Lou Monte provided "Elvis Presley for President," which sounded like a cross between a high school football cheer and a chewing gum commercial. Jerry Reed sang about "The Tupelo Mississippi Flash," a song about Beauregard Rippy, who came from Tupelo, Mississippi, wrote songs and sang like a bird, played licks on his gi-tar like you ain't never heard. A Jerry Lee Lewis-type piano accompanied Ivan Gregory's "Elvis Presley Blues," a song that said Elvis had affected not only his girl friend but him as well. And for Christmas, Mary Kaye told a moving tale of a little girl who promised to brush her teeth and pick up her clothing without reminder if she found Elvis under the tree ("I Don't Want a Bracelet or Diamonds, I Just Want Elvis Instead"); and Little Lambie Penn and Marlene Paula sang slightly different versions of "I Wanna Spend Xmas with Elvis."

Most of the songs offered the same rockabilly beat established by Elvis, but only a few were popular enough to appear on any of the best-seller lists.

Elvis's second album came out in October, carrying his first name as its title and a collection of twelve songs rather like those included in the first LP. Again Elvis paid his respects to his roots, recording "So Glad You're Mine," another Arthur (Big Boy) Crudup song; "How's the World Treating You," a country ballad by Chet Atkins and Boudleaux Bryant; and the song he performed as a boy, "Old Shep." Others included three of Little Richard's biggest hits—"Ready Teddy," "Rip It Up" and "Long Tall Sally"—"Love Me" by Jerry Leiber and Mike Stoller; and "Paralyzed" by Otis Blackwell, who'd written "Don't Be Cruel."

Within a couple of weeks the album was number one, meaning Elvis Presley again was the only name at the top of every important chart—also making it laughable when in the same month *Colliers* magazine, among others, intimated Elvis might be slipping and that another singer was gaining on him. This was Pat Boone, who had been a winner on Arthur Godfrey's *Talent Scouts* in 1954, shortly before Elvis was turned away by the same program. Like Elvis, Pat was a religious man, but Pat was married and the father of three, while Elvis was a polite yet enthusiastic womanizer who was quoted as saying about marriage, "Why buy a cow when you can get milk under the fence?" Pat had juggled his personal appearances to permit a straight A average at Columbia University (he would get his degree the following June), and Elvis considered himself lucky to squeak through Humes High. Their choice of material was different too, as Elvis generally picked gutsier songs than those Pat recorded, remaining more respectful of the material's origins. Both Elvis and Pat recorded rhythm and blues hits, but Pat's "covers" did little more than homogenize or neutralize the power of the originals. Pat's musical links were to the past and Elvis pointed the way to the future.

On October 18, there was an incident in a Memphis gas station. Witnesses said Elvis—just returned from Hollywood—had pulled into the station in his white Continental Mark II and asked the station manager, Edd Hopper, to check the gas tank for leaks. Elvis was recognized by passers-by, and a crowd formed. Traffic was blocked and Hopper asked Elvis to move on. Elvis said he would, but he apparently delayed long enough to sign a few more autographs, at which point, witnesses told police, Hopper slapped Elvis on the back of the head and said, "I said move on!" And so Elvis got out of his car and slammed Hopper with a right cross that cut a half-inch gash at the corner of his left eye.

In court a few days later Hopper appeared with one eye swollen almost shut, the left side of his face puffed, bandages covering the cut. He said he had asked Elvis to leave three times and pushed him only when Elvis made a move to get out of the car and go for him. Then Elvis was called to the stand to give his side of the story, which was confirmed by the police officer present. He said Hopper had swung first and then had pulled a knife on him.

Acting City Judge Sam Friedman listened patiently—fans in the courtroom had disrupted testimony with groans and cheers—and after suggesting that Elvis take into consideration the fact that he had a large following and should cooperate fully with businessmen in order to avoid "disruptions," he fined Hopper $25 and lectured him about "taking the law into your own hands." Next day the service station's owner fired Hopper. Elvis intervened, telling newsmen later, "I asked him not to fire him. The man has a family. It was one of those things that happen in life. We regret it, but it's too late." The station owner wasn't listening. Business had fallen off drastically and he was afraid if he hired Hopper back the kids would boycott him.

A month later, on November 23, nineteen-year-old Louis John Balint took a swing at Elvis in the Shalimar Room of the Commodore Perry Hotel in Toledo, Ohio. Balint was an unemployed sheet metal worker and he said, when questioned by police, that he was recently separated from his wife and he resented her carrying a picture of Elvis in her wallet instead of a picture of him. After pleading guilty to a charge of disturbing the peace, he was fined $10, plus court costs. He couldn't come up with it and went to jail, where he said the whole thing was staged—he had been paid $200 to start the fight.

Other fights were breaking out among songwriters and publishers over songs Elvis had recorded. The first battle had been over who wrote "Heartbreak Hotel." The next was over who wrote, and who published, "Hound Dog." And then there was a fight over "Don't Be Cruel."

It's obvious why so many were willing to take expensive legal shots at Elvis and his empire and those who surrounded him. Writers' and publishers' royalty percentages were small, usually a penny apiece per 45-rpm record sold. When you're talking about an Elvis Presley record, though, this penny could represent a small fortune.

The end of October, Elvis returned to New York for his second appearance on *The Ed Sullivan Show*. However much controversy continued to bob in his wake, Elvis now seemed in control, more relaxed. He had brought four of his friends with him (including Nick Adams) and they accompanied him to the show's rehearsal and live broadcast, and to the unveiling of a forty-foot-high cut-out poster that was part of the Paramount Theater marquee in Times Square, where *Love Me Tender* would premiere in about two weeks.

He also held a press conference, telling reporters, "Teenagers are my life and triumph. I'd be nowhere without them." He said he wished he could talk with the parents who criticized, "because I think I could change their minds and their viewpoint. Ever since I got to be a sort of name, I've examined my conscience and asked myself if I led anybody astray even indirectly, and I'm at peace with my conscience.

"I read my Bible," he went on, "and this is no story just made up now. My Bible tells me that what he sows he will also reap, and if I'm sowing evil and wickedness, it will catch up with me. I'm right sure about that . . . and I don't think I'm bad for people. If I did think I was bad for people, I would go back to driving a truck, and I really mean this."

Returning to Memphis, Elvis was joined by Natalie Wood for what the newspapers called a "motorcycle romance." Everything Elvis did was watched closely by newsmen hungry for the latest gossipy tidbit, and so when Elvis bought a new motorcycle on October 31, the United Press knew about it, and when the "Big E" from Tennessee (the "Chief" was another nickname he picked up in 1956) took Natalie for a three-hour ride on that motorcycle that night, the United Press knew about that too. And the United Press knew about it when Elvis's buddy Nick Adams went along on a second bike the next day. One newspaper, the *Nashville Tennessean*, headlined the U.P. story, "Natalie's Jeans Grip Tight As Cycle Romance Deepens."

Jordanaire Neal Matthews said, "The only time he could get out, really, was at night, if he had the night off. He'd rent a skating rink or a movie house and rent it for the whole night and he and whoever'd be around would go to the skating rink and skate all night until they'd just drop over. Or they'd see two, three movies, after the movie theater had closed. That's the only kind of entertainment he had. He couldn't go out.

"One time I was talking to him about playing golf. I told him how relaxing it was. I said, 'You ought-a come play golf with me one day.' He said, 'Man, I sure wish I could. I just can't.' Or tennis, or anything. Anybody else I could say, 'Hey, come out to the house, play some tennis.' I got a tennis court out the house. But if he did that, it wouldn't be fifteen minutes until everybody in the neighborhood was over there. He can't be a person like anybody else. It's bound to have an effect."

Elvis was amply paid for this loss of privacy. By now, he had sold over ten million singles for RCA (worth about $450,000 in royalties), representing two-thirds of the label's singles business. At the same time that the Colonel announced the new contract, promising Elvis $1,000 a month for twenty years, *Variety* adjudged him a millionaire based on record sales, movie income, song publishing, and live and television appearances—a feat unprecedented in the entertainment business.

Usually two to three hundred prints of a film were released at a time, but when *Love Me Tender* was ready for the nation's theaters, some five hundred and fifty prints were ordered so it could open in nearly double the usual number of theaters. In New York, they called out thirty-five cops, hired twenty extra ushers and notified the city's truancy department when three thousand teenagers—mostly girls—were lined up outside the Paramount Theater by eight a.m. It had been advertised that the first two thousand in line would get their choice of an Elvis Presley scarf, hat, lapel button or charm bracelet—items among those on sale inside for the latecomers. In New Orleans there was a girl who sat through forty-two showings of the film, just as she had sat through forty-two showings of the previous week's movie to see Elvis in the previews of coming attractions. Within three weeks the million dollars that had been sunk into the movie had been recovered. Never before had any

Hollywood film got its money back so rapidly.

The critics welcomed Elvis less ecstatically. The *New York Times* credited him for his enthusiasm, but used words like "turgid" and "juicy" to describe his characterization and, noting the film was a horse opera, said Elvis's "dramatic contribution is not a great deal more impressive than that of one of the slavering nags." The *Los Angeles Times* said, "He pales by comparison when pitted against the resonant inflections of Egan, of course, but who came to watch Elvis act?" Certainly not *Time* magazine, whose critic apparently *ran* all the way back to his typewriter to write one of the trashings of all time:

"Is it a sausage? It is certainly smooth and damp looking, but who ever heard of a 172-lb. sausage 6 ft. tall? Is it a Walt Disney goldfish? It has the same sort of big, soft, beautiful eyes and long, curly lashes, but who ever heard of a goldfish with sideburns? Is it a corpse? The face just hangs there, limp and white with its little drop-seat mouth, rather like Lord Byron in the wax museum.

"But suddenly the figure comes to life. The lips part, the eyes half close, the clutched guitar begins to undulate back and forth in an uncomfortably suggestive manner. And wham! The mid-section of the body jolts forward to bump and grind and beat out a low-down rhythm that takes its pace from boogie and hillbilly, rock 'n' roll and something known only to Elvis and his Pelvis. As the belly dance gets wilder, a peculiar sound emerges. A rusty foghorn? A voice? Or merely a noise produced, like the voice of a cricket, by the violent stridulation of the legs? Words occasionally can be made out, like raisins in corneal mush. 'Goan . . . git . . . luhhv . . .' And then all at once everything stops, and a big trembly tender half smile, half sneer smears slowly across the CinemaScope screen. The message that millions of U.S. teen-age girls love to receive has just been delivered."

Most other critics felt little different. For someone who wanted to be an actor—and, incidentally, had memorized not only his own lines but the entire script before filming began—it was difficult stuff to take.

On the Christmas cards mailed from Memphis that year—and received by film critics all over the country, as well as by disc jockeys and fans—it said, "To wish you all a Cool Yule and a Frantic First and a billion thanks to everyone." Signed: "Elvis"—in big letters—"and the Colonel"—in smaller letters.

Elvis started work on his second movie role during the holiday season, in *Loving You* at Paramount. This was Hal Wallis's first film with Elvis (the first of nine) and the first of several which were especially written for Elvis and based rather loosely on his own rags-to-riches story. In this one, Elvis was Deke Rivers, a small-town boy who became an overnight sensation when he was signed by a lady press agent (Lizabeth Scott) to sing with her ex-husband's (Wendell Corey's) country music band. At first Miss Scott and Corey show little more than greed in their interest in young Deke, but when they learn of his life as an orphan, they tear up the early contract to dedicate themselves to seeing Deke is happy as well as successful.

It was in the preparation of this film that it became evident that the Colonel, acting through Hill and Range Songs, had constructed an enormous music machine that would guarantee Elvis a broad selection of material. For this was the first film whose script was distributed to Hill and Range songwriters.

"We would give out dozens of scripts to writers we had under contract or I thought would do well," said Freddy Bienstock. "All the spots where songs went were marked. We asked the writers to submit songs for as many of those spots as they wished. That way, we would always have three or four different songs for each spot in the movie."

There was no guarantee the song or songs submitted by any writer would be used. The songwriters were told other composers had scripts too and that everything was to be sent to Elvis in the form of demonstration records and that he would select which ones would go into the film and, subsequently, on an album.

There were seven songs in *Loving You*, enough to fill up one side of what would be Elvis's first album for 1957 (to be released with the picture in July), and it was presumed that this album would sell at least as well as the first two, so the songwriters didn't balk at the unusual arrangements. Writing for a Hollywood film produced by a major studio never was done on speculation; some of the composers' guilds and unions even forbade it. In the past, composers who wrote for Hollywood musicals not only did so on assignment rather than on speculation, they also did so on salary. Not so with Elvis Presley flicks. When you wrote for Elvis, it was write now, pay later. Maybe.

Still, it was rare when a songwriter didn't submit some material once given the opportunity. Mike Stoller said, "The writer felt that if the song was done, the royalty that would come from the record would be great enough compensation, and actually that's the way it worked. If there are, say, twelve songs in a film and you pro-rate each song, on a flat fee it might come out to, I don't know, fifteen hundred or two thousand dollars a song in terms of the budget, the going rate at the time. But if Presley recorded a song and it came out in an album, it was good for a lot more than that."

Asking writers to produce on speculation was one thing. Asking them to share their royalties with Elvis and the Colonel was another. Almost always the songs were published by one of Elvis's companies, which meant if the writer had his own publishing company, he couldn't use it and sacrificed any publisher's royalties. Worse, there were several instances when Elvis was given partial writer's credit and so the composer gave up another bite.

For example, the authorship was changed on the songs Elvis sang in *Love Me Tender*. Composers credited for these songs were Vera Matson and Elvis Presley, neither of whom had anything to do with the actual composition. They were, instead, written by Vera's husband, Ken Darby, who served as the film's musical director. They were put in his wife's name because Darby was an ASCAP (American Society of Composers, Authors and Publishers) writer, and at that time Elvis had but one publishing company and it was a member of rival BMI (Broadcast Music, Inc.); although soon after, an ASCAP company, named for Elvis's mother, was formed—Gladys Music, Inc. Elvis was listed as co-author with Darby's wife, an insider said, "at the Colonel's suggestion."

Robert (Bumps) Blackwell was co-author of several of Little Richard's hits, two of which, "Rip It Up" and "Ready Teddy," originally were published by Venice Music, Inc., a Los Angeles-based company. But before Elvis included them in his second album, half the publishing rights (meaning, ultimately, half the publishing royalties) were transferred to Elvis Presley Music, Inc.

"Either we agreed to that or they said they wouldn't release the songs, Elvis wouldn't record the material," said Bumps. "It didn't bother us. Why should it? Do you know how many records Elvis sold? 50 per cent of several million records is much tastier than a 100 per cent of zero. We weren't upset. We were happy."

Friends say Elvis wasn't aware that any advantage may have been taken. They say that when he asked why his name was listed as an occasional composer, he was told his contribution in the studio in terms of arrangements and the occasional word changes he made entitled him to royalties and writer's credit. In fact, this is an arguable point, although Elvis once said he didn't think he could write a song if his life depended on it.

Friends said that once Elvis learned what was going on, he ordered an end to the practice.

Hill and Range was further fattening the Elvis calf in the winter of 1956-57 by buying other music publishing companies for Elvis. The first of these was American Music, one of the stalwarts in the country music field, listed as the American Division of Elvis Presley Music, Inc. Among the copyrights acquired were "Divorce Me C.O.D.," "Smoke, Smoke, Smoke [That Cigarette]" and "So Round, So Firm, So Fully Packed," all three being big country hits written by Merle Travis in the mid-forties. Others were "The Cry of the Wild Goose," a country hit in 1950; "A Dear John Letter," a hit in 1953; and one of the biggest country music copyrights of all time, "Sixteen Tons."

Although long past their peak in sales before Elvis bought them, these songs, along with many others, were well worth picking up. As country standards, they were included in dozens of later albums, and when those records sold, of course Elvis (and Hill and Range) got the publisher's slice of the pie.

During a long Christmas holiday in Memphis, Elvis paid one of his infrequent visits to the Sun Studio, where he found Sam Phillips working with Carl Perkins, backed up by his two brothers and a young piano player from Louisiana named Jerry Lee Lewis. After clowning around, they naturally began to sing. Sam already had everything set to record, so he did and when it seemed the impromptu jam session was going to go for a while, he called another of his young singers, Johnny Cash, who dropped by with his wife. Sam refused to admit that he'd recorded the "Million Dollar Quartet," as it came to be called, and it would be years before the tapes were released.

Then on January 4, 1957, four days before his twenty-second birthday, Elvis reported at Kennedy Veterans Hospital in Memphis a few blocks from his home for his pre-induction physical. Elvis went to the examination center with Dottie Harmony, a show girl from Las Vegas then staying with the Presley family as a house guest, and Cliff Gleaves, one of his salaried sidekicks. Gleaves drove the Cadillac, and Elvis and Dottie rode in the back.

When he might be drafted depended on several factors, Army hospital spokesmen said, ranging from the local draft board's quota to the number of volunteers. In any case, newsmen and fans were assured the call probably would not come for at least six months, perhaps for as long as a year, and during that time Elvis could enlist in any branch of the military armed forces he chose.

Elvis was the only potential recruit to be poked and prodded that day. Normally the Army moved men through in groups of forty or more, but given two days to ponder what might happen, the Army decided that forty men plus Elvis plus all the newsmen and curious employees would be a bit much. As it was, doctors had to chase photographers who were trying to snap Elvis in the raw.

A few hours after the examination Dottie boarded a plane for Nevada and Elvis and several friends boarded a train for New York, where he was to make his third and final appearance on Ed Sullivan's show.

"They had the streets blocked off for seven or eight blocks around the theater," Neal Matthews said. "The side street by the theater was packed. I'd say five thousand kids standing around screaming. They had policemen on horses directing, trying to keep crowds from getting out of control."

Neal said this was the time they used a decoy to get Elvis inside. "They'd use decoys a lot," he said. "Send a big black limousine up to the stage door, have somebody that sort of looked like him and dressed like him. All the kids would come over there and Elvis'd slip in the side door."

Elvis appeared in a gold lamé vest with a black satin lining and a velvet shirt and he introduced a religious song that was to be on his next extended play recording, *Peace in the Valley*. It was his last television appearance for more than three years.

The following week, on the eighth, Elvis's birthday, the Army recruiters in Memphis held a press conference, during which Captain Elwyn P. Rowan said, "Physically he's an A-profile and that's as high as you can go." Mentally? "Can't give you the exact score," the Captain said, "but Presley's score was about average."

Of course it couldn't remain as simple and uncluttered as all that. There were published accounts hinting that Elvis might be given preferential treatment if and when he was inducted—that, specifically, he might not have to get his hair and sideburns clipped. "Relax, girls," was the way the Associated Press started a story, quoting an unnamed Army spokesman as saying Elvis probably would go into the Special Services branch and could, as someone who would entertain troops and perhaps serve in a publicity/recruiting capacity, wear khaki but forgo the GI haircut required of the ordinary soldier.

As might be expected, there were those who objected to the thought of such favoritism. So much so, in fact, that several veterans in Miami wrote blistering letters to their Senator, George Smathers, who kicked the complaints over to the Pentagon with a request that he be informed whether the published reports were accurate. Said the Pentagon: "Many were present [when Elvis took his physical] and it is possible that numerous conjecturable remarks and off-the-cuff comments were expressed by military personnel, cameramen and reporters. It must be emphasized that these remarks, if made, do not represent the official position of the Department of the Army."

It was added that if Elvis was drafted, he would receive his basic training at Fort Chaffee, Arkansas—where the press went to Captain John Mawn, the post's public information officer, who said, "No one gets preferential treatment at Chaffee. All recruits get a military haircut the day they arrive." Asked what that meant, the Captain said it bore a striking resemblance to a "peeled onion."

That same week RCA released "Too Much," another in the long line of lurching rockabilly songs that went right to the top of the sales charts and Elvis returned to Hollywood to begin shooting his second feature film.

Arriving a few days early, Elvis spent his first weekend in the recording studio. This was his first RCA session in three months and the label again was desperate for material. Elvis's goal was to record four religious tunes, but Paramount wanted the new film's title tune and RCA needed a follow-up single for "Too Much." Elvis delivered on all fronts, in two days finishing not only the hymns (including "Peace in the Valley" and "Precious Lord, Take My Hand"), but also "That's When Your Heartaches Begin," originally an Ink Spots song, and a new composition by Otis Blackwell, "All Shook Up."

On Monday, he reported for makeup and wardrobe tests. Elvis believed that actors with dark hair seemed to have the most durable careers and when the makeup man said he thought he would photograph well, he dyed it. Elvis kept it dark for the rest of his career.

Once again, it was a Hal Wallis production, but this time for Paramount. Hal Kanter, a onetime writer for Bob Hope who had written the screen version of Tennessee Williams's *The Rose* as well as one of the then popular Martin and Lewis comedies (both for Wallis), had visited Elvis in Memphis at Christmas and accompanied him when he completed his *Louisiana Hayride* contract. Kanter was making his directorial debut. The stars were Wendell Corey, who played a country-western singer, and Lizabeth Scott, a publicist who discovers gas station attendant Elvis and promotes him to stardom. The movie's original title, *Lonesome Cowboy*, was changed to *Loving You* after Jerry Leiber and Mike Stoller wrote a song of that name expressly for the film. It would do well when released as a single, as would another slipped into the script, "Teddy Bear."

*Loving You* was not as lightweight an effort as this description makes it sound, when compared to most of the rock exploitation films that came from Hollywood during the same period, such as *Rock Around the Clock* and *Don't Knock the Rock*. Colonel Parker and Hal Wallis, who would go on to produce nine films with Elvis, did not regard him as a phenomenon to be forgotten in a few years, but intended to give the singer what he wanted: a career in the picture business.

For Elvis, one of the more cherished parts of filming came in the last scene when he sang "Got a Lot O' Livin' to Do" and his parents and two of their friends, who had flown in from Memphis for a long vacation, were shown on camera in the audience.

The Colonel then called a small press conference in his cluttered office in Madison to say that his boy would be making his third movie beginning the first of May. It was also to be filmed at Elvis's third studio, M-G-M, he said, and it was called *Jailhouse Rock*. The only other thing he had to announce was Elvis's price tag: $250,000 plus 50 per cent of all profits, unheard of for someone who'd had but one film released.

This was followed by the release of "All Shook Up," which became a part of the teenage vocabulary about the same time it sold its millionth copy.

Usually the Colonel went on Elvis's tours. There weren't that many now and the Colonel enjoyed them because it allowed him to relive his carnival days, mix with the crowd, and sell product. Moe Weisel who sold pictures of movie stars by mail in those days, said, "I got a call from the Colonel one day and he wanted five thousand prints of Elvis in a hurry. That sonofabitch. He chiseled me down and chiseled me down. I finally let him have them for five and a half cents apiece. Somebody else had said six cents, right? And I agree to five and a half, so I get the order. And I get them out in time, all five thousand, delivered like I promised.

"The next week I go to Long Beach for an Elvis concert with my sixteen-year-old daughter and there's the Colonel at the door, selling my eight-by-tens for fifty cents. I said, 'Not this . . . you don't need *this*!' Elvis had just had his sixth or eighth or tenth gold record and he'd signed a contract with RCA guaranteeing him a thousand dollars a week even if he goes fishing that week, and the Colonel's out there hustling eight-by-tens. He said, 'I'm only filling a need. These people want autographed pictures and I'm providing them. I'm not cheating them, am I? I'm giving them what they want and I'm asking a fair price. I could charge a dollar, you know."

Inside the auditorium it was even more bizarre.

"The real shows were in the audience, not on the stage," said Gordon Stoker. "I can't express that experience, being on a stage with as many as thirty thousand people screaming and hollering. He had a way of crooking his little finger and wiggling it. He'd do that and they'd scream. He didn't really understand the audience reaction to him and so he'd have fun, he'd put them on. He'd burp and they'd scream, then look at us and grin.

"We'd get so engrossed in what he was doing, we'd forget to come in vocally," Gordon said. "He never planned any of his moves and they fascinated us. You never knew what was coming. He didn't do the same thing at the same place in a song. So we'd be watching, and we'd be watching so hard we'd blow the part, we'd forget to come in with the 'ooooowahhhh' and he'd turn around and give us the lip—you know the way he moves the left side of his mouth in a cocky sneer—or he'd say something like 'oh yeah?' or 'sum-bitch.'

"He always wanted us in as close to him as possible. Scotty and Bill too. He wanted the protection. Those kids broke through police lines in Kansas City, Missouri, once and he said, 'Run for your lives.' We ran. We got into a car just as the kids reached us. They stole our instruments, our music, everything. He never could do any curtain calls or encores. This is what saved him. He'd disappear as the last notes were hit. Those kids would think he'd come back and he'd be gone.

"It was always a large show—with a dancer, a soloist, a juggling act, a comedian and a full orchestra. There'd be five to eight specialty acts. An hour and a half would pass before Elvis came on. By that time the audience was out of its mind.

"Elvis'd do 'Hound Dog' as his grand finale. The girls were in a fever pitch by the time he got through that. They were to a climax. And they wouldn't dare leave as long as he was on the stage. Sometimes he'd do sixteen choruses of that song, and all the time it kept building. One concert they were begging for something he owned and he threw his coat into the audience. It was like throwing a pound of meat to a pack of hungry dogs. They tore it to shreds."

Feeding Elvis's fondness for outrageous clothing, the Colonel had a famous Hollywood tailor who catered mainly to country and western singers make a $2,500 gold lamé suit. Elvis wore it on the brief tour that followed completion of *Loving You*, but tired of it, focusing instead, at tour's end, on a new and more exciting extravagance, the acquisition of a new home.

This was an eighteen-room southern mansion that included a seventy-five-foot-long parlor, situated on eighteen-plus acres of land on the road south leading to Mississippi. Elvis purchased the property from Dr. and Mrs. Thomas Moore, the latter of whom had inherited it as part of a hundred-year-old Hereford cattle farm. Named Graceland for one of Mrs. Moore's aunts, she previously had sold much of the land for the development of a shopping center and residential subdivision and the adjacent four acres for the construction of the Graceland Christian Church. What years later became one of the most famous homes in the world, and the second most visited private residence in the U.S. after the White House, cost Elvis $102,500. The extensive remodeling began.

On May 1, Elvis showed up at the MGM studio in Culver City, outside Los Angeles, to begin the recording sessions for *Jailhouse Rock*. Gordon Stoker said, "I don't remember what time it was, but it was morning and Elvis went to the piano and began to play spirituals, his first love. We all fell in with him, all the Jordanaires and Bill and Scotty and D. J. We sang all morning with Elvis, probably not even thinking about the songs for the film, certainly not rehearsing or recording them. And then we broke for lunch.

"That was when one of the studio officials called me over and said it was costing the studio a fortune and not to fall in with him in the afternoon if he tried to sing spirituals again. He said we had to get down to work.

"So we came back from an hour-and-a-half lunch break and Elvis went right to the piano again, starting right where he left off. I had talked with Hugh and Neal and Hoyt and we didn't join him. We refused to sing along. When that happened, Elvis stopped playing and looked at us. He called me over and asked me what was happening. I told him, 'Elvis, they told us not to sing spirituals. They told us we have to cut the songs for the film.'

"That did it," Gordon said. "Elvis blew up. He didn't make a scene. When he blew up, he blew up inside. And he walked out, taking his six or seven cronies with him. The day was canceled. Elvis didn't come back.

"It was really unfortunate. What the studio didn't realize was that Elvis hadn't sung in a studio in some while and this was his way of warming up, getting in the mood . . . that he might have done all seven songs that afternoon, or perhaps by the end of the following day. In that way he still would have finished the tracking in far less time than most singers would. They should have given Elvis his head, let him do what he wanted. Most singers could have taken at least two weeks." He returned the following morning and everything ran smoothly.

Although the movie's plot recalled that of *Loving You*—again a young, unknown singer became an singing success—and the script contained lines that now seem ludicrous—when Elvis's promoter and love interest (played by Judy Tyler) fends off an unwanted kiss and says, "How dare you think such cheap tactics would work with me?" Elvis kisses her again and says, "That ain't tactics, honey, it's just the beast in me"—*Jailhouse Rock* had much to recommend it.

The plot was a bundle of clichés, as well, with an old jail cellmate who taught Elvis how to play the guitar turning up to claim 50 per cent of all his earnings once Elvis was successful, Elvis turning into an ungrateful lout, and, finally, hit in the throat in a fistfight and told he'll never sing again. But of course it all ended well, and along the way Elvis showed a glimmer of real acting potential and emerged as a more polished and confident dancer, while the musical soundtrack included some of the strongest performances of his movie career.

Where in the past, Elvis was "just acting natural" in the way he moved while singing, now he had some new friends in his camp. Russ Tamblyn, the dancer and actor, coached him in how to "throw" his knees in a way that made the film's opening scene—a choreographed performance of the title song—an instant classic, and once Jerry Lieber and Mike Stoller, who had been contracted to write most of the songs, got over thinking Elvis was an "idiot savant" (Lieber's words) who didn't know much about the blues, they became mentors, too. The famous songwriting team, who had hated Elvis's rendition of their best known composition, "Hound Dog," now gave him not only "Jailhouse Rock," but also "(You're So Square) Baby, I Don't Care," one of the film's highlights.

Oddly enough, on May 14, just two weeks into the shooting schedule, Elvis swallowed a porcelain cap from one of his front teeth during a dance sequence, and when he experienced some pain in his chest the next day, he was rushed to the Cedars of Lebanon Hospital. There, X-rays showed he'd not swallowed the cap but inhaled it and it was lodged in one of his lungs. Thus the pain in his chest. The cap was removed with forceps and bronchoscope and after resting for a couple of days he returned to *Jailhouse Rock*.

In June, another single was released, combining the two best songs from *Loving You*, which was about to go into the nation's neighborhoods and drive-ins. On one side was the Leiber-Stoller title tune and on the other, a song Kal Mann and Bernie Lowe said they wrote because of Elvis's fondness for teddy bears, as demonstrated by his ability to win so many by tossing baseballs in amusement parks—typical publicity fluff for the time. It occupied the number one position in July and August.

As for the film, Jim Powers of the *Hollywood Reporter*, who didn't like Elvis in *Love Me Tender*, actually thought he wasn't bad in *Loving You*. Even if he did have to see the picture along with several hundred fan club members—invited by the Colonel—who screamed every time Elvis appeared on screen. "Presley . . . acts naturally and with appeal," Powers wrote. "He would be attractive to a member of the older generation if the picture could be seen without the maddening female chorus. Kanter [Hal Kanter, the director] has anticipated some of this by ingeniously using the massed feminine juvenile effects on screen so that at times you are not sure if it is the on-screen or off-screen females who are creating the din. Wendell Corey and Lizabeth Scott are handicapped by speaking their lines into the teeth of a hurricane . . ." The appraisal was typical.

And Elvis Presley teddy bears with Elvis's autograph began appearing in dime stores and supermarkets all across America.

Elvis took a three-week summer vacation, beginning in July when he finished *Jailhouse Rock*. Part of the vacation was spent supervising the Graceland remodeling and relaxing with his friends.

"We'd rent a roller rink and play football on skates," Alan Fortas said. "That was out at the Rainbow. We used to rent the fairgrounds here, the amusement park, ride these rides till we were sick. There was one favorite that we always ended up on. This'd be the last treat, the bumper cars. Here in Memphis they call 'em the 'dodge-'ems.' We'd choose up sides, ten to a side, and we'd have a war. It got so we had to have pillows around our waist, gloves . . . we'd really actually wear blisters on our hands from these dodge-'em cars, from ridin' 'em so long.

"We'd have a ball. The people who came didn't have to pay for anything. I mean, hot dogs, pronto pups, hamburgers, popcorn, candied apples, anything you want. Elvis being from Memphis, it was a special favor to him through the Park Commission, I'm sure. They would keep four or five operators there who could operate the different rides. They would stay open and they'd charge Elvis so much per ride or for the operators on an hourly rate.

"Elvis wouldn't turn anyone away. If they were people who just wanted a good time, he didn't care. Sometimes a friend would bring a friend or somebody would drive by and stop and say, 'Can I come in?' He wouldn't refuse anybody."

He added a swimming pool to the house and told friends he wanted to make his bedroom the "darkest blue there is, with a mirror that will cover one entire wall." He said he was going to decorate the entrance hall with a facsimile sky—clouds painted on the ceiling for daytime, little lights that blinked for stars at night. Over the mild objections of his mother—it was said—he ordered purple walls with gold trim for the living room, dining room and sun room, with white corduroy drapes. And the whole house outside was lighted with soft blue spots, making the limestone seem to have a life of its own, glowing in the dark like a phosphorescent birthday cake.

Down from the house, at the ten-foot wrought-iron Graceland gates that had larger-than-life-size metal figures of Elvis playing the guitar, the fans were in constant attendance. Some youngsters in a car with Arkansas plates had tried to steal Elvis's lawn furniture once and Elvis had to chase them several miles in one of his Cadillacs before he forced them to the side of the road. The same month that happened, two other fans, Helen Magyar and Alice Steinhauer, both nineteen, spent $250 each to get to Memphis from St. Paul, Minnesota; it was worth it, because Elvis saw them and, as they put it to the newspapermen afterward, "He let us run our fingers through his sideburns."

No matter where Elvis was, there were fans—in hotel lobbies, outside studio gates, backstage, at his home, anywhere he went. All over the United States, whenever a youthful runaway was reported by parents to police, if the missing teenager was female the police checked the mob of girls outside Elvis's house in Memphis before doing anything else. In Hollywood, outside the Knickerbocker Hotel, when Elvis was registered, there was a group called the Hotel Hounds. To be a member you had to have been kissed by Elvis and sing "Heartbreak Hotel" backward. Once when Elvis had tried to take a girl to the movies in Memphis, he was spotted by fans, and although he ducked inside the theater to the safety of a reserved booth, the fans found his Cadillac and in their worshipful enthusiasm jumped up and down on the hood and fenders, shredded the upholstery for souvenirs and wrote pledges of undying love all over the white paint with lip-sticks and nail files.

It got crazier farther away from him. In Boston a disc jockey named Norm Prescott offered seven strands of Elvis's sideburns for the seven most absurd reasons for wanting one—and in one week received 18,400 entries. In Forth Worth, Texas, high school students carved his name on their forearms with pocketknives. In Russia, Elvis recordings which otherwise were unavailable were cut on discarded hospital X-ray plates.

When Elvis finished his vacation, he went back on the road again, this time to make his first appearances in the Pacific Northwest. On September 1, he was in Vancouver, British Columbia. "We had the stage set up at the end of this huge, huge stadium," said Scotty Moore, "and the people that were on the field were at the twenty-yard line and we were at the other end. It was impossible to see, so they started moving forward."

"We were all scared," said Neal Matthews. "They turned all the lights on. They warned the crowd over the loudspeaker: If you close in any more, we're stopping the show. It didn't do a bit of good. They kept closing in, moving in. They were wild-eyed. Elvis said, 'I'm cuttin' out, man,' and he quit right in the middle of a song and he took off. He left us all stranded there. We just barely got out. They turned the stage over, they turned over the instruments. It was pretty bad."

Scotty said, "It took us an hour or two to get away. They'd ask us where he was and we'd point over that way and they'd take off running. Then they'd come back and we'd point off in another way, and they'd take off screaming again."

Elvis broke all records in the Pacific Northwest, grossing $147,000 for five half-hour performances. The biggest date was Vancouver, where $44,000 was taken in at the box office; other stops were in Spokane, Tacoma, Seattle and Portland.

The same weekend Elvis was making this brief tour, posters went up all over northern Mississippi and Alabama announcing his return later that month to Tupelo for the "Mississippi & Alabama Fair & Dairy Show," a benefit for what was described as "Elvis Presley's Youth Recreation Center to be Built in Tupelo."

Tupelo Mayor Jim Ballard explained that the city wanted to make a memorial of the birthplace—then still sitting on the same swampy snake-infested hillside—and a park of the surrounding property, with a swimming pool and community building. It was stipulated in the agreement with Elvis, when he said he would appear, that none of the money would go toward purchase of land. The city would cover that. The benefit money was to go to development of the property once the city owned it. Tupelo passed a bond issue to raise money of its own, bought thirteen acres and commissioned an architect to draw up some plans.

Not all was well. Some old friends were slipping away. Back when Elvis was making *Jailhouse Rock*, he was visited on the set by Dewey Phillips. Elvis greeted him warmly and, grateful for the start the Memphis disc jockey gave him, he played a test pressing of "Teddy Bear," which wasn't to be released—or broadcast—for a few weeks. Dewey took the dub with him and played it on the air, thus severing all ties with not only the Colonel and RCA, but Elvis, too.

About the same time, Oscar Davis approached Elvis's backup musicians and suggested they cut their ties with the Colonel and let him promote them as a band. So it was no surprise when Oscar became another persona non grata on the Colonel's list and Scotty and Bill didn't appear with Elvis in Tupelo; they'd quit, telling reporters they weren't being paid enough.

When Elvis read their letter of resignation, at first he was reported to be furious. He then issued a statement saying, "Scotty, Bill, I hope you fellows have good luck. I will give you fellows good recommendations. If you had come to me, we would have worked things out. I would have always taken care of you. But you went to the papers and tried to make me look bad . . ."

A week after the Tupelo fair, Elvis took the boys back on a per diem basis, but it was never the same.

"Elvis is the star and we know it," Scotty was quoted as saying at the time. "I didn't expect to get rich on this, and I certainly don't begrudge him any of the success he has had or what it's brought him, but I did expect to do better than I have and to make a good living for my family."

Scotty said he and Bill had been getting a hundred dollars a week at home and two hundred a week while on the road, plus a thousand-dollar Christmas bonus. The hundred dollars came in every week, whether or not they worked, but they also were responsible for paying all their own traveling expenses. Scotty said he told Elvis he wanted a raise of fifty dollars a week, plus ten thousand in cash, "so I could clean up my debts and have something to show for these four years.

"It wasn't a good salary, you have to admit that, and like any group that lives together you build up these little things . . . so Bill and I quit. We weren't away but a month or so and he wasn't touring that much anyway. He had one recording session during the period, but he was using a lot of Nashville musicians in addition to our own group at the time, so that was no problem. We never did go back on the payroll. We just booked it by the day. We'd just hire on and then go do something else until he needed us again."

The touring continued sporadically the next six weeks as Elvis concentrated again on recording and making movies. Scotty and Bill rejoined him for two appearances at the Pan Pacific Auditorium in Los Angeles. The shows were like most others: Elvis was accompanied by a full carnival of novelty acts, including a trio of tap dancers, a juggler, four acrobats, a comedy violinist and the Jordanaires; nine thousand girls screamed continuously and wet their pants and fainted, the local vice squad told Elvis he'd better clean-up his act or he wasn't doing a second show, and Elvis pocketed about $56,000. Even the press—and Hal Wallis—had to pay for tickets; by now the Colonel was giving *nothing* away.

The harsh criticism never stopped. Frank Sinatra was quoted in a book called *Anti-Rock*, saying, "Rock 'n' roll smells phony and false. It is sung and written for the most part by cretinous goons and by means of its almost imbecilic reiteration, and sly, lewd, in plain fact, dirty lyrics . . . it manages to be the martial music of every sideburned delinquent on the face of the earth . . . [It] is the most brutal, ugly, desperate, vicious form of expression it has been my misfortune to hear."

When asked for a response, Elvis politely disagreed. "I admire the man," he said. "He has a right to say what he wants to say. He is a great success and a fine actor, but I think he shouldn't have said it. He's mistaken about this. This is a trend, just the same as he faced when he started years ago."

At the same time, Jack O'Brien of the *New York Journal-American* compared his Pan Pacific performance to "a terrible popular twist on darkest Africa's fertility tom-tom displays" and Dick Williams wrote in the *Los Angeles Mirror-News* that, "If any further proof were needed that what Elvis offers is not basically music but a sex show, it was proved last night." His performance, Williams wrote, resembled "one of those screeching, uninhibited party rallies which the Nazis used to hold for Hitler."

Next, Elvis made his first visit to Hawaii, to perform twice in one day in the Honolulu Stadium. The Colonel flew to Hawaii first to supervise arrangements, which included rehearsing an American Legion band, which would provide the accompaniment to Elvis's arrival at the airport. The Colonel positioned the band in a fenced enclosure not much larger than the band itself, and when the plane landed, he began barking his marching orders. Within moments the musicians were hopelessly snarled—trombone players slamming trumpeters in the neck; drummers on their knees, feet and hands stuck through their drum heads; the entire woodwind section rammed up against a fence, bleating for help. And the Colonel stood proudly at attention—suppressing a smile—saluting the King of Rock 'n' Roll.

"Jailhouse Rock" had been released by now—first the song, and then the film. "Teddy Bear" was still in the top ten. His third album, *Loving You*, which carried the seven songs from the film and five others, including Fats Domino's hit "Blueberry Hill," was number one in album sales. There were three records ("All Shook Up," "Teddy Bear" and "Paralyzed") on the British charts, and his 45 EP of religious songs was the best-selling record in that category. When "Jailhouse Rock" was released, it was, quoting *Billboard*, "a smash in all markets"; and by November 1 *it* was number one.

As for the film, it was greeted about the same way the first two were—with critical reservation and audience adoration. In many cities it was released as the top half of a double feature—over *Action of the Tiger*, a slow-moving adventure starring Van Johnson. Probably there was no actor on earth who could deliver a line like "That ain't tactics, honey, it's just the beast in me" and get away with it.

George Klein and Alan Fortas were part of Elvis's entourage now. George was a Humes High School classmate, president of the senior class and editor of the school yearbook, who worked as a disc jockey for a while, but lost his job when his station dropped rock and roll. Alan was an all-city tackle from Central High, a university drop-out working for his father when George took him to Graceland.

George told Peter Guralnick that when Elvis went on the road, Elvis's mother told George to look after him. "He has some bad habits," Elvis's mother said, "so please watch him because he's my baby." George explained that she was giving him advice what to do when Elvis walked in his sleep. It was George who introduced him to Anita Wood, a nineteen-year-old beauty queen who became Elvis's more-or-less steady date for a couple of months in the fall. When George asked Elvis what he was supposed to do, Elvis merely said he was his "traveling companion."

Alan wrote in his book, *Elvis*, that the singer's respect for his mother determined the mood. "It never got wild at Graceland," he said. "People respected Graceland as the Presleys' home. And the language never got (too) rough around there either. If anybody said 'goddamn,' he erupted in a rage. 'You can use any other word you want, but you can't use the Lord's name in vain!'"

In October, Milton Bowers, the draft board chairman in Memphis, said that because of reduced draft quotas, probably it would be another year before Elvis got his call. But it was only two months later, on December 20, when the government's greetings were delivered in person, by Bowers, to Elvis at Graceland, where he had returned for the Christmas holidays.

Rumors had been circulating despite the October announcement, so much so that earlier in the week Army and Navy recruiters visited Elvis to offer him special enlistment opportunities. The idea was that if he enlisted instead of waiting for the draft, he could pick the branch and probably the specific job he was to have the next two years. The Navy even went so far as to say it would form an "Elvis Presley Company" with boys from Memphis if Elvis would sign Navy enlistment papers. Elvis thanked everybody and said he'd take his chances.

After all this—every bit of it covered in depth by the press—it was almost anticlimactic when the notice finally arrived, ordering him to report to the Memphis draft board office January 20, 1958. Most of the controversy had come a year earlier, when veterans, fans and senators alike all reacted so noisily to the no-haircut rumor. Now not even Elvis was ruffled. He was going to miss his mother and father, he told newsmen, but "I'm kind-a proud of it. It's a duty I've got to fill and I'm gonna do it."

Elvis then added, "My induction notice said for me to leave my car at home. Transportation will be provided. They tell me just to bring a razor, toothbrush, toothpaste, a comb and enough money to hold me two weeks."

If Elvis was treating everything matter-of-factly, Paramount Pictures and Hal Wallis in Hollywood were not. Elvis had been scheduled to report for his next film the same week the Army wanted him, and between $300,000 and $350,000 already had been committed to the project, all of which would be lost, they said, if Elvis went into the Army before March. In making this announcement, studio production chief Frank Freeman said he had sent a letter to Elvis's draft board asking an eight-week delay.

That was December 21. The letter arrived two days later, and the draft board bumped it back, saying such a request would have to come from Elvis not Paramount. So on the day before Christmas, Elvis wrote his letter. He said he hoped they understood that he was acting not in his own interest but on behalf of the studio. Paramount had helped him at the start of his career, he said, and now he felt it only fair to go along with the studio's request, "so these folks will not lose so much money, with everything they have done so far." Elvis closed his note with a Merry Christmas wish to the board.

The three members held a special meeting December 27 and voted unanimously to grant Elvis a sixty-day deferment, meaning induction would be delayed from January 20 to March 20. Elvis said he was grateful—"for the studio's sake"—and the Colonel described the deferment as "very kind."

Of course there were others who felt differently. In the last days of 1957, Milton Bowers and his two fellow draft board members may have been among the most unpopular men in all America. Elvis's fans wrote letters and called to complain about Elvis being drafted at all, while those who didn't like Elvis called to complain about giving him a deferment. It was the Christmas season, a time of peace on earth and good will toward men, but not at the Bowers house.

Bowers was one of the city's civic leaders, a former Democratic state legislator and onetime president of the Memphis School Board, as well as the head of a family-owned welding shop and metal works. He said he had expected some criticism for his board's actions—after all, what draft board *isn't* disliked by an individual or two occasionally?—but nothing like what he got.

SPEER
©'77

10212-59

*Opposite above: Elvis and Debra Paget on location for his first movie,* Love Me Tender, *1956. Opposite below and left: Elvis as Deke Rivers in his second film,* Loving You, *1957. Below: Vince Everett and friends in* Jailhouse Rock, *1957.*

*The idol at Graceland, Memphis, 1957*

*Left: Elvis with Hollywood actress Natalie Wood, in 1956. Below: Elvis and Liberace switch roles backstage at the Riviera, Las Vegas, in November 1956. Elvis wears Liberace's gold lamé jacket and carries his candelabra, while Liberace wears Elvis's striped jacket and plays his guitar.*

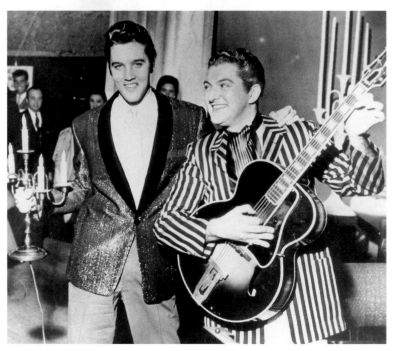

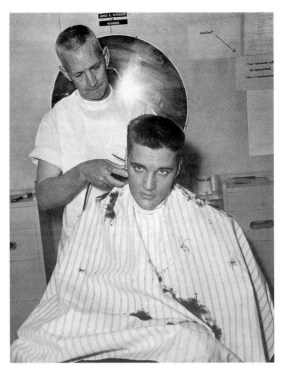

*Opposite above: Elvis at the gates of Graceland. Opposite below: G.I. Elvis at the gates of his Graceland mansion, with fans. Left: the army haircut: "Hair today, gone tomorrow." Below: beginning his eight weeks of military training at Fort Hood, Texas.*

*Above: waiting for news of his
mother in a Memphis hospital,
with (from left to right) Alan
Fortas, Lamar Fike, George Klein,
Billy Smith and Louis Harris,
1958. Left: his mother's grave;
nearby is a stone reading, "She was
the sunshine of our home."'*

"I'm fed to the teeth," said Bowers as 1958 began. "I eat, sleep and drink Elvis Presley. In fact, I talk Elvis Presley more than I sleep. With all due respect to Elvis, who's a nice boy, we've drafted people who are far, far more important than he is. After all, when you take him out of the entertainment business, what have you got left? A truck driver."

A comment that caused cheers from one side, boos and hisses from the other. And the controversy staggered on.

*Elvis' Christmas Album* had been released in mid-November, along with a Christmas EP, and both soon appeared at the top of all the popularity charts. The selection of songs was reasonably broad, including Gene Autry's "Here Comes Santa Claus," Irving Berlin's "White Christmas" (Berlin went on record as hating Elvis's version), a number of sacred songs that had appeared earlier on the *Peace in the Valley* EP, a couple of songs by writers Elvis had used previously ("Santa Claus Is Back in Town" by Jerry Leiber and Mike Stoller, "Santa Brings My Baby Back to Me" by Aaron Schroeder and Claude Demetrius), and some carols. It was the carols "O Little Town of Bethlehem" and "Silent Night" that caused the second peculiar controversy of Elvis's holidays.

In Los Angeles, disc jockey Dick Whittinghill at KMPC said he had been getting requests to play songs from the album, but he refused, saying, "That's like having Tempest Storm give Christmas gifts to my kids." And when Al Priddy at KEX in Portland, Oregon, played one cut, he was fired—because, according to station management, the album was in "extremely bad taste." The album was similarly banned at almost all Canadian stations—even after a jockey in Kingston, Ontario, Allen Brooks of CKWS, started playing the album and asking listeners to call in their opinion, and 93 per cent (including several who identified themselves as clergymen) heartily endorsed it.

Then during Christmas week Victor released another single, still another song by Leiber and Stoller, "Don't." Once again advance orders exceeded a million.

Elvis returned to Hollywood by train in January to begin work on *King Creole*, taking almost a dozen people with him, including his new "employee" Alan Fortas, who said, "Every town we passed through, no matter what time of morning or night, the whole station was jam-packed. These people knew as soon as Elvis finished this movie, he was going in the Army, so most of them considered it the last time to see him. As soon as he got on the train here in Memphis, it hit the wire, it got in the papers and on radio. People knew and they were lined up along the tracks all the way across America."

Elvis's fourth film was based loosely on the Harold Robbins novel *A Stone for Danny Fisher*. In the book the hero was a prize fighter, in the film a singer. The story also was moved from New York to New Orleans, where Elvis worked as a busboy in the King Creole, a honky-tonk on Bourbon Street. It was in this club that he met a prostitute (Carolyn Jones) and three bush league hoodlums (Walter Matthau, Vic Morrow and Brian Hutton), who swept Elvis into their miserable little underworld, eventually to plan a robbery of a store owned by Elvis's father. With the help of a demure, virginal dime-store clerk (Dolores Hart), Elvis extracts himself, is reunited with his father, and sings eleven songs, enough to fill out another album. *King Creole* was at that time, and remained, Elvis's favorite film. Thanks in large part to the director, Michael Curtiz, and flashes of brilliance by Miss Jones and a few others, it also was one of Elvis's best.

It was Hal Wallis's second film with Elvis and the first to utilize location shooting. Once Elvis had completed recording sessions and all the studio work in Hollywood, he and his gang—augmented by some of the cast and crew, producer Aaron Spelling (then Carolyn Jones's husband) and Nick Adams—took another train cross-country. Alan Fortas said that once again the tracks were lined with fans. As, of course, were the streets of New Orleans.

"We left the French Quarter one day and there were so many people they almost turned the taxicab over," Alan said. "There were thousands of people. Hal Wallis couldn't believe it. The Colonel told him before we went down there, 'You're gonna need a whole lot of security.' And Hal Wallis said, 'Oh no, we can handle it. I had Dean Martin and Jerry Lewis at their peak and nobody ever bothered them.' The Colonel said, 'Okay, but you never had Elvis Presley. You watch!' I got news for you," said Alan, "I never saw so many people in my life. They declared it Elvis Presley Day and let the kids out of school and it took us two hours to get back to the hotel no matter where we were, even from across the street."

As when Elvis stayed in Hollywood, he had taken an entire floor of a hotel—the Roosevelt, situated half a block from the French Quarter—and elevators were not permitted to stop at that level. "Once we got to the hotel, security was good," Alan said. "One time after we finished filming we got on the elevator and we said, 'Tenth floor, please.' The elevator operator said, 'No, sir, I can't stop on the tenth floor. Mr. Presley is up there and we just can't stop.' Elvis was on the elevator with us and he said, 'Yeah, I know. I'm Elvis.' The elevator operator looked straight at him and said, 'I'm sorry, sir, I can't stop on that floor for anybody.' We had to go to the eleventh floor and walk down."

Then when the film company moved to Lake Pontchartrain for a scene in a house on stilts over the water, the crowd on the adjoining beach got so huge and unruly, Elvis was forced to exit through a rear door in the structure, board a motorboat and travel several miles down the lake to a waiting car.

Elvis returned to Hollywood at the end of February.

"Here we were, only four hundred miles from Memphis," said Alan. "But we had to go back to California to get a release. They had to run the picture, make sure there was nothing they had to do over again, because once they give you a release they can't call you back. So we went back to Hollywood by train, Elvis got his release and we got back on the train to come to Memphis. Now this was our fourth train ride in a month and it was getting pretty boring. All you can do is sleep and eat and after a while you get tired of sleeping and eating. We were young and we didn't drink. We'd just sit and talk, try to write songs, try to sing. You know, just typical ol' boys. But it got to us by the time we got to Dallas. We couldn't take it any longer. So we got off that train and rented some Cadillacs and drove the rest of the way home."

Elvis was pleased with his performance in *King Creole* and his co-stars were flattering as well. Upon his return to Memphis, he told a reporter for the Memphis Commercial Appeal that the role "was quite a challenge for me because it was written for a more experienced actor." Jan Shepard, who played his sister in the film, said he may have been just beginning his acting career, but he had "a great sense of timing, there was great honesty in his acting." And Walter Matthau, who played the heavy, in an interview with the BBC, called Elvis an "instinctive actor" who "was quite bright, too. He was very intelligent. Also, he was intelligent enough to understand what a character was and how to play the character simply by being himself *through* the means of the story."

Elvis had just ten days at home before induction. Eight nights he and his friends went to the skating rink. Another night they went to see *Sing, Boy Sing*, another movie about the making of a young rock star, this one written specifically for Elvis; previous commitments forced the Colonel to turn it down, so the starring part went to Tommy Sands, one of the Colonel's young protégés, and, to Elvis's delight, the role of the singer's sidekick went to his friend Nick Adams.

Finally, he let all his salaried buddies go off to fend for themselves. He gave Anita Woods an automobile. And on the final day, he stayed up all night at Graceland, saying goodbye to friends.

# Chapter 10

# THE ARMY

On the cold, rainy Monday morning of March 24, Elvis arrived at Local Board 86. It was 6:35 A.M., and although he was nearly half an hour early, already dozens of newsmen and photographers were waiting. He looked a little sleepy-eyed but was filled with cheerful wisecracks. With him were his parents and Judy Spreckels, the blond former wife of a sugar millionaire, who said she was not a girl friend but "like a sister," and Lamar Fike, who tried to enlist but was rejected because his 270 pounds were considered more than the Army could handle in a single recruit. The Colonel was there too, of course, handing out balloons that advertised Elvis's up-coming film, *King Creole*. And although several Army spokesmen kept saying Elvis's induction was "routine," it was clearly anything but.

Elvis and his fellow recruits boarded a bus for Kennedy Hospital, where blood tests, mental examinations, the signing of loyalty oaths and the like took much of the rest of the day. Photographers trailed along, popping flash bulbs every time he stepped before another examining officer. Then Elvis was sworn in, designated US53310761, and at five o'clock boarded a chartered Greyhound bus for Fort Chaffee, Arkansas.

The bus crossed the Mississippi River and stopped in West Memphis, Arkansas, at the Coffee Cup, a small restaurant where the Army had hoped to feed its small band of new privates. They hadn't counted on the dozens of fans who soon arrived, and as Elvis began working his way through a plate of spaghetti, they stormed the cafe. In the rush to get back to the bus, Elvis lost a fountain pen, had his clothing torn, and behind him waitresses were arguing over who'd keep the chair he'd used.

Said Tennessee's Governor Frank Clement in a telegram to the recruit: "You have shown that you are an American citizen first, a Tennessee volunteer, and a young man willing to serve his country when called upon to do so."

Much thought, and newspaper space, was given to Elvis's entrance into the service and what it meant to his career.

On one side were those who said it was the end of his reign as pop music king. Not only would he take a rather noticeable cut in pay—from over $100,000 to $78 a month—he also would be unable to defend his position against other singers who were not so rigidly restricted. He would be unable to make any movies and it was unlikely he could do any concerts. And when dealing in the vagaries of popular culture, two years was a long, long time.

Not so, said the Colonel. There was that thousand dollars a week coming in from RCA. Paramount owed him 50 per cent of all profits from *King Creole*, as yet unreleased, and it was regarded as a sure thing that it would gross millions, it being the only way Elvis was going to be seen until 1960. There were several songs already recorded and ready for release as singles.

Besides, the lipstick and T-shirts and other novelties continued to sell, and now that Elvis was in the Army, that only increased the already broad range of product possibilities. When a group called the Three Teens released a song called "Dear 53310761" and Trinity Music, the publisher, made up fifty thousand Elvis Presley dog tags as giveaways to disc jockeys, for instance, the Colonel immediately claimed proprietary rights, licensed someone to merchandise the tags and took a juicy royalty. They were available in gold or silver plate, were stamped with Elvis's name, rank and serial number, along with his blood type (O), a facsimile signature and an etched-out picture. They cost one dollar.

By now there were several new novelty songs about Elvis; "Bye Bye, Elvis" by Gennie Harris ("I know I'll cry the day you go / My friends and I will miss you so"), "All American Boy" by Bill Parsons ("And then one day my Uncle Sam / Said—*thump thump*—here Ah am"), "Marchin' Elvis" by the Greats, and "I'll Wait Forever" sung by Elvis's latest sweetie-pie, Anita Wood (on the Sun label, of all places). The Colonel couldn't claim a penny of royalties from these records—Elvis was, after all, a public figure and therefore open to public comment—but the records did help strengthen the Elvis market.

As for that massive drop in income—which some said would cost the United States $400,000 in taxes alone—the Colonel said, "I consider it my patriotic duty to keep Elvis in the 90 per cent tax bracket." The Colonel's first order of business, of course, was to coordinate all the hooplah that was to accompany Elvis's reception and indoctrination at Fort Chaffee.

Private Presley was dressed and making his bed by the time a sergeant flipped on the lights in the barracks to wake the men at 5:30 the morning of March 25, Elvis's first full day in the Army. He and his fellow recruits had arrived at Chaffee late the night before and it meant he'd had little sleep. (He'd also been greeted by a crowd of at least three hundred girls when the bus drove past the camp entrance.) He then marched to the mess hall for breakfast, where he was met by Colonel Parker, who seemed to be using his honorary title to pull rank on Captain Arlie Metheny, the post public information officer.

"Let the boys take all the pictures they want," the Colonel said, pointing to no fewer than fifty-five reporters and photographers, exceeding by five the number of recruits being fed. And before the Captain could react, the boys moved in, preserving on film Elvis's every forkful of egg and sausage, every chew of toast and every swallow of coffee. Finally one of the reporters asked the Colonel what he was doing there and he said he was hanging around to "look after the boy . . . see that he gets everything he needs." Captain Metheny stood by, perhaps remembering with some peculiar sense of nostalgia one of his earlier assignments—handling the press when troops were brought into Little Rock during the crisis over integration.

Following breakfast, Elvis and the other inductees were marched off for five hours of aptitude testing, the results to be used in determining what assignment they'd be given once past basic training, also whether or not they were eligible to take another test for Officers Candidate School. (Next day Elvis said he didn't take the officers' examination, indicating he hadn't scored high enough in the preliminary tests to qualify. "I never was good at arithmetic," he said.) As Elvis passed a barracks on the way to take these tests, several soldiers standing on the steps greeted him with catcalls.

At lunch it was the same thing all over again. The reporters and photographers swarmed around Elvis so much, Captain Metheny resumed command and ordered a five-minute reprieve so Elvis and the others could eat in peace.

One of the recruits sitting next to Elvis, Benny St. Clair of Texarkana, Arkansas, looked at Elvis and said, "Is it always like this?"

"Yep," said Elvis, stuffing his mouth with mashed potatoes.

"Doesn't it bother you?" the private asked.

"No," said Elvis. "I figure I better start worrying when they don't bother me any more."

The Colonel stood to one side beaming.

Next the rookies and newsmen trooped over to a post theater, where the chaplain welcomed Elvis and his buddies to their new home. And from there it was right into the main event—the haircut that had been making headlines for so long.

As it happened, Elvis had his hair trimmed twice before this, removing an inch of sideburns in Hollywood for *King Creole* and some from the top and sides during his final week as a civilian in Memphis. It's not likely he expected it was enough, and if he did, he was mistaken.

Elvis sat down in the chair and barber James Peterson of Gans,

THE ARMY                                            135

Oklahoma—himself a lean, smiling crew-cutter—threw a towel around Elvis's
neck. He plugged in his electric clippers and taking careful aim, holding for the
photographers momentarily, neatly peeled one sideburn off with one swipe.
Then he took the other. He threw the sideburns into the air, went up the back
of Elvis's head with the clippers and then started leveling the top.

Elvis caught some of the falling hair in one palm and blew it toward the
cameras. "Hair today, gone tomorrow," he said, grinning a little woodenly.

Elvis paid sixty-five cents—the Army's going rate for a clipping—and
walked away as the barber shook the smock and let the hair mix on the floor
with that of the other recruits. The Colonel explained how much that hair was
worth and how many thousands of letters they'd received from fans wanting a
little of it. And then Elvis went into a telephone booth to call his parents. He
hadn't talked with them yet that day.

One more meal and his first day was done. Elvis returned to his barracks
and the press returned to nearby motels.

Wednesday, the second day, began with the issue of seventy-five pounds of
uniforms and other gear. It was the usual noisy, crowded affair, with recruits
stepping gingerly over a carpet of flash bulbs and around the post commander,
a brigadier general who said he wouldn't have missed it for anything.

Elvis was given a pair of size twelve combat boots. (He was then wearing
some low-cut motorcycle boots, along with the same plaid jacket and dark
pants he'd worn the past two days.) He said thank you, sir. Then he was given
his fatigues. Again he said thank you, sir. Before he was through, he had sirred
one private first class, one corporal and one sergeant.

The Colonel stood there, still beaming, and tried to sneak a Southern string
tie into the pile of clothing in Elvis's arms.

That afternoon a press conference was called, during which the General
announced to the anxious world that Elvis would be going to Fort Hood in
Texas for basic combat training with the Second Armored Division. Elvis had
been vaccinated against tetanus, typhoid and Asian flu only minutes before the
announcement and was rushed from the infirmary to the hall where all the
newsmen were. Asked what he thought of the assignment, he said he was
happy about it.

"You name it, I been all over Texas," he said. "I got my start in music
around Houston."

He was asked next about his barracks buddies. "They've been swell to me,"
he said. "The only GIs I've seen are the ones in the barracks. They treat me like
anyone else, though. That's the way I want it."

Finally, the press was cleared out. Enough was enough, Captain Metheny
said. After all, the boy did have to have some time to acclimate himself to his

new environment. And so the platoon of reporters and photographers scattered, moving through the camp slowly, interviewing anybody and everybody who had anything to say about Elvis. Nearly every one of them said something nice. One even called him "wholesome."

And then on Friday, March 28, Elvis and eighteen other buck privates boarded a bus at dawn for the 425-mile trip to the middle of Texas. No, the Army was sorry. It couldn't release the names of towns and restaurants where the bus would stop. Security, you know. Security against the "enemy"—teenagers.

The public information officer at Fort Hood was a woman, Lieutenant Colonel Marjorie Schulten, and she, along with several other high-ranking officers at the post, had received mysterious calls from the Commanding General, who said only that "I have information that would be of interest to you." They hurried to his office and were told Elvis was on the way.

The WAC officer didn't quite know what to say and in the hours that followed she met first with her fellow officers and then with Colonel Parker. Newspaper writers and photographers, television cameramen, magazine writers, editors from New York—the press was as thick as the dust in the area. She called a brief press conference the afternoon of Elvis's arrival.

"He has a mission and we have a mission," she said, standing on a table. "We expect to perform them mutually. Hereafter there will be no more interviews or picture taking during his training."

Elvis arrived at 4:34 P.M. (newsmen still were chronicling the operation minute by minute as if it were a military operation), and was assigned to 'A' Company, Second Medium Tank Battalion, Second Armored Division. Reporters were thanked for their attention and concern and gently asked to leave.

This didn't make Colonel Schulten's job simple. Even if no interviews were granted, still there remained the mail and the telephone calls. Elvis received two thousand fan letters at Fort Hood the first week and no one ever tabulated the hundreds of calls. Each, the WAC colonel said, deserved a personal response.

Then, of course, when it became apparent the lady wasn't kidding about interviews, the press wanted to interview her. That's right, she said patiently, Elvis is a prompt riser. Yes indeed, he was standing up well under the strain. Why just the other day Elvis's drill instructor, Sergeant William Fraley, *and* his superior, Master Sergeant Henry Coley, *both* said they were impressed.

In actual fact Elvis *was* behaving himself; he *was* being an exemplary recruit. Much of Army training is based on a philosophy of competitive gung-hoism, whereby trainee is pitted against trainee, company against company, battalion against battalion, in a constant quest for medals, ribbons, citations and grades. This was a philosophy that appealed to Elvis and recognizing his vulnerability, knowing there were millions of adults waiting for his first show of impatience, Elvis probably tried harder than many others.

Removal of the press was a help, certainly, but that represented only slight relief. Still Elvis had to contend with his fans, who swarmed over the post on weekends, hoping for a glimpse of their hero. And he had to live with his fellow soldiers, who rode him good-naturedly but endlessly. If he wasn't ducking back into a barracks to escape being seen by girls zipping up the company street in convertibles, he was forcing grins at comments like "Maybe you'd like some rock 'n' roll instead of reveille" and "Miss your teddy bears?" and "By the right wiggle—march!"

Elvis went through the standard indoctrination program—orientation to Army life, history of the service, military courtesy and justice—and then into basic instruction in equipment maintenance and small arms. In most courses he was as adept as any in his class, and when he failed to qualify on the pistol range, he signed up for additional instruction, given during his off-duty time.

Outside, back in the civilian world, many who'd once criticized Elvis were now lining up to offer praise. In Florida, the state that once had banned his wiggle, Congressman A. S. Herlong asked Elvis to appear at a celebration sponsored by the De Leon Springs Chamber of Commerce.

This invitation came in the middle of April, as Elvis entered his third week of boot camp, and it was quickly rejected, not by Elvis or the Colonel but by the Army. "Private Presley is currently undergoing his initial cycle of training," the Army said. "It is contrary to Department of the Army policy to interrupt this important phase of his training except for compassionate or emergency reasons."

It also was becoming apparent by now that Elvis wasn't going to appear anywhere for the Army either. Sometime earlier, of course, there had been talk of Elvis's going into the Army's Special Services branch to sing his way through his tour of duty. The Army never made much of it publicly, but it was made abundantly clear that it would be flattered if Elvis marched to the same drummer heard by Eddie Fisher and Vic Damone when they served. They had been inducted during the Korean conflict and entertained the fighting troops. Damone even took on a special assignment to help recruit women for military service, recording a song called "The Girls Are Marching." It was thought by the Army brass that Elvis should serve in the same way—appearing in television commercials to boost enlistment, entertaining at military installations, selling a few bonds.

The Colonel never talked much about why he finally said no to the Special Services. About all he said publicly was that Elvis didn't want any special treatment, didn't want to take "the easy way out." Undoubtedly, this was true. But the Colonel also knew this path served his own purposes, that if Elvis carried a rifle or drove a tank or marched for two years, rather than sang, the adult acceptance he was picking up could multiply.

"You can't imagine how much trouble the Colonel's decision caused," said someone then close to Elvis. "It's never been printed, but the Colonel was fighting with the Army constantly. Even after Elvis had completed his advanced training and had been on the job driving a jeep in Germany, the brass kept after him, wanting him to do this, do that. One General in Germany wanted Elvis to sing at his daughter's birthday party and when Elvis said he didn't think he was allowed to do that, the General would have to talk with the Colonel, the General practically made it an order. The Colonel finally said Elvis would sing, but the General would have to invite every man in Elvis's unit to the party too. That ended that, but it wasn't easy on Elvis."

There was some little known comfort coming from some of his instructors, however. One of them, Sergeant Bill Norwood, told Albert Goldman that when he saw how homesick Elvis was, and how worried he was about his mother's health, he told the recruit he could come to his house to "let it all out. Do whatever you want to, and don't worry about anything. But when you walk out of my front door, you are now Elvis Presley. You're an actor. You're a soldier. So, by God, I want you to act! Don't let nobody know how you feel on the inside." Norwood also made a room in his home available later in the training cycle to Anita Wood when, at Norwood's invitation, she came to visit Elvis.

Elvis found another home away from home in that of Eddie Fadal and his family in Waco. Elvis had met Fadal during a swing through Texas in 1956 and when he now went to the post to say hello, Elvis remembered him. Elvis took Anita to the Fadal home on a weekend pass.

At the end of his eight weeks in boot camp the Army announced Elvis would be granted the usual two-week leave, then report back to Hood for another fourteen weeks of training, eight in advanced individual training as an armor crewman and six of unit training. It was also announced that in September he and 1400 other soldiers would be sent as replacements to the Third Armored Division in Germany.

Elvis may not have been on public display during this period, but it didn't mean his popularity was diminishing. If anything, attention only increased.

Elvis wasn't in the Army a week when *The Phil Silvers Show* offered a half-hour burlesque called "Rock and Roll Rookie," in which a look-alike actor named Tom Gilson played a guitar-picking sideburned draftee named Elvin Pelvin who owned eleven Cadillacs and a hound dog, while Silver, as Sergeant Bilko, sang "You're Nothing but a Raccoon" and "Brown Suede Combat Boots." As was noted in *Billboard*: "Gilson played it straight and with sympathy, thereby safeguarding the sponsor from the easily aroused wrath of you-know-who's fans."

The same week, RCA released two more records—*Elvis Golden Records*, what was to be the first in a series of his greatest hit albums, and his twenty-second single, "Wear My Ring Around Your Neck" backed by "Doncha' Think It's Time?" Advance sales for each again topped the million mark.

And then in late May *King Creole* opened, just in time for Elvis to get back to Memphis on the leave that followed basic training and attend a preview with his parents.

His mother was not well, but in every other way it was a joyous homecoming. Anita Wood was there to join him in late-night roller-skating parties when Elvis again rented the Rainbow Rollerdrome, or to sit at home with him and watch television and talk. A couple of weeks later it would be reported that Elvis and Anita were engaged; both denied it, although Elvis had given her a diamond ring surrounded by eighteen sapphires. His fans continued to flock to the Graceland gates, something Elvis always regarded as a little odd but reassuring. And wonder of wonders, the critics greeted *King Creole* not with the sneers usually reserved for Elvis on screen but praise.

*The Hollywood Reporter*'s critic Jim Powers said the film made "extraordinary use of locations," called it exciting, said it dramatized juvenile delinquency rather than glorified or exploited it, and said Elvis showed real promise. *Billboard* said it was Elvis's "best acting performance to date," taking special note of the scenes between Elvis and Carolyn Jones. Howard Thompson in the *New York Times* opened with this: "As the lad himself might say, cut my legs off and call me Shorty! Elvis Presley can act." And closed with "Acting is his assignment in this shrewdly upholstered showcase, and he does it."

Elvis was ecstatic. Friends say the reviews, especially that in the *Times*, made Elvis happier than they'd ever seen him before.

So it was in good spirits that he and some of his old buddies drove to Nashville on June 10 to record a few new songs, the first sessions in Elvis's recording career when Scotty and Bill were absent, their places taken by Nashville studio pros. Elvis returned to Memphis three days later to rent the Rainbow again and invite about thirty friends, Anita Wood among them, to join him in a farewell whirl. And then on Saturday he got into a red Lincoln convertible he had bought to celebrate and leisurely returned to Fort Hood.

Vernon and Gladys Presley followed less than a week later. Elvis, or perhaps the Colonel, had studied Army Regulations during the first eight weeks and it was determined Elvis could sleep off post if he had dependents living in the same area. Usually the word "dependent" covered wives and children, but in that Elvis's parents were dependent upon him for food, shelter and spending money, they qualified in the strict reading of the rule. So Elvis rented a three-bedroom trailer and then traded that for a three-bedroom house in the nearest town to the post, Killeen. The house was to remain in the custody of the Presley family for just two months, until the owners, a judge and his wife, returned from their vacation. By which time, of course, Elvis was to be nearly finished with his advanced training and packing for Germany.

Some time later Elvis explained to a friend his real reason for moving off post. "Without taking anything away from Elvis's love of his parents," the friend said, "it was essential that he should have a 'retreat' because, you understand, while he took all the guff that is Army issue, and knocked himself out to be just one of the guys, he was denied the one inalienable right that soldiers hold most dear—the right to bitch. Had he at any time complained about anything or anyone, some s.o.b. would have passed on the comments, and they would have been reported unfavorably by some angle-hunting reporter. So he just took whatever was handed out, and kept his mouth shut—at least until he was at home with his family."

July was ordinary. A twenty-four-year-old secretary in Washington sued Elvis for $5000, claiming she had suffered whiplash injuries while riding in a car that was struck from behind by one of Elvis's automobiles—in 1956! "Hard Headed Woman," a song from *King Creole*, replaced a novelty tune called "Purple People Eater" at the top of the charts. Elvis was clocked at ninety-five miles an hour in a sixty-mile zone in Fort Worth, trying to elude pursuing fans, and was given a ticket. Then he began advanced unit training, his final classes before shipping out.

August was something else. That was when Elvis's world collapsed like a sand castle into the boiling sea.

His mother was still ailing. It had been difficult for her to walk and to concentrate and to carry on a normal life. She had lost most of her enthusiasm and sprightliness. Elvis and his father decided she was too ill to remain in Killeen and that she should return to Memphis and the family doctor. Elvis drove her to the train on Friday, August 8.

In Memphis, doctors said she had hepatitis and she was given a private room at Methodist Hospital, one of the city's newest and most modern facilities. Hepatitis is an infection of the liver, one of the vital organs. In three days the doctors placed a call to Elvis in Texas. They said he should come home as quickly as possible.

Elvis obtained an emergency leave and went against his mother's wishes and boarded an airplane. He arrived in Memphis Tuesday night and went right to her bedside. The doctors said his presence improved her spirits tremendously but didn't much affect the odds. Her condition remained "serious."

All through the night Tuesday and all day Wednesday and Wednesday evening, Elvis and his father took turns sitting at the bedside. Sometimes Elvis sat with his pals, Alan Fortas, Lamar Fike, George Klein, and some of his cousins. At three in the morning Thursday, Vernon was in the hospital room and Elvis was asleep at Graceland. Vernon said his wife began "suffering for breath." And then she died. Vernon called Elvis and told him what had happened.

The doctors later announced that Mrs. Presley had died of a heart attack.

A close friend of the Presley family's explained what happened. "Mrs. Presley loved white beans, corn bread and buttermilk," he said. "She was a half-a-dozen-eggs-and-a- stick-of-butter woman. She never got used to having money. Even when she was in Graceland, she bought twenty-five-cent bottles of shampoo and the smallest tubes of toothpaste available. That's not criticism. That's just the way she was, even when Elvis bought her Cadillacs.

"She tried very hard," said the family friend. "She really did. She wanted to be what she thought Elvis wanted her to be. She wanted to look good for Elvis, to be thin and attractive. But she was not supposed to be thin, and she stayed heavy, began to put on more weight. So she began to take pills. Diet pills. I guess they became a habit with her. And then she switched to alcohol.

"It was sad. Sometimes she couldn't even see across the room. She didn't even recognize me once, couldn't even see I was standing in the same room with her.

"All she wanted was to make Elvis proud. She just wanted him to be proud of her. And of course he was proud of her. But she kept on taking those pills, and drinking . . . and finally her big ol' heart gave out."

She was forty-six.

Elvis wanted the service to be held at Graceland, but when the Colonel said security would be a problem, he agreed to have a family viewing there instead, then have the service at the funeral home. Dr. Charles Clarke, Gladys's physician, told Peter Guralnick that when he arrived, "The expression of grief was just profound. He and his dad would just be pacing around, walk up to the front door with their arms locked around each other, and I remember the father saying, 'Elvis, look at them chickens. [The Presleys kept free-range chickens on the Graceland property.] Mama ain't never gonna feed them chickens no more.' 'No, Daddy, Mama won't never fed them chickens anymore.' Just short of abject grief.'"

Anita Wood flew in from New York and she recalled later that Elvis practically forced her into the parlor where his mother was laid out in a glass-topped coffin, telling her to look at her "precious feet." Nick Adams arrived from Hollywood and set up a bed in Elvis's bedroom so he could keep an eye on him overnight. Finally, Dr. Clarke gave Elvis a sedative and when the Memphis Funeral Home took the body away the next morning, he was still sleeping.

Vernon had called James Blackwood to ask if the Blackwood Brothers would sing at the service, and when James said they were contracted to appear in North Carolina that evening, the Presleys chartered a plane to fly the gospel quartet back and forth. The Blackwoods had been one of Mrs. Presley's favorite spiritual groups, as well as the group Elvis once hoped to join, and it was important to have them present.

The service was to be limited to four hundred invited guests, but by the time it began, some three thousand people had filed past the casket and thousands more stood outside the funeral home. Chet Atkins was there, but Scotty and Bill were not. The Reverend James Hamill delivered the eulogy. The Blackwoods sang "Rock of Ages" and Mrs. Presley's favorite, "Precious Memories." Elvis stood next to his father crying. Outside in the Memphis street were three thousand fans, standing in prayerful silence.

From the funeral home the procession moved slowly to Forest Hill Cemetery, on Highway 51 south of Memphis in low rolling countryside three miles toward the city from Graceland. There wasn't much to distinguish Forest Hill from most other cemeteries, except it seemed somewhat better tended than many. Mrs. Presley was buried on a hillside several hundred yards back from the highway, near one of the asphalt roadways that wound through the property, where a modest marker read:

GLADYS SMITH PRESLEY
APRIL 25, 1912-AUG. 14, 1958
BELOVED WIFE OF
VERNON PRESLEY
AND MOTHER OF
ELVIS PRESLEY
SHE WAS THE SUNSHINE OF OUR HOME

There were sixty-five city policemen hired to handle the traffic and pedestrian problems at the service, as reporters, photographers and fans crushed forward, pushing rudely, taking in every sob and mumbled syllable. Elvis was inconsolable.

Elvis was given a five-day extension on his emergency leave, during which time more than a hundred thousand cards, letters and telegrams of condolence arrived at the official Elvis Presley address, the Colonel's office in Madison.

On Sunday, August 24, he flew to Dallas, where he told newsmen who greeted him at Love Field that his father would be accompanying him to Germany. "One of the last things Mom said was that Dad and I should always be together," Elvis said. "I'll report back to Fort Hood in the morning. Wherever they send me, Dad will go too. Before I went home, I was scheduled to leave for Germany about the first of September. Mom and Dad and I often talked about going to Europe. I guess that's where we'll go now—the two of us." Friends then helped him load his luggage into a car and they drove off.

The remaining weeks at Fort Hood passed quickly as Elvis rapidly completed his training, and then he was shunted from line to line to line, from form to form to form, going through all that any soldier experiences in leaving any military post—return of equipment, final inspections, and so on—while preparing to go overseas. On September 19, he and his unit began the bumpy stop-and-go train ride to their port of embarkation, the Military Ocean Terminal in Brooklyn.

There was, however, a final damp hometown farewell—held when the train bearing Elvis and others from Fort Hood pulled into a switching yard in Memphis. There, Elvis was greeted by about forty girls who had raced across town from Union Station when they learned the train would remain in the yards for a brief period. He was permitted to speak to them and kiss a few goodbye.

Then it was north and east, where Elvis was to be given still another farewell, this one from what seemed to be half the press of New York. The Army was there in brassy attendance, too, flanked by Navy braid. The crew of the troopship U.S.S. *Randall* was tending to final departure details. Colonel Parker was there, of course, along with Jean and Julian Aberbach and Freddy Bienstock from Hill and Range, and Steve Sholes heading up a large contingent from RCA. Among other reasons, RCA was there to record the press conference for eventual release as a commercial EP called *Elvis Sails*, a record that remained available and sold for many years.

Finally Elvis appeared, dressed in khakis and wearing a garrison cap pulled down over but not hiding hair that had been bleached in the Texas sun. He saw the photographers practically surrounding him and grinned, taking the nearest WAC in his arms. For five minutes there were cries of "One more, Elvis!" and "Grab the WAC again!" Then Irving Moss stepped forward to break it up. He represented the terminal command and said, "All right, give him a chance. If everybody will sit down, maybe Elvis will sing a song."

It was an absurd suggestion—Elvis had neither plans nor inclination to play or sing and there was no guitar around anyway—but it worked. And so the questions began. What was it he wanted to do most when he got to Europe?

"The first place I want to go when I get a pass is Paris," he said. "I'd like to look up Brigitte Bardot."

(A day later, in an attempt to keep this angle going, wire-service men in Paris tracked Miss Bardot to get her reaction—which was that she was quite content with the singer-musician she already had, Sacha Distel. Then, of course, Elvis was pressed for his reaction to that, and he said what the hell, it was just an offhand remark, or words to that effect.)

Did he think his following had diminished in size or loyalty since he entered the Army?

"No, I'd say my fan mail has doubled. I've been getting around fifteen thousand fan letters a week and it's been driving them crazy down at Fort Hood." And then he added, looking at the Colonel, "Now they're sending them to the Colonel for answering."

Someone suggested rock 'n' roll might die and what would Elvis do then?

"I'd probably starve to death," he said. "If it ever did happen, and I don't think it would, I'd make a serious try to keep on top in the movies. That would be my best chance."

Was it true he was taking his family to Europe with him?

"My father and grandmother are following me to Germany in a few weeks. They'll be living in a house near the post where I'll be stationed. I guess we'll get one of those small German cars. I still have three Cadillacs and a Lincoln, but they stay home."

And his mother? The press was sorry about her death, but would Elvis make some comment now, in that he hadn't said anything since the funeral?

"I was an only child," he said. "She was very close, more than a mother. She was a friend who would let me talk to her any hour of the day or night if I had a problem. I would get mad sometimes when she wouldn't let me do something. But I found out she was right about almost everything. She would always try to slow me up if I ever thought I wanted to get married. She was right. It helped my career not to be married."

And from that, right into a question about Jerry Lee Lewis, who recently had been drummed out of England when it was learned he had married his thirteen-year-old cousin.

"He's a great artist," Elvis said diplomatically. "I'd rather not talk about his marriage, except that if he really loves her, I guess it's all right."

What kind of girl did Elvis want?

"Female, sir."

He told them no, the guys in his unit hadn't been rough on him, but they had given him some unprintable nicknames. He mentioned a few of his favorite songs—"I'll Never Walk Alone," a hymn, among them. He held up a book he said he had been reading, *Poems that Touch the Heart*, and called it "wonderful stuff."

"All right, you people," Irving Moss broke in. "That's gonna have to do it. Private Presley has a schedule to keep." Then, with the Army band doing its best to make "Hound Dog" and "All Shook Up" sound as if they'd been written by John Philipps Sousa, the press departed and Elvis and approximately 1300 soldiers slowly moved toward Bremerhaven, Germany, where the whole thing would begin again.

# Chapter 11

# GERMANY

E lvis was no stranger in Germany. His records sold briskly to German youth. His signature was worth a little under a dollar on the teenage auto-graph market, a signed picture equal to ten of his nearest local competitor, nineteen-year-old Peter Kraus, who admitted he took his style from Elvis's movies. There was even a magazine—*Bravo*, which became one of the world's largest youth publications—started because of his popularity.

"Our bomb shelter generation revolted against the stiff, straight old ways," said Werner Goetze, a German disc jockey who at first destroyed Elvis's records on the air, but changed his mind when overruled by his listeners. "They threw away their lederhosen for blue jeans and started standing and walking like cowboys. They were bored with 'O Tannenbaum' and skipped 'Ach du lieber Augustin' to hear rock 'n' roll. Elvis Presley was just what they were looking for—an American Pied Piper to lead them to excitement."

Of course, not all Germany was thrilled about Elvis's prospective visit. Some, in fact, made it sound as if he would be as welcome as other American soldiers who had arrived in 1945, when Americans crossed the Rhine River in World War Two. Goetze hadn't just broken Elvis's records—he had called him "the whiner," "yowling boy" and "the lovesick stag." And Ferdinand Anton, a respected German archeologist, went on the Armed Forces Radio Network and said Elvis was a throwback to the Stone Age.

In a special report in the *New York Times Magazine* five months before Elvis's arrival, the paper's Berlin correspondent, Harry Gilroy, wrote, "Undoubtedly the liveliest youth movement in Berlin and surrounding central Germany—even allowing for the Communist, Socialist and Christian Young People's organizations—is rock 'n' roll. Here, just as in the United States, it looks like a route of Dionysus." Gilroy then described the maniacal demand for blue jeans (about all Elvis actually wore in his first two films, which were all the Germans had seen so far).

It was, as the walls soon would proclaim in paint splashed there by his German fans, *Elvis über alles!*

There were five hundred screaming teenagers waiting at the dock in Bremerhaven on October 1, and Elvis was spotted coming down the gang-plank, even though he, like all the others, was dressed in Army fatigues and carried a heavy duffel bag. But only a few photographers got close enough to take a picture. The Army had positioned a troop train near the ship's unloading area and Elvis was rushed from one to the other without so much as a single teenage kiss. The train then sped to Elvis's permanent station in the rolling hills outside Friedberg, a village of 18,000 not far from Frankfurt, in the Hesse section of central Germany. At Friedberg, Elvis's fans again were disappointed, as the train passed right through the station where they'd gathered near a siding inside the gates of the Army post. Here, Elvis's home would be at Ray Kaserne, a barracks for German SS troops during World War Two.

The press reception was, essentially, a rerun of earlier meetings, the only difference being that now there was an international press corps, with the same old questions coming in half a dozen accents. For three days newsmen and anxious feature writers were given reasonably free reign over the post and were told to get everything they wanted or else figure on doing without, because once the "open house" ended October 5, Elvis and the post would be off limits to civilians.

The press also was told that Elvis would be serving the next sixteen months as a "scout" jeep driver. Originally he was to have joined the crew of a medium Patton tank. Why the change? No, said the Army, it wasn't special privilege or favoritism.

"The assignment of scout jeep driver is given to soldiers of above normal capability," said the post information officer. "The soldier must be able to work on his own, map-read and draw sketches, know tactics and recognize the enemy and enemy weapons."

It was explained that jeeps, and their drivers, may seem unimportant next to tanks and their crews, but tanks relied on information those in the jeeps obtained. So Elvis had been given more responsibility, not less.

By then, of course, Elvis's father and 68-year-old grandmother arrived and Elvis spent his first pass (issued just four days after his arrival) with them in a luxurious hotel in Bad Homburg, a resort spa a few miles from Friedberg—moving soon to the Hotel Grunewald in nearby Bad Nauheim, another spa, where they occupied an entire floor for the next three months.

Once again, Elvis was taking advantage of the Army rule that allowed its soldiers to live off base with dependent family members, but he also had two of his pals with him, the obese and faithful Lamar Fike and the feisty ex-marine Red West. Neither was on salary, both knew they were there as Elvis's friends, but when Elvis told his father to give them a reasonable allowance, he gave them just a few marks a day. For the present, they grumbled but accepted it.

They also welcomed one of Elvis's fellow recruits into the "family." This was Charlie Hodge, a onetime member of the Foggy River Boys on Red Foley's TV show *Ozark Jubilee*, who had met Elvis backstage at Ellis Auditorium in Memphis in 1955 and reconnected on the train that took them both from Memphis to Fort Chaffee. They became friendly again aboard the U.S.S. *Randall* when asked to organize a talent show to help pass the long days at sea. He was embraced by the others immediately, often joining Elvis in singing and giving Vernon what others said were his first laughs since his wife died, with a constant string of jokes.

Nor was Elvis lacking for female companionship. When a sixteen-year-old German girl named Margit Buergin approached him for an autograph and kissed him, Elvis had Lamar get her phone number and they started seeing each other, usually at the hotel with his family present or at her home with her family. Another autograph-seeker, Elisabeth Stefaniak, a nineteen-year-old German girl with an American Army sergeant as a stepfather, was next and it was with her family he spent Thanksgiving day. Then she moved into the hotel suite as a secretary.

Rex Mansfield, after Charlie the fellow recruit who became his closest Army friend, later quoted Elisabeth as saying, "There would be at least two girls a week, more on the weekends . . ."

Anita Wood, to whom Elvis wrote letters saying he was homesick during his first days in Germany, seemed to be slipping into his past.

Not long after arriving in Germany, Elvis went to see Bill Haley perform in Frankfurt Stuttgart, and occasionally he and Lamar and Red would sneak out to a movie, arriving and leaving late to avoid hassles. Most evenings they stayed in the hotel, amusing themselves with pranks. One night, when Red was chasing Elvis with a can of shaving cream and Elvis locked himself in his room, Red pushed some newspaper under the door and set fire to it. Panic ensued but they extinguished the blaze. Vernon said Elvis's friends were going to get everyone, including Grandma, thrown out of the hotel; Elvis discovered his father was still giving the boys just a few marks a night.

That's when the boys went on a sort of "salary" and in order to insure some residential stability and more privacy, Vernon started house-hunting. In early February 1959, everyone moved into a three-story, five-bedroom house not far from the Grunewald Hotel.

"It was just an ordinary middle-class German house," a family friend said. "A bit larger than many, but by our standards hardly better than his old

Memphis home on Alabama. And it needed repairs, which Elvis told me he had
to pay for. Although he was paying an exorbitant rent, the landlady claimed
that all the damage, which was obviously the wear and tear of the years, was
caused by him and his fans. To avoid any unpleasantness or embarrassment to
himself or the U.S., he paid, as the landlady had known he would do. It was a
sort of blackmail that celebrities must often know, I suppose."

It wasn't all fun and games. From the start, three months before, Elvis's
weekdays began early, usually at five or five-thirty, in order to be at the post by
seven, traveling at first in a Mercedes taxi contracted to take him back and
forth, and later in a BMW with Lamar at the wheel. He returned usually by six,
unless his unit was returning from field exercises or it was Friday, when everyone remained on base until nine or so, scrubbing the barracks and latrines for
the regular Saturday inspections.

His immediate "boss" was Master Sergeant Ira Jones, a career non-com
from Missouri who sat next to Elvis as they made their rounds or went wherever the day's orders took them. Often, they explored the back roads around
the base, so that in the event "the balloon went up"—Army slang for an
unplanned incident—they would be prepared to lead the unit in response.

Elvis also was responsible for the vehicle's maintenance and performing in
all the usual unit drills. According to Jones, he "scrubbed, washed, greased,
painted, marched, ran, carried his laundry, and worried through inspections
just as everyone else did." Off-base, in the evenings and weekends, Elvis's life
was far different from that of his fellow recruits, but during the week he was
exactly what he said he would be: just another grunt.

His second month in Germany, Elvis joined the 32nd Tank Battalion in
Friedberg on a convoy to the maneuvers area at Grafenwöhr, not far from the
border separating Germany from Communist Czechoslovakia. During the
exercises, which lasted a couple of weeks, Elvis was tested on the location and
observation of "enemy" positions, instructed in map reading, and practiced
rifle marksmanship. It was also during maneuvers that Elvis was introduced to
amphetamines, synthetic stimulants used to suppress appetite, control weight,
and treat a variety of disorders, but also to enhance performance within the
armed forces as an anti-fatigue pill for pilots and others in situations requiring
vigilance and alertness. It was harmless, Elvis was told, and it would give him
extra energy and help him stay awake while on guard duty. At the time, it
seemed unimportant.

Perhaps it was only coincidence that, as soon as he approached the Iron
Curtain, the Communists began an anti-Elvis campaign. Joseph Fleming of
United Press International tried to explain the attack: "It appears that youths

in Eastern Europe are expressing their distaste of the existing order in the only way they can. All free political expression is barred to them. Their press and radio are censored. All organizations except the church are run by the Communists. They are regimented in school, at work and in sports. Their only outlet is to wear their hair too long, use too much makeup, dance too wildly, and adopt as a symbol an American singer they are told they should despise—Elvis Presley. The Communists know this is a form of resistance and it has them worried."

Meanwhile, the Communists claimed that the leader of a juvenile gang arrested in Halle, East Germany, had purchased several Presley records and displayed a signed picture of Elvis in his living room. In addition, police in Leipzig arrested members of another gang, called the Elvis Presley Hound Dogs, who they said had committed anti-state acts.

Knowing—or suspecting—a good thing when they read about one, State Department officials in the U.S. again asked if Elvis wouldn't like to entertain the troops and perhaps do a little propaganda work. The Colonel again said no.

All through his Army years, although he didn't cut a record or appear anywhere, Elvis remained a highly commercial property that the Colonel represented quite masterfully. Elvis had been in Europe only a month when the Colonel told the papers in Nashville that Elvis earned $2 million in 1958, despite his being in the Army almost all that time. And he said he figured 1959 would be even better.

One of the problems facing RCA was the lack of unreleased material. Thus, the few songs remaining had to be issued sparingly. The first was the *Elvis Sails* EP. It sold far more copies than most novelty items, but didn't do nearly so well as some of the other EPs then available. The two from *King Creole*, for example, remained high on the EP record sales charts through most of 1959, making the records bestsellers for more than eighteen months.

It was in February—as Elvis was getting settled in his new house—that RCA released another album, *For LP Fans Only*. This was an unusual album, because all ten cuts on it were at least a year old, some of them nearly five years old. The most recent was "Playing for Keeps," which had been the B side of "Too Much," a hit during the winter of 1957. The tracks that had been around longest were four of the ten that originally had been released by Sun.

By late February there were no Elvis songs in *Billboard*'s Hot 100 singles chart—the first time this had occurred in nearly three years. In March, RCA issued "A Fool Such as I" and "I Need Your Love Tonight," two otherwise anonymous songs that (according to RCA) earned Elvis his nineteenth consecutive million-selling record, the tunes going to the number two and four chart positions, respectively.

The Colonel seemed little concerned by this and he continued to rebuff RCA, even when the company said it would send a recording team to Germany. He merely told RCA that he didn't want to flood the market. This was true, but it was also obvious that he was playing a game to make it clear who was in control, while holding firm to his decision that Elvis's long-term career would best be served by his refusing to perform, thus avoiding even the slightest chance of criticism.

The Colonel's continuing negotiations with Hal Wallis and Paramount, 20th Century Fox and MGM regarding Elvis's future films were even more heavy-handed. By planting false stories in the Hollywood trade papers, he played the studios against each other, increasing his demands from each until he had firm commitments for three pictures to be shot in the final three months of 1960—one for Wallis and Paramount, two for Fox—that would guarantee Elvis a half a million dollars.

With the approach of spring in Germany, in the Presley home it was getting chillier. In the first month after leaving the hotel everyone relaxed, and during off-duty hours the party went round-the-clock—thanks in part to the endless supply of amphetamines that Rex Mansfield said Elvis was now purchasing at the PX by the quart. All the latest recordings were available from the same source and the girls came and went by the droves.

Even Vernon began to act like a soldier on leave, getting involved with an American woman who had invited Elvis and Vernon to have dinner with her and her husband, an Army sergeant. Elvis didn't go, but Vernon did. One thing led to another and Vernon began sleeping with Dee behind her husband Bill's back.

Elvis disapproved, told his father it was too soon after Gladys's death. Red West was at Vernon's neck, too, and at the same time told Elvis he was getting tired of polishing his boots and kissing his butt. Finally, in late April, after a drunken yelling match at the Stanley home, Lamar and Red carried a protesting Vernon to the car and a week later Red was on a plane returning to the States.

Once back in Memphis, when Red was interviewed by George Klein on his radio show, he said only nice things about everyone concerned, but when Elvis called Alan Fortas to see if he'd take Red's place, Red told him, "Whatever you do, don't go. I promise you, you'll hate it, and you and Elvis will never be the same." Elvis's next call went to Cliff Gleaves, who said he was on his way.

In June, the last of the unreleased material was pressed. This was "A Big Hunk o' Love" backed by "My Wish Came True." Predictably, the record was a million seller. At the same time, the *King Creole* and *Love Me Tender* albums and

EPs were selling again, thanks to renewed interest caused by the re-release of the films as a summer double feature. And during the first week of August, RCA issued another of its repackaged albums, *A Date with Elvis*. It was, of course, precisely what every young girl wanted.

This album was the second to include songs from his early days at Sun, all previously unavailable on an album, but now more than five years old. Others included three songs from *Jailhouse Rock* and one from *Love Me Tender*. And with that, RCA hit the bottom of the barrel. Not that the material wasn't good. It was good. Except for one previously unreleased country ballad, that also was the end of it.

To make the package more appealing, several Elvis "extras" were added. The album sleeve doubled in size when opened, displaying a 1960 souvenir calendar (with Elvis's Army discharge date circled), there were four color photos on the cover at the top of the calendar, and inside there was a "complete picture story of Elvis's departure overseas" and a personal message from Elvis in Germany. The album went onto the charts immediately.

"It's a tribute to his staying power that he continues on such a powerful level," said Sholes. "And we don't sell his records on a guarantee basis, you know."

What this last meant was when a record shopkeeper ordered five hundred (or however many) copies of Elvis's latest record, he couldn't return them if they didn't sell. This ran against general policy in the record business and only because Elvis had such an exceptional sales history would retailers stand for it.

In August, it was announced that Elvis's first film following his discharge would be—quite naturally—about a tank sergeant in the U.S. Army stationed in Germany, called *G.I. Blues*. The producer was Hal Wallis, who went immediately to Frankfurt to begin shooting background scenes. For these he used tanks provided by the Third Armored Division, but he did not use Elvis.

"We prefer not to put him in front of cameras here," Wallis said. "We don't want any criticism and it might be misunderstood in some quarters. If we had asked, we could have had him."

This didn't halt the criticism. Paramount was offered cynical congratulations for not taking Specialist Fourth Class Presley from his jeep, but the same newspapers also asked how much it was costing the U.S. taxpayer to provide the tanks and tank crews.

Stan Brossette, a publicist who later would work with Elvis and the Colonel on ten pictures, told a story about how anxiously Wallis was awaiting Elvis's discharge: "In his contract, he still had four or five pictures to do with Elvis and for two years he was counting the money he was going to put in the bank. Then when it got close to when Elvis was to return, the Colonel had one of those fake front pages made to say 'ELVIS RE-ENLISTS.' And in smaller letters underneath: 'Wallis Collapses.' He wrapped the page around Wallis's morning paper about two weeks before Elvis was to get out and put it on Wallis's front steps. So when Wallis came down for the paper that day—and he'd already begun shooting backgrounds, remember—and he saw that headline, he collapsed before he saw the smaller headline that said he had."

All RCA could do for the Christmas season was re-release Elvis's Christmas album from the previous year and assemble still one more repackaged album, *50,000,000 Elvis Fans Can't Be Wrong, Elvis Gold Records—Volume 2*. This contained ten songs, all previously released in 1958 and 1959 as singles. On the cover there were several pictures of Elvis in the $10,000 gold lamé diamond-studded suit the Colonel had ordered but Elvis had worn only once, for a publicity shot in 1956.

While Wallis was dodging criticism and directing the movement of tanks, the Colonel was vacationing in Hawaii, where he met with Tom Moffatt and Ron Jacobs at the island's top rock station—who had MC'd Elvis's shows in Honolulu in 1957—and said if they could get 10,000 signatures, he'd make sure Elvis performed his first post-Army concert in Hawaii. "We took one of those long rolls of teletype paper like the wire services used in our newsroom and set up a table at the brand-new Ala Moana Center," Moffatt remembered. "We got many more than 10,000, believe me, and it didn't take long."

At the same time, the Colonel negotiated a new contract with RCA giving Elvis a 25 per cent increase in publishing rights for every song he recorded in which the company had a copyright interest . . . and announced that Elvis's first television appearance on his return to the U.S. would be as guest star on a Frank Sinatra special called *Frank Sinatra's Welcome Home Party for Elvis Presley*—quite a coup considering all the unflattering remarks Sinatra made when Elvis first appeared on the music scene. For singing just two songs, the Colonel added, Elvis would be paid $125,000, the largest sum ever paid for a TV guest appearance.

Back in Germany, meanwhile, it was business, and pleasure, as usual, and sometimes a nonsensical mix of both. Wally Beene, a staff writer with *Stars and Stripes* who interviewed Elvis, said, "Elvis talked about what it was like to go on maneuvers when it was the 'NATO forces' versus the 'aggressors.'" Not only was Elvis pursued by a battery of civilian reporters and photographers, troops opposing Elvis's unit were offered fifty dollars reward and a thirty-day pass if they captured Elvis. "A G.I. from the Twenty-fourth Division almost nailed me," Wally quoted Elvis as saying. "He spotted me on the road and started to take me prisoner, but about that time a string of our tanks rolled up behind him and he ended up as the prisoner."

"There was a fierce loyalty the guys in his outfit had for him," Beene said. "It was incredible how protective they felt toward him. I think it was because they sensed he was a regular fellow. He sat in the snow with them, ate the lousy food, and the fact that he lived off post and commuted in a fancy car didn't bother them. They lived in reflected glory to a certain degree. They had stories to tell back home. 'I was in the Army with Elvis Presley!' They were prepared to put the knock on him at first, but it reversed itself. In the end, they were impressed by Elvis."

If during the week he was an exemplary soldier, being praised for his map reading skills and self-effacing manner, evenings and weekends continued much the same, with the little pills from the PX being distributed to the gang of regulars and stream of visitors at parties in the home and on excursions to Weisbaden, Munich and Paris. On a two-week furlough to Paris with Lamar, Charlie and Rex, Elvis slipped easily back into his pre-Army routine, sleeping most of the day, eating a huge breakfast at 8 p.m., then going out, to the Carousel or the Folies Bergére and then to the Lido, where Elvis was especially drawn to a chorus line of beauties from England called the Blue Belles. One night, he and his pals took the entire line back to the hotel and the club's owner had to call the following night to remind them that they had a show to do. Elvis told Art Buchwald, the Paris-based syndicated columnist, "Paris reminds me of the life I used to live before I went into the service."

In Germany, there was a new girl in Elvis's life. He was still exchanging letters with Anita Wood and sleeping every night with Elisabeth Stefaniak, who still had a room in the house, but when Elvis met Priscilla Beaulieu, the fourteen-year-old daughter of an American Air Force captain who arrived with his family in Weisbaden in August, everyone else had to step aside. After charming her parents and assuring them she'd be chaperoned, Elvis entertained her at his home, often five and more evenings a week.

"I really felt I got to know who Elvis Presley was during this time," Priscilla told Peter Guralnick. "Not with ego—not the star he felt he should portray. I saw him raw, totally raw, I saw him as he really was after he lost his mother. We talked so much, he shared his grief with me, he was very insecure, and he felt betrayed by his father, that he would even fall for such a woman [Dee Stanley, whom Vernon had followed to the U.S.]. He was his most vulnerable, his most honest, I would say his most passionate during that time."

By mid-January 1960, Elvis had been elevated to sergeant and was commanding a three-man reconnaissance team for the Third Armored Division's 32nd Scout Platoon. But not for long, because it was announced that Elvis probably would be discharged not in March as planned, but in February. Quickly the media began to pump themselves up for the welcome home.

Series of newspaper articles reviewing the past and previewing the future began running in newspapers from coast to coast. A writer for one of the wire services even went so far as to ask many of the women whom Elvis had dated in Hollywood if they would consider dating him again. Most said they would. A reporter from Louisville, Kentucky, had written a small book about Elvis's Army career, *Operation Elvis*, which was to be published the same month Elvis returned. Fan magazines were announcing contests offering Elvis's uniform as prizes. Two hundred prints of *Jailhouse Rock*, which had grossed close to $4 million the first time around, were rushed to movie theaters for an early March reopening. WNEW radio in New York spotlighted "The Return of Elvis Presley" on its *News Close-Up*, calling the homecoming "a musical, cultural and military phenomenon of our time," while other stations in other cities planned special programs that took the appearance of Elvis marathons. Again there was a rush of novelty songs, including "I'm Gonna Hang Up My Rifle" by Bobby Bare and "The King Is Coming Back" by Billy and Andy ("The king is coming back / Get your guitar off the rack / Trade your khaki for black slacks"). And although Elvis hadn't even recorded the songs yet, RCA ordered an initial pressing of one million copies of his first single, with plans to ship half that number within seventy-two hours of release.

The excitement was motivated honestly. Elvis *was* still the reigning monarch of the pop music charts, and it *was* a triumphant return to the U.S. Of course, as *Billboard* noted, Elvis hadn't really been away; during the time he'd been in the service he continued to sell a million or more records with every single release, a mark that was unprecedented, and it became abundantly clear even to his detractors that almost all alone he was responsible for shifting the course of popular music.

During his absence much had happened. Jerry Lee Lewis had been banished by the prudish public and Little Richard had thrown his jewelry from a bridge into Sydney's harbour and gone into a seminary. Buddy Holly, Ritchie Valens and the Big Bopper were dead. Rock 'n' roll was reeling from a payola probe. The big album sellers in the winter of 1959-60 were Ricky Nelson, Fabian, Frankie Avalon and Bobby Darin—Elvis imitators. No one—absolutely no one—had come along during Elvis's tour of duty worthy of taking his throne.

The day before Elvis left Germany, the Army staged a monstrous press conference. Elvis's old friend from Sun Records, Marion Keisker, now a captain in the Women's Air Force and assigned to Armed Forces Television in Germany, was there. It was the first time she had seen Elvis in more than two years.

Marion remembered, "They were in a gym with all the klieg lights and tape recorders and thousands of people running around saying, 'At twelve-oh-two he will . . .' Ecccchhhh. I went to the other end to a bar where they were serving coffee. I looked up and there was a door just a few feet away. Suddenly it flies open and in steps Elvis in this ridiculous thing they had on him with red stripes and gold braid, an MP on either side. I said, 'Hi, hon.'

"He turned around and said, 'Marion! In Germany! And an officer! What do I do? Kiss you or salute you?'

"I said, 'In that order.' And I flung myself on him.

"The Public Information Officer was enraged. He said he was going to report me, have me court-martialed. He said, 'I certainly expected this sort of thing from some of the magazines, but not from a member of the Armed Forces.' He accused me of staging it. I said I was there officially, representing the Armed Forces Television station, of which I was the assistant manager. He said, 'Would you please leave.' I refused, of course.

"Finally, Elvis got free and he came over and he said, 'Captain, you don't understand. You wouldn't even be having this thing today if it wasn't for this lady.'

"The Captain said, 'This WAF captain?'

"Elvis said, 'Well, it's a long story, sir, but she wasn't always a WAF captain.'

"Through the rest of the press conference he was determined I wasn't going to get thrown out. So I stood there behind him and he kept reaching back to see that I was there." *Life* magazine published a picture of her waving goodbye and captioned it, "Girl He Left Behind."

The next day Priscilla went with Elvis to the Frankfurt airport. He kissed her goodbye and then with seventy-nine other GIs and their families he boarded a four-engine military air transport plane for the States.

The plane landed at McGuire Air Force Base in New Jersey, adjacent to Fort Dix, the Army post where he was to be discharged later that week. It was six-thirty in the morning and a snowstorm was approaching blizzard proportions as he stepped outside to bravely look into a twenty-five-mile-an-hour wind for five minutes, waving and smiling dutifully for cameramen. (The Colonel previously had asked *Life* magazine for $25,000 for the exclusive rights to photographs of Elvis's last days, and when *Life* declined, the Colonel invited everyone.) And then he was rushed to one of the post ballrooms for still another press conference.

It was little different from all those which had preceded it in Elvis's life. Frank Sinatra's oldest daughter Nancy, then nineteen, was on hand to provide a little glamour, giving Elvis a box of dress shirts from her father. But the rest of the morning was predictable. The matter of his marital eligibility was covered half a dozen times, his hair and sideburns at least four or five times. He said he probably wouldn't grow the sideburns back—a statement that sent wire service reporters sprinting for the telephones. He said that he had brought back a couple of German guitars, that he liked "Dean Martin, Mr. Sinatra, Patti Page, Kitty Kallen and quite a few others," that he didn't have nineteen Army public relations men assigned to him in Germany—only one, a captain who represented the whole division—that if rock 'n' roll died out, which he didn't think would happen, he and a lot of other people would have to find something else to do. Asked if his superiors had chewed him out in the Army, he grinned and held up a Certificate of Achievement that recognized his "faithful duty and service, etc." This kept the photographers pushing and shouting for a good five minutes. Finally it came to a blessed end as someone quoted a lady reporter as saying Elvis was "the sexiest man I've ever seen," and what about that, El?

Elvis looked the questioner straight in the eye, grinned his lopsided grin and said, "Where is that young lady now?"

At Elvis's feet, sitting on the floor and chewing on a cigar, was Colonel Parker. Jean Aberbach, Steve Sholes, Tom Diskin, Freddy Bienstock and Bob Kotlowitz, a Victor publicist who would stay with Elvis the first six weeks, were standing to the left and right. Outside, in the blizzard, scratching on the windows and shouting pledges of undying love, were a couple of hundred teenagers. A sergeant went out to tell them to be quiet, but they wouldn't.

Two days later, on March 5, he was a civilian again, and as Tennessee Senator Estes Kefauver was inserting a tribute to Elvis in the Congressional Record, Elvis went to Memphis to rest.

# Chapter 12

# HOMECOMING

The trip to Memphis by train gave some indication of what the next few months would be like. At every stop—at Bristol, Virginia, in Johnson City and Knoxville, Tennessee, at Chattanooga—and at many stations between, day and night, there were hundreds of fans gathered with welcome-home signs. When he arrived in Memphis early Monday morning, the crowd was so large that police had to escort him to Graceland, where all up and down the highway more fans had brought traffic to a halt. Gary Pepper, a Memphis boy Elvis's own age, held a sign aloft that said, "Welcome Home Elvis, The Tankers," the Tankers being a fan club he had organized in Elvis's absence. Gloria Martinez, twenty-one, and Sharlene Magee, nineteen, said they had hitchhiked in from Gary, Indiana. And Laura Driver, nineteen, from Brooklyn, said she had kissed Elvis at Fort Dix and flew to Memphis for another kiss, because she liked the first so much. The police car carrying Elvis whisked through the mob and disappeared up the sloping Graceland drive. No kisses. No autographs.

The first few days were spent calling friends, reassembling the old gang, putting several of the good ol' boys back on the payroll, lying around, looking at the house he hadn't seen in more than eighteen months, making plans for remodeling. Then on March 20, he and some of the boys drove to Nashville for the first recording session.

The Jordanaires were there, of course, and so were pianist Floyd Cramer, drummer Buddy Harmon and guitarist Hank Garland, Nashville studio musicians who had played for Elvis previously and would make up the core of his Nashville band for several years. Along with Scotty Moore and D. J. Fontana, naturally. The only one missing was Bill Black, who had formed his own group, the Bill Black Combo, and by then had had two instrumental hits, "Smokie" and "White Silver Sands." Among the seven songs recorded in that all-night session were "Stuck on You" and "Fame and Fortune," ballads for which there were more than a million orders even before Elvis opened his mouth.

The next day Elvis got on another train, this one for Miami Beach, where

Frank Sinatra would be videotaping his show. "In every little town along the way, the tracks were lined," said Scotty Moore. "Twenty-four hours a day. The whole trip. Photographers. Cameramen. Kids. I don't know where they came from." In some towns the Colonel had Elvis stand on the train's rear platform, as if he were running for President, and wave and sign a few autographs.

This was the fourth and last Timex special for Sinatra; and the third broadcast, a Valentine's Day tribute starring Juliet Prowse, a South African dancer who'd dated Sinatra, had been only average in terms of audience response. In his final show Sinatra was determined to better that mark. Thus he had agreed to pay Elvis $125,000 for minutes on camera. Said Sammy Cahn, who had long been one of Sinatra's best friends and top songwriters and was then serving as the show's executive producer: "You should make in a year what Frank is losing on this show. But he wants to prove he can go big on TV." It was no secret that Sinatra was galled by the price the Colonel asked.

Elvis was in rehearsals, meantime, and showing considerable nervousness, along with the usual courtesy, calling his host "Mr. Sinatra." It was agreed that Elvis would wear a tuxedo and stand still while singing.

Despite the Colonel's efforts, it wasn't an all-Elvis crowd, of course. More than half the audience was composed of affluent middle-aged Sinatra fans. Which gave the press in attendance the angle they wanted. Here, after all, were idols from two generations, joined not only in television booking convenience but also in song. Elvis sang both sides of his new single and then sang one of Frank's big songs, "Witchcraft," after which Sinatra sang one of Elvis's, "Love Me Tender," with Elvis joining him in harmony. Eighteen years had passed since Sinatra's bobby-soxers swooned in the aisles of the Paramount Theater in New York, two had gone by since Elvis was causing riots. Now they were together.

A month later, on May 12, the special proved Frank had achieved what he wanted—he had become, for one hour, "big on TV." At least so far as numbers were concerned. Sinatra got a rating of 41.5, stomping all the competing shows. Critically, it was received less ecstatically. "The expected dynamite was, to put it politely, a bit overrated," said Ren Grevatt in *Billboard*. "The impression lingers . . . that Presley has much to learn before he can work in the same league with pros like Sinatra, Joey Bishop and especially Sammy Davis, Jr., who just about broke up the show with his chanting and impressions. Presley has a distracting habit which gives the impression he's never at ease. Let nobody touch his singing. That's fine as is. What he needs is a lot of coaching on how to stand and how to talk." The *New York Times* was rougher. "The recent liberation from the Army of Elvis Presley may have been one of the most irritating events since the invention of itching powder," John Shanley wrote. "While he was in the service he lost his sideburns, drove a truck and

apparently behaved in an acceptable military manner. But now he is free to perform in public again . . . Although Elvis became a sergeant in the Army, as a
singer he never left the awkward squad. There was nothing morally reprehen-
sible about his performance, it was merely awful."

Following the Sinatra special, Elvis returned to Nashville for another all-night
recording session lasting twelve hours and during which he recorded twelve
songs, all of them released a week later on an album called *Elvis Is Back*. The
record was typically Elvis, a collection of songs with no particular theme, no
one direction. Some were ballads composed with Elvis's soft warbling style in
mind, others were rooted in the blues or rock. There were a couple—"Soldier
Boy" and "I Will Be Home Again"—that smacked of exploitation, but none
were offensive. Many of Elvis's regular songwriters were represented—Stan
Kesler, Jerry Leiber and Mike Stoller, Otis Blackwell—along with two other
respected blues writers, Jesse Stone and Lowell Fulson. The fans greeted the
album the same way they'd greeted Elvis—ecstatically. Throughout the summer it was in the number two or three position, kept out of number one by the
Kingston Trio, and sales passed the million-dollar mark.

Elvis returned to Hollywood in style—traveling with seven friends from
Memphis and two new buddies from his Army days in a private railroad car
that reportedly cost him nearly $2500 for the trip. He had the car parked on a
siding and welcomed the press in a tuxedo and black suede shoes. And then he
was driven to Paramount.

   *G.I. Blues* had as its hero Tulsa McLean, a tank gunner in Germany who
accepted a $300 bet that he couldn't break down the resistance of a standoff-
ish night club dancer named Lili (Juliet Prowse). Elvis did his best to win the
bet, and in the process, of course he won the girl. From that premise Elvis
ambled through less than two hours of script, stopping often enough to sing
eleven songs.

   Visitors to the Paramount set during shooting included the wife and daughter of the Brazilian president, the king and queen of Nepal, the king and queen
of Thailand, and princesses from Denmark, Norway and Sweden. All claimed
to be avid Elvis fans.

   (*G.I. Blues* was not the only entertainment exploiting Elvis's army career.
The same year, *Bye Bye Birdie*, a musical whose story revolved around the
induction of a rock 'n' roll singer named Conrad Birdie and the effect this had
on Birdie's manager, opened on Broadway, running for nearly two years.)

On July 3, Vernon Presley was married to Dee Stanley in a private ceremony in the Huntsville, Alabama, home of her brother, Richard Neely, who served as the couple's best man. She recently had been divorced from her Army sergeant husband and had custody of their three sons, Billy, Ricky and David, all years younger than Elvis. The wedding was described publicly as "secret" and "sudden." Elvis did not attend.

That same week RCA released Elvis's second post-Army single, "It's Now or Never" backed with "Mess of Blues," and both were credited with million-plus record sales, although it was the onetime operatic aria that occupied the number one spot for five weeks. Because it was a non-rocker, it was played on many more stations than were accustomed to playing Elvis records, a fact that must have been noticed by RCA and the Colonel, because the next single released was even further away from the rock 'n' roll beat, the recitation "Are You Lonesome Tonight." Some people were saying Elvis was deserting rock 'n' roll.

If there were any doubt, one only had to spend two dollars to see *G.I. Blues*, which was released simultaneously in more than five hundred theaters in October, or spend a few dollars more and get the soundtrack recording. In the film Elvis not only worked with puppets but with small children. And although there were a few rockers in the "score," most of the songs sounded as if their roots were in Tin Pan Alley or 1940s Hollywood musicals rather than in country blues. Even "Blue Suede Shoes," reprised in the film, lacked the gutsy dynamism Elvis had given the song four years earlier.

"When they took the boy out of the country, they apparently took the country out of the boy," Jim Powers wrote in *The Hollywood Reporter*. "It is a subdued and changed Elvis Presley who has returned from military service . . . [and the picture will] depend on the loyalty of Presley fans to bail it out at the box office." Bosley Crowther in the *New York Times* chimed in, marveling at how wholesome Elvis had become, saying he had honey in his veins instead of blood.

The critic from *The Hollywood Reporter* was well off target in his appraisal of the film's economic potential. *G.I. Blues* was one of the year's box office champs, grossing $4.3 million in rentals in the U. S. and Canada alone, equal to the amount grossed by *Lost Weekend*, *The African Queen*, or *Days of Wine and Roses*. But there wasn't much argument about the "new" Elvis. The days of "Hound Dog" and *Jailhouse Rock* seemed to be sliding into the past.

By the time *G.I. Blues* was released, Elvis was at 20th Century-Fox, where *Flaming Star* gave Elvis his first "acting" role. In it he played a half-breed son of a Kiowa Indian (Dolores Del Rio in her first film role in several years) and a white rancher (John McIntire) caught in the middle of white-Indian warfare in West Texas in the 1870s, a conflict Elvis tried to resolve. Elvis, like his parents in the picture, died—after singing only two songs.

*Flaming Star* was shot in forty-two days, mostly at the Fox studios with some location filming on the sprawling Conejo Ranch in the nearby San Fernando Valley, the 8000-acre spread where much of television's *Rawhide* and *Wagon Train* were made.

Elvis had high hopes for this film—not merely because of the reduced dependence on music, but also because the scriptwriter was Nunnally Johnson, who had written *The Grapes of Wrath*. But the director, Don Siegel, who had made the original *Invasion of the Body Snatchers* and who would go on to direct numerous Westerns that came to be regarded as classics, never took Elvis seriously (he said they didn't communicate well) and Elvis never seemed to settle into his role. No one said anything at the time, but hindsight could point to the increasing use of the pills that continued to fuel the evening and weekend parties that got him evicted from the Beverly Wilshire Hotel and, during breaks between scenes, the football games that Elvis and his buddies played in the blistering summer heat.

The film was rushed into release faster than any other, opening nationwide just in time for the Christmas school holidays, a pattern that would become as much a part of the Colonel's policy in the release of future films as his reluctance to grant any interviews. The Colonel was processing thirty thousand Elvis Presley fan letters a month in 1960 (there were five thousand fan clubs worldwide) and he knew that many of these letter writers went to see Elvis's films time after time after time. Release timed to coincide with a school vacation would make it easier for these fans to attend the movies on weeknights as well as on weekends.

From *Flaming Star* Elvis went into *Wild in the Country*, the last film he would make at Fox. Here he was a potential literary talent who had to overcome his rural beginnings, a lack of education and a personal history of violence. (He brains his brother, played by Red West, with a milking stool in the first scene.) Elvis also had to deal with a spiteful uncle (William Mims), whose ward he became, and his uncle's immature sex-crazed daughter (Tuesday Weld), along with the son of the town's richest citizen (Gary Lockwood). The rich kid hates Elvis, and before the picture ends, Elvis is accused of murdering him. There was even a suicide in the script for a while, but apparently that was considered too much for an Elvis audience to take, so the final scene was re-shot so that a social worker (Hope Lange) who'd helped Elvis would not die by carbon monoxide but be saved by her smoldering-eyed hero. It was as if the gifted playwright Clifford Odets, who took credit for the script, had transferred Peyton Place from New England to Virginia.

Several records were released as the film was shot, including an album of spirituals and religious songs and some singles designed for the foreign market.

It was logical that Elvis would record an album of church songs and hymns because this was his favorite music. Gordon Stoker said Elvis and the Jordanaires and his friends and family often sang such songs for as long as six or eight hours at a stretch. Elvis himself once said he thought he knew every hymn ever written. Besides, the *Peace in the Valley* EP that Elvis recorded in 1957 had been a consistent seller over the years. So the album *His Hand in Mine* was sort of a long-delayed follow-up. In it there were twelve songs, all featuring the Jordanaires and including several standards such as "Joshua Fit the Battle" and "Swing Down, Sweet Chariot," both of which Elvis arranged and adapted. The album was an excellent one, giving Elvis a chance to share the songs he liked to sing around the piano at home. It also showed how great a debt Elvis owed his favorite gospel groups.

Johnny Rivers, who had met Elvis by now and was joining him in occasional informal song, said: "One of his idols when he was young was a man named Jake Hess, who was the lead singer for the Statesmen Quartet. If you'll listen to some of their recordings, you'll hear some of that style that is now Elvis Presley's style, especially in his ballad-singing style. He was playing some of their records one day and he said, 'Now you know where I got my style from. Caught—a hundred million records too late.'"

*His Hand in Mine*—which pictured Elvis in a dark suit, dress shirt and tie, sitting at a white piano—never was what might be termed a smash hit, but sold briskly for almost a year, remaining on the charts long enough thereafter to qualify (eventually) as a gold record.

The other records released in the last months of 1960 were mostly from the *Elvis Is Back* and *G.I. Blues* albums, and none was issued in the U.S. From the first album, for instance, "The Girl of My Best Friend" was a hit in England; and from the movie soundtrack, "Wooden Heart" was the number one song in Germany, appearing on the charts under the German title "Muss I Denn Zum Stadtele Hinaus." In fact, "Wooden Heart," which was based on a 200-year-old German folk song and sung by Elvis partially in German, became a hit over much of Europe by February of the following year.

*Billboard* named "It's Now or Never" the vocal single of the year. The National Academy of Recording Arts and Sciences, gave Elvis five Grammy nominations—three for "Are You Lonesome Tonight" and two for *G.I. Blues*. He had been awarded another row of gold records. Two motion pictures had been completed and released and a third was in preparation. (He would finish *Wild in the Country* after the holidays.) He had received the highest price ever paid a television guest star and his motion picture salary was moving toward the million-dollar mark.

On February 25, Elvis was in Memphis to headline two benefit shows in the Ellis Auditorium. The proceeds, along with those from a $100-a-plate luncheon at the Claridge Hotel, were to be divided among several local charities and ongoing work on an Elvis Presley Youth Center near his birthplace in Tupelo. The Colonel paid for ninety-eight tickets to the luncheon, pushing the take to $17,200. Among those there: Abe Lastfogel, the Colonel's good friend and head of the William Morris Agency and Elvis's personal agent; Jean Aberbach from Hill and Range; several RCA executives; Mayor Henry Loeb; Governor Buford Ellington; and the master of ceremonies, George Jessel.

Jessel also introduced Elvis at the afternoon and evening shows, which featured the Colonel's standard line-up of supporting acts—a singer, a comedian, and a juggling act. Playing behind Elvis were his old friends Scotty Moore and D. J. Fontana, with Floyd Cramer on piano and Boots Randolph on saxophone, and, of course, the Jordanaires. Elvis sang seventeen songs at each of the two shows, including his new single, "Surrender"—an updated version of "Sorrento"—and closed with the same song he'd used in all his early tours, "Hound Dog."

Scotty Moore said, "We never ever really tried to top that song. Elvis felt 'Hound Dog' was the one they wanted and 'Hound Dog' was the one he gave 'em. And they always reacted the same way. If they weren't tore up by then—and of course they always were—why, 'Hound Dog' would just lay them out. He'd say, 'You ain' nothin' but a houn' dog,' and they'd just go to pieces. It'd be a riot every time."

There were nearly four thousand at the matinee, when tickets were three dollars, and more than five thousand at night, buying five-dollar tickets. Counting the luncheon, total receipts were nearly $55,000.

Elvis remained at home for the next week and then went to Nashville on March 8 for a non-singing appearance before a joint convention of both houses of the Tennessee State Legislature. He had been invited to attend the special session by Senator Lewis Taliaferro of Memphis, after legislators had passed a resolution paying tribute to Elvis for bringing so much fame to Memphis and Tennessee, as well as for his many charitable contributions.

Elvis made his entrance with the governor's daughter Ann on his arm and, after an introduction that was so flowery it sounded like somebody reading Valentines, went to the podium. He looked at the politicians and their families before him and then at the hundreds of teenagers who had packed the two galleries above.

"Governor Buford Ellington, members of the legislature—and those who skipped school—good morning," he said, getting a big laugh at the reference to the hundreds of truants present. "I'm not permitted to sing, and I can't tell any funny stories like Tennessee Ernie Ford"—who had been there a week earlier—"but I can say sincerely that this is the finest honor I have ever received.

"People frequently want to know if I plan to settle down eventually in Hollywood. Now, I like to go out there to play [laughs] . . . er . . . er . . . work. But my home is in Memphis, Tennessee, and that's where it's gonna be." Elvis and the two buddies he'd driven to Nashville with returned to Memphis that afternoon and four days later Elvis went to Nashville again to record some more songs at the Victor studios. And a week following that Elvis flew to Hawaii to his second public appearance of 1961 and his last until 1969. This was another benefit, to raise money for the Memorial Fund of the U.S.S. *Arizona*, the battleship that had been sunk by Japanese dive bombers almost twenty years earlier.

Minnie Pearl said, "I was asked to be on the same show and I flew over with Elvis and his group. They'd had a big to-do in the Pan Am room that morning and Elvis, as always, was very kind to me. I've never had much conversation with him, because of the age difference, but he was always so courteous. We were on the plane and Jimmy Stewart was on the plane. Elvis had the stewardess ask Jimmy if he could speak to him for a minute. Jimmy and I talked about it later and said how much Elvis made us feel like grandparents."

She describes the arrival in Honolulu: "They held us in the plane until everybody got off. There were twenty-five hundred screaming women at the airport. Jimmy Stewart got off and they didn't even recognize him. They were pushed up against the fence. Elvis went along, shaking their hands. They lined the streets all the way to the hotel. They'd shout, 'Ellllvviiissss!'

"Tom Parker, who was with us, said to stay with Elvis. He wanted me in the pictures. We pulled up at the Hawaiian Village Hotel, which has a sort of lanai [covered patio] out front—the lobby isn't enclosed. There were five hundred women there and as we got out of the taxi, Elvis grabbed my arm and the women broke and mobbed us. I felt my feet going out from under me. My husband was behind me trying to get to me and he was screaming, 'Get out . . . get out!' I just knew I was gonna be killed. I never felt so close to death. You know, everyone wants to be number one, but that one experience was enough to convince me I don't want it."

The show was to be in the 4000-seat Bloch Arena in Pearl Harbor, not far from where the sunken battleship *Arizona* lay. Ticket prices were scaled for everyone, rising to a hundred dollars apiece for the ringside seats.

"Naturally all the generals and admirals came at the Colonel, trying to get to Elvis," said Ron Jacobs, one of Honolulu's leading disc jockeys, a position he held when Elvis last visited Hawaii for a concert in 1957. "And so the

Colonel started snowing them about how important they were to the security of the world and how patriotic and so on, and if they'd line up, why he'd give them a little something from Elvis. So they lined up, all these guys in charge of the Pacific and parts west, and Parker went over to a trunk and carefully, almost secretly, pulled some tiny color pictures out and very stingily doled them out, one to each admiral and general.

"Later he showed me the inside of the trunk. It was full of eleven-by-fourteens in color, eight-by-tens in color, calendars, record catalogues, you name it. He told me he thought all the brass deserved was little pocket calendars.

"Then one of the admirals came to him asking for complimentary tickets and the Colonel said no—even if Presley's father came to the benefit he'd have to pay his way in, why even Elvis bought his ticket. Then the Colonel made sure the Negro chauffeur he'd been assigned was given two free tickets right up front next to all the brass."

It was true, Elvis *had* bought his own ticket to the show, the first of the hundred-dollar seats. Elvis and the Colonel also absorbed the cost of transporting and paying all the musicians and backup acts. They had read about the memorial committee's need for help in raising money and volunteered to stage the benefit only if every penny taken in at the box office actually went to the building fund. As a result, the committee received $47,000, to which Elvis and the Colonel personally added another $5,000.

As for the show itself, Elvis outdid himself. He sang nineteen songs, his longest show ever, and according to Gordon Stoker, at one point Elvis dropped to his knees and slid twenty feet to the front of the stage with the microphone in his hands, never missing a note. "We thought he was going right off the edge," said Gordon. "Ray Walker [who'd replaced Hugh Jarrett as the Jordanaire's bass] was so surprised he didn't come in harmonically where he was supposed to. He just stood there with his mouth open, and nothing was coming out."

Elvis remained in Hawaii following the benefit to begin location shooting of his next film for Paramount, *Blue Hawaii*, another for Hal Wallis and Norman Taurog. This had him playing a rich man's son who returned from the service and much against his parents' wishes took a job with a tourist agency. Angela Lansbury played a convincing mother, Joan Blackman an appealing heroine and love interest, Nancy Walters an older woman seeking romance while vacationing in the islands. According to Ron Jacobs, the high points were the scenes involving the Colonel, none of which, sadly, were filmed.

"There had to be fifty-seven technicians and directors and script girls and makeup men and all the rest standing around with reflectors, waiting for the clouds to clear so the light would be just right for a matching shot," he said. "Finally the sun comes out and they have twenty-six seconds to shoot. Elvis is ready. Everybody is ready. The director calls action and Parker comes out of the bushes, on camera, screaming for Hal Wallis. Wallis comes rushing up. The shot's been blown. He's furious, but he's trying to keep control, even if his face is purple. He asks Parker what's wrong and Parker said Elvis is wearing his own gold watch in the shot and the contract doesn't call for his providing wardrobe, but that's okay, so long as they come up with an additional $25,000 for the use of the watch.

"And the next day the Colonel has taken one of those aluminum tubes cigars come in and punched holes in it so it looks like a microphone, then run wires from that—wrapped with tire tape—into his hand-tooled valise, another wire from that into his ear, a pineapple in the valise for bulk, and he's walking around the lobby of the hotel interviewing people for what he said is the Pineapple Network."

Elvis apparently wasn't having so much fun. Minnie Pearl said she and her husband stayed at the Hawaiian Village for nearly a week following the concert and "the whole time we were there, Elvis never got out of his room except to work. They say he came down in the middle of the night to swim. He couldn't come down during the day. He had the penthouse suite on top of that thing there and we'd get out and act crazy, having the best time in the world, and we'd look up there and Elvis would be standing at the window, looking down at us."

# Chapter 13

# THE MEMPHIS MAFIA

E lvis may have been lonely, standing at the window of that Hawaiian hotel, but seldom was he alone. From the time he left the Army onwards, he had an impressive entourage, a group of seven to twelve—it varied—young men approximately his own age, all of whom were on salary. Most went wherever Elvis went and, except for two with whom he served in the Army in Germany, all were from the Memphis area, so newsmen began calling them the "Memphis Mafia." It was the "Mafia" that gave Elvis security, comfort, and companionship.

They were also there as party pals. "None of us slept more than a few hours at a time," Joe Esposito said in his book *Good Rockin'*, recalling the antics that led to their being asked to leave the Beverly Wilshire Hotel. "We lived on amphetamines. We woke at five o'clock each morning to report to the set, then spent the rest of our time screwing around. Music blared continuously . . . We ferried Hollywood starlets up and down in the elevators all day and all night. Elvis was breaking boards in his suite and trying to teach the rest of us karate . . . [and] when we weren't trying to break boards, we were running around the halls, waging water-gun fights that escalated into full-scale battles."

Elvis leased a house on Perugia Drive in Bel Air, a neighborhood just west of Beverly Hills favored by millionaires and movie stars. And into it he moved his boys. They may have been paid only $150 to $250 a week, but there was no heavy lifting when it came time to work and even the silliest expenses were all paid.

After Rex Mansfield said no to Elvis's offer to be his major domo, Joe Esposito grew into the role. He had accompanied Elvis to Paris when they were in the Army together and kept track of expenses poorly, the Colonel said, but Joe was schooled in accounting and, joining Elvis following their discharge, in time he was given responsibility for handling payment of Elvis's personal bills and serving as a buffer between Elvis and the most of the rest of the world. A Chicago boy, he was the only Yankee member of the "Mafia."

There was Alan Fortas, who had been a scholarship football player at

Vanderbilt University before he met Elvis. He had gone to work for him as a companion-bodyguard in 1958 during the filming of *King Creole*, had worked in construction while Elvis was in the Army and had returned to Elvis in 1960.

"My job was I took care of his travel arrangements when we'd drive from Memphis to California," said Alan. "I took care of making sure everything was ready for these trips. We'd go right out Route 66, never stop except to sleep in one of the Holiday Inns. We'd just pile into the cars and drive, and they had to be ready. When you have a lot of cars, they break down. Not from use, but non-use. Tires go flat and batteries go dead. They get dirty. When it came time, I made sure they were ready to go."

Helping Alan watch over this fleet of vehicles was Delmar "Sonny" West, who at one time dated Elvis's cousin Patsy Presley but then argued with Elvis, leaving in 1961 to turn his rugged good looks into an acting career, returning to the payroll in 1970. He was a cousin of Red West.

Charlie Hodge was one of the two not from Memphis, and on salary since he'd met Elvis in Germany. His contribution, besides his voice and sense of humor, was his almost puppy-like worship of Elvis. His assignment was to supervise the musical aspects of Elvis's personal life, keep track of Elvis's huge record collection and sheet music during recording sessions. He remained with Elvis well into the 1970s.

Helping Charlie with the music was Elvis's tall broad-shouldered high school friend, Bobby (Red) West. He was Elvis's movie fight "opponent," and off camera one of his karate partners. By 1961, the year he married Elvis's secretary Pat Boyd, he was writing songs, several being recorded by Pat Boone and John Burnette. Elvis was given co-composer's credit when he contributed the song's title, "I Forgot to Remember to Forget." He left Elvis in 1968 to become a full-time songwriter and record producer in Memphis, and a sometime actor in Hollywood, usually playing tough guy supporting roles.

Lamar Fike, who had joined Elvis in Germany, remained on the payroll throughout the early 1960s, later taking his family to Nashville, where he headed the branch office of Hill and Range Songs. He returned to the Presley payroll, operating the lights, when Elvis appeared in Las Vegas. Elvis called him the "Great Speckled Bird" and made him the butt of his jokes.

Marty Lacker knew Elvis slightly during their high school days. Following two years in the Army, he worked in radio in Knoxville and New Orleans. He returned to Memphis and went to work for Elvis in 1960 and was the only married member of the group at that time. Until he left Elvis in 1967, he was Elvis's personal bookkeeper and secretary.

Jerry Schilling was another old friend from the neighborhood, who played football with Elvis and his friends in a park when he was a teenager and who, following graduation from college, worked for Elvis off and on for thirteen years, as a bodyguard, photo double, personal trainer, and co-executive producer of a karate film, as well as becoming a confidant.

Elvis's cousins Gene and Billy Smith, who had grown up with him in Tupelo and had become a part of his entourage while he was recording for Sun, were short and dark and wiry, and they favored wardrobe and hair styling that matched Elvis's. Billy took care of Elvis's clothing, saw that it was clean and hung neatly, and helped him with his shopping. At Graceland the wardrobe at one point was a sixteen-by-twenty-foot room. Gene helped wherever he was needed but had little specific to do outside provide companionship.

"I have no need of bodyguards," Elvis once said, "but I have very specific uses for two highly trained certified public accountants, an expert transportation man to handle travel arrangements, make reservations, take care of luggage, etc., a wardrobe man and a confidential aide and a security man who will handle safety arrangements in large cities where crowds of people are involved. This is my corporation which travels with me at all times. More than that, all these members of my corporation are my friends."

"The boys were lovely," said Yvonne Craig, an actress who was in two films with Elvis and dated him in 1963. "They changed periodically, but all of them were polite. They're charming. They didn't swear around you, they pulled out your chair, there were six people lighting my cigarettes and asking me if I wanted a Pepsi. They were like brothers to him.

"You could tell they worked for him. Joe Esposito you could tell less. But there was a difference. When I say to my brother, 'When you get a minute, would you do such-and-such?' that's another tone of voice. They're pals, but they're always conscious of his likes and dislikes. Like, around Sinatra: Are his shoulders up? That means he's angry, or whatever. They're more conscious of his temperamental changes, however slight they may be, than your own brothers would be. He can be honking around with them, playing, and then say something in a slightly different tone and you know they work for him."

Even so, the way the boys told it, much of the time was spent having fun. What Yvonne calls "honking around" often took on the appearance of a young boy's fantasy come true.

"There was one time," said Richard Davis, "we went to Beverly Hills and bought out three photo shops of all their flashbulbs, every bulb in all three stores, and then bought a half a dozen BB guns. We went back to the house, threw the flashbulbs in the swimming pool, where they floated, and then started shooting. Every time we hit one, it'd explode and sink. We did that three nights running. It took me two solid days to clean the pool after, but it was worth it.

"Another time, back in Memphis, I got the job of buying tractors. First I bought the little ones and graduated to the big diesels. We had the carpenter build a trailer that held fifteen or twenty people and we'd drive around Graceland as fast as we could, pulling that trailer full of people, see if we could throw everybody off. I think it was Billy Smith suggested we strap a saddle on the tractor, ride it like a horse. By now the yard behind the house looked like a field plowed by a drunk, all ruts and bumps. We'd take turns driving the tractor fast across the ruts, trying to buck each other off. We did that for several days.

"To us these things weren't crazy," Richard said. "They were just new and different and fun. Elvis liked to try new things, liked to try everything once."

Of course there was some method to the madness. Hal Blaine, a drummer who worked most of Elvis's recording sessions in Hollywood, recognized the value of the horseplay. "We'd go anywhere from eight in the morning sometimes to four the next morning without letup," he said. "And if Elvis seemed to get uptight at all, that was sort of their cue to start fun and games. Somebody'd come over and throw a karate punch at Elvis, he'd throw a kick back and pretty soon we're all drinking Cokes and he'd be telling stories about overseas. They went out and bought about a dozen of those butane lighters, cut the little nipple off the end, so when you opened it, it shot a tremendous flame. They used to chase each other around the studio with them. It was one of those things to keep Elvis loose. Everybody gets uptight sometimes and they'd been with him long enough to know the inflection of his voice on a particular matter. They knew it was time for fun and games."

And of course there were all the vehicles. Occasionally Elvis would get on his Harley-Davidson and lead a pack of Triumphs around the Bel Air hills—causing newsmen to call them "El's Angels" and the neighbors to call the police. Other times Elvis and the guys would go riding in the Cadillacs or the Rolls Royce. Going to the studio each day, the Cadillacs were driven nearly bumper to bumper. The real treat was to take the "Solid Gold Cadillac" for a spin.

Essentially, it was a 1960 Cadillac 75 limousine, one of the models that remained a favorite with Elvis for years afterward. He took it to George Barris in North Hollywood, then the top car customizer in the world. The top was lengthened and covered with a coarse-grain white pearl naugahyde material and the body was sprayed with forty coats of a specially prepared paint that included crushed diamonds and fish scales from the Orient. Nearly all the metal trim was plated with twenty-four-carat gold. There were gold records in the ceiling. Gold lamé drapes covered all the rear windows and the glass that separated the chauffeur from the passengers. There were dual gold flake telephones, one for the chauffeur who took incoming calls and announced the caller's name on the intercom. Within Elvis's reach were a gold vanity case with gold electric razor and gold hair clippers, an electric shoe buffer, a gold-plated television set, a phonograph, a multiplex amplifier, an AM-FM tuner with loudspeakers mounted under the front fenders, air conditioning, an electrical system for operating any household appliances, and a refrigerator that made a tray of ice cubes in exactly two minutes.

He bought a Dodge mobile home and then had a bus customized for the trips back to Memphis, where he still kept his mother's pink Cadillac locked away in a garage. And on nearby McKellar Lake there was a twenty-one-foot-long Century Coronado with a 325-horsepower Cadillac engine for water skiing.

They developed their own language. "They'd spend hours, days, thinking up lines to throw back and forth," said a close friend. "Things that didn't make any real sense. If there was a minor beef, somebody'd say, 'Big scene.' For a while they went through a period of 'I gotchers.' They'd say, 'I gotcher book. I gotcher message. I gotcher coat. I gotcher joke.' There were key words and phrases that only they understood.

"They'd bug him sometimes," the friend said. "He took his likes and dislikes out on them and they'd do everything but wipe his ass. He could say, 'Boy, it's a nice day,' and it might be raining out, but they'd start snapping their fingers and elaborating on how great the day was. There was one recording session, Lamar came up to him and said he thought the song Elvis had just sung was the greatest thing he'd ever heard. 'Ten million,' he said. Elvis said no. Lamar said, 'Five million. For sure—five million.' Elvis said no. Lamar said, "Three. Three—easy.' Elvis said he didn't really like the song or the way he did it. And Lamar said, 'Now that you say so, it wasn't so good after all.'"

Jerry Schilling wrote in his book *Me and a Guy Named Elvis*, "Elvis loved to tease—the voice that could expertly mimic Peter Sellers in *Dr. Strangelove* could also perfectly imitate anybody around him, and he had a way of finding one inflection or mannerism in our speech you didn't want anyone to focus on and turn it into a whole routine. Of course, we enjoyed going right back at him. Everyone was fair game for a well-delivered gibe: Elvis's neck (he thought it was too long), Lamar's weight, Alan's ears, my romantic 'inexperience,' or the way Marty looked in the Fred Segal black stretch pants that he insisted on squeezing into. There was a brutal honesty among us that was a real key to the relationship."

The boys lived with Elvis's moods—some brought on, apparently, by dieting. "He always had the weirdest eating habits I ever saw," said a friend. "Burnt bacon, olives, vegetable soup and peanut butter and banana sandwiches—that was about it. Sometimes he'd get on a jag of some kind, eating nothing but yogurt, but usually he didn't eat much at all. He could go through four recording sessions without eating. The rest of us would eat three meals and all he'd have was a bowl of soup and maybe a glass of milk. This was to keep his weight down. He'd run his movies and watch himself in a screening room, slumped way down in his seat, cringing, saying, 'No . . . no . . . too fat!' He worried about his weight all the time.

"He also worried about his hair. He went into seclusion. He wouldn't be seen. People he loved would go to the Graceland gates and he wouldn't see them. If his hair wasn't right or his eyes weren't right, he'd hide. He was still dyeing his hair black, but once he hadn't dyed it and he let it grow out. It was blond and he looked great. We said we thought it looked just great and he said he thought he'd leave it that way. Next time we saw him it was dyed double black.

"The temper was the hardest thing to take," the friend said. "One day he'd be the sweetest person in the world, the next day he'd burn holes in you with his eyes. It was hard on the guys. One time he fired every one of them, told them to get their asses back to Memphis, and they packed and left. By the time they'd got to the airport, Elvis changed his mind, so he had one of the boys paged and when he came to the phone, Elvis told them to get their asses back, they were on the payroll again."

It was the same temper that often caused the destruction of property. Back in 1957, he hurled an expensive guitar out of his hotel room into a hallway, splintering it. A visitor to one of his Bel Air homes told a story about the time he demonstrated his reaction to a Lee Dorsey record by heaving a heavy glass ashtray through the front of the jukebox. Over the years, he destroyed several television sets; when the lights didn't work properly on a bumper pool table, he took a pool cue and beat the table into pieces; and on at least two occasions, when his uncles strayed from the Graceland gate, Elvis ordered his limousine backed across the highway and driven at high speed *through* the gate.

The Mafia never complained.

Of course it was not without precedent for a celebrity to have a faithful entourage. Frank Sinatra, in fact, had two. One was formed in the late 1940s with songwriters Sammy Cahn and Jule Styne, his arranger and conductor Axel Stordahl, his manager Hank Sanicola and several song pluggers who generally served as "go-fers," the show business errand boys. The second clan—the rat pack—was formed rather more publicly in the 1950s with Dean Martin, Sammy Davis, Jr., Joey Bishop, Peter Lawford and others. Dozens more in entertainment have had similar groups, even if they were composed of just managers, publicists and office help: the conventional show biz claque. There were many Hollywood movie stars who had salaried companions. But most were like Sinatra's, somewhat remote; certainly they weren't members of a group that "lived in." Elvis's group lived in; they were, as Richard Davis said, on twenty-four-hour call, seven days a week, 365 days a year.

Alan Fortas said this presented unique problems: "All the guys stayed at the house and that was a big hassle. We had to find one that was big enough for all of us—five bedrooms at least. And most people do not like to rent to five, six, seven, ten, maybe a dozen boys, no matter who you are. Anybody has a house that size, they don't need the money so bad they're gonna take a chance of getting it tore up. It was tough finding a house with five, six bedrooms, four and five baths and a big den."

The quasi-Oriental home at 565 Perugia Way was one of them. This was the first of three homes he rented in the expensive mountain community. It was built in a semi-circle, one side fronting a small lushly planted drive-court, the other facing the Bel Air Country Club greens. In the center of the house was a garden, which the landlady had ripped out at Elvis's suggestion; Elvis thought a second den should go there, and he built a fireplace where a waterfall was. The house was furnished comfortably, but did little to project the tenant's personality.

Ellen Pollon, who at ten had been standing outside the Knickerbocker Hotel as one of the "Hotel Hounds," was thirteen now and something of a regular visitor. "It was a very strange scene up there," she said. "Nobody'd talk. All these guys he was in the Army with and some that were from Memphis. I could tell there was a pecking order. The girls would sit around and they'd ball this one or that one. They go to Lamar maybe and from that to Sonny and finally you'd get to Gene, who was Elvis's cousin, and from Gene you were supposed to get to Elvis, although it never worked out that way."

Said another visitor to the Perugia Way home in 1962, when she was eighteen: "A friend of mine was going with one of the guys and she asked me to go to the house with her, and she explained the ground rules. She said if one of the guys took a fancy to me, I better take a fancy to him if I wanted to be invited back. And above all else, I had to be ladylike. So my girlfriend asked for the one she was dating, he came to the door and invited us in. We were offered soft drinks and given the run of the house. I found Elvis in a back room, seated at the center of a horseshoe-shaped couch, feet up on the coffee table, captain's hat on his head, with half a dozen girls seated on the couch on each side of him."

"You could hear them plotting," said Ellen Pollon. "There were twenty or thirty there every time he had one of those parties, which really was a sort of open house. And the girls were always jockeying for position. Sitting on the couch, not too close, but close enough, within eye range. You'd see Elvis looking around and he'd look at a girl and she'd smile. Or if he looked as if he were *about* to look at a girl, she'd smile. As soon as he looked away again, she'd drop the smile. No one ever talked to each other. I went over to one girl to admire her boots and she wouldn't talk to me. Then I realized you can't talk to someone when they're working, and these girls were working.

"Most of the girls were in their twenties. Some were sixteen and I was the child in the group. Some of them were starlet types. Not the Tuesday Weld variety. More like Jana Lund. She was one of them. Supposed to be Elvis's girl friend. For a while anyway. You know the type—the ones who played the 'bad girls' in all the *Rock Rock Rock* movies. But they weren't in the movies, just that type.

"It was weird. We'd sit around watching television—that's what we did 75 per cent of the time—and nobody'd ever laugh at anything unless Elvis did. If Elvis laughed, everybody'd just roar. Not more than Elvis laughed, but just as much."

Other gatherings at the Presley manse were more relaxed, when Elvis had a date. "It was when I did *It Happened at the World's Fair* with him [in 1963] that Elvis asked me out—or in, as the case may be, because he doesn't go out," said Yvonne Craig. "It was odd, because I think Elvis actually did the asking. Usually Joe Esposito does the asking and if you say yes, Elvis makes the arrangements. But it was Joe who came to my door to escort me to the car, and there's Elvis sitting in his white gold-dusted Cadillac—this crazy-looking thing. He said very apologetically, 'I brought this because . . . uh . . . I thought you'd . . . might . . . want to see it.' And then he pushed all the buttons for me as Joe drove us to the house. We had dinner and we were the only two people sitting in his dining room and it was so quiet I could hear me chew. Then we went into the living room and all the henchmen were there with their dates watching television, so we went to his quarters. That was when I gave him a lecture. I said, 'Elvis, I have to tell you something. I think this is a dangerous move for you.' He said, 'What?' I said, 'Well, you're just lucky that I'm the way I am, because you have no idea, I mean you're living in Hollywood now, it's a terrible trap, if you're to take a girl alone back here to your quarters, she can say anything: rape, scream, carry on, and the court will say uh-huh, he did it. There'll be a lot of publicity and you'll be in trouble.' And he's sitting there saying, 'Yes, ma'am yes, ma'am . . . I'll certainly be careful about that.'

"I felt like a dummy the next day, but I did feel protective. He makes you feel that way. Elvis encourages a motherly interest. It isn't a weakness, it's just that he's so quiet and Southern and sweet."

Yvonne, an attractive bubbly brunette, said she dated Elvis again while they were co-starring in another film, *Kissin' Cousins*. This time she said he fell asleep on her. "We were watching an old movie on television," she said. "He fell asleep, so I turned out the lights, turned off the TV and tiptoed out of the room. I went to get Joe and said, 'Elvis is asleep, you better get him undressed and to bed and I've turned out all the lights.' So Joe said, 'You didn't turn out *all* the lights?' I said. 'Yeah, yeah . . . I'm not his mother.' Joe said, 'He likes to have one light on.' I said, 'Well, go turn one light on.' How was I supposed to know that? Anyway, so we walk out the front door and there's not one, but five Bel Air patrol cars—cops all over the lawn. Joe said to me, 'You didn't touch a button, did you?' I said, 'I touched every button in the room trying to get the lights to shut off.' What I'd done was call the Bel Air patrol. The next day Elvis said, 'I understand you had some trouble with the police last night.' He'd slept through the whole thing."

Chapter 14

# HOLLYWOOD: 2

For seven years Elvis stayed on his Bel Air and Memphis hilltops and horsed around with his pals, played football and rode motorcycles, dated pretty girls, drove around in expensive automobiles, stayed out of sight most of the time, worried about his weight and hair, cut records and made movies.

Mostly he made movies. From the spring of 1961 to the summer of 1968—the date of the videotaping of his first television special, which marked the beginning of a return to public performance—Elvis starred in no less than twenty-one films, an average of three a year.

*Blue Hawaii*, the film made following the Pearl Harbor benefit, was released for the Thanksgiving-Christmas holidays, and when it completed its run in five hundred or so theaters in the U.S. in early 1962, it had grossed $4.7 million, equal to *Gunfight at the OK Corral* or *Pal Joey*, and was on *Variety*'s list of all-time box office champions. The soundtrack album became the fastest selling album of 1961 and occupied the top position on all album sales charts for much of 1962, eventually racking up more than $5 million in sales.

By the time this film was released, Elvis was the well-meaning but bumbling pride of a shiftless family of crackers living off the government in Florida in a film called *Follow That Dream*. Arthur O'Connell played his father, Jack Kruschen and Simon Oakland a couple of inefficient mobsters trying to take advantage of our hero, Anne Helm his love interest, Joanna Moore a sexy but menacing welfare worker. Although Elvis was sympathetic enough in the role, the film did little to change the Hollywood hillbilly stereotype and little to advance his career, even though it was the first to take advantage of his natural flair for comedy. For what seemed to many to be little more than a vacation in Florida, where it was filmed, Elvis was paid $600,000 plus 50 per cent of the profits.

No sooner was *Follow That Dream* in editing than Elvis had turned boxer to appear in a remake of 1937's *Kid Galahad*. Elvis's karate training and some boxing lessons from Mushy Callahan, a former world welterweight champ, made the fight scenes credible enough, and Joan Blackman was there to listen to Elvis sing while the Kid's hard-drinking manager (Gig Young) tried to double-cross him, but the film needed more than that to put it many notches above the preceding one. The movie was, incidentally, the third in a row in which Elvis often appeared stripped to the waist, something producers apparently believed was an important plus.

Elvis's third movie role in 1962 took him back to Hawaii, where he played a charter boat captain in *Girls! Girls! Girls!* The picture had, oddly, only two girls in it, Stella Stevens and Laurel Goodwin, but there were thirteen songs, including another in the long line of title tunes by Jerry Leiber and Mike Stoller, and another by Otis Blackwell, the million-selling "Return to Sender." Sadly, the plot was so flimsy and most of the songs so lame, Elvis appeared to be walking through the scenes in his sleep.

In 1963 Elvis made four musicals, the first taking him to Seattle for *It Happened at the World's Fair*. Now Elvis was a crop duster whose co-pilot and partner (Gary Lockwood) kept getting into gambling trouble, while Elvis chased Yvonne Craig around a couch and then went after and—with the help of little Ginny Tui—landed Joan O'Brien, while singing ten new songs. One of them, "One Broken Heart for Sale," still another Otis Blackwell tune, sold the usual million-plus copies when it was released as a single.

*Fun in Acapulco* was a more substantial film, giving Elvis a solid story line about a trapeze artist (Elvis) afraid of heights following an accident in the States. In sunny Acapulco—and the scenery was terrific; this was something many of Elvis's films offered—he becomes a singing lifeguard who is followed around by a young Mexican boy (Larry Tomasin) and the usual flock of pretty girls, Ursula Andress and Elsa Cardenas among them. In the end, after warbling about a dozen songs, Elvis dives from a monstrous cliff, thereby dissolving his acrophobia and establishing himself as one hell of a gringo. There were no singles released from the film, but the soundtrack album joined the others in gold on the wall in the den in Graceland.

The third film shot in 1963 was also filmed on location, *Viva Las Vegas*. In this, one of his better musicals—and certainly his most successful, grossing $5.5 million in the U.S. alone—Elvis was a race car driver trying to raise money to buy a new engine for The Big Race. He also was competing with an Italian racing champion (Cesare Danova) for the attentions of a swimming pool manager and night club dancer (Ann-Margret). Before it was all over, and Elvis had won the race and the girl, the cast and crew visited every picturesque background within fifty miles of the Vegas strip and Elvis had sung several appealing songs, one a duet with Ann-Margret.

Social note: There was much made of the off-camera duet between Elvis and his redheaded leading lady in this picture, most of it a publicist's puffery.

Ann-Margret even went so far as to say Elvis had given her an enormous bed. It was not true, yet when Elvis was asked he graciously said, "Anything the lady said, anything the lady said." And then he stopped seeing her.

It was now as predictable as a sunrise and sunset. Just as there were such easily identified formula films as "the Jerry Lewis movie" and, before that, "the Abbot and Costello movie" and "the Bing Crosby/Bob Hope road movie," and the Busby Berkeley musical, and movies celebrating the Hardy Boys and the Three Stooges and the Marx Brothers, in the 1960s there was something called "the Elvis Presley movie."

Even by the time *Blue Hawaii* was made in 1961, Elvis's films were becoming so individualized, they were a category unto themselves, most appearing to be little more than an excuse to get Elvis into a recording studio to produce another soundtrack album. Such recordings would comprise most of his prolific outpouring of song until he returned to public performance in 1969, and because he often cranked out three and sometimes four films a year, frequently the music was as weak as the cinema.

Critics of his films consistently have wrung their hands in dismay, expressing the shared belief that had Elvis been given better material and supported in his desire to become an actor rather than an amiable yet innocuous entertainer, his career, and popular image, would have taken a different turn. And, in retrospect, most blamed the Colonel for the joke that Elvis became.

But the Colonel had never made a secret of his plans for Elvis. Knowing how fleeting fame was in the recording industry—especially in pop music (as opposed to country music, where fans are more inclined to remain faithful)—he wanted to give Elvis what he'd always said he wanted, even when he was telling Marion Keisker about his dreams that day he walked into Sun Records to cut two songs for his mom. He wanted to be a movie star.

And so the Colonel created a sort of machine called "the Elvis Presley movie," where the film promoted the soundtrack album and the album promoted the film, and both were enormously successful. Three times a year, it seemed to work without fail and as everyone knows about any machine, if it ain't broke, don't fix it.

It should also be noted at this time that if Elvis was not always inspired by the material, he invariably went along. Jordanaire Gordon Stoker was quoted in Ernst Jorgenson's *Elvis Presley: A Life in Music* as saying, "He always tried to make the best of any situation. Sometimes he'd walk over to us and say, 'Man, what do we do with a piece of shit like this?' Most of the time, he would console himself with the idea of, 'Well, regardless of what I say, [they're] just going to demand that I do this song, so I'll just do the best I can.'

Such was Elvis's attitude when he made the follow-up to *Viva Las Vegas*.

*Kissin' Cousins* was the first to be produced by Sam Katzman, known in Hollywood as the "King of the Quickies." He'd just completed *Hootenanny Hoot*, a revue that had showcased fourteen musical acts (Johnny Cash among them), in eight and a half days and was working on *Your Cheatin' Heart*, the story of the late Hank Williams, starring George Hamilton and shot in fifteen days. It was then that he met Colonel Parker.

According to Gene Nelson, Katzman's director, Katzman allowed the Colonel to tell MGM how to distribute the Williams film, and it subsequently became one of the studio's biggest grossers. Then, Nelson said, "over a cigar and a cup of coffee, Sam and the Colonel made a deal. The Colonel told Sam, 'Instead of making four-million-dollar pictures like we have been, we want to make a picture the way you do it.'"

"With me being a frugal producer, the Colonel figured we could save a few dollars," Katzman said. "I saw a few of Elvis's pictures and some I liked, some I didn't. I knew Elvis at heart was a country boy, so I thought we better put him back in the woods, put him back in the country where he belonged. So I assigned a writer [Gerald Drayson Adams] to write an original story for him."

Later the script was rewritten appreciably by Gene Nelson, who said, "As we were writing it, when we came to a spot where a song was needed, we wrote down four to six suggested song titles and sent the scenes and titles to Freddy Bienstock in New York, who then sent them to his writers. And then we sent the script to the Colonel with a note: 'Before we send this to Elvis, we wanted you to see it.' The Colonel sent it back with his note: 'Thank you for the script, Gene. But if you want an opinion or evaluation of this script, it will cost you an additional $25,000.'"

Gene said the Colonel later explained, "We don't know how to make pictures. We have you for that. All we want is songs for an album."

The story was about as flimsy as most but offered the twist of having Elvis in a dual role, playing an Air Force officer trying to persuade a hillbilly family to allow construction of a missile base on their land, and also the part of his cousin, one of the Smoky Mountaineers. Both characters—one brunet, the other blond—danced and sang and, except for the hair of course, sounded and looked exactly alike. As the hillbilly he again had Arthur O'Connell as a father, Glenda Farrell as a mother and Yvonne Craig and Pam Austin as sisters. In his role as the officer he had Yvonne as his romantic lead.

"Things got tense on *Kissin' Cousins* because of the tight schedule," Gene Nelson said. "He'd never worked this way before. The Colonel explained how he'd make more money on the 50 per cent of profit deal he had [in addition to $750,000 in salary] and I said it was like shooting a television show and to pretend it was that instead of a film. Elvis went along.

"Nonetheless there were times when Sam leaned very, very hard. He was always on the set and I hadn't learned the patience and control I think I have now and I'd get uptight, and this upset Elvis. He came to me the last week and he said he didn't like to work this way, it wasn't worth it. He said he knew what pressure I was under and he volunteered to get sick or show up late if it would help. I thanked him and said to hang in—it was my problem, not his."

There were other problems too, not the least of which was the blond wig Elvis had to wear whenever he played the hillbilly cousin. "It was really trauma for him," said Yvonne Craig. "He didn't want to come out of the dressing room with the blond wig on. I figured other things were happening and I said to Gene Nelson, 'What's the hang-up this morning?' And Gene said, 'Well, it's a problem. Elvis feels that he looks odd in the blond wig and really he doesn't have the guts to get up and get out here yet. But don't anybody make any remarks like "Gee, you sure look funny with the blond wig on."' Elvis never said anything about the wig, except that he didn't care for it. But he dyes his hair. That's no secret, you know. And I thought, could it have something to do with that?"

There also was an accident when the cast was on location for a week at Big Bear, a ski resort a couple of hours from Los Angeles. Glenda Farrell broke her neck during a scene when she was to flip Elvis from the porch of a house. Actually, Elvis flipped himself in the stunt and on the first take it worked perfectly. But on the second take she didn't let go and she went down, hitting her neck on a step. The rest of the picture she wore a brace until it was time to go on camera.

The final problem came in shooting the final scene, when Elvis and Lance LeGault, who was doubling him, were circling each other. "Marvelous Sam Katzman," said Yvonne Craig. "Lance was supposed to stand with his back to the camera and as he moved, Elvis with black hair was moving up and as Lance made the turn, they were to lock off the camera and switch them, putting Elvis in a blond wig, Lance in a black wig. But somebody blew it and in the final scene you see Lance looking right into the camera. You could see it wasn't Elvis. Clearly. And Sam Katzman said, 'Nobody'll even know.' It was too expensive to shoot it again and that's the way it went into the theaters."

The film was completed two days late, but still in under two and a half weeks and at a total cost of $1.3 million, about a third to a fourth of what the likes of *Blue Hawaii* cost. *Kissin' Cousins* apparently had all the right ingredients too, appealing to MGM so much the studio released it before *Viva Las Vegas*, in time for the Easter school holidays.

Elvis's first film in 1964 was *Roustabout*, which told the tired old tale about cold-hearted business types moving in to shut down a fumbling carnival. Elvis was a vagabond singer who fell in with Barbara Stanwyck, the show's owner, and then fell in love with Joan Freeman, daughter of Leif Erickson, the temperamental boss of the show. There was a blow-up caused by the romance, Elvis took his guitar to a rival show, and then returned as the sheriff was moving in for foreclosure. Sue Ann Langdon was on hand as the female menace to the Presley-Freeman romance, there was a belly dancer—giving reason to unwrap a five-year-old classic by Leiber and Stoller, "Little Egypt," originally sung by the Coasters—and Elvis was permitted to ride a Honda around the dusty hillsides of Thousand Oaks, California, where the film was shot. None of the eleven songs was released as a single, but the soundtrack album was another million-seller.*

After *Roustabout* Elvis made *Girl Happy*, in which he was a nightclub entertainer who found love and reason to warble eleven new songs in Fort Lauderdale during the annual Easter college migration. The picture's producer, Joe Pasternak, previously had made *Where the Boys Are* in the Florida beach city and admitted that when he arrived with Elvis the city was less than thrilled, because his first film had "brought down ten times as many college boys the next year and it almost wrecked the town." Elvis had three sidekicks in the movie backup band—Gary Crosby, Joby Baker and Jimmy Hawkins—and the girls he chased were Shelley Fabares and Mary Ann Mobley. The single released from the film was a typical mid-sixties dance number, "Do the Clam."

Elvis's third, and last, film for 1964 was *Tickle Me*, his first for Allied Artists, one of Hollywood's studios then staggering toward bankruptcy. It had Elvis playing a singing rodeo rider who got a job on an expensive dude ranch that apparently catered almost exclusively to voluptuous girls who spent most of their time in peek-a-boo bathing suits.

The story line: Elvis and the girls (Jocelyn Lane, Julie Adams) go hunting for hidden treasure and find it. Said the *New York Times*, rightly: "This is the silliest, feeblest and dullest vehicle for the Memphis Wonder in a long time."

Next came his second quickie for Sam Katzman, Elvis's first "costume" flick, *Harum Scarum*, a weak and muddled musical adventure that had Elvis running around some mythical Arab kingdom in robes and on dromedaries. The story had him playing an American movie star who was kidnapped during a sort of State Department tour in the Middle East. Mary Ann Mobley was the daughter of a king and somehow, following some foolishness involving political assassins and the like, everybody moved to Las Vegas, where Elvis entertained everybody.

---

*The only other noteworthy feature—in retrospect—was a scene that had two pretty girls taking an outdoor shower behind one of those board walls that cover from knee to neck. Billy Barty, a midget, came along to peek at the girls and then Elvis arrived to break up the resultant chaos. One of the girls was Raquel Welch, making a Hollywood debut she never talks about.

All Sam Katzman said about this one was "It didn't do so good as *Kissin'
Cousins*." The director, Gene Nelson, believed Elvis never looked better, but
said the script was "a bad choice." (At one point the Colonel suggested adding
a talking camel, but no one was listening. It might have helped.) The film was
shot in eighteen days, Elvis was paid a million dollars, one of the first
Hollywood stars to be paid so much (plus the usual 50 per cent of profits), and
it was released in several cities as part of a double feature with a witless
Japanese horror film, *Ghidrah, the Three-Headed Monster*.

The next film, *Frankie and Johnny*, had Elvis, a riverboat gambler, romanc-
ing Donna Douglas, then starring in the *Beverly Hillbillies* television series.
Nancy Novack played Nellie Bly in the film and for those who didn't see it, and
remember the tragic ending in the popular legend upon which the movie was
based, United Artists studio had everybody happy and alive at the end. It was
a confusing film and not an especially entertaining one, although Elvis did look
quite handsome and comfortable as a Southern gambler. "Even compared to
some previous Presley turkeys," said the *New York Times*, "this one almost
sheds feathers from the start."

Then came *Paradise, Hawaiian Style*, sort of a remake of *Blue Hawaii*, in
which Elvis played an airline pilot whose inordinate interest in girls gets him in
trouble with his boss, so he returns to the islands, where he convinces a buddy
(Hawaii native James Shigeta) to set up a charter helicopter service. Suzanna
Leigh was Elvis's girlfriend and several of the scenes—dances and songs, primarily—were shot at the Polynesian Cultural Center on Oahu where Elvis's
dressing room was a replica of a native royal palace from Hawaii's more primitive and natural past. The soundtrack album of nine songs—plus one of the
"bonus" tunes that were added to many sound-track LPs as filler—sold about
as well as that of the preceding film—moderately, but profitably.

The pictures continued to appear as regularly as the school holidays. In
1966, he made *Spinout*, his second with Joe Pasternak and sixth with director
Norman Taurog. This was another one about fast cars and only slightly slower girls (Deborah Walley, Diane McBain, Shelley Fabares). Each of the three
girls used a different ploy to land Elvis—Shelley her dad's money, Diane a
book she was writing, while Deborah was trying to get him to recognize her as
something more than one of the four guys in his backup band. (He was a
*singing* race car driver.) There were nine songs in the flick, and on the album
there were three bonus songs, including "Tomorrow Is a Long Time," one of
only two Bob Dylan songs Elvis ever recorded.

*Double Trouble* was a little better, but not much. Elvis was a tuxedoed rock
'n' roll singer who was supposed to be in love with two girls at the same
time—hence the title—an aggressive tease (Yvonne Romain) and a naïve

English heiress (Annette Day). Elvis leaves for a tour of Europe and is followed by Miss Day, who is pursued by her murderous uncle and two bumbling but occasionally amusing hoodlums. There are also three comical foreign policemen in trench coats—played by former vaudevillians, the Wiere Brothers—and eight songs, one of them an updated "Old MacDonald's Farm."

The final film made in 1966 was *Easy Come, Easy Go*, in which Elvis played a Navy frogman searching for a sunken treasure ship. There were two girls—Dodie Marshall, a descendant of the treasure ship's captain, and Pat Priest—and three songs. Unfortunately, the only real moments of entertainment came when Elsa Lanchester appeared briefly as a wacky yoga cultist.

Elvis next appeared in *Clambake* as the son of an oil millionaire who wanted to be loved—by Shelley Fabares—for himself and not his money. So he exchanges places with a Florida ski instructor (Will Hutchins) and wins a ski boat regatta, beating his rival in the film (Bill Bixby). Elvis acquitted himself in his usual competent manner—while singing seven songs—but the film was another in that long gray line of musical clinkers. Said the *New York Times*: "What do we see over his shoulder when the star drives Miss Fabares to the Miami airport and professes true love? Mountains, real Florida mountains."

Essentially they were all fantasies, totally unrelated to reality, or to anything outside Elvis's world. Not even when a twist number, "Rock-a-Hula Baby," was inserted at the last minute in *Blue Hawaii* or "Bossa Nova Baby" was shoehorned into *Fun in Acapulco* or "Do the Clam" was shoved into *Girl Happy*, all to capitalize on current musical or dance fads, did Elvis seem in touch.

A footnote: In 1965, as Elvis celebrated his thirtieth birthday, the number one song in the U.S. was "I Feel Fine," the fifth consecutive number one song for the Beatles. Later in the year the Beatles visited Elvis at his Bel Air home, joining him in an awkward jam session, while the Colonel played roulette with Beatles manager Brian Epstein on a table brought into the house for the occasion. Although the Beatles said Elvis was what inspired them, their inspiration didn't have any number one songs from the spring of 1962 to the winter of 1969. Elvis was lost in Hollywood.

Lance LeGault, the talented blues singer from Louisiana who doubled Elvis or plotted his choreography from 1960 through 1968, said, "We shot *Kissin' Cousins* in seventeen days and I think that film was the turning point in Presley films as far as shooting. Up until that time certain standards had been maintained. But it seems to me from *Kissin' Cousins* [1963] on we were always on short schedule. That's where we noticed there was no rehearsal for all the numbers.

"Now I don't remember how long we were on *Viva Las Vegas*," Lance said, "but it seems it was ten or eleven weeks. A long time. That was the picture just before *Kissin' Cousins*. We weren't off a week or two weeks when—boom—we jumped right back into *Kissin' Cousins*, which was shot in seventeen days. From then on, once they realized they could take this guy and do a film that quickly, we were on quick pictures."

Lance was a tall, husky blond who met Elvis when he came to a club where Lance was singing.

"He always had a thing—six o'clock, he was through. But many times I stayed and worked with him late. On his own time. Because we had the number to do the next morning and there hadn't been time for him to learn it. More times than I can tell you there was no lunch break. Because when everyone broke for lunch was an ideal time to use the stage, the actual place where the scene was to be shot. And we'd rehearse all the lunch hour, except for the last ten or fifteen minutes of it. That time he would use to get ready for the first scene. Because he'd be wringing wet, his hair'd be messed up. Because we'd worked thirty-five or forty minutes—hard! You know. Get this damn number cookin'. That's how the schedules were set up. There'd be six or seven or eight songs to do where he had to move and there'd never be any time on the schedule for him to rehearse properly. It was a bear, man."

Lance blamed the studios. "The first time I noticed it for real was in *Roustabout*," he said. "Elvis rode a Honda in it. Which is pretty silly, when you think about it, because Elvis rode Harleys. Yet in the film they put him on a 350 Honda. And this is a guy who's playing the part of a drifter whose only mode of transportation is his bike. This is a guy who supposedly goes across country on a machine that's about right for the driveway, a 350 Honda.

"That's just a little, simple example. They never used Elvis to his full capacity in the situations in these films . . . in these songs that were given to him to do . . . never, never used the guy. I always had the feeling; Okay, here's a schedule and because it's Elvis we're gonna make so much money with the film regardless of whether he rides a Honda or he rides a Harley-Davidson, whether he sings a groovy tune like 'Don't Be Cruel' or 'All Shook Up,' where you had the real Elvis, as opposed to any piece of crap you want to name that he sang in the film. If you were there and saw it time after time . . . I never counted up the films, but I think I did between twelve and fourteen, fifteen films, plus the NBC special . . . and I kept seeing incident after incident after incident of taking somebody and treating him like it's good enough because it's Elvis and it's in color. And so we're gonna make two and a half times negative cost, plus another two and a half times . . . y'see?"

Dozens of others agreed, picking on the choice of directors or the script or some other aspect of the films. A former studio executive who watched Elvis make more than a dozen films said, "Directors usually handle Elvis with kid gloves. There was one picture that was thirty minutes late in starting, which is a lot of time when you're on location. They were late because Elvis wasn't there. And Elvis wasn't there because the director was afraid to send somebody to knock on Elvis's dressing room door. His best performances have been with gutsy directors, but there haven't been very many of them. They're afraid of alienating Elvis or the Colonel."

Gerald Drayson Adams, who wrote *Kissin' Cousins* and *Harum Scarum*, said, "There never were any story conferences. They consisted of money—first act, second act, third act money. And all were conducted by Colonel Parker."

"*Clambake* was one of the really, really awful ones," said Jack Good, the Englishman who had produced the *Shindig* television show before taking a small role in the picture. "There was a party after the film was completed, with Lance LeGault's band playing. And Elvis wouldn't sing. Slowly, Lance got him into a blues thing, 'Let It Roll.' And he was terrific. And I thought what a shame he doesn't do that sort of thing in the film."

Joe Pasternak said, "Elvis should be given more meaty parts. He's thirty-five years old, he's a man, he's got guts, he's got strength, he's got charm. He would be a good actor. He should do more important pictures."

Many felt Elvis was talented. Even the hard-to-please Bosley Crowther of the *New York Times* had said, "This boy can act," about his portrayal in *King Creole*. Others concurred. Don Siegel, the director of *Flaming Star*, said Elvis had switched from Little Richard to Stanislavsky, had become a Method actor who "jumps out at you from the screen." Yvonne Craig said she'd seen but one other actor more at ease while doing scenes, Spencer Tracy. Excusing some of his sadder efforts, even Hedda Hopper came to Elvis's defense, saying, so what if he wasn't a trained actor, neither was Gary Cooper; he learned on-camera too. Bill Bixby said, "He is a performer, he is an actor. He is worth considerably more than people have given him credit for. Frank Sinatra once said the best singers are the best actors and I think he's absolutely right. He's a good example. When Frank decides to act, man, stand aside. Elvis Presley has the same kind of presence. There is a presence. That's the only word I can think of. They both have it and I am not making a comparison. When they take stage, they take stage. They are it." And Gene Nelson said, "He always could handle more than he ever took on."

Elvis apparently disagreed in 1963, when he said, "I've had intellectuals tell me that I've got to progress as an actor, explore new horizons, take on new challenges, all that routine. I'd like to progress. But I'm smart enough to realize that you can't bite off more than you can chew in this racket. You can't go beyond your limitations. They want me to try an artistic picture. That's fine. Maybe I can pull it off someday. But not now. I've done eleven pictures and they've all made money. A certain type of audience likes me. I entertain them with what I'm doing. I'd be a fool to tamper with that kind of success."

Perhaps so. But Elvis was being unduly modest and in a few years' time the audience, the success, changed. Gerald Drayson Adams said the Colonel once told him there were a quarter million dyed-in-the-wool Elvis Presley fans who'd see every picture three times, that Elvis transcended any material given him.

This point is an important one. Elvis *did* transcend all the medium-to-lousy material he was assigned; when lines formed outside the theaters, those in the lines were there to see Elvis and no one or anything else. This had changed by 1966. Elvis had put on weight and his dyed hair was sprayed with so much lacquer you could bounce rocks off it and even the loyal fans who wrote for *Elvis Monthly*, a British publication, stopped going to the pictures. One called the films "animated puppet shows for not-overbright children." And Elvis began to wonder about the product he was turning out, first showing boredom and then occasional pique.

Red West, who continued to work as Elvis's stand-in, said, "At first it was something new for him. After a while it got to be the same, a pickup from the last movie. It really got so he didn't enjoy doing them. At first he liked making movies, but when it didn't get any better . . . the scripts didn't get any better and the songs were all the same, it kinda got bogged down. Actually, some of the films he couldn't wait till they were through. Most of 'em. He liked *Wild in the Country* because there was a good story there. He liked *King Creole* and he liked *Flaming Star* and I can't think of too many more he enjoyed doing."

Gene Nelson said that after they'd finished *Harum Scarum*, Elvis came to him and said, "Maybe one day we'll do one right." And a former executive at MGM said that after Elvis had completed one of his pictures there, he approached the director and said, "Hey, there were some pretty funny things in this script. I'm gonna have to read it some day." He wasn't smiling.

Jack Good said, "I said to Elvis, 'Why do you keep making these rotten films? Why don't you do something really exciting, like *King Creole*?' He said he left all that to the Colonel, but that the Colonel promised something really exciting soon, real soon."

# Chapter 15

# THE COLONEL: 2

The funny thing about it was that while turning out so much pap, Elvis became the highest paid entertainer in history; as the quality of the films went down, Elvis's earnings went up, until they began to average out at between five and six million dollars a year. Other performers may have been wealthier—thanks largely to wise investment—but none was paid so much for performing. Elizabeth Taylor, Cary Grant and Audrey Hepburn were in the million-dollar-per-picture category, but Elvis stayed ahead because he was getting a million dollars *plus* 50 per cent of the profits, and for the better part of his career all the films were profitable.

"They don't need titles," said an MGM studio man who worked on five of them. "They could be numbered. They would still sell."

Elvis also contracted to do more pictures per year than any other superstar. The Grants and Taylors and Hepburns of the business insisted upon script approval and they were picky about what they'd do, but Elvis would amble (sing) through anything he was given, and few pictures were so complicated that they required more than five or six weeks to shoot, so Elvis did a lot of them.

A breakdown of his 1965 income:

—Salary for *Harum Scarum*: $1,000,000.

—Salary for *Frankie and Johnny*: $650,000. (This and other sums were under a million because of early contract dates.)

—Salary for *Paradise, Hawaiian Style*: $350,000.

—Percentage of profits from *Tickle Me*: $850,000.

—Percentage of profits from *Girl Happy*: $850,000.

—RCA record royalties: $1,125,000.

—Music publishing royalties: $400,000.

All of which came to more than $5 million and did not include income from non-performing activities such as royalties on Elvis Presley products still being carried by several large chains and mail-order businesses.

And if these figures weren't enough to impress, others were released the same year. It was when Elvis and the Colonel celebrated their tenth anniversary together that the Colonel said the seventeen films released to date (April 1965) had grossed between $125 and $135 million. Then, not to be outdone, RCA said Elvis had sold 100 million records valued at $150 million.

How did it happen? A look at what was titled *Colonel Parker's Special Promotion and Exploitation Campaign*, prepared for *Kissin' Cousins*, shows how this worked. Although it is only sixteen mimeographed pages long, it could be considered the definitive text in its field. Some of the bases the Colonel touched in the report, in the order given:

1. Every piece of outgoing mail from RCA and MGM and the Colonel's office carried literature about *Kissin' Cousins*, was rubber-stamped with a "*Kissin' Cousins* Is Coming" type of message, and carried an Elvis Presley pocket calendar.

2. Interviews were set with Elvis (rarely) and other cast and crew members (less rarely).

3. Photographs were taken whenever Elvis was visited on the set by celebrities.

4. A regular series of bulletins were issued to the leading fan clubs, with special attention paid to the hundred or so that offered their members fan club newsletters.

5. Radio spots employed the drawls of two of the Colonel's favorite disc jockeys, Biff Collie and Squeakin' Deacon, and emphasized what the Colonel called "the fun and frolic of the hoedown and mountain folk humor."

6. The standard RCA tie-ins were planned—covering preparation and makeup of the album and singles to be released; scheduling of release (some of the dates had to be staggered so the album would appear in the stores the same week the film appeared in local theaters); preparation and distribution of streamers, display racks and other point-of-sale devices to be shipped to the 12,000 record dealers in the U.S. (all cross-promoting the film, of course).

7. Window displays were planned for lazy or unimaginative record store owners, along with disc jockey promotions and radio contests.

8. The MGM field men and the five hundred movie house managers, the RCA field men and the record retailers, all were told to get (a) friendly and (b) busy. They also were told how.

9. A special RCA campaign was launched: ELVIS MONTHS—APRIL AND MAY.

10. Just before *Kissin' Cousins* was released, press kits offering a wide assortment of pictures, feature stories, plot synopses, ads, etc., went to the Colonel's full list of columnists, wire service and newspaper writers. Wires and cables were sent to leading show business personalities, and personal contact was made with a list of disc jockeys and radio executives. "In short," the Colonel said in his report, "people in the trade were sensing that something was going

on and they were watching with interest for the public reception."

11. Fan club presidents were written again and given means and materials with which to make everyone in their own communities and in the cities of all their members what the Colonel called "*Kissin' Cousins* minded." (Send the disc jockeys requests to play the title song, etc.)

"With the release of the picture and the first positive indications of a most enthusiastic public reception, these activities were continued and enlarged upon, carrying much the same excitement and interest of the election returns night," said the Colonel. "The bandwagon was starting to roll and everyone was being encouraged to get on board."

Before it was all over, the following promotional material had been distributed: 3,000,000 wallet-sized calendars; 15,000 *Kissin' Cousins* single-record streamers; 15,000 *Kissin' Cousins* album streamers; 5000 *Kissin' Cousins* lapel buttons for use in radio contests and distribution at record hops; 3000 eight-by-ten color photos; 1500 photo albums; 150,000 copies of "Kissin' Cousins" sheet music; 400 souvenir kits to writers; 1000 special promotional kits to exhibitors; and 15,000 fan club president kits, one to each club.

"What this all comes down to," said a former associate of the Colonel's who worked with him in promoting some of the movies, "is the Colonel goes in ahead of Elvis and gets things stirred up. Elvis is catered to out of proportion to his size, when compared to anyone else of like or approximate stature."

This was the keystone to the Colonel's philosophy and it played a key part of his enormous success.

In 1963, Jon Hartmann was an aspiring actor who took a job in the mail room of the William Morris Agency, thinking it would give him invaluable contacts in terms of advancing a film career. Jon decided two weeks later to stick with the agency; the power thing involved in selling talent appealed to him. Six months after that he was given what was thought to be the "shit assignment" for William Morris employees—he was sent to join Colonel Parker's staff for two weeks. There he was to be the Colonel's "go-fer," to fetch him coffee on demand, to drive his car for him, to do whatever he asked. At the end of the two weeks the Colonel didn't so much as say thanks but said instead, "Why don't you come back on Monday?" Jon stayed for another six months, saying later that that was his managerial apprenticeship.

"The game of artist-manager is a very tricky game because the artist's manager, outside of the talent agency level, is a non sequitur," Jon said. "He doesn't have a union. He is a manager only because he and the talent say he is. He doesn't have any other qualifications. It's a bastard art. His responsibilities can be whatever he determines they are. And the way I see it, the way the Colonel

ran things, a good manager had to believe there were no rules or regulations—you can make your own rules so long as you can get away with it, and
that's what makes a good manager.

"Once the Colonel saw what Elvis was, which was probably the first time
he ever saw him, the Colonel probably was with Elvis constantly until Elvis
was totally under the hypnotic control of his personality. Because a manager
doesn't trust the artist. He's always afraid the artist is going to blow it. That's
why he's the manager.

"What this is, is psychology at its highest level. What the Colonel is, is a
superpsychologist to a superstar. He didn't see Elvis too often, but I don't think
that Elvis would do anything without checking with the Colonel first."

Spyros Skouras, former head of 20th Century-Fox, once tried to get Elvis
to make a public appearance against the Colonel's advice. "If you can get Elvis
to do it," the Colonel said, "you can *have* him." Elvis stayed home.

Jon Hartmann said, "He made it totally easy on his client, y'see. Elvis floats
on a cloud of adoration. He never witnesses any pressure. He just has to appear,
that's all. He's totally free. He's freer than any other star. All the other stars are
being called all the time for benefits and so on. Well, by the time I was with the
Colonel, 1963 and 1964, it had been firmly established that Elvis did nothing. It
was no to everything. No other star had, or has today, the freedom Elvis had."

Jon said the Colonel kept Elvis "loose" so subsequently Elvis would do
anything he wanted him to. Jon said this may sound Machiavellian but isn't so
nasty as it sounds, because most artists have no inkling how to operate a business and if the artist wants to be successful economically, he has to believe in a
businessman as much as the businessman says he believes in the artist. And one
of the keys to this arrangement is keeping the artist comfortable.

"The Colonel's comfort campaign includes having people next to Elvis who
are the people he likes and who can keep other people away," Jon said. "That's
why the Mafia was so close to him. That's why others couldn't get through.
They weren't needed. Elvis had all the companionship he wanted."

Another thing Jon said he learned about was success and how it is assured
through salesmanship.

"There's regional success and there's world success, and those are the two
smaller kinds," Jon said. "Both of those are economic successes. There's
another level of show business that transcends economic success. That's media
success, media power.

"The Colonel doesn't sell Elvis to the public, dig? He sells Elvis to the people who sell the public, and those are the media people—the television and
motion picture personalities, the executives and businessmen who control the
networks, the important radio people. It's like an endless trip for the Colonel.

Elvis, as a product, always is in the state of being sold.

"He communicates with these people regularly and he draws on their energies, pulling them along with him. He makes it fun for them and that's why they go along. He makes them members of the Snowmen's League. He works one of his elaborate practical jokes. He sucks them in. I'll give you a small example. When the Colonel came into his office in the morning, there'd be a list of names on his desk. These were the people whose birthday it was that day. Most of them got a telegram: 'Happy birthday . . . from Elvis and the Colonel.' Somebody heavy he'd call to wish a happy birthday personally. On one occasion I suffered the indignity of having to stand in front of a microphone that was hooked into the telephone and sing happy birthday to a 20th Century-Fox executive, along with the other guys in the office, in four-part harmony.

"The executives, or stars, or whoever, at the receiving end of this would think it was just terrific. Most of them even felt they owed the Colonel something in return, which of course is what the Colonel had in mind to begin with. Now they were on his team and the Colonel had them selling for him, selling Elvis to the public. It was amazing to watch. Every day the Colonel'd do something like this. And the team just kept getting bigger and bigger and bigger."

Jon mentioned the Snowmen's League. This preposterous organization occupied much of the Colonel's spare time over the years (dating back to the fifties) and its membership, in fact, formed a large part of the "team" Jon and others talk about. In the words of a slickly assembled booklet the Colonel distributes with a membership certificate and card to members, the organization was formed for those "skilled in evasiveness and ineptitude." The members—probably uncounted, according to the Colonel's friends—included dozens of the country's top executives and two, perhaps three, U.S. Presidents.

There are dozens of what seem to be apocryphal stories told about the Colonel, most of them told by the Colonel himself, but apparently many if not most were true and virtually all concerned the means by which he made his deals. Any visitor to his suite of offices in the 1960s was treated to several, making it appear, at times, as if building his own image were as important as building Elvis's.

Hubert Long, the Nashville talent manager who worked for the Colonel twenty years earlier, said, "When Elvis was going to do that film at the World's Fair, they were after him to do a personal appearance in a stadium that held thousands, and the Colonel was asking an enormous price. The Colonel said okay to everything and the promoter said okay to everything and then the promoter said, 'There's one thing we forgot, Colonel. This is outa-doors and what happens in the event of rain? Do we get another date?' The Colonel said, 'Wait a minute, you mean there's no roof on that building?' The promoter said, 'Oh no, it's a stadium.' The Colonel thought a minute and said, 'In the event of rain, we will have the concession to sell umbrellas.'"

An executive at 20th Century-Fox tells another: "The studio wanted Elvis to sing some additional songs in one of the films and the Colonel said it would cost the studio another $25,000. The man the Colonel was dealing with was aghast. He said absolutely not. Without blinking, the Colonel reached into his pocket, pulled out a pair of dice, tossed them on the man's desk and said, 'Tell you what—we'll roll the dice, double or nothing.'"

Other times when the Colonel got a call for Elvis to do something, he'd say the boy was tied up for the next three and a half years, but he'd be pleased to rent the gold lamé suit for the weekend for $5000. The gold Cadillac was leased to RCA and RCA put a man on staff full time to travel with the car, exhibiting it for charity. When asked if Elvis would do a walk-on on *The Joey Bishop Show*, the Colonel said yes, for $2500 and when the producer asked why so little, the Colonel said it would cost another $47,500 for Elvis to walk back off.

When Elvis's RCA contract expired and was renegotiated, RCA executives complained to friends that the Colonel got everything but the dog in the company trademark. One friend said that, among other things, RCA agreed to press one million copies of each record, no matter what the record's quality or public interest in it. Another friend quoted the Colonel as saying that RCA must print at least a million Elvis pocket calendars each year, distribute them without charge, and pay a royalty on each one of them for the use of Elvis's picture.

"I'd rather try and close a deal with the devil," Hal Wallis said. Sam Katzman calls the Colonel "the biggest con artist in the world" and a critic describes him as "the toughest manager since Cardinal Richelieu."

However unflattering many of the stories sounded, Jon Hartmann was quick to the defense. "None of the Colonel's shit is evil," he said, "because even where he's laying it out heavy, he's giving those people something that they wouldn't get otherwise. He never takes anything unless he's giving something. He may have embarrassed me occasionally and made me angry, but sometimes he'd hand out hundred-dollar bills for no reason, or radios and records, and I regard the whole thing as an education. The Colonel understands people better than most men, y'dig? He knows how to give them what they want and get what he wants and make everybody happy.

"The only good deals are where everybody's happy. If anybody came out ahead of the other guy, then it wasn't a good deal. And the Colonel has a way of getting people to give him stuff, because he makes them feel he has it coming. It was never leverage used in a negative way. It was 'Look what I did for you, now what are you gonna do for me?' And the guy said, 'Anything you want, Colonel.' And the Colonel said, 'Okay, give me this and give me that.' Next day a crate of cigars or television sets or maybe a matched set of ponies arrives at the Colonel's office. And the guy who sent them *still*, somehow, thinks he owes the Colonel a favor."

At the time Jon Hartmann was the Colonel's flunky he reported to a suite of five incredibly cluttered rooms on the Paramount studio lot, one of the fringe benefits that came with the nine pictures Elvis made for Hal Wallis there. The office was to Parker and Presley, in terms of memorabilia, what the Smithsonian Institution is to America. Walls were covered with photographs of Elvis—from wallet-size to larger-than-life-size—and posters from his movies, in all languages. Another room was wallpapered floor to ceiling with autographed pictures of celebrities, from Charles de Gaulle to Bob Hope to Richard Nixon. In the kitchen there was a huge table for meetings and again the walls were covered—with gold records. In Parker's huge office itself there was an elephant's-foot trash basket and small elephants covered his desk. He was inordinately fond of elephants, ponies and midgets. There were enormous snowmen and teddy bears and bubble gum machines and neon displays, and on the wall behind his desk were dozens of framed certificates presented to the Colonel for his "non-artistic artistic help" in producing the predictable Elvis album art. (All album covers offered at least one large color photo and never—never—pictured anyone else or credited a record producer.) It was as if he'd never thrown anything away. Jon Hartmann said that when the Colonel moved from Paramount to MGM in 1964 he and the others on the staff had to do the moving, and it took weeks.

There was also a public address system in the office, with a horn on the Colonel's desk that squeaked. "He would call us by squeaking the horn and we'd all have to come running," Jon said. "He'd squeak the horn into the P.A. or just squeak it until everybody was in there at attention. It was just a game we were playing. It was the Elvis Presley Game."

A chain of command had been established in the organization that ran the Elvis Game. The Colonel was the Colonel, and Tom Diskin was the only other officer, perhaps equivalent to a lieutenant in rank. Said a former associate: "He's the one who's paid to do all the worrying." Said Jon: "Elvis had the Colonel to screen out all the unnecessary bullshit, to keep him isolated and comfortable . . . and the Colonel had Diskin. I would guess that the Colonel only heard about 10 per cent of the calls that came in and none of the minor problems. The Colonel spoke for Elvis and Tom Diskin spoke for the Colonel." Diskin never married. He was reported to be a millionaire and had at least one major operation for ulcers.

According to Jon, Jim O'Brien was next in line, serving as a kind of sergeant-at-arms. He was the Colonel's private secretary, what Jon called an "efficient motherfucker who handled all the lower-level stuff." Like Diskin, he remained with the Colonel well into the 1970s. Grelun Landon was a former press contact for Hill and Range who then worked as a freelance publicist in Hollywood with the Colonel as one of his occasional clients and then moved over as manager of West Coast public affairs for RCA. He was a genial, easy-going father of three who went along with more nonsense than most of his friends expected he would. He enjoyed a long career with RCA and was an active member and sometime officer of the Country Music Association, but always spent up to twenty hours a week with the Colonel.

Irving Schecter was another former mailroom boy from William Morris. He worked for the Colonel for four years, although the Morris Agency continued to pay his salary. Along with Jon, Irving was at the bottom of the totem pole and was, among other things, called upon to move the Colonel's belongings from one house in Palm Springs to another when, Jon said, they discovered Elvis's gold suit in the Colonel's closet and gleefully tried it on.

Every day at nine, these six would report, and if the Colonel needed any more, he had only to call the Morris Agency or RCA or Paramount or MGM.

"Sometimes we'd draft some of the Memphis Mafia," said Jon. "Sometimes we'd pull them in to help with a special mailing. They hated that. If the Colonel put them to work, they thought that was the grossest bummer of all time, the worst part of their job working for Elvis."

The Colonel's office routine was a basic one, Jon said. If the Colonel wasn't there, as was the case on all Mondays and most Friday afternoons, when the Colonel went to Palm Springs to spend the weekend with his wife, it was relaxed. If the Colonel was in town, "there was a state of tension until the Colonel left. And based on that tension, everybody was supposed to look busy even if they weren't busy. Like, O'Brien would wander around and say, 'Do something.' Y'know? So we'd feign working and go through bullshit changes, to make the Colonel happy, to play the Elvis Presley Game."

Still another former associate goes so far as to say, "The Colonel treats his office staff like shit, especially if there's anybody visiting. All it is, is 'Get the Colonel a cigar! Light Mr. So-and-So's cigarette. Do this! Do that!' And all the time he's winking at you." This same source said the willingness to comply was based on fear and that the fear stretched to the office the Colonel maintained through the years in Madison. There, he said, the women who ran the office (some of them Tom Diskin's sisters), who filed, kept the Complete Elvis Presley Scrapbook, posted checks, etc., were "so fearful the Colonel might put in an unannounced visit they keep all the pencils sharpened and the same length and everything in every drawer just so. Keep 'em crawling—that's the Colonel's philosophy."

Said another former associate: "When the Colonel was behind his desk, nobody relaxed. The MGM, the RCA, the Morris people who were there—every one of them was keyed up. The Colonel's a master at keeping people keyed up. There was one picture the Colonel walked onto the set and coughed. It wasn't intentional. He just coughed—once—and the stage went so quiet you'd-a thought it was the beginning of the world."

Said Ron Jacobs: "He used to carry a ballooning leather hand-tooled souvenir-of-Phoenix valise. And he'd walk into the Morris offices, where everybody was dressed in the dark suits, polished fingernails, everything very proper and cool and just the correct amount of hip and they're sitting around talking about Charlton Heston this morning four million dollars, right? And Parker walks in with his dishevel, socks down around his ankles, carrying that hand-tooled valise and every one of those guys just fall apart."

On the office directory in the lobby of the William Morris Agency in Beverly Hills there were just two names, that of the agency president, Abe Lastfogel, and that of Colonel Thomas Andrew Parker.

Jon said the Colonel liked to have him serve as chauffeur, driving him around in the beat-up old convertible Jon owned at the time. "The Colonel liked to sit in the back seat, with me at the wheel of this rotten old car, holes in the top and everything, and when we'd be passing through the gate and run into one of the studio executives, the Colonel would reach out through a rip in the top and shake hands, saying, 'Hello, how are you, how do you like my new car?'"

It wasn't all fun and games. "There was the fan club," said Jon, "and it was always serviced. At the time, it was run by the people in the Colonel's office in Madison. The Colonel was very much in tune with fan mail, making sure it was all answered, giving it personal attention, even when it was thousands of letters a day. He was so into this, making sure it was covered, he had arranged to have a mailbox in the mail rooms of the three other studios where Elvis had made pictures. Part of my scene was to go around once a week or so and collect that mail, package it and send it back to Madison."

It was also during this time, Jon said, that the Colonel made one of the biggest Elvis Christmas mailings in a history of Presley-inspired post office gluts. Not only did it carry the usual holiday wishes—to a million-plus recipients—on an eight-by-ten-inch card, it included an eight-by-ten Elvis Presley calendar, a small four-color chromatone postcard photograph, a mimeographed letter bringing all the recipients up to date on Elvis's activities, and one of those notched wooden sticks with a propeller on the end—when you rub a straight stick along the notches, the propeller spins—with the name of Elvis's latest movie, *Fun in Acapulco*, stamped on the side.

"Instead of feeding it down to the Paramount mail room a piece at a time, he waited until it was all done and then had us take it down all at once—ten trunks of the stuff—just to blow their minds in the mail room. That was the vibration the Colonel liked to project," Jon said. "He blew minds. His day consisted of getting everybody high on Elvis, whether it was the mail-room guys at Paramount or the head of 20th Century-Fox or one of his big-time Southern politicians. Everything he did, it was for Elvis."

Often the Colonel helped others in the business. It was when Sonny and Cher had five records in the Hot 100 that he called their managers in to tell them—without charge, without tangible obligation—how to negotiate. Said one of the managers, Charlie Greene, "I'd been getting Sonny and Cher $2500 a night. After I left the Colonel's office I got on the phone and got them their first $10,000 gig."

He also talked several times with Brian Epstein, the Beatles' manager, providing guidance, especially regarding crowd security. So when the Beatles were sneaked through a mob of fans in a laundry truck and they took rooms in several hotels and Brian considered taking the Beatles through lying on couches that were covered with canvas, looking like so much furniture—it was because the Colonel had conceived and executed these same security measures in 1956 and 1957 when Elvis was touring the U.S.

The Colonel was charitable in many ways. In Nashville Mrs. Jo Walker, executive director of the Country Music Association, said the first contributions to start the city's country and western music museum and hall of fame came from the Colonel and Elvis: checks for $1000 apiece. She said the Colonel, one of the fifty original lifetime members of the CMA, also provided an imaginative fund-raising campaign. Elsewhere in Nashville the Colonel's old friend and advance agent, Oscar Davis, was partially paralyzed by a stroke in 1963, and when his friends held a benefit party, the Colonel said rather than contribute anything to it, he'd send Oscar a hundred dollars a month for life. Still elsewhere in the same city, Minnie Pearl said the Colonel has been sending her a big check each Christmas to be given to one of her pet charities, a home for unwed mothers. "He helps people," she said. "He hears of a widow who's gonna lose her home and he'll pick it up."

Once he was settled at MGM, the Colonel began staging what he called "moving drills." That meant if the Colonel ever encountered any friction from the studio, he could have every last eight-by-ten autographed picture, carved elephant and stuffed teddy bear packed in trunks and ready for a move to another studio in twenty minutes.

"Everybody ready to move?" the Colonel would shout.

"Yes, sah!" said someone back.

"Somebody grab the pitchas!"

"Yes, sah! Yes, sah!"

# Chapter 16

# PRISCILLA

Over the years, Elvis's name had been linked with dozens of women, some well known, some not so well known, many of them his leading ladies—Juliet Prowse and Tuesday Weld among them. Almost all the relationships, no matter how superficial and innocent—as most apparently were—were heavily publicized, either by an eager actress's press agent or the nosy fan magazines. For years, from 1956 through the period when Elvis was churning out so many films, the stories in these publications were of the "Why Elvis and I Can't Marry Now by Anita Wood" and "Why Troy's Women Prefer Elvis's Kisses" and "The Night Ann-Margret Confessed to Roger Smith, 'I Can Never Forget Elvis'" variety.

Occasionally Priscilla Beaulieu was mentioned, but even though it was commonly known that she continued to live at Graceland, most didn't take her too seriously. She was still young, after all, and friends said Elvis enjoyed being a bachelor, as was abundantly clear from his open dating in Hollywood.

At the same time, Priscilla did grow up, completing high school, taking classes in a "finishing" school and karate, eventually taking LSD with Elvis and Jerry Schilling and his wife and another friend, part of Elvis's interest in spiritual growth.

So there came a time when Elvis stopped taking girls to Memphis between movies, when he and Priscilla started wearing matching rings, and in January 1967, when Elvis's sixteen-year-old cousin Brenda Smith was hospitalized, she received flowers with a card signed "Love, Elvis and Priscilla." Even some of those closest to Elvis hadn't realized that the relationship had moved past the point expressed in his early song, "Baby, Let's Play House."

On Sunday, April 30, the Colonel sent telegrams to his closest friends and associates: Abe Lastfogel, head of the William Morris Agency; Harry Brand, head of publicity at Fox; Grelun Landon and Harry Jenkins, both of RCA; Stan Brossette, the MGM publicist who'd worked with the Colonel on the past several pictures, among them.

"He asked us all to go to the airport and he told me to bring two photographers who could be trusted," said Stan Brossette. "And at the airport we were asked to go to Las Vegas. Rona Barrett had been on the air saying Elvis was getting married in Palm Springs, but we didn't think that was right. Or we wouldn't have been going to Vegas. We thought that's why the Colonel wanted us, but we really didn't know. He didn't tell us and we didn't ask. We were just doing what he wanted done."

It was three o'clock the following morning when Elvis and Priscilla and four members of the wedding party arrived from Palm Springs in Las Vegas in Frank Sinatra's Lear jet. Friends met them at the airport and drove them immediately to the Clark County courthouse, where Elvis paid fifteen dollars for the marriage license. There was no blood test, no waiting period in Las Vegas. They then were driven to the Aladdin Hotel on the Vegas Strip, where Elvis and Priscilla and their parents went off to separate suites to get ready, and the rest of the party saw to the catered breakfast that was to follow the wedding ceremony a few hours later. It was soon after that the newsmen began to arrive from downtown Las Vegas and Los Angeles—some of them diverted from Palm Springs.

"We were met at seven," said Stan, "and taken to the rear entrance of the Aladdin and put in separate rooms. Then we were told to meet the Colonel in the coffee shop. By now the hotel lobby was packed with press, but the Colonel wasn't talking. We had breakfast and then were returned to our rooms and told to call no one. Shortly after that he finally told us. I still don't know why the mystery. It was just something the Colonel did."

The double-ring ceremony began at 9:41 A.M. in the second-floor private suite of Milton Prell, the principal owner of the casino and hotel and a longtime friend of the Colonel's. It lasted eight minutes, was conducted by Nevada Supreme Court Judge David Zenoff and had Elvis and Priscilla promising to "love, honor, cherish and comfort." The word "obey" was not used.

Joe Esposito and Marty Lacker, the only two members of the Mafia present at the wedding, were dual best men, although Lacker, at the time, knew he would soon be let go; all the others who'd flown to Las Vegas at Elvis's invitation were barred at the last minute, the Colonel claiming that his friend's suite wasn't large enough to accommodate all, and not wishing to show favoritism, he excluded all. Priscilla's only sister, Michelle (she had four brothers), was her maid of honor. Altogether, there were but fourteen persons present.

If the ceremony was simple and traditional—forgetting for the moment the rather bizarre location; one would have expected a church in Memphis—what followed it was not. As soon as they said their "I do's" and kissed, they were escorted under guard to the Aladdin Room, where there was a five-foot-high six-tiered wedding cake decorated with pink and white frosting roses, and a breakfast for one hundred (including press, although the photographers had to leave their cameras outside) that reportedly cost $10,000.

Elvis and Priscilla and their families sat at a long head table, the guests at nine round tables, all covered with pink tablecloths. The food was served buffet style—although there were twenty waiters in white gloves serving champagne and tending to the smaller details—and included ham and eggs, Southern fried chicken, roast suckling pig, Clams Casino, fresh poached candied salmon, Eggs Minette and Oysters Rockefeller.

Circulating through the huge ballroom was a string trio playing romantic ballads, including "Love Me Tender."

Following breakfast there was a brief press conference. One of the photographers shouted, "El, give her one more kiss on the cheek and slide over a bit, please. Big smile now—look happy!"

Elvis replied, "How can you look happy when you're scared? I'm a little bit nervous, you know. There's no way out of it. We appear calm, but Ed Sullivan didn't scare me this much."

"Why did you give up bachelorhood?" a reporter asked.

"Bachelorhood," Elvis said.

And then the Colonel jumped in and said, safely, "Can't give it up without gettin' married."

"Why did you wait this long to get married?"

"Well," he said, "I . . . I just thought . . . the life I was living was . . . too difficult, and I decided it would be best if I waited till I . . . I really knew for sure. And now I'm really sure."

Following that the photographers began calling orders again, urging Elvis and Priscilla to shove cake into each other's mouth, and the Colonel called a merciful end to it.

Elvis and Priscilla went to their rooms, changed clothes, reappeared at two-thirty, got into a chauffeured Lincoln Continental and returned to Palm Springs for a four-day honeymoon in the great circular house that Elvis had leased. Then they flew to Memphis to spend some additional time at Graceland and on a nearby ranch Elvis had bought.

Elvis had purchased the 163-acre ranch near Walls, Mississippi, in February. He had become a familiar figure riding horses on the Graceland grounds and occasionally had gone riding at local stables, but neither seemed suitable; there wasn't room enough at Graceland, nor privacy anywhere else. So he paid $250,000 for a one-story one-bedroom board-and-brick residence, some cattle barns and the land, and immediately had it surrounded by an eight-foot cyclone fence.

The ranch—called Twinkletown Farm and soon to be named the Circle G (for Graceland)—was situated five miles south of his Memphis home, just below the Mississippi state line. The land formerly had been used for growing cotton. In recent years it had been in pasture as a cattle ranch, and once Elvis took over—hiring a local cowhand to look after it—he bought some horses, cattle, tractors, trailers and trucks.

When Elvis and Priscilla returned to Los Angeles, shortly before Elvis was to begin work on his next film in June, Elvis faced two problems—resolving the turmoil within the Memphis Mafia caused by the sudden marriage, and finding a new home. The first was trickier than the last.

In a sense it was too late to soothe all the hurt feelings caused when Priscilla came between Elvis and his buddies. It was no secret that some didn't care for Priscilla, that she didn't care for some of them. It was also logical to expect Elvis wouldn't want a bunch of grab-assing menservants thumping around the living room once he'd selected a wife. Nor was it odd when Priscilla expected the payroll to be cut—and not for budgetary reasons. But that didn't halt the trumpeting and quarreling, and when it was all over, there were only two remaining on salary in California—Joe Esposito, who continued as Elvis's secretary-bookkeeper-confidant, and Richard Davis, who served as his valet and began working more closely with Elvis in his films. Alan Fortas stopped taking care of Elvis's cars and went to the Circle G Ranch to help with the livestock. The others either remained in Hollywood as extras and stunt men or returned to Memphis to go into the recording business. Marty Lacker became general manager of Pepper Records, for instance, and Red West eventually found himself on the staff of the American Recording Studios as a producer-songwriter. In time the size of the Presley household staff—not counting the usual maids and cooks—would increase to four or five again, but the Mafia was part of the past.

Elvis had promised his wife a new home and the one finally settled on was a huge multileveled house pitched on the topmost slope of a mountain in the Trousdale Estates, at 1174 Hillcrest Road. Trousdale was then one of the newest, and certainly one of the most expensive, of several sumptuous real estate developments undertaken in Southern California in the 1960s. The house originally had been built, on one of the choicest lots, for $169,000, but the next owner sank $200,000 into it, building in all the furniture and keeping workmen there for nearly eighteen months. It was in a California version of French Regency styling and had a huge pool, four cavernous bedrooms, half a dozen baths, a large living room with an adjoining bar decorated in black glass, and offered (when the smog cleared) a breathtaking sea-to-city view. There also was an expansive brick patio behind electrically operated gates—first metal, later wood—and another of Elvis's high storm fences. Additional privacy was provided by the stand of Tuscany cypress trees. For a while Harry Karl and Debbie

Reynolds lived up the street, and Hal Wallis owned the vacant lot next door, but most of his neighbors were industrialists, businessmen, doctors and developers. The house was only six years old when Elvis and Priscilla moved in and because the owner wanted to vacate immediately, he let Elvis have it for $400,000.

Only Elvis's personal life and California mailing address changed during the first half of 1967. Everything else remained much the same, as the drooping film scripts and weak musical material continued to come his way.

Perhaps it was in the music that the story was most embarrassing, for it was in recording that Elvis got his start and generally was regarded as being strongest. When he married in May, he hadn't had a number one record in more than five years. And although many still had sold in excess of a million copies, several of *those* were songs recorded years earlier. The last million-selling record he received, for instance, was for sales of "Wooden Heart," but this was a song originally recorded in 1960 as a part of the *G.I. Blues* soundtrack album, when it became a monstrous hit single in Europe—*and* it had been released in the U.S. not once, but twice, in 1964 and 1965. It was as if RCA was determined to make it a million-seller because Elvis was getting so few.

The second most recent million-selling record was "Crying in the Chapel," released in April 1965, but recorded, according to Gordon Stoker, *before* Elvis went into the Army. He said legal problems kept it from being released sooner. Nearly all the other gold singles awarded from 1962 to 1965, when they stopped, were from the *Girls! Girls! Girls!*, *It Happened at the World's Fair*, *Fun in Acapulco*, *Kissin' Cousins* and *Viva Las Vegas* soundtrack albums. Most were as bland as the movies.

Nor were things improving on the movie front. Elvis reported for work in *Speedway* in June, and it was essentially the same as all the rest. In this picture, director Norman Taurog's eighth, Elvis was a hotshot stock car driver from Charlotte, North Carolina (where some of the racing footage was filmed), who because of his manager's (Bill Bixby) fondness for horse racing, owed the Internal Revenue Service $150,000. The IRS sent an undercover agent (Nancy Sinatra!) after Elvis and it was touch and go there for a while, but Elvis won the race, paid his manager's debt with his winnings and got the girl. Of course the racing champ and the lady tax agent sang a few songs along the way, enough to fill up one side of an album.

Said the *New York Times*: "Music, youth and customs were much changed by Elvis Presley twelve years ago; from the twenty-six movies he has made since he sang 'Heartbreak Hotel,' you would never guess it."

Elvis was prankish by nature and his friends say the tedious film assignments only made him more capricious on the set. Jack Good said of his experience on *Clambake*: "You could tell he was being bored out of his mind doing these pictures. That was the reason, I suppose, he was so ready to gag around a bit. Because what else was there to do? Nothing. Same old stuff. Elvis in boat. Elvis waving at girls. Elvis driving up. Elvis driving away. Elvis hitting somebody. Somebody hitting Elvis. That's about all it was, wasn't it? And Elvis sort of warbling away in that curious baritone voice. What a shame."

And so they joked. Red West said of the same film, his last with Elvis: "It was the wildest we ever done. We'd get up on the rafters, Richard and I and Billy, and we started out throwing water balloons down on the people, then it got to pies filled with shaving cream. Arthur Nadel, the director, came on the set one day with an ol' rain hat, coat and rubber boots. He said 'Roll 'em,' and somebody hit him with a water balloon. Another time, when somebody was supposed to come through a door, they put blood all over me like I'd been in a fight. They started the cameras and Elvis was acting his foot off when I come staggering in the door and fell down. He broke up."

Bill Bixby said, "In *Clambake* they all had water pistols. You'd come around a corner and you'd get it. And then it was a small glass of water and the next thing you know it was a hose. I remember once when we were on a sound stage doing the water ski shots and it went from water pistols to buckets. It was all over the stage, and afterward we had to get everything in one take so we wouldn't fall behind. And then in *Speedway* it was constantly cherry bombs. My dressing room door would fly open and in would come a cherry bomb and there I was in an eight-by-eight room with the door shut.

"It wasn't Elvis that threw the stuff most of the time," Bill said, "but you knew that the guys only did what pleased him, did things he inspired or suggested."

The jokes are not the only thing Bill recalled. "First I found him to be a gentleman and then a gentle man," he said. "I found he could be sensitive to small issues. For someone of his stature there is very little for him to notice, y'know? He's so insulated by the people who surround him and by his own popularity. And yet Elvis will still find little things. He'll take the time to be very gentle with people. Especially with children. The fact that you can perform with a child doesn't mean you're going to act with that child in the same way personally, and Elvis did. And he certainly didn't have to.

"At that time I knew how much Elvis wanted a baby. When I was doing that picture, Elvis had gotten married, snuck off as it were. It was very, very private. But after it was announced, he talked an awful lot on the set about how much he wanted a baby."

Elvis had good reason to be talking about babies, and wanting one, because Priscilla was pregnant by then, something Elvis announced in July. "We really hadn't planned to have a baby this soon," he said. "But less than a month after we were married [and before Elvis started *Speedway*] Priscilla came back from the doctor in Memphis and told my father and me the good news. I was so shocked I didn't think I could move for a while. Then it began to dawn on me that this is what marriage is all about."

As for the Colonel, who always had something to say, he said he already had a contract drawn up "for the new Presley singer."

The news had been withheld for six weeks, Elvis told a writer at the time, because they weren't sure. "We'd been back there [Memphis] a while when Priscilla went to the doctor and he made a test and told her the results were positive. Isn't that right? Isn't it positive? Or is it negative? Anyway, he told her it looked as though she were pregnant but he couldn't be absolutely sure, because an early test isn't always accurate. The excitement of the wedding and all might have affected the results. She went back to the doctor for another test and that one was positive too. Still she wasn't sure. She went to the doctor a third time and he told her, 'You've flunked this test three times. You're pregnant.'"

Bill Bixby said, "After he found out, he was ecstatic. Elvis was happier than I had seen him." Bill said Elvis always wore his wedding ring, right up to a take, then put it into his pocket, replacing it afterward. "He seemed totally content. I remember him whistling and humming. He was thinner and everything seemed to be falling into place."

It was just before Elvis went into his second film of the year, in September, that he used his fists again. It was on a Sunday, September 17, in Memphis, when a former yardman at Graceland went to Vernon's house to see about getting his job back. Vernon told him the job wasn't open, that he had known it was a temporary job for four months only, while the regular man, who was African-American, was sick. The yardman Troy Ivy said he thought it was "pretty raw" to give a black man his job, and left.

About a half hour later, Ivy appeared at the Graceland gates and, according to Elvis's report to the sheriff, the man was "drunk, belligerent, arrogant, cursing loudly and he took a swing at me." The way Elvis told it, Ivy missed and Elvis responded, knocking the man to the ground with one punch.

Elvis returned to California for *Stay Away, Joe*, a film in which he played a shabby Navajo Indian brave who returned from the rodeo circuit to his Arizona reservation with twenty heifers and a bull he had promoted from his Congressman. The idea was that if Elvis and his Indian father (Burgess Meredith) were successful in raising cattle, the U.S. government would help the whole reservation. Of course Elvis barbecued the bull and sold the cows to buy some plumbing and other home improvements and then, for good measure, started chasing the girlfriends of his fellow braves.

"I look at my old movies and I can pick up on my mistakes," Elvis said at the time. "There's a lot I'd like to change. I want to grow up on the screen. When I see my old movies, something is always happening to me, someone's always telling me what to do. Girls are chasing me. Bad guys are after me. Now I'm getting away from that. In this picture I'm a kind of sharp Navajo, a wheeler-dealer who's always promoting something. It's a more grown-up character—part Hud, part Alfie. He's a man, not a boy, and he's out looking for women, not just waiting for them to stumble over him.

"In most of my pictures I'm singing in every other scene, but in this one I do only three songs and I get to do a lot more acting. There isn't a guitar in the whole picture."

Elvis completed the picture in November, about the same time *Clambake* was released to the usual mixed reviews, and returned home to Memphis to supervise the auction scheduled for November 5 on his ranch. From the thousand or so items put on the block: a battered guitar, a hundred doors and a blue bathtub taken from Graceland in a recent remodeling, several pairs of boxing gloves, two catcher's mitts and, pointedly, five house trailers that Elvis had bought to house the members of the Mafia when they stayed at the ranch; the auctioneer reported at day's end he had collected more than $100,000.

This was, by now, the sum that Elvis was giving to charity each year. Even back in the hysterical 1950s Elvis was—like the Colonel—a charitable man, usually giving rings and cars away. Although sometimes he was more imaginative, as when he contributed a trunkful of teddy bears to be auctioned by the National Foundation for Infantile Paralysis and gave a kangaroo he'd received from an Australian fan to the Memphis zoo. Then in 1961 he headlined a benefit show for Memphis charities at the city auditorium. Since then Elvis had contributed money rather than do any more benefits, always matching, and often exceeding, the sum he would have raised by singing. The two local newspapers, the *Commercial Appeal* and the *Press-Scimitar*, supervised a massive collection each Christmas and usually Elvis or his father took the checks down personally. Almost always each check was made out for $1000 and often there were more than a hundred of them. They went to, among others, church building funds, the YWCA, the Boy Scouts, Baptist and Catholic children's homes. Goodwill Industries, the Salvation Army, the Memphis Heart Association, a home for incurables, homes for the aged, the Muscular Dystrophy Association, Jewish community centers, day nurseries and schools for retarded children.

Nor were the Christmas checks the end of it. In 1964 he bought the yacht President Roosevelt used during World War Two, the *Potomac*, for $55,000 and, following a comedy of errors that had the March of Dimes and the Coast

Guard Auxiliary in Miami refusing it, he gave it to St. Jude's Hospital in Memphis. In Hollywood in 1965 he gave $50,000 to the Motion Picture Relief Fund and a year later pledged 2 per cent of his salary for one picture to the same fund—which brought his total contributions to the hospital and home for failing movie people to $240,000. And he still was giving cars as gifts, the way some people buy flowers.

His philanthropic activities were not totally secret, of course; when Vernon or Elvis walked into the Memphis newspaper offices with a fistful of $1000 checks every Christmas, it was not the sort of thing the press easily overlooked. So the city tried to respond by naming something after him.

Over the years, various Memphis agencies and bureaucrats had nominated nearly a dozen buildings, parks and roads—even the Lauderdale Courts—to carry the Presley name. At one point Mayor William Ingram took it upon himself to rename the Mid South Coliseum the Elvis Presley Coliseum, but even that was overruled when a city commissioner said Park Commission policy provided that buildings be named only for the deceased.

Elvis was showing himself to be a religious man too, even if he had long ago given up attending church services. An album of spiritual songs, released in March, *How Great Thou Art*, was played on nearly 350 radio stations in fifty states, without commercials, paid for by Elvis and the Colonel. (The album won a Grammy the following year for Best Sacred Performance.) And for Christmas the stunt was repeated, this time including some of Elvis's earlier Christmas songs and more than 2000 radio stations were used.

He was a millionaire possessed of unfailing politeness and an unimpeachable love of God, mother and country, and he had a beautiful, gracious Southern *pregnant* wife.

He began appearing on the best-dressed lists.

Album titles of the early movie period: *Something for Everybody* (1961), *Elvis for Everyone* (1965).

Even Hedda Hopper, who slapped Elvis around verbally in the fifties, loved him in the sixties, devoting several Sunday columns to saying how swell a fella he'd become.

Said a movie executive who worked closely with the Presley camp for several years: "The Colonel didn't want Elvis to come out sounding like Jesus. It's pretty bland. But everybody assumed that's what the Colonel wanted, and that's exactly what he sounded like, and maybe that's what he had become."

Elvis Presley once may have represented some sort of threat to the American Way, but now he was a part of the Establishment.

# Chapter 17

# CHANGES

E lvis remained at Graceland all during January 1968, Priscilla's last month of pregnancy, and at eight-thirty the morning of February 1 Elvis and Priscilla got into a blue 1968 Cadillac driven by Charlie Hodge and were taken to Baptist Memorial Hospital. They were followed by a black Cadillac carrying Richard Davis and Jerry Schilling, with Joe Esposito at the wheel. The second car was a reserve vehicle, in the unlikely event Elvis's car should break down.

Within half an hour Priscilla had been admitted and two uniformed but unarmed off-duty city policemen were stationed at the entrance to the maternity ward. Elvis was then taken to the doctors' lounge to wait, where he was joined by Joe, Charlie, Jerry and Richard, and later by Patsy and Gee Gee Gamble, Marty Lacker, Jerry Schilling's wife, Lamar Fike and George Klein, and finally Vernon and Dee, whose telephone had been out of order and therefore were among the last to be notified.

Outside the hospital, reporters were swarming all over the steps.

Eight hours later, at 5:01 P.M., the child was born, weighing six pounds fifteen ounces, and named Lisa Marie, a name Elvis and Priscilla said they picked from a baby book, although the Colonel's wife's name was Marie. Vernon and Dee were dispatched to tell the reporters the news. Elvis sent one of the boys for cigars, called his grandmother, who was bedridden with a broken hip at Graceland, tried to reach the Beaulieus in California, and then went to see his daughter.

It had been nine months to the day since he and Priscilla were wed.

The guards remained on duty outside Priscilla's room the four days she stayed there, keeping hundreds of fans away. Priscilla, meanwhile, had a closed circuit television set placed nearby, giving her a round-the-clock view of the hospital nursery. Downstairs at the switchboard the calls came in from all over the world. At Graceland thousands of cards and hundreds of pink booties and dolls and blankets and dresses arrived.

Elvis's first film in 1968, started a few weeks after Lisa Marie was born, was *Live a Little, Love a Little*, another bit of fluff from the MGM mattress. In it Elvis was a photographer with two bosses, the publisher of a *Playboy*-type magazine (Don Porter) and a high-fashion advertising executive (Rudy Vallee!). It was, vaguely, based on Dan Greenburg's novel *Kiss My Firm but Pliant Lips* and was shot for the most part in an authentically garish estate that seemed much like those in Trousdale. And Vernon had a bit part but no lines.

At first glance it seemed the pattern was unbroken. But there had been a shift of direction—made when Elvis did *Stay Away, Joe*. It was in that film the dialogue implied Joan Blondell had been an "older woman" in Elvis's life and he was, besides that, actually seen romping (if clothed) on a bed with Quentin Dean, a teenager. In *Live a Little, Love a Little* the script included several "dammits" and one "how the hell" and had Elvis rising from a bed recently shared with Michele Carey, the shapely starlet who pursued him through most of the movie.

Not too many months before, an MGM executive was quoted as saying, "He has never made a dirty picture. They never go to bed in a Presley picture."

"I don't think I'm changing my image," Elvis told a writer at the time. "I think you have to mature a little bit."

No matter what he said, his image *was* changing and in the next picture, *Charro*, filmed in the summer of 1968, Elvis abandoned several more "trademarks." Usually in his films Elvis was given a nice wardrobe, but in this one, a western, he wore the same greasy leather pants throughout. He also appeared in the film unshaven, looking much like the former outlaw type he was supposed to be. Not only was his face partially hidden in the scruffy beginning of a beard, his hair was covered by a hat. Nor were there any pretty girls in bikinis. And he didn't sing.

"A different kind of role . . . a different kind of man" was the way the advertising read.

In the next picture, capriciously titled *The Trouble with Girls (And How to Get into It)*, Elvis was the manager of a Chautauqua troupe that gets mixed up in the affairs of one of the towns it visits. Elvis does get into some "trouble" with girls (Marlyn Mason and Nicole Jaffe), but nothing to warrant the film's title. In fact, Elvis didn't even appear in the picture until halfway through. It was a bad film, even if Vincent Price and John Carradine had bit parts, and Elvis sang a couple of songs and looked great in long wide sideburns and an ice cream suit and hat. But there was a nod toward the new image. It came when Elvis was massaging Marlyn Mason's shoulders and suggested they continue their conversation in bed.

Something else happened in 1968 to change the Presley image more than any cinematic propositions could. It had been announced by the Colonel in January that NBC-TV would finance and produce a one-hour special to be broadcast during the Christmas holidays and later would finance and produce a motion picture as well—a combination making it possible for the Colonel to keep the salary near the million-dollar level. Elvis's films had been dropping in popularity, and profit, lately and unless the Colonel agreed to do a film *and* a special, probably the million-dollar figure would not have been met anywhere in Hollywood. Whether or not the move was forced, however, it was one of the most astute made by the Colonel in years. It initiated what afterward came to be called Elvis's "comeback."

Steve Binder had directed a late night series for Steve Allen and NBC's popular rock show *Hullabaloo*, along with *The T.A.M.I. Show*, a concert film with James Brown and the Rolling Stones, among others, that went into theatrical release. He also produced and directed a Petula Clark special—during which there was an incident over guest star Harry Belafonte touching Petula on the arm—when he got the call to serve in the same categories for Elvis. At the time, his partner was Bones Howe, the record producer who'd worked with Elvis in the late 1950s and early 1960s, and it was understood he would supervise the music on the show. The call came from Bob Finkel, who had produced *The Jerry Lewis Show* for ABC and who was to be executive producer in title, the vice-president in charge of keeping Colonel Parker amused in fact.

"The way I felt about it," said Steve, "was I felt very, very strongly that the television special was Elvis's moment of truth. If he did another MGM movie on the special, he would wipe out his career and he would be known only as that phenomenon who came along in the fifties, shook his hips and had a great manager. On the reverse side, if he could do a special and prove he was still number one, he could have a whole rejuvenation thing going."

"And," said Bones, "we both felt that if we could create an atmosphere of making Elvis feel he's part of the special, that he was creating the special himself—the same way he was organically involved in producing his own records in the old days, before the movies—then we would have a great special. People would really see Elvis Presley, not what the Colonel wanted them to see."

Both Steve and Bones seemed miffed at the Colonel in retrospect. They say he had his ideas of what the special should be like and he wasn't moving: Elvis would come out, say "Good evening, ladies and gentlemen," sing twenty-six Christmas songs, say "Merry Christmas and good night." Steve and Bones felt this would be disastrous and said Elvis should talk more and perhaps sing only *one* Christmas song.

"I in no way wanted to do a show full of Christmas songs," said Steve. "I wanted to leave that to the Andy Williamses and the Perry Comos, the people who you know do weekly television and sing Christmas songs at Christmas time. The one thing I knew that I wanted was Elvis to say something—let the world in on that great, great secret, find out what kind of a man he really was."

For weeks it went back and forth, and even when the conceptual differences were settled and it was agreed Elvis would sing only one holiday song, there were other problems. Elvis's friend Billy Strange, who had done the music for *Speedway* and *The Trouble with Girls*, was fired as the show's musical director and replaced by Billy Goldenberg, who previously had worked with Steve but at first was convinced he had nothing in common musically with Elvis. Steve wanted some new songs written and talked about Elvis singing songs already recorded by other singers, and the Colonel insisted Elvis sing only material *he* published. There was a battle over whether there'd be a soundtrack album and if so, who would pay for it. Elvis normally paid for all his sessions, providing RCA with a completed master tape, but in this instance NBC paid for the sessions and *then* the Colonel claimed the tape was his and Elvis's. NBC had its own huge orchestra and objected when Steve and Bones said they wanted to hire extra musicians, people Elvis knew. Sponsor representatives from Singer worried about (Steve's words) "offending the little ladies in the Singer Sewing Centers across the country."

The show was to tell the story of a young man leaving home and what happens when he enters the outside world. "The first thing the boy does," said Steve, "he walks into a whorehouse. It did not say whorehouse. There was no suggestion that he was physically going to take one of the girls and go to bed. In fact, it was pointed up that the girl he zeroes in on is Purity, the girl with no experience, and before the moment of truth, the place is raided and he's back on the road to his next adventure. That scene was taken out in editing. It happens to have been the best scene I've ever been responsible for. If I didn't say I was doing a bordello sequence, and said I was doing a number with twenty girls and Elvis, there would have been no fuss. I made an error and said what I was doing. It was that special moment in the show. People would have remembered it for years. At the same time, of course, Dean Martin can play with a girl's boobs on the air and people say it's great clean American fun."

And then Steve decided to take out the one Christmas song, confronting the Colonel with his decision with Elvis present. "The Colonel was furious," said Steve, who was being called "Bindel" by the Colonel now. "He said Elvis *wanted* to do a Christmas song and so we were going to *do* a Christmas song. Elvis was just sitting there, head hanging down, and the Colonel said, 'Isn't that right, Elvis?' Elvis just nodded, and when the Colonel left, he looked up and said, 'That's all right . . . we'll take it out.'

"With all his hollering and threats and the rest of it, the Colonel let the show be done. He's a sly old fox. He is the wizard in *The Wizard of Oz*. He *is* Frank Morgan, the guy behind the big black velour with lots of gadgets and neon signs lighting up and all, and he's putting on the whole world. So there were showdowns. Everything was meetings. If a microphone was placed six inches to the left and it was supposed to be six inches to the right, there was a meeting to discuss it."

The meetings with Elvis were more relaxed—so relaxed, in fact, Billy Goldenberg said, he was convinced the time to tape the show would come and they'd still be sitting around telling stories and plunking guitars. The first several of these were held in an office Steve and Bones shared on the Sunset Strip.

"When I sat down with Elvis," Steve said, "I wanted to find out where he was at musically, because a lot of people who are said to be part of today can never really get past yesterday. I said to Elvis, 'Would you do all the songs you have done in the past again?' He said 'Certain ones I would do, a lot of them I would never do again.' I said, 'If I brought you "MacArthur Park" today and nobody had touched it yet, would you record it?' He said yes. I knew we were home free. If Elvis would think of 'MacArthur Park' for himself, I knew he wanted to be part of what's happening right now."

One day, Steve said, he asked Elvis what he thought would happen if they walked out on the Strip. Elvis seemed apprehensive, but he said he was willing to find out. "So we did it," said Steve. "Four o'clock in the afternoon and there we were, standing outside the Classic Cat [a topless bar]—Elvis, Joe Esposito and me. We stood there to the point of embarrassment. Kids were bumping into us and saying 'excuse me' or not even saying that. Elvis started talking louder than normal, trying to be recognized or noticed or something. But nothing happened. Nothing. Zero."

Finally the meetings ended, with several ideas down on paper, and Steve went to the Colonel to say he was having Billy Goldenberg start writing music for the show.

"The one thing I'd always felt about Elvis is that there was something very raw and basically sexual and mean," said Billy. "There's a cruelty involved, there's a meanness, there's a basic sadistic quality about what he does, which is attractive. You know the story *In Cold Blood*? I've always felt Elvis could very well play one of those guys, that he is that kind of person. Most of Elvis's movies have shown him as the nice guy, the hero, but really that is not where he shines best. He's excited by certain kinds of violent things. The karate is just one example. It's all over him. I thought, if there was a way we could get this feeling in the music . . ."

Billy also told a story about sometimes finding Elvis alone in a studio playing Beethoven's "Moonlight Sonata." "He'd get to a certain point and he'd not know how to do it and I'd show him the chord and he'd do it over and over again until he got it. And then some of the guys would come in and he'd stop, as if it were a sign of some weakness."

With the musical direction formed, there were two other decisions made that gave the show much of its subsequent power. The first came as a suggestion from Bill Belew, the costume designer, that Elvis wear a black leather suit. Elvis never had worn leather before—that was Gene Vincent's trip—but Bill thought he had, and it was approved. The other decision was Steve's, and that was to assemble a number of the guys from Elvis's present and past—Lance LeGault, Scotty Moore, D. J. Fontana, Alan Fortas—and to surround Elvis with these guys during rehearsals and, perhaps, during a part of the show itself. The Jordanaires were asked, but the invitation came so late, they'd already committed themselves to thirteen studio sessions that week in Nashville. The idea was to keep Elvis comfortable during rehearsals and to see if the interaction between Elvis and his friends could be translated into program content. Said Steve: "I thought it would be an excellent way to get Elvis talking, sitting there with the guys he knew, but it was an experiment only. We weren't really sure what would happen."

"A whole week we were there," said Scotty. "We did our rehearsing at night, if you would call it rehearsing. What it amounted to was we'd set up the guitars in the dressing room and everybody'd set back and start yakking. Just bangin' around. It was like old times. First somebody'd think back on a good story on the other one, tell it, then maybe sing a couple of songs."

The sessions in Elvis's dressing room that would inspire the show's first half hour lasted four and five hours and audiotapes reveal them to be as spirited as they were directionless. There was a lot of laughter, with lines about executive producers and waitresses and people standing naked in windows, and Elvis sang and sang and sang. Many of the songs, like the people around him, were from his past: "Love Me," "When My Blue Moon Turns to Gold Again," "Are You Lonesome Tonight," "I Got a Woman." That was what Steve and Bones had been looking for.

By now the recording sessions for the production numbers that would provide the show's second half largely were completed. The days were long, beginning at noon and usually running until after midnight. With musicians Elvis knew from previous sessions—including some of the best studio rhythm men in Hollywood: Hal Blaine on drums, Don Randi on piano and organ, Tommy Tedesco and Mike Deasy on guitars, Larry Knectal on bass—Elvis seemed quite comfortable.

"It was like a live performance," said Bones. "I gave him a hand mike and when he sang he performed. He didn't just stand there. He worked out—complete with twists and turns and knee drops."

There was one more battle to be fought—over how the show would end.

"I wanted Elvis to say in his good night something about who he was," said Steve. "He could say, 'Peace . . . good will toward men,' anything he wanted. And the Colonel would have no part of it. He still wanted Elvis to sing 'Silent Night' or some other Christmas song, and say good night, and I kept saying everybody does a Christmas song at the end of their show and when Elvis ends that show, it's got to blow everybody's mind. So I got Earl Brown, who was my choral director, and I took him aside and said, 'We're under the gun now and I want you to go home tonight and write me the greatest song you ever wrote to close the show.' And I explained what I wanted Elvis to say. Next morning at seven o'clock Earl woke me up and said, 'I've got it.' I rushed to the studio and Earl played for me 'If I Can Dream.'"

Steve took the song to Bob Finkel, who said the Colonel would "blow his stack." So Steve next went directly to Elvis, took him into a quiet room with a piano, and once again Earl played and sang "If I Can Dream." The song was, essentially, a plea for peace and understanding—key lines were "If I can dream of a better land / Where all my brothers walk hand in hand"—certainly not a message alien to a show planned for December broadcast. But it did represent another shift in direction for Elvis, a move toward making the personal—social—statement Steve was looking for.

"After Earl played it, Elvis said to play it again," Steve said. "Earl played it six times for Elvis and Elvis sat there. And then he said, 'I'll do it, I'll do it.' Unbeknownst to us the Colonel was saying at that very moment to Finkel and Tom Sarnoff and all the rest, 'Over my dead body will Elvis sing an original song'—right there in the next room. So now I open the door and say Elvis has a new song for the end of the show. I couldn't have said a worse thing. But nobody wanted another confrontation. And Elvis had already said yes. So they said, 'Let's hear it.' And before it had been played all the way through, one of the guys from RCA had the title registered in one of Elvis's publishing companies."

All during this time, of course, the Colonel was up to his usual tricks—some of them expensive enough, Steve said, to warrant his having a special slush fund in the show budget to cover them.

"It was a sideshow with the Colonel carrying on with Finkel," said Bones. "The Colonel would say, 'Finkel, give me twenty dollars.' Finkel isn't about to *not* give the Colonel twenty dollars, so he reaches into his pocket and peels a twenty from his gold Florentine money clip. The Colonel puts it on the table and said, 'I'm thinking of a number between one and ten. What's the number?' Finkel said, 'Four.' The Colonel said, 'Wrong number. Seven.' And he puts the twenty in his pocket. So now Finkel is sucked into the game called Honesty. The Colonel said, 'It's called Honesty, Finkel. I got to be honest with you. Give me another twenty and tell me what number.' Of course Finkel wins a couple of times. But the Colonel took Finkel for about six hundred dollars in Honesty money before the special was over. The Colonel has tremendous insight to people's personalities. He knew somehow that Finkel's weak spot was money."

Another time, Bones said, the Colonel pulled a trick on Finkel he said he normally reserved for freeloaders who came around looking for favors. "The Colonel had this incredibly delicious champagne and offered Finkel a glass. And Finkel expressed genuine enthusiasm. So the Colonel said, 'Really like that champagne, huh, Finkel? I gotta see you get some.'

"And two days later there's a full case waiting for him at home. Finkel chills it and tells his wife the Colonel has given him a case of the best champagne he's ever tasted. They light candles, do the whole bit, and they sit down to have a glass before dinner and it's water. Every bottle in the case is filled with water."

The production numbers were taped first. And in some of these the supporting cast was huge, with dancers and singers all over the place. (At a get-acquainted party held at the start of rehearsals there were so many people—thirty-six dancers, thirty-five musicians, a total of eighty performers in the "Guitar Man" opening alone—everyone wore name tags, including Elvis: "Hello! My Name Is Elvis. What's Yours?") In one number, there were several wardrobe changes for Elvis. In another, his name in lights formed a background twenty feet high.

The day of the live videotaping, before an audience, Elvis was not so sure of himself. "He was really frightened," said Bones. "He sat in makeup sweating. He said, 'I haven't been in front of those people in eight years.' He said, 'What am I gonna do if they don't like me? What if they laugh at me?'"

"Of course he'd performed on movie sets," said Scotty, "and sometimes there's three, four hundred people there, but that's different."

"That's right," said D. J. "Those people are working, they're paid to laugh and scream. But those people out there in the studio were real live people, man."

The ticket holders—including Diskin and his family, who had to wait with all the rest—filed into the NBC studio and took seats on bleachers arranged around three sides of a fifteen-by-fifteen-foot white stage rimmed in red. At the last minute the Colonel suggested the prettiest girls in the audience be moved close to the stage, even to sit on the edge of it.

"That was a stroke of genius on his part," said Bones. "'Get them close to Elvis,' he said. The Colonel was moving around the crowd like a carnival barker, picking the faces he wanted, saying, 'Who here really loves Elvis?'

"So Elvis finally came out in that leather suit, all his guys were there on the fourth side of the stage, and when he reached for that hand mike, his hand was actually shaking. You could see it on the camera. But then he started singing and it was all over. He was terrific."

Lance LeGault was seated to Elvis's right, with a tambourine. Charlie Hodge was there with a guitar, along with Scotty Moore. Alan and Lamar and the others were there too, laughing, talking, feeding Elvis lines and reacting to those he contributed himself. The songs came naturally and powerfully, including many of the early hits: "That's All Right [Mama]," "Blue Suede Shoes," "Heartbreak Hotel," "Love Me," "Are You Lonesome Tonight," "Lawdy, Miss Clawdy" and, pleasing the Colonel, "Blue Christmas."

And they talked—about the time the crowd destroyed D. J.'s drums and when Elvis was censored at the Pan Pacific Auditorium in Los Angeles. They shouted, whistled, and echoed one of Elvis's favorite expressions: "Mah boy, mah boy!" Charlie remembered the time when a girl got into the house and got on the intercom and said, "I'm in the house, where's Elvis?" Elvis came right back: "I told her, I said, 'If you're lookin' for trouble . . . you came to the right place . . .'"

It was like the evening sessions in the dressing room, only now Elvis was performing—moving across the stage as some sweaty, sexy fertility god, hair the color of India ink, black leather shining in the strong spotlights.

"He was so frightened when he went out and so with it once he got there," said Bones, "he was shot when it was over. He came off the stage, we practically had to carry him off. While we were slapping each other on the back. It was like we'd won a football game."

Altogether, counting both audiences, Steve taped nearly four hours of this. Most of it was thrown on the floor and in the edited show, ready three months later in September, the "live" segment was under a half hour long. But it opened the show and was the most impressive part of it. The "experiment" had worked.

"After it was all over," Steve said, "Elvis asked me what I thought as far as the future was concerned. I said, 'Elvis, my real, real feeling is that I don't know if you'll do any great things you want to do. Maybe the bed has been made already, maybe this'll be just a little fresh air you'll experience for a month. Maybe you'll go back to making another twenty-five of those movies.' He said, 'No, no, I won't. I'm going to do things now.'"

The show was broadcast Tuesday night at nine o'clock, December 3, opposite *Red Skelton* and *Doris Day* on CBS, and *It Takes a Thief* and *N.Y.P.D.* on ABC, swamping everyone, and was followed by a Brigitte Bardot special that gave NBC the evening. The same week, the soundtrack album was released. Elvis had gone back into the studio after the show to re-cut the vocal to "Memories," but the rest was as it had been pre-recorded for the production numbers and sung live for the sections with an audience. Both the special and the album were received favorably.

"There is something magical about watching a man who has lost himself find his way back home," said Jon Landau in *Eye* magazine. "He sang with the kind of power people no longer expect from rock 'n' roll singers. He moved his body with a lack of pretension and effort that must have made Jim Morrison green with envy. And while most of the songs were ten or twelve years old, he performed them as freshly as though they were written yesterday."

"It wasn't the old Elvis, trading on the nostalgia of early rock and obsolete Ed Sullivan censorship," said the writer in *Record World*, "it was a modish performer, virile and humorous and vibrating with the nervousness of the times."

The *New York Times* said that Elvis "helped bring the pop world from illusion to reality" and called Elvis "charismatic."

Two other Elvis stories appeared in the same December 4 edition of the *New York Times*. One reported that readers of the *New Musical Express*, England's top music paper, had voted Elvis the number one male vocalist of the year. And Mike Jahn quoted Tom Diskin in an interview as saying Elvis's movie income was dropping noticeably enough for the Colonel to consider some personal appearances.

"For the time that goes into it," Diskin told Jahn, "it's more profitable for him to appear in public. It takes Elvis fifteen weeks to make a movie, on the average. If he appears for ten weeks, one concert a week at $100,000 each, he can do much better."

Diskin said Elvis had two more films to do, but that they were "keeping open" the possibility of a concert tour in eight or nine months. Such a tour, he said, would take that long to plan properly and, besides, it would be better to wait until summer, so concerts could be staged comfortably in baseball parks, then thought to be the only locations where $100,000 a night could be guaranteed.

Elvis himself said in 1968, "I'm planning a lot of changes. You can't go on doing the same thing year after year. It's been a long time since I've done anything professionally except make movies and cut albums. From now on I don't think I'd like to do as many pictures as I've done—almost three a year. Before too long I'm going to make some personal appearance tours. I'll probably start out here in this country and after that, play some concerts abroad, probably starting in Europe. I want to see some places I've never seen before. I miss the personal contact with audiences."

There was another noticeable shift in 1968 and that was in the recordings released. There were several besides the soundtrack albums. There was a grab bag of leftovers called *Elvis Sings Flaming Star and Others*, an album released by Singer to promote the special, and Volume Four of the *Elvis' Gold Records* series, which contained twelve songs released over an eight-year period, only three of which actually sold a million copies.

But if these albums were disappointments, most of the singles released in 1968 were not, beginning in January with the gutsy foot-stomping version of Jerry Reed's "Guitar Man." For those looking for meaning in song lyrics, this one seemed precisely right for Elvis: "I've come a long way from the car wash / Got to where I said I'd get / Now that I'm here I know for sure / I really ain't got there yet / So I think I'll start all over / Sling my gi-tar over my back / Gonna get myself back on the track / Ain't never, never gonna come back."

In March Elvis released another of Jerry Reed's country rockers, "U.S. Male." This was followed by three others—"You'll Never Walk Alone" for the Easter season, "Your Time Hasn't Come Yet, Baby" and "A Little Less Conversation," all somewhat disappointing in sales. But then in October, near-ly a full two months before the television special was aired, RCA released "If I Can Dream." By December it had reached the number twelve position in *Billboard*, his highest position in five years. "If I Can Dream" also gave Elvis his first million-selling single in more than three years.

And then in January 1969, Elvis walked into a recording studio in Memphis for the first time since he had left Sun fourteen years earlier. To many it meant that Elvis had gone "home."

Chips Moman and his American Recording Studio in Memphis were in the middle of a long winning streak, although you couldn't tell it by looking at the facilities. The cluttered orange-and-black studio was in a state of continual breakdown and repair and the offices were next door over a restaurant, with the only entrance at the top of a rickety fire escape, situated in one of the city's poorest, blackest neighborhoods. The boulevard that ran past the studio may be named for Danny Thomas and many top recording stars may have record-ed here, but the glamour of Hollywood was far away.

Still, when Elvis entered the studio January 13, Chips, one of the owners, was as a producer-engineer working his way through what would be a string of ninety-seven chart records in a period of just twenty-eight months. A group Chips found and recorded, the Box Tops, accounted for several, and some oth-ers were by Dionne Warwick, Joe Tex, Wilson Pickett, Joe Simon, Roy Hamilton, Neil Diamond and Merilee Rush. Chips said there had been so many hits, not because the funky studio had any special "sound"—as many claimed—but because the house band was so good. It was this backup group, he said, and the experience every man in the band had, that attracted Elvis.

Some of the musicians Elvis had known for years, even if he hadn't worked with them. Reggie Young and Bobby Emmons, a guitarist and organist, were in the late Bill Black's combo. (Bill had died in an automobile accident.) Gene Chrisman, the drummer, worked with Jerry Lee Lewis. Bobby Wood was a piano player who had a few small hits of his own. Mike Leech was a bassist who'd worked in local clubs for several years. And helping Chips with production was one of the top guitarists and bassists in the country, Tommy Cogbill. For the sessions with Elvis, Chips added some brass—Wayne Jackson, Ed Logan, Bob Taylor—and brought in part of the string section of the Memphis Symphony Orchestra, along with several backup singers, including Ronnie Milsap, a white blues singer Chips produced for Scepter Records. The names weren't well known outside Memphis, but the sound was.

Elvis booked the studio for ten days and had laryngitis on four of them. But with sessions beginning at eight at night and running until dawn, he still cut thirty-six songs, enough material to fill two albums—*From Elvis in Memphis*, released in May, and half of the *Memphis/Vegas* set released in October—account for several singles, and still have songs left over. It was, flatly and unequivocally, Elvis's most productive recording session ever. It also made it abundantly clear that the days of the "Fort Lauderdale Chamber of Commerce" and "No Room to Rhumba in a Sports Car" movie sound-track songs were over.

There were unadorned country songs such as "Long Black Limousine," which told the story of a hearse bringing a girl friend home, and Eddy Arnold's composition "I'll Hold You in My Heart (Till I Can Hold You in My Arms)." There were raunchy blues songs: "Power of My Love" and "After Loving You." There were lush ballads, Neil Diamond's "And the Green Grass Won't Pay No Mind" and Burt Bacharach's "Any Day Now," as well as John Hartford's modern country classic, "Gentle on My Mind." And there were some more songs by Mac Davis, a young Texan who said he was moved to write his first song after seeing Elvis perform in Lubbock in 1954.

Elvis had recorded three of Mac's songs already—"A Little Less Conversation," "Memories" and "Charro," the last two to be released in March—and was working with Billy Strange when Chips called for material.

"Chips said he wanted some country songs," said Mac. "I didn't know what he meant, so we sent a tape with seventeen of my songs on it. The first two songs on the tape were 'In the Ghetto' and 'Don't Cry, Daddy.'"

Mac said he had played "Don't Cry, Daddy" at Elvis's house months earlier and that Elvis's reaction was that he wanted to do it sometime because it made him think of his mother. And "Ghetto," he said, had been rejected by Bill Medley, who "thought he'd already done enough protest-type material."

After the session, Elvis and Priscilla went to Aspen, Colorado, for a month's vacation, and Elvis learned to ski.

The movie *Charro* was released in March and only a few critics seemed to believe Elvis's first non-musical represented much of an improvement. The title song, backed with "Memories" from the television special, barely limped into the top forty. In April, two more singles were released—Elvis's annual Easter record, pairing the title songs from his two religious albums. *His Hand in Mine* and *How Great Thou Art*, and the "protest song" that Bill Medley had rejected. For Elvis it exploded.

"In the Ghetto" told the story of a child born in the ghetto, a child who was "gonna be an angry young man someday" and learn how to steal and fight. The child grew up, bought a gun and got killed in a robbery attempt, the world looked the other way and next day another child was born in the ghetto. Many seemed stunned when Elvis released the song, but they shouldn't have been. It was really a logical extension of "If I Can Dream." Still, disc jockeys who had in the post-Beatle/post-Dylan days become somewhat "hipper than thou" as regards Elvis, began to play *this* record more than any Presley record of recent years. And it went to number three, selling a million and a half copies, fast.

Coincidentally, as "In the Ghetto" was becoming a hit, Elvis was in Hollywood, making a film (his thirty-first) about a ghetto. This was an improbable property called *Change of Habit*, taking its title from the fact that Elvis, playing a doctor working in the slums, falls in love with one of his nurses, who is, unbeknownst to him, a nun. If that premise wasn't enough to boggle the minds of Presley fans, what the three screenwriters did with it proved more than adequate. Elvis's nurse-nun-love interest, played by Mary Tyler Moore, was but one of three nuns who had changed to street clothes to work in the ghetto, and each had her moment—Moore when a speech defective being treated in Elvis's clinic tried to rape her, Jane Elliott when she was forced to slug a cheating grocer, and Barbara McNair when she confronted some of the local black militants. But it all worked out in the end. Elvis asked his nurse-nun-love interest to marry him, and although it wasn't spelled out, the viewer was left with the impression she was going to leave the order and do so. Elvis sang three songs in the film and was sporting a new hairstyle, longer and bushier.

After this, Elvis and Priscilla went to Honolulu with Patsy and Gee Gee for two weeks, then returned to Memphis, where he sold the Circle G Ranch and moved the horses back to the Graceland stables. Elvis's visits home now followed a rigid but comfortable pattern. Elvis would rise from bed in the afternoon, go for a swim in his pool, eat breakfast, and at five-thirty or six ride down to the front gate to sign autographs and talk with visiting fans. Occasionally, when the crowds got so unwieldy as to cause the state police to send cruisers to sort out traffic, Elvis had the gates opened, so everyone could come in. Then maybe some of the guys would come over for some pool or television, until midnight, when Elvis's Midnight Movies began at one of two theaters downtown.

The Midnight Movies had become a tradition. "It's what Elvis did after he stopped renting the Rollerdrome and the amusement parks," said Alan Fortas, who soon was to leave the Presley employ, now that the ranch had been sold. "Paul Shafer at the Malco Theater set it up for him. Every night Elvis wants to see movies, Mr. Shafer reserves the Malco from midnight on, however late Elvis wants it, and gets the pictures Elvis asks for. Usually they're all the latest movies, whatever's current. And he'd go down there with as many friends as'd be around, plus others who knew about it, fan club presidents and so on—maybe as many as forty or fifty people some nights. And we'd run the pictures one right after the other all night. They sit there sometimes from eleven o'clock, midnight, to five o'clock, maybe six in the morning."

On July 5, he left Graceland for Los Angeles to begin rehearsals for what was to be his first public appearance in over eight years.

# Chapter 18

# LAS VEGAS

I got tired of singing to the guys I beat up in the motion pictures," Elvis said the night he opened in Las Vegas.

The offers to do more movies weren't being made, either. What counts in Hollywood is not how big a star you are, it's how much your last picture made. So, as Elvis's box-office figures began to fall, encouraged by the reaction to the NBC special and with Elvis's assent, the Colonel negotiated a contract with the International Hotel, a thirty-story building that was to be the largest hotel (1519 rooms) in Las Vegas but then was still under construction. It was, on completion, the first major Las Vegas hotel built off the Strip. It cost $60 million, and at 346 feet was the tallest building in Nevada. It had the world's largest casino, and in the middle of its eight-and-a-half-acre rooftop recreation area was a swimming pool that held 350,000 gallons of water, the largest man-made body of water in the state, aside from Lake Mead. It had 240 miles of carpeting, more than 2500 employees, an eighteen-hole golf course, a convention hall that seated 5000, six major dining areas (not counting the Showroom Internationale, which seated 2000 and was to be Elvis's showcase for a month), a thousand slot machines and a computer-operated reservation desk.

Since then, Vegas hotel developers have exceeded such superlatives many times over. But at the time, there was nothing that came even close to the International and many thought it too big to fly. It seemed a suitable place for Elvis to use for his public return.

The Colonel made his deal with Bill Miller, the talent booker who had been the first to gamble then-unbelievable salaries on Red Skelton, Ray Bolger, Donald O'Connor and other stars who hadn't performed publicly in years, and then was the first to bring in the fleshy spectaculars. He was in semiretirement in the Caribbean when he was asked to book the International, to go after the names that would fill a showroom twice the capacity of any other in town.

As a rule, Miller didn't talk about the deals he made, but when Barbra Streisand opened the Showroom on July 2, it was generally known that her manager had negotiated a complicated million-dollar stock and capital deal for four years. Nick Naff, the International's publicity head, said the original deal with Elvis was for five years, one engagement a year, on an option basis. "But contracts like that don't mean much to the Colonel," Nick said at the time. "The Colonel likes to do it one show at a time." It is believed that Elvis was promised a million dollars too. And so that the Colonel could say he got more than Miss Streisand, the Presley-Parker forces were given more "extras," such as rooms and transportation.

The Colonel hired Sammy Shore, a noisy, hardworking comic who depends upon smoky barroom humor. Elvis picked the backup singers and found someone to organize the band. The male vocalists he selected were the Imperials, a quartet that had backed Elvis on the *Spinout* album and one of his religious LPs, *How Great Thou Art*. (Again the Jordanaires had been asked, but they felt they couldn't afford to leave Nashville for that long; Gordon Stoker called this one of the biggest disappointments in his life.) The four girls were the Sweet Inspirations, then under contract to Atlantic Records. And the bandleader was James Burton, one of the best and most popular of studio guitarists in Los Angeles.

"First I got a call from Tom Diskin," James said, "asking if I'd be interested in putting a group together. I said yes and then I got a call from Memphis. It was Joe Esposito on the line and I'd never heard of Joe Esposito and all he said was, 'There's somebody here wants to talk to you.' And Elvis said hello. We talked, kicked it around, and after about forty minutes, I felt I knew what he wanted."

What Elvis wanted, James said, was a rock 'n' roll band, and the four men he hired were, if not always the first asked, among the best available.

James's roots, like Elvis's, were in country rock. He grew up in Shreveport and remembered seeing Elvis on the *Louisiana Hayride* Saturday nights. The first record he played on, when he was fifteen, was Dale Hawkins's "Suzie Q," in 1957. He then went to Hollywood to make an exploitation film with country singer Bob Luman (*Carnival Rock*) and there met Ricky Nelson, who asked him to join his band, which he did soon thereafter. He even moved in with Ricky and his brother David and their parents Ozzie and Harriet for a year. The past several years he had done almost nothing but studio work, always turning down tours and personal appearances. He once refused three months with Bob Dylan because the money didn't match studio work. He recently had bought a big home in the Toluca Lake section of Los Angeles, not far from Bob Hope's old place. He preferred his 1949 Cadillac over his other half dozen cars, was married and had two children.

Jerry Scheff, the blond, mustachioed bassist, was raised in northern California, spent four years in the Navy band playing string bass and tuba, then traveled for two years with what he calls "two-bit, small-time Dixieland and lounge groups," finally coming to Los Angeles to become a studio musician after his instruments and clothes were burned in a Palm Springs night club where he'd been working. Four years as a studio man came next, with six months out in 1969, touring as one of Delaney and Bonnie's friends. He was married and a father of two.

Ronnie Tutt, the bearded drummer, was another of Delaney and Bonnie's friends and was from Dallas, where he was a bass singer and sometime percussionist for a company that produced commercial jingles. He was moving his wife and six children to Los Angeles when he got the call to audition for Elvis's band and, in effect, stopped in Vegas for a month *en route* to California, where he became another busy studio musician.

Larry Muhoberac, who backed Elvis on piano, organ and electric piano, got the call to join the band from Tom Diskin, who remembered him from ten years of working with Elvis off and on—dating back to when Larry was the youthful musical director of the benefit show Elvis did in Memphis in 1961. Larry also had played with the Woody Herman, Hal McIntyre and Ralph Flanagan bands and served as an executive in the jingle factory Ronnie worked in. Larry was raised in New Orleans, was married and had four children.

The only member of the band who couldn't be tagged a studio musician was John Wilkinson, who was essentially a vocalist, signed, like Elvis, to RCA Victor. He provided what James Burton called "basic rhythm guitar" and like most others in the band, although none of them was miked, added some back-up harmony.

Serving as an ex-officio member and combo factotum, and playing acoustic guitar, was Elvis's buddy from his Army days, Charlie Hodge.

The boys had a lot in common. They were, most of them, Southern, or were rooted firmly in the basic country and blues traditions from which Elvis had come. In fact, every one of them named Elvis as a major reason they were in the business. They were somewhat older than many of their contemporaries—in their late twenties to early thirties—and possessed a certain reserve, a maturity that matched Elvis's. They were, most of them, family men: settled.

Elvis rehearsed with his band for two weeks in Los Angeles, playing and singing more than a hundred songs, picking twenty or so that he would use as the core of the show, including nearly a dozen of his old hits, the rest more recent songs, with a small selection of songs made known by other vocalists. He worked on the "choreography," which because he never really choreographed anything in the traditional sense, meant there were some karate-like moves he wanted to incorporate. And then he took the band to Vegas, where they rehearsed another two weeks with the Imperials and the Sweet

Inspirations and finally with the hotel's twenty-five-piece orchestra.

One of the members of the band, Larry Muhoberac, would be replaced for the next Vegas engagements by Glenn D. Hardin, who said, "Elvis likes to rehearse himself, and he likes to hang around guys and sing. So he don't rehearse just the songs he's gonna do. He likes to rehearse anything anybody can name. If you take off playin' 'Stagger Lee,' he enjoys that and he'll just sing it, man, for about an hour and a half. He gets a big kick outa that. And by doin' that, when you get on stage with him, you feel like you done ever' song in the world. 'Cause he may just jump inta one of them one night. He feels very comfortable. I think he's figured all that out: He can bust inta anything he wants to and the band'll be able to play it."

When rehearsals were finished, Elvis had lost fifteen pounds and he had never looked better.

"We were opening a new hotel," said Nick Naff, "and we read all the signs. We figured Barbra Streisand was the hottest entertainment property in the world. She'd just won an Oscar, she had three pictures going, her name was fantastic. And Elvis was an unknown stage property. We weren't sure. We knew he'd be a draw, but my God . . ."

"With Streisand," said Glenn D. Hardin, "they couldn't keep the sumbitch full. But with Elvis it was full, full, full. Elvis was the magic word."

The fans had come from Europe and Australia. Hotel employees were taking calls from all over the country from people begging for reservations that no longer existed. The opening week was sold out and the rest of the month nearly so.

Still, no one was taking risks. There had been something of a "rock revival" going on in the last months of 1968 and much of 1969—a popular reaction to the over-intellectualization of rock music that had set Dion, Rick Nelson, Little Richard, Bill Haley, Fats Domino, Carl Perkins, Chuck Berry and others striding along the comeback trail. Elvis had been getting some promising press as well, thanks in part to improved record material and the television special, but also because of the renewed interest in rock's roots. Elvis had even been praised at length and often in the underground press, which surprised even the Colonel. So it was agreed that no reporter, whether he represented the *New York Times* or the *Los Angeles Free Press*, couldn't attend the opening if he wanted to. To make it easier, Kirk Kerkorian, the hotel's owner, made available his private plane, reportedly the first DC-9 in private ownership, remodeled to accommodate twenty luxuriously.

"Who could turn down such an offer?" asked Robert Christgau in *The Village Voice*.

The Showroom Internationale was a masterpiece in ostentation, a monstrous multileveled restaurant and balcony that seated two thousand nearly comfortably and offered as part of the decor a phony Roman colonnade, some larger-than-life-size figures in Louis XIV velvet and lace, paintings of Greek ruins which made a travesty of artistic perspective, and hanging precariously above all this, some scattered cupid-like angels. The menu offered a narrow but gout-inducing selection of wines and foods that began with *Fonds d'Artichauts Farcis Walewska* and closed with *Savarin Glace Napoleon*.

Finally a disembodied voice: "Ladies and gentlemen, welcome to the International Hotel and the Elvis Presley show with Sammy Shore, the Sweet Inspirations and the Imperials."

The gold lamé curtain rose, tucking itself away in the ceiling, to reveal the Bobby Morris orchestra in tuxedos, the four Sweet Inspirations bopping toward the audience, looking much like a road show version of the Supremes, singing show tunes. Sammy Shore came next. He knew the invitation-only crowd was there to see Elvis and he aimed some of his material that way: "The Colonel came up to me and said, 'I like your kind of humor.' I said, 'Why, thank you. I like your chicken.' And the Colonel said, 'You do? Well, lick my fingers.'" And then he said, "Youth is wasted on the young. Give us what the kids got and you know what you'd have? A lot of old people with pimples."

As Sammy was keeping the older folks laughing—boring or antagonizing the younger ones—Elvis stood in the wings. He was drumming his fingers against his thighs nervously. He watched Sammy, probably not seeing or hearing him, then disappeared farther backstage to talk to one of the boys positioned there for security, then he reappeared again, still drumming his fingers.

Sammy closed with a routine that used evangelism as its base, blue humor and a lot of tambourine-banging as its means of delivery, and got off. The curtain fell, there was a frantic moment rolling out the piano and drum kit and getting set, musicians and singers scuttling back and forth, stagehands moving microphones, and then the curtain went up again.

The band was pounding out a rolling, thunderous "Baby, I Don't Care" rhythm and without a word from the disembodied voice, Elvis sauntered to center stage, grabbed the microphone from its stand, hit a pose from the fifties—legs braced, knees snapping almost imperceptibly—and before he could begin the show that he had pushed through three full-dress rehearsals that afternoon, the audience stopped him cold. Just as he was to begin his first song, he was hit in the face with a roar. He looked. All two thousand people were on their feet, pounding their hands together and whistling, many of them standing on their chairs and screaming. And he hadn't even opened his mouth.

Finally the ovation subsided, the band picked up the beat and Elvis hit the pose again: "Waaaaaaaal, it's one for the money . . ."

The leg snapped.

"Two for the show . . ."

The leg snapped again, and he thumped his acoustic guitar.

"Three to get ready, now go cat go . . . "

It was as if the audience had fallen through a time warp, leaving the sixties for the fifties, appearing somewhere on the biting edge of memory that went with high school and the beginnings of rock 'n' roll. It was a shortened version of "Blue Suede Shoes," lasting only a minute and a half, and as the audience was applauding, Elvis walked to his right, toward Charlie Hodge, who handed him a glass of water.

"During the show you'll see I drink a lot of wa-wa," he said, using his daughter's word for water. "That's because the desert air is very dry and it affects my throat. I've also got some Gatorade. It's supposed to act twelve times faster than water." He held the bottle aloft. "Looks as if it's been used already to me . . . but if it aids my gator . . ."

The comment was made offhandedly in the familiar slurring drawl that had come out of Mississippi and gone through so many movies, emerging nearly fifteen years later as the voice of a relaxed yet polished performer. Backstage, the boys were laughing at the joke. "Gatorade . . . used already . . . whew!" Haw haw haw.

Elvis went into his second song, "I Got a Woman," and then, almost as an afterthought, something he'd forgotten, he said, "Good evening, ladies and gentlemen. Welcome to the big, freaky International Hotel, with those weirdo dolls on the walls, and those funky angels on the ceiling . . . and, man, you ain't seen nothin' until you've seen a funky angel."

The next song was "Love Me Tender" and this was for the fans. Elvis spotted a pretty girl near the edge of the stage and knelt down and kissed her. He kissed a second, and a third, and a fourth, working his way along the stage. Still singing.

And from that right into a medley of his early hits—"Jailhouse Rock," "Don't Be Cruel," "Heartbreak Hotel" and "All Shook Up." Here and there the lyrics were altered slightly, as if Elvis was playing with the songs, not regarding them so seriously as perhaps he did in the 1950s.

Then, mock serious, he said, "This is the only song I could think of that really expresses my feelings toward the audience."

He sang "Hound Dog."

It was just the way it had been in the fifties, when "Hound Dog" was the song he used to *close* his shows. The same gutsy power was there, along with just a shade of parody. Elvis was singing the song because he enjoyed it and because he thought it funny. Later in the month he would tell the audience, as he went to get some water, "When I drink wa-wa, just say to each other, 'Is that him, is that him? I thought he was bigger than that.'" Elvis knew there was something that was bigger than reality involved: the image. And Elvis was ready to laugh at it.

The next song was "Memories."

After which he looked at the floor and spotted the letters "B.S." in marker pen. "It said 'B.S.' here," he told his audience. "Do you think they're trying to tell me something?" There were scattered chortles. "Oh . . . maybe it stands for Barbra Streisand." There was a roar of laughter.

Right into "My Babe," an up-tempo song that had been a hit for the Righteous Brothers.

Then "I Can't Stop Loving You."

The audience was reacting—creating and distributing energy in massive waves—and Elvis was reacting to that. His voice was deeper, richer, more sensual then it was in ten years of soggy films, gutsier even than nostalgia gave it credit for being before the soggy films began. And behind and all around it was the tight, basic yet soulful rhythm of James Burton and his good ol' boys, and the scaling, precisely timed harmony of the Imperials and the Sweet Inspirations, filling in every musical crack, building a melodic yet roughhouse wall of sound.

"I'd like to do my latest release," he said, catching his breath and drinking some Gatorade. "It's been a big seller for me." And then he added modestly, "Something I really needed."

"In the Ghetto."

And from that right into the song he said would be his next single, "Suspicious Minds." Elvis was forty minutes into his show and the audience was in disarray. Bouffants were tilting, neckties askew. People were sweating. Women were wriggling on the edge of their seats, debating whether or not to make a dash for it. Elvis was wearing a modified karate suit, tied at the waist and slashed down the front, all black. With all that black, black hair covering the tops of his ears, shaggy, almost Beatle-length, the lean features of his face, and the moves—the legs spreading, stretching, actually *vibrating*—it was enough to make any female itch. All that was needed was a final push.

A six-minute version of "Suspicious Minds" provided it. In this, a heavy production number utilizing the full orchestra, Elvis told the story of getting "caught in a trap," loving a girl and knowing it couldn't go on—with suspicious minds. He also turned the stage into a karate mat, kicking and slashing and tumbling like a man fighting his way out of the most incredible Western brawl ever devised in Hollywood. Never missing a note.

There was another standing ovation.

Elvis was panting now, gulping for air, trying to swallow more Gatorade. And grinning.

"Yesterday," he sang, "all my troubles seemed so far away . . ." It had come full circle. Elvis, who had been the inspiration for the Beatles, now was singing a Beatles song. And then he sang a second one, "Hey Jude." Not the entire song. Just the title and the rhythm sounds ("Na na na na nanana na . . ."), over and over again. If before, the showroom resembled an orgy scene, or at least a Pentecostal revival at fever pitch, now it was a giant sing-along.

As Elvis finished the next song, "Johnny B. Goode," an old Chuck Berry hit, many were calling requests. Elvis nodded his thanks but went on, diving into one of his earliest songs, "Mystery Train," which ran directly (same rhythm line) into "Tiger Man."

"I'm the king of the jungle," Elvis sang, "they call me Tiger Man . . ."

He closed with "What'd I Say" and two thousand people were on their feet. Elvis bowed and left and came back and sang the song he intended to close with anyway, the song he would make his permanent closer, "Can't Help Falling in Love."

The critics were ecstatic. "Elvis Retains Touch in Return to Stage," *Billboard* headlined, pointedly placing the review on its country music page, where Elvis first appeared exactly fifteen years earlier. Said David Dalton in *Rolling Stone*: "Elvis was supernatural, his own resurrection . . ." Ellen Willis in *The New Yorker* said that if Elvis continued to perform, and "Suspicious Minds" was as big as it should be, he again would have a significant impact on popular music. *Variety* called him a superstar, said he was "immediately affable . . . very much in command of the entire scene," while proving himself to be one of the most powerful acts in Vegas history. "There are several unbelievable things about Elvis," said *Newsweek*, "but the most incredible is his staying power in a world where meteoric careers fade like shooting stars."

If there were any doubts remaining, the hotel extended its option for a second booking the day after the opening, raised his salary to $125,000 a week, then extended the contract to two performances a year for the next five years, guaranteeing Elvis $1 million for eight weeks work per year through 1974.

As the month wore on—two shows a night, seven days a week—Elvis relaxed more. Friends said he was extremely nervous opening night, quoting him as saying he wasn't sure he could "cut it" any more. They said he also was aware that many of those coming to see him were doing so because they figured Elvis was some kind of freak, pushed on stage once each decade now, and that it was a bizarre curiosity rather than an interest in him or his music that attracted them. But from the first night, it became absolutely clear that Elvis would do more than serve as a contemporary version of the two-headed cow, or any other act in a sideshow.

Elvis changed the songs each night. Seldom, if ever, were the same ones sung in the same order. Sometimes he sang a Bee Gees song, "Words," other times the eight-year-old Del Shannon smash, "Runaway," or a song that was one of the first really popular rhythm and blues hits, "Money Honey," or some of his own early hits ("Love Me," "Loving You," "That's All Right [Mama]") or some that he'd recorded recently in Memphis. But usually the songs were familiar. And always "Suspicious Minds"—released two weeks later—was the one that caused the greatest excitement.

He added a mini-autobiography that sometimes rambled so much he sounded stoned: "Like to tell you a little about myself. I started out . . . in childhood. I started out when I was in high school, went into a record company one day, made a record and when the record came out a lot of people liked it and you could hear folks around town saying, 'Is he, is he?' and I'm going 'Am I am I?' . . . whew [out of breath] . . . Elvis deterioratin' at the Showroom Internationale in Las Vegas . . . where was I? . . . oh, anyway, made a record, got kinda big in my home town, few people got to know who I was, that's w-u-z, was. See, so I started down in the wuz . . . ah shucks, what I mean to tell you is I was playin' around these night clubs, alleys and things. Did that for about a year and a half, then I ran into Colonel Sanders . . . Parker, Parker . . . and he arranged to get me some [blows nose] Kleenex . . . he arranged to get me . . . whew, I'm tellin' you . . . shot to hell, this boy can't even finish a sentence straight . . . anyway there was a lot of controversy at that time about my movin' around on stage so I . . . cleared my throat again, looked at my watch and ring and the guy said . . . the guy said? . . . the guy said nothin' . . . I'm the guy! I'm telling you, you better get this together, boy, or this is gonna be the last time they let you up on a stage.

"So, as I said, I went up to New York, did the Jackie Gleason show three times . . . whew, sure has been a long time . . . anyway, did that couple of times . . . had pretty long hair for that time, and I tell you it got pretty weird. They used to see me comin' down the street and they'd say, 'Hot dang, let's get him, he's a squirrel, get him, he just come down outa the trees.' Well, anyway, did the Ed Sullivan show. They just shot me from the waist up. Ed's standing there in the wings sayin', 'Sumbitch! Sumbitch!' I didn't know what he was sayin' so I'd say, 'Thank you very much, Mr. Sullivan.'

"Next thing they dressed me up in a tuxedo and had me singin' to a dog on a stool. You know I'm singin' to this dog and the dog is goin' 'Whhhoooaaaugh!' and I'm goin' 'Whhhoooaaaugh!' Then I got into the movies—*King Creole, Jailhouse Rock, Love Me Tender, Loving You,* loving her . . . so I done four movies and I was feeling pretty good with myself, had a pair of sunglasses and was sittin' there in my Cadillac going, 'I'm a movie star, hot damn!' and the driver's goin', 'Whew, watch that squirrel, man, he's just outta the trees.' I was livin' it up purty good there for a while and then I got drafted, and shafted and ever'thing else. One thing I found out, though, is that guys really miss their parents in the Army, they're always goin' around callin' each other 'Mother.' When I got out I did a few more movies, and a few more movies, and I got into a rut, you know there's this big rut just the other side of Hollywood Boulevard . . . POW! . . . you know they let me do my thing here for a while and then they put me away for another nine years . . ."

Elvis, who had—according to the myth—never said more than "yes, sir" or "yes, ma'am," couldn't shut up. It boggled the mind.

Elvis amused himself—as well as his audience—in many ways. He mopped sweat on borrowed napkins, once even blew his nose, and returned them to their ecstatic owners. He changed a word in "Yesterday" so he sang, "Suddenly, I'm not half the *stud* I used to be." He walked over during a song and goosed one of the Sweet Inspirations. He introduced Charlie Hodge as Kate Smith. And the kisses became as much a part of the performance as "Suspicious Minds" and karate chops. One night, when one of the women said she wanted seconds, he practically lifted her off her feet, bit her playfully and threw her back to her husband.

Once during all the kissing, Priscilla ventured forward. Elvis kissed her along with the others and said, "Don't I know you?"

At the end of the month-long run, the hotel announced that Elvis had attracted 101,500 customers, far more than Barbra Streisand had, and more than anyone else would.

The night after he closed, Elvis went to Nancy Sinatra's opening in the same showroom—with Mac Davis on the show with her—and backstage gave her the printing plates from the ad he had taken out in the local newspaper advertising her show. He then flew to Los Angeles and from there went to Palm Springs to relax for three weeks, flying to Graceland on September 23. And then, before leaving in October for three weeks in Honolulu and two more in Nassau with Priscilla, Patsy and Gee Gee, he spent two days in Nashville, re-recording most of the vocals for what would be released in November as the first of his "live" Vegas albums.

In the late autumn and winter months—with no movies scheduled, nothing to do until he went back to Vegas the end of January—the product continued to pour out. By now "Suspicious Minds" had gone to the top of the record charts, giving Elvis his first number one record in nearly seven years, since "Good Luck Charm" in 1962. It was followed by "Don't Cry, Daddy," the weeper Mac Davis had written more than a year earlier and which Elvis had recorded in Memphis in January. It went to number six and was, like

"Suspicious Minds," certified a million-seller.

And then in December Elvis's thirty-first movie, *Change of Habit*, was released. Because of the enthusiasm over his Las Vegas appearances and renewed interest in his recordings, the film was practically—and kindly—overlooked. And where it was noticed, it was criticized sharply or laughed at, a ghost from Elvis's past.

Elvis was back at Graceland for Christmas, resuming the Midnight Movies and spending some of his days planning the annual New Year's Eve party he'd been hosting the past few years. This year it was to be at T.J.'s, the supper and music club managed by Elvis's old buddy Alan Fortas. (Richard Davis was on the door.) Lamar Fike and his wife Nora came down from Nashville. Joe and Joanie Esposito were there, of course, along with Patsy and Gee Gee Gamble, Red and Pat West, Sonny West and his date, and Charlie Hodge. Other guests included Gary Pepper, one of his biggest fans, and several of the city's top musicians. Ronnie Milsap, who'd been making the club home base the past six months, performed and was joined by some of the people Elvis had worked with earlier, Chips Moman, Tommy Cogbill, Reggie Young. Even Mark James, who'd written "Suspicious Minds," got up and sang.

Five days later Elvis returned to Los Angeles to begin rehearsals for his second Las Vegas performance.

When it was announced Elvis would return to the International Hotel in January 1970, some said it was too soon, that he should have waited a year, as suggested in the original contract. They said the winter engagement would only disappoint those who recalled so vividly his return from "retirement." To go back in only five months, and to do so during the slack season, would be a mistake. But by mid-January, a week before opening, all but seven days of the twenty-nine had been sold out—nearly four thousand seats a night—and hotel and reservation clerks had been instructed to say further reservations could be made only by guests staying in the hotel. This wasn't a move to prop up sagging occupancy, but to give guests first crack at seeing Elvis, as is Las Vegas custom.

"Elvis changes the entire metabolism of the hotel," Nick Naff said at the time. "And he is singularly significant in one regard: there is constant occupancy. Tom Jones, they fly in, see the show, fly out again. Elvis has such a following, so many fans, for him they fly in, check in and stay two weeks, going to every show."

Most of the changes in the show were minor. Glenn D. Hardin took Larry Muhoberac's place at the piano and organ and began arranging some of Elvis's material, giving the hotel orchestra a more noticeable role in the show. Ronnie Tutt had gone to work for Andy Williams and was replaced on drums by Bob

Lanning. Elvis's wardrobe was somewhat flashier, with the addition of a couple of dozen macramé belts hung with semiprecious stones. The only major change was in the selection of songs.

Elvis had decided, wisely, that for his first engagement he would concentrate on his own hits, songs that were immediately recognizable as his—perfect for a return. The second time around much of the emphasis was shifted to songs made popular by other vocalists. So on opening night, a Monday, January 26, after he'd sung "All Shook Up" and "That's All Right [Mama]," Elvis said he wanted to sing songs not his own. He glanced at Dean Martin, seated in the booth next to that occupied by his family, and mimicked him: "Everybody needs somebody . . ." and then—bang!—into a version of "Proud Mary" that came on with the power of a trainload of gospel singers. (The Sweet Inspirations and the Imperials were back, along with the predictable Sammy Shore.) And later in the show he sang "Walk a Mile in My Shoes," "Sweet Caroline" and "Polk Salad Annie"—hits in the past year for Creedence Clearwater Revival, Joe South, Neil Diamond and Tony Joe White, respectively. Along with Ray Price's "Release Me," "See See Rider" and "The Wonder of You," this is the music that would form the centerpiece not only of the performances, but also a live recording, *On Stage—February 1970*. The rest of the material was from his own catalogue.

"I've never seen anything like it," said Emilio, the *maitre d'* at the International and an eighteen-year veteran of Vegas showrooms. "The phones ring all day and people begin lining up at ten a.m. for reservations. The response is stronger than last summer."

Elvis seemed more relaxed, even when the flu and a persistent cough hung on for the final days of the engagement. Often he would be hit with what those around him called the "sillies," sometimes laughing all the way through a show. Several times he toyed with women, teasing them. He'd unzip part of his jump suit, quickly zip it up again, and grin devilishly. Other nights his frenzied movements would cause the macramé belt to work its way around him until the ends were hanging down in front, whereupon Elvis would notice them, look embarrassed, grin, and with a quick movement swivel the sash ends to the side again and wink.

"He'd play a few tricks on the orchestra too," said Glenn D. "They'd be right in the middle of an orchestrated thing and he'd suddenly skip a verse. On purpose. He's got a thing about gettin' locked in—got to do this verse, that verse—and he'll take a notion he don't wanna do that tonight and so he'll skip one, leavin' them up there playin' somethin' where he ain't."

There were three songs during the month that took Elvis to the piano. He played and sang the raucous Lloyd Price hit, "Lawdy, Miss Clawdy," and for two other slower songs he merely played: "Blueberry Hill" and "Old Shep."

Elvis closed February 24, a day later than originally scheduled. The members of the band drove their cars to Los Angeles and flew back to Vegas on the twenty-sixth, boarded Kirk Kerkorian's DC-9 with Elvis and the singers and flew to Houston. It was there, in the Astrodome, that Elvis was to perform six times, the featured attraction of the annual Houston Livestock Show and Rodeo.

Like the International Hotel, the Astrodome was a logical choice, even if the acoustics in a sports arena—enclosed or not—always leave much to be desired. It was, like the hotel, a monument constructed of superlatives. For the three evening performances—there also were to be three matinees—the field was lighted by three hundred foot-candles, one third more than had been used before. There were 44,500 armchairs, sufficient number for over a hundred movie theaters. The temperature was a constant seventy-two, a one-mile-an-hour breeze provided circulation, and a smoke detector checked visibility and pollution, feeding information to a weather station computer in the roof, the first system of its type ever developed. Some of the box seats—which are leased for five years for $15,000 a year—were seven stories above the playing field. The eighteen-story Shamrock Hilton Hotel could be positioned in the middle of the field and not touch the dome or its walls. Even Billy Graham, a recognized expert on magnitude, was impressed, pronouncing the Astrodome "one of the great wonders of the world."

"The Astrodome was a purty crummy gig," said Glenn D. Hardin. "The Astrodome is just a big ol' giant terrible place to play. We rehearsed there for a minute to see how it was gonna sound one night and Elvis told ever'body, 'This is gonna be rather atrocious, so don't fight it, go ahead and play.' So we did. We just rolled out there on a trailer each night to do our number, and then split.

"They had wires and networks that run out in the field and the cowboys would just hook the trailer to a jeep. They'd dim the lights, they'd roll us out there and plug us in, and they'd put Elvis in a brand new red jeep with white seats. He'd ride all around and ever'body'd freak and he'd get on the trailer and bust inta 'Blue Suede Shoes.' You could hear the echoes bouncing all over the place. It definitely wasn't made for any serious giggin' inside. So he'd just sing it, knowin' it was terrible, and we'd go home."

Even when Elvis had engineers flown in from Los Angeles and Las Vegas to work on the sound system, it never was what it should have been.

However unfortunate the booking aesthetically, in other ways it made sense. Economically, of course, it was sound. Elvis was guaranteed $100,000 a show, plus a percentage of the box office. Because he broke so many records—playing to 207,494, nearly doubling the Vegas figure in one tenth the

number of appearances—he walked away with a reported $1.2 million. Glenn
D. said one of the reasons the Colonel agreed to the concerts was to pick up
enough money to cover the cost of paying everyone for the month in Vegas and
certainly this figure was adequate.

The engagement was important largely because it marked Elvis's first
appearance outside Vegas, which some took to mean a tour—or at least several other concerts—might be forthcoming. Otherwise it wasn't so extraordinary. Elvis held a short press conference; Priscilla flew in, partially dispelling
rumors that she and Elvis had separated; and the security was what it always
was—massive and airtight. Before Elvis returned to Los Angeles he had collected another box of awards for his trophy room—five gold records, a gold
deputy sheriff's badge (the Colonel got one too), a Stetson, and a King Midas
Rolex watch that was valued at $2500 and looked as if it had been carved from
a solid bar of gold and shaped to Elvis's wrist.

In March, the Colonel announced that Elvis would do a nationwide closed circuit television show that would bring him the largest sum—a million-dollar
guarantee—ever paid an entertainer for a single performance. Elvis was to
appear in the 5000-seat Las Vegas Convention Center a few days before opening again at the International Hotel next door, and the concert was to be
broadcast simultaneously to 275 cities, with a potential audience of (that magic
figure again) one million. Of course the idea was the Colonel's, but he called
two young Los Angeles concert promoters to implement it: Jim Rissmiller, a
former William Morris agent, and his partner Steve Wolf, who had a background in television. They both were in their middle twenties but had been
promoting concerts for three years, presenting, among others, Bob Hope and
the Rolling Stones.

They had been after Elvis for a fifteen-city tour, and when Tom Diskin told
them no, they presented an offer for one concert at the Anaheim Stadium,
home of the Angels baseball team. This time Diskin told them to be at the
Colonel's Palm Springs home the following Saturday.

As soon as they arrived, the Colonel, dressed in a turquoise T-shirt and a cap,
glasses pitched at the end of his nose, took them to the bedroom he'd converted
into an office. It was, like his office at MGM in Culver City, cluttered with photographs and mementos. Occasionally one of the Parker cats came in, or the
housekeeper arrived with cookies and milk. "It was," said Steve, "very folksy."

The meeting was equally casual. "We were going through our speech and
he was going through his press clippings," said Jim. "He was reading, saying
three hundred thousand this, four hundred thousand that, and passing the clippings to us as we talked. The more he showed us, the more excited we were get-

ting. And after we got through talking ourselves blue about Anaheim, he said he wasn't interested. He told us he owed the International to keep Elvis out of the area. And then he said what he wanted to do was a closed circuit show. He knew we had tried to set one up with the Rolling Stones and that, plus our Anaheim offer, made him think of us. We said okay, let's talk."

"We were prepared to negotiate," said Steve. "But the Colonel gave us the deal he had in mind and that was it, take it or leave it. We were to give Elvis a million. He also said he wanted us to pay costs of producing the show—musicians, singers and so on—approximately a hundred thousand more. It was fair deal, everybody would have made money, but he threw it out so fast we had to keep asking him over and over and he kept saying, 'I told you boys—now for the last time, this is the deal.' He really hits you. He doesn't sit back and let it sink in. You're almost sorry you asked."

Rissmiller and Wolf, who called themselves Concert Associates, went to their bosses, Filmways, with the deal they'd made, and the Filmways people "fell off their chairs. The scale was so large," said Steve. "The logistics of the thing were staggering."

A second meeting was called, during which Steve and Jim gave the Colonel a check for $110,000 representing one-tenth of the guarantee, the deposit the Colonel had asked. "The condition was we wouldn't get the money back if it fell through," said Steve. Those present at this meeting, all crammed into the same small bedroom office, included Diskin, the Colonel's secretary Jim O'Brien, George Parkhill of RCA, Steve and Jim of course, and two nervous Filmways executives.

At ten o'clock in the morning, less than a week later, when Steve and Jim entered their Beverly Hills offices, they were told the Colonel wanted to see them at eleven-thirty. This was for a meeting with Irving Kahn, president of TelePrompTer, the company that would provide the closed circuit equipment. The cast was otherwise the same, with the addition of Joe Esposito and a William Morris mail-room clerk who was responsible that day for serving the fried chicken, hot dogs, and hard-boiled eggs. The meeting was held in the Colonel's MGM office kitchen, "the cookhouse."

Apparently much of the meeting passed with Parker and Kahn, a flamboyant former press agent with 20th Century Fox, flattering each other. Then when they began to talk business, Kahn made a huge undertaking monstrous by suggesting the show also be sent to Japan and Europe by Telstar. Steve and Jim confessed to being somewhat bewildered by talk *that* big, but they agreed generally to everything that was discussed. And it was understood there would be future meetings.

"When Irving Kahn left," said Steve, "the Colonel told us what we'd done wrong in the negotiating. He also told us where he thought Kahn's strengths and weaknesses were. He wasn't telling us what to do, but he kept saying, 'If I were you . . .' And when he said that, that's when you get the pencil out."

The Colonel additionally made it clear that advertising for the concert and broadcast would *not* read "Concert Associates Presents Elvis." He said, "Let's get it straight who we're promoting here—Elvis or you." He told them when they advertised for local promoters in the two hundred-plus cities not to accept any collect calls "because if they can't pay for the call, you don't want them." This, the Colonel said, would eliminate 90 per cent of the dead wood. And when they said they'd make an announcement in April, he said they had the date right, but *he* would do the announcing. "I'll have the boy there and we'll do it right," they quoted the Colonel as saying.

Then on March 19, the story was given considerable space in the *Los Angeles Times*. The writer, Robert Hilburn, had the facts correct and gave what appeared to be a logical reason for the Colonel to concoct the scheme: "To maintain his image as 'King,' Presley needs 'super engagements.' By appearing in Las Vegas' biggest showroom and in the Astrodome, he had just that. But what else was there." Answer: " . . . the closed circuit package is a first for the entertainment field. It is a match, both financially and in artistic prestige, for the Las Vegas and Houston engagements. In fact, it would, if ticket sales match expectations, exceed them both."

But that was the last ever heard of the project. Steve Wolf and Jim Rissmiller ducked the question when asked, but it was apparent *they* broke the story and the Colonel reportedly was purple with rage. Besides, fairly good sources said Filmways made some additional demands not accepted by the Colonel.

In any case, said Steve, "It kept being tabled and finally it was tabled past the date when there was sufficient time to organize. There were some phone calls, but there never was another meeting."

The Colonel did return the $110,000, however.

At the same time this was going on, the Colonel was negotiating with the people at the International. All the kitchen workers had gone on strike in Las Vegas in March and the hotels were empty. Nick Naff at the International said there was a meeting of all the hotel administrators to determine what might be done to bring the business back as quickly as possible, once the strike ended. Nick said it was unanimously agreed that the personality who could get the action going in Vegas fastest was Elvis, and the International was asked if it would try to get Elvis back for a week or ten days. Nick said a deal was made with the Colonel all right, but the strike ended sooner than they thought and it was impossible to assemble the show so quickly. Others contend the act already booked into the

International, the Gene Kelly show, refused to be bumped for the ten-day peri-od. And so Elvis did not return to Vegas until August, as scheduled.

Opening day, the Colonel was supervising the decoration of the building's entrance, watching half a dozen men climb ladders to hang hundreds of little colored flags on strings. The flags said it was an "Elvis Summer Festival" and they gave the entrance to the huge hotel the look of a used-car lot.

Inside, on the carpeted steps leading to the casino, stood a pretty blonde hawking Elvis Presley photographs (one dollar) and picture books (a dollar and a half), and beyond her every dealer and pit boss was wearing an Elvis Presley scarf (three-fifty, available at the hotel's gift shops) and a white Styrofoam skimmer with a colorful band that once again proclaimed the month an "Elvis Summer Festival."

Elsewhere in the hotel—in the six restaurants, by the bay-sized pool, in the half-dozen bars, in the youth (babysitting) hostel—were hung posters and autographed pictures and scarves and banners and flags. Outside the Showroom entrance the hotel's professional decorator was stapling this stuff to everything that wasn't moving.

At the reservation desk there was a line thirty feet long, and an attractive redhead was telling the day's three hundredth caller (her estimate) that no, there wasn't any room at the inn—every one of the hotel's rooms was full. (Herb Alpert was told he could bunk in with record producer Lou Adler or go somewhere else.) The Showroom itself was reported sold out for two shows a night, seven nights a week for nearly the entire engagement.

Giving the scene a final bizarre touch was a forty-man camera crew from MGM, there to continue shooting for the documentary the Colonel wanted in the theaters by Thanksgiving. So regularly were they in the casino—inter-viewing the bell captains, the dealers, the *maitre d'*, the bartenders, the change girls, the chefs, the fans—that the gamblers paid them no mind, even if they *were* hauling and shoving huge Panavision cameras between the rows of slot machines.

Already the filming of a documentary had begun in Los Angeles, as Elvis started rehearsals at an MGM rehearsal hall and the documentary's Oscar-winning director, Denis Sanders, visited some of southern California's top Elvis fans. It had been more than a year since Elvis finished *Change of Habit* and with no interesting offers, the Colonel agreed to a documentary that would go behind the scenes as well as include live concert footage.

"What we're trying to do," said Denis, "is capture Elvis the entertainer, from the point of view of the fans, the hotel and the audience." He explained that about half the film—fifty minutes to an hour—would be edited from Elvis's first five performances in the Showroom, the rest would be in scene and interview.

"What I'm shooting is a musical documentary and I'm not just talking about the concert segments. Everything in the film will be musical. Just as Elvis, or any other performer, alternates fast numbers with slower numbers, say, or creates moods, so will I. We'll have a sad scene, a happy scene, another sad scene, and so on."

If this sounded not at all like the predictable Elvis Presley flick, it was because Denis Sanders was not the predictable Elvis Presley director. A six-hour documentary he directed for National Educational Television won the 1970 Cannes Film Festival prize for the best news film. He wrote the ninety-minute television special *The Day Lincoln Was Shot*; directed segments of television's *Naked City*, *Route 66*, *Alcoa Premiere* and *The Defenders*, and wrote the screen adaptation of Norman Mailer's *The Naked and the Dead*. His *Czechoslovakia, 1968* won the Academy Award for best documentary in 1969. His motion picture short *A Time Out of War*, which he wrote, produced and directed, also won an Academy Award, in 1954.

Denis said he doesn't know why he was called to direct the Elvis film. He'd never even met the Colonel or Elvis and the only contact he'd had with MGM was in 1959, when he was kicked off the lot after working just two weeks as director of *The Subterraneans*. At that time, he said, MGM accused him of turning Jack Kerouac's story into an "immoral film."

However unsuitable Denis seemed to be on the surface, probably he was the perfect choice. Elvis's films hadn't been making the fortunes claimed, and it was logical that with his return to personal appearances there should have been a concurrent shift in the film direction. Making a documentary—as opposed to another cream-puff musical—was a means of realizing this shift. Making a *good* documentary cinched it.

Budget for the film was between $1 million and $1.3 million, surprisingly little of which went to Elvis. Denis said half went to cover the "above the line," or creative, costs, which meant Elvis had taken nearly a 50 per cent cut in pay.

Elvis had a new orchestra leader for this engagement, Joe Guercio, a seasoned professional who'd worked with mainstream vocalists like Patti Page, Steve Lawrence and Eydie Gorme, and Diahann Carroll before settling down in Las Vegas. At first, he said, he was unimpressed by the lack of musical arrangements and Elvis's carefree approach to rehearsing, and when Joe Esposito later asked him how he felt it went, he said, "It was like following a marble falling down concrete steps."

The next day, Joe had trouble opening his dressing room door. "I finally push it open," he said, "and there must have been three thousand marbles on the floor and a sign on the mirror: 'Follow the marble . . . Me.' From that day on, it was like I was one of the gang."

When Joe then saw Elvis in performance, he became a fan, saying, "I've been onstage with a lot of stars and I hate to let the air out of their balloons, but they have no idea what a star is. Jesus Christ! It was unreal. It was just a group of songs, very little production—it wasn't as organized as a lot of Vegas shows. But, boy, if you want to talk about going out and grabbing people, Elvis was a happening, and what he had going will never be again. There was a vibe you could pick up in the audience—it was unbelievable. I'm not going to say to you that musically it was the best in the whole world. It was charisma. He just loved to put other people around his little finger and do it, and he did."

When the Colonel gave Denis his last-minute instructions, he said, "Now don't you go winning no Oscar with this pitcha," he said, "because we don't have no tuxedos to wear to the celebration."

# Chapter 19

# ON THE ROAD

I n the late summer of 1970, as Elvis completed an engagement in Las Vegas, there was no personality on the planet who could claim greater fame. Before going to this desert city, Elvis had been little more than an interesting curiosity left over from another era, and now he was the definition and embodiment of the word Superstar. Such creatures are rare. It was inevitable that Presley's manager, Colonel Tom Parker, would put this phenomenon on tour.

People had been after the Colonel to do this for years, ever since the Beatles did for the sixties what Elvis had done ten years before that. After all, hadn't the Beatles said Elvis was their inspiration? Hadn't John Lennon said, "Before Elvis there was nothing?" But the Colonel wisely rejected all offers, fearing the possibility of failure due to premature release. In no way did he want Elvis to be regarded as another oldie-but-goodie on the comeback trail. When Elvis began touring again, the Colonel wanted him to be bigger than anything else then occasionally available—bigger than Bob Dylan, bigger than the Rolling Stones, bigger than Frank Sinatra. So he gambled on Las Vegas as the place where Elvis could establish his superiority. He gambled and he won. Now, after only three engagements in just over a year's time since Elvis had emerged from relative obscurity in Hollywood, the Colonel, and Elvis, were ready to conquer the rest of the North American continent.

The first meeting with the people who ultimately booked nearly all of Elvis's road shows was held in 1969 before Elvis even went to Vegas, when the Colonel invited two energetic promoters named Jerry Weintraub and Tom Huelett to his office at MGM. Other meetings followed, over dinner, or in the steam room of the Spa in Palm Springs. The Colonel loved the steam room, was able to spend hours in one without wilting, and enjoyed holding meetings in them because those he was negotiating with were unable to match his stamina.

Both Weintraub—who was married to singer Jane Morgan—and Huelett were promoters who had established their names and reputations during the heavy rock years of the sixties, when Weintraub, operating from Los Angeles, booked Eric Clapton and Cream, and Huelett, working in Seattle, handled tours for Jimi Hendrix. Joining forces, they began promoting national tours and by 1969, when the Colonel began considering them seriously, they were known as honest, ambitious, efficient, and tough.

Modestly, six widely scattered concerts were set, in Phoenix, St. Louis, Detroit, Miami, Tampa, and Mobile, beginning just two days after Elvis closed in Nevada on Labor Day 1970. It was a sort of test run, a shakedown tour to see how Weintraub and Huelett—and Elvis—worked together. Elvis worried about the audiences. Everyone else worried about logistics. They *knew* the shows would be successful. Tickets sold out only hours after they went on sale. If he and his management had wanted him to, Elvis could've performed in a hundred cities. What caused concern was organization, not appeal.

"It was pretty funky compared to what came later," said Joe Guercio, the orchestra leader who had taken the baton in Las Vegas the previous month and who would conduct for Elvis for most of the next six years. "Most of us were traveling in a Granny Goose airplane. We called it Greyhound Airlines. Oh, it was pretty together, but we didn't know how much equipment we needed and we had different pickup musicians in every town. We were doing a show every day and when you're rehearsing new horns and strings every day, you want to cut your wrists."

"We weren't organized," said Joe Mescale, leader of the Imperials, the gospel quartet that Elvis used as backup singers. "We didn't even know we needed an announcer until we got out on the road. So Al Dvorn, who was in charge of the souvenirs, told *me* to do it. He told me to get up there and tell 'em we got these pennants and teddy bears, it's their last chance to get 'em before we start the show."

These were minor problems and the overall impact of Elvis on tour far outweighed them, in fact swamped them in a tidal wave of what looked like the 1950s revisited. Each of the auditoriums held at least 10,000 persons, who paid $5, $7.50, and $10 apiece to see the show (giving Elvis individual concert grosses ranging up to nearly $100,000). In every city, after the Sweet Inspirations and the Imperials and comic Jackie Kahane performed and Elvis walked out, there was an incredible flash of energy and light as everyone present let out a roar and thousands of Instamatics went off. Long minutes passed as Elvis bathed in the wash of applause and the stroboscopic twinkle of tiny flash cubes, while behind him rumbled the rhythmic thunder of his backup band. There he stood, center stage, his arms outstretched, showing off his jeweled cape, a popular god reincarnate, a sort of comic book hero come to life.

"That first tour was exciting," said Joe Mescale. "We felt like history was being made. It was loose, the organization wasn't together yet, but nobody cared, because it was so darned exciting. When we got to a town, the people were waiting for us. They were at the hotels. They were in the restaurants. They were at the auditorium all day long, waiting."

There was a story that Elvis himself told over and over in the years to come that captured the spirit of the time: "We flew to Mobile and the hotel didn't have any air conditioning, man, and that's a no-no. Gotta have that air conditioning. Anyway, on the way into town we passed a Holiday Inn, so I said, 'Let's go there, to hell with this goddamned sweat-hole.' I got on the phone and called the Holiday Inn and said, 'Ma'am, I'd like some rooms and I'm comin' right over.' I didn't tell her who I was. She said, 'I'm sorry, sir . . . no rooms.' I tol' her she didn't understand and, I needed thirty rooms right away. She said, 'I'm sorry, sir, there aren't any rooms. H'nt you heard . . . Elvis Presley's in town?'"

Elvis loved the tour and for days afterward in Memphis he talked excitedly about all the things he'd seen and done, laughing now about the bomb threat in Phoenix and the limousines that didn't show up. "'Member," he said, "the godawful yellow Merc we got?" Then he told the story about the Mobile Holiday Inn again.

He also fell into a post-tour physical and mental depression and disorientation, caused by a recurring eye problem that later would be diagnosed as glaucoma, and on top of that, the symptoms that come with the regular dosage of chemical stimulants and sleeping potions.

"We lived a fast life," said Jerry Schilling. "Not only Elvis, but the rest of us, too. We lived long hours, slept in the daytime and lived in hotels. We started taking a sleeping pill to make it easy. After awhile one wasn't enough. Sometimes for a weight problem or to wake up for an early studio call, we'd take a diet pill. Over a period of time, one diet pill wasn't enough either."

The pills weren't considered a problem in 1970. That would come later. Elvis's dependency was growing. There were signs that drugs *could* become a problem in his life, but this early no one worried about it. Drugs were a part of the music scene, as much a part as guitars and girls. No one paid much attention. If anyone thought about it at all, they might have commented on how few drugs Elvis took.

A week after returning to Memphis, on September 22, Elvis flew to Nashville for what was supposed to be a week of recording. His eyes began hurting, so the session ended the same day it began with only four songs completed. Two of these, "Snowbird," a faithful copy of the recent hit by Anne Murray, and a sloppy version of Jerry Lee Lewis's "Whole Lotta Shakin' Goin' On," were included in a country album released a few months later, in January 1971, and the other two, "Rags to Riches" and "Where Did They Go, Lord?," were released as a single in March.

With Elvis going home after only one day, that left four days of recording time open for James Burton to record *his* album. Elvis's guitarist and an old-time Southern rocker from the 1950s, Burton had received $6,000 to produce an instrumental album for A&M Records, and so he did, with Elvis paying for the studio time. According to musicians who played the sessions, everyone got ungodly drunk. (The result was released by A&M but it wasn't popular.)

Back in Memphis, Elvis was officially on vacation.

Back in Los Angeles, a hundred yards from the Colonel's office, Denis Sanders' documentary—now being called *Elvis: That's the Way It Is*—was being rushed through post-production for a November release to coincide with Elvis's second tour.

For the Colonel, coordinating a promotional campaign that included more than one element was a piece of cake. In the past, it was usually a movie and a soundtrack album. Now it was a film and an album and a tour. Every day dozens of calls were made, to Sanders and to the publicity offices of MGM. The studio's poster—"FILMED AS IT HAPPENED, 'LIVE' ON STAGE IN LAS VEGAS"—was rushed over for the Colonel's approval.

(The Colonel was also making it very clear to MGM's boss, Jim Aubrey, which scenes in the rough cut had to be deleted. There were too many fan interviews, he said, and the negative remarks about *Blue Hawaii* and *G.I. Blues* had to be cut. More of Elvis's performances had to be put back in.)

Photographs were selected. Meetings were held with representatives of RCA to make sure there would be an adequate supply of records in the cities where the movie and Elvis went. Press kits were sent to record stores, theater owners, and auditorium managers; in many cases these were followed up with telephone calls.

There were nine concerts in seven days in this second tour and with the exception of Oklahoma City and Denver, all were on the West Coast, so in early November Elvis moved to his home in California. It was from there, on the eleventh, that he left by charter jet for shows in big coliseums in Oakland, Portland, Seattle, San Francisco, Los Angeles, and San Diego.

Everywhere the shows were sold out just hours after tickets went on sale, setting new attendance records. At the Forum in Los Angeles, where he performed afternoon and evening shows, 36,000 tickets sold in less than two days, with the more devoted fans camping overnight in front of the box office. Everywhere Elvis was greeted with a roar that sounded like the ocean and thousands of rippling flash cube pops. It was, as one writer put it, the world's best light show, and the Colonel didn't have to pay a penny for it.

No matter what Elvis sang, or did, the audience lapped it up. Elvis was like no other, for with him there seemed to be no foreseeable market saturation point. Even when the "Elvis industry" seemed to be producing at a runaway pace, still there was an audience ready to consume it happily. Each year, for example, RCA proudly published an updated pamphlet entitled *The Complete Catalog of Elvis Records and Tapes*. In 1970, there were thirty pages of albums, eight-track stereo tapes, cartridges, cassettes and stereo reels, all of it "available at record dealers everywhere." That meant the stuff still sold sufficiently to keep the material in stock and to give it precious warehouse space, although much of it was of mediocre quality and some of it fifteen years old.

What made this even more amazing was that so many of Elvis's records were "repackages," records that were released more than once with only slight changes in the packaging. For example, in August, while Elvis was still in Las Vegas, the fifty songs that the Colonel claimed as million-copy sellers were pressed onto four discs and put in a box with a photo book, confidently called *Elvis' Worldwide 50 Gold Award Hits, Volume One*. And just two months later, a double album, *From Memphis to Vegas/From Vegas to Memphis*, originally released only a year earlier, was re-released as two separate LPs, called *Elvis In Person at the International Hotel* and *Elvis Back in Memphis*.

However arrogant this approach to marketing may have seemed, the stunning thing was that it worked. Such repackaged product seldom made the record charts, yet Elvis's loyal audience was large enough—while still others were suckered in, thinking the albums were new—to insure that each was comfortably profitable. His was an audience that crossed all lines. Elvis spelled legend to rockers and rednecks alike and if they were fanatically adoring, they were also well behaved. People just weren't arrested at Elvis Presley concerts. Elvis didn't cause riots, only excitement. He didn't bait the police who ringed the stage—when he borrowed an officer's cap for some clowning, he returned it with a polite thank you. His bumps and grinds still caused female bladders to let go, yet even when he dangled the ends of his fringed and beaded macramé belt between his legs suggestively and curled his lip, the effect was self-mocking. Elvis was sexy, but he wasn't ever threatening.

The tour ended in Denver, where Elvis was feeling high and fit. Elvis and his touring group stayed in the hotel where the Playboy Club was located. "You know what end-of-the-road parties are like," said the Imperials' Joe Mescale. "Well this one was wild, just wild . . . and you can't print any of it!"

The natural high continued in the weeks following as Elvis relaxed in California, watching a lot of television and wandering into Hollywood and Beverly Hills to spend $38,000 on guns and $80,000 on cars for Christmas gifts. This, in turn, led to a fight with his father on December 19. It was Vernon's job to write the personal checks and when he came at Elvis with a handful of bills, shaking his head the way he always did, Elvis mumbled, "Fuck . . . here we go again.''

"Lookit, Elvis, I know you don't like me sayin' anythin' about your money, but I just got these in from California and I wanna check 'em with you. There must be a mistake, because this one's from Kerr's and it said you charged \$38,000 in guns there this month.''

"Christmas shoppin', daddy. That's all.''

"Now, Elvis, how many times I got to say it? Vegas pays you real good and the Colonel said now you're tourin' again, there's gonna be good money there, too, but we just not makin' that kinda money these days to spend so much as this and . . .''

Usually Elvis tried to keep his temper in check, but tonight Priscilla joined Vernon; she hated his wild spending, too. When Elvis wanted, he could be the model of Christian patience. His fury also was legendary. When the gates to his Graceland estate weren't opened promptly enough by his gatekeepers—most of whom were relatives—he was famous for ordering the limousine driven *through* the gates. How many times had he angrily humiliated the guys who worked for him? How many television sets had he shot out with his Derringer? There were many things that aroused his ire and being told what to do was one of them.

"Lookit, goddammit,'' he said, "it's my fuckin' money and I can do whatever in goddamn hell I want with it!''

When the shouting had stopped and a taut silence had constricted the room, Elvis aloofly stalked out of the mansion, wearing a purple velvet suit and cape, gold belt buckle, amber glasses; carrying a jeweled white cane and a .45 caliber pistol in a shoulder holster. He then drove one of his cars to Memphis International Airport and for the first time in his life, he bought a ticket on a commercial airliner and flew to another city *alone*.

Elvis had never done anything like this before. At age 35, he'd never even been in a bank. When he was young, he was poor; when he was older he had people to take care of such things. Surrounded by salaried lackeys for nearly fifteen years—even through his army duty in Germany—he was effectively isolated from ordinary life and society. And now he was on his way to Washington, boarding not a chartered jet but a commercial airliner.

There was purpose and determination in making this flight and Elvis had planned it for some time, although only John O'Grady knew about it. O'Grady was a tough ex-narcotics cop, now a private detective who had been hired by Elvis's attorney for help in a paternity suit. Sometime after that, O'Grady said, he started Elvis collecting police badges.

"I was a cop for twenty years, a sergeant in charge of the Hollywood narcotics detail. I knew when people were doped up and Elvis was strung out on pills. Now, I'm not saying he didn't have prescriptions for those pills, but he was strung out. If you know what to look for, the eyes, the slurred or speeded-up speech, I mean, twenty years and I *knew*, so I figured if he started carrying badges around, maybe he'd stop taking that shit. I was in Hawaii talking about industrial security at a cops' convention in 1969 and I met John Finlator, the deputy U.S. narcotics director. Elvis said he wanted a U.S. narcotics badge to add to his collection. I set up a meeting. I thought it might help."

Of course, Elvis had his own reasons for meeting the nation's number two narc. He carried a pistol almost everywhere he went these days—sometimes even to bed, stuck into the waistband of his custom-made silk pajamas or in the pocket of his robe. He and some of his boys had deputy sheriffs' badges and permits to carry side-arms in Memphis, courtesy of his friend Sheriff Bill Morris, and in Palm Springs. Elvis believed that if he had a federal badge it would allow him to go armed everywhere in the United States.

There was another reason he wanted the badge. For Elvis, the word "drugs" meant heroin. "He talked with other performers in Vegas," said Jerry Schilling, who was, ironically, the most liberal of his sidekicks. "They were junkies and after he talked to them, they stopped taking drugs. I know that sounds far out, but it's true. I personally know of two individuals who stopped taking heroin. Elvis figured if he had a federal narcotics badge, he could maybe scare some other entertainers into kicking dope."

Elvis reported to the American Airlines check-in counter in Memphis, where he was sold a ticket and whisked into the V.I.P. lounge, and then boarded on the flight to the capital apart from the other passengers. Thus he didn't go through the security check for weapons and his pistol wasn't discovered. He also was traveling under the name John Burroughs, a name he'd used for years for personal mail and telephone calls. In Washington, he hailed a taxi to the Washington Hotel. What happened on the way was one of the stories Elvis would tell and retell.

"He had the driver stop at one of those ghetto donut joints on the way to the hotel," said T. G. Sheppard, another friend. "He had his diamonds on his fingers and he had his gun and one of the people there said, 'Allll-visss Presley—lookit them diamond rings on you hands, man, Lord have mercy!' And Elvis said, 'Yeah, man, an' I'm gone keep 'em too;' and he pulls the .45 outa the shoulder holster. He'd laugh when he tol' this story. He had the deepest laugh I ever heard. He laughed all the way down to his soul."

Once at the hotel, Elvis made a number of calls, the first to Gerald Peters, a fiftyish Englishman who'd recently begun chauffeuring Elvis in Los Angeles. When the operator told him "Mr. Burroughs" was calling, and there was no response, Elvis broke in and whispered, "Sir Gerald . . . it's me . . ."

Elvis told Gerald he was in Washington and said he was coming to Los

Angeles. Twenty minutes later he called to say he'd changed his mind and thirty minutes after that he called another time to say he was arriving on Trans
World Airways flight number 85, at 1:17 A.M. He swore Gerald to absolute
secrecy regarding his present whereabouts and plans and then called Jerry
Schilling. Jerry then called Gerald and together, in secrecy in the middle of the
night, they drove to the airport to meet The Boss.

The picture Jerry described was executed in a mix of bold and subtle
strokes. 1:30 in the morning and there's Elvis exiting the plane still wearing his
cape and purple velvet suit, a stewardess on each arm. Jerry also notices that
Elvis's face is swollen up . . . and then he sees that Elvis is carrying, besides the
cane, a small cardboard box. Jerry looked into it and counted a toothbrush,
small complimentary-size toothpaste and soap, a little washrag. Elvis
explained, "I had to get some stuff for traveling."

Elvis had Jerry call a doctor to meet them at his home and then, on the way
in from the airport, they took the girls home. It was then that Elvis told Jerry
the story about what had happened in Washington when he told the airline ticket agent he was boarding with a pistol. The agent followed him onto the plane.

"I'm sorry, Mr. Presley, but you cannot fly on this plane with a gun."

Elvis angrily left the plane, fairly running down the staircase. The pilot, who
was watching, followed him and ran along behind on the tarmac, calling, "Mr.
Presley, please come back. This is the pilot, please accept our apology . . ."

Elvis finished telling the story as they rode up the drive of his new estate in
a rich section called Holmby Hills. The doctor was waiting at the gate and after
he gave Elvis a shot, he slept for eight hours.

At noon Sunday when he woke up, Elvis hollered for Jerry and when Jerry
came running, he said, "I want you to come to Washington with me." He did-
n't tell Jerry why.

"Aw, Elvis, look, I just took this job at Paramount and if I go to Washington
tonight I'll miss work tomorrow, this is important to me . . ."

"Don't worry about it. I'll charter you a jet."

"Elvis, there's no way I can make it there physically and get back to work
in time."

Elvis looked down at his feet, a little boy toeing the ground, and said,
"Okay, I'll go by myself."

Jerry sighed resignedly and began making arrangements for the trip. He
called the Washington Hotel and reserved two rooms—yes, they remembered
"John Burroughs"—and then booked two seats on a flight leaving about ten
o'clock that night. Now Elvis was traveling under another alias, Dr. John
Carpenter, the name of the character he'd portrayed only a year earlier in
*Change of Habit*. On the way to the airport, Gerald stopped at the Beverly Hills

Hotel so Elvis could cash a check for $500. Jerry and Elvis had had no cash between them and Jerry assured Elvis that "you can charge plane tickets and hotel rooms and meals to credit cards, but you really can't travel properly unless you got money for tips and incidentals." Elvis looked at him as if he didn't know what he was talking about, but nodded his approval.

By now, Elvis had been gone from Memphis for more than twenty-four hours and his family and friends were frantic. At first they thought he'd merely gone for a ride to cool off following the fight. Then they began to make casual inquiries. Joe Esposito and Charlie Hodge, two of Elvis's hired hands, both started calling around the country. Gerald was one of many who got calls: "Uh, by the way, you haven't heard from Elvis, have you?" Gerald of course said no.

When Elvis boarded the plane in Los Angeles, every seat was full. Christmas was only five days away and in 1970 that meant every plane heading east from California was carrying soldiers on leave from Vietnam. About half the passengers on the flight were in uniform. Elvis, seated on the aisle, struck up a conversation with several of the men. It was late, but the mood was up, people were in the aisles laughing and talking.

"Elvis and I settled down," Jerry said, "and pretty soon he tells me he's going to write a letter. Now, I think Elvis in his whole life only wrote about three or four letters. He tells me he's going to Washington to get a federal narcotics badge from John Finlator and he is writing a letter to the President of the United States, President Nixon. He asked me to proofread the letter."

In the letter Elvis expressed freely his ideas about Jane Fonda and Communism and especially drugs, showing concern about the role popular musicians and singers played in this. He said he wanted to do something positive and wanted to talk to Nixon about that. He told the President he was staying at the Washington Hotel under the name John Burroughs, gave his room number, and suggested he call his personal public relations man, Jerry Schilling, to make an appointment.

"Well, first of all," Jerry said, "there was a lot of grammar and stuff that probably could've been changed. But I knew where his heart was in the letter and I liked it the way he wrote it, so I said, 'Elvis, it's perfect the way it is.'"

Jerry returned to his book after reading the letter, and Elvis started talking to another G.I. After a few minutes, he poked Jerry in the ribs. "Jerry," he said, "where's the money?"

"I got it, it's safe . . . why?"

"Jerry, give it to me."

Both men were whispering. Jerry said, "Elvis, this is our expense money. You can't . . ."

Elvis said, "Jerry, this soldier's going home for Christmas and I want to make it a good one for him and his loved ones."

"Elvis, we won't have any money for tips and . . ."

Elvis gritted his teeth and said, "The guy . . . just . . . got . . . back . . . from
. . . Vietnam." So Jerry gave him the $500 and Elvis gave it to the soldier and
said, "Merry Christmas."

The plane arrived in the capital Monday, December 21, at 6:30 A.M. Elvis
had eaten a half-box of candy that someone had given him and again his face was
swollen. Jerry saw Elvis to the waiting limousine and called the hotel, telling the
desk to get a doctor. Elvis said he wanted to go to the White House first.

"Elvis, it's 6:30 in the morning. Let's check with the doctor first and clean
up . . ."

"Godammit, Jerry, we're going to the White House now!"

They rode silently to 1600 Pennsylvania Avenue as Elvis took out his pen
and covered a portion of the envelope containing his letter: "Personal—For the
President's Eyes Only." Driving to the guard gate, Elvis got out of the car and,
extending his hand with the envelope, he said, "Sir . . .?" The guard looked
right through him, as if Elvis didn't exist.

Elvis glanced back at Jerry as if he didn't know what to do, as if his feelings
were hurt at not being recognized. Then he remembered his mussed clothing,
shoulder-length hair, and tinted glasses.

"Oh," he said to the guard, "uh, uh, I'm Elvis Presley and I have a letter for
the President and . . ."

The guard snapped to and smiled broadly, apologizing, and when Elvis
explained his mission, he said he'd see the letter was delivered as soon as Nixon
was in his office. The limousine then took Elvis to the hotel.

After the doctor left, Jerry asked if he could call Memphis. "Elvis," he said,
"you've been gone for two days and I'm very worried about your father and
Priscilla. They must be going crazy. I gave you my word and you know me, I'm
not going to break it. But can I call down there and say you're with me and
you're okay? We don't have to say where you are . . . and I've got to get back
to my job, so I'd like to have Sonny come up here."

Elvis agreed and told Jerry to stay at the hotel to take the President's call.
He then left the hotel alone to take the limousine to John Finlator's office, leaving Finlator's number with Jerry.

Finlator was expecting "Mr. Burroughs" and, leaving a wake of startled secretaries and intermediaries behind him, Elvis was ushered quickly into the
deputy director's office. Elvis got right down to business. He said he wanted to
donate $5,000 to Finlator's department. Finlator was startled by the offer, gra-
ciously refusing it, explaining that his department was funded by the taxpayers,
so Elvis already was a contributor. Elvis wasn't certain how to handle this

rejection, so he told the deputy director how he'd already talked two entertainers into getting off heroin in Las Vegas.

Elvis then asked for a badge. Finlator said he'd be pleased to arrange for an honorary badge. Elvis then produced his deputy's badges from Memphis and Palm Springs and said he wanted the real thing. Again Finlator turned Elvis down. It was impossible, he said. There were regulations. It was not a choice. It was out of his hands.

"Elvis was depressed when I got him on the phone in Finlator's office," Jerry Schilling said, "and before I could say anything he said, 'Jerry, I can't do any good here, I'm coming back to the hotel.' I interrupted him. I said, 'Why I'm calling, Elvis, is the President wants to see you right away.'"

Amazingly, the letter had reached Nixon and he cleared twenty minutes in his schedule. Elvis told Jerry he'd pick him up in the limo and before leaving asked Finlator one more question.

"You won't mind if I ask the President for the badge, will you, sir?"

Finlator chuckled and said no, go ahead, because that was the only way the department could give him one.

When Elvis returned to the hotel he found Jerry waiting and Sonny checking in. Together they went to the White House, where they were met by Egil "Bud" Krogh, Nixon's top enforcement officer, later convicted as one of the Watergate conspirators. When they told him they were armed, he advised them to leave their pistols in the car. Except for one. This was a gold-plated commemorative World War II Colt .45 that Elvis had picked up while in Los Angeles as a gift for the President. This was given to Krogh, who checked to see that it was empty, whereupon Elvis finally was sent into the Oval Office.

Jerry and Sonny were disappointed when Elvis left them behind. Krogh explained that it required more security if more than one person went in.

"Well," Sonny said, "I know Elvis and he'll ask the President to let us in."

"It doesn't matter if he asks or not," said Krogh. "It's out of the President's hands."

"Well, Elvis is a pretty hard guy to say no to."

At that moment the interoffice telephone buzzed. It was the President, asking that Jerry and Sonny be allowed in. At the same time, Elvis appeared at the door and said, "Come on in, guys, I want you to meet the President."

Elvis was grinning broadly, as excited as a small boy. As soon as Elvis met Nixon he explained his need for the federal badge and Nixon told Krogh to take care of it.

Jerry and Sonny hesitated at the door to the President's office, clearly nervous about entering. Elvis laughed and said, "C'mon, c'mon . . ." For years afterward he would retell the story of this meeting and always tease his bodyguards about their timidity.

Nixon came forward and shook their hands stiffly. "Elvis, you got a couple of pretty big guys here. It looks like Elvis is in pretty good hands with you two. You guys play football?"

The small talk continued for a few minutes as the White House photographer snapped several pictures, one formal shot of Elvis and Nixon, other more candid shots around the President's desk. Then Elvis said, "Mr. President . . . you know that Presidential button you gave me?"

Nixon started and said, "Oh yes . . ." and pulled two more lapel pins from a drawer, coming around the desk to hand them to Jerry and Sonny.

"Uh . . . sir . . ." Elvis said. "They've got wives, sir."

The President started again, returning hurriedly to his desk to get two brooches.

Nixon then walked the trio to the door, patted Elvis awkwardly on the shoulder and told Krogh to take the boys on a tour of the house. The badge arrived twenty minutes later.

By Christmas all was calm again at Graceland and if Elvis reviewed the year he must have been pleased. Just when he'd begun to tire of Las Vegas, was growing slightly bored, the tours had begun, giving him another opportunity to test his power. And he'd done well. Both tours were short, only sixteen shows in all, but every concert was a sell-out. Travel expenses were high, yet so were the grosses, showing the Colonel that in the American heartland it was possible to make money faster than in Nevada.

Elvis also liked *Elvis: That's The Way It Is*, enjoyed watching it in his Graceland screening room, reading some of the more flattering clippings forwarded to his home. Said Howard Thompson in the *New York Times*: "The powerhouse drive that used to flail about wildly is shrewdly disciplined and siphoned until it explodes into his extraordinary sense of rhythm. Tired? Elvis? He's ferocious. Most impressively of all, he comes over as a genial, reasonably balanced guy . . ."

Even his albums were accepted graciously—especially the movie soundtrack.

Then to cap it off, only a week before, the President had given him a U.S. narcotics badge.

So on New Year's Eve, just before midnight, Elvis fairly strutted into T.J.'s, a popular Memphis nightclub that he'd rented for his annual party. Alan Fortas and Richard Davis were behind the bar and at the door. Ronnie Milsap, the club's regular singer, was on the stage.

"Hey, E," came the greeting over and over that night, "great party, man,

Happy New Year!"

Priscilla was on his arm and nearby stood his daddy. Vernon's brother Vester, a guard at the Graceland gates, was trading stories near the bar with Sterling Pepper, another guard whose son Gary, seated at a table nearby, was president of the International Elvis Presley Fan Club. At another table sat George Klein. Red West was there with his wife Patty, and so was Billy Smith, another cousin. Jerry Schilling and his brother, Billy Ray, were over against a wall, talking with Sheriff Bill Morris.

Elvis stood near the edge of the room, his back to the wall. (He hated to have his back to anyone.) He looked around and puffed on his thin cigar and grinned at Priscilla. "Happy New Year, babe," he said. "Believe me, it's gonna be all right."

Elvis was riding a giant wave at the start of 1971. He was 36 years old on January 8, and eight days after that the national organization of Junior Chambers of Commerce held its annual banquet in Memphis and named Elvis one of seven young men of the year.

"I'd tried to get him to take that honor several times, but he wouldn't accept it," said Bill Morris, who was instrumental in getting Elvis's name before the national Jaycees organization. "This would have been the last year that he could have accepted it, because of his age. I talked to him about what the Jaycees were really doing and the effect they had on the leadership of this nation and he finally said, 'Hey, that's keen, I might just do that deal.' It was the first public function that he ever attended."

The place: the Municipal Auditorium concert hall, the same huge room where as a teenager Elvis attended all-night gospel sings. With Elvis at the ceremony were his family and closest friends. When his name was called, he walked briskly to the podium, wrapped in the warmth of applause.

He adjusted the high collar of his dark blue suit and touched the bridge of his tinted glasses, then grabbed the microphone nervously: "I, I, I'd like you folks to know that I was the hero of the comic book. I saw movies and I was the hero of the movie. So every dream that I ever dreamed has come true a hundred times. And these gentlemen over here . . ."

He looked at the other Young Men of the Year. Ron Zeigler, who was President Nixon's press secretary, was one of them. In previous years, they included Nelson Rockefeller, Howard Hughes, Ted Kennedy, Ralph Nader, Jesse Jackson, and Leonard Bernstein. For a man who, only fourteen years earlier was lambasted from the pulpit for his performances, that was pretty heady company.

". . . these type of people who care and are dedicated, you realize that it's possible they could be building the kingdom of heaven. It's not too farfetched from reality. I'd like to say that, ah, I learned very early in life that without a song, the day would never end . . . without a song, a man ain't got a friend . . . without, without a song . . . so I just keep singin' the song. Good night."

Cloaked again in applause, Elvis returned to his seat.

The speech was perfect. In just forty-four seconds he had summarized everything he believed and lived, giving his audience precisely what it wanted to hear. While acknowledging the realization of his fantasies, he acknowledged his co-nominees in a way that included him in a group of young men that was engaged in "building the kingdom of heaven" on earth. Abruptly changing the subject, Elvis then rhapsodized the role of song in his life. He was modest. Humble. The effect was reassuring.

# Chapter 20

# TROUBLES

E lvis went to Las Vegas on January 24. The threat came the same day by telephone. A male voice told Sonny West, who answered the call, that a madman was planning to kill Elvis during one of his upcoming hotel performances. For $50,000 in unmarked cash, the unidentified caller said, he would reveal the assassin's name. A few hours later a menu from the hotel showroom was found in Elvis's mail and message slot behind the hotel desk. Elvis's picture on the front of the menu was defaced, a pistol was drawn pointing to his heart, and at the bottom was the message: "Guess who, and where?" When the local FBI agent saw the menu, he shook his head and said, "We have to take this one seriously."

Over the years, Elvis had been threatened many times, dating back to the 1950s when jealous, macho boyfriends took pokes at him for making their girl-friends squeal. This was one of the reasons Elvis had gone into seclusion. As a rule, since then, threats against his life were handled without his knowledge. Those around him believed, rightly, that most were cranks and Elvis didn't need to know about them. This time, however, he was told and, given his love of police adventure, he was caught up in the drama immediately. At the same time, he was terribly frightened; if the FBI was worried, so was he, and as the federal agency made its plans for his protection, Elvis began taking inventory of his personal entourage.

The payroll was smaller than usual, an attempt on his part to pacify Priscilla, who was becoming extremely tired of having so many of the boys around the house all the time. When Jerry Schilling had quit to become a film editor at Paramount, for instance, Elvis hadn't replaced him. Now, in Las Vegas in late January 1971, all he had were a handful of faithfuls, with Jerry coming in on the weekends. So he put in a call to his cousin, Red West, who was working for a recording studio in Memphis, and another to Jerry in Hollywood.

"I arrived there," Red later wrote in his own book, *Elvis: What Happened?*, "and Elvis just stumbled into my arms and hugged me. There was no doubt that he was taking this very seriously."

When Elvis called Jerry, he didn't say why he wanted him instantly, in the middle of the week, and Jerry didn't ask why. He was on the next plane to Vegas.

"There's a very serious threat on my life," Elvis told Jerry when he arrived. "I think the guy is either insane or, I don't know what the deal is, the FBI's been contacted on it and I *need* you . . ."

Jerry said, "I'm here. Whatever you need."

With Jerry and Red and Sonny, and a part-Hawaiian karate instructor named Ed Parker, Elvis felt somewhat better. Hotel security, doubled whenever Elvis played the hotel anyway, was bolstered even more. FBI agents were positioned strategically throughout the showroom opening night. An ambulance and surgical team were standing by.

Just before going on, Elvis looked around his dressing room. "The hotel's told me I don't have to do this show," he said, "but I'm going to do it. I'd rather die on stage than in bed . . ."

His voice trailed off and he was silent for a moment, then he added, " . . . and I don't want any sonabitch running around afterward saying, 'I killed Elvis Presley!' What I want you to do is if some guy shoots me, I want you to rip his fucking eyes out!"

With that, Elvis stuck a Derringer into his right boot and into his waistband he pushed a .45. Then, allowing Charlie Hodge to place his jeweled cape on his shoulders, he strode off to do the dinner show.

"It'd been decided," said Jerry Schilling, "that if Elvis heard a shot during his performance, he would hit the floor and someone would jump on top of him, whoever was closest, while the others went after the gunman. So the show was very tight and stiff, until right in the middle, from up in the balcony a guy hollers, 'ELVIS!' Now, this was very unusual. Usually it's the girls who holler."

At the sound of the strange male voice, Elvis dropped to one knee, peering into the darkness beyond the footlights, as applause from the preceding song died out. Sonny and Red peered over the amplifiers, moving their hands toward the weapons they were carrying.

Elvis remained on one knee in the silence and answered the call: "Yeah?"

"I mean," Jerry remembers, "we all thought that this was *it*.

"Then this guy in the balcony said, 'Can you sing, "Don't Be Cruel?"'" And Elvis jumps up and sings it. And as a rule, he *never* takes requests."

During the following weeks Red cruised the audiences along with the hotel security and FBI plainclothesmen, while Sonny and Jerry and Ed remained on guard on stage. Nothing more was heard from the extortionist, however, and on February 23, Elvis returned to Memphis, where he again went into a post-performance depression and physical decline that would extend into recording sessions scheduled for three weeks later.

There was never anything boring about one of Elvis's recording sessions, because they were so unpredictable. Sometimes he went into the studio and recorded song after song after song—getting thirty-four songs down in just five days in June 1970, for example—and other times he blew it all away very quickly, growing bored himself and getting stoned (usually on sedatives, prescribed by his doctor) or sick, and canceling after only a day or two and mostly fooling around during that time, with nothing much to show for it. The only thing predictable was unpredictability.

The first 1971 session was set for middle March in Nashville's RCA studios. It'd been six months since Elvis had recorded any new material and although RCA had enough material to get through the year, there was talk of another Christmas album and nothing had yet been scheduled for release in 1972. So Harry Jenkins, RCA's "vice president in charge of Elvis Presley," began urging the Colonel to get his boy motivated and the Colonel, working directly with Elvis and through Elvis's number-one aide, Joe Esposito, began passing RCA's wishes along. Initially, Elvis wasn't excited about the Christmas album: Why didn't RCA just re-release the first one, from 1957?

Eventually he agreed and lackadaisically chartered a jet for the twenty-minute flight to Nashville. There he was greeted by a studio full of familiar faces, including the guitarist he believed he couldn't sing without, James Burton (who made $5,000 a week when he worked for Elvis); the rest of the rhythm section handpicked from the best Nashville had to offer (guitarist Chip Young, bassist Norbert Putnam, drummer Jerry Carrigan, pianist David Briggs, Charlie McCoy on harmonica); and twelve backup singers, including the familiar Imperials from his Vegas and road shows, the Nashville Edition, Millie Kirkham (with whom he'd recorded for fifteen years) and three other female voices.

Also present and showing somewhat more nervousness were Felton Jarvis, a big jovial Tennessean who worshiped Elvis like a brother and "produced" the sessions, the sober-faced representatives of Elvis's song publishing companies and RCA, and half a dozen members of his personal entourage. According to drummer Jerry Carrigan, it was the latter group that pretty much set the mood inside the studio.

"The first couple of times I went to work for him," Carrigan said, "people told me, 'Man, when he smiles at you, you smile back or he'll think you don't like him.' I said, 'I'm not a man that smiles all the time.' They said, 'Well, if he said somethin' funny, laugh, man.' I said, 'Well, if it's not funny to me, I'm not gonna laugh.'

"Well, one night they brought a big quart milkshake cup of dill pickles and sat 'em on the little console. Now I'd seen several guys go over there and get a pickle, man, and they'd eat it. So I went over there and just as I got my hand over the cup, one of his guys went, 'No, no!' I said, 'What?' He said, 'Those are Elvis's pickles! Don't you touch 'em!' Now, no way Elvis would mind me having a pickle. It was these yes-men, they ran his whole life. Charlie McCoy started to go into the restroom and they said, 'Don't you go in there!' Charlie said, 'What?' They said, 'Don't go in there!' Charlie said, 'But I have to go to the bathroom.' They said, 'You'll have to wait—Elvis is in there.'"

The March session lasted only one day, when Elvis recorded four songs, including an old hymn that'd been a hit a few months earlier for Judy Collins, "Amazing Grace," and a song of Gordon Lightfoot's that'd been a hit for Peter, Paul and Mary in 1965, "Early Mornin' Rain." Elvis sounded tired, his performance of the material was listless (although regarded good enough to be released) and the remainder of the week's sessions were canceled the following day. The musicians and singers were told that Elvis's eyes were bothering him.

Dr. George Nichopoulos ('Dr. Nick') flew in from Memphis and with Dr. David Meyer, a retina specialist, Elvis was given a shot of Cortisone directly into the ailing eyeball to relieve the pressure that had built up. He was then admitted, against his wishes, to the Nashville Baptist Hospital, where further tests showed he was suffering from iritis and a type of secondary glaucoma. He was discharged a few days later—following a visit from the Tennessee governor—and returned to Memphis, where he was attended by another of his recurring girlfriends for several days.

The next session began exactly two months later, on May 15. RCA was planning a September release for the Christmas album and now was willing to get the album any way it could. Thus, this week of sessions was programmed with Elvis's assistance but without his fulltime presence. He delivered a "scratch track," a rough tape of the songs Elvis recorded at the piano, which was designed to keep the musicians together, who then went in and laid down the instrumental portions, listening to Elvis's previously recorded voice on earphones. Later Elvis and the backup singers went in and recorded the vocal parts and after that, in June, strings were added in Hollywood.

Not all of the material recorded was done so mechanically, however. One of the Christmas songs, "Merry Christmas Baby," for instance, was a sort of lazy jam that ran for nearly six minutes and Bob Dylan's "Don't Think Twice, It's All Right" *was* a studio jam, running eight minutes and unintended for release but recorded anyway and released after Elvis's death. For these songs, and several others, Elvis *was* present. After the session ended, Elvis also sat down at the piano and played "I'll Take You Home Again, Kathleen." It was a paste-up, patchwork

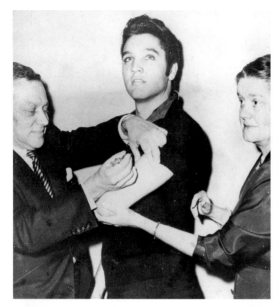

Left: taking his shots. Below left: spinning a record at his off-base home at Bad Nauheim, Germany. Below right: out on maneuvers with the Third US Armored Division. Opposite above: 14-year-old Priscilla writes a letter to Elvis in her Wiesbaden home, with his picture in front of her, March 1960. Opposite below: Elvis signs autographs for fans in Germany.

*Left: with Stella Stevens and Laurel Goodwin in* Girls! Girls! Girls! *1962. Below left: in* Kissin' Cousins, *with and without the blond wig, 1964 and right: astride a Honda in* Roustabout, *1964. Opposite above: enjoying a "harem holiday" (the movie's European title) in* Harum Scarum, *1965. Opposite below: sharing a ride with Dodie Marshall in* Easy Come, Easy Go, *1967.*

*Left: Elvis wears his spectacular gold jacket to perform, 1961. Below: Elvis and Priscilla Beaulieu at their Las Vegas wedding on May 1st, 1967.*

*The Happy Couple and the Cake at the champagne breakfast following their wedding.*

way to work, but not without precedent in recording and the end result was thirty-five songs, more than enough material for three albums, although typically for
Elvis some of the songs wouldn't be released for many years.

Elvis wanted to rerecord two of the songs from May, one of them for the
Christmas album, and to record a few more songs for his third gospel album so,
two weeks later, on June 8, Elvis made his last spring visit to Nashville. Jerry
Carrigan remembered it unfavorably.

"Everybody was drinkin', man, going outside and smoking dope. Nobody
was straight. And there was so damn many people in the studio we didn't have
a place to sit. The gospel quartets were spread all over the place, his guys were
running around, and Elvis was telling stories, so we'd just wander off, go outside, drink a beer, we'd talk, play us some cards. Then one of his guys came out
and said, 'Hey, you're gonna have to come back in, you're supposed to be
workin'!' Finally I said, 'Look, you want us to come back in there, you're gonna
have to clear some of those people out and bring us some chairs so we can sit
down.' So they brought us some chairs and we listened to Elvis tell his stories."

All night they were there and eventually they recorded four songs, and the
next night they recorded another four. Elvis was genial, relaxed during most of
both sessions, easy to please, usually accepting whatever came out the first or
second time. He demanded nothing more than the group's attention. But as the
second evening wore on, his mood changed radically, and the Presley temper
was revealed.

"One of the backup singers wasn't paying attention," said Carrigan, "and
he threw the biggest fit and took the microphone and THREW it down on the
floor and STORMED out. He said, 'I've run this damn song fifty times and you
all *still* don't know your parts!'"

Elvis's entourage scrambled after him, scowling at the singer who had upset
their boss.

"Hey, E," one of them cried after the disappearing figure, "hey, E, let's go
get some cheeseburgers, man, I know an all-night place that . . ."

In the studio the producer's voice came over the intercom:

"Okay, that's it, wrap it up . . ."

"What about tomorrow?" someone called.

"That's okay, that's it, the session is canceled, thank you and good night."

Elvis sat slumped in his limousine, head sunk into his high collar, staring
through tinted glasses, speeding for the Nashville airport.

Back home in Memphis, life returned to "normalcy," which meant going to bed
at eight in the morning and getting up in the middle of the afternoon to have
breakfast at five or six, then rent the Memphian Theater for an evening of

movies, or on special occasions rent the Memphis Fairgrounds to ride the roller coaster ten times in a row. By 1971, Elvis's normalcy was, by "normal" standards, downright weird. It was a kind of Alice-through-the-looking-glass life, where nothing could have made much sense to the outsider. Of course it made perfect sense to Elvis. Ask a small child his heart's desire and he might say he wished to banish bedtime and stay up all night. Elvis did that, taking logical refuge behind the argument that fame and its attendant bothersome fans made it impossible to go out in the daytime, or to go to movie theaters and amusement parks when others did. Similarly, when he wanted to buy a small fleet of German sports cars as Christmas gifts, the Mercedes agency was thrilled to open its doors at two in the morning. His favorite jeweler in Memphis, the man in California who designed his flashy costumes, no matter who you were, or where, if you were a part of Elvis's life, the calls came after midnight.

"Hello? This is Joe," said Joe Esposito matter-of-factly at 4 a.m., "Elvis wants to talk to you . . ."

Some of the guys who worked for Elvis still lived with him, sharing his lifestyle while serving him. Because Elvis was a longtime aficionado of karate, they took karate lessons too. When Elvis went on a yogurt kick, they ate yogurt until it came out of their ears. They took the same pills he did. They laughed when he laughed and they walked around on eggs whenever The Boss was uptight. Some might have killed for him. All believed they would die for him.

He drove only when he wanted to, he never placed a telephone call, he let them find girls for his lonely evenings away from home. On tour and in Las Vegas they protected him from unruly fans and potential assassins.

Most still had specific assignments. Joe Esposito continued to carry Elvis's personal checkbook and serve as the gateway through which anyone, including the other guys, had to pass. The puppy-like Charlie Hodge passed him his Gatorade and scarves during his performances. Lamar Fike, who sometimes ran the lights, mainly was there as a whipping boy.

Lamar could talk back, but never was allowed to win. There was a time he and Elvis were going to Tupelo with some others and they began trading insults. Lamar called Elvis a no-good singer, Elvis started shooting off one-line jokes of the sort Henny Youngman would tell: "You're so fat, Lamar . . . your toilet is so big there are whitecaps on the water."

Another time, Lamar fell off the toilet at Graceland and got wedged between the bowl and the wall. Laughing hysterically, Elvis had another one of the boys call the fire department to come get Lamar unstuck. Elvis never let Lamar forget that one.

The other guys would sit around listening to Elvis humiliate Lamar, almost as embarrassed as Lamar himself. Other times the guys would be jockeying for position. When Elvis took one to the store with him and bought him a new .38 with pearl grips, the next day he'd show it off to the others who then would see what they could do to get the first one in trouble. Elvis encouraged this. He deliberately spent more time with a new addition to the personal staff, knowing it would send the long-timers into a fit of jealousy. All of them, even Joe, competed ardently to be what one insider called "the Number One boy of the week."

In talking about Elvis's guys, it was easy to forget that their boss was married during this time. By the early 1970s, with Elvis returned to the public spotlight, it was his wife Priscilla who wore the mantle of mystery. She attended Elvis's openings in Las Vegas, and many of the closings too, the teased, dyed hair and black eye makeup of an earlier time replaced by her natural colors and simple, if expensive, dresses, purchased in Beverly Hills boutiques or at some of the nicer Memphis stores. Except for this, little was known about her. This was as Elvis wanted it.

Because she had moved into Graceland when she was fourteen, it was easy for her to turn her life over to Elvis, and the first seven or so years of their relationship, she did exactly what he wished. In time, however, this changed. She attended a finishing school, studied ballet, design, and modeling. And she became something Elvis never became: an adult.

It became harder and harder for her to accept some of Elvis's demands. When they'd married, he'd let most of the guys go, but now that he was appearing publicly they seemed to have drifted back into their lives. Joe Esposito and his wife, and Charlie Hodge, actually lived in Graceland with them. It wasn't that she disliked any of these people. She merely wanted privacy and space.

She also began to want an identity apart from being "Elvis's wife." A pleasant and unusually attractive young woman with an exploitable name, she'd often been asked to consider an acting career. She found herself more and more interested in design. Little Lisa Marie was three. A nocturnal lifestyle didn't fit any of this.

Outwardly, the relationship was good; both parties acted according to long-established guidelines: Elvis was protective and Priscilla feathered the nest. When Elvis saw a photographer with a telescopic lens standing on a hill overlooking his Los Angeles home, for example, he pictured a rifleman on the same hill and, fearing for his wife and child, sold the house. Just before they moved into the new one, Priscilla redecorated it with the kind of big, bulky furniture that Elvis liked.

Although Elvis and Priscilla agreed on most things, there were important areas where they didn't. Permitting Lisa Marie to stay up until ten or eleven o'clock and then sleep through much of the day like her daddy might be acceptable now, but what about when she reached school age? Priscilla also believed that Elvis spoiled the child.

Priscilla thought Elvis spoiled himself, too, believed he was too free with his money. When they argued about it, she objected most fiercely to his giving gifts to strangers. Friends and family, she understood, but when strangers were given cars and jewelry, it made her mad.

Most significant was her concern about Elvis's recurring "illnesses" and the "medicine" he took to relieve the many symptoms. But whenever she brought that subject up, he got defensive, or said he didn't want to talk about it or, more winningly, played the wounded little boy.

Harder for Priscilla to take were the other women. When she returned home from Vegas, or she wasn't in the same house with her husband—in Los Angeles, Palm Springs, or Memphis—beautiful young women passed through his bedroom doors like aspiring actresses auditioning for a Hollywood film. As always, there was a succession of regulars, too. Besides Kathy Westmoreland, his companions included a 23-year-old starlet who had been on the arm of MGM head Jim Aubrey at one of Elvis's Vegas openings and a twenty-five-year-old member of the House Armed Services Committee whom he'd also met in Vegas and later saw in Washington. Both were flown from wherever they were to be with him off and on for many months; one of them got pregnant, had an abortion, and later wrote a book.

If trouble was brewing inside the Graceland gates, outside Elvis's stardom was rushing through the skies, gathering momentum. In February 1971, Elvis was named the world's top male singer for the twelfth time in thirteen years by Britain's weekly *New Musical Express*. This wasn't particularly surprising, for in England Elvis held a godlike position. What was more noteworthy was the attention he began to get in the U.S. In the months following his being named one of the Young Men of the Year by the Jaycees, that part of Highway 51 that ran past his Memphis house was renamed Elvis Presley Boulevard, and while he was appearing in Las Vegas he joined Frank Sinatra, Duke Ellington, Ella Fitzgerald, and Irving Berlin as a recipient of the prestigious Bing Crosby Award, recognition granted by vote of the national board of trustees of the National Academy of Recording Arts & Sciences, for his "outstanding creative and artistic contributions of long-lasting duration in the field of phonograph recordings." In music, there was no higher honor.

He also set records in Nevada. In Tahoe, he played the Sahara, a club too small to afford Elvis and still ask a reasonable price for tickets, so several other hotels chipped in to meet his price, knowing their business would benefit from his presence; all existing showroom attendance records were shattered when 3,400 persons attended the dinner and midnight shows on Saturday, July 17.

A month later, back in the International in Vegas, they packed in 4,428 people in two shows, a figure that will never be topped because fire safety laws were broken to achieve it. (The room only seated 2,000.)

The International Hotel in Las Vegas had changed hands since Elvis was there in February. "My first meeting with Colonel Parker was five hours after Mr. Hilton took over the hotel," said Henri Lewin, the German-born Hilton vice president. "I came in at noon and had a meeting with Colonel Parker at five, so you can imagine how important he was. Tom Jones, Engelbert Humperdinck, Barbra Streisand, they are all great stars. But there is only one who when you announced his name he is sold out for the duration of the engagement. Never before and never again do I think that will be possible.

"Colonel Parker flew in right away from Palm Springs. He had in his contract a clause that if the hotel should be sold it would be up to Elvis and the Colonel whether or not they would extend the contract to the new owner. The Colonel said, 'I did business with [Kirk] Kerkorian [the former owner], I liked him, and I have no reason not to trust that you will be as good, or better.' This time we assured him we would be as good. Later the Colonel made it better. He accepted the same contract. It was not renegotiated. That was later, the renegotiation."

Elvis and the Colonel were perfect for Nevada. This was a state—more of the mind than of geography—that understood carnival, and by 1971, Elvis was America's best-known and most easily exploited sideshow act, a performer who demanded superlatives, personified exaggeration, attracted the bizarre and extreme.

For months ahead, all rooms in the hotel were reserved. Every day lines started forming before breakfast for the dinner show, with friends spelling each other for trips to the bathroom and meals when they remembered them.

Twice a night they filled every seat, paying $15 apiece to let their steak go cold and squeal and pray for a kiss. After the show they went to the powder room to exchange their soiled panties for fresh ones. "We never stocked women's pants except for an Elvis engagement," a powder room attendant said.

"I watched the audience as he walked out on stage," said Bill Jost, the showroom's assistant *maitre d'*, "and so many had their faces in their hands. They'd sit there and cry. It was almost biblical, as if the clouds had parted and down a shaft of light came the angels."

Jost's analogy is not extreme, for it was with this engagement that Elvis made his entrance to the rumbling, heraldic score of Richard Strauss's "Also Sprach Zarathustra," better known as the theme from the movie *2001: A Space Odyssey*, used in that picture's dramatic sunrise scene. This was followed by a drum-roll of controlled frenzy and an audience reaction of uncontrolled frenzy, as Elvis strode quickly onto center stage, a tall, handsome figure in a suit of black and white and gold appliqué.

"Waaaallll, it's all right, li'l mama . . ."

Still, Elvis wasn't as thrilled with Vegas as he used to be. After all, fifty-six shows in twenty-nine days is no performer's idea of fun, even if he's being paid more than anyone else in town. It was doubly hard to take because now he stayed in his penthouse suite of rooms, afraid to venture out in public. Only six months before he had FBI agents crawling all over the hotel looking for an assassin, an experience he remembered clearly and uncomfortably.

Yet, Elvis did enjoy himself, often laughing out loud at the antics of his most ardent fans. For example, when he sang "Teddy Bear," one of his 1950s hits, at the Colonel's suggestion he tossed several stuffed bears into the audience, always causing dozens to crash and dive for them, knocking over tables and drinks. By the end of the month, he was trying to heave them into the balcony, winding up and tossing them with a drum roll provided by Ronnie Tutt. Then he'd walk offstage and bring back a teddy that was fully six feet tall and about as big around as the portly Colonel himself. This one he rolled into the audience near the stage and with a signal to the band, began the next song, seemingly oblivious to the pandemonium he caused. Elvis barely could contain himself as two and sometimes three songs later, the fans sitting near the stage still were wrestling and tugging and screeching for possession of the big bear. This was typical behavior for Elvis. A man of boyish extreme, he would do anything for a laugh, so long as no one was hurt.

In Vegas in July 1971, Elvis hosted parties in his room to amuse himself. At one of them circumstances gave Elvis a chance to play one of his favorite roles. The Imperials, the gospel quartet that sang behind him in his show, were singing around the piano with Elvis when the phone rang. Sonny West answered it and said to Joe Mescale, a member of the quartet, "It's your wife . . ."

She was calling from their motel room and told Joe that a neighbor back home in Franklin, Tennessee, had called to say their house was burglarized. Joe's wife sounded extremely upset, so he said he'd go back to the motel immediately, then he told Sonny, "Don't say anything to E . . ."

Joe exited the suite and Sonny went right to Elvis to give him a full report. Whereupon, Elvis strode swiftly to the door, threw it open and called out to Joe, who was waiting for the elevator: "Mescale, goddammit, come back here!"

Elvis's orders continued to bark through the suite as Joe meekly returned. "Sonny, call the airport and get the plane warmed up! Red, get my guns! We're goin' home, we gone find that sonabitch! Tonight!" He turned to Linda Thompson, a girl he had with him, and shouted, "Darlin', get your coat. We're goin' on a posse!"

People were jumping all over the room, making arrangements, collecting a small arsenal of rifles and .38s. Only his date, who wasn't used to Elvis's sense of police drama, stood still. Elvis suddenly looked at her and said, "DARLIN', GODDAMMIT, GET YOUR COAT!" She got her coat and like a bunch of angry cowboys they rode over to the Bali Hai Motel in a pack of white Cadillacs.

All the way Elvis kept up a running monologue about the burglary. "Gotta tell your wife, Joe, that everythin' gonna be all right, probably just some kid broke in, took the TV for dope . . ."

Joe finally uttered some resistance to the idea of going. "It's not necessary, I appreciate your concern, E, but the police can handle it, and besides, we have a show tomorrow . . ."

Elvis was determined. "We gone get that sonabitch, Joe, we gone get him!"

The three limousines rolled into the motel parking lot and Elvis, wearing a white leather coat with a mink collar and cuffs and a big floppy "Superfly" hat, a thin cigar clenched in his teeth, followed Joe up to his room.

Joe's wife was stunned. She was wearing only a nightgown and her hair was in curlers. Elvis hugged her and told her, "Now don't you worry, I'm gone replace everything that's been taken, I'll replace it with better than what you had . . ." Then he went to the telephone and began a marathon series of calls, telling his producer Felton Jarvis, who lived in Nashville a few miles from the Mescale house, to get over there to supervise; calling the local police; calling the FBI.

"Okay," he said finally at six o'clock in the morning, seeming to have tired of the game, "that's it! Let's go back to the hotel."

Elvis didn't say a word about the incident again and no one said anything to him.

"It was just something he did to have some fun," Mescale said. "He wanted some excitement. He was organizing a posse. The little boy wanted to have a good time. Yet he really cared and this was the way he showed it."

It was also that he was growing bored again. The first few engagements in Las Vegas were challenging, but now they were predictable. This didn't go unnoticed. "Uninspired Elvis Delights Vegas" is the way *The Hollywood Reporter* described the month. "As performances go," the critic wrote, "Elvis Presley's show at the Las Vegas Hilton is sloppy, hurriedly rehearsed, uneven, mundanely lit, poorly amplified, occasionally monotonous, often silly, and haphazardly coordinated. Elvis looked drawn, tired, and noticeably heavier—weight-wise, not musically—than in his last Vegas appearance. And do you know what? The packed to over-capacity audience . . . positively couldn't have cared less . . ."

Elvis never saw this review—such things usually were kept away from him—and two months later he took the same show on the road again. Fourteen shows in twelve days, zigzagging all over the East and Midwest, starting in

Minneapolis, going to Cleveland, Louisville, Philadelphia, Baltimore and Boston, then heading west and south to Cincinnati, Houston, Dallas, Tuscaloosa, Kansas City, and Salt Lake City. In each venue he played to sold-out auditoriums—never outdoors; Elvis knew he could draw larger crowds in stadiums, but hated the acoustics. Total take for the tour, his first in a year, was close to $1.5 million dollars.

With so much time to plan it, this tour ran more smoothly than the first two in 1970. A year before, only the orchestra leader, Joe Guercio and two of the horn players went along and pick-up bands were assembled in each city and quickly rehearsed for what was in large part a spontaneous show. It didn't work well, Elvis was not comfortable and he let the Colonel know that he wanted familiar faces in the orchestra, so in 1971 the pick-up band concept—a popular one with many touring singers—was dropped and now Joe Guercio began taking not two but twelve musicians. With Elvis's six friends in the rhythm section, eight backup singers, the comedian who was in his show, half a dozen in his personal entourage, the sound men and people who drove the trucks of equipment from city to city, the Colonel and *his* entourage (including people from RCA), there now were nearly fifty in the group. The logistics were impressive. The number of plane tickets, bus seats, and hotel rooms handled each day—not to mention the number of tickets sold—made it clear that behind the scenes were at least another hundred, perhaps several thousand or more individuals who kept the machine running.

In each city there were bus and limousine drivers, ushers, souvenir salesmen, food concessionaires, box office representatives, telephone answerers, auditorium staff members. In Minneapolis, a small company paid all its overheads with the money earned from the production of Elvis Presley pennants. How many secretaries and executives at RCA earned salaries directly linked to the success of *their* Number One Boy? How many lawyers and accountants and booking agents (and *their* secretaries!)? How many fan magazine writers and editors and sneaky photographers trying to get a picture of little Lisa Marie? How many people *were* there tied into Elvis's career, dependent on his continuing success?

It cost Elvis money to keep this industry going. There were agents' and manager's commissions and other sums were paid to the concert promoters, the picture-book publishers, and the makers of scarves and teddy bears. The huge six-figure daily grosses dwindled rapidly. It was abundantly clear to anyone keeping track that being a giant star was costly. With taxes on top of expenses, it was a good month when Elvis managed to keep one dollar out of every ten he earned.

There were other problems too.

The first was brewing in August, in Las Vegas, when the Imperials, part of Elvis's backup chorus, decided they wanted more money and a solo spot in the show. They believed that musically they were at least as good as the Sweet Inspirations who opened the show and when Joe Mescale, who also served as the quartet's manager, admitted he'd asked for too little money in the beginning, the other three insisted he confront the Colonel instantly. Nervously, Joe approached the hulking Colonel, who was sitting at the roulette table. Standing next to him, protectively, was Tom Diskin, the Colonel's number one lieutenant and whipping boy.

"Uh, Tom," said Joe, "I'd like to talk to the Colonel for a minute. It's important."

Diskin waited until the play was finished on the table and said, "Colonel, Joe Mescale wants to talk to you."

The Colonel didn't even look around. He said, "Tell Mr. Mescale I'm busy."

"Tom," said Joe, "the Colonel has to understand that we need more money, or at least he has to pay for our motel rooms, or our outfits. We're just not making enough to cover it. We're staying in crappy motels and . . ."

The Colonel interrupted, but still refused to turn around. "Tell Mr. Mescale," he said to his assistant, "that he's not gonna get it, he's wastin' his and my time."

Diskin turned to Joe and said, "The Colonel said you're not gonna get it and there's no way you can change the deal in the middle of an engagement."

"Well, we can't live with it."

Diskin relayed that message: "Joe said he can't live with it, Colonel."

And so it went for fifteen minutes. Both the Colonel and Joe talked through Tom Diskin; neither one ever made direct contact with the other, although they stood within arm's reach. Finally, Joe walked dejectedly away.

The Colonel may have handled the confrontation brusquely, even rudely, but he felt somewhat justified in turning Joe away, believing that Elvis had been more than generous. The Imperials also had been working with Jimmy Dean and, in fact, for part of the Vegas engagement Elvis had agreed to let them sing for Dean in Arizona, then flew them to Vegas in time to make his second show. Their pay wasn't cut during this period and Elvis paid for the plane tickets.

Soon after that Mescale went to Elvis and told him the Imperials wouldn't be going with him on the fall tour. Jimmy Dean had offered them the same money and a chance to open the concerts, as well as a feature spot on a television show. Elvis was hurt.

"You gone with that *cowboy?*" he said. "That *sausage-maker!* You're not gone have any fun with him."

He then asked Joe who he'd recommend to take his place. Joe suggested the

Oak Ridge Boys or J. D. Sumner's Stamps. J. D. was the godfather of the gospel field. Elvis had worshiped him as a child and so it was the Stamps who next went on the road with him.

At the same time, it was an open secret in Las Vegas that the Colonel was addicted to the roulette table, a man who was, hotel manager Alex Shoofey later said, "one of the best customers we ever had," good for at least $1 million a year. In addition, the Colonel was known to take everything from salted peanuts to sides of beef back from the hotel pantry to his homes in Tennessee and Palm Springs. There also was talk of his Dutch birth in the fan magazines and rumors in Los Angeles that said he was talking with Tom Jones's manager about selling his Elvis contract.

Worse than changing four backup singers and a problematical manager was what came to a head in November, the same month Elvis finished his tour—a widely publicized paternity suit. Over the years Elvis was the subject of more than a dozen such suits, but this one was the first to reach the courts and the press covered each tiny development as if the future of western civilization depended on it. For more than a month Rona Barrett made it a lead item in her network television reports and lawyers argued on newspaper front pages—as well as in court—about whose blood test meant what.

Eventually the girl's case was dismissed for a lack of believable evidence, but the repercussions of the suit were significant, because the party scene she described was accurate and never really denied. Worse, the details of the Vegas evening now were a matter of public record, printed in publications and broadcast by radio and television stations.

Priscilla and the other wives had had their suspicions about what went on. Elvis's prodigious appetite for sex was well known and only a fool would have been surprised to learn that many of the guys in his entourage helped themselves to the overflow. Still, as one insider said, "Priscilla and the other wives didn't like having their noses rubbed in it. They started asking questions. Some insisted on going on the next tour. And when they were told it wasn't practical, which it really wasn't, that only made it worse. What it all came down to was that when the shit hit the newspapers, it also hit the fan."

Of course it had been building for a long time. For years Priscilla and Elvis had been drifting slowly, subtly apart. Back at Graceland following the December tour, they tried to pretend nothing was wrong and it seemed in most ways to be a typical Presley Christmas and New Year's.

For the whole month of December, the big house and winding drive were outlined with thousands of tiny blue lights, a large tree went up in the living room, and Elvis settled into his habit of renting a movie theater for the after-midnight screenings that he held for himself and friends. The movies he saw reflected his fascination with police and violence and included some that were among his all-time favourites—James Bond in *Diamonds Are Forever*, the bloody Sam Peckinpah thriller *Straw Dogs*, and Clint Eastwood's portrayal of a macho San Francisco cop in *Dirty Harry*.

For little Lisa Marie and others, Elvis and Priscilla presented a compatible facade. She accompanied him to the movies and they exchanged expensive gifts. (When she refused a new car, he gave her ten new thousand-dollar bills.) And they hosted a party a few days before Christmas at Graceland. Ironically, it was at that party that it became clear to everyone that the seams of the marriage were pulling apart. It was as if Priscilla had decided to drop the front.

All night long, Priscilla virtually ignored Elvis as she chatted amiably and somewhat smugly with some of the wives present, hinting at an affair that Elvis still didn't suspect. "This," Priscilla told the girls, "was the year that I came out." Puzzled by her behavior, Elvis slumped into depression and even began to drink, something he ordinarily never did.

Suddenly, smoke began filling the room. Vernon and Jerry Schilling traced it to a wall and knocked a hole in the plaster with a sledgehammer, snipping the wiring that had heated up. Elvis watched them dejectedly and grumbled, "That's the funniest thing I've seen all night."

Priscilla left for California with Lisa Marie the following day, to be away from Elvis and near her new man. The story would be kept from Elvis for another two weeks and Elvis, in all innocence, still suspected nothing. He merely thought she was tired of his lifestyle, was fed up with all the boys in his life, and weary of all the girls.

# Chapter 21

# UPS AND DOWNS

At midnight one night soon after Priscilla left, Elvis told Charlie Hodge to turn on the lights in the well-house behind Graceland and set up some targets. Another of Elvis's hands was sent upstairs to Elvis's bedroom to collect an assortment of rifles and handguns. He returned with such a load of weaponry that he bent over backward as he walked. Meanwhile, Charlie had erected a man-sized target against the well-house door. Elvis picked one of the army-issue automatic rifles—illegal for a private citizen to own—and said, "Charlie, put up a row of clay ducks. See if I can get 'em with one burst."

First, they warmed up with some of the handguns and rifles. Finally, Elvis put the machinegun-like Browning automatic rifle under one arm and, like John Wayne spraying an enemy pillbox, he fired forty or fifty rounds into the well-house, sending bits of clay and wood flying in all directions, and setting the old structure aflame.

Elvis doubled over laughing as his father rushed to smother the flames with his jacket. "Oh, Daddy," Elvis finally said, still laughing, "let it burn. It's only money."

As usual when Elvis and his boys began banging away in the middle of the night, Graceland was visited by the police. By now, of course, the guns had been put away and when asked about all the noise, Elvis and his pals denied hearing anything, or said, "Musta been a truck backfirin'." The policemen knew better, but never followed through, choosing to tell Elvis to keep it down as they left with a smile on their faces. After all, they'd got to meet The King. And a king can get away with anything.

New Year's Eve he decided to stage another, slightly quieter but possibly more dangerous war. He and eleven of his friends pulled on heavy gloves and jackets and football helmets and went into the yard, where they chose up sides and Elvis distributed over a thousand dollars worth of roman candles, fire-crackers, and cherry bombs. No one was hurt, but when the play ended, the air stank with the smell of scorched wool and cotton and melting polyester, and everyone's clothes were gaping with blackened holes.

The diversion was short-lived, the mood shattered when early in the New

Year Priscilla returned from Los Angeles to share her secret: She was in love with someone else. Elvis was crushed. It would've been bad enough if she'd fallen for a total stranger, but the man, Mike Stone, was a friend! When Elvis and Priscilla had been trying to prop up their sagging partnership a year earlier, it was decided that she would begin taking karate lessons, to give them another common interest. The instructor Elvis selected was Ed Parker, one of his own teachers, and Ed passed her along to Stone, who was, like Ed, part-Hawaiian. He was also an international champion, then running a karate school in a Los Angeles suburb and separated from his wife.

Soon after they met, Priscilla's brown Mercedes was often to be seen parked behind the Sherman Oaks studio and she became one of Mike's most attentive students. After a while Mike and Priscilla agreed that her presence in the big classroom seemed to upset some of the other students, so private instruction began. Priscilla began sneaking letters and small packages into the mail, giving them to the secretaries at Graceland to post. While Elvis was in Las Vegas in August, the two began going to chic Los Angeles restaurants together. It seemed as if she were determined to let Elvis know, without directly telling him. The degree of Elvis's isolation is shown by the fact that he never heard a word of it from anyone.

Priscilla didn't torture Elvis with details about her romance with Mike. She merely said she had been seeing him, liked him a lot, and wanted a separation, and then she returned to California.

Elvis's reaction ranged from hurt to fury and according to those around him, he alternately sulked and raged. His friend Ed Parker, who had introduced Mike and Priscilla and who was still on Elvis's security staff, wrote in his book *Inside Elvis*, "The biggest setback in his life was the death of his mother, but the biggest threat to his ego was the loss of his wife. Had Priscilla died, he could have coped, but to lose her to another man was a mortal blow. There is no way to forget the night he took me aside at his home in Beverly Hills and told me of his impending divorce. He poured out his soul that night, and I saw him cry for the first time.

"'She has everything money can buy, Ed—cars, homes, an expense account. And she knows that all she has to do is ask, and I'll get her whatever she wants. I can't understand, Ed. I love that woman.'"

No matter what his personal state, another Las Vegas engagement was only a week off. Traditionally this was a time for him to—literally—get his act together. First, there was the matter of new costumes. Ironically, it was Priscilla who'd started Elvis wearing capes, starting just over two years before when she gave him the one he wore when he met Nixon. A year later, Elvis told his costume designer, Bill Belew to make him a black brocade suit and red-lined cape. Now, in January 1972, Elvis was ready to add a flowing, full-length cape to his

Vegas costume, an act that made him appear, as he stood in front of the mirror and looked at himself, more than ever like a hero from a Marvel comic book.

This was also the time for him to add new material to his showroom repertoire, requiring rehearsals. One of the new songs would fit the cape perfectly. This was a medley called "American Trilogy," three songs successfully pieced together a few months earlier by a singer named Mickey Newbury.

Although the original arrangement was little changed in Elvis's hands—only made flashier, somewhat more dramatic—"Dixie," "The Battle Hymn of the Republic," and "All My Trials" in time would assume the proportions of a personal anthem.

There was another new song added during this Las Vegas engagement and in its lyrics Elvis opened a small window into his carefully guarded personal life. "You Gave Me a Mountain This Time" was a ten-year-old song written by Marty Robbins whose second half seemed ripped from Elvis's own life:

> *My woman got tired of the hardships,*
> *Tired of the grief and the strife;*
> *So tired of workin' for nothin',*
> *Tired of bein' my wife.*

In Vegas, Elvis's moods soared and plummeted erratically. He thought about how he'd loaned Mike money to start his own studio at the same time Priscilla was getting serious about her new relationship. He felt as if he'd been set up and he sought refuge where he often did, moving from the uppers he had taken to lose weight the last few days before opening, to the wide assortment of sleeping pills that doctors had prescribed, allegedly to combat his insomnia.

His performances were affected. Some nights, when he decided to "show her" and be the biggest rock-and-roll-superhero-movie star-sex-idol-in-the-sunny-West, he was a consummate performer. Other nights the show was not so good. Reviews by the two Los Angeles newspaper critics presented divergent views. His reaction to the reviews revealed much more.

Frank Lieberman, the chatty entertainment writer for the *Los Angeles Herald-Examiner*, made Elvis a friend when he wrote a review that included such phrases as " . . . has finally got it together . . . devastating showman; confident, compelling and in control . . . power and thrust reminiscent of the glory days . . . sensitive, emotionally assertive presence . . . creative artist and craftsman . . . electrifying, rambunctious, resourceful and perceptive . . ." Elvis was so pleased that he had Lieberman summoned and, when asked, gave the first interview that he'd given in several years.

Two days after Lieberman's review appeared, the *Los Angeles Times'* man,

Robert Hilburn, said he was disappointed. He said Elvis was no longer a leader, but a follower in singing so many songs previously recorded by others. Besides "AmericanTrilogy," he noted Hoyt Axton's "Never Been to Spain" recorded by Three Dog Night, and Buffy Sainte-Marie's "Until It's Time for You to Go." It was, he said, an "alarming" trend. Hilburn previously had been one of Elvis's favorites and was granted several brief audiences in the past. Never again. Now Hilburn was on the Elvis shit list.

More personally damaging was the appraisal made by Joyce Bova, the one-time House Armed Services Committee staffer who had been an off-and-on part of his life. She made her last visit to Vegas at this time and said in a book she wrote years later that she confronted him about his drug abuse. She had shared Elvis's spiritual search and talked to him on that level.

"We all have divinity inside us, Joyce," she quoted him as saying. "Some of us just understand it more."

"I took the plunge," Joyce wrote. "'Elvis, if we're gods, or at least have this "divinity" in us, why do we need drugs?'"

"'Silence is the resting place of the soul. [Elvis said.] It's sacred. And necessary for new thoughts to be born. That's what my pills are for . . . to get as close as possible to that silence.'"

Joyce left him the following morning before he was awake, thinking, "What a small, dull, shitty way for it to end."

Priscilla moved out of the Los Angeles house on February 23, 1972, the same day Elvis closed at the Hilton.

Elvis had only a little time free following the Vegas engagement before reporting to MGM in Culver City for what would be his final film, another documentary, originally titled *Sold Out*, ultimately called *Elvis on Tour*. The filmmakers suggested by the studio, Bob Abel and Pierre Adidge, had met the Colonel and then Elvis backstage after one of the February shows at the Hilton.

Abel was a young intellectual who'd worked on David Wolper's prize-winning film about Bobby Kennedy, and with Adidge he'd just made a documentary about a Joe Cocker tour, *Mad Dogs and Englishmen*. "At that time," he said, "music was where it was really at. To me, it was the great artistic statement of our time. With the other great artistic statement of its time, film—what an incredible marriage. I felt like Alan Lomax out there recording Woody Guthrie. I was recording for posterity this great phenomenon. *Woodstock* had just hit and everybody was suddenly aware that it was an incredibly artistic, social revolution going on and I'd always wanted to trace its roots and I'd always wanted to make a film on Elvis. Then, again, I think it was partly ego. Because I saw all the films that'd been made, all the records that'd been made, and it was all pretty shoddy. I couldn't believe this crap that was turned out by various studios. I think Don Siegel did a good job with *Flaming Star* and there were some things about *King Creole* and *Jailhouse Rock* that I liked, but for the most part it was utter drivel. So when Pierre and I went backstage, we didn't know what to say."

At first there was small talk. Elvis was charming—a relaxed and congenial host amid a welter of suspicious yet anxious-to-please employees who remained pretty much in the background. Finally Elvis said, "The Colonel told me you're gonna make a film . . ."

"Possibly so," Abel said. "*Hopefully* so. If the mood and atmosphere are right, if the conditions are right, I have the desire, but not the commitment."

Elvis looked puzzled. "What d'you mean?"

"Well, I'm a documentary filmmaker and I'm really interested in the man who makes the music, not just in recording the music, although I'd like to get your real music on film, too, because I haven't been too impressed by the music you've put on film so far. If we can develop an interest in you, it might be an interesting film to make . . ."

Elvis interrupted: "Do you like my music?"

Abel said he did, delivering a monologue that focused on Elvis's music in the 1950s. He once took a long train ride with Willie Mae "Big Mama" Thornton, he said, and talked with her about how hard it was for blacks to get certain songs played back then and about how this guy Elvis Presley came and stole their music. He talked about the two top songwriters of the period, Jerry Leiber and Mike Stoller, who'd written many of Elvis's early hits ("Jailhouse Rock," "Love Me," "Hound Dog," etc.). Abel said that during the 1950s, "I really wanted to take a punch at you." Elvis rocked back in his chair and laughed. "A lot of people did take punches at me . . ."

"It's true," Abel said. "I admired you on the one hand, and yet on the other hand I was trying too hard to get a girl to kiss me or to let me get my hand under her sweater, when I knew that any girl would have pulled her pants down for Elvis Presley. I hated you for that. Because you had total access to their pants and I couldn't even get access to their lips."

Now Elvis practically fell off his chair with laughter. "That's . . . that's . . . that's the funniest fuckin' thing I've ever heard."

"I didn't like the first documentary," Abel said later. "Denis Sanders did a hatchet job on Elvis, quite frankly. There's a part of me that's a missionary and I think the world deserved a better image of Elvis than cross-cutting him with a guy who's cutting up the meat eating dinner. When the Beatles met Elvis, there was this incredible silence across the room. Then John Lennon came forward and said, 'Until there was you, there was no one.'

"And that's how I felt. I told Elvis that everybody had photographed and filmed Mount Rushmore and the Washington Monument, but no one had done him yet. I told him there was no lovely, permanent record that we could refer back to in a positive way. I said I thought it was about time someone did something, since we were all getting along in years.

"I liked him," Abel said, "I really did. There was an ingenuous quality about him. There was a brightness and an awareness, and a vulnerability and a sensitivity about him that I really liked. I said, 'Look, if we make a film, we'll have to get access to old pictures, we'd want to talk about your childhood.' Later that was a problem, but at the time he said he'd talk to the Colonel, and we left."

A week later Abel and Adidge were told they probably, but not definitely, had the assignment—the Colonel played his game this way—and while Abel organized crews and equipment in Los Angeles, Adidge, the more gregarious of the two, went on a 72-hour jet tour with Parker to look at the auditoriums Elvis would play in April, to see which ones were best for filming.

Before going on the road with Elvis, they then filmed in MGM's Culver City recording studio, where on March 27, 28, and 29 Elvis and his show band rehearsed and joked around for the cameras. Although Elvis had used these musicians in live recording in Las Vegas, this was the first time he'd taken all of them into the studio together.

Elvis and his musicians recorded seven songs in the three days and less than a week later left for Buffalo, New York. Abel and Adidge had picked four cities in the South for major filming and Abel went along to Buffalo to familiarize himself with Elvis's repertoire and stage movements.

"He came out on stage, in total blackness. The orchestra went into 'Thus Spake Zarathustra.' I'm sure he hadn't read Nietzsche or understood his concepts, or knew about [Richard] Strauss and the Third Reich, but it was the perfect piece of music for him. So, there was total darkness, then this blinding flash of light. I'm not talking about the super trooper—the big spotlight—but the 15,000 flashbulbs from the Instamatics going off simultaneously.

"I saw a woman run down the aisle at full speed and launch herself like a SAM missile, like an Evel Kneivel motorcycle . . . From four rows back she just took a leap and sailed through the air and landed with a splat, skidding across the stage the way you'd see a seal or a walrus at Marineland. Elvis saw her coming and sidestepped her and she slid right into the drums. I knew then that that was the kind of stuff we had to put into the movie."

Buffalo was still thawing after a bitter winter, and from there Elvis and the fifty or sixty persons in his entourage went to Detroit and Dayton, then dove into the South, where they knew the weather would be warmer, and also the audiences. There were two shows—afternoon and evening—in Knoxville, another two in Hampton Roads, individual concerts in Richmond, Roanoke, Indianapolis, Charlotte, and Greensboro. Double concerts followed those in Macon and Jacksonville, then there were evening shows in Little Rock and San Antonio. The tour closed in Albuquerque. Nineteen shows in fifteen days, in huge arenas and coliseums. Again all the shows were sold out, leaving Elvis with grosses of about $100,000 for each show.

"I took a 3/4-inch Sony Portapack with me when I previewed the show in Buffalo to videotape the concert so we could study the music and study all his moves," Abel said, "so that when we went in to shoot we'd know the entire choreography of the show. It was mandatory that any cameraman who was to work for us had to watch the tape I'd made to know all the moves. We knew that by the time we got to San Antonio and the music started it'd be so loud we couldn't maintain communication with any of the cameramen."

Incredibly, even after they began filming in Hampton Roads April 9 they didn't have a final go-ahead from the Colonel, so they took no chances and went out of their way to please. They rehearsed the camera moves during the matinee and filmed that night, then Abel rushed the film to Hollywood where he had it developed, meeting the Colonel the following day in Charlotte to show it to him, without sound, on a 16-mm projector in the local auditorium. At the time, Abel thought his beard might have made the Colonel wary.

"Hollywood guys with beards were suspect," he said. "It wasn't that long after *Easy Rider*. The Colonel said he'd watched us and he'd gotten reports about us and he was confident we were doing a superb job. He said he'd misjudged us and we could shoot anything we wanted up on the stage and he didn't want to impede us and we had his blessings."

"I feel honored," Abel told the Colonel. "There is one thing we need. We need more access. We have to get closer to Elvis."

The Colonel looked at Abel for a minute and said, "If you deliver, I'll deliver." So saying, he lifted his cane and slammed it down on the auditorium floor near his chair. Abel and Adidge got up and left, to begin planning the next day's filming. Abel was a worrier with a tendency to over-shoot. "Hampton Roads was fabulous, the best we ever got. Everything worked and what we filmed that first night was most of what we used in the film. The night he wore the powder-blue jumpsuit. It was a magic night. We wanted something more. A good concert doesn't make a good film. Throughout, I experienced a general despondency about not having enough."

As a consequence, Abel and Adidge and their pack of cameramen followed Elvis virtually everywhere, once he exited his hotel rooms—backstage, into his dressing rooms, into the limousines after the shows, and then into his chartered jet. The mayor of Roanoke presented him with a key to the city, shaped like a guitar; Elvis, dressed immaculately in one of his dark blue, high-collared suits, accepted the honor most graciously. In this and in every other public and semi-public situation, Abel said.

Elvis revealed little more than his politeness and a good-natured, macho camaraderie with those in his personal entourage. Once he was unfailingly kind to an aggressive, obnoxious fan, refusing, as Abel put it, to "spoil that person's moment." Another time, when Adidge got into a limousine with a small tape recorder stuck into his pocket, he asked Elvis about the night before and Elvis, slumped in his seat, wearing the dark glasses he wore all the time now, mumbled, "Sheeeeet, last night I had my face buried in a beaver." Joe and Sonny and Red laughed loudly in response.

"I heard the same jokes and small talk over and over," Abel recalled. "After every show, you knew what was going to be said in the limousine. He'd be sweating, a towel around his neck, and breathing hard, very nervous. In Jacksonville, I remember he'd cut his finger when a girl from the audience had rushed the stage and grabbed for a ring. The boys fussed over the cut. Elvis didn't care about that. He wanted to know, 'How'd it go?' 'Good show, boss!' they said back to him. And then I caught a moment, I think. He said the people had started coming at him as he left, the security wasn't good enough. He felt he hadn't given a good performance. The guys started talking and Elvis tuned them out and started gazing out the window. It was just a sliver of film out of maybe 100,000 feet of film that we shot, about fifty hours in all, and it was that unguarded moment that I was looking for. He got a faraway look in his eye. They were going over a bridge. He'd done this hundreds and hundreds and hundreds of times and I wondered what it was like when he was seventeen. When I got back to Hollywood I asked James Burton to do a funky, slowed-down version of 'Don't Be Cruel' for the soundtrack. I grease-penciled the position of Elvis's face on the Movieola and sifted through hundreds of old pictures we'd collected until I found the shot that matched, from when he was seventeen. He was on a train, looking out of the window. And I did a match dissolve. The point I wanted to make was that this man had been doing this for seventeen or eighteen years. What loneliness he must've felt!"

Each day the film was flown to Los Angeles for processing, so that a day after the tour was complete, editing could begin. At the same time, a research staff was collecting more photographs from the 1950s, along with early television film, from Steve Allen, Jackie Gleason, and Ed Sullivan, while still others began cutting out all the romantic scenes from Elvis's movies to create a montage of Elvis kissing his leading ladies. Initially, Elvis and the Colonel opposed the use of old pictures. Elvis had worked to remove the anti-establishment stance of his past and this wasn't an image he wished to project, even as part of a historical retrospective. Finally, Jerry Schilling, who'd gone to work for Abel and Adidge as an assistant film editor, went to Elvis and asked him to reconsider. Jerry caught him alone at home, brushing his teeth, and after Jerry made his appeal, Elvis relented.

Another time Jerry went to Elvis, this time with Joe Esposito present, to ask Elvis to let Adidge and Abel do an interview. "What they want to do, Elvis, is get your thoughts about performing and rehearsing and stuff and then use your voice over the pictures and some of the film." Elvis didn't like interviews and it was against the Colonel's policy. Again he relented, however, and the first week of May he and Red, Sonny, Joe, and Charlie Hodge entered a small dressing room at MGM where Pierre and Bob were waiting with a cassette tape recorder.

Afterward, transcripts of the two-hour interview were guarded like high-level war plans and Adidge was quoted in *Rolling Stone* as saying Jerry Schilling learned more about his boss that afternoon than he had in seven years. Stan Brossette, who worked as Elvis's publicist on many of his MGM movies, said much the same thing. A year after Elvis's death the transcript was still being talked about in whispers and when finally a copy was produced, it was handed over with the strongest plea to keep the source unknown. Never was anything controversial said. Even the questions were friendly, almost patronizing. The good-guy image held, the modesty seemed real, unshakable.

Life wasn't all smooth. Elvis may have given a relaxed and reflective interview and between sellout concerts occasionally he may have found himself face-down between someone's thighs—as he so bluntly phrased it for Pierre Adidge—but in between all of that, he remained depressed about the formal and final split with Priscilla.

"For six months after Priscilla left, he wouldn't allow our wives or girl-friends around," said T. G. Sheppard, the country singer then working as a promotion man for RCA. "I was going by my real name. Bill Browder, then. I went to work for RCA in Memphis; I was their promotion manager and if you're a promotion man and you have an artist in your area, you're there to assist that artist with anything he may need as far as business is concerned. Far as RCA was concerned, if Elvis wanted anything, I had to pick up the phone and call RCA. And if Elvis wanted me to go somewhere with him and I'd say, 'I can't, I have to go to work tomorrow,' he'd say, 'Hey, wait a minute, I *am* RCA!' If he said go, I'd go. Over the years, we got close. I remember, after Priscilla moved out, we'd get calls from Charlie Hodge to tell us that Elvis was wanting some company up to the house, at Graceland. Because I was married to Diana and I knew Elvis liked her and all, I'd ask Charlie, 'Do we bring the wives?' And Charlie always said, 'No, no women.'"

According to Becky Yancey, then a secretary at Graceland, "He tried to be cheerful during those days and occasionally he stopped in the office to talk. Now and then he warned us to watch out, because he was a swinging bachelor again. But he didn't fool us. He was terribly hurt . . ."

T. G. Sheppard agreed: "I saw so many hours of sadness and hurt and bewilderment, as to life in general, as to maybe what was happening to him. When the marriage failed, it was such a damaging blow. Here's a man who was brought up in a Southern, Christian environment, where marriage was labeled forever. It was very special. You got married, you had kids and you grew old together. Divorce didn't happen. Marriage was very sacred. I think when that failed, it was a turning point in his life. Things seemed to change. It never was the same. The health problems came, the problems that didn't seem to appear before. Seemed like life became more difficult. It didn't flow like it did before.

"After a while, he began to let the girlfriends and wives come back. He talked about his marriage a lot to my wife and myself. He'd say, 'I don't want you two to ever split up.' And his voice would crack sometimes. I could see he was hurtin'. And this wasn't just after she moved out, it was years later too, after I'd started singing. He'd say, 'Bill, you don't know what's in store for you . . .'

"What do you mean, Elvis?"

"'You gone be successful and it's gone be tough on your marriage. Always remember, if you leave your home and walk away from that door and that woman is smiling, it can make your day or your night real easy. But if you walk away and she's unhappy, it can make it very miserable. So always take that extra few minutes to leave your home in order. Take the time with your wife. Don't take her for granted.'"

T. G. said, "He always preached to my wife and me the importance of staying together and working things out, never divorcin' because of the music industry. He would turn to Diana and say, 'Try to understand what he'll be goin' through. Stay with him, because he's gonna need you.' Then he would always slide over into religion or go in another direction. You could see he was gettin' so deep into it, he'd have to shrug it off and go in another direction. And we had this conversation often."

T. G. was not alone. Others agreed with his assessment. "After he and 'Cilla split up, he lost control," said Dee Presley, his stepmother from soon after his army days until she and Vernon separated in 1974. Almost to a man, Elvis's hired hands now say the same thing. "It was as if he took the third strike," said one. "His twin brother died at birth—that was strike one. Then his mama died—that was strike two. Number three was Priscilla divorcin' him."

The songs he sang showed the same melancholy. One he had included on the tour—the first featured in the documentary, in fact—was one that would be released as a single. "Separate Ways" was written by Red West, and it probably seemed the most autobiographical of his career. although it was composed before the split-up.

Songs like this and "You Gave Me a Mountain This Time" and others that followed in the next year or so represented a significant departure for Elvis. In the past, very little of the personal side of Elvis showed through in the material he selected for performance and recording. In the 1950s they were, with rare exception, predictably macho ("Baby, Let's Play House," "Hound Dog," "Treat Me Nice") or reflected what then was called teenaged lovesickness ("Don't Be Cruel," "Love Me Tender," "Wear My Ring Around Your Neck"). Then in the 1960s they became as bland as the movies most of them were recorded for.

Now in the 1970s, following his separation from Priscilla, Elvis was taking an inward look, so once again the texture and tone of his songs took a turn. There were critics who said Elvis never really showed his soul except in his gospel songs. That may have been true in the early years. In the final years, Elvis was hurting and he didn't seem to care who knew it.

This didn't go unnoticed by the Colonel. While touring, he and Elvis saw each other daily, even if only for a few minutes at the airport and then again just before beginning the evening show. (The Colonel then flew on to the next city to begin advance work for the following day's concert.) Between tours, they communicated less frequently and usually by telephone. Sometimes they talked directly, other times it was through the Colonel's lieutenant, Tom Diskin, and Elvis's Man Friday, Joe Esposito. In this way, the news that another one of Elvis's records had been certified a million-seller sometimes reached Elvis after it first had been passed from the Colonel to Diskin and finally to Esposito.

This didn't mean the Colonel didn't know what was going on. If he didn't get it directly from Elvis, or Joe Esposito, or Vernon, there was always someone else. "I kept him up on a lot of things," said Ed Hookstratton, Elvis's attorney in Beverly Hills, who handled almost all of his personal matters, including the paternity suit in 1970 and then the divorce. "I made regular reports."

Sometimes it seemed as if the Colonel were anticipating the command, predicting his boy's needs, and preparing for them. He may not have spent much actual time with Elvis, but the Colonel believed he knew him well. He saw the way Elvis got bored—and then fat—first in the movies and then in Las Vegas, so he conjured up new challenges to keep Elvis excited, exciting, and slim.

It had almost worked for the *On Tour* film. Elvis ate voluminously and compulsively in the weeks after Vegas then crash-dieted to look good for the MGM cameras. This was a pattern that had started many years earlier, in Hollywood, when he worried about how he looked on the movie screen. "He was overweight and pale on the tour," said Bob Abel. "We lighted him carefully. We used a lot of flesh tones. We used reds and ambers and golds and things like that to try to give him better color. We used camera angles and lighting tricks that would make him look better. He'd taken off a little bit of weight, but he was paunchy and he looked bloated. So we tried as much as we could."

The Colonel had another challenge planned: the most prestigious hall of all in a city Elvis had never played in his life, Madison Square Garden in New York, the first stop on the spring (1972) tour. If Elvis said stage fright was part of every concert on the road, the series of four shows the Colonel scheduled in two days in Manhattan had him downright scared. This was where all the journalists and critics and editorial writers who'd attacked him in the 1950s worked. Friends say Elvis was certain they'd tear him apart again.

"He really wanted to be accepted by everybody," said Jerry Schilling, who was on the tour. "It stemmed back to the early days when he wasn't. He always tried to make up for that, he tried to set that right."

He needn't have worried. New York was waiting for him not with animosity, but affection. In 1972 a nostalgia craze was forming. The media were developing and exploiting an interest in 1950s American kitsch, and many thought Elvis was a prime subject.

Elvis sweated and worried and dieted and exercised and took a big handful of diet pills every day for nearly a week before opening the tour June 9, so he looked pretty good. Not great—he was still overweight, his eyes were heavily lidded and there were bags underneath. Still, his mood was light and the press conference was as smooth—and bland—as grits. Elvis was the master of the Nothing Rock and Roll Press Conference, saying nothing, doing nothing, grabbing headlines anyway. It was a style he had perfected in the 1950s, a style the Beatles used later for *their* meetings with the press: cotton candy "news."

*Elvis, why have you waited so long to come to New York?*

"Well sir, we had trouble finding a good building. And once we found one, we had to wait our turn."

*Mr. Presley, why have you outlasted all your competition?*

"I take a lot of vitamin E. No, actually, honey, I suppose I've just been very fortunate."

*Elvis, are you satisfied with your image?*

"Well sir, it's very hard to live up to an image."

*You seem to have less grease in your hair these days.*

"Yes sir, I've stopped using that greasy kid stuff."

*Elvis, we're told that deep down you're really very shy and humble.*

"What do you mean shy?" Elvis said, grinning widely and standing up to pull back the folds of his powder-blue jacket to reveal his $10,000 gold belt buckle, a gift from the Las Vegas Hilton. It was a moment of braggadocio that

captured his boyishness perfectly, and Bob Abel decided to use the scene in the
*On Tour* documentary for just that reason.

Pretty soon after that the Colonel jumped onto the stage and said, "I'd like
to live up to my reputation of being a nice guy. This is it, folks."

With that, Elvis and his father, who had sat next to him through the affair,
were whisked away.

The first show was the most difficult—because it was the first, also because
it was the first time that an audience turned against Elvis's friend, comedian
Jackie Kahane.

"To begin with, his material was no good," said columnist Chris Chase in
the *New York Times* a week later. "And when the audience began to turn on
him, he whined . . . But the catcalls and boos were building, along with shouts
of 'We want Elvis!' and the comic shared his self-pity with the audience. 'You
are 20,000, I am one . . . that's pretty rough odds.' Nobody cared. They howled
until he gave up. 'You win,' he said, quitting the stage."

Backstage, when Elvis was told what had happened, he was furious. "Fuck
'em!" he barked. "Just plain fuck 'em! If they can't be polite, I'm not gonna sing
for 'em." Elvis was pacing nervously. His bodyguards were upset, running in
several directions, seeking the Colonel. Finally the Colonel appeared and
calmed Elvis down.

"At 9:15, Elvis appeared, *materialized*, in a white suit of lights, shining with
golden appliqué, the shirt front slashed to show his chest," the *Times* reviewer
wrote. "Around his shoulders was a cape lined in cloth of gold, its collar faced with
scarlet. It was anything you wanted to call it, gaudy, vulgar, magnificent . . ."

This—from the *New York Times*, mind you—was typical. "A stone gas,"
said *Billboard*'s writer. "Elvis has nothing really to do with time. To our everlasting love and envy, he has transcended the exasperating constrictions of time
and place." "Pure entertainment," said *Cashbox*, the other music business
weekly; while *Variety*, the "bible" of show business, said, "Presley is now a
highly polished, perfectly timed, spectacularly successful show business
machine. He performed about twenty numbers with supreme confidence in
routines which were better constructed and choreographed than the terping of
most Broadway musicals."

The Lively Arts writer for *New York* magazine went farther out on the same
limb: "The performance he gave us was a spectacular triumph of insight into
the mind of our mindless era. No demagogue of fact or legend has ever seen
more keenly into the blackest depths of his followers, or grasped them in so
many ways. He knows what ails and uplifts us, he rubs each of our dirtiest little secrets until it shines brightly in the dark, hollow arena of our souls."

One wonders what Elvis could have thought if he had read such analysis.

Chances are, he didn't see it. As such stuff was being written in New York, Elvis was back on the road moving from the Garden into the humid, summer gray Midwest, with shows in Fort Wayne, Evansville, Milwaukee, Chicago, Fort Worth, Wichita, and Tulsa.

In RCA's offices in New York and Los Angeles, meanwhile, dozens were readying the release of an album that Elvis didn't even know about. The decision to record some of the Garden shows was made less than a week earlier. "I don't know why Elvis wasn't told," said Joan Deary of RCA. "Maybe they thought it would make him nervous."

Like many others on the Presley team, Joan had been around for a long, long time. In 1954, she was secretary to RCA's Steve Sholes, the brilliant record producer and talent scout who authorized payment of $35,000 to buy Elvis from Sun Records. In 1972, she was an assistant to Harry Jenkins, the RCA vice president "in charge of Elvis Presley." That meant the Colonel was one of his primary friends and associates. It also meant that Joan Deary was part of the RCA Presley fire squad.

"We recorded two of the shows," Joan said. "The first was a dry run. The second was what we put out. We recorded on Saturday and Sunday. You never knew with Elvis what order anything was coming in. It was spontaneous. You'd have a list of songs that he thought he would use, a list he prepared for each show and sent down a few minutes before he went on—Charlie Hodge would bring the list to the guys in the band and the orchestra.

"We started mixing on Monday and decided to produce the record without any 'bands' or silent space between the songs. We knew that would make the disc jockeys mad, because they couldn't cue up to the beginning of any song, but we didn't have a choice. We'd have had to drop the level and we wanted to keep it up for the excitement. A week later we mixed another version for the radio stations, banding it.

"On Monday night we approved the lacquers and they were shipped to the plants so we could begin pressing records on Tuesday. We were in the stores on Wednesday. We went from actual concert onto the street in under three days."

For the four New York shows, Elvis grossed $730,000 and the album sold the by-now predictable million-plus copies at six dollars apiece. Elvis got to keep about a third of the concert money and a sixth of the record take. That eventually came to about $1.2 million for six hours of singing.

The Colonel had set up a month-on, month-off schedule in 1972—Vegas in February, tours in April and June, back to Nevada in August, the final tour of the year in November.

It was a schedule designed to get the most from Elvis, without taxing him.

Even so, Elvis usually played as hard as he worked. Following the April tour, for instance, he took a bunch of his boys and went to Hawaii to watch a karate demonstration, and a few days before the Fourth of July he took some of the same guys over the Tennessee-Mississippi border to buy $500 worth of firecrackers and roman candles for a re-enactment of his New Year's backyard shootout.

"He liked to watch movies," said T. G. Sheppard, "and he'd watch the same ones over and over again. Sometimes he stopped the film and had 'em run it back to a particular scene and watch that scene all over again. Sometimes we watched the same scene five or six times in a row."

"Other times," said Diana Sheppard, "he'd run a movie thirty minutes and if he didn't like it, he'd turn it off and you might like it, it didn't matter, that was it. You were left hanging."

"There were lots of movies I never got to see the end of," said T. G. "And sometimes people'd fall asleep. After all, it was the middle of the night, maybe even getting on to breakfast time. Diana'd fall asleep. And George Klein would too, but he'd snore and get caught. Others would do the same and Elvis would get on 'em. He'd say, 'Who's asleep? Who's sleeping? Charlie! Find out who's sleeping and wake that sucker up!'"

In assembling a picture of The King at play, the images loom big and bright, like the garish rings and buckles he wore. Lowell Hays, a Memphis jeweler who sold Elvis nearly a million dollars worth of "sparklers" (as Elvis called them), recalled when they first met. It was two in the morning, Lowell said, and Elvis was wearing a full-length ranch mink coat and kneeling in the mud behind Graceland, banging away with a .45 caliber pistol at a target pinned to the side of his father's office.

Elvis *liked* guns, really liked them. Living on Audubon Drive in Memphis back in 1956 after his first records hit and before he bought Graceland, Elvis broke a thousand pop bottles with an air rifle. In Hollywood some years later, whiling away time between movies, he and his hired hands fired at flashbulbs floating in the swimming pool; they not only exploded, they flared into light, making this a popular night-time stunt. Nowadays, Elvis always carried a Derringer in his boot, or in the pocket of his robe, and liked nothing better than to shoot out the front of television sets when he didn't like the programming; Robert Goulet was shot more than once—Elvis *hated* Goulet.

Personal paranoia explained part of his fascination with guns. In an era of growing terrorist violence, airplane skyjacking, and political assassination, much of the Third World and all of the modern West was becoming paranoiac. Everywhere one looked there were plots and threats and conspiracies. Elvis had experienced his share of them.

More than that though, for Elvis, guns were toys. When he became an excellent shot, it wasn't because he was in training, but because he enjoyed shooting guns and insisted upon being good at anything he enjoyed.

Thus he drove motorcycles and automobiles well, and got so he could stand up in the front car of the roller coaster and go the full ride without holding on. He may have held the unofficial world's record for the number of cheeseburgers consumed at one sitting. When he got into pills, and religions, he knew all there was to know about them, too.

Elvis was the ultimate expert. He bought (and gave away) more cars and took more drugs and hired more bodyguards and sang more songs and entertained more girls and collected more awards (and badges) than anyone.

"He was really into the police," said John O'Grady, the private detective who worked for Elvis's attorney. "He'd watch stories on TV about police officers being injured or killed and he'd give me money to take to them. One time he called up Kelly Lang, the newsgirl at NBC in Burbank, when she reported on one of these stories, and he had her take money to the policeman's wife.

"When he wanted to know about something, he'd go to experts. I explained the penal codes over and over, until he understood them. He really liked the idea of being a police officer. I think he could have been happy at that, except for one thing. I remember him asking me once what kind of salary a policeman made. I told him what I made as a sergeant in Hollywood. He laughed. He said, 'Christ, that wouldn't pay my water bill.'"

Another record he may have set was in the number of recordings released in a year. Where most artists were generally pleased to release two albums and two singles a year, Elvis and RCA managed to release more than double that. This was true throughout his career. And so it was now, in Elvis's eighteenth year as a recording star. New records appeared with the predictability and frequency of holidays—usually with the same kind of hoopla and noise.

In 1971 there were seven album releases, one of them a four-record set. A year earlier RCA had repackaged fifty of Elvis's best-known songs, calling it *Elvis: Worldwide 50 Gold Award Hits, Volume I*. The boxed set—it came with a picture book—rose to the number 45 position on *Billboard* magazine's "Hot LP" chart and remained on bestselling charts for almost six months. So, in 1971 RCA marketed another four-record package of old songs, the flip sides of the previously re-released million-selling hits. This was *Elvis: The Other Sides, Worldwide 50 Gold Award Hits; Volume II*, and it, too, sold well, despite its $20 price tag.

The other albums released in 1971 offered more substance. The first was *Elvis Country*, drawing its repertoire of songs mostly from the 1950s and 1960s country charts, hits by Billy Walker ("Funny How Time Slips Away"), Stonewall Jackson ("I Washed My Hands in Muddy Water"), Patsy Cline ("Faded Love"), Jack Greene ("There Goes My Everything"), and Eddy

Arnold ("I Really Don't Want to Know" and "Make the World Go Away").

Paying visual tribute to his country roots, the album cover showed a picture of Elvis at age two, the perfect 1930s urchin. On both sides of the album sleeve were the words—in quotes—"I'm 10,000 Years Old." This was a song Elvis had recorded and asked to have cut into bits and pieces and inserted between all the other tracks on the album. It contributed nothing artistically to the album, but Elvis wanted the people to know where he felt he was sometimes. Many of Elvis's friends say this is the way he often felt, that this is the way Elvis chose to share that feeling with others.

The rest of the albums released in 1971 were a disparate and generally undistinguished lot, including *The Wonderful World of Christmas*, comprised of the holiday songs recorded earlier in the year, and four collections of nine or ten songs apiece, stitched together from the recent and distant past. Three of these—*You'll Never Walk Alone*, *C'mon Everybody*, and *I Got Lucky*—were released on the budget Camden label, a subsidiary of RCA. The final—seventh—was called *Love Letters from Elvis* and was the only one offering new material, and with the exception of one or two cuts (such as "Got My Mojo Working") it, too, left much to be desired. It didn't matter. They all went onto the bestselling album charts.

Three of the five albums released in 1972 were little better, seeming to be held together with the weakest mucilage and defying ordinary reasoning. Released on Camden, for example, was something called *Burning Love and Hits from His Movies, Volume Two*. The title of the album said it all. "Burning Love" was Elvis's first gold record in more than two years and his best rock and roll performance in probably ten. Most artists would have included this song–it went to the Number Two spot in the late summer of 1972—on an album of recent material. Not Elvis. If you wanted "Burning Love" on an album, you had to buy it as part of a hodgepodge of forgettable songs like "Guadalajara" and "Santa Lucia." These performances were turkeys like "When the Saints Go Marching In" and "Old MacDonald," which were included in *Elvis Sings Hits from His Movies, Volume One*, released by Camden the same year. One wondered why the Colonel, who orchestrated these albums, did it, save for the fact that income from all Camden LPs were shared fifty-fifty with him. Both albums hit the bestseller charts. The one with "Burning Love" went up to Number Twenty-Two and remained on the list for six months. Perhaps this is the only way Colonel Parker could've slipped so many turkeys back onto the marketplace and not only get away with it, but make money on it, too.

One could ask many questions. The "greatest movie hit" idea was valid and with more than thirty musicals behind him, Elvis had a lot of good material to draw from. One wondered, then, why the dogs were dragged out of the closet instead of songs like "Love Me Tender," "Hard-Headed Woman" (from *King Creole*), "Blue Hawaii," and "Jailhouse Rock?" With very little effort an excellent package of recycled songs could've been created. Why, then, these duds?

At the time, John Wasserman pointed a finger of accusation at the Colonel in his column in the *San Francisco Chronicle*: "On the back cover of the album (*Elvis Now*) is 'Elvis—Now—Now', which is almost the trademark of Colonel Tom Parker, his manager. Remember 'Fifty Girls Fifty' at the vaudeville shows? Well, that's where the good Colonel's head is still at. He was a carny barker once, and a good one. He is still a carny barker but Presley is not the bearded lady, I sincerely hope."

Lest all this make Elvis's early 1970s album production sound dismal, or worse, keep in mind that there were highs to match the lows. "Burning Love" *was* an exciting single release, sung somewhat in the Vegas/Tom Jones style—Elvis liked Jones—and worthy of the sales success it got. A gospel album, named for the song "He Touched Me," took many of its arrangements from previously recorded albums by the Imperials and was recorded when that quartet backed him up in performance; it went on to win a Grammy Award—Elvis's first, and only—for best gospel album of the year. And an hour of Elvis live from Madison Square Garden was another natural for the Colonel's excitation machine, *and* Elvis's performance came across well on the record as well as in concert.

"This is a damn fine record, friend, and you're going to like it whether you like it or not," said Bob Palmer in *Rolling Stone*. "There's Wagnerian bombast, plenty of your favorite songs, some jukebox music and some Las Vegas lounge music. There's even some old fashioned rock 'n' roll. And most of all there's lots of Elvis, doing what he does best, strutting his stuff before his adoring fans." Elvis had come through superstardom, Palmer said, "without forgetting what it means to rock, that's the important thing. Now I personally feel that he could save a lot of money and tighten up his act by firing his orchestra and making do with a couple of timpanists and the Memphis Horns, and if he just did stuff like 'Polk Salad Annie' and 'That's All Right' and forgot about Las Vegas for awhile, I'd like that too. But there's lots of people rocking and rolling to Elvis who wouldn't be caught dead at a Faces or a Stones concert, people who don't know the difference between Sun Records and Sun Ra, but who will be more than happy to tell you what they like. And what *they* like is remembering sock hops and looking forward to that big Vegas vacation. So everybody gets enough of what they want to get what they need."

At the same time, it was as if Elvis were in quarantine, as if he were the modern equivalent of literature's "man in the iron mask," a sort of opposite bookend to another famous Las Vegas recluse, Howard Hughes. The time spent locked away in a heavily guarded penthouse suite, the whispered stories of his appetite for sex and drugs and guns, the eccentric generosity, all this came together to give Elvis a mythic persona almost equal to that of Hughes. In fact, his persona was perhaps stronger. By going on the road and singing in Las Vegas and Lake Tahoe, Elvis gave his public a peek, leaving them wanting more. It was almost magical; now you see it, now you don't.

In August 1972, Elvis returned to Las Vegas. Each night before he did his noisy dinner show, Elvis met with the Colonel, who told him if there'd be any celebrities in the audience and then passed along the day's news. On August 4, for example, the day Elvis opened, the Record Industry Association of America announced that retail sales of Elvis's Madison Square Garden album had passed the million-dollar mark. Elvis was presented with a gold record. Pictures were taken.

On another night the news passed along to Elvis was not festive. This was on August 18, halfway through the engagement, when he was told that earlier that day his attorney in Beverly Hills, Ed Hookstratton, had appeared in Santa Monica divorce court. The lawsuit filed was typical for the time; the male (Elvis) was doing the suing, claiming "irreconcilable differences," a standard California catch-all of the time, and Priscilla got custody of Lisa, who was then four years old. Priscilla was given a lump payment of $100,000, plus $1,000 monthly spousal support, and an additional $500 in child support. Hookstratton said he had tried to talk her into taking more, but she refused. When the Colonel passed along this news, alone with Elvis in his dressing room—having dismissed the bodyguards—Elvis merely nodded.

On still another night, the news was cause for celebration. This was just before closing, when Elvis was given a copy of a press release that would be issued by RCA the following day, September 4, announcing an hour-long concert would be televised in Honolulu in January and broadcast around the world by satellite. The show was to be televised at 1 A.M. Hawaiian time to allow the live performance to be viewed in prime time in Australia, Japan, Korea, New Zealand, the Philippines, Thailand, and to U.S. forces in Vietnam. The following night the show would be shown in twenty-eight European countries via a Eurovision simulcast, and NBC-TV would show the concert in the United States still later. Ultimately, this concert would be seen by an estimated one-and-a-half billion people.

That wasn't all. Within days of the concert, RCA expected to release a two-record album, simultaneously throughout the world.

Elvis finished reading the press release and handed it back to the Colonel. This time he smiled.

# Chapter 22

# ALOHA!

Obviously, The Colonel and others had been at work for some time, booking the 8,500-seat Honolulu International Center, getting NBC-TV's agreement to pay much of the production cost in exchange for the right to broadcast the concert twice, getting RCA to provide further backing and agree to release the two-record set practically overnight.

As the Colonel and his staff supervised the setting of details for the show, and incidentally began planning a November tour, Elvis's health and habits went downhill again. Years later, three of his bodyguards would write a book that emphasized the darker side, *Elvis: What Happened?* The singer's separation from Priscilla and the subsequent divorce action, they said, resulted in a "yo-yo" pattern of behavior.

"Man, we were going through tough times," said Sonny West. "Elvis's diet was going mad. He would eat whole gigantic cakes all by himself. He would get mad at us after he ate the stuff, and if we hid it from him he would get mad again."

Elvis's diet had never been good. That is, at best he preferred the simple things—meat and potatoes, and never anything fancy. Occasionally, Jerry Schilling's devotion to "health foods" would rub off on Elvis, or Elvis would go on a yogurt kick. But generally he ate sweets and starch—hamburgers by the stack, ice cream by the half gallon, bacon a pound at a time, a dozen devilled eggs, bags and bags of potato chips.

"When Elvis was troubled," Ed Parker wrote in his book, *Inside Elvis*, "all of his resolve would fly out of the window. Without consciously realizing what he was doing he would consume cheeseburgers, french fries, pizzas, ice cream, popsicles by the box, banana and peanut butter sandwiches, Pepsi-Cola and a stomach-wrenching assortment of junk foods. It was as though he were trying to comfort the spirit within by stroking it with food."

As Elvis's bodyweight increased, as his moods swung wildly, in Los Angeles the Presley machine ground feverishly on. The Colonel received weekly reports from Memphis, when Joe Esposito called. By now, he'd learned to read between Joe's lines, as Joe always said Elvis was fine, "No problems,

Colonel . . . " The Colonel, and others at RCA and in the Colonel's office, knew what that meant. They also knew that Elvis always rose to a challenge, and if an audience of more than a billion wasn't a challenge, what was?

In offices at RCA, artwork was being readied for the album and time was being reserved at the pressing plant; initial reports indicated that orders for the record would go well past the one-million album mark. Across town, in the Colonel's circus of offices at MGM, his staff was hammering out final details of the tour schedule that would climax in Honolulu November 18, when Elvis would hold a press conference personally announcing details of the satellite show. The Colonel also was on the phone daily to NBC-TV in New York, talking to Bob Sarnoff, the network president, about who would produce and direct the show.

The man suggested by Sarnoff was Marty Pasetta, a Californian then in his late forties whose forte was the entertainment special. An independent who didn't work for any network, he had a forceful personality and a proven ability to juggle many complicated details simultaneously, a claim backed up by his directing the Emmy, Grammy, and Oscar shows for television. He also had produced and directed five Don Ho specials in Hawaii, so he knew the islands fairly well.

"The way I got it," Marty said, "Elvis had liked the first NBC show, the one he did in 1968, but he wasn't knocked out by all the production. He wanted the pure sense of a concert. NBC called me and I went to look at Elvis in performance in Long Beach. I expected to see a gyrating person moving all over the stage. He was far from that. He was staged, quiet. In fact, I was wondering how I was going to make an hour-and-a-half show sustain without anybody else on it with what I saw. I went back to discuss it with NBC and they said, 'You're on your own—discuss it with the Colonel.'"

Elvis had lost some weight for the tour, but not much. His face and torso were still bloated, his movement on stage sluggish, as Pasetta noted. The performances also were, for Elvis, short—lasting just under an hour in Oakland, for example, which is longer than most top-name performers were staying on stage, but represented considerably less than what Elvis gave his audiences when he felt and looked better.

The tour was one of Elvis's easiest, with short flights to Tucson, El Paso, and Oakland, and after that, leisurely drives from his Los Angeles home to the big auditoriums in nearby San Bernardino and Long Beach. The tour group then took a full day to travel to Hawaii and settle into—and throughout—the thirtieth floor of the Hilton Hawaiian Village on the sands at Waikiki. The press conference, Elvis's fourth in a dozen years, was held in one of the hotel ballrooms the day after his second Honolulu concert.

Elvis sat behind a mass of microphones, wearing a black corduroy suit and white shirt, silver-trimmed sunglasses, and a coral and turquoise necklace. He seemed rested, agreeable, at ease, and in control.

"What about marriage in the future?" he was asked.

"Uh . . . I haven't thought about it. I have a little girl, four years old. It's hard to put the two, marriage and the career, together."

"Are you a religious person, Elvis?"

"It's played a major role in my life, gospel music. I like it. We often go into our suite and sing all night."

"How do you account for your success after seventeen years?"

Elvis laughed: "A lot of praying, sir."

More seriously, Elvis announced that the broadcast would be a benefit for a local charity, the Kui Lee Cancer Fund, named for a beloved Hawaii singer who had died at age 34. Elvis had included one of Kui's songs, "I'll Remember You," on an album released in 1964, the year of the composer's death. This was suggested by Eddie Sherman, who had worked with the Colonel during the Pearl Harbor concert, wrote the Colonel and said that inasmuch as it wasn't permitted to charge admission to televised performances, perhaps he could ask for donations in Kui's name.

Once again Elvis had pulled it off, appearing somewhat jowly, but otherwise untouched by time, still the Southern gentleman, still boyishly innocent and ebullient, still generous.

After seeing Elvis in the Long Beach Arena, Marty Pasetta took a few sketches of stage design to the Colonel and said he wanted to build some excitement into the show. "I wanted to put a ramp in, I wanted to lower the stage, I wanted to get closer to the fans and the people, I wanted to generate excitement, so they could get to him," Pasetta said. "And the Colonel said no, no, no to everything. Finally he said, 'Well, you take it up with Elvis.' I said, 'Okay, I'll take my shot and go.'"

Elvis was vacationing in Las Vegas in October when Pasetta first met him. He went upstairs to Elvis's suite alone and Elvis was flanked by Sonny and Red and one other. As the producer sat down, the three took out silver-plated pistols and laid them down on the table. Pasetta was visibly shaken, but plunged ahead: "I saw your show in Long Beach and I didn't think it was that exciting . . . "

The three bodyguards sat forward in their chairs and Elvis just stared at Pasetta.

". . . but," Pasetta continued, literally sweating now, "I've got a lot of ideas about how to make it an exceptionally exciting television show . . . "

Elvis was amused by the producer's forwardness, and he began to laugh. They spent the next four hours talking and when Pasetta left, it was with Elvis's arm draped casually over his shoulder.

"Y'know," Elvis said, "this is the first time I've ever sat with a producer for longer than a half hour. Normally they come in and talk to me and they're out."

Pasetta said, "I felt I had to be honest in front or it wouldn't work. He understood what I was going for. I said, 'You're overweight, you've got to lose weight . . .'"

Elvis went home to Memphis after that and started "taking care of business," a phrase that was his motto and that was hanging around the necks of so many of his friends and associates. These gold pendants carried the symbol of a lightning bolt and the letters TCB, which meant do it right and do it now. Elvis was genuinely excited by the satellite challenge and once he was back behind the Graceland gates he began to exercise and diet like a man possessed. He increased the frequency of his karate workouts, often with Kang Rhee, his karate instructor since early in 1970. "Master Rhee," as Elvis unfailingly addressed him, was one of those recurring figures in Elvis's life to whom he turned for spiritual sustenance.

An immigrant from Korea, the fortyish instructor spoke in the uncertain manner of those still learning a new language, but his meaning was always clear. "My school in Memphis basically about self-refine, self-reform and self-respect. Not trying to raise champion, but help the weak and to build confidence, to make better human beings. I'm teaching here as an art, in the traditional manner. Anybody can fit this training. Some institutes, they emphasize power, breaking concrete blocks. Very, very few people can do this kind of power. Seems to me karate has to be, as long as they respect themselves, as long as they get better, that's what we try to do."

With Rhee around, it seemed Elvis read more in his well-thumbed Bible and other inspirational books—Chairos's *Book of Numbers*, Khalil Gibran's *The Prophet*, Linda Goodman's *Sun Signs*, various texts obtained from the Self Realization Felowship. Journalist Frank Lieberman recalls an incident in Elvis's hotel suite during the same period, when Frank was there with his fiancée, Karen.

"It was loaded with people, and we watched. All the guys were there with girls they'd picked up. Elvis knew they weren't there to be with the guys, but were using the guys to get to him. It was so damned awkward. Elvis disappeared after a while into the bedroom with a bunch of the girls. Karen and I were talking outside with Elvis's date and Karen was confused. Elvis's date said, 'Elvis is only reading the Bible to them.' We snuck up to the door and watched, and that's what he was doing. So many times I saw that happen."

It worked. As Elvis turned his thoughts toward his spirit, he also cleansed and tuned his body. He helped the process along with diet pills, but he also consumed large quantities of protein drink to make the number of karate and racquetball workouts reasonable. He drank only mineral water and began swallowing vitamin pills by the handful.

"He was fat and he had a lot of problems with his stomach, which just quit working," Sonny reflected in his book. "His body wasn't working. The pills were doing all the work, and yet when that television special came up, he dropped down to 165 pounds, thin as a rake and more handsome than ten movie stars.'

Quickly the pieces came together. Usually a new costume was designed only for Las Vegas, but Elvis wanted something special for Hawaii, so he asked Bill Belew to make an all white outfit with a huge eagle on the front of the jumpsuit as well as on the back of the full-length cape.

In Los Angeles, "We love Elvis" was being translated into the languages of countries where the concert was to be shown and the album sold; for this, RCA actually hired the Berlitz firm, while Marty Pasetta had the same phrases reproduced in neon and began designing a stage set that was so big it would cover 3,500 seats in the Honolulu auditorium.

Back in Memphis, although it was the first Christmas since Priscilla moved out, Elvis was feeling good. His daughter Lisa was present and would be visiting her daddy for two weeks. He also had Linda Thompson with him. In fact, Elvis and Linda had been inseparable for several months now.

They had met through their mutual friend Bill Browder, in August, six months after Priscilla left, when Elvis began dating again. While an undergraduate at Memphis State University, majoring in theater and English, she had held a few small beauty titles, then went to the Miss USA pageant as Miss Tennessee. She had finished four years at Memphis State, but still was twelve hours short of her degree and undecided about what to do when she met Elvis. Would it be Hollywood, where she wanted to act, or New York, where she thought she could model, or someplace else, as an airline stewardess? She said it was "my Prince Charming who decided for me."

From the start they were inseparable, and although there were many others who came and went quickly—including the actress Cybill Shepherd, another onetime Memphis beauty queen—Linda was the most important woman in Elvis's life for the next four-and-a-half years, until only a few months before he died. They had much in common, including a strong religious streak and a love of gospel music. As a youngster growing up in Memphis she sang in her Southern Baptist church choir and as a contestant in the Miss USA contest, she was teased by other contestants for reading her Bible daily. Linda said she took a girlfriend, Miss Rhode Island, for protection on the first date, "in case it got too wild and too Hollywood," and left her car parked illegally near the Memphian Theater entrance, "in case we had to make a quick getaway." After that it was pretty ordinary, she said, in a way that reveals her sense of humor, one of the things that Elvis liked in her. "He came and sat next to me and started getting a little friendly—you know, the old yawn and stretch of the arm behind the seat."

Linda would do practically anything to get him to laugh. That first Christmas together, Elvis was entertaining a bunch of his guys and their wives and girlfriends at Graceland, when he told Linda to go upstairs and put on her crown and Miss Tennessee banner.

"He was trying to show me off," she said. "He had bought me a full-length mink coat and had had one of his big diamond rings made over into a ring for me. He was happy to have a new love in his life. I was kind of embarrassed about it. He didn't know that, so I went up and put on an evening gown and put my banner on and then my crown, and I blacked out my two front teeth with mascara. Then I descended the stairs as if I were really into it, my beauty queen role, keeping my mouth shut. When I got to the bottom step, I smiled and said, 'Is this what you have in mind, darling?'"

Elvis's laughter rocked the room. One of the things Elvis's hired hands worried about in the final years was his mood. "How's his mood today?" they'd nervously ask each other. Linda did her best for the next four years to keep it cheerful.

January 1973 began with final fittings for his jewel-encrusted white costume and the shipment of tons of equipment from Los Angeles to Honolulu. Several days ahead of Elvis's departure, Pasetta and his crew flew over to begin filming big waves, misty mountain ridges, flowered trees, Diamond Head and coconut palms—footage that would be edited into the satellite show to expand it to ninety minutes for telecast on the Mainland. At the same time, RCA's Rocky Laginestra decided that the album would be recorded and released in quadraphonic sound, the process that recorded sound for four speakers, rather than stereo's two. Finally, on the tenth, two days after quietly celebrating his thirty-eighth birthday with Linda at Graceland, Elvis flew to the islands.

There were problems right away, one of them caused by Elvis, when he gave the belt to his costume to actor Jack Lord, star of television's long-running *Hawaii Five-O*. Bill Belew was called in a panic in Los Angeles and told to make another, fast. "But we've used the last of the rubies," he cried. "We'll have to get more from Europe . . ."

A second problem involved Elvis when he saw the stage for the first time, with individual risers, or platforms, for the members of his backup band, scattered widely.

"I'm sorry, sir," he told Pasetta, "but I like to have my boys with me. Isn't there some way we can keep everybody together?"

Pasetta crumbled before such manners and the risers were taken away. The rehearsals went without a hitch. The musicians and singers, who had arrived a few days before Elvis, were given books when they arrived, giving them their schedules for the next eight days, through the videotaping on the fifteenth.

"We rehearsed at the Honolulu International Center for seven evenings—singers one night, us the next," said John Wilkinson, Elvis's rhythm guitarist. "We had our days clear. We'd check with Tom Diskin and then lie around on the beach or go shopping, rent motorcycles and ride around the island, we rented paddle boats, we went on the Hilton luau cruise. Some of the guys brought their wives and girlfriends. It was a vacation, it really was."

For the Honolulu media, it was a field day, and now that Elvis remained in one place for longer than it took to sleep for awhile and then do a concert, he began to see some of the stories. All were filled with praise. And on the thirteenth, the mayor of Honolulu declared an "Elvis Presley Day."

Elvis enjoyed himself. His rehearsals were held secretly in the Hilton Hawaiian Dome, a geodesic dome on his hotel's front lawn; he wore some of his most outrageous outfits, including a long mink coat and white "Superfly" fedora, telling everyone that he was "in disguise." When he wanted to go shopping, one of his boys made the call for him and the store was opened at two o'clock in the morning. When Pasetta filmed his "arrival" at the Hilton's helicopter pad, more than a thousand fans were there. "It's just like the old days," Elvis said. Linda was at his side through it all.

An over-capacity crowd was squeezed into the big auditorium for the dress rehearsal Friday night. On Saturday the audience size was restricted and to accommodate those who were turned away, the Colonel arranged to have a virtual circus of entertainment outside—robots and clowns and high school bands.

Suddenly there were technical problems. Pasetta and the engineer from Hollywood present to record the album, Wally Heider, had brought so much electrical equipment with them, they ran out of power and two hours before going on the air they picked up a hum from the lighting system. "We thought we'd lose the album and had to go scrounging to the navy to borrow thick lead sheets to baffle the hum," Pasetta recalls. "They came in, sirens blaring from Pearl Harbor, and we got them in place just minutes before we started broadcasting."

They also discovered a ten-minute error in the timing of the show. When told about needing more material, Elvis merely nodded and sent Charlie Hodge out with the titles of three more songs for the orchestra.

From the moment he walked on-stage, wrapped in Richard Strauss and illuminated by thousands of Instamatics and hundreds of spotlights, Elvis was in total control, giving the viewer the appearance of looseness while adhering to a precise schedule.

After that, Elvis sang twenty-three songs, a wide assortment that swept up some of his distant past ("Love Me," "Blue Suede Shoes," "Long Tall Sally") and mixed it dexterously with the more recent ("American Trilogy," "You Gave Me a Mountain," "Suspicious Minds"), as well as a song he now shared with Sinatra, "My Way." Conforming to patterns long established now, Elvis leaned down into the audience so fans could kiss him and encircle his neck with hugs and leis. Behind him "We love Elvis" blinked and flashed in a dozen languages.

The backup band provided a thunderous beat, the audience a constant roar.

As he finished his traditional closing song, "I Can't Help Falling in Love with You," striking a dramatic pose, legs spread, head bowed, one fist thrown up and out, Charlie picked up his jeweled cape and, as Elvis slowly stood, draped it gently on his shoulders. Elvis stood with his head bowed for a moment and then took the cape and sailed it into the audience like a Frisbee.

Then, throwing up his hand in the Hawaiian, thumbs-up "shaka" sign—thumb and little finger extended simultaneously—he strode back into the off-stage darkness, leaped into a limousine and was whooshed back to his hotel.

"Great show, boss, great show," the guys seated around him in the Rolls Royce said. Linda snuggled into his side and purred, "Personally I was hoping you'd rip your pants."

The show went "on the air" by satellite at 12:30 in the morning Sunday. At that moment it was 7:30 p.m. Saturday in Tokyo and the show was the climax of a Japan-wide "Elvis Presley Week." The singer's popularity in that country was made clear when the station broadcasting the relayed program announced the next day that Elvis had broken all Japanese television records, capturing an astonishing 98 percent share of the audience.

The two shows also raised $85,000 for the Kui Lee Cancer Fund, $60,000 more than the goal set in November. In part, this was because of the Colonel's pressuring prominent figures, such as Jack Lord, to contribute $1,000 apiece to watch the show . . . while many children got in for a penny.

If Elvis was good for charity, he was better for business. According to Marty Pasetta, production of the satellite show cost $2.5 million. It was, he said at the time, "the most expensive entertainment special ever done." Elvis, of course, got a million of that, a figure far greater than any other performer had received for just two hours in concert. The rest was spread over a large area, providing work for hundreds of individuals.

Elvis took a half dozen of these with him as he left Hawaii, flying to Los Angeles and then to Las Vegas for a few days, and then on home to Graceland, partying all the way.

In the late winter of 1972-73 and on into the following spring it seemed that Elvis could do no wrong, that he was, clearly, the man with the Midas touch. In every medium—in film, television, and recording—he broke records and received prestigious awards.

The first accolades came following the release of the Adidge-Abel documentary, *Elvis on Tour*. Originally released to coincide with the fall tour, it remained in scattered locations for several months. According to Bob Abel, the film cost only $600,000 to make—not counting Elvis's million-dollar fee—and MGM got that negative cost back in the first three days in the theaters.

The reviews, on the other hand, were not so generous, what Abel called, sadly, "lukewarm." *Rolling Stone* exulted: "At last—the first Elvis Presley Movie!" But others cast the thing aside as if it were merely another in a series of Elvis Presley promotional pieces. Abel and most who worked on the film were surprised when it was nominated for a Golden Globe award and astonished when it won.

Elvis was in Las Vegas, following the hugely satisfying satellite show, when the Golden Globe awards banquet was held in the Hollywood Palladium. Elvis was between his 8:15 and midnight shows when the ceremony was broadcast, and he watched it on his bathroom television. A few of the guys were nearby, relaxing elsewhere in the hotel suite, when they suddenly heard Elvis yell.

"My God! Sonofabitch, we won!"

With that, Elvis came running out of the bathroom, pulling up his pants.

"We won," he said, looking around at the others, who had risen and started for the bathroom when they heard his shout. "We won the Golden Globe!"

It was also while in Vegas that Elvis was given two more gold records, for the four-record *Elvis: Worldwide 50 Gold Award Hits, Volume One*—a first of its kind, recycling earlier gold for newer gold—released two years before, and for *Elvis: Aloha from Hawaii*, available for less than a month.

In Las Vegas, of course, both shows sold out every night for a month.

Then, on April 4, NBC-TV broadcast the ninety-minute version of the *Aloha* satellite show, claiming, the following day, a 57 percent share of the audience, swamping the popular *All in the Family* and all other competition. The *Daily News* called the show "most impressive," the *Los Angeles Times*, "stunning . . . one of those rare television moments." Executives at NBC began talking about three more specials and Marty Pasetta decided that the first of these would have Elvis dropped into the Ginza in Tokyo by helicopter, the second would be in London, the third in Moscow.

As sweet as things were, they quickly turned sour. Even while in Las Vegas Elvis had begun to put weight back on again, as boredom returned and depression followed. More problems were caused by the increased use of pills, leading to throat and lung problems that drew doctors to his suite with the frequency of beauty queens. Five midnight shows were canceled, something that never had happened before. The Colonel apologized in writing to the hotel, said it would never happen again.

There was also an incident onstage when, according to Gene Dessel, the hotel's head of security, " . . . this guy next to the stage was trying to shake Elvis's hand all night and for some reason Elvis avoided him. He walked back to the band area where Charlie Hodge was at and got a drink of water. A girl ran up and before she could get to him, a bodyguard ran out. Elvis gave her a kiss and sent her back to the audience. The guy saw that and with Elvis's back to the audience, he jumped up on stage and started running toward Elvis. So Red West comes running off the side of the stage and grabs the guy and takes him offstage. Another friend of his sitting at the table gets up on stage to see where his buddy went. Well, Elvis thought they were coming after him. J. D. Sumner went to defend Elvis and Elvis stiff-armed the guy and he went flying back onto his table. They started cussin' Elvis out and Elvis started cussin' back at them. And the band kept playing. Elvis's dad and the bodyguards are holding Elvis. One of my guys was in front of Elvis and I was next to him. Then somebody else from that table tries to get on stage. My guy and I, we threw him offstage. My guards took him out along with the other guy who was knocked down. The insults went on for like a minute, minute-and-a-half, but it seemed like an hour. Elvis was so excited afterwards up in his room he didn't even know he had hit the guy."

It was also while he was appearing in Las Vegas that Priscilla hit him with a blockbuster that turned Elvis into a raging, shouting, vindictive man. She never said she exactly went along with the idea, but when she said her boyfriend, Mike Stone, thought it would be a good idea if Elvis didn't see Lisa Marie for awhile, Elvis started screaming. Priscilla had tried to word the notion tactfully, referring to Elvis's "demanding career" rather than making direct charges about his use of pills. This, according to Priscilla's friends, had become a major concern and she actually feared for Lisa Marie when Elvis was so often experiencing the effects of what he called "medication." Elvis reacted to the idea violently. He decided he wanted Mike Stone killed.

Ed Parker, the karate instructor still on the scene as a paid bodyguard during the Vegas engagement, recalled in his book that Elvis made such threats repeatedly. Red and Sonny West devoted an entire chapter in their book to an evening when Elvis walked back and forth in his suite and said, almost as a mantra, "Mike Stone must die, he must die. You will do it for me, you must, he has no right to live." During that awful night, the Wests said, Elvis actually pulled an M-16 army rifle out of the closet and pushed it into Sonny's hands and said, "The sonofabitch must go!"

Linda was the first to act. She suggested calling Elias Ghanem, the Lebanese-born physician who was building a reputation in Las Vegas for helping singers cope with "Las Vegas throat," a loss of voice caused by the hot, dry air. Elvis liked Elias, in time would give him expensive cars, over the years gave him tens if not hundreds of thousands of dollars, too. Whenever Elvis was in town, he was on twenty-four-hour call. He came and gave Elvis a sedative.

Red recalled that the rage continued for several days, with Elvis insisting that if Red refused to kill Stone, he must hire someone else to do the job. Red said he actually talked to someone who said he would do it for $10,000, and nervously told him, "I'll call you back." Then when he went to Elvis with his report, Elvis said, "Aw, hell, just let's leave it for now. Maybe it's a bit heavy. Just let's leave it off for now."

Red went to his friend Bob Conrad, the actor, and shared the incident. Conrad said he'd seen that same sort of reaction to amphetamines in others and told Red to humor his boss. This, essentially, is what Red and the others did for the following several years. However, they did make one significant attempt to dissuade Elvis from taking so much of his prescribed "medication." All had tried very casually to discourage his use of pills over the years, but always Elvis had ended up snubbing them, or cutting them out of the inner circle they all worked so hard to stay within. This time, Red and Jerry and Lamar Fike went to Kang Rhee. They knew Elvis respected the diminutive karate instructor and thought he would listen if he warned him.

"They ask me to tell him not to take any pills," Kang recalls. "Stop him take pill. At the same time, Elvis ask me to give him my certificate for sixth degree black belt in karate. I said, 'Let me think about it.' I ask Red and Sonny and the others come to my room. I was stay with Elvis in his house in Beverly Hills. I ask them, 'What should I do?' They said, 'As long as he wants it . . .' Ed Parker already give sixth degree to him and in the morning he expect the same from me."

The scene the next morning described by Kang and the others is a study in tension. Conversation between the bodyguards was minimal and forced, Elvis was nowhere in sight, remaining upstairs in his room because, according to Kang, "He afraid I say no when he comes down."

Finally Elvis appeared.

"When Elvis start to study with me in Memphis," Kang said, "I give every-body titles real quickly. Red West always walk behind Elvis, so I call him the Dragon. Sonny was always in front, so he is the Eagle. Joe Esposito is the Lion. Jerry Schilling is the Cougar. Elvis I call the Tiger. So when he come down that morning, I told him, 'You are the Tiger already and if you are going to be king of the jungle you have to lick yourself well, like a cat licking his wound.' I say, 'You should not depend on any pill or medicine to get well, you have to get well yourself.' I think he understood. And then I present the sixth degree black belt. Everybody standing around say, 'You know, Elvis, Master Rhee is right . . .'"

The feeling remained tense, but some of the tension disappeared as Elvis took the advice without reacting angrily.

That night, Elvis took Kang Rhee aside and showed him his badge from the U.S. Narcotics Bureau and said the Beatles were the ones who took drugs, not him.

A few weeks later there was another incident with another bodyguard, a blow-up over the use of Elvis's name to promote a karate competition in San

Francisco. This was the California State Karate Championship, probably the biggest karate tournament held anywhere in the Western world. One of the organizers was Ed Parker.

Elvis's interest in the martial arts was strengthening during this period, despite, or perhaps because of, the decline in his physical appearance and condition. The new television series in which David Carradine played a kung-fu master was one of Elvis's favorites. In performance, he continued to feature many moves from karate in his choreography and, after the shows, he still held classes or staged demonstrations in his hotel suites. So when Parker's big tournament was coming up, he invited Elvis, who accepted with glee.

Elvis organized the event as if he and friends were going on a safari. He had one of the boys charter a plane. He had others make calls for limousines and hotel rooms in San Francisco. He decided, carefully, what clothes he would take and supervised the packing. He bought Linda a new outfit. He invited Kang Rhee and had him flown into Los Angeles from Memphis. He also invited Joe Esposito, Charlie Hodge, Gee Gee and Patsy Gamble, and Jerry Schilling.

All went well, spirits were high. Though overweight, Elvis joked on the short flight up from Los Angeles, and sat back into the seat of the limousine, puffing on an expensive cigar. Then, on the way to the hotel, the mood changed. As they passed the auditorium, Jerry Schilling noticed that in big letters on the marquee it said, "Elvis Presley—In Person." He called it to Elvis's attention. Elvis jammed his cigar into the limousine ashtray and cursed.

"Those fuckers are doing it again! Godammit, Ed Parker knows better than that! Jerry, when we get to the hotel, you get your ass over there and you get my name offa that signboard, you hear! Charlie, you go with Jerry! Joe, you call the Colonel and then get us a plane to Los Angeles! Linda, I'm sorry, godammit, we're going home. The fuckers . . ."

As the limousine fell into a horrible silence, Elvis retrieved his mashed cigar and stuck it in his mouth. No one moved.

"Godammit," Elvis said, looking very foolish, "isn't anybody going to light my cigar!"

The Colonel was so mad you could hear him all over the hotel room through the telephone. Elvis stood listening impassively. There was a clause in Elvis's contract that forbade his appearing publicly anywhere within 500 miles of Lake Tahoe within six weeks of one of the singer's appearances there and Elvis opened in Tahoe in three.

Ed Parker blamed the local promoters, said they put Elvis's name on the marquee before he arrived and now the union people had gone home, so no one could touch it. Jerry and Charlie made it clear how unhappy Elvis was. Ed and one of his instructors took the letters down, violating union rules, and then hurried to the hotel to apologize.

Elvis wasn't ready to listen. "Okay," he said, finally, "we're going." And with that, he led the troupe out of the rooms and down the elevator, through the hotel lobby, into the limousines and back to the airport.

"We spent an hour at the airport," said Kang Rhee, "waiting for the airplane to be ready. Elvis was still mad, he couldn't control himself. I told him to give Ed a chance, I asked him to accept Ed's apology. He felt Ed was using him."

Jerry Schilling said, "It was a long time before we ever saw Ed again."

There was a short West Coast tour the last week of April, a dozen shows in nine days, in Phoenix, Anaheim, Fresno, San Diego, Portland, Seattle, and Denver. Five days after that, on May 5, Elvis was back in Lake Tahoe, thirty pounds overweight and looking tired. Then, on the sixteenth, four days short of his scheduled closing date, Elvis canceled all remaining performances and went home to California to rest. The announced explanation varied somewhat, from "throat congestion" to "pneumonia." What was bothering Elvis more than anything else was his accelerated use of drugs; the announcement of cancellation due to sickness was merely part of an ongoing cover-up.

If Elvis's habitual and aggravated use of prescribed medicines was effectively kept secret from his public, it was well known to those around him, and a growing source of worry. Already, Elvis's lawyer, Ed Hookstratton, had put private detective John O'Grady back on the job. This time Elvis didn't know. What O'Grady and another detective named Jack Kelly were hired to do was make a full-scale investigation into the sources of Elvis's drugs.

"His asking for our investigation was an obvious attempt to save Presley's life," O'Grady said much later. "Hookstratton hired us to investigate the doctors to see if we could scare them off."

For six weeks O'Grady and Kelly nosed around, confirming that not only were doctors prescribing depressants, painkillers and amphetamines directly to their patient, but they also were writing prescriptions for several of his employees, who then would pass the medicine along to their boss. Often, they found, the prescriptions were telephoned in by the doctors, then delivered to Elvis's homes and hotel rooms. Three doctors and one dentist were named by the detectives and, although the information was turned over to federal and state drug authorities, no immediate action was taken. Nor did any of the doctors concerned back off when confronted by O'Grady.

There were more problems for Elvis in May, when Priscilla hired a new attorney, Arthur Toll, who filed a petition on the twenty-ninth in Los Angeles Superior Court charging that his client was a victim of "intrinsic fraud" during the divorce settlement negotiations. Elvis, Toll said, had failed to make a full disclosure of his assets. California law gave her right to half of Elvis's "community property"—bank accounts, houses, cars, business, the works—but, the attorney said, Priscilla was tricked into accepting such a small settlement.

The picture she painted in her complaint wasn't pretty. She had lived with the Presley family from age fourteen, she said, and during that time had come to trust Elvis, his father, and their lawyers. She had, in fact, permitted Elvis's attorney, Ed Hookstratton, to select her first attorney, and then took Hookstratton's advice to tell that attorney that she had been fully informed about Elvis's finances. She did as she was told and when Elvis filed the original divorce complaint, she didn't contest it.

Now, nine months later, she said she wanted more money. Much more money. And to back up her claim she listed monthly expenses for herself and Lisa amounting to $14,900. This sum included, among other items, $400 for the telephone, $2,500 for clothing (and $500 to keep it clean), $1,000 for transportation (plus $500 for car expenses), $1,000 for food and household supplies, and $1,500 for "incidentals." Priscilla further said that although she had no idea how much Elvis was worth, his monthly income was "in excess of $200,000." Describing herself as a "housewife," she said she had no income of her own.

The negotiations would drag on for several months, delaying court approval of the final divorce decree and causing great strain in Elvis's relationship with Priscilla. The image projected publicly was that everything remained friendly, but during this period it was not, although Elvis told friends repeatedly that Priscilla could have anything she wanted. The lawyers, apparently, had negotiated with Elvis's "best interests" in mind, but without Elvis's full knowledge of what they were doing.

In the end, Priscilla improved her position enormously. Now she was to get $4,200 a month alimony for one year, $4,000 a month for the support and education of Lisa Marie until she became of age or married, half of the proceeds from the sale of their Los Angeles home (which Elvis then put on the block for $500,000) and 5 percent of the stock in Elvis Presley Music, Inc. and White Haven Music, Inc., two of his song publishing companies. Elvis also agreed to give Priscilla $750,000 in cash and another $720,000—payable at $6,000 a month—to discharge any further claims on community property. He also paid her $75,000 legal bill.

There was one other change in the settlement; whereas previously Priscilla had full custody of Lisa Marie, now the couple shared "joint legal custody," although the child continued to live with her mother. Priscilla additionally agreed that Lisa Marie could visit her father whenever it was convenient and always during the Christmas holidays.

One of the reasons she felt she needed more money, Priscilla told Elvis, was that she wanted to go to work—to open a Beverly Hills boutique with a new friend, designer Olivia Bis. The shop on Little Santa Monica Boulevard would be called Bis and Beau—for Priscilla's maiden name Beaulieu—and cater to young, rich Beverly Hills. That, Priscilla said, was why she wanted so much money for her wardrobe. She thought it was important to dress well in order to convince others to do the same.

Elvis nodded his approval as Priscilla talked. He'd watched her change much over the years. An innocent teenager when she moved in with him, she'd become a mature woman with, really, very little help from him. He'd given her an unlimited checking account and a purse-full of credit cards, paid for her lessons in karate—including Mike Stone's—and paid for her finishing and modeling school. Over the years an army sergeant's daughter had become a polished and graceful woman. Elvis had given 'Cilla a hard time, too—with a house full of loud, grab-assing bodyguards, a head full of pills, and a record of sexual infidelity. Yet, he loved her still—if not as a husband and lover, at least as a respected friend, and as one whose love he wished returned. For years after the separation and subsequent divorce, he gave her cars and fur coats and expensive jewelry. More than one friend remembers that whenever Priscilla visited Graceland, Elvis always shaved and dressed nicely and put on lots of cologne.

Elvis had gone through some changes, too. Following a long period of bitterness, rejection, and rage, he had literally gotten down on his knees and prayed to God and then scribbled out something he called "The Promise." In this, Elvis asked God to help him not do anything to hurt Priscilla, Mike, or Lisa Marie.

Besides that, Elvis didn't feel he had lost anything in the renegotiated settlement; he believed he had gained. Money meant little to Elvis and Lisa Marie meant everything. Having the threat of not seeing her removed—legally—allowed Elvis to relax around Priscilla, to switch from legal adversary to supportive friend. When it came close to the time her new boutique opened, for example, he called Frank Lieberman, the Los Angeles nightclub writer he'd befriended a couple of years earlier, now publicity director for the Tropicana in Las Vegas.

"He called me," Frank remembered, "and he wanted me to help however I could. He knew I knew people in the media, that sort of thing. I helped with who to invite to the opening, wrote some of her press releases. Elvis asked if she ever needed help, would I help? I said yes."

There was a two-week tour of the South and East in June—five shows in Atlanta, four more in Uniondale, New York, others in Pittsburgh, Cincinnati, St. Louis, Mobile, Nashville, and Oklahoma City, sixteen performances in thirteen days.

By now the Presley tour machine was finely tuned. The way the Colonel found it worked best was to arrive in a city in three waves. The first was led by the Colonel himself, with his staff and at least one of Elvis's representatives. This was the advance team, arriving in a city the night before a scheduled concert, to supervise last minute details and prepare for Elvis's arrival later the same night.

"Security was the first thing," said Jerry Schilling, who often went ahead with the Colonel when he wasn't working in Hollywood's film studios. "We'd check out the hotel and figure which entrance he could use to get to the room without using the lobby, avoiding the kitchen and employees if possible. Second priority was that his rooms be quiet and with adequate space to have all his personal people around. We'd take all the rooms on the floor, so we could have our security outside the elevator. That way no one could get on the floor except those people we knew. All doors to the floor, even to the fire escape, would be bolted or tied with bedsheets or barred with broomsticks. Room service would be told to deliver food to the elevator or to the door, but never go into Elvis's room. That was to avoid the inevitable staring and dumb questions.

"Then we prepared Elvis's room. That meant blacking out all the windows of Elvis's bedroom with aluminum foil. Elvis was a nocturnal person and this was to keep out the light so he could sleep the next day. It meant checking the air conditioning, to make sure it worked, because Elvis liked it cold. Cold and dark. Then we'd go down the list of people on that particular tour and assign rooms. The room assignments would be typed up by one of the Colonel's men, in an office we'd set up in one of the rooms."

The Colonel would then return to the airport in time to meet Elvis's plane, to hand out room assignment lists and room keys. Elvis and those in his immediate party would get into a waiting limousine and be taken directly to the hotel.

"Occasionally there'd be problems," Schilling said. "Sometimes we couldn't get an entire floor in the hotel and it'd be overrun with people, so that when Elvis came in, people'd be hanging out of the doorways. When Elvis came in at two in the morning, he didn't look his best and he didn't want to be seen by a lot of people. He was adamant about that. And the next day he didn't want to be seen on the way to a show. He wanted to be seen on the stage and that's it."

Elvis would come in the second wave, right after the concert. In the early tours, he went to a hotel after a show and flew on to the next city the following day, along with everyone else. But Elvis suffered a kind of insomnia common among entertainers; after completing an energetic performance, and experiencing the high degree of excitement that goes with it, he was "wired," as so many put it, and needed time to "come down" or relax.

"So," Jerry said, "rather than him stay up half the night and have to get up the next morning and fly to the next city, we found through experience to use that energy flying to the next city right away. This way you couldn't have people up to the dressing room after a show. Elvis wasn't real crazy about that scene anyway. So when somebody announced in the auditorium that Elvis had already left the building, it was true. He was on his way to the airport."

The next morning, as Elvis slept, the Colonel and his advance team continued to work their way down their checklist, seeing that the sound system had arrived, making a dry run with the driver of Elvis's limousine from the hotel to the auditorium and planning alternate routes, visiting local radio stations, picking up a cashier's check for the box-office receipts, leaving behind a cloud of cigar smoke and a sprinkling of what he called "Super Souvenir Elvis Presley Pitcha Books"—brochures produced by RCA that would, incredibly, be sold for five dollars apiece at the concert, although each was clearly marked, "Photo album—For record promotion only."

In the afternoon the third wave would arrive by chartered jet. "It was a big plane, an Electra 99, a four-engine workhorse," said guitarist John Wilkinson. "We took the seats out of the first class cabin and used that for cargo, all the sound equipment that didn't go on trucks, all the instruments, the luggage, a lot of the Colonel's promotional material, the pennants and posters he sold at the show. The rest of the plane was for the band, the Vegas orchestra, the singers, eight or ten roadies, the sound guys, the light crew, I guess maybe thirty-five or forty all told.

"There'd be buses waiting for us at the airport to take us to the hotel. And a luggage truck. When we checked out of a hotel, we just put our luggage outside our room an hour before we had to get on the bus and the luggage handlers took care of it. They also took care of it in the next city. All we had to do was walk off the plane and get on the bus again. We were given our room keys and the luggage would be delivered to our door within an hour. It was the smoothest operation I ever experienced, before or since."

Every night, just before Elvis went on stage, the Colonel nodded his hello and passed along any information he felt that Elvis should have, then left immediately for the airport, and the process began again.

After the tour, Elvis went home to Memphis where, on July 21, he was to begin a week of recording. It'd been sixteen months since Elvis had been in a studio, and that was only to record half a dozen songs at MGM, included in the *On Tour* documentary. A number of live albums had been released in recent months, and RCA was anxious for new material.

Hopes were high that this session would repeat the one in 1969 at the American Studios, when Elvis cut thirty-six songs in six days, three of them million-sellers, including "Suspicious Minds." Although he didn't use the same studio—this time going to Stax—there were reasons for the optimism. Both American and Stax were located in funky black Memphis neighborhoods and both were known for the number of hits produced within. At American, the studio had produced hits by the Box Tops, Neil Diamond, Dionne Warwick, Joe Tex, Wilson Pickett, Joe Simon, and Merilee Rush. Stax was known as home base for many other top performers, including the late Otis Redding, Booker T and the MGs, and Sam and Dave, predominantly rhythm and blues acts. When Felton Jarvis put the studio band together, he also used some of the same musicians from the American sessions, including bassist Tommy Cogbill, guitarist Reggie Young, and organist Bobby Wood.

In addition, Marty Lacker, who'd been instrumental in setting up the sessions with Chips Moman, now was working at Stax. More promise was placed in the studio's location, almost next to the First Assembly of God Church that Elvis attended as a teenager. It was also just five minutes from Graceland.

Elvis arrived five hours late, his ballooning body wrapped in a long black cape over a white suit, his "Superfly" hat pulled down over his eyes.

"I thought I'd dress for the part," he cracked.

The session that followed set the scene for those that followed. It was terrible. The studio was crowded with singers and musicians and hangers-on, much like the sessions two years earlier in Nashville, and Elvis didn't seem overly excited about recording. Nor was he any more prepared than he often was, hearing the songs for the first time after entering.

It was, to many around him, astonishing. Elvis had been recording for twenty years and still he didn't prepare his material beforehand, still he waited for his publishing representatives to show up with a stack of demonstration discs. This wasn't the way he always did it, but for Elvis to be doing it at all in 1973 was puzzling. This seemed an acceptable way to produce movie soundtrack albums, where songs were forced into creaking scripts to fit specific dramatic situations. But for the production of albums in the seventies? When Elvis's man from New York began playing demo after demo, waiting for Elvis to find one that he liked, the musicians in the studio looked at each other and shook their heads.

"The first night there were two drummers," said Jerry Carrigan, who was one of them. "Me and Al Jackson, who was the black drummer who usually worked at Stax. Elvis finally heard a song he wanted to record, called 'Three Corn Patches.' I guess maybe he just gave up and said he'd do it because he'd already broken several of the demos, just twisted them and broke them in his hands. You talk about pieces of junk, that was junk. It was so corny, Al Jackson listens to the song and looks at me and said, 'Shit, I cain't play that, I'se raised on chitlins . . . *you* do the song.' I said, 'Not me, man, I'm gonna watch you.' And he did it."

That's the way it went for four days. The musicians arrived at seven, and Elvis entered wearing his big white hat about five hours later, flanked by his good-natured, but doting and protective entourage.

"The second night," Carrigan recalled, "Felton Jarvis called some of us into the control room and said, 'Now, look, don't you guys yawn. It brings him down. If you feel like yawning, go outside and splash your face off or get a breath of fresh air, but don't yawn. It brings him down, okay?' They called Tommy Cogbill down because he was laying down on the floor, worn out and tired from playing bass all night. He was still playing, but laying down. They said, 'Don't you be layin' down on the floor and playin'. Set up in a chair, or stand up. No layin' down.'"

On the first day Elvis recorded three songs. On the second day, another three. On the third day, only two. Then three again on the fourth day, a final three on the fifth. The sixth and seventh days he never showed up and the musicians sat there, waiting. Finally they were told that Elvis was sick and they went home.

"He was just visibly miserable," said Carrigan. "And he did something I never saw him do before. He wore the same clothes two days in a row. Normally, his valet would bring clothes and he'd change during the course of the evening."

However depressed the scene at the time, the material produced during the sessions included several songs that either went on to be hits or, at the least, critically successful. One was "I've Got a Thing About You Baby," a song originally recorded by Billy Lee Riley using some of the same musicians that Elvis had in the studio with him. Elvis also followed the original arrangement, merely changing the guitar lead to an organ lead. This same approach to recording—putting his own distinctive voice on top of someone else's proven arrangement—previously had produced a hit in "Suspicious Minds" (a copy of Mark James's original version) and Elvis and Felton hoped this song could duplicate that earlier success. It didn't do nearly so well, but was a hit the following winter.

Thus Elvis's declining health and increasing dependence on drugs didn't seem to affect his career. No matter how low he got, he remained at the top in his field, able through sheer willpower, blessed with momentum, to continue his string of record hits and crisscross the country every year—when other top acts such as the Rolling Stones and Bob Dylan toured every three years or less frequently.

At the same time, the Colonel went on making his fabulous deals. Much to the music industry's surprise, he sold to RCA all rights to all the material recorded by Elvis through 1972. Obviously this represented a huge body of product—more than 350 recorded songs, nearly fifty albums' worth, almost all of it still in the catalog and selling slowly, but steadily. One RCA executive claimed the Colonel's motivation was "greed, pure and simple," saying the record company went for it only because it figured that eventually it'd get its money back and the big price tag the Colonel attached to the property was worth paying to keep Elvis and the Colonel happy. Others point to the Colonel's constant need to pay his gambling debts at the Hilton hotel.

At the same time, as Elvis's contract entered its final months at the Hilton, the Colonel had been courted both subtly and strongly to go to another hotel. Henri Lewin, the Hilton vice president who negotiated the Presley contracts, said, "The Aladdin offered him anything. He didn't even talk to them. They just opened their big showroom. He never came to me and said, 'I have an offer from the Aladdin, will you pay me more?' I know that they called him. The MGM Grand had good reason, because Kirk Kerkorian (the president of MGM) was very close with him. I said to the Colonel, 'I want to know one thing—when the MGM opens do I have to fight with you or do you stay with me?' He said, 'Henri, I will give you an opportunity in two months from now to make a deal with me, which will go over the opening date of the MGM Grand. If you make that deal, I don't go to MGM. If you don't make that deal, I might go anyplace.' The man never gave us an exclusive. He could have played another three days, four days, five days, or ten weeks at any hotel in the world, or in Las Vegas, but verbally he said, 'I don't do that.' I said, 'That's good enough, you don't have to put it on paper.'"

Eventually it *was* put on paper, of course, and during the last week of July the Colonel and Lewin agreed that Elvis would appear at the Hilton two times a year for the next two years. Elvis was also given the option of working the hotel only two weeks at a time instead of four. And he was to be paid $150,000 a week—more than any other Las Vegas performer—as well as get his room and "incidentals" picked up. Sometimes these "incidentals" added more than $25,000 to his cost. The hotel never complained.

"He was just as important to Vegas as he was to the hotel," said Bruce Banke, the Hilton's publicity executive. "It was like bringing in a major convention. Everybody reaped the benefits. His August 1973 engagement was his last full month in Vegas. He did two shows a day for twenty-eight days. That's 100,000 people a month. We've never seen anything like it and probably never will again."

If the fans remained loyal, the critics did not. "It's Elvis at his most indifferent, uninterested, and unappealing," said *The Hollywood Reporter*. "He's not just a little out of shape, not just a bit chubbier than usual, the Living Legend is fat and ludicrously aping his former self . . . Since his return to live performing, Elvis has apparently lost interest . . . It is a tragedy, disheartening and absolutely depressing to see Elvis in such diminishing stature."

After closing September 3, Elvis zigzagged around the country with Linda and his hired hands, flying to Memphis and then to Los Angeles and finally to his house in Palm Springs, as if looking for a comfortable roost. He bought cars in Memphis, jewelry in Beverly Hills, and ammunition for his guns in Palm Springs. He watched movies late at night on television wherever midnight caught him. Linda made him goodies—popcorn balls held together with caramel—and shoved them into his mouth like a mama bird feeding her young. He went through the motions of practicing his karate, but the efforts were little more than self-parody.

"Then to make matters worse," one close friend confides, "Elvis broke his wrist, so he had his arm in a sling. He tried, man; oh, he tried. But have you ever seen a one-armed man, greatly overweight, thrashing around in a karate suit, huffin' and puffin'? It was sad, man, very, very sad."

Despite all this, Elvis attempted to record in Palm Springs, using equipment taken right to his door by RCA. Working with his guitarist, James Burton, he struggled through two songs and then hung it up.

Two weeks later, on October 9, Elvis appeared in Santa Monica Superior Court with Priscilla in private session with Judge Laurence J. Rittenband, who granted Elvis's petition for divorce. They emerged from the judge's chambers arm-in-arm, kissed for the collected photographers, and then parted.

Only six days after that, Elvis checked himself into Baptist Memorial Hospital in Memphis for what the press was told was "recurring pneumonia."

"It's common knowledge now that Elvis had a number of chronic type medical problems," said Maurice Elliott, the hospital vice president who got the job of talking to the press when Elvis entered the giant medical facility, "but whenever he came in they'd say all they wanted said was that Elvis was in for rest, or had the flu. Now, I didn't want to lie, but I felt our first responsibility was to the patient, so we told the press basically what the doctor and Joe [Esposito] told me, even though I was aware it wasn't totally the truth. We didn't lie, but we didn't tell the total facts of the case. And that made it difficult."

The truth was, Elvis *did* have trouble breathing and congestion that bordered on pneumonia. These problems had caused him to cancel his Lake Tahoe engagement early in May. And he *did* need rest; recent events had exhausted him, psychologically as well as physically. The boredom in Las Vegas, the aborted recording session in Palm Springs, the divorce hearing in Santa Monica had created uncommon pressure. However, the real problem or problems he was experiencing were not caused by that pressure, but by how he attempted to relieve it. No one was saying so aloud at the time, but Elvis checked into the hospital October 15 to dry out. This was confirmed two years after Elvis's death, when Dr. Nick testified at a Tennessee Board of Medical Examiners hearing to determine whether or not he was guilty of prescribing drugs to Elvis illegally.

In fact, it was another doctor Elvis saw in California who had been giving him almost daily injections of Demerol. Elvis had become addicted and it was eighteen days before he was weaned off of drugs entirely, after detoxification that included the substitution of methadone, a drug often used to treat heroin addiction.

This was Elvis's first prolonged visit to a hospital, the only time he had been in one except to have a broken finger put in a cast—the result of a touch foot-ball game—and to attend the birth of Lisa Marie. Elvis didn't like hospitals par-ticularly, so everything was done to make it as much like home—or, more accurately, another hotel room—as possible.

"We put tinfoil on the windows first thing," said Maurice Elliott, "to keep the sunlight out and allow him to stay to his nocturnal habits. It affected nor-mal hospital routines a little bit, but with 1,900 beds in the hospital, we have at least 250 special diets a day and special requests like Elvis's weren't too much of a problem. The problem was that Elvis had no spokesman. It'd have been nice if Joe or Dr. Nick would have released the information, but they didn't."

The result was that as soon as word got out that Elvis was in a sixteenth floor suite of rooms, all hell broke loose. Newsmen from all over the world began calling, at all hours of the day and night, by telephone and in person. Get-well cards arrived by the tens of thousands, filling up the small hospital mailroom and piling ceiling-high in the hallways. There were enough flowers for almost every patient in the entire building.

The hospital did what it could. A private telephone line was installed, so that calls couldn't be made direct to Elvis's rooms, as was the case in all the other rooms. Hospital guards were assigned twenty-four-hour duty outside Elvis's rooms and given a list of those who were permitted to come and go. The switch-board was told what to say to the hundreds of daily callers. Fans were ejected from the hallways. When some on the hospital staff added to the problem by try-ing to visit or sneak a look, a policy decision had to be made about personnel.

To assure the star's comfort, hospital rules were waived to allow Linda Thompson to move into the room with Elvis, where she remained for more than two weeks. "I had a cot in there right next to his bed," Linda said, "and at night he lowered his bed to the height of the cot. Finally they brought in a hospital bed for me. Then they started treating me like a patient. I never got out of my night-gown. The nurses came and said, 'And how are our patients today?' I tried to go downstairs and look at the magazine rack. I was going stir crazy, so I got dressed and Elvis said, 'What're you doing?' I said, 'I'm going downstairs to look at the magazines.' He said, 'Oh, no, honey. If I can't have my clothes on, you can't.' He made me put my gown back on and get back into bed. He was just like a little kid and I was his little buddy. Whatever he had to go through I had to go through."

Elvis checked himself out of the hospital on November 1. During that time, he got rest and ate almost normally—although on his orders, his boys smug-gled in bags of cheeseburgers and fried potatoes. He was also visited daily by Dr. Nick, who continued to keep an eye on Elvis's medication.

It would be two full months at home before recovery was deemed complete.

Elvis spent most of the final months of 1973 in Memphis, where in November he watched a rerun of the NBC-TV *Aloha from Hawaii* satellite show and from December 10-16 returned to the Stax recording studio for RCA. Although this session was considerably more satisfying than the one in July—eighteen songs in seven days—in no way did it represent Elvis at his most productive. Or happiest. Still overweight and depressed about the year behind him, many of the songs seemed as autobiographical—and sad—as anything he ever recorded.

Some of the material reflected his general mood, such as in Larry Gatlin's composition, "Help Me," where Elvis literally dropped to his knees in the studio to sing the song.

Others were more specific, as in "Take Good Care of Her" where he seemed to be singing to Priscilla's new escort, Mike Stone. Perhaps the saddest of all—and ultimately most prophetic—was the mournful "Goodtime Charlie's Got the Blues".

Three of these songs would be released as singles in the next year and all would be included on his albums. There were up-tempo songs as well—including Chuck Berry's rocker, "Promised Land"—but it was the mournful ballads that set the tone and remained most memorable.

Christmas Eve 1973 was not the happiest of times. Again three stockings were hung on the staircase with Linda's name replacing Priscilla's. The usual bounty of gifts were exchanged. But many of Elvis's presents were still under the tree unopened a week later.

New Year's Eve was quiet, too, as Elvis held another party at Graceland rather than rent a nightclub, and pared the guest list to about thirty of his closest friends. There was champagne, but no food until someone went out and bought chips and dip at Pancho's, a Mexican fast-food takeout place not far away.

Elvis finally appeared at 11, freshly shaved and smelling of cologne, wearing an all-black fringed outfit, a knee-length coat and a wide-brimmed, floppy hat. Linda looked as if she had spent a lot of time making up and was wearing a silver lamé pants suit with a transparent top. They made one circuit of the room, greeting everyone cordially, then went back upstairs. Total time they were at the party was under fifteen minutes.

In their wake they left a disgruntled and deflated party. "I flew eighteen hundred miles for this?" Joe Esposito grumbled. "This is the greatest party on earth," said Lamar Fike. "Fun! This is really great."

At midnight, the men started playing cards and the women gathered in front of Elvis's closed-circuit television and waved Happy New Year to him. He had a monitor in his bedroom, but no one knew if he was watching.

# Chapter 23

# FALLING APART

Elvis may've been suffering emotionally, and it's undeniable that the negative reviews and comments were accumulating. Yet, the image prevailed; the momentum seemed unstoppable as, in January 1974, RCA released a well-researched and elaborately packaged album called *Elvis—A Legendary Performer, Volume One*.

"It was my idea," said Joan Deary, the person at RCA responsible for much of the nuts-and-bolts work of assembling Elvis's records, "and when I took it to Rocco [Laginestra], I thought its appeal was to the Elvis collector. And it went gold. It sold better than a lot of his regular albums." Eventually the series went to Volume Three and all sold enormously, prompting RCA to use the same packaging approach for other top artists.

The timing was perfect. In 1974, nostalgia for the 1950s was reaching a crest. This was the year Henry Winkler became an overnight star as television's Fonz in the hit TV series *Happy Days*; *Grease* was a smash on Broadway; and *American Graffiti* won an Academy Award. In Elvis's first *Legendary* album, Joan pushed the same nostalgic buttons, presenting a series of musical milestones in Elvis's career; his first single ("That's All Right, Mama"), his first million-seller ("Heartbreak Hotel"), his biggest-selling record ("Don't Be Cruel"), his first gospel hit ("Peace in the Valley") and his biggest selling movie record ("Can't Help Falling in Love" from *Blue Hawaii*). She also dropped in excerpts from a 1958 interview and several previously unreleased cuts, including some material Elvis recorded when he was still with Sun Records.

With this came a slickly produced book of historic photographs (Elvis with the Dorsey Brothers, Elvis singing to a hound dog on the Steve Allen television show, Elvis with Ed Sullivan, etc.), newspaper clippings, material from RCA's files showing recording dates, and other session information.

The album served Elvis in several ways. Besides giving him product that he didn't have to go into a studio to record, and giving his fans a well-produced nostalgia trip, it also gave the reviewers and rock pundits another Elvis "event" to use as a springboard for one of their by now predictable retrospective glances. Jim Miller wrote in *Rolling Stone*, "Elvis Presley remains the quintessential American pop star; gaudy, garish, compromised in his middle age by commercial considerations, yet gifted with an enormous talent and a charismatic appeal beyond mere nostalgia. Presley remains a true American artist—one of the greatest in American popular music, a singer of native brilliance and a performer of magnetic dimensions."

Greil Marcus went Miller one better in *Oui*: "If Elvis's genius is as simple as inborn talent, its result has been as complex as the U.S.A. His goal (if the idea that a hillbilly thinks is still a bit strange, you can call it his instinct) has been to make music that touches, takes, and personalizes virtually every positive side of the American soul; a completely innocent and mature delight in sex; a love of roots and a respect for the past; a rejection of roots and a demand for novelty; the liberating arrogance and sense of self-worth that grows out of the most commonplace understanding of what 'democracy' and 'equality' are all about (no man is better than me); the humility, piety, and self-deprecating humor that spring from the same source (I am not better than no man); a burning desire to get rich, to have fun; a natural affection for big cars and flashy clothes, the symbols of status that deliver pleasure both as symbols and on their own terms. There are a lot of contradictions there; Elvis, after all, has become one of those symbols himself. Perhaps that is why one of his earliest critics pronounced him 'morally insane.'"

The critics also loved the album itself. "Listening to *Legendary Performer* is almost like discovering Elvis for the first time," said Ed Ward in *Phonograph* Magazine. "What," asked San Francisco's *City* Magazine, "another Elvis reissue? Well, yes and, as it happens, it's one of the best ever." "RCA has at last recognized that some of Elvis's buyers are not just fans—or blind consumers ready to buy anything with the name on the package—but *collectors*, interested in the performer's social, historical and musical contributions," said the writer in the *Los Angeles Free Press*. And as for Greil Marcus, he believed that "*Legendary Performer* does justice not only to Elvis's talent but, dare I say it, to his vision."

By mid-January, Elvis was—using his phrase—gearing up for Las Vegas again, this time with less than the usual apprehension. This was because now Elvis would perform only one show a night during the week, instead of two—two on Fridays and Saturdays—for only two weeks instead of four. Thus, Elvis was cutting his commitment from fifty-five or sixty shows to half the number, without a cut in pay.

In the week or two before leaving Memphis, Elvis remained closeted with friends. Still practicing karate and dieting—that is, taking more than the usual number of amphetamines—he began to lose weight. New costumes were designed and fitted—the first without a cape and the first non-jumpsuit in years and, as the last days before he had to fly to Nevada approached, he began to sing more. Among those singing with him were three young men that Elvis had put on his personal payroll the previous summer, in time to record with him in Palm Springs.

"Anything he wanted he got, right?" said Tony Brown, the pianist for the trio, who later replaced Glenn D. Hardin in the backup band. "He allus wanted to be in a gospel group and there were a bunch of singers who were out of work—Donny Sumner, who was J. D. Sumner's stepson; Sherill Neilson, who used to be with the Statesmen and the Imperials, and was one of the greatest Irish tenor gospel singers in the world; and Tim Batey, a bass player who could sing, who played in the Stamps.

"Elvis let Donny arrange songs on the albums and cut two or three of his songs. Elvis catered to Donny. He offered to buy him a house outside Chicago. Elvis was always calling Donny to talk to, because J. D. allus treated Donny like a lamebrain, like he was dumb and stuff. I remember the night when Elvis told Donny, 'Pick out the land and pick an architect and build you a house.' He came and told me and I said, 'Donnnnneeeeee, God, do it!' And he said, 'I couldn't do it.' There were others who would've got right on the phone and called about the house. Donny just blew it off.

"Elvis was in awe of Sherrill's talent, but he didn't treat him as nice as Donny. He got featured a lot, got a lot of solos in Elvis's shows. He sang 'Softly, I'll Leave You' and 'Killing Me Softly' and Elvis sang a duet with him, 'Spanish Eyes.'

"Tim Batey was the weird one of us. He looked like a white black man—tall and lanky—and he could play anything. He was a rock and roller, really, and the Stamps had a school in Dallas and he took a job playing bass for the group because it was a job. Tim was good at karate. He was into all the books Elvis was into, he's the one turned me onto Elvis bein' heavy.

"He was into karate, Elvis, and it was into his head to teach us. Used to be every day at six we'd be at the house to take karate. Elvis bought us outfits. We studied with Dave Hebler, who was one of Elvis's bodyguards. Then we'd get into settin' around and seein' your aura and like that. He really was a heavy person. He had a stack 'a books all times. He was into numerology, psycho-genetics, all those kind of things. He'd take everybody in the group and get you in a room and read from one of the books and make you feel important. He told us what our number was—he was an 'eight' because he was born January 8—and then go on for an hour about what that meant.

"We were paid $10,000 a month for the group, plus all expenses. We had a Master Charge. We flew first class. Everywhere we went, everything was covered. We got bonuses—allus big bonuses. He gave us a $34,000 camper. After a while, some people started to get really pissed-off at us because they thought we were taking advantage of Elvis. But it was Elvis's idea all along. He *wanted* us there. He wanted us to come runnin' whenever he wanted, and that's what we did. When we weren't touring with him, we'd be off months at a time and we could count on ten days out of every month we'd get a phone call. Joe Esposito would call and say Elvis wants you to come to Palm Springs, so we'd go to Palm Springs from Nashville and check into the hotel until Elvis woke up and called. Some nights it'd be all hymns. Some nights it'd be all rock and roll. Some nights it'd be nothing. Sometimes we'd fly out to Palm Springs and check into the hotel and they'd call from the house and say, 'Elvis just went to L.A., go to L.A.' We had rent-a-cars, so we'd drive to L.A., we'd get there and check into a hotel, they'd call, say Elvis was in a bad mood, go back to Nashville. So we'd go back home. We never knew."

In Las Vegas in February 1974 there was an incident that had everyone talking for weeks. That was when Elvis fired his .22 caliber Savage at a light switch in his hotel suite and the bullet pierced the wall behind it, ripping through the bathroom and missing Linda Thompson only by a few inches. Some of the bodyguards who were present later recalled in their book, *Elvis: What Happened?*, that when Linda came panicking out of the bathroom seconds later, Elvis merely grinned and said, "Hey, now, hon, just don't get excited."

Another time, he started banging away at the chandelier. All the guys froze when that happened, relaxing finally when a dumbfounded Elvis said to them, "What'sa matter? We're in the penthouse. Nobody gonna get hit long as you shoot straight up." He then shot at the chandelier some more.

"It was somethin' to do," nearly all of the boys say. "You ever spent a month in a hotel room?"

After closing in Vegas, Elvis took his family of fifty dependents on the road again on March 1 and in the next twenty-two days performed twenty-five times in fourteen southern cities. It was a strange tour, crisscrossing eight states. Two of the shows were held in Houston's Astrodome. There he did matinee and evening performances to a total of nearly 90,000—the headline act for the annual Houston Livestock Show and Rodeo. Each show opened with the orchestra members, the backup band, the Sweet Inspirations, J. D. Sumner and the Stamps, Jackie Kahane, and the group Voice being towed aboard a portable bandstand to the middle of the Astroturf field. There they waited in place as the chuckwagon races were run around them, which just about freaked out the Sweet Inspirations. Then Elvis appeared in a jeep that circled the field twice, before depositing him by the stage to perform his fifty-minute Vegas set.

In Monroe, Louisiana, his shows were attended by the mayor and the governor of Louisiana and the fans nearly tore the motel apart. In Auburn, when he offhandedly tossed one of his scarves to a lady in the front row, she hugged the memento to her bosom and raced frantically across the coliseum, screaming. Elvis arrived in Montgomery on the sixth of March, midway through "Elvis Presley Week" in Alabama, proclaimed thus by Governor George Wallace, who attended the show with his wife. In Memphis, more shows were added until there were five in all, and RCA rushed mobile recording equipment to the Mid-South Coliseum to record an album, *Elvis Recorded Live on Stage in Memphis*.

All shows on the tour were sold out. Each grossed at least $100,000. Some went as high as four times that. In two road tours, Elvis grossed more than $1.5 million, contrasted with $400,000 paid for two 1974 engagements at the Hilton. In other words: touring, he grossed three times the money for half the number of shows. Even with his sky-high expenses, touring seemed the way to the future.

In May, Elvis was on the road again, performed four shows in California, then went into Lake Tahoe for two performances a day for eleven days. In two important ways, this was not the standard Nevada engagement. For this one, the High Sierra Theatre in Del Webb's Sahara Tahoe did away with dinner and presented "Elvis in Concert." This allowed the hotel to cut its expenses and give Elvis a larger slice of the box office. Tickets sold for $17, which included two drinks, taxes, and gratuities. Turning the dinner show into a cocktail show also allowed the hotel to move in smaller tables, thereby seating more customers.

More striking than the increased income was an incident that occurred one night outside Elvis's room. A few months later a land developer from Grass Valley, California, filed a $6 million lawsuit against Elvis as a result of that incident, also naming the Sahara Tahoe and Del Webb International Hotels. The developer, Edward L. Ashley, said in his district court suit that on May 20 he paid one of Elvis's hired hands $60 to be admitted to a party in Elvis's suite following the second show. When he knocked on the door and there was no response, he said, he threw some breaker switches he found on the wall in the hallway, turning off all the lights in the area. That, he said, was when Red West and one of Elvis's stepbrothers, David Stanley, and a former police sergeant from Palm Springs, Dick Grob, came rushing into the hallway.

"Who the fuck turned out the lights?"

"Who're you?"

"Hold this dude, David, let's get some answers."

More men were pouring out of the room, followed by Elvis himself. Someone found the breaker box and turned the lights back on. According to Ashley, Stanley and Grob and two others held his arms while Red West and two others beat him up severely. "All of which occurred," he said, "in the immediate presence of defendant, Elvis Presley, who refused plaintiff's request to stop the beating and did in fact participate in said beating."

Elvis was being attacked, too—critically. "It was a plump and sluggish Elvis Presley who gave a cookie-cutter concert at the Forum Saturday night," the critic in the *Long Beach Independent* wrote. Said a headline in the *San Francisco Sunday Examiner & Chronicle* of his Tahoe engagement: "The Pelvis Slows Down in a Show of Hokum & Ennui."

Otherwise, it was business as usual. Elvis went home to Memphis for two weeks and then embarked on a sixteen-city tour that began in Texas, zigzagged all over the deep South and Midwest and East, reaching as far as Rhode Island, closing in Salt Lake City, Utah. Everywhere he went, the Colonel was a step ahead of him, arranging the complicated logistics and choreographing the carnival-like atmosphere in which Elvis always played.

They came in Montereys and LTDs, in Gran Torinos and camper vans (making a weekend of it several hundred miles from home), wearing shined shoes and summer suits, new dresses and wigs just back from the hairdresser. And the smell in the auditorium was not of marijuana smoke—as at other rock concerts of the time—but of perfume, hair spray, and after-shave. Some paid ticket scalpers as much as $150 for a front-row seat. Many who paid only $7.50 for a seat on the last row paid another $9 for Elvis Opera Glasses.

The money came pouring in, and Elvis kept right on spending it.

One of the ways Elvis chose to spend his earnings in the summer of 1974 was in the production of his own film. This, like the hiring of his own group, Voice, was to cause friction within the Presley camp.

Jerry Schilling remembered, "Elvis'd go to the Memphian Theater and maybe see three karate films in a row, from the best, of which there were only a few, to the worst. Sometimes we'd sit through the WORST films! And he loved them. They were very basic. He could relax when he watched these films. There weren't any problems he had to deal with. Finally, after watching so many, he thought he could do his own."

Elvis had talked about doing such a film—either a documentary or an action adventure film—several years earlier, and made a tentative start several times, after talking it over with his various karate instructors.

In his book, *Inside Elvis*, Parker said that at first Elvis wanted an adventure film in which he might play the villain . . . and never play the guitar or sing. "I want to be," Jerry remembers Elvis saying, "the baddest motherfucker there is." Elvis called the Colonel with his idea, Ed said, and then hired a Lear jet to take them to the Colonel's home in Palm Springs. There the Colonel reportedly gave his tentative approval and said he would call around to see which major movie studios might be interested.

About the same time, Elvis called in one of Jerry Schilling's old fraternity brothers from Arkansas State, Rick Husky. Elvis first met Rick soon after he'd been discharged from the Army and was initiated into the fraternity as an honorary member. Through Jerry they'd stayed in touch and now Rick was a successful television writer and producer for such shows as *Mod Squad*, *Cade's Country* and *The Rookies*.

There was no animosity in the meeting that took place soon after, but no one remembered it as being particularly productive.

"Elvis was not a meeting type of guy," said Jerry, "so Ed [Parker] did most of the talking for him. The talk was mostly centered on action. Rick said that can be done, but karate films are over basically, they'd had their day. Rick felt Elvis could be a fantastic dramatic actor with the right script."

Husky recalled it much the same way. "My ideas differed from theirs. Elvis and Ed Parker talked karate shtick, they got up and demonstrated. I said, 'Great, but you need a story.' Elvis said, 'That's why you're here.' That was when I told him about his potential as an actor. I compared him to Frank Sinatra and said I'd bet he'd get an Academy Award nomination right off the bat. His response was he didn't want to talk about acting and Oscars, he wanted to do an action film.

"I couldn't get the discussion back to acting and drama. Ed kept saying, 'What Elvis means is . . .' I also felt he had to do the best karate film ever done because karate films were on the way out. I asked to write a treatment for the film and Elvis said okay."

In the thirty-page movie story that Rick wrote, Elvis was to play a retired CIA agent running a karate school. He had a friend who was murdered by drug dealers. (Naturally, they'd made it look like an overdose.) And Elvis, like the retired gunfighter in the Old West, went out to seek revenge. Rick brought it to Jerry, who took it and put it on Elvis's bedroom desk. So far, Elvis's investment in the film was minimal. In the months to come it would swell.

In the meantime, Elvis continued to write checks—or instructed his father to write them—to buy extravagant gifts for his friends. One such incident occurred shortly after Elvis reopened for two more weeks August 19 at the Las Vegas Hilton Hotel.

"I was still working as an assistant film editor for Paramount," said Jerry Schilling, "and I went to Vegas on Friday night after work and brought Elvis up to date on the karate film. We talked to about 3 A.M., then I said I was going to my hotel room. Elvis asked me to stick around. I said, 'Okay, I'll be downstairs [in the casino].' Thirty or forty minutes later Charlie Hodge came, found me and said Elvis wanted to see me.

"I went back up. It was just Elvis and Linda and me. He said, 'I want you to have a home.'"

Jerry had been house-hunting, but his salary at Paramount wasn't high enough to satisfy the customary bank demands to buy the house he wanted in the Hollywood hills. As it happened, the present owner was Jerry's friend Rick Husky, and with Jerry in the room, Elvis—at 3 A.M.—called Rick and woke him up.

Elvis was sitting on his bed, wearing a karate jacket and pants, his pistol on the table nearby, a cigar gone dead in the ashtray. Linda sat proudly at his side, hugging a pillow. Jerry sat about fifteen feet away in a chair.

"Hello, Rick," Elvis said, "did I wake you up?"

Rick shook himself and said it was all right.

"I wanna ask you some questions, do you mind?"

"No . . ."

"Look, is it a good house? Are you asking a fair price? Is it really right for Jerry? Tell me the truth. We're talking about a good friend, your good friend and mine."

Rick gulped and said yes to every question.

"We talked about the loan situation," Rick said. "Jerry had the down payment and needed $35,000 more in his account to get the bank loan. Elvis said, 'I don't want those bankers screwing around with Jerry and I've got my checkbook out here and I'm writing a check for the house, is that all right with you?'

"'Yes, of course.'

"'Well,' said Elvis, 'how soon can you get out?'

"'Jesus, Elvis, can I stay the rest of the night?'"

Of course this situation led to more friction. Jerry wasn't even on Elvis's payroll at the time and when those who were heard about it, they wanted houses, too, and began jockeying for position, dropping hints. Elvis liked keeping his boys on their toes—stirred up—and he ignored them all.

Two other things about this engagement in Las Vegas made it remarkable. One was a visit backstage by Barbra Streisand and her live-in boyfriend, a hairdresser named Jon Peters. Jerry Schilling, Joe Esposito, and Rick Husky were with Elvis in his dressing room when they entered. Following the cordial introductions and a few minutes of small talk, Barbra asked, "Is there any place we can talk privately?"

Elvis nodded and excused himself, then led them into the dressing room behind the backstage reception area. There, Barbra told Elvis that she and Jon were going to do a remake of the classic film *A Star Is Born*. She said she wanted him to be her co-star.

Although Rick Husky subsequently told Joe and Jerry and Elvis and several others on the team that the part and story were "fantastic," it never happened. While Elvis worried quietly about how well he could handle the competition of a big co-star like Streisand—used to playing opposite unknown starlets as he was—negotiations broke down between Jon Peters and the

Colonel. Peters, who was to be the film's producer, wouldn't meet the Colonel's salary demands.

More memorable and less interesting was the boredom that Elvis felt. Even though the Nevada engagement had been pared to about a third of what it had been previously, Elvis quickly tired of the hotel room/dressing room/show-room routine. He reacted by taking more sleeping pills to sleep longer, then needed more amphetamines to stay on his feet and alert on stage. Consequently, his onstage monologues grew longer and more discursive. From a tape recording of a typical performance:

"The other night there was a minister in town to raise money for a new Evangelical Church. He had an all-night telethon and J. D. Sumner and the Stamps went over and sang. The minister asked J. D. if maybe I would come by, and J. D. replied, 'If he does, I'll jump in the pool.' Later I called and told the minister that because of my contract I can't appear in Las Vegas outside of the Hilton. But I told him I'd donate $2,500 if J. D. and the Stamps did jump into the pool. And they did. I told the minister I'd give another $1,000 if he'd jump in the pool. They had to throw him in!

"I couldn't have a better audience if I stood outside and paid everyone $20 each to come in and listen. You're outtasight! You see him—that's Charlton Heston, ladies and gentlemen. He's made some dillies, hasn't he? *Ben Hur*, *The Ten Commandments*—I'll never forget that in my life. When he comes off that mountain, from Mount Sinai with those white tablets, and all that white hair. I'd like to talk to him sometime to find out what state of mind he had to get himself into to play that part. Can you imagine that? He had just talked to God, and came down the mountainside with those tablets under his arms and that white hair. I'd like to ask him how he got to thinkin' that part. Phew—it's tougher than a nickel stovepipe.

"See that ring? I wore this ring on the 'Aloha' special. It's not just one big diamond at all. The center stone is eleven and a half carats, and there are several diamonds surrounding it. It was a Christmas present to myself. I was looking for gifts for my father, my grandmother, and my daughter, and when the jeweler came—this just accidentally fell from his case. I was really suckered into buying it. It's the biggest diamond I've ever seen—I just thought I deserved it.

"You know I've never liked the way this showroom's looked—the interior decorating. It's too wide for a performer. I had this ramp made so I could come out a little closer to the audience. Put a spotlight onto the statues on that wall. Okay. That's nice. I don't know what it is, but that's nice. Tom Jones was in here the other night, and he's from Wales. I asked Tom who it was, and he said it was King Edward. King George, sorry, excuse me your majesty. Now take the

spotlight and put it on those angels. Just look at those dudes, boy! Big fat angels.
Put the spotlight onto this wall over here. You will notice a slight difference.
Those of the Caucasian race. That's what it is, isn't it? Caucasian? It was on my
army draft card. I thought it meant 'circumcised!' Anyway, the other night, I
came down here at about 4:30 in the morning with a couple of friends who work
for me—Jerry Schilling and Red West. Red is a second degree black belt in
karate—he's got a school in Memphis, and I'm very proud of him. Red wrote
'Separate Ways' and 'Why Can't Everyday Be Like Christmas' and 'If You Talk
in Your Sleep.' Anyway, he climbed the fence where they keep the supplies, the
paint and so forth, he climbed the fence, as high as this curtain; he went down
and got a little can of black paint. He put it in his belt, came back, climbed over,
and we went over there and stacked up two tables. I got up with the paint and
brush, and I was Michelangelo, or the guy that painted the ceiling in the
Vatican—the Sistine Chapel. I painted that statue—it took thirty minutes to do.
The hotel hasn't said a word. I just thought I'd share it with you."

Another night, the monologue started after he sang "You Gave Me a
Mountain": "I've been singing that song for a long time, and a lot of people kind
of got it associated with me because they think it's of a personal nature. It is not
. . . I just loved the song and it has nothing to do with me or my ex-wife Priscilla.
She's right here. Honey, stand up. Come out, honey. Come out, come on out.
Turn around, let them see you. Boy, she's . . . she's a beautiful chick, I'll tell you
for sure, boy. Boy, I knows 'em when I picks 'em. You know? Goddamn.

"Now, my little daughter Lisa, she's six years old. Look at her jump up. Pull
your dress down, Lisa. You pull your dress down before you jump up like that
again, young lady. And then at the same booth is my girlfriend, Sheila. Stand
up Sheila. Turn around, turn around, completely around. Sheila, hold it up.
Hold it up. Hold the ring up. Hold up the ring. The ring. Your right hand.
Look at that sonofabitch.

"No, the thing I'm trying to get across is, we're the very best of friends, and
we always have been. Our divorce came about not because of another man or
another woman, but because of the circumstances involving my career. I was
traveling too much . . .

"After the settlement, it came out about two million dollars . . . Well, after
that, I got her a mink coat. I know it. I'm talking about the mink coat. You hang
loose over there. The, the XKE Jag after the settlement, just gave it to her. She
got me, listen to this, tonight, a forty-two-thousand dollar white Rolls Royce.
That's the kind of relationship we have. It's not a bad setup, is it, fellas? I mean,
I got part of it back anyway . . . She bought the car just out of a gesture of love,
and she likes this Stutz that I have. It's not a car, it's a Stutz. No, wheeew! God
help me, no, it's called a stud, a Stutz. And she likes the stud. She likes the Stutz.

Mike Stone ain't no stud . . ."

Priscilla was appalled. The hotel wasn't happy, either.

These long monologues left little time for music and when Elvis did sing, often he didn't finish the song, or he walked through it as if he were bored to death. His abuse of prescription drugs already had caused cancellations. Now they were radically affecting the shows he did perform.

It was a bad time for Elvis. Everything seemed to be coming apart. First, his father and his father's wife of ten years, Dee, separated. "I'm a self-centered person," she said. "Vernon made me that way. He treated me like a child, he kept me in a cage. I was about the last to know about Priscilla and Elvis's problem. The business is something I never knew about. I started writing songs. I wanted a life of my own."

It was a familiar theme. Priscilla had felt suffocated, restricted, too. Now, as Dee was packing up and leaving Vernon's house nearby, Elvis saw his friend Linda Thompson move her things out of Graceland. Their relationship was an emotional one and there would be flare-ups off and on for years to come. Elvis was not one to remain alone, however, and when he went on the road only two weeks after closing in Las Vegas, he had a new girl on his arm, Sheila Ryan, another Memphis beauty queen who later would marry actor James Caan.

Elvis had also lost his longtime piano player, David Briggs, who was being paid $3,000 a week by Elvis, but wanted to return to the Nashville recording studios, where he knew he could earn even more.

His health plummeted as his weight ballooned. Never again would he be measured by his costume designer, Bill Belew. "That stopped sometime that year, 1974," Bill said. "After that I'd make the costumes by guess and take them to Elvis and leave them for him to try on. Joe Esposito would call and say they needed letting out, so I'd go back and pick them up, then take them back, pick them up and take them back, until we got it right. It was never explained why no measurements were taken. It was just understood. You didn't ask questions. Ever!"

Just how much weight Elvis had put on, and how quickly, became apparent when he arrived at the University of Maryland in College Park on September 27, just three weeks after closing in Vegas. So great was the change, some of the boys in the band say they had trouble recognizing him.

Tony Brown, the pianist for Voice, had taken Briggs's place in the backup band and he watched Elvis arrive. "He fell out of the limousine to his knees," Tony said. "People jumped to help and he pushed them away, like, 'Don't help me!' He always did that when he fell. He walked onstage and he held onto the mike for the first thirty minutes like it was a post. Everybody was scared. It was the talk of the . . . is the tour gonna happen? Is he sick? Is it gonna be canceled?"

SPEER © '78

*Left: Nine months after the wedding, in Memphis—leaving the hospital with Lisa Marie. Below: Elvis and Priscilla with a fellow Las Vegas performer, British singer Tom Jones, in 1971. Opposite above left: from the "live" segment of the NBC TV special, 1968, and right: performing in Las Vegas. Opposite below: at the International Hotel, Las Vegas, 1970.*

*Opposite: in rehearsal at MGM for the documentary on Elvis's third season in Las Vegas,* That's the Way It Is, *1970. Above: Elvis in his "American Eagle" jumpsuit at the* Aloha from Hawaii *concert, which was broadcast live via satellite around the world on January 14th, 1973.*

*Opposite above: floral tributes at Elvis's funeral. Opposite below: a devoted fan kneels at Elvis's grave on August 16th, 1978, a year after his death. Above: more than a thousand fans filed past Elvis's grave at Graceland on January 7th, 1978, on the eve of what would have been his 43rd birthday.*

*Above and below: The gravesite by the Graceland meditation pool. The inscription is by Elvis's father, Vernon. Above right: sign directing tourists to Graceland, and right: graffiti on the stone wall outside Graceland.*

Guitarist John Wilkinson was standing a few feet away on the stage. "The lights go down," he recalled, "and Elvis comes up the stairs. He was all gut. He was slurring. He was so fucked up. I looked at Kathy Westmoreland. She looked at me. What happened? It was obvious he was drugged. It was obvious there was something terribly wrong with his body. It was so bad the words to the songs were barely intelligible. You couldn't hear him hardly. College Park let it be known they wouldn't have him back. We were in a state of shock. Joe Guercio said, 'He's finished . . .' I remember crying. He could barely get through the introductions on the stage. He cut the show very short and it seemed like it went on forever."

The rest of the tour was, as Tony put it, "uphill." For three nights, in Detroit, South Bend, and St. Paul, Elvis seemed in control. His eyes were bright and the shows were energetic and musical, giving hope to those around him. Back in Detroit, he slipped again.

"I watched him in his dressing room, just draped over a chair, unable to move," said John Wilkinson. "So often I thought, 'Boss, why don't you just cancel this tour and take a year off . . . ?' I mentioned something once in a guarded moment. He patted me on the back and said, 'It'll be all right. Don't you worry about it.'"

The cities rolled by. Dayton, Wichita, San Antonio, and Abilene. The Playboy jet that Elvis had chartered for the tour flew in, and the Playboy jet flew out. Limousines and hotel rooms and huge auditoriums became the only environments he knew. Finally, on October 10, Elvis and his entourage pulled into Lake Tahoe to make up five days for the canceled engagement in the Sahara Tahoe a year earlier.

After that, Elvis didn't work for five months.

Back in Memphis—in the final months before his fortieth birthday—it wasn't his health but finances that caused the next crisis. In all categories, costs were rising alarmingly. The paternity suit that Elvis had taken so seriously finally was dismissed after blood tests and a private detective's confidential reports made it clear that the waitress was lying, but legal fees for this and the ongoing lawsuit involving the hallway assault in Lake Tahoe topped all previous years.

Three years later that lawsuit would require Elvis's accountants in Memphis, Rhea and Ivey, to produce a breakdown of his 1974 earnings and expenses. It was a fragmentary picture they drew, it didn't tell all the story, but even the boldest strokes were revealing. This was the first time that Elvis's finances emerged publicly.

He had earned lots, $7,273,622, in 1974—86 percent of it, $6,281,885, from Nevada and the grueling, carnivalesque one-nighters, the rest from record

ELVIS

sales ($416,864), publishing royalties ($278,360), and movie rentals to theaters and television ($133,529). But he also spent lots—$4,295,372 in what the accountants called "operating expenses" alone.

Where, and to whom, did the money go? Only tax deductible expenses were shown in the financial statement, yet these certainly are revealing enough. Colonel Parker, for instance, took as his share $1,720,067, while those on his personal payroll—an unspecified number, but probably about fifteen—split $467,599. Elvis also spent $24,300 on his wardrobe, $2,207 on cleaning and laundry, and $12,819 on telephone calls. The accountants said that they and the lawyers had earned $62,626.

On top of this, Elvis paid predictably high taxes, $1,484,867, leaving him with a net income of $1,493,384. That's not bad. Most small businesses wish they had that margin of profit. The trouble was, Elvis still managed to spend more than he made. According to the accountants' statement, he started 1974 with $2,640,355 in the bank and finished it with $1,928,746. That meant his year-end deficit was $711,609.

What *that* meant was that Elvis took in a million-and-a-half in 1974 and spent more than three . . . not on deductible expenses, but on *himself*. Jewelers and car dealers were given a lot of it, of course, and there was the matter of Jerry Schilling's house. Only the accountants knew exactly how much Linda cost; at least $250,000, according to the estimates of friends. Several rooms in Graceland were redecorated. Guns and ammunition ate up another small fortune. Television sets were blown apart and replaced. Some say the biggest expense was "medication." "Would you believe half a million dollars?" asks one insider. "It's possible, when you keep flying people to Las Vegas and Los Angeles from Memphis to pick up the prescriptions."

By the end of the year, Elvis had spent the better part of a month under the care of Dr. Elias Ghanem, a Las Vegas "doctor to the stars" who had put him on a "sleep diet" and said he had been treating him with placebos—this, after Elvis collapsed at the physician's home and called Jerry Schilling for help. Jerry wrote in his memoir that he confronted Ghanem after he returned "from a night on the town," telling him, "This is a proud man, and I better not see him like this again or I'll go all the way."

Not long after that, Linda confronted Elvis, telling him he was killing himself. In an interview with Peter Guralnick, she said she asked Elvis what he thought was his biggest character flaw. To her surprise, he said he was "self-destructive." "You do recognize that?" she said. "Yeah, I recognize it," he said, "but there's not a lot I can do about it." Linda said they never spoke of it again. Nor, apparently, did he admit this to anyone else.

It didn't get any better in 1975. On January 8 Elvis celebrated his fortieth birthday and that hurt in other ways.

The press had been taking shots for several months. In October, *Pageant* magazine asked on its cover, "Elvis at 40: What's ahead for the aging star?" then warned that Elvis could be on the brink of "male menopause," raising doubts about Elvis's vanity surviving his loss of youth.

The *National Enquirer* joined the assault a month later. Again Elvis was on the cover, pictured this time in concert in a ferociously unflattering pose that gave him a hunched back, thick waist, and a visage that was a cross between Sidney Greenstreet at his most sensual and Boris Karloff at his scariest. Under the photograph were the words, "Elvis at 40—Paunchy, Depressed & Living in Fear." Most of the sources for the story were employees of motels where he stayed on his last tour through the Midwest and local police assigned to his security. The impression they left was vivid. He was afraid for his life, feared being kidnapped or assassinated, the *Enquirer* said; in Abilene, where Vernon and Lisa flew in for a sort of family reunion—Linda was back, too—Vernon was quoted as being so upset by the way Elvis looked, he had Dr. Nichopoulos flown in from Memphis.

It wasn't much of a story, really. But many of Elvis's most avid fans read the *Enquirer* religiously and the effect was felt. Elvis's friends did their best to keep such stories away from him, but this was one that got through and Elvis was reported enraged as well.

Several other publications checked in that January to wish Elvis sardonic birthday greetings. *People* magazine also put him on the cover—by now it was clear to publishers that an Elvis cover sold magazines—and compared his "sybaritic reclusiveness" to that of Howard Hughes, his "ambivalent social consciousness" to the film character Billy Jack.

Robert Hilburn in the *Los Angeles Times* took a different, harder tack. "Elvis: Waning Legend In His Own Time?" was the title of an essay on the front page of the Sunday entertainment section that opened with the statement, "Maybe it's time for Elvis to retire."

"At 40," Hilburn—once a devoted fan—said, "his records are increasingly uneven, his choice of material sometimes ludicrous, and his concert performances often sloppy. Worst of all, there is no purpose or personal vision in his music anymore."

Hilburn went on to call Elvis's latest album, *Promised Land*, "bland and directionless." On the basis of this and other recent albums, he said, it would be difficult to convince a young music fan that Elvis was the most important figure in the birth of rock and roll. Elvis had refused to advance his music, Hillburn charged; he took the easy way, and when faced with an adoring audience that didn't seem to care what he did, or how well, came to his concerts and bought his records anyway, he put his career on "automatic pilot" and stopped growing. He weakened his standards. He *wasted* his talent.

The fans were there, to be sure. As quickly as the sea of public criticism rushed in, they sent Elvis avid confirmation of undying love.

There was a wonderful salute in *The Commercial Appeal*, Memphis's afternoon newspaper. It reported that although Elvis observed his birthday privately in "self-imposed seclusion," letters had poured in at the rate of about 600 a day for more than a week, along with hundreds of telegrams. A special "Happy Birthday Elvis" box was set up outside the Graceland gates for the wishes of the two thousand visitors who came by daily. Radio stations, the medium through which Elvis initially rose to fame, played Elvis records throughout the day, gave away birthday cakes and Elvis albums every hour, and conducted interviews with longtime Elvis friends and associates.

It wasn't enough. As Ed Parker told the story in his book, *Inside Elvis*, his friend called at 5 A.M. He said it was his fortieth birthday and it was clear to Ed that Elvis wasn't happy about it. He said he gave him a pep talk, said Sinatra was much older and still pulling them in. Elvis wasn't convinced. He was forty years old and it hurt.

Twenty days later Elvis was back in the hospital, this time with, among other problems, an enlarged colon. At least that's what the press was told. And it was true. But it was also true that Elvis was back in the hospital for another detoxification. This, too, would be confirmed years later by Dr. Nick. The way Nichopoulos told the story at the time, however, he merely stated that Elvis had been sick for several days but was reluctant to go to the hospital. He said it required several more days of talking before he submitted to the physician's wishes, during which time a suite was held for him on the Baptist Hospital's eighteenth floor.

Finally, on January 28 at 5 A.M., the telephone rang at the nurse's station. Dr. Nick said he was leaving Graceland with Elvis and would be arriving in fifteen minutes. Elvis was wearing navy blue pajamas and the start of a dark beard when he entered the end-of-the-hallway suite of rooms, with his father, Joe Esposito, Linda Thompson, and a few of his bodyguards trailing along behind him. Soon after that, Linda shaved Elvis and the hospital star routine began.

The first days were uneventful, as Elvis slept long hours in the always darkened room. When awake, he talked with the nurses assigned to him, one of them a recent graduate of the University of Arkansas who soon began dating one of Elvis's hired hands, another a middle-aged woman named Marian Cocke, who later also would write a book, *I Called Him Babe: Elvis Presley's Nurse Remembers*.

The enlarged colon and drug detoxification were two of several serious problems examined during his three-week stay. Another concerned his eyes. He had been experiencing headaches and optical pressure in recent months; eventually this would be diagnosed as glaucoma, the third major cause of blindness in the United States. There was no danger of Elvis losing his sight, the doctors reported, but before he went on the road again and exposed himself to bright lights in performance, tinted contact lenses would be made. He also was given medication for some time and ordered to continue wearing the tinted glasses he favored.

A more serious problem—one never discussed publicly—showed itself in the results of a liver biopsy. Later, Elvis would joke about the long needle that was stuck into his side to extract a sample of liver tissue, but the findings weren't at all amusing. There was severe damage to the organ and it was clear to attending physicians that in Elvis's case the probable cause was drug abuse.

The colon problem, Dr. Nick said, was caused by Elvis's poor eating habits. Elvis loved fried foods and sugar, he said, and needed a nearly complete change in his diet.

As usual, Elvis was cheerful and obedient, promising to mend his ways. It got worse before it got better during this hospital stay, when Vernon had his first heart attack and was rushed to the hospital's intensive care unit, where he remained for nearly a week. Vernon was then moved into the suite adjacent to Elvis's. Elvis was checked out of the hospital before Vernon, on February 14, but visited him often.

"Elvis would come and try to cheer him up," Jerry Schilling recalls. "It was the first time that Vernon had been in a hospital all his life. And both he and Elvis were scared to death."

"I was there the first time he went in to visit," said the hospital vice president, Maurice Elliott. "Elvis came out crying."

There was one other incident connected to this hospital stay. Elvis wanted to put the young nurse who had begun to date Al Strada on his payroll, to accompany him to Las Vegas in March and go on tour in April and May. When she accepted his offer, he gave her a thousand dollars to buy a new wardrobe. Quitting her job at the hospital, she went home to visit her parents in Arkansas.

Several on the hospital staff, including Dr. Nick, tried to change her mind, but she was convinced. When word of her hiring reached the Colonel in California, however, the tide turned quickly. He didn't believe Elvis needed a nurse with him—certainly not one that was going with one of the bodyguards—and thought her presence would be bad for Elvis's image. The Colonel called Joe and Joe talked to Elvis, who wanted to see that the nurse kept her hospital job. Joe saw that that was done and then broke the news to the young nurse.

The Colonel's relationship with Elvis had undergone considerable stress in the previous year. They'd been partners in this multi-million-dollar enterprise for exactly twenty years by 1975, and it's doubtful that any partnership survives that long without some pulling and tugging. Still, during 1974 and on into the following year, there were recurring rumors that Elvis and the Colonel were separating.

It's true that they often disagreed—over some of the tour dates that the Colonel approved, for example, when Elvis thought the cities were too small. Another time they fought over whether or not Elvis would do a ninety-minute-long gospel show on television: the Colonel wanted it; Elvis did not. Elvis also started grumbling over an album the Colonel had released first as a joke on his own Boxcar label and then had released by RCA; this was *Having Fun with Elvis on Stage (A Talking Album Only)*, a severely edited but still embarrassing collection of monologues and so on from Elvis's concerts—belches, burps, bad jokes, and all. More complaints were heard backstage when the Colonel suggested strongly that Elvis stop using so much karate in his act.

Their biggest fight resulted from something else that happened on the Hilton showroom stage. Elvis's favorite chef at the hotel had been fired, and he was so angry, he started badmouthing hotel management between songs. The Colonel had recently renegotiated Elvis's contract, giving the singer the same pay for less work, and after the show, he confronted Elvis outside his dressing room.

"You can't tell these people how to run their business!" the Colonel said, so angry that his jowls shook as he thumped his cane on the floor. "What right you think you got to say somethin' like that on their stage?"

Bang, bang, bang went the cane, and Elvis began shouting back. The Colonel saw an audience gathering and suddenly stopped, looking at Elvis and nodding toward the dressing room door. Silently, they went inside, where they again began to shout at each other, their words muffled by the door. A few minutes later the Colonel emerged and said, as he stalked away, still pounding his cane as he went, "All right . . . I'll call a press conference in the morning and say I'm leaving."

Elvis had to get in the final word. According to Red West, he shouted, "I'll call a press conference tonight!"

In his book *Elvis: What Happened?*, Red explained that what happened next was that the Colonel stayed up all night, figuring out how much money Elvis owed him. "I didn't see the figures," Red said, "but it was like a million due him for this and a million for that. Elvis showed Vernon the figures. Vernon was ready for the Colonel to leave, but then after looking at the figures, things seemed to quiet down."

# Chapter 24

# SPENDING SPREE

E lvis hadn't worked in five months when he returned to Las Vegas in March 1975 and although he still packed a lot of uncomfortable weight inside his jeweled white jumpsuit, his spirits were higher than they'd been at the start of a Nevada engagement in years. This was his twelfth visit and if he didn't view it with the nervous excitement of his first, at least for a change it didn't seem a boring prospect. Elvis may have been in a rut, the performances may have become more than a little routine by now, but Elvis needed them. Going face-to-face with an audience and moving it was what he was all about. A demonstration of power, a salve for wounded self-respect, it was Elvis's heaviest drug.

The first nights in Las Vegas were good. Even the reviewers, though they noted his bulkiness, talked mostly about how good his voice was and how much fun he seemed to be having. "Fat and Sassy," was the headline on one story. Much of his good humor took the form of self-parody, usually in the middle of "Hound Dog" or another of the 1950s songs that he was now very tired of singing. He feigned difficulty getting the left side of his upper lip into its famous curl, for example, poking it up with a finger and muttering, "When I was nineteen it worked just fine." Sometimes he pretended to be unable to get his legs to shake. These were bits of stage "business" that he used with great success for years, and they still seemed to amuse him.

This was an engagement that also was marked by changes in the hotel and in the way the audience was seated. A new $20 million tower containing 600 rooms was opened, allowing more Elvis fans than ever before to sleep under the same roof with their idol. There was a new policy in the showroom, too. Waiters no longer were required to present checks at the end of the show. Now tickets were sold. Cost of the show was now $20 a person, up from $17.50 charged previously. That gave the customers either two drinks or a half-bottle of champagne, and included tax and tip. This was true for both shows; thus it was Elvis's first performance in Vegas that didn't have a dinner show. Drinks were easier to prepare and serve, the margin of profit was higher in alcohol (and soft drinks for the under-aged fans) than it was in food, and replacing the dinner tables with smaller cocktail tables allowed the hotel management to increase the capacity of the room by 20 percent.

More money was being made on Presley product. As usual, all money from the sale of Elvis souvenir items in the hotel lobby went to a local charity, but that which was sold in the gift shops and boutiques went into Elvis's and the Colonel's pockets. Besides scarves, you could also buy pennants, picture books, and records.

The albums continued to appear with the predictability of the seasons, usually three or four a year, with the same number of singles. Those released in 1974 and 1975 showed clearly the aimless sort of career trajectory that Bob Hilburn referred to. Following the release of the inspired *Legendary Performer* album (in January 1974), there was an album (in March) called *Good Times*, a collection of songs from the autobiographical session in Memphis a year earlier ("Take Good Care of Her," "Goodtime Charlie's Got the Blues," etc.). Then there was the first of many live albums, a so-so double disc recorded during the March concerts at the Memphis Coliseum and released in June, and after that came the embarrassing "talking album."

In 1975 the same pattern of no pattern held steady. The first album, released in January, was named for his recent Top Twenty hit, "Promised Land," a rocker written by Chuck Berry. In March came a repackage of ten songs that had sold a million copies or more, called, unimaginatively, *Pure Gold*—a nice enough collection, but lacking in direction, including songs from three decades ("All Shook Up," "In the Ghetto," "It's Impossible"), with no connecting thread.

All went onto the bestseller lists, as did the four singles released in the same period.

Besides music and performing it in public, Elvis probably enjoyed spending money more than anything else, and 1975 was his year for spending it. It's unusual that a man's jeweler becomes a significant source of information in writing a biography. Again, Elvis was the exception to the rule. Elvis favored two jewelers. One had a shop in Beverly Hills that Elvis frequented the way other men frequent their neighborhood bars. The other, from Memphis, Elvis liked so much he took him on the road with him when he went touring—with the understanding that he always would have two sample cases full of trinkets for when Elvis got in the buying mood.

Sol Schwartz was a fast-talking former New Yorker with an eighth-grade education and a heart the size of the Beverly Hills Hotel. He met Elvis when the singer was making a movie with Nancy Sinatra, back in 1966. Sol's wife Betty had thrown a couple of handfuls of expensive rings and pins into her handbag and gone to Nancy's house so Nancy could pick out some gifts. Nancy bought about $7,000 worth of jewelry and Elvis, who was at the house visiting, doubled that. A few days later Elvis visited Sol's shop and soon after that offered to lend him $50,000 so he could upgrade his inventory.

"He'd be here every day, usually about four o'clock, and stand outside and hustle customers for the store," Sol said. "Everybody'd know he was in town. The fat old ladies from the department store down the street would be outside waiting for him. He used to come into the store and sit in my office with his feet up and shave himself with an electric razor. When he came in, I'd pinch him on the cheek and say, 'Hey, baby, you're gettin' fat.'

"I made Elvis a ring one day, one of Elvis's first big pieces, a coffee-colored marquise diamond ring, about five carats. It was a woman's ring in the window. His taste ran to women's jewelry. It was $18,000. He got hassled in the Hilton in Vegas two days later and one of the guards helped him. Elvis said, 'What can I do for you?' He said, 'I like your ring.' Elvis took it off and gave it to him.

"His buying habits were interesting. He used to ask me the price of everything. He'd look and ask the price, I'd put it back and then about five minutes later, before he'd leave, he'd say, 'I'll take that, that, that, that, that, that, and that.' He was like a kid in a candy store."

It was Sol's partner, Lee Ablesser, who designed the TCB neck charm that Elvis gave away to friends and people who worked for him. Sol said he sold Elvis five hundred of the chains and charms, and another five hundred charm bracelets. The "TCB" and the "Elvis bracelet," as they came to be called, cost Elvis $175 apiece.

"It was a mutual thing," said Sol. "Elvis wanted the jewelry and I wanted to sell him. And he never threw it up, like he was doing me a favor. Some of the stars, they aren't like that. Elvis musta spent half a million dollars with me, yet he didn't play the kiss-my-ass game once."

His Memphis jeweler, Lowell Hays, sold Elvis more jewelry than that, at least $800,000 worth. It was easy. After a while, Elvis not only took him on tour, he took him along on vacations, too. He met Elvis through Dr. Nick.

"The first time, they called me at home and said Elvis wants to see some jewelry. They said bring it to the Memphian Theater. I said, 'What does he want?' They said he likes big, flashy things. So I came by the store and opened the vault, took out the biggest, flashiest things I had, and went to the theater. The show was already on and I found Dr. Nick and he said sit down. A few minutes later he went over to Elvis and told him I was here and Elvis got up in the middle of the movie, looked at me and motioned with his finger and took off up the aisle. I followed him to the little boys' room. He locked the door and we sat there and went through the jewelry. He had one of his body-guards with him. He picked out Christmas gifts for several people, in the neighborhood of ten nice gifts.

"Another time they called me from Atlanta and said bring some jewelry up here, Elvis wants some. I got some jewelry together and flew to Atlanta where my instructions were to go to the top floor of the Staffer's Hotel. He told me he wanted to buy something for the Sweet Inspirations and he did and he ended up buying several other things. I asked him, 'Can I stay with the tour?' He said sure. From then on, my name was on that list and I had a room and I could come and go as I pleased and I did. I had my room like one of the boys, I had no obligations, I had all my expenses paid for everything. Many times I joined the tour in the middle or left and went back to Memphis in the middle and then I'd pay my air fare, but otherwise it was all on Elvis. I went on every tour he had for the last three or four years. There were a lot of tours and I was on every one of them.

"I called him one time and said I'd be coming in to join the tour. I didn't take any jewelry with me. I went just to go. Elvis saw me and said, 'Bring your case, I want to buy something.' I said, 'Elvis, I didn't bring it, I didn't come on this thing to solicit you, I just wanted to be here.' He said, 'Look, I don't consider you're soliciting me. Ever' time I see you, I see diamonds. From now on, you can come on all my tours with me, but from now on, bring your jewelry with you. Don't come along as dead weight. I expect you to have jewelry with you. When I see you, I think Lowell's got his jewelry with him, I want to see what he's got. If you don't bring it with you, I'm gonna teach you a lesson some time.'"

He did, too. After Lowell and Elvis and several others had gone to a football game in Memphis, Elvis flew them to Dallas and then to Palm Springs, where a department store opened in the middle of the night to him so he could buy everyone pajamas and toilet articles and hair dryers and a change of clothes, because they'd left Memphis on Elvis's whim and without going home to pack.

Relaxing at Elvis's Palm Springs home, Elvis told Lowell, "Bring your case."

"But, Elvis, I don't have it. We went to a football game, remember?"

Elvis glared at Lowell and said, "I told you to bring jewelry when you were around me." He then took Lowell with him as he visited a Palm Springs jeweler and spent a small fortune.

Lowell never forgot again.

Such highs in Elvis's life inevitably were followed by depression. Even before he left Las Vegas in April he was slipping. His pianist, Tony Brown, remembers that the closing-night party for that engagement was one of the biggest and best, but Elvis never even appeared.

That was followed by a two-week tour of the South (including a benefit for Mississippi tornado victims) and a three-day recording session in Los Angeles. The songs he recorded during those sessions were not particularly memorable, but Elvis's reaction to the album that came from the sessions was. RCA was anxious for a May release, and so rushed the tapes to New York for a quick "mix-down," returning the tapes to Los Angeles for Elvis's appraisal.

"Elvis was pissed, *really* pissed," said John Wilkinson, "because it didn't sound the same as it did when it left the studio in Hollywood. And he went into a *rage!* There was some guy from RCA in the booth when we heard the album and Elvis started saying things about RCA. He said, 'You know, if I was smart, I'd quit you sonsabitches and I'd go with White Whale (a small Hollywood record company) or somebody. I betcha I can find a job someplace. I betcha somebody'll hire me.' He put that poor guy through some shit. We took a break after listening to the album. Red or Joe suggested a break, said we'd been working too hard. I guess they talked to him and got him calmed down. But he was mad and he had a right to be mad. After that, he said, 'By God, none of them go to New York. They go to Memphis for the re-mix and that's where it'll stay!'"

Two weeks later, at the end of May, Elvis was on the road again for another sixteen shows in twelve days, again crisscrossing the South and going as far north as Cleveland, Ohio, and Terre Haute, Indiana. The tour ended on the tenth of June and six days after that, Elvis was back in the hospital again. However, this time it was a different hospital, the Mid-South, and the press was not advised.

Later, when a few facts leaked out, Elvis's people said the two-day hospitalization was for an eye examination, which made sense, considering the recent trouble he'd had with his eyes and the seriousness of the diagnosis. In fact, his eyes did play a role in the hospitalization. The plastic surgeon Elvis saw removed bags from under them.

Afterward, back at Graceland, after remaining in seclusion until the bruises around his eyes disappeared, he called one of his bodyguards into his bedroom. "Well," he said, "how do I look?"

The bodyguard said, "Good, good. Your eyes look clear, you look happy . . ."

"No," Elvis interrupted, "no . . . look here." He then lifted his hair back near his ears, revealing the stitches, explaining that he'd had a facelift.

The bodyguard just stared. He couldn't discern any change at all.

Another precipitous dive began three weeks following the operation, in early July when Elvis went back on the road. The tours were shorter now, seldom lasting more than two weeks, but they were coming more frequently; this was the third in just over two months. Over the years, Elvis had dated one of his backup singers, Kathy Westmoreland, who was now dating one of the band members. In Cleveland, Elvis introduced her to his audience, saying, "She will take affection from anybody, anyplace, anytime. In fact, she gets it from the whole band." She asked the Colonel's lieutenant, Tom Diskin, to talk to Elvis about it. Diskin made the mistake of mentioning it to Elvis just before he walked onstage in Greensboro in July.

He sang a few songs and then earlier than usual he introduced some of the singers. It was apparent to everyone that he was angry. First he went over to the Sweet Inspirations, who were standing behind him, and said, "I smell catfish! You girls been eatin' catfish?"

The girls didn't know what Elvis meant.

"I said, 'You been eatin' catfish?'"

They got it then and one of the three singers walked off the stage. Then Elvis introduced Kathy.

"This is Kathy Westmoreland . . ." He turned to face her and curled his lip. "If you don't like the way I introduce you," he said, "get off the pot."

Hearing that, she left the stage, followed by two of the Sweet Inspirations. The odd thing was, hardly anyone noticed, outside of those on Elvis's payroll. They were swiveling their heads and necks furiously during all this, shooting signals that said, "What the hell!?" Yet only ten yards away, no one was paying any attention to what Elvis was saying, or what he was causing to happen onstage. The crowd's collective attention seemed to be somewhere else instead; focused so intently as to seem mesmerized, blind to what was actually happening. Reading the audience accurately, Elvis introduced J. D. Sumner and the Stamps as if nothing out of the ordinary had happened, then walked over to the single remaining member of the Sweet Inspirations, Myrna Smith.

"Here," he said, taking off one of his big diamond rings, "you take this, I want ya to have it."

Myrna tried to give it back. Elvis refused. Then he resumed the show. Later, he did accept the ring from Myrna.

That night after the show he felt uncomfortable. He asked Jerry Schilling and others to apologize to Kathy and the Sweet Inspirations for him. They looked away and said they didn't think the girls would accept the apology from him.

That was on the twenty-first. On the twenty-second, the tour left for Asheville, North Carolina, for three concerts. A short hop from Greensboro, departure time was at 4:30, but at two, Elvis passed the word: "We're leaving now." Everybody rushed for the bus, carrying their own luggage. Then Elvis said he was staying a little longer. He told the others to go to the airport, he'd join them later.

"On the way to the airport," said Lowell Hays, "there was an ice cream parlor. We were all kind of unhappy about his hurrying us out of the hotel for no reason and we told the driver to pull over. We got off and got us some ice

cream. And who do you think passed us while we were standin' there? Elvis.
He was pissed, too. We saw his face as he went by. So we jumped on the bus as
fast as we could and headed for the airport. We hadn't even unloaded the luggage when he said, 'Anybody on that plane yet?'

"There were a couple and he said, 'Get 'em off!' He made everybody get
off the plane and he got on and said, 'If they can't do what I tell 'em, leave 'em
here!' And he took off. He left us standin' there in the middle of the runway."

In Asheville, getting into his limousine as if nothing out of the ordinary had
happened, Elvis ordered the plane to return for the members of his entourage.

When the plane returned to Asheville the second time, one of Elvis's boys
approached Lowell and said, "Elvis wants to see you right away."

According to Lowell, when he entered Elvis's hotel suite, he said, "I want
to buy everybody something."

"He bought everything I had and he said he wanted more," Lowell recalls.
"I was putting the stuff I had in envelopes and writing their names as fast as I
could and I had a *lot* of jewelry with me, but we ran out. He said, 'Do you know
any jewelers here in town?' I said, 'No, sir, but I can get the jewelry here from
Memphis in about an hour.' He said, 'Get it here.'

"I called Memphis, made arrangements for them to get the jewelry together, jumped on a plane, flew to Memphis, picked up the jewelry, and flew right
straight back. Elvis bought what I call a fortune in jewelry, practically a whole
jewelry store. He gave something to everybody in the group, everybody in the
band, all the backup singers, everybody who meant anything to him. I was in
the dressing room when he apologized to the Sweet Inspirations. He told them
it wouldn't happen again. He gave each one of them a $5,000 ring. Then he
called everybody else in."

Back in Memphis, the end of July, Elvis still couldn't purge the guilt he felt,
so he did what he always did in that situation—he went on another spending
spree. This time he bought fourteen Cadillacs and two airplanes.

The last ten years of his life, Elvis owned at least one hundred expensive
vehicles—usually eight to ten at a time and sometimes as many as fifteen—and
he bought and immediately gave away at least that many more. In ten years
Elvis gave away cars—to bodyguards, maids, nurses, friends, and
strangers—that cost him more than one million dollars.

On July 27, his second day home following the embarrassing incident on
tour, he and some of his boys drove down to the Cadillac agency on Union
Street, not far from the original Sun Records studio where Elvis had made his
first records. He'd been buying Cadillacs there for twenty years, since 1957,
from a white-haired, bankerish sort of man named Howard Massey.

"As a rule he'd bring the people in he was going to buy cars for," the sales-

man said. "He never asked you the price. And he always wanted them right
away. So we'd put the hubcaps on and deliver them if there were a lot going out
at once, then bring them back for servicing later. It wasn't a matter of having to
sell him anything. If he saw what he wanted, he took it. Usually they'd drive the
cars away themselves. He was always a perfect gentleman. He could buy as
many cars here as he wanted and we never worried about payment. I doubt that
I ever sold him less than three. He'd call me at home at nine, ten, eleven, one
o'clock in the morning and I'd meet him here. Anything he wanted here he
could get, day or night. As a matter of fact, the boss said, 'Hell, give him the
front door key if he wants it.' I guess he spent a half a million dollars here, easy."

On this day, Elvis set a record, for himself as well as for Madison Cadillac.
He bought fourteen cars, including one for a woman he didn't know who merely happened by. She admired one of the cars he had just purchased. Elvis
approached her and asked her if she liked it. She said she did. Elvis said, simply, "I'll buy you one." He then took her by one arm and courteously escorted
her into the showroom where he said, "Pick one out." She picked a gold and
white El Dorado, list price $11,500.

Elvis then told Joe Esposito, who was at his side, to write a check "to buy
some clothes to go with the car."

Elvis began to realize his dream to own a fleet of airplanes when he made a
bid of $1.5 million and put down a $75,000 deposit for a luxury Boeing 707 jet
purportedly owned by exiled financier Robert Vesco. Another party appeared
claiming ownership and Elvis withdrew and went to Nigel Winfield, who sold
airplanes nationally from an office in Florida. From him Elvis bought a
Convair 880, a former Delta Airlines plane, paying $1,000,000; he then ordered
a $750,000 remodeling. Elvis also bought a smaller, faster Lockheed Jet Star.
This was a four-engine jet, the type of aircraft popular with big companies; in
fact, he bought it from the Amway Corporation, paying $850,000. Over the
next six months, as the big Convair was being renovated, he used the Jet Star
to shuttle his friends from Memphis to Fort Worth to watch the progress.

"I'm building me the damnedest thing you've ever seen," he told his friends
over and over. "I'm building me an airliner."

Flying them to Texas in the middle of the night, he took them on a tour, at
first through a skeleton of a craft with all its seats and paneling ripped out. "It
was," said T. G. Sheppard, "like walking into a tunnel."

"This is gonna be a little sitting area where I can read my books . . . this is
where the living room gonna be . . . right here, gonna put me a little wet bar .
. . right here gonna put a dining room . . . then back here's where the bedroom
gonna be, then my makeup and wardrobe."

He said he was going to paint an American flag on the tail and under that paint his beloved "TCB" and lightning bolt. The jet would be named after his daughter; *Lisa Marie* would be written in script across the airplane's nose.

However extravagant their purchase, both of these planes got maximum use by Elvis and his organization. When you toured as much as Elvis did, it often made economic sense to own planes rather than charter them. Generally, the Colonel did his advance work in the sixteen-seat Jet Star and Elvis followed along behind in the *Lisa Marie*.

Elvis was still chartering planes for his tours to carry his musicians and singers, so in July he decided to buy a plane for them, at the same time buying a fourth plane for the Colonel. The Colonel's gift was bought on an egotistical whim; when he read that Elton John had paid $40,000 for a Rolls Royce for his manager, Jerry Weintraub, a friend of the Colonel's who promoted Elvis's concerts. Elvis laughed and said, "I'll show that sonofabitch . . ." Together the planes cost Elvis $1,300,000.

"Elvis, I got to talk to you."

It was Vernon talking and Elvis knew what he wanted and answered as he always did: "Daddy, I don't want to talk about it."

"Elvis, you got to listen this one time. Son, you're spending money faster than we're makin' it."

Elvis walked away from an argument with his father. Then he said nothing when the Colonel refused his gift. Nor did he say much when, soon after, two of the four airplanes were advertised for sale in *The Wall Street Journal*.

One of the secrets to Linda's staying in Elvis's life for as long as she did was her willingness to share him with others. Elvis dated freely, and quite often it was his friend George Klein he called to find someone new to keep him company. George was now a popular Memphis disc jockey, a position that gave him ample opportunity to scout the city's young women. One he provided was Melissa Blackwood, a former Queen of the Memphis Southmen. One day in July 1975 George called the eighteen-year-old Melissa and told her Elvis wanted to see her that night.

She fixed her hair and changed clothes four times and then waited until almost midnight, when she took off her makeup and dress, put curlers in her hair and went to bed. George called at 1 A.M. and told her to go to the Memphian. She said she couldn't, she was in bed. George said he understood and hung up, then started calling around for a replacement. In the meantime, Melissa changed her mind, flew into her clothes and drove her Cadillac that said "Queen of Memphis Southmen" on the side down to the Memphian Theater. By now it was two. She waited in the lobby.

After a while, Elvis appeared from inside the theater, greeting Melissa. She was shaking nervously and said, "How do you do, Mr. Presley?" He laughed warmly. He said he was sorry, but he had made other plans. He thanked her for coming and she left.

The next day Elvis had one of his boys call Melissa and, with Lisa playfully disconnecting them from time to time by pushing down the telephone receiver, they talked for over an hour. After getting much of her life story, Elvis told her he was going on tour the next day, so it was a month before she heard from him again. This time she abandoned a regular boyfriend to return his call at 2 A.M. Elvis came on the line and said he wanted to see her right away. She said it was too late. Elvis said he understood and would send someone to pick her up at seven in the morning, for breakfast. One of Elvis's boys showed up promptly in a Lincoln Continental and finally Melissa was taken to Graceland.

"We entered the house and I was told, 'It's at the top of the stairs, through the big gold doors.' I was sent up there alone. I went through two sets of doors and Elvis was in bed, wearing blue pajamas. And he just looked so tired. I think he was sick. He looked tired and hot, like he had a fever. He'd been up all night, of course, and he said, 'Come here and sit down beside me.' I think he could tell I was very nervous and he said, 'I want to tell you three things. The first thing I want you to know is that things may look a little odd, me in my pajamas in bed and all, but I want you to know I'm gonna be a perfect gentleman. I don't want you to think I'm a makeout artist . . .'"

She sat on the edge of the bed and in her sweet, tiny voice answered his questions about her life. He called her Brown Eyes and he played with a lock of her hair that fell across her forehead. "After a while," she said, "he told me to get out of my clothes and put these pajamas on, these pajamas he had draped over a chair by the bed. I looked at him, shocked at the suggestion. He added, 'I don't mean anything by it. You have to understand I'll be more comfortable if you're wearing those and you sit here with me, both of us and just talk and spend some time together. I want peace and quiet. You won't get your clothes all wrinkled up and I'll feel more like you're at home.' So I went into the bathroom and put them on."

This apparently was not what some may think. The pajamas Melissa put on were Elvis's and so big on her they had to be pinned in the middle, creating an image more funny than sexy. Elvis's physical condition also was an inhibiting factor. He wanted to eat some yogurt, he told her, yet "he was so sick he couldn't even hold his head up and feed it to himself. So I held his head in one arm and tried to feed him."

They continued to talk and finally Elvis asked her, "What kind of car do you have?" She told him her father didn't think she was old enough to own one. "Well," he said, "if you could have one, what would you like to have?" She drove a Cadillac as Queen of the Memphis Southmen, she said, and it was too big, it was hard to park and felt like "it oughta be my father's car." He told Melissa she should drive a white car and then excused himself and went to the bathroom, where he telephoned the local Pontiac dealership and ordered a white Grand Prix to be delivered to Graceland in half an hour. Then, after talking with Melissa for a while longer, he took her down to the front porch to watch the car delivered.

"What did I do to deserve this?" Melissa said, after the squealing had stopped.

Elvis looked at her beneath heavy lidded eyes and said, "You came today."

"Then we went back upstairs," Melissa recalls, "and he said he was really tired and wanted to go to sleep. That's when it got worse and worse. He took this bunch of pills and really started to sweat. They were all prescription pills and when he took them I had to hold his glass of water and just feed them to him. He was hot and uncomfortable, like a little child with a terrible fever. He was shaking and it scared me to death. I got mad and I took the pills away from him when he tried to take some more to go to sleep. He said, 'This is the amount I'm supposed to take, it's all right, I have the best doctors . . .' Finally he said, 'Will you stay here and hold my hand?' And he wouldn't let me leave. It was the strangest thing. He would sit there in bed, silent, with his eyes closed for the longest time, and I would think he was sound asleep but when I got up to leave, he'd claw my arm, saying, 'Don't go!' He wouldn't let go of my hand until he was really sound asleep."

Melissa finally tiptoed out of the dark bedroom and, still worried about Elvis, confronted the young man who'd driven her to Graceland several hours earlier. She said, "There's something terribly wrong with Elvis and I want you to call a doctor."

He said, "Don't worry about it. He's like this every day. He has to have these pills. He's under a doctor's care. Don't interfere, because you just don't understand. This afternoon he'll wake up and he'll be fine."

Melissa then drove her new car home to show it to her mother, returning to Graceland about three in the afternoon. Elvis was awake and greeted her at the door: "I give her a car and she leaves me in it." He was joking, but Melissa knew he was angry, too. "I wish you hadn't left," he said.

That night, late, Melissa went with Elvis and several others to Fort Worth in his Jet Star to see how renovations were going on the big 880 Convair. Elvis was full of himself, practically strutting along the length of the airplane. "How nice that you named it after Lisa," Melissa said. "Yeah," Elvis replied, "I wanted to impress Lisa and when I showed it to her, she yawned."

"Then we went back to Memphis and to Graceland," Melissa said. "By this time I was really worn out, I hadn't been to bed in two days. He didn't want me to go home. He said, 'I want you to stay here. I don't mean staying with me. I just want you in this house. I don't want you to leave.'

"I said, 'I can't stay. I don't have my things . . .'

"He said, 'Well, get your things. I have everything you need. You'll have your own place, your own bathroom, everything.'

"I said, 'No, I can't, this is too much for me, I want to go home and be in my own room and go to sleep in my own bed and then I'll come back . . .'

"He said he and the boys were going to the movies and he wanted me to stay at the house. He said, 'I've given you the car and I've done everything and . . .'

"I got upset and said, 'Well, if that's why you gave me the car . . .' and I gave him the keys back and he looked so hurt.

"He gave them back to me and he said, 'That's your car, I want you to have it. If you don't take it, I'm gonna park it on the street until you come and take it away.' And then I left the room and sat in a chair and cried. He came and put his arms around me and I said, 'I care, Elvis, but I just can't move in here.'

"He said, 'I care, too, babe.'

"He walked me to the door and that was the last time I ever talked to him."

There were other women who came and went—a Las Vegas showgirl named Sandra Zancan, the actress Cybill Shepherd (who saw Elvis off and on while still dating director Peter Bogdanovich), and another Memphis Southmen hostess, Jo Cathy Brownlee. All were given big new cars or jewelry, or both, in much the same way Elvis surprised Melissa. All tell similar stories. And then it was Linda's turn again. However many women Elvis saw—and he saw many after the divorce—it was Linda who returned again and again, it was Linda who was the closest.

Another reason Linda lasted so long was her vivacious personality, her willingness to do anything to get Elvis to laugh. In Vegas once after a show, she said, she was walking casually through the casino with Ricky Stanley, one of Elvis's stepbrothers, when someone who was visiting another of Elvis's bodyguards came up to her.

"The procedure was the guys would go around the casino trolling, go downstairs and invite girls up to the party after the show. That was a big line: 'Would you like to meet Elvis?' And it was used on me as I got on the elevator. He didn't know Ricky and he said, 'Hey, like to go up to the thirtieth floor, meet Elvis?'

"I went along with it. I said, 'Oh, you're kidding! You mean you could arrange that?' He said, 'Yeah, I know him, I'm going up there right now, to a party. You wanta go?'

"And I said, 'Oh, God, I'd be too nervous, I don't know what I'd say to him.' And Ricky was about to collapse laughing, but this guy didn't notice, he was so busy coming on to me and seeing his line was working, that he was oblivious to him. I said I'd love to meet Elvis, I kept it going all the way up to the thirtieth floor, when Ricky said, 'Do you know who this is?'

"He said, 'What do you mean?'

"Ricky said, 'This is Elvis's girlfriend.'

"The guy said, 'Oh, my God, are you Cybill Shepherd?'

"I said, 'Strike two, one more . . .' And then we went inside the suite. When Ricky told Elvis what happened, he died laughing. That became one of our classic stories. Elvis liked telling it."

Linda tells another story, one that recalls the time she blacked out her teeth to make Elvis laugh. This time it happened at a Vegas party, when Elvis and Linda entered Elvis's suite by a back entrance and changed before joining the large party elsewhere in the suite.

"We got all dressed up," Linda said, "and we'd blacked out our front teeth, but kept our mouths closed, sedate and stoic, and we descended the stairs and there was a hush. There were about fifty people there and you heard them say, 'There's Elvis, there he is! Oh my God, he's gorgeous! There's his girlfriend, isn't she pretty?'

"We got to the bottom of the stairs and people came up to us and we smiled. The funny thing was people were not sure if they should laugh or not, or pretend they didn't notice. It was dimly lit in the room and they couldn't tell, they didn't know if we took our teeth out and relaxed or were playing a joke. The people just had this quizzical look on their faces. And we just broke up.

"He told me I was the first girl he ever took on the road with him," Linda recalls. "Priscilla was the role of wife-mother, tucked away in the corner somewhere. She never went on the road with him. She came to Vegas at first on the weekends and after a while that stopped. Elvis told Priscilla, 'You don't take your wife to work with you.' That was his excuse for not taking her with him. She brought that up later, when Elvis and I were seeing each other. She said, 'You couldn't take your wife to work, but how come you take your girlfriend everywhere?'"

With Lisa back in Los Angeles with Priscilla, and Melissa and Jo Cathy driving new cars in Memphis, Elvis took Linda to Vegas for the annual "Elvis Summer Festival" on August 17. The way Red West told the story in his book, they almost didn't make it when, after taking some unidentified pills, his breathing became labored. They were over Texas in Elvis's new airplane at the time, Red said, and Elvis suddenly yelled, "I can't breathe! Drop the oxygen mask, drop the oxygen mask!" When that didn't help, Elvis got down on the floor of the plane and put his head near an air vent, finally gasping, "I'm not gonna make it. *Land!*" An emergency landing was made in Dallas, where Elvis was taken to a motel to rest. Five hours later he seemed all right again and the flight continued.

In Vegas it got worse. Much worse. His pianist Tony Brown remembers that "everybody hated rehearsals because by now Elvis usually canceled them at the last minute, or he'd be in a bad mood or only do two songs and split. This time he came to rehearsals and tried to sing two sad ballads and they weren't sounding right, so he stopped. He started making jokes, fooling with Red and the others, while the string players and the rest of us just sat there, waiting.

"Suddenly he turned to the orchestra and said, 'You know what? I feel sorry for you sonsabitches have to live in this shitty town. I hate this place! Charlie, I hate it!'"

Charlie stared back at Elvis, who then curtly excused himself, saying he'd be right back. The long minutes dragged past as everyone waited for Elvis's return. Five minutes. Then ten. Finally someone called from backstage, "That's it. Rehearsal's over. The first show's at eight. Be in your places at the usual time."

The show that night was so-so and the second night was worse. In fact, Elvis didn't even want to go on the second night. He wanted to make this announcement after the audience was seated and the Colonel confronted Elvis, telling him he could cancel the rest of his engagement for all he cared, but he wasn't going to tell that night's audience that Elvis wasn't going on. "Tell your father to make the announcement," the Colonel said. Elvis muttered an inaudible reply and finally went on and did the show. But that was it. Immediately after the show, he was driven to the airport and he flew back to Memphis.

"It was incredible," said Tony Brown. "The next day there wasn't a picture of Elvis or a pennant in the whole hotel. By morning all the stuff was gone. All of it. Gone. The Colonel had his men taking it down all night and the next day Peggy Lee was moved over from the Flamingo Hotel to take Elvis's place. She pulled about ten people and then they brought in Bill Cosby, who did a lot better, but it wasn't like what it was when Elvis was there. When Elvis was in town you couldn't get into any restaurant; if you wanted to eat, you had to eat off hours. Then, when word got out he'd left town, the place was empty. The Colonel kept us around for a couple of days, because it was always possible that he'd come back, you just never knew. But he didn't."

In Memphis, the aluminum foil was back up on the windows of Elvis's suite in Baptist Hospital, where this time it was announced he was under treatment for "exhaustion." The truth was far more complicated, and serious. Elvis was suffering from an under-functioning liver and intestinal spasms caused by his enlarged colon. He was also forty pounds overweight and the huge quantities of uppers and downers he took had his metabolic system gravely unbalanced.

"Elvis was a junk food junkie," his doctor, George Nichopoulos, said, "and instead of helping him break his bad eating habits, the cooks at Graceland prepared whatever he ordered. They had diet sheets in the kitchen, but it was hopeless. They mothered him to death. They couldn't believe they were doing him harm by making a fuss over him. He'd say fix a hamburger and fries and they'd send up enough for six people."

Dr. Nick talked with Elvis about alternatives. There was an operation called an intestinal bypass, or "shunt," where a large part of his colon could be removed, permitting him to pass food through his body before it was totally digested. Dr. Nick said he didn't recommend the surgery, merely mentioned it as a possibility. Elvis, no stranger to rapid and extreme weight loss schemes, said he wanted the operation that night. When Dr. Nick went on to explain the difficulties Elvis would have afterward if he didn't adhere faithfully to a special diet, Elvis began to lose interest. That night he made his decision. He'd let 300-pound Lamar Fike have the operation, then buy him a little bitty sports car once he was down to a size that would fit into it. To celebrate the decision *not* to have the operation himself, he had one of his boys go to a fast food place in the neighborhood and sneak back with a sack of bacon cheeseburgers and fried potatoes.

Dr. Nick had also talked with Elvis about hiring private nurses to be with him at Graceland, to keep him on his medical schedule. Elvis said he wanted Mrs. Marian Cocke and a young nurse named Kathy Seamon to report to Graceland during their hours away from the hospital. They leaped for the jobs when they were offered and agreed between them that they wouldn't accept any pay.

Now, in the hospital, as Elvis's body detoxified, his mood leveled. People who were with him then recall the calmness, the normality, the laughs. Linda talks about how she and Elvis became absorbed by the afternoon game shows on television, and watched the babies in the nursery on the closed-circuit channel. "The nurses knew he watched," Linda said, "and sometimes they'd put a little sign on one of the cribs that said, 'Hi, Elvis!' Sometimes they came up to the camera and waved."

Elvis's nurse, Mrs. Cocke—whom he had given a car soon after checking in—remembered Elvis's last night in the hospital. Good-naturedly he autographed a picture for her, marking it "To Mrs. Cocke, the sex symbol of the Baptist . . ." That prompted Jerry Schilling to make a wisecrack about the last names of Elvis's nurses, Cocke and Seamon.

"I reached over on the bedside table," she recalled, "picked up a full pitcher of ice water, walked over to Jerry, pulled the neck of his shirt out, and poured the entire contents of the pitcher down his shirt. Elvis laughed until he cried and said I was going to work out just great at Graceland."

Elvis left the hospital September 5. It would be three months before he returned to work.

Once again the old "routine" was established. Movie theatres were rented for all-night screenings of *Dog Day Afternoon*, *Westworld* and *The Towering Inferno*. He watched his favourite bunch of comedians in their first feature film, *Monty Python and the Holy Grail*, five times.

Other nights he flew his friends to Fort Worth to watch the *Lisa Marie* being readied for flight. A pilot with the unlikely name of Milo High was hired, along with a co-pilot and first officer. "His calls to warm up the plane usually came between 11 o'clock and 2 A.M.," Milo recalled. "And we'd be in the air an hour later."

Elvis continued to meet with Rick Husky and Ed Parker about his karate film, a project that was still limping along more than two years after Elvis had conceived it. Special costumes and patches were designed for a team that was sent to Europe and filmed, and later Elvis himself permitted a film crew to record him in demonstration, but there seemed to be no direction. "I remember when Parker and Husky came to talk about the film," said Jo Cathy Brownlee, who was still dating Elvis off and on. "They caught us as we were about to leave. We were sitting in Elvis's Stutz Bearcat with the mink rug when they came up. The motor was running as he talked to them. I sat there for almost two hours, watching the gas gauge go down."

The film also was being slowed by the Colonel's and Vernon's personal reluctance to spend money. Elvis, of course, had no such inhibition. Already well in the red for the second year in a row, a dozen automobiles and a small air force at his beck and call, still giving money and cars and jewelry away the way ordinary people send postcards while on vacation, surrounded by a staff of maids, cooks, gardeners, gate guards, secretaries, and round-the-clock nurses (not to mention the Memphis Mafia), in the autumn of 1975, Elvis devoted much of his time planning more ways to spend.

A recent convert to racquetball, he decided to build his own indoor courts at Graceland and traveled as far as Dallas to look at existing courts to get ideas. He also took possession of what probably was his most expensive ring, designed by Lowell Hays and nearly three months in the making. They woke Elvis up the day Lowell arrived at Graceland with it.

"He got up, one of the first times before dark," Lowell said, "came down and sat at the dinin' room table. He said, 'Where is it?' I gave it to him, he slipped it on his finger and looked at it and said, 'That's the most beautiful fuckin' ring I've ever seen in my life. God, won't Sammy Davis Jr. shit a brick when he sees this! How much do I owe ya?'

"I told him $55,000. He said, 'You got to be kiddin'!'

"'No, Elvis, it's got an eleven-and-one-half-carat diamond in it.'

"'Well, all right.' Elvis smiled, then looked at Lowell with his lopsided grin. 'I want to do something for you. What do you want?'"

Lowell looked at Elvis blankly and someone in the room said, "He'll take your car, E."

Elvis said, "My car? You cain't have mah car, 'cause that's a hoss and ain' nother one like it." Elvis was driving the first special edition Mark V with a brown and white interior. "I had to special-order this car," he said. "But if you want a Mark V, we'll go get you one. Ricky . . . go get my car ready!"

Ten minutes later Elvis was in late afternoon rush hour traffic. As he looked around at all the cars on the freeway, one of the boys with him said, "Isn't it fun to get up before dark, E? Everywhere you look, man, there are real people . . ."

# Chapter 25

# LOSING IT

On December 2, Elvis went back to work, traveling with his entourage to Las Vegas to make up the twenty shows he missed when he canceled out in August. Once again he turned Las Vegas around, this time doing what no entertainer has been able to do before or since.

The vice president of the Hilton hotels, Henri Lewin, said, "In December a Las Vegas showroom draws twenty or thirty percent of its capacity. That's the way it is. People stay home between Thanksgiving and Christmas and don't really come back to Las Vegas until after New Year's. Elvis Presley filled every show. You must understand that Tom Jones in the second week of December might lay an egg completely. Elvis sold out! Our slot machine revenue was *doubled*."

Next up: Pontiac, Michigan for New Year's Eve.

This was the first time Elvis had ever worked during the winter holidays. In the 1960s it was always written into his contract that he was not available until after his birthday, January 8. Why did he break tradition? Why did he agree to perform in the huge Silver Dome that seated 80,000, when he knew it would be like the Astrodome—too big to give his fans the show they paid to see? The answer, of course, was money. Elvis needed money, desperately. His bank accounts were empty and he had *borrowed* $350,000 against future earnings, using Graceland for collateral. As difficult as it was to accept, Elvis was broke.

The Michigan show was, every way except economically, a disaster.

The sound of "Thus Spake Zarathustra" filled the gigantic space, echoing off a roof so far away a fifteen-story building could have been put on the stage next to Elvis. As he entered, he looked confused. Where were his sidemen? Where were his singers? Finally he spotted them below him, on another level. He was surprised, then angry. Why hadn't anyone told him he had to sing alone?

In the middle of the show, his pants ripped, splitting at the seams because of his extra poundage.

The temperature made it worse. It was so cold, the members of his band were playing in their overcoats. "The trumpet players, their lips were so cold they could barely blow their horns," said guitarist John Wilkinson. "It was so cold our strings kept changing key. Oh, we were glad to get out of there."

On the way home, Elvis exploded, cursing and blaming everyone and anyone he could think of for the show. So black was his mood, Linda just sat there and let it happen. Normally she would have made a face at him, or fed him some gooey sweet and cooed him back to serenity with baby talk.

A few days later a story appeared in the entertainment trade papers reporting a gross of $800,000 for the concert, believed to be a world's record for a single night by a single artist, beating out the Beatles' take at Shea Stadium in 1964. Elvis kept about half of it.

1976 began with little planned, and quickly turned chaotic. His forty-first birthday was January 8, and Elvis took Linda and several of his boys to Vail, Colorado, to celebrate.

"Elvis really didn't like birthdays," said Jerry Schilling, one of those who went along, "but this time he seemed to want company."

Jerry made arrangements for the rental of three condominiums, talking a family out of a vacation to make the largest of them available for Elvis. Linda baked a cake. President Gerald Ford's daughter Susan was vacationing in Vail, and when she heard Elvis was in town she invited him to a party. Elvis's hired hands started making arrangements.

What followed was, according to those present, a nightmare.

Elvis was bothered by the ongoing lawsuits involving some of his bodyguards. Red and Sonny were among those with him in Vail and he turned on them, criticized them for getting so rough. They attempted to defend themselves.

"That's easy for you to say," Elvis shouted, "but I'm the one they sue!"

"Well," said Red, "they got our names on that lawsuit too, you know, boss."

"Damn right they do. It was you motherfuckers beat the shit outa that poor bastard."

And so it went. When the boys were present, he fought with them. When they weren't present, he told them to get their asses back on the premises. Susan Ford's invitation was trashed; if she wanted to meet him, he said, she could come to *his* condo. Then in the middle of the night he decided he wanted to move into the condominium that Jerry had gotten for himself and Myrna Smith, one of the Sweet Inspirations. He called Jerry and told him he was moving in immediately.

"Come on, Elvis," Jerry said, "can't it wait until morning?"

"Listen, Jerry, when I say jump, you jump . . ."

Jerry said nothing in response, and after a minute Elvis barked another command that began, "Listen, motherfucker . . ." Jerry cut in, "Look, Elvis, you can have the condo . . . because I fucking quit." The next morning Elvis called Jerry and apologized.

Of course there were brighter moments, when the mood-altering effects of the drugs Elvis took subsided somewhat. In the days that followed, Elvis and his remaining entourage—after Jerry and Myrna had left—rented snowmobiles for noisy, 3 A.M. rides through the snowy woods. Wearing a white woolen ski mask and bulky snowsuit, he also visited a luxury automobile showroom in Denver, arriving three hours after closing time with a large party, telling three in the group to pick out the cars they wanted. These were Captain Jerry Kennedy, head of the Denver vice squad, and Detective Ron Pietrofeso, who had been Elvis's police guards during concerts in Denver months before, and Dr. Gerald Starky, a police physician who had treated Elvis a day earlier for a scratch he said was caused by his ski mask. The $13,000 cars he bought the three men were his way of saying thank you.

Before he left Colorado, while watching the television news, Elvis saw one of the local anchormen report on the car-buying he had done, then look into the camera and say, "Elvis . . . if you're watching, I wouldn't mind getting a car, too." Elvis had a new Cadillac delivered to the station the following day and then went home to Graceland.

Elvis was losing control.

He hadn't recorded any new material in almost nine months and with RCA wishing to maintain its three-album per year release schedule, new songs were sorely needed. In fact, the last album released, *A Legendary Performer, Volume Two*, and the one set for the next month, *The Sun Sessions*, both were repackaged anthologies of old material. Elvis had ignored pleas to go to Nashville or Hollywood to record, said he didn't want to go back to Stax in Memphis, either. So in the first week of February 1976, RCA began moving $200,000 worth of recording equipment into Elvis's Graceland den. If Mohammed wouldn't go to the mountain, then the mountain would go to Mohammed.

Elvis's road band came too, flown in from Los Angeles, along with a number of the top Nashville studio men—David Briggs on piano, Bobby Emmons on electric piano, Norbert Putnam on bass. J. D. Sumner and the Stamps were there and so were Kathy Westmoreland and Myrna Smith. Everyone was waiting for Elvis to come downstairs to sing.

Felton Jarvis was producing the sessions, as usual, and he kept moving nervously back and forth between the den and the big RCA mobile truck parked outside. The string of jokes never stopped, but by midnight everyone was getting quite anxious. Elvis sent word that he was sick and had a doctor in attendance. Red and Sonny West and Dave Hebler explained Elvis's behavior in their book, *Elvis: What Happened?*, telling a sinister story about a plan Elvis had to kill the city's top narcotics dealers and contend it was this that kept Elvis holed up in his upstairs bedroom.

Red said Elvis summoned him to his room, where he had a dozen rifles, at least two dozen pistols, several automatic rifles and machine guns (illegally owned), a handful of rocket launchers and ammunition for all of it, strewn all over the floor. Most of this had been kept in his Los Angeles house, but once he sold the house, he had the arsenal moved to Graceland, where he liked to keep it handy in case he needed it. Now, he told Red, he needed it to wipe out all those "motherfuckin' drug pushers that got Ricky [Stanley] on heroin!"

Ricky was one of his three young stepbrothers, the sons of Vernon's second wife, Dee. Elvis doted on the boys, had spoiled them with lavish toys when they were younger and now had them on his payroll as valets, errand boys, and bodyguards when he traveled. When Elvis got heavily into pills, so, too, did they, as did many others on the Presley teat. Ricky caused the most trouble of the three. On five occasions he had run afoul of the police, the last time for forging a prescription for Demerol. Each time, Elvis bailed him out, got the charges dropped. In time, Ricky graduated to heroin, and Elvis was mad.

He handed a list of names and a packet of photographs to Red, given to him, Elvis said, by the Memphis police when he said he thought he and his guys could help get something on them if they knew who to look out for.

"Elvis had it all planned," Red wrote. "He wanted myself and Dave Hebler and Dick Grob, the former cop [who had gone to work for Elvis some years previously], to go out and lure them, and he said he was going to kill them."

Not long before, Elvis had watched a similar plot in a film called *Death Wish*. In the movie, Charles Bronson carried on a similar vendetta, a one-man crime assassination squad. Elvis identified strongly with the film, and Bronson's role, and told Red and Dave that he would use the recording sessions as his cover, or alibi. They'd set the target up—he told them—and he'd sneak out of the house the back way, make the hit, and then return swiftly to Graceland, where he then would go downstairs and sing.

Somehow, Elvis was diverted, chemically or conversationally. His fantasy was pushed aside. And the recording session finally began.

In seven days Elvis sang a dozen songs, ten of which appeared on an album in May called *From Elvis Presley Boulevard*. The lyrics, as a lot, were sad, and Elvis's performance, though adequate, showed clearly his failing strength and health.

The songs included Neil Sedaka's "Solitaire" ("There was a man, a lonely man, who lost his love . . ."); an old favorite of Elvis's, "Danny Boy" (". . . the summer's gone / roses dying. . ."); a song that said it all in the title, "Hurt" (his next single release); the old chestnut written by Fred Rose and recorded by Willie Nelson, "Blue Eyes Crying in the Rain"; as well as songs called, poignantly, "Bigger They Are, Harder They Fall" (by Larry Gatlin, one of Elvis's favorite contemporary composers); "I'll Never Fall in Love Again"; "The Last Farewell"; and "Moody Blue," a song written by Mark James, who had given Elvis "Suspicious Minds" several years before.

"Hurt" recalled, but weakly, the operatic drama of a much earlier hit, "It's Now or Never (O Sole Mio)." His reading of the hoary "Danny Boy" was uninspired; he didn't even try for the high notes. On several others he insisted that the backup voices be allowed to all but bury his own. His voice remained rich, a worthy match for any sort of material, but there seemed to be a lack of concern or confidence. The performance sounded lazy, uncertain.

The recording session over, Elvis unexpectedly returned to Denver. The younger brother of his policeman friend Jerry Kennedy, also a cop, had killed himself and Elvis, wearing a Denver police uniform he'd been given, attended the funeral. He then asked the police doctor for Dilaudid—a painkiller usually prescribed for cancer patients—to treat an ingrown toenail. The cops knew a man with a habit when they saw one and they confronted him, assuring him they were speaking as friends, offering to get him into a private sanitarium. Elvis insisted he didn't have a problem, said he could quit whenever he wanted, and angrily flew back to Memphis.

Elvis's moods continued to swing wildly. When he first saw the recording setup in his den, he said, "Let's leave it, I like it better this way than with the furniture." A few days later he stood in the den facing the huge playback speakers, his eyes glazed, pointing a shotgun. "The sound's no fuckin' good in those things!" he croaked. "I'm gone kill the motherfuckers and put 'em out of my misery." He cocked the shotgun and took unsteady aim. Some of the musicians got the gun away from him and a few minutes later the session was canceled. Other nights he didn't talk to his old friends in the usual way, he seemed remote, disconnected. Some nights he failed to show up at all. Finally, on February 9, RCA packed up its gear and returned to Nashville, happy to have what it had.

In the weeks that followed, Elvis tried to strengthen his loosening grip, tried to take control again. He not only took appetite depressants, he wore five-pound weights on his wrists and ankles during long, active rehearsals.

He went on yogurt and other "health" kicks. He fasted. He gobbled vitamin pills by the handful, drank mineral water by the gallon, and played racquetball even when he was exhausted. At one point he turned himself over to a doctor in Las Vegas who promised him he would lose thirty-five pounds in two weeks if he moved into the doctor's home and followed the "Sleep Diet."

This one got Elvis into trouble.

The phone rang at the Hilton Hotel, where some of Elvis's guys were staying. It was Elvis. He said he was alone at the doctor's house on his belly, on the floor, unable to get back into bed. He'd managed to knock the telephone over and dial, but had no more strength. Would someone come and help him back into bed?

The way the diet worked, Elvis would be given medication to make him sleep during the periods when he usually ate. That way he could literally snooze his pounds away. It was a faddish diet, one of many that gained some popularity in the 1970s and, according to most weight loss counselors, it seldom if ever produced lasting results.

One of Elvis's guys rushed to the doctor's house and lifted Elvis back onto his bed and, at Elvis's insistence, left him to continue the treatment.

On February 16, 1976, Elvis had the first of four meetings with a Memphis hypnotist. Six months after Elvis died, the hypnotist told his story publicly (in the *National Enquirer*). As was usual in such personal matters, Joe Esposito had made the arrangements.

The hypnotist, William Foote, said Elvis slurred his words—a strong indication that he was under the influence of painkillers or tranquilizers. Foote quotes Elvis as saying he was taking morphine for pain, Quaaludes to sleep. He said people were taking advantage of him. He said he had emotional problems.

Foote taught him a simple relaxation technique to relieve the stomach pain he said he had.

The following visits were unrewarding. Elvis refused to say much and, although he seemed "straight" the second and third times, on the last office call Elvis was slurring his words again. Foote gave him a strong hypnotic suggestion to build self-respect, he said, and Elvis "awoke refreshed—but he also seemed anxious to leave. He didn't mention another appointment, and I didn't press him."

Just before Elvis left his office, Foote said he turned and said, "Thanks, doc. I think I've got it now. I might be able to do it alone now. But I just don't know . . . if it will be enough to replace my medications."

Elvis went back on the road. This was the first of the really short tours—six shows in six days—that would characterize the remainder of his life. It was believed that this was as much as he could handle.

It was also his first with two new musicians in his backup band. Some time before he had lost Glenn D. Hardin on piano, a severe blow to Elvis, and when his replacement, David Briggs, also left, Elvis didn't know what to do. The loss of Ronnie Tutt, the drummer who'd been with him from the first show in Las Vegas, was an even greater jolt. James Burton also quit, but he returned, receiving a substantial jump in pay.

Why did they quit? They told Elvis they had better offers, offers they couldn't refuse. As much as Elvis was paying him—maybe more than any other pianist on the road—David Briggs could make even more at home in the studios. Both Glenn D. and James left to accept jobs with Emmylou Harris that offered them a percentage of the gate and a schedule that would allow them to pick up some of the same big studio dollars that David wanted. Ronnie Tutt said much the same thing, wanting to get back to the busy studios in Los Angeles.

"The short bursts seemed to work for a while, but it also screwed up the other guys," said guitarist John Wilkinson. "They were studio musicians and they lost too much work when they were always traveling. Studio time is booked a long time in advance sometimes and a lot of times for some reason they wouldn't tell us when the next tour was. We really griped and complained. They'd let us know a week-and-a-half ahead of time sometimes. I'd say, 'What! I've got a contract to sing in a hotel in San Diego . . .'"

There were other reasons, of course. "The newness had worn off," said Larrie Londin, the drummer who took Tutt's place. "They weren't that impressed anymore. They didn't have the edge that it takes to drive that type of performer, like he was used to being driven. They'd been with him almost six years, most of them, and they wanted to try new things."

The new band gathered at Graceland for a rehearsal before the March tour. "We just sat around and listened to records," said Larrie Londin. "Elvis came down about midnight or so, we did about four bars of this song and that song and he went back to bed. And we went back to the hotel and walked out on the stage the next day cold."

This began a year of tours that would recall the concurrent crisscrossing of America of the Freedom Train, a traveling museum of the country's history. It was 1976, America's bicentennial, a time for a burst of national pride and Elvis seemed up for it.

First stop: Johnson City, Tennessee, where Elvis performed three concerts; was somewhat grouchy with his new band members; coaxed out J. D. Sumner from the Stamps and told him to hold out his "Elvis hand," the one with all the rings he had given him (worth more than $100,000), and told a joke about the bumper sticker on the Cadillac that said, "I paid for this—Elvis didn't buy it." After he left, the owner of the motel where he stayed cut up the sheets he slept on and the aluminum foil from his windows and sold them in one-inch squares.

And so it went. A girl rushed on stage in Charlotte and kissed him so hard she cut his lip. In another auditorium a small boy in a tiny Elvis suit that his parents made was lifted onto the stage and Elvis tried to get him to shake his little legs and sing "Hound Dog." Yellow jacketed coliseum ushers were sent sprawling in Cincinnati by women rushing the stage.

Every city was the same on the April tour. He ordered the house lights turned on so he could see his audience. He joked about his road family, members of his band and backup groups. He accepted gifts over the footlights from fans and gave kisses and scarves in return. He sang patriotic songs, usually "America" or "God Bless America." He still entered the stage to the momentous "Thus Spake Zarathustra" from *2001: A Space Odyssey* and at the end, after singing "I Can't Help Falling in Love (With You)," he posed a final time, arms outstretched, smiling, smothered by the waves of energy rushing at him from the pounding band behind him to the roaring thousands at his feet.

There was a relationship between Elvis and his fans like no other in popular music. The writer in the *Los Angeles Times* put his finger on it when he described Elvis's Long Beach show (April 25) as "a combination of music and manner that often resembles more a visit among friends than a hard-edged concert performance."

Elvis was so good at doing this, he could do it in his sleep.

And sometimes he did.

"Sometimes," one of his former sidekicks said, "he just hung on the microphone."

And that was the other half of the story of Elvis on the bicentennial road. John Wilkinson said it "seemed like all the enthusiasm had just left. No matter how hard we tried to pump him up, Elvis would just stand there with his thumb hooked in his belt, it was like he was just there to sing a few songs and pass out a few scarves, but all the thrill had gone."

He suffered from memory loss, unable to remember the lyrics to some of his more recent hits. Occasionally there was locomotive loss and slurred speech. Tony Brown said some nights "he'd just stand there, four or five minutes—not do anything. The audience would be screaming out song titles or applauding or stomping their feet. Elvis would have his back to the audience, and he'd be gong like, 'Just listen to them stupid people . . .' He's just being Elvis out of control, saying, 'These people, they don't care if I'm good or bad. I can do anything and they'll still love it.'"

Elvis finished his second tour in Spokane on April 27, and opened in Lake Tahoe four days later. During the engagement, he was visited by John O'Grady, the Hollywood private detective that Elvis liked so much.

Given Elvis's love for cops-and-robbers stories, there had to be people like O'Grady in his life. (His head of security, Dick Grob, the former Palm Springs policeman, was another in that category.) Meeting O'Grady was like reading Raymond Chandler. He was a tough former narcotics cop with a list of Hollywood stars for a clientele and, since helping Elvis with his paternity suit, O'Grady had performed many personal services. When Elvis showed some interest in a woman, for instance, O'Grady had the job of checking her out.

"I did an evaluation of the women," he said. "Background, that sort of thing. And I would make an absolute calculated determination about whether they'd hurt him or not. I was right about Linda. I told him she'd happily take the money, but she would never gossip."

Elvis also pumped O'Grady for information about drugs. The detective knew Elvis was using—"and probably abusing"—prescription drugs as early as 1970. "I was a narc for *twelve* years, and you can tell. I *knew*. I shared my knowledge with him. He carried the Merck manual around with him."

The Merck manual, produced for doctors and pharmacists, describes all prescription drugs—chemical makeup, recommended dosage, side effects. Elvis's favorites were in the book. Hycodan. Demerol. Percodan. Valium. Placidyl. Phenobarb. He memorized every sentence that had anything to do with whatever he took.

"You gotta remember one thing," O'Grady said. "He had real pain. He had blood clots in his legs. He had hypoglycemia. He had an extremely enlarged heart. He had glaucoma. He was susceptible to respiratory ailments. His liver was three times normal size. He had a twisted colon . . ."

In May 1976, O'Grady's son, a graduate student, wanted to meet Elvis, so they went to Lake Tahoe. "He was bloated," O'Grady said. "His eyes were almost closed. He was fighting to make a good appearance. He was sick. I called Ed Hookstratton [Elvis's Beverly Hills lawyer, who first hired O'Grady] and I told him that I gave Elvis one year to live unless we got him into a hospital. We made quiet arrangements for a hospital in San Diego, the Scripps Clinic, which is known for drying out rich drunks and rich drug cases. He was to remain there for three or four months and then we were going to take him to a private estate in Hawaii on Maui, for the rest of a year, to recuperate. I had dinner with Priscilla and her sister, Michelle, and we presented the whole program. Priscilla agreed and she took it to Elvis and he rejected it. She flew to Memphis and he said he could handle it, he didn't need outside help. The next time I saw him, he said, 'I was okay in Tahoe. Really. It was the altitude.'"

Only seventeen days after closing in Lake Tahoe, Elvis was back on the road again, moving into extremely loyal middle American geography—starting in Bloomington, Indiana, on May 27 and going to Ames, Iowa (where the sold-out sign went up in forty-five minutes), then diving deep, to Oklahoma City and then to Odessa, Lubbock, Tucson, El Paso, and Fort Worth, closing in one of the true centers of deep-South Elvis fandom, Atlanta, on June 4, 5, and 6. There were a dozen shows in eleven days and Elvis was still hanging in there.

"The best show I ever saw him do was in Fort Worth in June," said pianist

Tony Brown. "He was singing on pitch, no jiving around, singing entire songs, not a blown word. He was just great. That show was a killer."

And the next night he was stoned again, giving the folks another kind of show. Slower, shorter, somewhat disappointing when compared to previous performances in the same cities, but still "The King," performing for a constituency that wouldn't desert him no matter what he did or didn't do. Thus, the box office never flagged. Profit for the March tour was $500,000, April grossed about the same, and eleven days in Tahoe brought another $315,000.

There was another tour in June and July, another twelve shows in eleven days. Every month now he was gearing up for another short run at the American heartland. It was then that the friction began.

"You can get along with someone very nicely when you're with them three times a year," said orchestra leader Joe Guercio, "but then when you're with somebody every two weeks, boy, then all those little faults they got absolutely like to kill you."

Even Guercio, who wouldn't have missed a show for anything in the early years, now was sometimes staying at home in Las Vegas to work in the hotels, sending the trombonist Marty Harrell out as conductor.

"He was surrounded by giants," Guercio said, "and if everyone there gave their all, it could be explosive. In the beginning that's what it used to be. It was great. As much smoke as would come out of the engine would come outa the back cars. It didn't happen so often later."

Elvis never lost his sometimes demeaning and often goofy sense of humor. When he introduced Larrie Londin, who weighed 350 pounds, it was before he sang "God Gave Me a Mountain This Time," saying, "I got me my own little mountain right here in the band." His fans, knowing his quirky sense of humor, gave him funny hats to wear; in one city, Elvis was handed a loaded water pistol and he promptly began spritzing J. D. Sumner and the Stamps. On Marty Harrell's first concert conducting, Marty's friend Pat Houston, the trumpet player, got everyone in the orchestra to agree to sit silently when Marty gave the downbeat. "I was nervous as hell anyway," said Marty. "I gave the downbeat and nothing happened. I looked at my hands. What did I do wrong? I looked over at Elvis and he was doubled over laughing. I gave the downbeat again and they started the show."

Sonny West was in his dentist's office when he got the call from Vernon. Dave Hebler was by his Memphis motel pool when his wife said he had a call. Red West was at the office of a private investigator.

Vernon told each of the three that he wanted to see them in person. They knew something was afoot by Vernon's sober tone.

"I told him I was a grown man and could handle anything he could tell me on the telephone," Sonny said.

"Well," said Vernon, "things haven't been going too well and we're going to have to cut back on expenses. We're going to have to let some people go . . ."

In their book, Red and Sonny and Dave say they were fired whimsically, a characteristically capricious decision of their former boss. "What pissed us off," Red said, "after all those years I had been with him, he never took the time to tell me himself. He just cut out and left it to his father to do. It was cold, man."

It *was* cold. Over the years, Elvis had "fired" Red and Sonny and Dave, along with all the rest, a dozen times or more apiece. "I'll fire your ass!" was a Presley cliché. Now, when it came time to fire three of his men for real, Elvis made the final decision, then ran away from it, holing up in Palm Springs.

But the decision was not whimsical or capricious. It came after much agonizing and advice from several of his most trusted associates. One of these, John O'Grady, in fact, takes credit for being the first to recommend that the three be dropped.

"I recommended Red and Sonny be fired because they were too rough with the fans. Red had punched a guy while Sonny held him. That sort of thing was resulting in a lot of unnecessary lawsuits. Elvis was spending a lot of money on lawyers and it looked like he was maybe going to lose some of the lawsuits besides."

Elvis was getting the same advice from the Colonel and Ed Hookstratton and his father: the bodyguards were not just expensive, but dangerously so.

On July 23, ten days after the "Tuesday Massacre," Elvis went back on the road again. And soon after that tour ended, he was back on the road still another time. Three weeks off and one week on. It was a schedule they thought Elvis could maintain.

Yet on the other hand were the inevitable sold-out concerts and consistently successful records. On August 21, RCA distributed a press release announcing that sales of Elvis Presley records had passed the 400-million mark, a figure light years ahead of any previous total for a single performer. Twenty years after his first million-selling song, "Heartbreak Hotel," through all the other various RCA greats (Jefferson Airplane, Waylon Jennings, John Denver, etc.), Elvis was far and away the biggest star the company had ever had, including Enrico Caruso.

# Chapter 26

# GINGER

lvis went on the road again August 27, floating through the South from
Hilton hotel to Hilton hotel, from one convention center or municipal
auditorium or coliseum or sports arena to the next, $100,000 and more in the
box office each night, several thousand more from the sale of pennants and picture books, sold-out houses everywhere, the same dazzling Instamatic flash.

Yet the image he projected to friends worried them. His pianist, Tony
Brown, remembers a grim matinee in the Summit in Houston: "He was worse
there than in Maryland. The sound truck turned over on the way to the gig and
they had to hire a new sound company. He had more monitors than any group
on the road. He was so loaded . . . I retract that. He was in 'one of his moods'
again and mumbling through his songs. And the new guys had piled the monitors on the stage blocking the view of some people seated behind him. Elvis
usually hung his monitors from the ceiling so they wouldn't block anybody. It
wasn't the right microphone. The sound people were doing their best, they
really wanted to impress Elvis, but he turned around and said, off mike, 'This
is the sorriest sonabitchin' sound system I've ever seen.' The guys turned
against him then. It wasn't much of a show. It was a sorry show. Every time
somethin' like that happened, people started talkin' about the tour getting canceled. And the next night . . ." Tony snaps his fingers. "Okay again."

Up and down. Up and down. But mostly down. Joe Mescale, leader of the
Imperials, crossed paths with Elvis a week later in Huntsville, Alabama. It was
the last time he saw Elvis alive.

"He was fat and sick," Joe said, "I went to his hotel and when I entered the
room, he cleared everyone else out. Sheila Ryan was with him. He was wearing a robe. I'd taken a *Living Bible* with me for him and I'd written something
in the front of it. He held me by the neck, just put his forehead to mine and just
hugged me. He said he was so sick. He said, 'I don't even want to be here.'"

The tour ended September 8 and a month later, on October 14, his seventh
tour of the year began, taking him deep into the Midwest. A month after that
came the eighth, a rapid swing through the West that ended with still another

fifteen performances in Las Vegas. He had two weeks off for Christmas and then went on his ninth tour of the year. Not since he started out with Sun Records, had Elvis toured so much.

The late summer and autumn months had been a disaster.

First came the dissolution of a partnership that Elvis had entered to build and operate a chain of fifty racquetball courts. Dean Nichopoulos, the son of Elvis's doctor, sometimes worked for Elvis on the road and was one of the fastest young racquetball players in Memphis. Elvis personally loved the game, so when Dean's father, Dr. Nick, asked Elvis if he'd like to be partners with him and Joe Esposito and a local real estate developer named Mike McMahon, Elvis didn't even consult the Colonel before saying yes.

Two months later Elvis suggested the name of the corporation be changed from Racquet Ball of Memphis, Inc. to Presley Center Courts, Inc. His partners were thrilled. To be able to put Elvis's name on the sign in front of the courts was, they believed, to become rich. Elvis was named corporate chairman and agreed to be liable for 25 percent of the finances. Construction of the first court began in Nashville. Then Elvis pulled out, scattering his relationships all over the landscape. Lawsuits were threatened; lawyers were hired.

Meanwhile, Red and Sonny and Dave were striking back at Elvis in another way. They didn't sue their former boss; they "wrote" a book. First they went to Rick Huskey, the television writer who was a friend of Jerry Schilling's, and asked him to help them. He said no, thanks. Then they asked Frank Lieberman, the one-time Vegas critic. He said no, too. But Steve Dunleavy, the Australian gossip columnist for the weekly tabloid *National Star*, said yes immediately, and a deal was quickly made, giving the three former members of the Memphis Mafia a hefty percentage of the book's earnings. They wanted to tell everything there was to tell, they said. They said they wanted to warn Elvis. "He will read it and he will get hopping mad at us because he knows that every word is the truth and we will take a lie detector test to prove it," Red later said. "But, just maybe, it will do some good."

The three began calling around, asking questions about dates, telling people they were writing a book and wanted it to be accurate. Many thought they smelled a rat and refused to help. Word got to Elvis and he was furious. He sent John O'Grady to say he'd had second thoughts about the firing, didn't know they weren't given any severance pay, and so was prepared to give them $50,000 apiece, if in return, O'Grady said, they wouldn't write a book. Red, Sonny, and Dave said no. Two days later, Elvis called Red at his motel in Hollywood. The conversation was tape-recorded and part was included in what came to be called "the bodyguard book."

In November, Elvis had Joe call Jerry Schilling to say Elvis wanted to see him. He said he was at Linda's apartment.

"We talked at length about the bodyguard book," Jerry said. "He told me he really appreciated that I didn't get involved. I said, 'Jesus, that's no big thing . . .' He said, 'It's a big thing to me and I'll never forget it.' He wasn't worried for himself. The concern he had for that book was the friends and family around him that could've gotten hurt. He told me, 'Jerry, everything that could possibly be written about somebody has been written about me already. But what about my family and friends, my doctor . . . ? These are good people that I don't want hurt.' He was extremely concerned about Lisa. If I'd 'a been in the situation Elvis was in, I'd 'a never been able to handle it as gracefully as he did."

If the firing of Red and Sonny and the collapse of the racquetball courts were stunning, what happened to Elvis's relationship with Linda put them in the shade. They had been drifting for months. To the outsider it became noticeable when Linda unglued herself from Elvis's side on the tours and in Las Vegas and began playing cards with the boys in the band. And that led to a relationship with Elvis's piano player, David Briggs.

"The real thing that was most difficult to accept and probably the primary reason why I ultimately left," Linda said, "was that there was no room for personal growth. Your life revolved entirely around Elvis's. It was not conducive to personal, individual growth. I couldn't be assertive as an individual. I felt like an appendage, which was not his fault. He had an overpowering presence. Not that he even meant to do that to people but somehow when you were with him you knew how great his needs were and you were willing to give up yourself. I think that essentially I just grew up. I think it amounted to that. I finally thought, 'Hey, I'm an individual entity, too. I have a right to my own feelings, my own desires, my own life. And I wasn't having that. My life revolved around him. I felt stagnant.

"Wanting my own life came on slowly," Linda said. "It wasn't like I woke up one morning and said, 'I'm leaving.' It was a long time coming, it was a long, painful, drawn-out process. Because I loved him dearly, and still do. But there's a great tragedy sometimes in the realization that you can love someone and not be able to live with him, not be able to live their lifestyle and grow and prosper as an individual.

"After so many years being around the same people all the time and then being together so much, it was more intimate than a marriage. He often used to say we had spent more time together in four-and-a-half years than a lot of married couples spent in twenty years. We were together twenty-four hours a day. I went to every concert. I never sat one out. I think that would have really hurt him if I had not shown an interest in every show. I was out there pulling for him. I had to give him critiques after the show. He would say, 'Did you see such-and-such?' He wanted that communication. He wanted to know you were with him. I was pulling for every high note and low note and watching every movement. That was ingrained with me. That was the kind of dedication you gave Elvis. He expected that of the others, too. Not just be there, but pay attention.

"From the very moment we met, we felt a true affinity for each other. We weren't just lovers, we weren't just mates, we were partners. I was his sister and he was my brother. I was his mommy and he was my baby. He was my daddy and I was his little girl. We were lovers, we were friends, we were everything to each other. It was an all-encompassing relationship for an awfully long time. There's a line from a Kim Carnes song: 'Sometimes the love that burns the brightest/burns itself right out in time.' There's so much highly charged energy sometimes within a relationship that it's almost too much. I really feel sometimes that I loved him too much, that he loved me too much."

Of course it wasn't so uneventful as that. There was friction. That much togetherness wears thin and as Linda rediscovered the assertiveness and competitiveness that made her a successful beauty queen, she began peppering her baby talk with criticism and advice. They fought sometimes, over his demands for her fidelity when he left her at home to go on the road with other women, and over his subsequent sexual boasts. They also had what Linda described as "horrible fights" about the pills he took, usually after she had stayed awake while Elvis slept so she could watch his breathing. More than once she had called for help from Joe and the others on duty downstairs when Elvis apparently took too many sleeping pills.

Finally she wrote him a letter, saying she still loved him and always would, but adding that she had to leave. Then, before returning the Master Charge card that Elvis had given her—with unlimited credit—she went out and charged $30,000 worth of stuff, a third of that in airline tickets.

Only Vernon was really upset. Elvis was somewhat amused and laughed.

Linda left the first week of November and within a day or two, George Klein was calling around Memphis for a replacement. Ginger Alden was one of the names he had on his list and he called her November 19. Ginger was the daughter of a woman born in Arkansas and a retired career army sergeant who had been present in the Memphis recruiting office when Elvis was drafted in 1958. Ginger was twenty.

"When Ginger was growing up," her mother said, "we'd go stand outside the Graceland gates when we read that he was in town and watch him ride his horse or his golf cart. We got invited to the Fairground when Ginger was five and Elvis patted her on the head. We stayed until four o'clock in the morning and Ginger rode the roller coaster with him."

Ginger's older sister Terry was Miss Tennessee in 1976, the same year Ginger was named Miss Mid-South and then went on to be first runner-up in the Miss Tennessee-Universe contest. She also had won the Miss Traffic Safety title and was a Duchess in the Cotton Carnival. She was a pretty girl, almost painfully shy, with long, teased dark hair and dark makeup that made her look very much like Priscilla did in the bouffant 1960s.

The first night she was taken to Graceland, she waited for between three and four hours downstairs with the boys. She said George told her Elvis was upstairs practicing karate. "Finally," she said, "I was told to go upstairs and turn left into Lisa's room. I met him there. I stayed that night. We read some religious books. And then he had one of his aides drive me home. The next night he took me to Las Vegas for one night and on November 28 I joined him in San Francisco on tour. He had his personal pilot, Milo High, pick me up in the Jet Star for that. Then when he went to the Hilton hotel in December, he flew my parents, my sisters and my brother and me out."

That was when Elvis bought his first big gift for Ginger, a white Mark V Lincoln Continental with white upholstery.

The shows were predictably mixed, reflecting not only Elvis's use of drugs but also mood shifts affected by events. On December 9, Vernon was hospitalized with what appeared to be another heart attack. It was not, but the day that Vernon was released, Larry Geller, who was back on the scene, found Elvis literally hanging from the drapes in his room to keep from falling, sweating profusely, crying out, "This is it . . . I'm going out . . . I, ah, took too much, or someone gave me the wrong thing, I'm going. I'm leaving my body. I'm dying."

The final day of the engagement, Elvis was visited backstage by Rex Humbard, the televangelist. Elvis asked him if he should continue singing or give it up to serve the Lord. Humbard told him to do what he could do best, sing. Elvis started rambling about Armageddon and the Second Coming of Christ and, according to Humbard, "I took both his hands in mine and said, 'Elvis, right now I want to pray for you.' He said, 'Please do,' and started weeping."

The following two weeks were spent quietly at Graceland and then Elvis went to Pittsburgh for a New Year's Eve concert. "A few hours before the concert," said Marty Harrell, the trombonist and sometime orchestra leader. "Four of us in the band were playing cards. We took a break as one of the guys—Howard Struble, one of the horn players—went down to get more booze. It was snowing and about five degrees, with at least eighteen inches of snow on the ground. There was a little park down below the hotel and Howard stamped out in twelve-foot letters a message to one of the other trumpet players, Pat Houston; FUCK YOU PAT.

"And then he came up to the room again. We called Elvis and Ricky [Stanley] answered the phone. He said Elvis was lying on the floor laughing.

He'd watched Howard do the whole thing."

That night, Elvis put on one of his best shows ever. "He was bright-eyed and bushy-tailed," said John Wilkinson. "It was a great show. He never sounded better."

Taking care of business was his motto and there was little he liked to do more. So when Ginger's mother's father died, Elvis started making plans and issuing orders to get everyone to the January third funeral in Harrison, Arkansas. The Memphis sheriff took Ginger and her mother and sisters to Graceland at the same time a rented Lear jet was flown in from Nashville to accommodate those who couldn't be transported in the Jet Star. (The runway in Harrison was too short for the *Lisa Marie*.) Joe Esposito and Charlie Hodge and Ricky and David Stanley went along to drive the cars Elvis rented to take them to the church. He wanted to buy the fanciest coffin and didn't only because Mrs. Alden insisted that her father was a humble man, who had picked out his own before he died.

Two days later Elvis took Ginger and her sister Rosemary to Palm Springs, where they remained for more than a week. While there, one of Elvis's doctors from Beverly Hills, Max Shapiro, came to visit him, accompanied by his fiancée. Max was a dentist who later would admit that he had provided Elvis with prescriptions for some of his drugs, and over the years they had become friends. In fact, Max had designed an artificial heart and Elvis had talked about providing money to build the prototype, planning to give one to his father, another to Ginger's mother.

Max told Elvis that he had been planning to get married, but didn't know where or when. He already had the license, he said, and produced it for Elvis to look at. Elvis suggested they get married right away at Elvis's house, so they did, with one of Elvis's friends, Larry Geller, performing the ceremony.

A week later, back in Memphis, Elvis was planning his own marriage. The story of his proposal to Ginger is another that shows how those around Elvis dropped everything when he called.

Elvis had one of his guys call Lowell Hays about one o'clock on the morning of January 26. He said he'd consulted *Cheiro's Book of Numbers* and this was the day he was supposed to get engaged and he wanted a ring right away.

"Yes, sir," Lowell said. "Tell Elvis I can bring out a selection from the store. I can be there in . . .

"Low'll . . . listen a minute. Elvis wants the diamond in the ring as big, or bigger, than the one you put in his TCB ring."

Lowell was aghast. "That's impossible! That diamond's eleven-and-a-half carats. I don't have any diamonds that size and there's no way of getting one in the middle of the night. Will you tell Elvis that?"

Five minutes later Elvis called back and said in an authoritative tone, "Low'll?"

"Yessir?"

"I've got to have this diamond and I've got to have it by tonight. If you don't have it, where can I get one?"

"I have no idea, Elvis, and you won't get one tonight."

Elvis shot back, "The hell I won't. Watch me."

Lowell went back to sleep, only to be awakened again an hour later. It was Elvis again. "Low'll?"

"Yessir?"

"What if you went to New York? Could you get me one then?"

"I doubt it, Elvis. They keep those things in bank vaults. No one's gonna have a diamond like that at home where they can get to it . . ."

Elvis interrupted: "Will you try?"

Lowell said he would and called "a couple of millionaire diamond brokers" he dealt with in New York, waking them to make his unusual request. Was there any way, he asked, to get such a diamond immediately? They said no, not even in New York. Then, just before Lowell started dialing a friend who had a diamond that size to see if he would let him "borrow" it, he thought of the TCB ring. He dialed the Graceland number.

"Elvis," he said, "I've talked to everybody I know in New York and there's no way to get an eleven-carat diamond tonight. What if you give her the diamond in the TCB ring and I'll put another diamond in your ring later?"

Elvis went for it and Lowell rushed to Graceland to retrieve the big ring, drew a sketch of the suggested mounting, rushed to his store and woke one of his employees, got him to come to work immediately, and the finished ring, worth about $70,000, was delivered to Elvis on time. Elvis then called Ginger into the big bathroom adjacent to his bedroom and proposed. When she said yes, he gave her the ring.

Ginger said she didn't want to go to Nashville when Elvis told her he was going to record. He said she didn't have any choice about it; she was going and that was final. Normally shy and retiring, Ginger remained firm, telling Elvis that she didn't like Nashville and he was a gruff old bear for making her go. She questioned his love. Of course he loved her, he said; he didn't have to prove that.

This wasn't the first disagreement. Once, Ginger stalked out of the house and Elvis came running after her with a pistol, firing it into the air over her head. Later the media would say Elvis was trying to scare her into returning. Ginger saw it another way. Elvis was just proving how great his love was. She turned around and walked back to Graceland. But she still refused to go to Nashville.

For three days, his road band waited. James Burton, John Wilkinson, Ronnie Tutt, Kathy Westmoreland, and Myrna Smith from Los Angeles;

David Briggs and Tony Brown from Nashville. Finally, Elvis went to Nashville, flying with only a few bodyguards in his Jet Star. They checked into a motel. The musicians and singers continued to wait.

On the third day Joe Esposito called the studio to make the arrangements to get everyone home, to arrange for cars and planes. Then Elvis flew back to Memphis to be with Ginger.

RCA was frustrated and unable to do anything. If the company was to maintain the output of Presley product they planned, they believed they needed more songs immediately. Only one album of new material had been released in a year and seven months, and that was the weak collection of sad songs recorded for the most part at Graceland in April 1976. RCA and the Colonel decided that again the mountain would go to Mohammed. A session was scheduled for Graceland for the first week of February, 1977.

Elvis hadn't forgotten the lousy sound he heard in his den, so this time the microphones and monitors and instruments and so on were set up in his big indoor racquetball court, which if anything was even more of an acoustical mistake than the den.

Again the musicians and backup singers waited, this time in their motel rooms. One, two, three days passed, just as they had in Nashville. Finally the call went out and Elvis appeared. Not to record, however.

"He didn't like the sound," said John Wilkinson. "He may've been using that as an excuse, because he didn't want to record. He told them to pack the speaker up and send it back to New York. He said, 'They're wrong! They're all wrong. Send 'em back. Get new stuff!' They tried to fix them and he still found something wrong. He finally called a halt to the whole thing. He gathered us around and he said, 'I'm really sorry about this. My throat doesn't feel right. We can't record with this kind of equipment. That mobile truck is no good. We'll do it again. No big thing. We need some other engineers and stuff.' And then he started talking about the bodyguard book. He just couldn't believe Red and Sonny'd do that to him. He had big huge tears in his eyes behind his glasses. He was visibly upset. He said he loved them like brothers and he couldn't understand why they'd want to stab him in the back. He'd bought cars for them, he'd bought houses for them, he'd given them jobs when they couldn't get jobs any place else. He went on and on and pretty soon he just stopped talking.

"Finally he asked how we wanted to get home. He was gonna take the *Lisa Marie* and fly all the L.A. people there on it and fly the others to Nashville on the Jet Star and have limos take everybody to their houses. Joe Esposito didn't like that and J. D. [Sumner] said he could have his wife meet him. Elvis said, 'Joe, give J. D. the keys to that white one out front.' A big white limousine went to J. D. Elvis flew us home. J. D. went and got in the car and drove off with the

Nashville people. That was the last time we were in the house." It was also the last time Elvis attempted to record.

On February 12, Elvis began one of his shortest scheduled tours—nine shows in nine days, about half of them in Southern cities where he'd never appeared before; in Miami, West Palm Beach, and Orlando, Florida, and in Augusta, Georgia, and Columbia, South Carolina. It was as if the Colonel wanted a pin in every city on the U.S. map.

Although Ginger and her family accompanied him, the tour was otherwise undistinguished. Elvis was overweight, nearing the 225-pound mark. Only a few of his costumes fit now, and often he wore the same one every couple of days. By now he rarely learned the words to a new song, preferring to read them from a typed lyric sheet, and his performances were listless. The knee drops and high karate kicks were long past; now Elvis merely teased his fans with a slight shake of his beefy hips, his bay window noticeable as it hung over the top of his huge jeweled belt buckle. Elvis looked bored.

It was also on this tour that he learned about Linda and David Briggs. So it was with great relief when he'd performed the last date and began planning a vacation trip to Hawaii.

At first, no one paid much attention to Elvis's infatuation with Ginger. They'd seen it too many times before, and no one thought she held even the dimmest candle up to Linda Thompson; Ginger seemed such a child, and a petulant one at that. When Dr. Nick and others expressed their doubts, Elvis dismissed them. When Billy Smith suggested he might look for someone closer to his age, Elvis snapped, "What in hell could a forty-two-year-old woman do for me?"

Elvis told Dr. Nick there was something about the girl that reminded him of his mother. Others thought that the attraction lay in Ginger's playing hard to get. Whatever it was, he seemed hooked, and those closest to him were left to shake their heads.

Before leaving for the islands, however, there was one matter of business—the signing of his will. It had been drawn up by his Memphis attorney, Beecher Smith, and was taken to Graceland for Elvis's signature on March 3. In it, he named three principal beneficiaries—his daughter Lisa Marie, his father Vernon, and his grandmother Minnie Mae. The will also granted absolute control of the estate to Vernon, naming him executor and trustee. Vernon was to have discretion to provide financial assistance to other of Elvis's relatives "in need of emergency assistance." This generosity was to end with Vernon's death, however. No charitable organizations were mentioned, nor were Priscilla or Ginger or any of his longtime employees.

When the thirteen-page document was given to Elvis in his bedroom, he nodded his thanks and asked to have Ginger and Charlie Hodge sent up to witness his signing. A third witness, Ann Smith, wife of one of his cousins, tagged along and added her signature under Charlie's. Elvis then returned the will to his attorney and began making final plans for the Hawaii vacation. Elvis took thirty-one others with him, and had Joe Esposito reserve more than a dozen rooms in the Hilton Rainbow Tower and rent a house on the beach.

The beach house, in Lanikai, about half an hour's drive from Waikiki, was for Elvis and Ginger and her sisters, plus one bodyguard, the former Palm Springs policeman Dick Grob. The others stayed in the hotel and came over during the day or joined Elvis on his rare public forays. One evening they were sneaked into the Polynesian Cultural Center to watch the Polynesian show. Other times, he took Ginger and her sisters and some of the others to one of the small shopping centers in Kailua, buying presents for everyone and, on one occasion, paying the bill for a stranger who was making a purchase for his wife.

Most of the ten days in Hawaii were spent close to home, sitting on the beach, playing ping-pong at the house, or touch football on the sand. Those who had been with Elvis for some time said later that his health improved during the vacation, said his color was better, his eyes brighter and clearer.

There was another observer who hadn't seen Elvis in some time, and he was shocked. Kalani Simerson, a onetime performer who operated a successful limousine service, had known and worked for Elvis since the early 1960s, when Elvis made his first films in Hawaii. The last time he had seen Elvis was when he weighed a trim 170 or so for the satellite television show. As before, Kalani was again called to make some of the arrangements for Elvis's visit, and because of his long-standing friendship, he was invited to join Elvis on the beach socially.

"We played football," Kalani said, "and it was sad, very sad. Elvis was overweight and just unable to function normally. I guess it was all that medication they said he took. Somebody'd throw him the ball and he'd catch it and start running and he couldn't stop. He just wasn't able to control his own body. One time he ran right into a cyclone fence and cut his hand."

On the fourteenth day, Elvis got some sand in his eyes and abruptly the vacation was ended. Five days after that he was back on tour again.

This time, the dates included some of the cities where his oldest and most loyal constituency lived—in Phoenix and Amarillo and Norman and Abilene and Austin and Alexandria. This was the territory he traveled when he drove from city to city with Scotty Moore and Bill Black ("The Blue Moon Boys") to appear in noisy, crowded honkytonks and on the backs of flatbed trucks. This is where he was a young star on the *Louisiana Hayride* radio show. It was this region—in the panhandle of west Texas, in Arkansas, in north Louisiana—that gave little Sun Records an entire galaxy of stars besides Elvis: Carl Perkins, Roy Orbison, Conway Twitty, Charlie Rich, Jerry Lee Lewis, and Johnny Cash. It was a sound that defined the time and the musicians and singers it influenced went on to define the time to come. Buddy Holly and the Crickets, Buddy Knox, Leon Russell, and Mac Davis were only a few of the faces in his early crowds.

More than twenty years had passed and, to the people who lived in the region, Elvis epitomized the American dream. They too were, or had been poor; generally were part of the working class. And they wished to get out of their box, to live the fantasy life that Elvis had come to represent. He was what every woman wanted and every man wished to be, and it didn't matter that he was fat. They'd grown up with Elvis and weren't they fat, too? When you lived, or tried to live, the good life, wasn't fat one of the penalties?

At first the tour was like all the recent rest. Some shows were good some were fair, and some were miserable. Elvis did his best, but nowadays his best was much less than it was when he played that city as a youngster. Some concerts, Elvis performed like an old man. At times it seemed he had only the loosest control of his voice and muscle coordination. He dropped lyrics, mumbled introductions, and very nearly *stumbled* around the stage.

On March 31, following a so-so show in Alexandria, Louisiana, Elvis's private plane took him to Baton Rouge for a concert at Louisiana State University. As was customary, the show started before he was to leave the hotel for the coliseum. All the usual acts performed. First the Sweet Inspirations; then J. D. Sumner and his youthful Stamps; then Jackie Kahane, with the predictable jokes. Elvis usually arrived during the intermission that followed Jackie's monologue. Tonight he didn't.

There was chaos backstage. Elvis's hotel room was called.

"Well, Joe?"

"I don't know, Charlie. Maybe . . ."

A half-hour passed. There were more calls. Finally it was decided to cancel the rest of the show, to say Elvis was too sick to go on, that he was under a doctor's care and was being flown back to Memphis to be hospitalized.

It was from a very peculiar position that Dr. Nick watched Elvis dry out once again in the hospital, because he knew that some of the pills Elvis was so strung out on had come from him. As early as January, Dr. Nick had become Elvis's primary supplier. It wasn't greed, or ego, that put this small, white-haired physician in that place. Up until January, Elvis had solicited his prescriptions from dozens of doctors, stretching from Beverly Hills and Palm Springs to Elvis's Graceland neighborhood. Dr. Nick, who had been one of them, figured that if he could become his patient's only source, he could gain control and with care and time could wean Elvis off drugs completely.

# Chapter 27

# FINAL TOURS

In April, only days after checking himself out of Baptist Hospital, a story appeared in the popular weekly tabloid, *The National Star*, that made Elvis appear foolish and over-the-hill. On the cover was his picture, sweating and overweight, a suspicious, spaced-out cast in his eyes, along with the provocative headline: "Elvis, 42, fears he's losing his sex appeal—psychologist explains Presley's tantrums and why, at 230 pounds, he craves young girls and jelly donuts."

Two weeks later, another unflattering photograph showing Elvis's double chin appeared on the cover of the *National Enquirer*. Now the come-on headline read: "Elvis' Bizarre Behavior and Secret Face Lift." Again a publication broke all previous sales records.

Elvis's name and face had sold two decades of wishy-washy movie fan magazines. In those days, the dirtiest it got was "The Night Ann-Margret Confessed to Roger Smith, 'I Can Never Forget Elvis.'" Now it was "Elvis—fat, feisty and 42 . . ." There were stories of how he fired guns in the air and how he talked about his mother's presence walking the Graceland halls at night. Motel keepers were interviewed about his diet; they said he ate like a family of four. His extravagances were reported disparagingly; once he dispatched his pilot and private plane from Memphis all the way to Dallas for a sack of hamburgers from an all-night snack bar he liked. Nothing, no matter how trivial or personal, was left out.

Nor did it get any better when Elvis went back on the road April 21 on a tour of thirteen performances in thirteen days. There'd been critical reviews in the past, but nothing to compare with these. It was as if the press, usually adoring of Elvis and his performances, or at least forgiving, had turned into a bloodthirsty pack of dogs, snapping at the singer's shaky legs.

A writer in Detroit was especially critical. Describing Elvis as an "old idol," he said, "Let me tell you something, gang; when I say old, I mean old. That turkey needs a feather transplant. It is damning Presley with faint praise to say that he stunk the joint out. If he appeared live and in concert tonight in my backyard, I wouldn't bother to raise the window shade. As it was we got stung

$15 a seat to listen to his aging voice crack and to hear him stumble over lyrics he should have memorized twenty years ago. I couldn't get close enough to see his eyes or smell his breath, but the dude had to be either high or stiff when he came on stage—late, of course. Presley is old, fat and virtually immobile. At best, he is a parody of himself. At worst, a bad imitation of Burl Ives. It was a merciful gesture when Presley left the stage following his brief and disappointing performance and refused to make a curtain call."

Because Elvis still moved on to the next city immediately following a concert, he still missed seeing such reviews. Not so the members of his backup band, however. They read the reviews and were hit with the force of a blow. "The Green Bay paper and the Detroit paper were vicious and nasty," said John Wilkinson. "The *Green Bay Chronicle*, April 29, 1977, I'll never forget it. It was sick."

"There was one guy, he panned it so bad it was like he was pissed off," said Tony Brown. "We got panned nine times out of ten. He was still packin' 'em in, but we got panned anyways, because he was overweight: 'Elvis ain't like he used to be, blah, blah, blah.' The really bad one was in Detroit. We were staying way out in the country, forty-five minutes from the auditorium, and on the bus Jackie Kahane wrote an answer to the review: "Dear So-and-So, I was reading your review, sitting in the John, and it stunk up the place worse than anything I was doin'.' At the end he said, 'Well, that's all I have to say about your review. There's no toilet paper and I guess there's only one thing to do with it. Signed: Jackie Kahane.'"

Even the news reports were negative. In one, the Colonel was reported to be planning to sell Elvis's contract to a consortium of California businessmen, to pay off his gambling debts in Las Vegas. (The debt was real, but the story was not.)

Two weeks on, two weeks off, and in May it was time to go back on tour. This time Elvis faced fourteen shows in fourteen days, starting May 20 in Knoxville, then working his way north and east into Maine, finishing in the deep South. The first part of the tour was uneventful, but it was clear that Elvis's health was not good.

His eyes hurt. He used eye drops to protect them from the glare of the bright stage lighting, but when the sweat ran into them, they stung. He'd pulled a hamstring muscle and it hurt to strike any of the karate-styled poses that once were such an important part of his choreography. The enlarged and twisted colon, the high blood pressure, the ravaged liver, the shrinking arteries and enlarged heart—none of it went away.

His eyes were lidded during most performances, his speech slurred. In one city he forgot the words to a song. Everywhere he looked tired. He complained aloud about his intestinal problems and a sprained ankle. A crisis was approaching. It arrived in Baltimore's Civic Center in front of 13,000 people on May 29.

Later there were reports that he collapsed on stage and had to be carried off by two of his bodyguards. This wasn't true, although he did leave the stage for nearly thirty minutes. The early part of the performance was rough. His voice was weak and he mumbled the lyrics, or dropped them. He also dropped his microphone and had one of his aides hold a microphone in front of him while he played at his guitar for a few minutes. Then he introduced one of his favorite singers, Sherril Neilson of the Stamps, and asked him to sing "Danny Boy." While he was singing Elvis left the stage and, leaning on friends for support, he went to his dressing room. Right behind him was Dr. Nick.

"Bodyguards stationed themselves and nobody was allowed inside," said Larry Collins, the Civic Center's publicist, who rushed backstage, worrying about whether he'd have to refund the $200,000 box office. "The doctor came out, then went back inside with his medical bag. Thirty minutes later, Presley reappeared looking refreshed, went back on stage and sang four or five songs . . ."

John Wilkinson remembered: "He asked J. D. and the guys to sing a couple of numbers and Charlie Hodge emceed while he was gone. I got the impression he had to go to the bathroom. When he came back, he thanked everybody and apologized. He said, 'But when you gotta go, you gotta go.' And then under his breath I could hear him over the microphone. He said, 'Sometimes it hurts me so fuckin' bad . . .' It was like his insides were just being torn up. I also saw him wince as he walked a couple of times, as if it was hard for him to move. Hence no more stage movements. It was tragic to see."

From Baltimore the planes flew to Baton Rouge. "The show started," John said. "Jackie and the Sweets and the Stamps did their thing and the intermission went on and on and on. All the bigwigs were talking: 'What do we tell the audience?' Because you could have yourself a riot. Elvis never left the hotel." The Colonel had to refund the money for that show, and for the one scheduled the following day in Jacksonville. By the time Elvis limped back into Memphis a couple of days after that on June 2, following listless appearances in Macon, Georgia, and Mobile, Alabama, his concert promoters on the West Coast were talking about Elvis dying.

"How many more times," they asked, "can Elvis be pointed onstage and be expected to perform? How many more times can he even be expected to *find* the microphone?"*

---

* It was a cold description, sounding cruel, but it was accepted as a realistic appraisal. So seriously was it taken, in fact, that I was called by the radio syndicater for whom I'd adapted my first Elvis book. He'd talked with Elvis's concert promoters and on the basis of what they'd said, he wanted me to start thinking about lining up interviews so we could add a thirteenth hour to the series when he died.

It was so ironic. As Elvis's health slid rapidly, and even as the gossipmongers and critics closed in for the kill, in many ways his career seemed unaffected, his great success remained untouched.

The same week Elvis lay recuperating from his tour in Memphis, his records were selling in greater numbers than they had in several years. In England, for example, RCA Records had reissued sixteen Elvis Presley singles simultaneously. All had been number one hits in Great Britain at the time of their initial release and included such songs as "Return to Sender," "Jailhouse Rock," "It's Now or Never," and "All Shook Up." All sixteen went onto the British charts again.

In the U.S., his new single was the prophetic "Way Down," a song from the Graceland sessions a year before.

The record was a hit on the Easy Listening, Country and Popular charts, and was followed by the album *Moody Blue*. The press release from RCA for the trade publications showed the Colonel was still at work:

"The album will initially be released as a limited edition, pressed on blue, translucent vinyl with a sticker calling attention to the fact that 'Way Down' is contained in the album.

"RCA's blitz campaign on the single and album began in the trades and will continue there and in consumer publications through the months of June and July with special emphasis in cities Elvis will be visiting on tour and where the single is having the greatest market impact.

"Marketing aids will include two radio spots, one featuring 'Moody Blue' and 'Way Down' and the other featuring 'Moody Blue' and Elvis' entire RCA catalog on which a special program will be running throughout the summer.

"A five-foot standup display of Elvis will be the chief accessory among the merchandising items. Others will be a 'Way Down' streamer, a 'Moody Blue' poster featuring a blowup of the album cover, Elvis calendars and a die-cut display.

"Heavy advertising, window and in-store campaigns and other special localized promotions, are planned throughout the campaign."

It was as if nothing had changed. As ever, the Colonel was the master of the "tie-in" campaign, the guru of the market blitz.

That's not to say the Colonel was callous in his control of the Presley empire, willing to kill the golden goose. Not at all. In fact, following the tour that was to begin June 17, the Colonel had nearly two months set aside with nothing for Elvis to do but rest. And it should be noted that most of the promotional activity involved with any Presley campaign—whether it was to sell a movie, a record, or a concert tour—was handled not by Elvis but by publicists, record distributors and retailers, concert hall managers, and hundreds more whose incomes came all or in part from the Presley mint. At no time was Elvis ever required, or even asked by the Colonel to do anything more than a rare press conference.

Still, it was clear to the Colonel that Elvis needed more than rest. He also needed a new challenge and however much he may have wondered if Elvis was up to meeting one, by late spring of 1977 the Colonel was planning not one, but two "events." One was another documentary film, this one for the CBS television network. This was to be filmed—in concert—when Elvis went back on tour in June. Elvis also was scheduled to open the Las Vegas Hilton Hotel's new Pavilion, a convention hall and sports arena that seated 7,000. This was to be Elvis's only Las Vegas appearance in 1977. The regular showroom engagements were canceled to further whet the appetite.

"We did not put Elvis in the hotel before that," said Hilton vice president Henri Lewin, "because we wanted it to be the greatest opening ever. It was to open in October."

First came the CBS documentary. The Colonel had Elvis's agent, Larry Auerbach at the William Morris Agency, call CBS rather than NBC because the Colonel wasn't happy with NBC. In the past, NBC had loomed large in Elvis's career, with the "comeback" Christmas special in 1968 and the satellite show from Hawaii in 1973. Ratings for both shows were extremely satisfying, but when the satellite show was rerun, the audience was much smaller and subsequently NBC went cool on suggestions to do some follow-up specials. Auerbach called Bill Harbach and Gary Smith, two seasoned television producers, who were also represented by the Morris Agency, sending them to Las Vegas to meet the Colonel.

"The Colonel told us Elvis wasn't interested in doing anything that required anything special of him," said Gary Smith. "He said Elvis would do it while touring rather than in a studio. He also said Elvis didn't want to attend any meetings. So we flew to Chicago in May to see him in action. He was overweight and his voice was only fair, but the electricity in that audience was something."

In the weeks that followed, the Colonel seemed almost defensive in explaining why he had made a deal that seemed so risky. Sometimes he insisted it was for the challenge that he thought (hoped?) Elvis would meet, but other times he made it sound as if he had asked for so much money, he thought CBS would say no, and when the network brass said yes, he couldn't back out. It called for a $750,000 payment that was to be spilt down the middle between Elvis and the Colonel, with full ownership to be shared by them after a single repeat broadcast. This would be the first time that the Colonel put into play the full partnership agreement Elvis had signed with his manager a full year earlier. The Colonel also made it clear to Elvis that the two thirds/one third division of profits from touring that continued to be observed was temporary and that all money due under the January 1976 contract would be due by the end of the year.

Gary and Bill returned to their Hollywood offices to begin logistical planning that eventually involved their own production team of twelve, a six-man film crew, and about twenty more from CBS. They surveyed the cities that Elvis would visit during his June tour, starting in Springfield and Kansas City, Missouri; going on to Omaha and Lincoln, Nebraska; Rapid City and Sioux Falls, South Dakota; Des Moines, Iowa; Madison, Wisconsin; Cincinnati, Ohio; finishing in Indianapolis, Indiana.

"We picked Rapid City for filming because it was Elvis's first concert in that hall," said Gary. "He'd never been to Rapid City before. We wanted to avoid any possible audience disappointment over his being overweight."

How did Elvis feel about appearing on television overweight? Reports are mixed. So, perhaps, were his feelings. Tony Brown said, "It didn't seem to bother him that he was overweight. He seemed to be excited about being on TV again. He said, 'People want to know what I'm doing.'" In his book, Ed Parker saw another side: "As we drove to the auditorium where Elvis knew that the CBS cameras would be waiting, he turned to me and asked, 'How come I get placed in these situations?' He looked out of the window, bit his lip and said, 'Ah . . . hell, I guess it's show business.'" A few days earlier, a fan handed Elvis a caricature that emphasized his bulging waist and Elvis held it aloft and asked, "Do I look like that?" It was Ed's opinion that he'd been shaken by that incident and was experiencing "controlled white knuckle panic" about the bright lights and unblinking cameras of CBS.

Whatever his feelings, the Omaha show was a disappointment. They were staying in Lincoln and on the drive back to the hotel after the show, Elvis slumped quietly in the right rear seat of his limousine, staring into the Midwestern night. A few collected in his room to go over what they'd done and not done. Elvis sat on his bed in his pajamas. His cousin Billy Smith and Charlie Hodge were nearby.

Elvis asked Joe Guercio, his orchestra leader, "Well, what'd you think?"

Joe said, "It was a fair dress rehearsal."

Elvis said, "Yeah, you're right."

Elvis went on a crash diet, fasting and consuming greater than usual quantities of his favorite appetite depressant, Ionamin. Gary Smith said that when he saw Elvis again two days later in Rapid City, "it looked like he'd lost ten pounds." Elvis also put on a much better show. One reason may have been that he was under the influence of stimulants now, rather than staggering under the weight of painkillers and sedatives, which were responsible for wrecking so many of his recent shows. Another reason was that Elvis rose to what little challenge he saw in being on TV again. So he tried harder. As a result, only one song from Omaha, "My Way," appeared in the edited, hour-long show and all of the rest of the music came from Rapid City.

"I thought the show in Omaha was very bad," said John Wilkinson. "He was pale and unsteady. I don't even know if he knew where he was. Maybe he did. And yet the other show, which made up most of that special, it was pretty good. His voice was strong. Physically he looked awful, but he was steady on his feet, and in Omaha he was not."

The finished show, broadcast after his death with a tacked-on message from Vernon, showed John's appraisal correct. Elvis *did* look awful, and much of what could be said positive about the performance had to be couched in phrases that hinted at how much worse he could have been. His movements, however steady, were slow, restricted. His voice, however strong, was never daring.

Yet the show caught a special moment in Elvis's time. Fans were interviewed about how much they had sacrificed to make the trip (of sometimes hundreds of miles) to see Elvis; car mechanics and postal workers and their overweight, spray-haired wives told stories about emergency surgery and house fires, yet still they came to see their King.

There were scenes showing the aging, gray-sideburned Al Dvorn, selling Giant Photo Albums and Portraits on Portrait Paper for $5, Elvis Forever Lapel Pins for $2, the same price for a twelve-inch by fourteen-inch color photograph. Binoculars went for $5, a popular item because so many sat so far away.

Elvis wore his white suit with the Mayan calendar design. He had two of them and alternated wearing them every night of the concert tour, sending his staff scrambling to clean them between shows. They were the only two of the more than fifty he'd had made that still fit. His eyes bulged slightly, slitted under puffy lids. His face was swollen. His cheeks melted right into his neck. There was no chin line. His hair was sprayed. In close-up it looked as if someone had stuck the distinctive wide, flat nose and bee-stung lips onto a balloon face.

The camera followed him up the stairs and onto the stage. He moved slowly, like an older man, as if he were fragile, feeling his way almost a step at a time. He was breathing heavily while singing "C. C. Rider." Occasionally he hefted his wide belt over his midsection, calling attention to his bulk. Throughout his performance, sweat rolled off his face in sheets. Still, it wasn't a bad show. He sang "Jailhouse Rock" and "How Great Thou Art" and "Early Morning Rain." A little something for everyone. He introduced his father, mentioning how sick he had been. He introduced Ginger. He gave away scarves and kissed his fans. At the end of the show he held out his beefy arms in a Christ-like pose for another Instamatic flash. It really did appear that he was having a good time.

His next-to-last concert was in Cincinnati where, at three o'clock in the afternoon, the air-conditioning unit in his room stopped working. Elvis liked his rooms as cold as it was possible to get them. Angry, he stormed out of the hotel and started off down the street in search of another. One of his stepbrothers, David Stanley, saw him leave, raced along behind Elvis and half a block from the hotel was joined by Ed Parker, who was returning from a late lunch. Then the Colonel spotted Elvis and, according to Larrie Londin, "like to swallowed his cigar." Because Elvis never did anything like that. He didn't like the hotel, so he left. "And the Colonel was runnin', hoppin' along after him."

Elvis was wearing a jogging suit. His black hair was askew, his tinted glasses sliding down his nose because of his heavy sweating. People on the sidewalk stopped to watch him pass. The clerk in the next hotel was startled, too, and as a crowd began to gather in the lobby, Elvis was taken into the manager's office while another of his security aides, Dick Grob, arranged to book two rooms, one for Elvis, the other for his bodyguards. Shortly after that, Elvis announced they would return to Memphis after the show and not stay in Cincinnati at all. Which is what they did, flying on to Indianapolis the following day for Elvis's final performance.

In the beginning, after the *2001* opening and "C. C. Rider," Elvis did what he often did, teased the audience, played it like an instrument. "Wull, wull, wull . . ." he'd say, amused by the screams his silliest grunts returned, sliding into "I Got a Woman" and from it directly into a prolonged chorus of "Amen" with the ten backup singers he had with him. After that, Elvis joked with the audience for five minutes, using J. D. Sumner's voice as a toy, getting him to sustain long low notes to the crowd's amusement. He sang a final chorus of "I Got a Woman." Then came another few minutes of offhanded small talk and goofing around with the audience and his first real oldie of the evening, "Love Me."

And so it went for an hour and seventeen minutes. He sang a handful of his early hits, including "Jailhouse Rock," "Teddy Bear," "Don't Be Cruel," and the inevitable "Hound Dog." There were dramatic renditions of "I Can't Stop Loving You," "Bridge over Troubled Water," and "Hurt," songs that had worked in the past as records and in performance, with Elvis stretching for and reaching the high notes. He tossed the customary dozen scarves to the bleating, writhing women who clamored at the lip of the stage throughout the show. No matter what he sang or said or did, or didn't do, the frenzied response was constant, reminiscent of the reaction he got when he first shook his hips at the Overton Park Shell in Memphis more than twenty years before.

He introduced "the guys in the back, the number one gospel quartet in the nation," the Stamps, flattering each one individually, and then featured each member of his band in a song, and then Joe Guercio and the orchestra. He introduced his daddy (did Mick Jagger or Paul McCartney or Bruce

Springsteen or the Bee Gees ever take *their* parents on tour?) and "my girl-friend, Ginger" and her mother and sister, and Dr. Nick and three cousins, several sound engineers and his producer Felton Jarvis. It sounded like an Academy Award acceptance speech.

"Most of all I'd like to thank you and I'd like to say this is the last day of our tour. And we couldn't have asked for a better audience. And you've really made it worthwhile."

He closed with "Can't Help Falling In Love," the song he always sang last, and finally held out his arms, strutting around the stage for a final time, disappearing into the darkness as the band began its thunderous vamp. The voice of one of the Stamps came booming into the big arena.

"Ladies and gentlemen, Elvis has left the building. Thank you and good night."

There was a slight pause and the voice continued. "We'd like to remind you that following this evening's concert the Elvis Super Souvenir Concession Stands will be open for a short while. If you didn't get your souvenir of your evening with Elvis, be sure that you do so before you leave. We thank you for coming. Be careful driving home. Good night."

"We played Indianapolis three times," said John Wilkinson. "The first time the sound wasn't right and the audience was rude and the second time it wasn't much better. But the last one was really good. The place came unglued, like they were really glad to see him. It was a dynamite show, rock and roll all the way. But he looked whipped when he came around the corner to get off the stage at the end of the show. He really looked tired."

# Chapter 28

# THE END IS NEAR

E lvis returned to Memphis immediately at the end of the tour, arriving in the pre-dawn hours of June 27, and went into virtual seclusion, a bear in summer hibernation, collapsed on his grandiose bed, two television sets in the ceiling, Ginger at his side, often going several days without seeing anyone else, except when the regular meals and packets of medicine arrived, brought by his maids and hired hands.

Elvis's sky began to darken at the end of July when the first copies of *Elvis: What Happened?* by Red and Sonny West and Dave Hebler went into the bookshops, supermarkets, drugstores, and airports across America, and simultaneous with the book's release, lurid excerpts appeared in *The Star*, the tabloid whose entertainment editor, Steve Dunleavy, had ghostwritten the book. The first installment told the story of Elvis's mad wish to have Priscilla's boyfriend killed.

Suddenly, through much of the western world, big headlines and dripping prose revealed Elvis's abuse of drugs and guns, told of late-night conversations he had with his mother, said he was a man obsessed with religion and psychic powers (his own) and law and order and probable life after death. The overall picture a reader got was of a fat and stoned-out, aging rock star locked away in a Southern mansion, venturing forth only on rare occasions to a movie theater kept open from midnight to dawn for his personal use, living his life by the numbers in his numerology book, a machine gun cradled in his ample lap.

The authors, once among the closest of Elvis's friends, said they wrote the book in an attempt to shock their former boss into doing something about his drug habits, as its title *Elvis: What Happened?* indicated. But in the end it sold three million copies, losing the selfless explanation some credibility.

That said, there was truth in the book—however narrow its scope—and Elvis was wounded by it. For hours, day after day, he talked about Red and Sonny and Dave. Dave he could forgive, or forget, he said, because he hadn't been around long. But Red and Sonny were *family!*

He called Priscilla and said he was worried about what Lisa Marie would think if she ever read the book, or heard her friends talking about it. Elvis told Priscilla he was going on the road soon and asked, "Would it be all right if Lisa Marie comes to visit first?" Priscilla thought it would help take Elvis's mind off the book and agreed happily.

At the end of July Elvis sent one of his hired hands in the *Lisa Marie* to Los Angeles to collect his daughter for what would be her longest visit at Graceland since Elvis and Priscilla split up. During the next three weeks, he spent time with her nearly every day, leaving her to amuse herself or be entertained by Ginger and the maids and cooks when he remained in his room, sleeping long hours or too sedated to move around.

In Lisa's room nearby there were dolls and toys and a television set (one of sixteen in the mansion) and behind the house in the garage she had a miniature electric golf cart that Elvis had bought for her. Always accompanied by one of the help or bodyguards—Elvis feared for her safety always, terrified of a kidnaping—she often took the cart down the sloping driveway to the gate, whooping with laughter as her adult companion ran breathlessly along beside her.

On August 7, Elvis planned a special treat. A year earlier the old Fairgrounds amusement park that he had rented so often in earlier years was reopened as Libertyland, a theme park. It was here that he had ridden for hours in the fifties on the dodgem bumper cars and in the sixties on the roller coaster, standing up, always riding without holding on. It was a slower, fatter, less daring Elvis who rented the park on this night. His friends remember him as a proud father, somewhat solemn but fun loving as he accompanied her from ride to ride with the other children and adults he had invited to go with him.

On August 10, he took a group of friends to the United Artists Southbrook 4, renting the theater and paying the projectionist for an after-midnight showing of the latest James Bond movie, *The Spy Who Loved Me*. Elvis loved James Bond, usually took his gold-plated PK Walther with him; that was the gun Bond usually carried.

The second week of Lisa Marie's visit, Elvis saw friends occasionally, or talked on the telephone when they called. He played racquetball in the court behind his house with his cousins and stepbrothers and Dean Nichopoulos, who almost always let Elvis win, no matter how hard it sometimes seemed for Elvis to move around the court. He watched gospel shows on television. He talked with Joe Esposito about the tour that was to begin on the seventeenth in Maine and invited his father to go along; Vernon had stayed home on some of the tours this year to rest and to be with his girlfriend, a warm and generous nurse named Sandy Miller, but this time he said yes. Ginger said they continued to make wedding plans, claiming he was going to make an announcement at a concert at the end of the tour in Memphis in two weeks. He read in his Bible and in his numbers book. He ate his cheeseburgers and took his pills.

On August 14, he started a fast, something he often did to lose weight quickly before going on tour. Oddly, he didn't take any Ionamin, the appetite suppressant that he had favored for so long. Perhaps he believed the racquetball and fasting were enough. Besides, what difference did it really make? At 250 pounds, he was grossly overweight and in two days how much could he lose?

On August 15, he awoke at four and after breakfast played with Lisa on the grounds, laughing as she ran around and around in her electric cart. She was going home to Priscilla the next day.

In the early evening, some of his guys reported to him that they were unable to get the projectionist at the Ridgeway Theater to stay past midnight that night, so he'd have to see *MacArthur* another time. Soon after that Elvis called his dentist at home and, apologizing for the time of his call, he asked if he and Ginger could see him. Dr. Lester Hofman had been the subject of Elvis's generosity many times; he drove a Cadillac that Elvis gave him. He told Elvis that yes, 10:30 that night at his office would be fine.

Elvis arrived in his customized Stutz Bearcat with Ginger and Billy Smith and Charlie Hodge jammed into the small rear compartment. Dr. Hofman had never met Ginger. Elvis introduced her, using his pet nickname "Gingerbread," and after the dentist x-rayed her teeth he turned to Elvis and filled an upper right first bicuspid and an upper left molar. As was the custom, the fillings were porcelain. Elvis had many fillings and he didn't want a flash of gold when he opened his mouth to sing.

There was a lot of Elvis-styled small talk. Elvis invited the doctor to come out to Graceland to see his new Ferrari, and the doctor said the next time Elvis went to California he'd like to go along so he could pop in on his daughter and surprise her. Elvis said sure, there was always room on the *Lisa Marie*.

Three hours passed. It was now Tuesday, 1:30 A.M. and Elvis was back at Graceland, where he called one of his security men, Dick Grob, and handed him a list of songs he had decided to add to his concert repertoire. He told Grob to locate the words and music and chord changes for the new material, so he could brief his band before they went on (and would have the lyrics for himself onstage in case he needed them). Grob later said he and Elvis talked about public reports of his health and reaction to "the bodyguard book." This was his first public appearance since the book had been published and this must have worried Elvis much more than he allowed friends around him to see. Grob said that as he left the room Elvis said, "Dick, we'll just show 'em how wrong they are. We'll make this tour the best ever."

By two or two-thirty Elvis had changed into a striped workout suit and was on his racquetball court with Ginger and Billy Smith and Billy's wife Jo. They played loosely, without much enthusiasm, as if Elvis were merely warming up. Then Ginger and the Smiths drifted away to one side as Elvis began clowning around with the ball. Ginger said she was hoping the play would help Elvis relax enough to fall asleep easily. Elvis called it quits about four and after working out leisurely for a few minutes on the exercise cycle he had positioned at one end of the gym, he and Ginger retreated to his bedroom.

There is disagreement over what happened next. Ginger said they merely talked about their wedding and when the tour was mentioned, Elvis reportedly grabbed his flabby midsection in his hands and said, "The boy's not in shape, Gingerbread, the boy's not in shape. It's been too long since the last tour. Too long . . ." Others who were in the house say Elvis and Ginger fought over whether or not she would go with him on the tour; reportedly he wanted her by his side and she wanted to stay in Memphis to spend some time with her family.

Whatever the truth, Ginger soon fell asleep, leaving Elvis alone, reading a book on the bed beside her.

Between eight and nine o'clock in the morning of the sixteenth, Elvis's Aunt Delta knocked on his door, delivering the morning newspaper and a glass of ice water he'd requested. Elvis told her he was going to sleep until seven that night, then leave for Portland, Maine, about midnight. Between getting up and leaving, he said, he wanted to see Nurse Cocke to say goodbye; would Aunt Delta call the nurse and ask? Aunt Delta did and soon after that Elvis called Marian Cocke himself. She said she'd come to the house when she finished work.

At nine, Ginger awoke to find Elvis still reading. She said he told her he couldn't sleep and was going into the bathroom to read. Ginger knew that meant he was going to take some of his medication. Elvis's syringes were in the bathroom and so was some of his personal pharmacy.

"Okay," Ginger said, "just don't fall asleep." And with that, she rolled over on the big bed and went back to sleep herself.

Elvis went into the bathroom with a book, his finger stuck into it as a marker. He may've glanced at himself in the mirror. Blue pajamas. Puffy eyes and face. Bad color. No one knows, but it's likely he helped himself to something from his pharmacy, because as the autopsy would later show, he now had as many as ten different drugs coursing through his body, taking control of his brain, his heart. Four of the drugs were in what the medical examiner would describe as "significant amounts." These were codeine, an addictive opium derivative, commonly prescribed for severe pain; ethinamate and methaqualone, two strong sedatives; and unidentifiable barbiturates, which are depressants. The others were also "downers." He had taken an unidentified number of Placydil and Valium capsules, both tranquilizers, and unknown quantities of Demerol and Meperidine, both painkillers. Bringing the amazing total to ten were morphine, which is an illegal substance and probably was the natural result of the body's absorption of codeine; and chlorpheniramine, an antihistamine which by itself would make its user sleepy.

Elvis sat staring at the open book in his lap, his eyes glassy, his body motionless. Then his chin dropped to his chest, the big body slumped imperceptibly, then shifted and toppled out of the big cushiony chair, the noise of the fall muffled by the thick brown shag carpeting.

The room was silent except for the sound of his final breath. Ginger slept on the other side of the bathroom door and downstairs in the mansion the rest of the household, which included three maids and two cooks, went about their daily routine. Joe Esposito was present, along with Al Strada. Charlie Hodge was in the kitchen drinking coffee. Uncle Vester Presley was at the Graceland gate. Vernon was in his home less than a hundred yards away.

The Colonel, meanwhile, was in Portland, Maine, where it was Tuesday afternoon and he was meeting with the auditorium manager and watching Elvis's sound crew move equipment into the backstage area. Members of his band and orchestra were in Los Angeles, Las Vegas, and Nashville, packing or waiting for the *Lisa Marie*, which would take them to Portland. Elvis was to follow along behind in the Jet Star. The thirteen-city tour was a sellout. The crates of posters, pennants, and picture books were on the way by truck. The local record stores had been serviced by RCA to accommodate the certain demand for Elvis's records that followed all his concerts. Elvis's limited wardrobe of his bigger costumes was packed, along with several hundred scarves. Dick Grob had the music together, except for one song, which was driving him nuts.

Ginger awoke sometime between one and two in the afternoon. Seeing the bed empty beside her, she walked quickly to the bathroom door.

"Elvis?" Ginger called timidly. "Elvis, darlin'?"

There was no answer, so she entered, finding Elvis on the floor, his face in a puddle of vomit. She ran gulping from the room and called downstairs. Al Strada answered the phone and came rushing up, with Joe Esposito right behind him. Together, and with some effort, they rolled Elvis onto his back. The flesh was stiffening and cold and when Strada saw that Elvis wasn't breathing, he leaped for the phone in the bedroom and called the nearest doctor to Graceland, Dr. Perry Holmes, while Joe started pounding on Elvis's chest, suspecting a heart attack brought on by an overdose of drugs.

"They sent me out of the room," Ginger said, "but I went back in and I tried to beat on his chest, too. I was praying: 'Oh, please, God, don't let Elvis die!'"

"Mr. Presley arrived and they pried open Elvis's mouth with something. He'd bitten down on his tongue. Mr. Presley was on his knees and saying, 'Elvis, speak to me! Oh, God, he's gone!'"

"Lisa Marie came in. She said, 'What's wrong with my daddy?' I pushed her away and closed the door. I said, 'There's nothing wrong, Lisa,' and she ran around to the other door into the bathroom and saw Elvis on the floor."

The doctor Al Strada called wasn't in and Al hung up abruptly. One of the doctor's associates was in, however, and when he was told that Strada seemed extremely upset, he called Graceland, reaching Elvis's Aunt Delta. She said her nephew was having difficulty and asked the doctor to make an emergency house call. The doctor suggested that Elvis be taken to a nearby clinic.

Meanwhile Sam Thompson—Linda's brother, still on the payroll as a bodyguard—had arrived to take Lisa Marie back to Los Angeles on a commercial airliner. On the way up the drive, he passed David Stanley, one of Elvis's stepbrothers, on his way down to the gate. David hollered something unidentifiable as he passed. Sam continued on up to the house and was met at the front door by Lisa Marie.

"Sam!" she cried. "Sam! My daddy's dead! My daddy's dead!"

Joe was now administering mouth-to-mouth resuscitation. Dr. Nick was on the way and so was a fire department ambulance. Vernon was in the bedroom with Ginger, who was sobbing uncontrollably. Someone took all the syringes and pills out of the bathroom. Graceland was in panic.

Finally Ginger and Vernon and Aunt Delta retreated into Grandma Minnie Mae's room to pray, as Dr. Nick and Joe and David Stanley went off with Elvis in the ambulance.

Resuscitation attempts continued all the way to Baptist Hospital without result. At the hospital Elvis was wheeled into one of the emergency department's "trauma rooms." A call went out on the hospital intercom, ringing through every hallway and room: "Harvey Team report to E.R. (Emergency Room). Harvey Team report to E.R. Harvey Team report to E.R." This was the signal for the hospital's team of resuscitation experts, who literally ran through the corridors when they got the call. When the heart stops beating, only eight minutes remain before there is irreparable brain damage.

"Whenever Elvis was admitted to the hospital," said vice president Maurice Elliott, to whom fell the job of press relations again, "there always were rumors that he was dead. It got so I took it with a grain of salt. I was in my office and I got a call from Miss Bingham, the nursing supervisor in the emergency department. She said, 'We're doing a Harvey Team on Elvis and it doesn't look good.'

"I went to the emergency department. He was in the first trauma room, which is a small operating theater. There were several doctors in attendance, a respiratory therapist, a nurse-anesthetist, a number of people. They were working at both ends of the table. Elvis was nude and his head was over the edge of the table. My first impression was that he was dead. His head was blue.

"I went into the Number Two trauma room and waited with Al Strada, Charlie Hodge, and two or three others. They worked on him for about thirty minutes and then Dr. Nick came in, his head down. He said, 'It's over. He's gone.' You could see tears come to his eyes and everybody there started crying.

"Joe came to my office to make some calls. He didn't want anything said to the press until Dr. Nick had gone back to Graceland to tell Vernon. So for thirty minutes we had to hold the press off. They were there before Elvis was, because they heard it on the fire rescue radio. So what we did was say he came in in severe respiratory distress and that they were working on him right now. And that was true. At least I rationalized it was true. He was obviously in severe respiratory distress. He wasn't breathing."

After Joe called the Colonel in Maine and the tour organizers in California, and after he got word from Dr. Nick at Graceland, he went to meet the press. He choked up, unable to say anything. "You do it," he said to Maurice Elliott. "I can't do it. You do it."

Within minutes, thanks to the media that had aided Elvis so greatly in his meteoric climb, it was known throughout the world that the king of rock and roll was dead.

Several of Elvis's band members and backup singers had been picked up in Los Angeles and Las Vegas, and were on the way to Maine when the pilot got a message to return. No explanation was given. The fuel level was low and it was decided to continue on for refueling in Pueblo, Colorado, where Marty Harrell called the Presley office to find out what was happening.

"We'd all gotten out of the plane and were wandering around when Marty came back," said John Wilkinson. "Marty stood on the stairs of the plane, everybody gathered around and he said, 'I hate to be the one to do this, but Elvis died this morning.' Marty was crying. He was hanging onto the rail. We were all just wandering around in a daze. The band and two of the Sweets, Kathy [Westmoreland], the Las Vegas guys, nine or ten of them, twenty or twenty-five people altogether. I've never been through anything like that before. Myrna broke down and cried as hard as I've ever seen a woman cry. We were all so shocked. Elvis Presley doesn't die. I die, you die, but he doesn't. And he damn sure did. Someone asked, 'Marty, what happened? Car wreck? Suicide?' It could've been anything. Marty said, 'Something about respiratory failure combined with a heart attack, I don't know. All I know is we're going home for the last time.'"

In Nashville, the rest of the musicians were at the airport waiting for their flight to Portland when Felton Jarvis got a page to come to the courtesy phone. All he said when he rejoined the others was, "Tour's off. We may call you later. You know how Elvis is." Tony Brown hung around for a while and heard someone in the airport say, "Elvis is dead!" He found Felton and told him. Felton said yes, he knew.

On the *Lisa Marie* returning to the Coast, James Burton said to no one in particular, trying to brighten the solemn mood, "Well, I guess I'll have to call and see if John Denver needs a guitar player."

James meant it as a joke. No one laughed.

Elvis's body was moved onto a gurney and taken to the hospital pathology department for autopsy under the direction of the department chief, Eric Muirhead. A representative of the coroner's office was present when they began.

Said Maurice Elliott, "Our pathologists were concerned, without it being said, that with the controversies that surrounded John and Robert Kennedy's autopsies, they wanted to be sure that the hospital wasn't embarrassed and that this was done very thoroughly and professionally. They were very detailed and the autopsy took three or four hours and then the body was released to the funeral home."

At eight o'clock that night, the coroner, Jerry Francisco and Dr. Nick held a press conference to disclose their preliminary findings. Some said later that this is when "the whitewash" began.

Death was due to "an erratic heartbeat," the medical examiner said. "There was severe cardiovascular disease present. He had a history of mild hypertension and some coronary artery disease. These two diseases may be responsible for cardiac arrhythmia, but the precise cause was not determined. Basically it was a natural death. It may take several days, it may take several weeks to determine the cause of death. The precise cause of death may never be discovered."

Francisco was asked to explain "cardiac arrhythmia." It was just another name for a heart attack, he said; it meant Elvis had an irregular heartbeat and it stopped beating. This explanation was subsequently endorsed, and given credibility, by Elvis's great aunt, Vera Presley, who told reporters, "The Presleys all had such bad hearts . . ." No one contradicted her, recalling Elvis's mother's death by heart attack and the recent attack that put Vernon in intensive care.

There were questions from the press regarding Elvis's use of drugs, prompted by the garish headlines running that week in *The National Star* and by the stories in what was now being called "the bodyguard book." Francisco denied that there was any indication of drug abuse. The only drugs found in his body, he said, were those prescribed by his physician for the hypertension and a long-standing colon problem.

However true that may have been, literally, the quantity and variety of drugs prescribed by Dr. Nick alone challenged all credibility. Two years after Elvis's death, a computer check of prescriptions in the Memphis area showed that in the final seven months of Elvis's life, George Nichopoulos, M.D., prescribed 5300 uppers, downers, and painkillers for Elvis. That's an average of about twenty-five pills or injectable vials a day.

At the same time, when Shelby County medical examiner Dan Warlick entered Elvis's bedroom as part of his investigation, he found the bed stripped and remade, the bathroom carpet cleaned, and while two empty syringes were found in the bedroom, no other trace of even the most common household remedies were found. The medicine cabinet was bare. So, too, a black bag that looked like a doctor's bag, all of the interior drawers empty as well. Warlick commented that not since he examined the home of a Christian Scientist had he witnessed a death scene so clean.

The days that followed were as strange as any in Elvis's life.

Tuesday night the body was taken in a long white hearse from the Baptist Hospital to the Memphis Funeral Home, where the body was to be prepared for an open-coffin viewing the next day at Graceland. Already the fans were gathering. Less than an hour after the death had been announced Tuesday afternoon, a crowd formed outside the mansion gates. Many carried portable radios, all broadcasting a constant parade of Elvis's record hits, interrupting with news bulletins whenever another bit of information or another interview was obtained. By now, the media was covering Elvis's death the same way it covered his life—in great and lurid detail.

Hundreds of daily newspapers sent reporters. All the television networks scheduled instant specials and assigned their best feature men; Geraldo Rivera was there for ABC, and so was Charles Kuralt, whose popular *On the Road with* series had run for so many years on CBS. The wire services, *Time, Newsweek* and the *National Enquirer* sent teams of reporters. (The *Enquirer* alone had twenty on the story.) When word came that Caroline Kennedy was at the Graceland gates, she was escorted to the house, but when it was learned she was working as an intern for a New York newspaper, she was asked to leave. *Rolling Stone* sent people not just to Memphis, but to Tupelo, and two days before going to press threw out half of their pages and started filling it with Elvis material, calling upon writers on three continents. All over Memphis anyone who had known Elvis or who had been near him when he died was being interviewed.

In the Midwest and deep South, fans began traveling to Memphis to pay homage to their king. Hour by hour, the crowd grew, right on through the night. By lunchtime Wednesday, there were thousands standing in a slow mist, waiting for the hearse that would bring Elvis from the funeral home to Graceland, where the informal, open-coffin service for family and friends was scheduled for 2 P.M. Shortly after noon the caravan of police motorcycles and the long white hearse, lights flashing, sirens blaring, swept past the Graceland gates and entered the estate by a side entrance to avoid the milling crowd.

Vernon decided to let mourners file past the open casket from three until six, and literally miles of his fans lined up. The sun returned and in the 90-degree heat and high humidity, dozens fainted, to be tended by doctors dispatched to the scene, along with platoons of police. Eventually, National Guardsmen were called out, as the crowd swelled to an estimated 75,000.

Inside the high rock walls, a press compound had been established with telephone lines and tables with typewriters. Next to it was the medical area and farther up the hill, closer to the house, were all the flowers in Memphis. Every florist
in the city ran out. Eventually 3,166 floral arrangements were sent by everyone
from the Soviet Union to Elton John to the Memphis Police Department, many
of them in the shape of guitars, crowns, hound dogs, and hearts.

Inside the house, just past the National Guardsmen standing at stiff attention at the door, at the end of the foyer, Elvis lay at rest inside a 900-pound cop-
per-lined coffin, beneath a crystal chandelier. He wore a white suit, a light blue
shirt, and white tie. As is true with most corpses laid out in such a manner, there
was too much makeup and hairspray, creating a sort of grotesque mask.

For more than three hours the fans filed past, thousands of feet scuffing
over the white linen spread on the Graceland rug. Across the street, oppor-
tunists were selling out of the trunks of their cars Elvis "memorial" tee-shirts
and lapel buttons that they'd had made up overnight.

When Priscilla and Vernon and the others inside the house watched the ten
o'clock news that night, there was an outpouring of tributes from entertainers
and politicians alike. "We lost a good friend," Frank Sinatra said. "There's no
way to measure the impact he made on society or the void that he leaves," said
Pat Boone. Even President Carter issued a statement, saying the death
"deprives our country of a part of itself." Elvis's music and personality, Carter
said, "permanently changed the face of American popular culture." Flags were
lowered to half staff throughout Mississippi and Tennessee.

For four hours starting at 9 A.M. a hundred vans—from nearly every flower
shop in Memphis—transported the thousands of floral tributes from Graceland
to the Forest Hill Cemetery three miles away, where Elvis was to be entombed
later that afternoon following a private service for family and close friends.

There were about 150 gathered in the Graceland music room at two o'clock for
a service that was scheduled to last half an hour and went for nearly two. Priscilla
sat in the front row, flanked by Vernon and Lisa Marie. Linda and Ginger sat farther
back and in between were the Smiths and Presleys and dozens of former employees
and friends, along with actor George Hamilton and Ann-Margret. Colonel Parker,
sitting at the back in his shirtsleeves, was making his first public appearance since
the death was announced. When he arrived, he was wearing a tie and one of Elvis's
concert promoters, Tom Hulett, told him to take it off, because he'd never worn one
when around Elvis when he was alive. The Colonel did as he was told.

First, Kathy Westmoreland sang "My Heavenly Father Watches Over Me"
and then a singer Elvis had claimed was a major influence on him, Jake Hess,
stood up with two members of the Statesmen gospel quartet to sing "Known
Only to Him." James Blackwood sang with the Stamps the title song to one of

Elvis's albums, "How Great Thou Art," and finally the Stamps alone sang "His Hand in Mine" and "Sweet, Sweet Spirit." This was followed by remarks from C. W. Bradley, pastor of the nearby Whitehaven Church of Christ, a longtime friend of the Presley family; Rex Humbard, the television evangelist from Akron, Ohio; and the comedian Jackie Kahane.

"We are here to honor the memory of a man loved by millions," Bradley said in the main eulogy. "Elvis can serve as an inspiring example of the great potential of one human being who has strong desire and unfailing determination. From total obscurity Elvis rose to world fame. His name is a household word in every nook and corner of this Earth. Though idolized by millions and forced to be protected from the crowds, Elvis never lost his desire to stay in close touch with humanity.

"In a society that has talked so much about the generation gap, the closeness of Elvis and his father, and his constant dependence upon Vernon's counsel was heartwarming to observe. Elvis never forgot his family. In a thousand ways he showed his great love for them.

"But Elvis was a frail human being. And he would be the first to admit his weaknesses. Perhaps because of his rapid rise to fame and fortune he was thrown into temptations that some never experience. Elvis would not want anyone to think that he had no flaws or faults. But now that he's gone, I find it more helpful to remember his good qualities, and I hope you do, too.

"Thus, today I hold up Jesus Christ to all of us. And challenge each of you to commit your heart and life to Him. May these moments of quiet and thoughtful meditation and reflection on Elvis's life serve to help us also reflect upon our own lives and to re-examine our own lives. And may these moments help us to re-set our compasses. All of us sometimes get going in the wrong direction."

It was an honest eulogy, franker than some might have expected, alluding to Elvis's "temptations," asking those present to remember the positive side but also to learn from the more troublesome side.

After the last words were spoken, friends and family gathered in small groups, talking softly, moving toward the door. Then the caravan, led by a silver Cadillac followed by the white Cadillac hearse with Elvis's body and seventeen white Cadillac limousines, rolled slowly down the curving drive and onto Elvis Presley Boulevard to the cemetery. A brief ceremony followed in the white marble mausoleum where Elvis was entombed. The huge coffin was slid into place, Vernon stood quietly by it for a moment, then walked slowly away, as workmen entered to cover the opening with concrete and cement.

The following morning, Friday, an estimated 50,000 fans visited the cemetery, each taking home a single flower at the wish of the Presley family.

Not even the Colonel, who'd already created a slogan, 'Always Elvis', for the posthumous marketing, could foretell the strange turns ahead.

# Chapter 29

# LOVE ME (IN LEGAL) TENDER

No one should have been surprised when Iain Calder, the longtime editorial director of the *National Enquirer*, confessed in his personal history of the scandal-mongering tabloid that when Elvis died he sent twenty-five reporters to Memphis with $100,000 in cash to spread around for exclusives.

Calder, in his book *The Untold Story: My Twenty Years Running the National Enquirer*, said $18,000 of that went to one of Elvis's cousins to sneak a camera into Graceland and take the infamous photograph of Elvis's corpse in his open casket. The next issue had the picture on the cover and it became the largest and fastest selling issue of all time.

Calder also reported that Elvis's stepmother, his father's wife Dee Stanley Presley, showed up at the *Enquirer*'s Memphis hotel rooms offering her story for a price. Next came Ginger Alden and while she was weeping her way through her account, the two ambulance drivers who transported Elvis to Baptist Hospital said they just wanted to tell their story, but didn't want any money. They were flown to Florida, where the *Enquirer* has its offices, so no one else could get to them.

The tsunami of memories-sold-for-cash was on its way, its explanation no more clearly expressed when one of Elvis's closest, longtime pals, George Klein, was the guest lecturer at the University of Memphis. He was telling some of his favorite Elvis anecdotes to a class in popular culture when he noticed someone in the classroom taking notes. George recognized the man as someone who had written about Elvis. He stopped talking.

"What are you doing?" he asked.

"Taking notes," the man said. He looked perplexed.

"Well, stop it. I don't want any note-taking in here."

Already a movie company had paid Klein to share these memories. He was also planning a book and he didn't want anyone stealing what he now considered his property.

Within two years of Elvis's death, it seemed that almost everyone who had been close to him felt the same way. In that short time, there were more than a dozen books, several movies and television specials, and dozens of other projects, nearly all of them launched by Elvis's friends and relatives—to set the record straight, they said, or to pay tribute to The King.

Uncle Vester Presley, Vernon's brother at the guard gate all those years, self-published a slender, trivial volume that he autographed and sold by the thousands to fans who made pilgrimages to Graceland each week. Ed Parker, the karate instructor and sometime bodyguard, wrote an answer to Red, Sonny, and Dave, defending his former boss, insisting there was no use of drugs. No way, said Vernon's now ex-wife Dee, who along with her three sons, Ricky, Billy, and David, received $100,000 from a New York publisher, producing a manuscript called *Elvis: We Love You Tender* that in Dee's words "made the West [bodyguard] book look like a kindergarten class." Another longtime hired hand, Lamar Fike, hooked up with the author of a sensational Lenny Bruce biography, Albert Goldman. Because of Albert's name, they got $225,000 from another New York publisher and then set out to write a book that told even more of the "truth" than the others did, and to imply that Elvis committed suicide.

At the same time, Charlie Hodge sold his advice to Dick Clark for a television movie in which Kurt Russell took the title role. After that, Charlie designated Dick Grob, who was still head of Graceland security, as his "manager" and began (1) working with an Elvis impersonator, (2) selling subscriptions to a newsletter at $10 a year, and (3) appearing at Elvis fan gatherings—a new phenomenon, sometimes attracting as many as 10,000 in a weekend. At these, Charlie sold copies of a little picture book he threw together about Elvis's last vacation in Hawaii and then posed with the fans for a Polaroid snapshot. Dick Grob took the picture and then sold it for $5, while J. D. Sumner began displaying the stretch limo that Elvis had given him, charging $1,000 a weekend at flea markets and shopping mall openings. Ginger Alden became an "actress," starring in a movie about a pop singer who had trouble with success (as her mother sued the Presley estate for $40,000, claiming Elvis had promised to pay off her mortgage).

When a Memphis promoter named Buddy Montesi bought Elvis's old ranch in Mississippi and began selling seven-inch pieces of the board fencing, it was Billy Smith who authenticated the pieces of wood on a certificate bearing his signature. Billy also promised to donate all his cars and furniture and guns— gifts from Elvis—to a museum that Montesi was planning for the property; in return, Billy would get a lifetime job working in the museum.

The first two years following Elvis's death there must have been several hundred entrepreneur-privateers like Montesi. When he and some partners bought the ranch soon after Elvis's death, he said, "My plan was to sell it an inch at a time to the fans. We made up certificates of transfer, individual deeds, the whole shot. If we sold an acre at five dollars a square inch, we could've made a bundle." He said he was selling the portions of the fence to make payments on the property until the "bundle" came in.

Others were more successful. The body wasn't in the ground before several singers began recording musical tributes. One of these, "The King Is Gone," established Ronnie McDowell as a star in Nashville and earned him a job singing the tracks for Elvis in the Dick Clark television movie. Paul Lichter, an Elvis collector in Pennsylvania who had written one book about his hero—a picture book called *Elvis in Hollywood*—immediately began writing another, also produced a calendar, and watched his Elvis Unique Record Club, a mail-order operation, double in size to 200,000 members. Within a year, Paul was the largest retailer of Elvis records, as well as the biggest merchandiser of pre-1977 Elvis memorabilia. His wife, Janice, admitted that Paul "has a lot of guilt feelings—all of a sudden he feels like a whore to cash in like everybody else. Still, there was that $30,000 a month in the mail."

Steve Goldstein was another record retailer, using television. He recalled that as soon as he heard about Elvis's death, he took an album that had been selling for $2.98 in the stores, increased the price to $6.98, bought a $100 telephone order ad on a New Orleans television station at 3 A.M. Next day, he said, "There were 150 orders. I told my people, 'Buy every television market in the U.S.! Buy the world!' Orders were so heavy we shorted out phone systems in Little Rock, Cleveland, Memphis, and Nashville."

The next couple of months, Goldstein picked up another four albums, charged $10.66 for each—although all were available in shops for $7.98—and using the same advertising techniques, moved 665,000 records. Goldstein also quickly published a news-stand picture magazine, selling 270,000 copies in under a month, and bought a Cadillac Elvis once gave a girl in Denver and started taking it to Elvis fan gatherings, charging $3 to have a picture taken at the wheel. "We were making $3,400 a day," he said.

Elvis always had attracted bootleggers. In Memphis by the second anniversary of his death, there was an entire shopping center of stores directly across the street from Graceland offering more than seventy different Elvis products—ashtrays, coasters that looked like the original Sun record labels, guitar-shaped hairbrushes, pennants, pillows, picture books, replicas of the TCB pendant, lapel buttons, postcards, bumper stickers, candle holders, Christmas tree ornaments, key chains, posters, plastic drinking cups, trash baskets, wall clocks, wristwatches, scarves, pencils, statuettes (four sizes), belt buckles, pen knives, pocket mirrors, even what was claimed to be "dirt from

Graceland" and "Elvis sweat," both sold in tiny glass vials. One shop gave away a replica of Elvis's driver's license with every purchase. Another allowed visitors to punch up their favorite Elvis song on a jukebox in the foyer. Petrol stations and the nearby Howard Johnson restaurant carried a full line of Elvis tee-shirts.

By mail from Memphis it was possible to order a "Complete Elvis Memorial Package" that included copies of the last will and testament, marriage certificate, and medical examiner's final report, along with a handful of cheap jewelry, $9.95 plus $1 for postage. Gray Line Tours was running an Elvis Memorial Tour, taking busloads of fans to see the renovated Sun Recording Studio, Nathan Novick's Pawn Shop on Beale Street where Elvis bought some of his early clothes, Humes High School (now a junior high school), Loew's Palace where he worked as an usher, Graceland, and the Crown Electric Company where he drove a truck—$7.50 for adults, $5 for children. All up and down Elvis Presley Boulevard, shops and motels and restaurants started using the address in their names (i.e., Elvis Presley Boulevard Inn, 3765 Elvis Presley Blvd. Souvenirs). The Memphis newspapers combined all the stories about Elvis published the week following his death into a single special edition and sold more than 250,000 copies.

As the gossipy books appeared, embarrassing bits of information were revealed. David Stanley said his job accompanying his stepbrother on the road had been to carry an attaché case full of pills and rolls of $100 bills. Following a computer check of all prescriptions filled in Memphis, state health officials said that on the day before Elvis died he received 160 tablets and 20 cubic centimeters of the painkillers Percodan and Dilaudid, 262 pills of the depressants Amytal and Quaalude, and 278 tablets of the stimulants Dexedrine and Bipetamine, apparently part of his preparations for the tour. For years the controversy raged on. At first Dr Nick just had his wrists slapped, being suspended from practice for three months and put on probation for three years. But finally—in 1995, eighteen years after Elvis's death—his license was revoked and he was never permitted to practice medicine again.

These revelations, and others, meant little, as larger-than-life-size statues were erected in downtown Memphis, at the Las Vegas Hilton, and in Tupelo, the latter depicting Elvis as a boy of twelve, holding his first guitar. Beside the birthplace, which was given a fresh coat of paint, an $80,000 chapel was dedicated. In Nashville, a "memorial" exhibit was opened, featuring a thirty-meter cyclorama. And John Bakke, a communications professor at the University of Memphis in 1979, began a series of annual seminars "to make the point that Elvis was a worthy subject for serious study. Our mission was also to educate the community about its musical heritage."

In the face of all the ridiculous Elvis-is-alive reports in the media that would continue through the 1980s, Elvis also was being taken seriously, soon to become the darling of the academic world.

The Colonel wasn't asleep all this time. When he was told Elvis was dead, he was shocked but unsurprised. Already he was talking with an East Coast promoter about the merchandising rights that in death would become worth millions. Immediately, he returned to Memphis where he convinced Vernon that if they didn't act right away and get authorized product onto the marketplace, the sleazy vendors would move in.

Vernon signed a letter empowering the Colonel to act on his behalf and the Colonel then flew to New York where he met with Harry "The Bear" Geissler, the 47-year-old owner of Factors Etc., Inc. Geissler, who took his nickname from the town where he had his factory—Bear, Delaware—was a third-grade dropout, a former steelworker and just the man to head up the posthumous marketing, the Colonel decided, because he already had a multi-million dollar business and the experience to handle something big, yet he wasn't so big he wasn't still hungry. Geissler had made it into the big leagues earlier that year when he put up $300,000 for the Farrah Fawcett-Majors tee-shirt rights. By the time Elvis was dead, he earned enough to pay an additional $400,000 in royalties to Farrah's agent as well as purchase merchandising licenses to *Star Wars* and *Rocky*.

The second thing that attracted the Colonel to Geissler was his somewhat shadowy past. Just before taking on Farrah, Factors paid $100,000 to companies that claimed Geissler was a bootlegger. This, the Colonel figured, gave the Bear and his aggressive 27-year-old son, Lee, an edge when it came time to go after the bootleggers already a part of the Presley market and sure to drain away a part of it in the future.

The man who later would take over operation of what became Elvis Presley Enterprises, Inc., Jack Soden, said that some people called the Colonel a "heartless bastard" for doing this, but also quickly added that "while everyone else was paralyzed by grief, with Vernon's approval, the Colonel did what he always did, take care of all of Elvis's business."

In the days following the funeral, the Colonel's office was like a war room, as orders went out to RCA and staggering sales reports came back, as the Colonel demanded the return of all rehearsal tapes sent over the years to Elvis's backup musicians, a move aimed at stemming the bootleg tide. The Colonel had a rubber stamp made that said ALWAYS ELVIS and used it on every piece of mail that left his offices.

"It's still Elvis and the Colonel, but now it's Elvis and Vernon Presley and the Colonel," he said. "Elvis didn't die. The body did. We're keeping up the good spirits. We're keeping Elvis alive. I talked to him this morning and he told me to carry on."*

When Elvis died, his will named his father as executor and trustee. Beneficiaries were his grandmother Minnie Mae Presley (who was in her eighties and still lived at Graceland), his father, and his daughter Lisa, nine. Vernon died in 1979 and if there were some who wanted the Colonel to continue as the estate's money manager, others clearly did not. When the Shelby County Probate Court appointed Priscilla, Elvis's longtime accountant Joe Hanks, and the National Bank of Commerce (the bank Elvis had used for years) as executors and trustees on behalf of Lisa, it further ordered Blanchard Tual, an attorney who was the child's guardian ad-litem (routinely appointed when a minor's residence was out-of-state; Lisa then lived with her mother in California) to take a close look at the estate's financial bottom line and its management.

The report, submitted to the court in 1980, shocked everyone. Elvis may have been one of the highest-paid performers in history, but at the time he died, the estate was worth less than $500,000 and likely headed for bankruptcy. (The house and fourteen-acre property on which it stood was valued at $350,000 and, at the time, Priscilla said maintenance and taxes came to more than $500,000 a year.) The report squarely blamed the Colonel, saying he not only made poor business decisions, he also acted in his own financial interests. When Elvis died, RCA tied up most of the country's pressing plants to keep up with orders, clearing every record store in the nation in twenty-four hours, selling an astonishing 200-million records the first year. The Colonel had sold most of those recording rights to RCA for $5.3 million when Elvis and Priscilla divorced in the early 1970s, so the estate received only publishing royalties after that. (Even from the sale, after taxes and the Colonel's 50 per cent share were taken out, Elvis benefited little.) The attorney's report to the Probate Court accused the Colonel of self-dealing, overreaching, and violating his duty to Elvis and his estate. The report, which also confirmed rumors that the Colonel was a Dutch citizen, further recommended that all agreements with the Colonel be terminated and that the estate sue RCA and the Colonel in an attempt to recapture "unfairly obtained gains."

---

* A personal footnote: My first Elvis biography had also been turned into an internationally syndicated radio series of twelve hour-long episodes. When Elvis died, a thirteenth show went into production and my first day on the job, the Colonel called me. This was the first time I'd talked with him and he said, "Mr. Hopkins, so long as we keep one thing in mind, that we're both in this for the dollar, we won't have any problems."

During the year that followed, as a blizzard of lawsuits froze all relationships between the estate, the Colonel and RCA, initiating a three-sided legal squabble that would continue for five years, the estate's new executors tried to find a solution on their own, meeting a creative, young television writer-producer named Andrew Solt who had worked with Jacques Cousteau in Paris and was now associated with David Wolper, a New York-based documentary filmmaker known for his *Biography* series on television.

The son of refugees from Communist Hungary, he had grown up in South Africa and following migration with his family to the United States graduated from an American university. In 1981, less than a year after the blockbuster court report, Solt was at Graceland scouting locations for *This Is Elvis*, an unusual feature release that mixed documentary footage with sequences of actors playing Elvis at various stages of his life. It was the first time filming had been permitted inside the Graceland gates and during his visit, Solt was approached by Joe Hanks, who asked him if he would go to Wolper and Warner Brothers, the studio backing the documentary, to see if they'd be interested in buying Graceland. Stunned, Solt asked Hanks what he wanted. Hanks said $10 million.

Wolper had gone to grammar school with the Warners boss, Steve Ross, who said no, theme parks weren't what his company did. He suggested they go to Universal, already running its own successful studio tours, as well as Yosemite National Park.

The same year, 1981, everything turned around again. This is when Jack Soden, a stockbroker and financial planner employed by a Kansas City firm, met Priscilla, who had been using the firm to handle some of her earnings from a, by now, successful acting career. On a visit to Kansas City, she asked Soden if he thought he could help. Soden later insisted that "it would be wrong to say Graceland was one step from the auction block," but when he took a look at the Probate Court report and Priscilla told him about the cost of keeping Graceland going, it was clear that the estate was in serious jeopardy. Soden said Priscilla wanted to improve the situation, creating an estate for Lisa when she grew up. Priscilla was "speaking from the heart," he said, and she didn't want to sell Graceland and its artifacts, because Lisa might "grow up and have regrets that everything had been sold."

Soon after that, it was decided that opening Graceland's gates to the public might be the best way to go. The estate went to the City of Memphis for support. The City funded a feasibility study and said no, believing that Elvis's memory would fade. Next they went to the man who ran Opryland in Nashville. He wasn't interested, either. Priscilla asked Jack Soden to do some research.

"People in Memphis were too close to the story. It was hard for them to see how big it already was becoming. I was new to the story and from somewhere else so it was easier for me to see the long-term possibilities. No one saw Elvis's long-term viability," Soden recalled in 2006. "I did. She asked me to meet the bankers, who were dubious about hiring a money manager. I had a great fear of screwing up, but they told me to take a look around at the possibilities.

"I met with the curator of the Smithsonian Institute who had asked for something to display along with Fonzie's jacket and Archie Bunker's chair. We felt Elvis deserved a whole hall at the Smithsonian, not a jumpsuit next to Archie's chair."

The Smithsonian curator agreed, saying that he felt Elvis was the single greatest influence on American music in two hundred years, but they didn't have room for more than a suit or cape.

To see how it was done elsewhere, Soden visited the White House, Mount Vernon, Monticello, the Hearst Castle in California, Thomas Edison's home and laboratory in New Jersey, and some of the presidential libraries. Returning to Memphis, it was decided to restrict the public to the mansion's first floor—the music room, the dining room, the TV room, the billiard room, the kitchen where all those banana and peanut butter sandwiches were fried, and the "Jungle Room" where Elvis recorded parts of the *Moody Blue* and *From Elvis Presley Boulevard* albums. Taking strangers upstairs was regarded as "disrespectful and inappropriate" and not something that Priscilla would remotely consider. Besides, adding the upstairs to the tour would require changes to the structure of the house. Also out of the question. Eighteen "stations" were established and staffed with guides and the home was opened on June 7, 1982. Soden and Priscilla were there to greet 3,024 fans who paid $5 each.

"I figured I'd go back to Kansas City when it was up and running," Soden said, "but I was always making lists of things to do. I saw a picture of Elvis's jet, the *Lisa Marie*, and I decided I wanted to find it. And the mall across the street was a tacky zoo. I told the executors we had to get control of the property and change it. From 1982 on, every day was a discovery."

The bank rejected Soden when he asked for a loan to buy the mall property, so with the reluctant permission of the estate he put together a group of investors in Kansas City who agreed to buy the land and mall and lease it to the estate for ten years and then sell it to the estate for the 1983 price. (Soden said this was his most satisfying accomplishment.) Upon assuming management, the unauthorized product was replaced by that produced by licensees. The last of the original shop leases expired in 1987 and Graceland began an overall facelift. In 1993, the property was purchased and renamed Graceland Plaza.

Well before this, dating back to when the Colonel was still in charge, he had "The Bear" start what became a continuing barrage of lawsuits and threatening letters to gain legal control over the estate's key asset, the Elvis Presley name, image, and likeness. When Elvis died, this legal "right of publicity" ended at the time of an individual's death and in the next five years, following the Colonel's lead, the estate went after an illegal poster manufacturer and an Elvis impersonator who sold bogus Elvis product at his shows, among others. Following mixed results in the courts, in 1984, after lobbying from the EPE, the Tennessee State Legislature passed the Personal Rights Protection Act, decreeing that the rights of publicity survived a person's death and passed on indefinitely to his or her heirs and executors, so long as continuous use was made of that public persona. New York and California followed—along with many other states, over time—and a subsequent EPE case in 1986 was victorious in a federal appeals court, sending the concept toward becoming the law of the land.

Everything was falling into place. In 1983, at the Probate Court's direction to end the three-way fight, RCA said it was offering $2 million to the estate and the Colonel, take it or leave it—leave it and we go back to court—and the Colonel, still telling the estate that it couldn't fire him because he was part-owner, said he'd take it all and relinquish all claims and genuine ownership. By which time, Soden said, he and the Colonel had become good friends, the Colonel calling him "the day Graceland opened to say if I ever wanted someone to bounce ideas off of, he'd be there."

Soden located the *Lisa Marie* and, subsequently, the *Hound Dog II* JetStar that Elvis's father had sold in 1978 and in a joint venture with the current owners, both airplanes were added to the Graceland tour on land adjacent to the mall that had been acquired by Elvis several years earlier and never developed. The Graceland Christian Church and land that formed the north boundary with Graceland was also acquired—"essential to protect Graceland's security and integrity," Soden said—and turned into the estate's corporate offices. In 1989, the Elvis Presley Automobile Museum was opened adjacent to Graceland Plaza. A year after that, Jack Soden, still making lists, was named the organization's CEO.

The same year, Soden also supervised the purchase and transport of the Colonel's archives that had remained in storage since Elvis's death in Madison, Tennessee. "I remember exactly how much stuff there was," Soden said. "The eighteen-wheelers bringing it to Memphis passed through a state-operated highway weigh station and it came to 70,000 pounds. It took us most of the nineties to go through it. We were fortunate. Both Vernon and the Colonel were pack rats. They never threw anything away and the estate now has full use of all of it."

More paper was generated by relatives, friends and onetime associates whose names appeared on the ongoing torrent of books. June Juanico and Becky Yancy (girlfriends from Humes High and the first years of his career), Joe Esposito, Alan Fortas, Larry Geller, Marty Lacker, Rex Mansfield (from his Army days in Germany), Charlie Hodge, Scotty Moore, D. J. Fontana, Donna Presley (a cousin), Harold Lloyd (another uncle who served with Vester Presley at the Graceland gates), Gene Smith, Kathy Westmoreland, Wayne Carman (a karate partner), Mary Jenkins (Graceland's cook for fourteen years), Nancy Rooks (a maid for ten), Sara Erwin (a neighbor), even Priscilla—all these and many, many more were authors now.

There were books about the Colonel and the Memphis Mafia. There were collections of Elvis interviews, along with exhaustive recording session chronologies. There were numerous heady academic tomes, as well, including a collection of essays by the University of California, Berkeley's Greil Marcus called *Dead Elvis*. As "American Studies" and "Popular Culture" gained support from universities, Elvis became an established subject for serious investigation in universities around the world.

There also was an accompanying descent into trivial pursuit and speculation. A fan who followed Elvis on his May/June 1975 tour slapped together a sort of scrapbook of seventeen shows that included personal photographs and newspaper clippings from every city. Someone else argued that Elvis forged his own death certificate and listed Elvis sightings around the world as evidence he was still alive and another, inspired by the television series *The X Files*, would write *Elvis Files: Was His Death Faked?* Inevitably, there was an Elvis cookbook with recipes for triple bacon cheeseburgers and other heart-stoppers.

The Elvis estate could do nothing to slow this frequently salacious, sometimes ridiculous, occasionally puzzling, and usually saccharine tide except decide which books would or would not be sold in Graceland Plaza and, just to the north, a neighboring shopping center called Graceland Crossing. This second, smaller mall was built in the late 1980s and was independently owned (until the estate bought it in 1997), but it generally went along with whatever Soden and his increasingly powerful organization decreed.

In 2003, David S. Wall, Director of the Centre for Criminal Justice Studies at the School of Law at the University of Leeds in England, wrote an article for a legal journal called *Entertainment Law* in which he said, "The aspects of Elvis's celebrity culture in which there lies an intellectual property right (trademark, publicity rights, copyright) are now so jealously guarded that his name is almost synonymous with litigation." The estate was, he said, "widely regarded as one of the most effective organizations of its genre," sometimes referred to as "the Darth Vader of the merchandising-licensing business."

Soden was proud of the legal victories, but scoffed at the *Star Wars* comparison, calling the estate's past legal position something more like a "Fonzie strategy." In other words, be the toughest guy in town but stay out of senseless brawls. The marketplace knows we will fight to protect our rights which, hopefully, will reduce the number of actual battles.

That said, there were some incidents that made Wall, not Soden, seem correct. In 2004, when a story appeared in newspapers worldwide that Elvis's ancestors may have come from a village in Aberdeenshire, Scotland, where Andrew Presley was born before migrating to the U.S. in 1745, it was speculated that Elvis's fans might wish to visit and some entrepreneur might open a guesthouse called Heartbreak Hotel. The estate reacted by issuing its customary warning, a reminder that it owned all the intellectual property rights in his name and image, as well as his songs, including the trademark use of the words "Heartbreak Hotel."

Indeed it did, having purchased a small hotel property adjacent to Graceland Plaza and, following a complete remodel, opened it in 1999 as Elvis Presley's Heartbreak Hotel. Here, 128 rooms and suites were decorated in blue-and-gold carpeting, drapes and bedspreads, two of the dominant colors Elvis used at Graceland. There were vintage black-and-white photographs of Elvis on the walls and the blond wood furniture evoked the same era. All rooms came with a refrigerator and microwave and the themed suites slept up to eight. (The Burning Love Suite was done in reds.) Rooms started at $99 a night, double occupancy suites from $520.

The music was not forgotten or neglected. However much the media seemed preoccupied by Elvis's increasingly bizarre and larger-than-life-sized image, and as Graceland began to attract hundreds of thousands of visitors a year, as many as 3,500 to 4,000 a day during the peak summer season, and hundreds of products bearing the singer's name and likeness were licensed and sold worldwide, the music remained at the core of the business, just as it always had. This presented new challenges.

For years following the settlement between the Colonel, the estate and RCA, the relationship between EPE and RCA was poor and in 1987, after managing the Beach Boys for ten years, Elvis's old friend Jerry Schilling proposed to the estate that he try to get everybody working together again. He also wanted to suggest some ways to promote Elvis through the creation of new documentaries that would feature the music. He got the job, which he admitted didn't exist before he applied for it—the title was Creative Affairs Director—and the next day he met with Andrew Solt to see if he had any ideas.

Solt proposed a show called *Elvis: The Great Performances*, saying, "We tell Elvis's story in the show, but let the music have the loudest voice." In 2007, Solt recalled, "It was about keeping the image alive. It's important for any estate, keeping the artist in the public eye." Schilling easily sold the notion to the board, of which he was now a member. But when Solt asked the Ed Sullivan estate about the rights to Elvis's appearances in the 1950s, he was told he could have a maximum of five minutes for $26,000 for each, thirteen times what he'd paid in 1972 when he worked on *Elvis on Tour* in charge of research.

"I was in a state of semi-shock," Solt said. "There was no way we could handle that. I asked if they had any plans for the entire Sullivan library. That casual remark led to my buying all the Sullivan shows and I never made the last *Great Performances* payment because by then I owned the shows myself." (There were three DVDs in the boxed set, the third one narrated by Bono, another longtime Elvis fan, refusing remuneration and asking that his fee be donated to a charity.)

As this was going on, Schilling negotiated a deal between RCA and EPE whereby the estate got a percentage of all future royalties. "It wasn't a fifty-fifty deal," he said, "but the estate got to keep all rights to any projects using the music." And immediately following the show with Solt came *Elvis in Hollywood*, when Schilling worked with the studios and RCA, producing a documentary about his old boss's early movie years; after that, Schilling co-produced with his old fraternity brother Rick Husky a dramatic series of thirteen hour-long shows for ABC TV called *Elvis*, starring a young actor named Michael St. Gerard—Priscilla was executive producer.

"Disney sent a script about Elvis called *Heartbreak Hotel* and I turned it down," Schilling said. "I got a call from Jeffrey Katzenberg [longtime Disney boss] and Priscilla went to the meeting with me. He said he had fifty lawyers who said he could do the movie without permission and fifty more who said he couldn't. But he wanted the estate's cooperation. We said okay, but we had to have script approval. He gave it to us and made all the changes we asked."

A later Disney project represented a breakthrough for the estate. That came when the empire that Mickey Mouse launched wanted to put the *Aloha* satellite show on the Disney Channel. "Conventional wisdom said Elvis's fans were getting older and eventually would die off and that would be that," Soden said. "This was in the late 1980s and I recall an argument over how much to charge for licensing. I said if we were smart, we'd give it to Disney for a dollar and let them have unlimited use. Because for introducing Elvis to seven-, eight-, and nine-year-olds, we should be paying them! Ultimately I won the argument. Fully half of the visitors to Graceland are under thirty-five and we want to keep it that way."

The same thinking prevailed when Disney came again to the estate about *Lilo & Stitch*, an animated film planned for a 2002 release. In it, Stitch was an extraterrestrial and Lilo was a young Hawaiian Elvis fan who carried her idol's photograph everywhere. Disney wanted the rights to use the picture, along with several Elvis songs for the soundtrack. The estate got an up front licensing fee but didn't push too hard for a share of the profits. "If we had been unreasonable," Soden said, "they could have turned her into a Don Ho fan."

Such films—inspired by Elvis or dependent on his music—were beginning to pile up like the movies that Elvis himself made in the 1960s, and by now a longtime Elvis fan named Gary Hovey was supervising the estate's music. One of his cousins was dating Priscilla and he sent her to Hovey's father's automobile agency in Gardena, a Los Angeles suburb, when she was looking for a new car. Later, when she bought one for Lisa, Priscilla met Hovey, a recent college graduate. He then met and in 1984 married Priscilla's sister Michele and in 1990, Priscilla asked him if he would come to work for the estate.

"They wanted someone to take charge of the music," Hovey said, "and they wanted someone they could trust."

Over the years, there were so many movies and television shows that used Elvis's music, Hovey said, he had no idea how many, but the most important, besides *Lilo & Stitch*, included *Honeymoon in Vegas*—a preposterous but charming film that had Nicolas Cage deciding to marry Sarah Jessica Parker in Las Vegas, where he lost her in a rigged poker game to James Caan, all of which took place against the backdrop of an convention of Elvis impersonators. The soundtrack was to comprise entirely Elvis songs, performed by everyone from Billy Joel to Bono.

"The producers approached us and we said no," Hovey recalled. "The script called for a 'Korean Elvis,' a 'Midget Elvis' and a 'German Elvis.' 'What is this?' we said. 'A joke? What's a "German Elvis impersonator" mean? He has swastikas on his cape?' They said, 'Oh, we would never do that?' I said, 'Well, it doesn't say in the contract you won't.' Rob Reiner, one of the producers, was at the meeting and he promised to show us the final movie and if there was anything we didn't like, he'd take it out. We gave him our permission."

Hovey said he generally took a hardnosed stance. People came in with a script, looking for a license to use some of Elvis's music, he said, believing the license from the estate would make it easier to find financing and get bonding and insurance for the film. "We told them to get the financing first and then come back," Hovey said. "It was a 'Catch 22,' they needed one to get the other, but we figured if it was a good script with good people behind it, they'd find the financing. We rejected far more films than we accepted. But Jack [Soden] always said, 'You make a bad movie using Elvis's music and the next year, we're still in the Elvis business and you're making some other movie.'"

Hovey was also disapproving of much of what RCA did to the music, repackaging the recordings they owned so frequently and unimaginatively, releasing the same songs over and over again and throwing in one or two previously unreleased alternate tracks and maybe something new, and sometimes using badly mixed tracks, all the while rarely consulting the estate on anything. In the late 1990s, Hovey said, there was something that prompted them to go to RCA with their attorney.

"In the UK," Hovey said, "there was a competition to pick the Top Song of the Twentieth Century, and it looked like it was going to come down to Elvis's 'If I Could Dream' and John Lennon's 'Imagine.' RCA wanted us to give them the video track of 'Dream' to promote that song. We said they had to pay us. They refused and we didn't let them have the footage. 'Imagine' was named Number One."

Another conflict occurred in 2001 when a Japanese record company made a deal with Sony/BMG, now RCA's parent company, to release a collection of Elvis songs titled *Junichiro Koizumi Presents: My Favorite Elvis Songs*, twenty-five tunes that RCA owned. The plan was to put Koizumi's photograph on the CD cover, however, and that was something the record company didn't have a right to do. Because Koizumi, who claimed to be a lifelong Elvis fan, was Japan's prime minister, Hovey said this time the estate responded more gently. The CD was released only in the Japanese market and proceeds went to a charity.

RCA and EPE locked horns again in 2002 over "A Little Less Conversation" when Nike wanted to use it in a commercial in Europe, after it had been "remixed" by a Dutch disc jockey. "This was leading up to the World Cup and Nike had already hired the DJ and he'd made all the changes and they didn't tell us until after the fact," Hovey said. "RCA owned the original recording, but they didn't have the right to alter it in any way without our permission and we also owned the publishing. Then, when we learned that a cover version of the remix was planned by some other artist, we settled with both RCA and Nike, who had to pay us a royalty. We also told them to put the remix out as a single and it went to Number One in twenty-six countries. Another remix, released a year later, didn't do so well."

The music was used on the stage as well, one of the earliest shows produced in 1993 when the Memphis Symphony Orchestra devoted its annual "Rock and Roll Pops" concert exclusively to Elvis's hits. "My project was putting that show together," said the estate's Todd Morgan. "I'd seen Dick Clark use Elvis in one of his specials, isolating his voice from the original multi-track recording and playing a video with that track, accompanying it with a live band. We decided to do the same thing and used his medley 'American Trilogy' with J. D. Sumner and the Stamps and Fusion and the orchestra backing him up. We continued to work with the Memphis Symphony Orchestra and the next year he did three songs and the year after that, six.

Todd Morgan came to Graceland as a guide the summer of the year it opened, when he was a marketing major at the University of Mississippi. He had grown up on a rice farm in Arkansas and was an Elvis fan, so he returned to Memphis when he graduated and took a "first-rung management position." Twenty-five years later, in 2007, he was the estate's Director of Media and Creative Development. "We knew we had to do something special for the twentieth anniversary show for Elvis Week in 1997. We decided to put together as big a reunion as we could, of everybody who'd worked with Elvis on stage in the 1950s, 1960s, and 1970s. We got Scotty Moore, the Jordanaires, J. D. Sumner and the Stamps, Millie Kirkham, the Imperials, Voice, the Sweet Inspirations, the TCB Band [guitarist James Burton, drummer Ron Tutt, pianist Glenn D. Hardin, bassist Jerry Scheff], and Joe Guercio and put them with the Memphis Symphony Orchestra, with Elvis singing lead on interactive video performance."

Guercio recalled, "I said to Ronnie, 'Man, this is going to be weird. I haven't seen some of these people in twenty years. You know what's going to happen, Ronnie—all these old folks are going to walk in!' Then that door opened and damn! You know—who had lost their hair, and all that stuff. It was like doing a guest shot on *The Twilight Zone*. Imagine going back twenty-five years and doing exactly what you did with the same people. Isn't that cool?

"So we started the first rehearsal and someone said at one point, 'It was like we closed two days ago in Cleveland.' Everybody just got into the notch. We were coping along and then we got to 'Bridge over Troubled Water' and the girls lost it. I called a fifteen-minute break. The Sweets could not get through it. It's an emotional song and there he is on a screen, and here are all the original guys, so they just lost it. We took a break, we came back, and we've been laughing ever since."

By now, the original scores from Elvis's concerts had been discovered in the mass of material from the Colonel's archives, eliminating the need to write new ones and making a fusion of Elvis's voice a more perfect match with the backing sound. Morgan said they also decided to add Priscilla and Lisa to the show. "Lisa told her mother she didn't want to talk," Morgan said. "Instead, she wanted to sing a duet with her father on a video. The song she picked was 'Don't Cry, Daddy.' We decided to keep this on a need-to-know basis. We wanted it to be a surprise to everyone.

"Jack said the audience is going to be too shocked to comprehend it, so we need to be ready to roll it again. So it was agreed that Priscilla was to come out first and talk to the crowd. Which she did and then she talked about Lisa a little bit and said, 'Before I bring Lisa out, there's something she wants me to share with you.' We then ran the video, and then Priscilla came back out with

Lisa and, knowing the audience was in shock, she said, 'Wouldn't you like to see that again?' We then ran the video a second time."

There wasn't a dry eye in the audience.

Radio City Music Hall in New York had been looking for a show for the following spring and asked Randy Johnson, a stage director, if he had any ideas. Stig Edgren, a West Coast producer who worked with the estate on the Memphis show, invited Johnson to see the concert and he was so impressed, talks began the next day to take the show to New York.

The format was as simple as it was difficult to explain. In the center of the stage was a vertical screen some ten meters high, where excerpts from the MGM specials, *That's the Way It Is* (1970) and *Elvis on Tour* (1972) and *Elvis: Aloha from Hawaii via Satellite* (1973) were projected. Two smaller horizontal screens on the sides showed the live action on the stage below, as two roving cameramen captured Elvis's original back-up band and singers and a sixteen-piece orchestra conducted by Guercio as they provided—twenty years after his death—a live soundtrack to Elvis's recorded voice.

A particularly poignant moment came when, in the original footage Elvis introduced the members of his band, who as they were shown in the center screen with Elvis they simultaneously were shown on the smaller screens live, as they appeared twenty years later—fatter, hairier, or less hairy or gray—while playing the same music, note for note.

The show, called *Elvis Presley in Concert*, did a ten-date tour leading up to the three-day engagement in New York, then remained on the road for two to three months a year for ten years, crisscrossing the United States (the March 1998 tour included Elvis's "return" to the Las Vegas Hilton with eight shows) and going to Europe, Australia and Asia, thus giving Elvis his first international tours. Five times the show toured Europe and twice it played to sellout audiences in London's Wembley Arena. *The Guinness Book of Records* called it the "First live tour headlined by a performer who is no longer living."

(Another stage show, *All Shook Up*, an $11 million musical based on Elvis's songs and, amazingly, Shakespeare's *A Midsummer Night's Dream*, debuted on Broadway in 2005. Whereas Shakespeare had a magic flower spread love, pitting gods against mortals, *All Shook Up* had a magical jukebox that inspired a love for music, pitting residents of a small 1950s town against a leather-jacketed guitar player. It was one of numerous shows of the time, called "juke box musicals," featuring the music of ABBA, Queen, Billy Joel, Johnny Cash, Pink Floyd, the Beach Boys, and John Lennon, to varying degrees of success.)

However easy it was to control the musical product and licenses for the music's use in other media, there were some areas where the estate either couldn't or declined to go. For example, when dozens of countries used Elvis's name

and image on postage stamps. Grenada was the first, in 1978, and dozens followed—there were 58 in 2006 and still counting—many of them tiny, little
known nations desperate for the revenue. This practice had been common for
small, poor countries for more than fifty years, when unusually attractive special issues were designed and marketed—all actually printed by a company in
New York—for sale to collectors. With Elvis fans added to this niche market,
the practice increased. Thus, there were postal issues from Burkina Faso,
Gambia, the Central African Republic, Comoros Islands, Laos, Antigua and
Barbuda, Guyana, Marshall Islands, Palau, Tadjikistan, and Madagascar—but
also from Russia, Germany and the United States, the latter conducting its
first-ever write-in campaign to determine which image should be used: the
rocker from the 1950s, the movie star from the 1960s, or the somewhat hefty
concert king from the 1970s. The rocker image won and more than half a million stamps were sold, three times the usual print run.

The Elvis impersonators, or "tribute artists" as they preferred to be called,
were in another no-go zone. They began to appear in nightclubs before Elvis died
and after his death they multiplied like mushrooms following a rain, becoming an
entertainment staple. From the mid-1980s onward, in almost every major city in
the world there were Elvis fans who let their sideburns grow, combed their hair
into elaborate pompadours, and climbed into high-collared, spangled white
jumpsuits and became, for an hour or so on Friday and Saturday night, The King.

"Our policy was one of benign neglect," Soden said. "There were so many
First Amendment rights involved. You don't need permission to mimic an
artist. So we didn't give it much of our attention. I did notice, though," he
added, "that ten to twenty years ago, they tended to give me the creeps. They
didn't look like Elvis but they all looked like each other. Happily, that's
changed and there's an Elvis festival in Canada that has a contest that attracts
50,000 people each year. We're going to have our first international contest in
2007 hosted by Graceland at the Cannon Performing Arts Center in Memphis."
Nor did they go after people like Ron DeCar, a licensed minister who made his
living in Las Vegas marrying people while dressed in an Elvis suit, and offered
a room in the hotel behind the Viva Las Vegas Wedding Chapel that had a bed
built into the front half of a 1954 pink Cadillac. "Do you both agree to adopt
each other's hound dogs," he asked the about-to-be-betrothed, "not to wear
your blue suede shoes in the rain, to always be each other's teddy bear, and to
never have a blue Christmas without one another?" How could you sue someone like that, even without the First Amendment getting in the way?

There was so much weirdness attached to the Elvis phenomenon it sometimes seemed that the legacy had been turned over to the writers of *Saturday
Night Live* or Jay Leno. Churches—religions!—were begun in his name

online, some of them as parody, some of them not. Peter Whitmer, a clinical psychologist in Princeton, devised an elaborate theory around the fact that Elvis's twin brother, Jesse Garon, died at birth. Other "twinless twins" included Diego Rivera, Thornton Wilder, Philip K. Dick, and Liberace, Whitmer said, convincing him the "syndrome" might be a creative driving force. And when one of Elvis's hairdressers offered clippings from his haircuts for sale, others suggested that Elvis might be cloned from them.

Jack Soden said the strangest phenomenon, for him, was the widespread belief that Elvis wasn't dead. "A *USA Today* poll said 16 per cent of the American population believed he could be alive," Soden said. "We're not talking Jimmy Hoffa here. Twenty-five thousand people walked past the open casket!"

Even the establishment went along with the weirdness, notably in 2001 when *Forbes* magazine began listing the "Richest Deceased Celebrities." For five years, Elvis outdistanced all his competition, among them at various times *Peanuts* cartoonist Charles M. Schulz, John Lennon, Theodor "Dr. Seuss" Geisel, James Dean, Andy Warhol, Marilyn Monroe, J. R. R. Tolkien, Bob Marley, Robert Ludlum, and George Harrison. (Kurt Cobain topped the list in 2006 only because his widow, Courtney Love, sold 25 per cent of Nirvana's song catalog that year.)

One wire service story put it, "Surprise! He's worth more dead than alive." Where during his best years in Hollywood and on the road in his final years Elvis grossed between $5 and $6 million, now he was making ten times as much. Another headline writer exclaimed, "He ain't nothin' but a cash cow."

Or so it seemed. Yet, another crisis loomed. Annual revenue had flattened near the $45 million mark, leaving profits of about $10 million, and Lisa, becoming the estate's sole legal owner at age twenty-five, was spending $5 to $7 million of it, leaving little to reinvest. One insider said, "She's her daddy's daughter, alright. She not only looks like him, she inherited his money gene."

Added to this was the costly failure of Elvis Presley's Memphis, a restaurant and nightclub that opened in 1997 on the site once occupied by the Lansky Brothers clothing store on Beale Street, where Elvis bought his first pink-and-black suits. In the 1980s, a concept pioneered by the Hard Rock Café, merging dining with entertainment, seemed to point the way to the future, with Planet Hollywood and others in quick pursuit of the new themed restaurant market. So it wasn't surprising when the estate debuted what it thought would be the first of a chain of "cultural embassies," creating places in foreign countries where the Elvis "brand" could be espoused to expand "retail opportunities," to quote Soden.

The building was completely renovated, state-of-the-art sound was installed for live entertainment, millions of dollars were spent. It opened in

1997 and closed four and a half years later, by which time profits from other businesses were used to keep it going. Not even a free shuttle service between Graceland and Beale Street helped much.

"We were over-confident," Soden admitted. "I spent way too much money. The public started to see the themed concept as expensive teeshirts and mediocre food. I couldn't believe it when Planet Hollywood announced in a press conference that they were in the entertainment business, not the food business. We wanted to be both a great restaurant as well as a tourist destination and the winters in Memphis are too long. In the end, Planet Hollywood went down and so did we and all the memorabilia we had on display went back into the archives."

Another problem was that there seemed to be little new the estate could do to expand its marketing. Besides all the product and tours, the estate provided facilities, catering, decorating and planning services for private events, including weddings in the Chapel in the Woods on the Graceland grounds. "Christmas at Graceland" offered musical, animated e-cards, a Christmas music video, and an interactive holiday trivia game. For the computer user, there were wallpapers and screen savers. There was an "Elvis Kids Site" on the Web and for adults, an Elvis Visa card ("For Takin' Care of Business"). If you couldn't actually visit Graceland, there was a virtual tour. With more than one hundred licensees churning out product, and RCA creating its endless repackages, and all the new television specials and Hollywood movies and commercials and the like, what was left to do?

By now, Lisa had become a darling of the tabloids. Following a six-year marriage to musician Danny Keough, with whom she had a son and a daughter, she married Michael Jackson (two weeks after divorcing Keough). Cynics said he wanted to add Elvis's songs to the Beatles catalog he already owned and she married him for his money or to recruit him into the Church of Scientology, to which she and Priscilla were introduced by John Travolta. They were married for twenty months, divorcing in 1996. Then in 2002, she married Nicolas Cage, the star of that film with all the Elvis impersonators in Las Vegas; they separated after four months.

She was a close friend of her father's onetime girlfriend Linda Thompson and in 2003, Thompson's record producer husband, David Foster, suggested Lisa re-start a singing career that had faltered three years earlier when her then-producer dropped out of a recording project. Her first album, *To Whom It May Concern*, reached Number Five on the *Billboard* 200 albums chart, was certified gold, and given respectful reviews. For many, she had inherited her daddy's musical gene, too.

Despite Lisa's warm welcome from critics and her music peers and the increasing visitor count at Graceland and all the other success, the estate was still struggling, running as fast as it could to stay in place, leaving Soden and the board to anguish over what to do. In February 2005, Lisa did what she thought would fix things. She sold nearly all of her inheritance.

Lisa retained 100 per cent of the house and grounds, as well as all her father's personal effects, along with 15 per cent of Elvis Presley Enterprises. What she gave up was 85 per cent of EPE, including all trademark rights to the name, likeness and image of Elvis Presley and all EPE-owned intellectual property, currently used in all those licensing and merchandising deals. She also sold the estate's massive collection of photographs and archival documents, publishing rights to 650 songs, record royalty rights to the material Elvis recorded after 1973, royalty rights to twenty-four Elvis movies, the Graceland visitor center complex including the two malls, the airplane and automobile museums, Heartbreak Hotel, and all other real estate investments now spread over one-hundred acres in the Graceland neighborhood.

In exchange, Lisa was to receive $50 million in cash and $26 million in common and preferred stock of the new parent company. Another $25 million went to pay off debts, including operating debt typical of a business its size, mortgages for land purchases, and what was still owed from the restaurant debacle. In addition, Priscilla was to get $6.5 million for use of the family name, although the buyer wasn't obligated to do that because she was divorced from Elvis at the time of his death. This was what is called in the merger and acquisition game, payment for "good will."

Some greeted news of the sale with stunned disapproval. "What's wrong with a 20 per cent profit?" one observer asked. "Most businesses would kill for that margin. She sold the golden goose!" Others expressed doubts about the buyer, a man known for acquiring entertainment properties, building them up and re-selling them; "flipping" is what the practice is called. Would Elvis be "flipped" as well?

Even *Forbes* magazine was dubious, headlining a news story about the sale and the questionable involvement of the buyer's banker, Bear Stearns, "A Deal Unfit for The King."

The estate's new boss was Robert F. X. Sillerman, the son of a pioneering radio executive who went bankrupt when his son was thirteen. He grew up in New York's Bronx, graduated *magna cum laude* from Brandeis University in 1969, a child of the sixties who identified with counterculture politics and rock music. Forming a partnership with one of New York's top disc jockeys, "Cousin Brucie" Morrow, in the mid-1970s, he followed his father's footsteps and started buying radio stations, Sillerman teaching the sales staff, Morrow coaching the on-air personalities. By 1985, they had seventy stations, which they sold for $50 million.

When the Federal Communications Commission loosened restrictions on how many stations could be owned by one individual or company, Sillerman and Morrow bought more stations and sold them to Westinghouse in 1989 for $389 million. He then set up a company called SFX, acquiring another seventy stations, selling them for $2.1 billion.

Next, he started buying concert halls, from Roseland in New York to the Fillmore West in San Francisco, creating a network of 120 stages, selling that exposure to commercial sponsors (Smirnoff vodka, Kendall-Jackson wines, Levi's, etc.) and becoming what a writer in *Fortune* magazine called "the single big fish in the concert business," as well as a "corporate gorilla." After buying a sports agency (representing Michael Jordan, among others), he again sold out, this time pocketing $3 billion.

Over time, his philosophy shifted from distribution (radio stations, concert halls) to product, so he formed a new company called CKX, the CK standing for "content is king," and started looking around for a name to buy. "We thought there were only three rock acts worth owning," a source in Sillerman's camp told *Fortune*, "Elvis, the Beatles and the Rolling Stones. Elvis was available."

Both Lisa and Soden defended the sale. Lisa said, "First off, companies merge all the time and while it is true that EPE has been successfully holding its own for twenty-five years, myself, my mother and the board came to realize that in order to take the business to a whole different level, merging with another provenly successful team would accomplish that."

"We were quietly looking for an investor to buy a significant portion of the estate to assure Lisa and her family of a secure future," Soden added. "If we found the right one, we thought it would allow us to grow—into Las Vegas, into Europe, into Asia. At first, we thought Bob Sillerman had too many businesses and couldn't manage the estate. We'd talked to four or five others and it was his plan for the future that seemed the most imaginative."

Sillerman's personality was another factor. He may have been a fast talker and a formidable negotiator, but he also had a true love of music (he put Bob Dylan and Paul Simon on tour together even though they disliked each other, because they were the two most important American singer-songwriters of the sixties) and an *Animal House* sense of humor that would have appealed to Elvis. (He was known to pop out of bushes at his Southampton estate at parties to scare people and once with Morrow, stripped naked and ran back and forth in front of one of their radio disc jockeys to get him to loosen up.) He was a party guy, vacationed in Paris and Cuernavaca, and owned a resort in Anguilla; he once flew several friends to Ireland on his ten-seat Challenger jet and rerouted the flight on the way home for a Rolling Stones concert in London. He also was a triathlon athlete, a fierce competitor on volleyball and basketball courts with his friends, had beaten cancer, had his own charitable foundation, and served as a generous benefactor and provost to a Long Island university.

Within months of announcing the EPE purchase, Sillerman made his next big product acquisition, paying $196 million for 19 Entertainment, a British company owned by Simon Fuller, who had created the Spice Girls and the interactive on-air talent contest *Pop Idol*, giving Sillerman the proprietary rights to the television franchise, including the *American Idol* series in the U.S. and local adaptations of the format in over 100 countries. He then acquired an 80 per cent interest in the name, image, likeness and all other publicity rights of Muhammad Ali.

At the same time, he was looking for a way to exploit Elvis's name and in 2006, his company formed a creative partnership with the Cirque du Soleil to "develop, produce and promote Elvis Presley projects including touring and permanent shows as well as multimedia interactive 'Elvis experiences' throughout the world." The Cirque du Soleil, a modern theatrical troupe based in Quebec, Canada, figured it would follow the success of its *Beatles Tribute*, a show that featured live musicians and singers, video projection, dance, multimedia sound and lighting, and it was announced that Elvis would return to Las Vegas in 2009 in one of the showrooms of the new MGM Mirage's Project City Center, a massive development covering 66 acres and encompassing a 4,000-room hotel and casino, two 400-room non-gaming hotels, 2,800 luxury condominiums, and half a million square feet of commercial space. Cirque du Soleil also outlined plans for at least one touring Elvis show for Europe and/or Asia and one permanent attraction for each of the succeeding six years.

In 2006, the Cirque du Soleil had collaborated with the surviving Beatles and heirs to the estates of John Lennon and George Harrison to adapt for the stage an album produced by Giles Martin, the son of the group's original producer, George Martin—what is called a "mashup," where two musical entities are mixed together, in this case limiting the musical choices to the original Beatles material: no outsiders allowed. No one was saying Elvis might get the same treatment, but given how the bottom of the barrel was being scraped for Elvis recordings, it wouldn't be a surprise.

"There is no way that we could ever have established a partnership with Cirque du Soleil like the one that has been crafted by CKX," Soden said. "We did not have the financial resources. The way we were structured we would have remained financially limited. The CKX ownership has given us breathing room. The ability to earn more and keep more has allowed us to purchase the remaining key real estate pieces of our campus and, with CKX resources, to master-plan the long term future of Graceland whose managers fifty years from now will thank us."

Time passed. The Colonel died in 1997, at 87. So have Charlie Hodge and Richard Davis and virtually everyone from the early days: Bob Neal, Sam Phillips, Marion Keisker. J. D. Sumner and two of the Jordanaires, Hoyt Hawkins and Neal Matthews, have died too. Jerry Schilling continued to work in film and TV, remaining close to Priscilla and Lisa (he was the only non-family member in the special that accompanied the book *Elvis by the Presleys*) and in 2005 finally published his own memoir, *Me and a Guy Named Elvis*. George Klein, the only insider who never got around to writing a book, had a weekly Elvis show on the Elvis satellite radio channel and worked as the casino host at the Horseshoe Casino in Mississippi just south of Memphis. Joe Esposito, who was selling his books and autographed pictures on a web page, also worked as a casino host, at the lavish Wynn Resort in Las Vegas. Red West, Sonny West, Billy Smith, Lamar Fike, and Marty Lacker operated the Memphis Mafia Store on the Internet. Scotty Moore had a web page, too, but it was less focused on Elvis and more on his own career—although he, too, had a book for sale. Lisa married for a fourth time (in a traditional Japanese ceremony in Kyoto, Japan, with Priscilla giving her away and her first husband, who was still in Lisa's backup band, in attendance) and nominally presided over the Elvis Presley Charitable Foundation, an umbrella organization that provides homeless families with free rent, child day care, and counseling, as well as a scholarship program at the University of Memphis. While Jack Soden—who said the estate's mission statement remained "Don't screw it up"—was named to the boards of the Memphis Area Chamber of Commerce, the National Civil Rights Museum Foundation, and the Regional Medical Center at Memphis, as well as inducted into the Society of Entrepreneurs.

Priscilla had carved out a career for herself, co-hosting the ABC series *Those Amazing Animals* with Burgess Meredith, acting in the television series *Dallas* for five years, starring opposite Leslie Nielsen in the *Naked Gun* movie trilogy, serving on the board of MGM, launching lines of signature perfumes and bed linens, and despite a twenty-two-year-long relationship with a man with whom she had a son (born in 1987), nonetheless was perceived as her ex-husband's "virtual widow," Graceland her virtual Memphis home.

It was a role she filled with pride and dignity, appearing in or serving as a producer of at least eight Elvis television specials, writing her autobiography (*Elvis and Me*, a bestseller) and co-authoring with her daughter *Elvis by the Presleys*, both books being made into TV specials. Graceland was remodeled under her direction to look as it did when she lived there and when it was opened to the public, she was at the door. For many years, she served on the EPE board. When Graceland was named a National Historic Landmark in

2006, she made the announcement with Interior Secretary Gale Norton. When the design house Dolce & Gabbana staged an Elvis-themed fashion show in Milan, she was there too (with Lisa and her daughter, Riley Keough). As a member of the board of CKX, it's clear that she will continue in this role.

Memphis had changed as well. Graceland had become far and away the city's most popular tourist destination, currently drawing 600,000 visitors a year, fifteen million since Elvis's death—including President Bush and his guest Junichero Koizumi, the prime minister of Japan (who played air guitar at the Graceland gates), Bruce Springsteen, Jerry Lee Lewis, and the entire cast of the Boishoi Ballet. The city had also added other attractions, including B. B. King's Blues Club on Beale Street, the (original) Sun Studio, the National Civil Rights Museum, the Memphis Rock N Soul Museum, and the Stax Museum of Soul Music, a tribute to the artists who recorded for Stax.

In January 2007, in the chill Memphis winter, the crowds were seasonally smaller at 3734 Elvis Presley Boulevard, but went up the first week for the annual birthday celebration (January 8), one of the two festivals that fill the Memphis streets with families in RVs, and the hotels with visitors from around the world. This year, things kicked off with an Elvis Birthday Dance Party, with Argo, one of the disc jockeys on the all-Elvis satellite channel taking breathless and teary requests. The next morning, the annual gathering of the presidents and officers of some of the 625 or so active Elvis fan clubs convened at the Memphis Marriott East to ask questions of estate representatives and hear a guest speaker, this year Lance LeGault, the actor who helped choreograph many of the songs in Elvis's Hollywood movies. That night, the Memphis Symphony Orchestra presented an 'Elvis Presley Birthday Pops,' lead vocals by Terry Mike Jeffrey, a popular tribute artist, and special guest vocalists the Imperials. LeGault and the Imperials appeared informally again on the third day when they met members of the Elvis Insiders, who, for a membership fee, are given access, to "rarely seen Elvis Presley photos, Graceland artifacts, Elvis video clips, and rare documents from the Graceland archives," along with "confidential information, exclusive updates, and news about Elvis before any-one else!"

The final day, on what would have been Elvis's seventy-second birthday, featured a military color guard ceremony at Graceland at which the estate was given "a special certificate and medal, earned but never received by Elvis, in recognition of his service with the army." This was followed by the cutting of a birthday cake. More cake was available to all comers at a party at a restaurant on Beale Street, a $5 cash donation going to Humes Middle School, formerly Humes High School, Elvis's *alma mater*.

"Elvis Week," marking the anniversary of his death (August 16) is even more elaborate, closing each year with 10,000 or more celebrants gathered along Elvis Presley Boulevard for a candlelight service. The description of one such week, published in the *Los Angeles Times*, captured the mood: "The man loitering along the stone wall says he'd recently been in a mental hospital, and no one doubts his word.

"Before the doctors cured him, he believed himself to be Elvis Presley. Now, he merely wishes that he was. The wish is written all over his face, not to mention his back and shoulders. Much of the man's torso, in fact, is covered with tattoos of Elvis's visage, and his soft, hairless midriff is given over to a painstakingly rendered portrait of the Graceland estate, just beyond the wall, where Presley died twenty years ago on August 16, 1977.

"What makes the man so remarkable, however, isn't his fanatical love of the King, or his fondness for king-sized tattoos. What makes him stand out is the way he blends in. Only during something called 'Elvis Week,' only now, only here, could such a man say, 'I belong.'"

"We're never mean to these people," Soden said. "They've all been touched in some way. It's like *Close Encounters of the Third Kind*, where all those people were drawn to that mountain and they didn't know why. People are drawn in the same way to Graceland."

Most of the time at the annual events is left open for touring Graceland and shopping. Much of the product for sale in the shops (and online) consisted of everyday items, including every sort of clothing, luggage, umbrellas, coffee (including Love Me Tender, a light roast) and hot chocolate and mugs to drink it from, soap dishes, tooth brushes, refrigerator magnets, handbags and belts, sewing kits, lunch boxes, mouse pads and memo pads, salt and pepper shakers, air fresheners, wrist and pocket watches, bookmarks, ash trays and Zippo lighters ("Elvis & Zippo—two American icons, one perfect team"), personalized checks and checkbook covers, personalized return address stickers, cosmetic cases, pot holders, doormats and placemats and the like.

Other items were recreational. There were pool balls and cues, guitars and guitar picks, shot glasses and ice buckets, bicycles, bowling balls, jigsaw puzzles, CD cases and cell phone covers, pinball machines, playing cards and poker chips, music boxes, cameras, bean bags, darts and dart boards, candy (including a peanut butter and banana crème Elvis Reese's Cup), board games, and wine.

Much was more unusual. There were engraved pistols and a rifle from a company that also sold weapons honoring everybody from Gene Autry and Roy Rogers to Generals Patton and Custer. There was a fully functional table-top jukebox right out of the 1950s that came bundled with a CD of Elvis's hits or gospel favorites, your choice. There was a fabulous rubber duck. For the Elvis impersonator or the fan with more money than sense, there was a black leather outfit like the one Elvis wore on the 1968 NBC special ($1,300 tailor-made, $800 off the rack), a gold lamé jacket, shirt, pants and tie ($1,900), and a copy of the *Aloha* satellite concert costume (suit, cape, and belt, $3,300).

There were talking key chains, Elvis and Priscilla wedding dolls, and for your teddy bear a full wardrobe that included the jeans outfit that Elvis wore while singing "Jailhouse Rock" (same TV special), a gold lamé suit, a white jumpsuit, and a motorcycle jacket. There also was an animated telephone with an Elvis figure on it that gyrates and hollers when it rings.

Over the top? Yes. But it seems appropriate, because from the time he favored wide black trousers with a pink stripe down the side, a pink draped jacket, wore eye makeup and combed his dyed black hair into an elaborate ducktail and pompadour, to the time when he marched into the Oval Office at the White House to meet President Nixon wearing a velvet suit and cape, cinched around the waist with a belt buckle the size of a Cadillac hubcap, carrying a jeweled cane, blasted TV sets with his sidearm and sent someone to Houston in his private plane to pick up a bag of cheeseburgers, Elvis epitomized the phrase "over the top."

America is weird and kitschy, too, worshiping at the same altar of excess. So perpetuating this in Elvis's name doesn't degrade or demean his memory so much as it makes him appear to be a typical American, just on a bigger scale and a little bit less inhibited.

(Some say that the tackier merchandise cheapens the King's legacy and Soden does not disagree. "However," he says, "we have a genuine challenge in this regard. If we ignore these categories of less expensive merchandise then unauthorized vendors who care nothing about quality quickly sweep in to fill the void. While infringement is a measure of a brand's value, it still represents a plague of legal and financial problems. If we can stay reasonably involved in that segment of the market we can protect our trademarks and at least have control over the quality. Nonetheless, in licensing, you'd be amazed by how much we turn down. Only 2 per cent of licensing applications are accepted.")

What do you say in conclusion about someone who sold an estimated one billion records worldwide, more than anyone in record industry history—the individual whose following makes pilgrimages to the house where he lived in a spirit that seems half groupie and half devotional celebrant?

John Bakke, now a University of Memphis Professor Emeritus, said he thought Elvis was now "acknowledged as a social phenomenon and change agent who made the waves out of the still but deep waters of the fifties and touched off a youth movement at the same time he revealed a youth market. More than that, however, I believe that Elvis and especially his image (or both of them) will be the cultural icon noting the cultural revolution that is ongoing.

He is a symbol of cultural freedom, at the same time he is the outsider who never fit in, and who as such was always an object of derision. He is at once the symbol of the hero and the guy who was so out of place he didn't even fit into the movement he started. He will remain to a large extent a mystery and that's why he'll always be of interest.

"There really is no one to compare him with. Not Valentino, not James Dean, not John Lennon, and not Princess Diana although she may have come the closest. Elvis was controversial in so many ways that a lot of us took sides and thus invested a part of ourselves in him. I don't think people do that now. The only name to rival Elvis's might be Ali."

To understand Elvis fully, perhaps it's necessary to return to Tupelo, where the two-room house where he was born has been furnished with period furniture, including a porch swing that was never there before. There's also a disagreement about the wall covering. Right now, there is period wallpaper, a flower print; some say the Presleys used newspaper. Bare bulbs hang from the ceiling, and because there are only two small rooms, each measuring just four and a half meters square, only a few can visit at a time. Admission is $2 and the mood is reverential.

The six-hectare Elvis Presley Birthplace Park that includes the tiny structure, located at the end of what's now called Elvis Presley Drive, is open seven days a week. There are trees and grass and a neatly bricked pathway leading to a museum, gift shop, and a chapel in the back. Just a two-hour drive south of Graceland, straight down U.S. Highway 78, it attracts about 100,000 of the devoted pilgrims and the simply curious each year, three times the town's population.

There is also that bronze statue of Elvis at age twelve (his age when his family left Tupelo), and in town there are concrete markers with copper plaques at the two schools Elvis attended, the site of a grocery store where it's believed he sometimes socialized with neighbors, a restaurant he is said to have liked, and the hardware store where, at eleven, his parents bought his first guitar. Behind the counter, near the door, is a framed letter from the store's former owner, Forrest Bobo, who made the sale.

"I am proud to have had a little part in Elvis's life," he wrote.

So, too, were so many more.

# INDEX